More praise for

Making Classrooms Better

"This book exceptionally translates up-to-date scientific studies into useable knowledge and practical tools to be utilized by anyone concerned with optimizing learning outcomes in individuals of all ages and within many contexts. A stimulating resource full of solid information for improving learning and understanding."

> —**Stephanie Peabody**, PsyD, Neuropsychologist, Course Director: Mind, Brain, Health and Education, and Course Director: Neurobiology of Positive Psychology at Harvard UES

"This is a must-read for every educator who is willing to question and enhance their practice to deliver a better, research-based curriculum with improved methods for the benefit of their students. It blends learning theory and research (the why) with strategies for clearly identified instructional goals (the how). A worthy goal for every teacher would be to add one of the 50 best practices to their repertoire until they finish the reading."

> —**Elizabeth Helfant**, Upper School Coordinator of Pedagogical Innovation at the Mary Institute and St. Louis Country Day School (MICDS), Missouri

"As a true transdisciplinary diplomat, Tracey Tokuhama-Espinosa invites us to participate in her 'interactive feature film' about MBE Science, bringing education to the center of the fields of pedagogy, neuroscience, and psychology."

> —**Renata Menezes Rosat**, MD, PhD, Professor, Department of Physiology at the Federal University of Rio Grande do Sul, Brasil

"This book is fundamental for anyone who cares about increasing the benefits that students can reap from education as well as improving their experience while in school. Teachers, education leaders, policy-makers, graduate students, researchers, parents, and others interested in improving education are extremely lucky to have access to this wealth of up-to-date, research-based information in such an enjoyable read."

> —**Daniela Bramwell**, Master's student, University of Toronto

Making Classrooms Better

A Norton Book in Education

Making Classrooms Better

*50 Practical Applications of
Mind, Brain, and Education Science*

Tracey Tokuhama-Espinosa, PhD

W. W. Norton & Company
New York • London

Dedication

Best life teachers: my parents, husband, and children.

> *The direction in which education starts a [wo]man will determine [her] future life.*
> —Plato

Best guides, who have shown me how the love of one's profession ignites and is ignited by passion: Mary Helen Immordino-Yang, David Daniel, Lisa Cirieco, Monserrat Creamer, Xavier Bellpratt, John Hattie, Daniel Ansari, David Lansdale, David Perkins, Kurt Fischer, Stanislas Dehaene, Diego Quiroga, Gonzalo Mendieta, Carlos Montúfar, and Santiago Gangotena.

> *The best teachers are those who show you where to look, but don't tell you what to see.*
> —Alexandra K. Trenfor

Best inspiration: the thousands of humble, devoted, dedicated teachers around the world who I have had the pleasure of meeting.

> *I have come to a frightening conclusion. I am the decisive element in the classroom. It is my personal approach that creates the climate. It is my daily mood that makes the weather. As a teacher I possess a tremendous power to make a child's life miserable or joyous. I can be a tool of torture or an instrument of inspiration. I can humiliate or humor, hurt or heal. In all situations it is my response that decides whether a crisis will be escalated or de-escalated, and a child humanized or de-humanized.*
> —Haim G. Ginott (as cited in Martin & Loomis, 2006, p. 222)

Contents

Acknowledgments   xix

Preface   xxiii

Introduction   xxxi

    What Is Mind, Brain, and Education Science?   xxxiii

        Complex, but Not Necessarily Complicated   xxxiv

        Levels of Analysis   xxxv

    Using Mind, Brain, and Education Science to Structure Learning   xxxvi

    Keeping Things in Perspective   xxxvii

        Strong Learning Communities   xxxvii

        Great Teachers   xxxix

        Biology   xli

    What's to Come?   xliii

    Suggested Readings and Videos   xliv

        John Hattie's *Visible Learning*   xliv

        Excellent Community Education Initiatives   xliv

            Geoffrey Canada and the Harlem Children's Zone   xliv

            Japan's Community Learning Initiatives   xlv

            Finland's Community Learning Initiatives   xlv

        Recommended Films About Great Teaching   xlv

PART I
From the Classroom to the Lab and Back

Chapter 1. Great Minds Don't Think Alike: 1
The Transdisciplinary Mind, Brain, and Education Approach
   A Unified Vision   1
   Catching Up With the Times   8
   Teacher Training in the Context of Mind, Brain, and Education Science   9
     Do No Harm   14
     Order   15
     Form   16
     Content   16
   Crossing the "Bridge Too Far": From the Classroom to the Lab and Back   17
     The People   17
     The Science   19
     A Final Analogy: Connections Through People, Connections Through Synapses   22
   MBE Concepts, Principles, Tenets, and Guidelines   23
     Principles that Great Teachers Follow   25
     The Tenets of MBE   36
     The Instructional Guidelines of MBE   37
     "Proven" in Education but Not in Neuroscience?   37
   Suggested Readings   40
     "A Bridge Too Far" Commentaries   40
     Differentiation   41
     Executive Functions and Self-Regulation   42
     Mind, Brain, and Education Science   44
     Transdisciplinary Fields   45

Chapter 2. "Brain-Based Learning 2.0" and the Messiness of the Classroom: 46
What Really Influences Student Achievement
     10 Categories of Teacher Influence on Student Learning   47
       1. Student Self-Efficacy and Self-Concept   47
       2. Teacher Credibility   48
       3. Student Attitude Toward Interventions   51
       4. Constructivism   53

5. Evaluation and Assessment Practices 58
6. Teacher Self-Reflection on Practice 61
7. Appropriate Methodologies 64
8. Communication 67
9. Learning in Groups 69
10. Classroom Management 70
Moving On 73
Suggested Readings 73
Student Self-Efficiency 73
Teacher Credibility and Self-Efficiency 74
Attitudes Toward Academic Interventions 75
Constructivist Designs 75
Evaluation and Assessment Best Practices 76
Teacher Self-Relfection 77
Teacher Communication and Clarity 78
Classroom Management and Engagement 78
About Math and Science (Challenges) 79

Chapter 3. Why Do We Teach?: Models of Education that Create Usable Knowledge 81
The Actors and Locations of Learning 82
The Goals of Great Teaching 83
Thinking About Teaching and Teaching to Think 84
Cultivating Good Thinking Over Time 86
What's Worth Learning? 87
Strong Teaching Models 90
Beyond Bloom's Taxonomy: LOTS and HOTS 90
Fink's Significant Learning 95
Wiggins and McTighe's Six Facets of Understanding 98
Costa and Kallick's Habits of Mind 101
Premack and Woodruff's Theory of Mind 103
Gardner's Five Minds for the Future 105
Where the Thinking Models Point Us 109
What Deep Thinking Looks Like in the Classroom 111
Is There an Ideal Teaching Model? 113
Suggested Readings 114
Great Thinking Frameworks of the 20th and 21st Centuries 114

PART II
*50 Best Classroom Practices
Using Mind, Brain, and Education Science Principles*

Chapter 4 Filters: Electing the Best Planning, Evaluation, and Activities   **119**

Planning Lessons   121

Best Classroom Practice 1. Plan Activities That Grab Attention   122

Best Classroom Practice 2. Plan Activities That Stimulate Memory   125

Best Classroom Practice 3. Plan to Use Spaced Versus Massed Learning   128

Best Classroom Practice 4. Plan to Incorporate Repetition   132

Best Classroom Practice 5. Take Advantage of Variation and Transdisciplinarity   134

Best Classroom Practice 6. Plan Authentic Lessons   138

Evaluation   139

Best Classroom Practice 7. Implement Formative Evaluation   141

Best Classroom Practice 8. Use Product, Process, and Progress Evaluations   143

Best Classroom Practice 9. Test to Improve Learning   144

Best Classroom Practice 10. Develop Shared, Explicit Learning Objectives   145

Best Classroom Practice 11. Strive for Clarity and Immediacy   148

Best Classroom Practice 12. Provide Feedback for Mastery Learning   151

Best Classroom Practice 13. Nurture Teacher-Student Relationships   155

Best Classroom Practice 14. Believe in the Role of Plasticity
and in Your Students   156

Instructional Design: Methods, Techniques, Strategies, Actions, and Activities   158

Best Classroom Practice 15. Foster Metacognition and Mindfulness   160

Best Classroom Practice 16. Employ Zemelman and Colleagues'
Best Practice Filter When Selecting Activities   168

Best Classroom Practice 17. Develop Students' Ability to Identify
Similarities and Differences   178

Best Classroom Practice 18. Develop Students' Summarizing and
Note Taking Ability   179

Best Classroom Practice 19. Reinforce Effort and Provide Recognition   179

Best Classroom Practice 20. Provide Purposeful Homework and Practice   180

Best Classroom Practice 21. Prepare Students to Set Personal Objectives
and Give Themselves Feedback   181

Best Classroom Practice 22. Teach Students to Generate and Test Hypotheses   181

Best Classroom Practice 23. Use Cues and Triggers   183

Summary   184
Suggested Readings   185
   Memory and Attention   185
   Spaced vs. Massed Learning   186
   Repetition and Learning   187
   Authentic Learning   188
   Evaluation   188
   Mastery Learning   189
   Student-Teacher Relationships   190

Chapter 5. What Has Always Worked and Why:
What Traditionally Happens in Great Classrooms   **191**
Ancient Methodologies in a Modern World   191
   Best Classroom Practice 24. Use the Socratic Method   191
   Best Classroom Practice 25. Cultivate the Art of Questioning   201
Small-Group Learning   202
   Best Classroom Practice 26. Incorporate Problem-Based Learning   203
   Best Classroom Practice 27. Incorporate Cooperative Learning   207
   Best Classroom Practice 28. Incorporate Reciprocal Teaching   208
   Best Classroom Practice 29. Incorporate Case Studies   211
Methods for Teaching All Subjects and All Ages   213
   Best Classroom Practice 30. Harness the Power of Analogies   213
   Best Classroom Practice 31. Implement the 5Es: Engage, Explore, Explain,   216
      Elaborate, Evaluate
Summary   219
Suggested Readings   220
   The Socratic Method   220
   Questioning   220
   Problem-Based Learning   221
   Cooperative Learning   221
   Case Studies   222
   Reciprocal Teaching   222
   Analogies   222
   The 5Es   223

Chapter 6. What *Could* Work in the Classroom and Why: 224
  Getting Teachers (and Administrators) out of Their Comfort Zones
    A Teacher's List of Habits   224
      Best Classroom Practice 32. Improve Student Self-efficacy   225
      Best Classroom Practice 33. Maintain High Expectations   227
      Best Classroom Practice 34. See Learning as Fluid   229
      Best Classroom Practice 35: Appreciate the Role of Affect in Learning 230
      Best Classroom Practice 36. Take the Lead in Social Contagion   234
      Best Classroom Practice 37. Award Perseverance and Celebrate Error   235
      Best Classroom Practice 38. Motivate   237
      Best Classroom Practice 39. Never Work Harder Than Your Students   239
      Best Classroom Practice 40. Be Passionate!   240
      Best Classroom Practice 41. Design Engaging Classrooms   242
      Best Classroom Practice 42. Manage   244
      Best Classroom Practice 43. Use Thinking Routines   247
        Interpretation and Articulation   248
        Guiding Inquiry   248
        Decision-Making   249
        Synthesizing and Summarizing   249
        Understanding One's Own Understanding   249
        Metacognition   250
        Empathy   250
        Limiting One's Own Presumptions   251
      Best Classroom Practice 44: Keep Abreast of Technology and Flip   251
        the Classroom
    School Design Choices That Impact Student Learning   256
      Best Classroom Practice 45. Adjust for Ages and Stages   257
      Best Classroom Practice 46. Improve Nutrition   258
      Best Classroom Practice 47. Get Students out of Rows   260
      Best Classroom Practice 48. Begin Year-Round Schooling   261
      Best Classroom Practice 49. Change The School Day   263
      Best Classroom Practice 50. Stop Using Tests as Indicators of Higher Thinking 263
    Summary   265
    Suggested Readings   266

Student Self-Efficacy   266
Thinking of Learning as Fluid   267
Affect, Emotions, and Learning   267
Perseverance   268
Teacher Passion   268
Motivation   269
Technology   270
The Flipped Classroom   271

Conclusion   **272**

Appendix A: Members and Commentators on the Original Delphi Panel Outcomes   279
    on Mind, Brain, and Education Science
Appendix B: John Hattie's *Visible Learning*: 150 Influences that Impact   283
    Student Learning Outcomes
Appendix C: 47 Interventions Mentioned by Hattie that are Interpreted to be   289
    Within the Teacher's Realm of Influence
Appendix D: The Goals in Mind, Brain, and Education Science   291
References   295

FIGURES

Figure I.1 Principles and Tenets of Mind, Brain, and Education Science   xxxvi
Figure I.2 Instructional Guidelines of Mind, Brain, and Education Science   xxxvii
Figure 1.1 Education Is Behind the Times Compared to Other Social Institutions   2
Figure 1.2 Disciplines and Subdisciplines in Mind, Brain, and Education Science 3
Figure 1.3 Scaling Up Interventions Gradually   6
Figure 1.4 Results of a Bad Diagnosis   6
Figure 1.5 Mind, Brain, and Education Science: A Transdisciplinary Field   7
Figure 1.6 Growth in the Mind, Brain, and Education Field Over the Past Decade 10
Figure 3.1 Performance Verbs for Learning Outcomes   85
Figure 3.2 The Goals of Formal Education   88
Figure 3.3 Bloom's Taxonomy Now and Then   91
Figure 3.4 Ms. Green's Categorization Game   92
Figure 3.5 Ms. Potts' Categorization Game   92
Figure 3.6 How to Meet Objectives at Each Level of Bloom's Taxonomy, According 95
    to Surgey (2012)
Figure 3.7 Fink's Significant Learning   97
Figure 3.8 Wiggins and McTighe's Six Facts of Understanding   98
Figure 3.9 Gardner's Five Minds for the Future   108
Figure 3.10 An Ideal Model?   113
Figure 4.1 Backward Design Steps   121
Figure 4.2 Baddeley's Phonological Loop   133
Figure 4.3 Sample Mind Map   134
Figure 4.4 Student Motivation Is Linked to Teacher Clarity   146
Figure 4.5 Terms for Instructional Practices   159
Figure 4.6 Performance Checklist: Metacognition   165
Figure 4.7 Zemelman and Colleagues' Best Practice Activities and Associated   168
    MBE Concepts, Principles, Tenets, and Instructional Guidelines
Figure 4.8 Cycle of Innovation   182
Figure 5.1 Problem-Based Learning and Cooperative Learning   205
Figure 5.2 Analogy Examples   214
Figure 6.1 The Intersection Between Emotion and Cognition   232
Figure 6.2 You Are What You Eat   259
Figure 6.3 Which Classroom Layout is Better?   260
Figure 6.4 Year-Round Schooling   262

TABLES

Table 1.1 Neuromyths Still Prevalent Today   12

Table 1.2 The Guiding Principles, Tenets, and Instructional Guidelines of   24
    Mind, Brain, and Education Science

Table 2.1 Mr. Peters' Email to His Statistics Class   54

Table 2.2 A Teacher's Reflective Journal   62

Table 3.1 Performance Verbs Associated with the Six Facets of Understanding   100

Table 4.1 Strategies for Developing Metacognitive Behaviors   166

Table 4.2 MBE Intersections With Zemelman and Colleagues' Best Practice   169

Table 4.3 Singing About Math vs. Acting Out a Play About Formulas   177

Table 4.4 Summary of Best Classroom Practices 1–22   184

Table 5.1 Progression of the 5Es Instructional Model   217

Acknowledgments

It is the supreme art of the teacher to awaken joy in creative expression and knowledge.
—Albert Einstein

Numerous new books and journal articles over the past few years have finally moved from talking about the potential of using brain science to improve learning outcomes to concrete recommendations. The genre of Mind, Brain, and Education (MBE) science literature, joining the forces of neuroscience, cognitive psychology, and education, has grown, and almost all major publishers are scrambling to get more information out to the general public. University degree programs, courses, congresses, conferences, and workshops on the subject are increasing in number. These are exciting times for teachers.

I am indebted to the giants in MBE, educational neuroscience, neuropsychology, and related fields, who selflessly support me and others like me in our quest to teach better by replying to our innocent emails, sharing studies, and most of all, posing intriguing questions. Daniel Ansari, Mary Helen Immordino-Yang, David Daniel, Paul Howard-Jones, Adele Diamond, and Stanislas Dehaene have been particularly generous in sharing their expertise. Similarly, colleagues on the expert panel to redefine teachers' pedagogical knowledge for the Organisation for Economic Co-operation and Development (OECD), Johannes König, Sonia Guerriero, Marilyn Leask, and Daniel Ansari have offered a seemingly endless amount of evidence related to best classroom practice from international comparative studies and enthusiastically applauded MBE's debut in this context. John Hattie, whose *Visible Learning* (2009, 2012) and *International Guide to Student Achievement* (2013) have impacted the educational world, kindly responded to my queries and entertained my proposal to unify his excellent contributions with MBE to help move the teaching profession forward from the classroom to the lab and back. Jay McTighe, who has changed the face of instructional design, also offered encouragement for this book and animated feedback. I thank Patricia Wolf and Judy Willis not only for their guidance, but also for their ever-contagious cheerleading as MBE inches forward toward mass acceptance. I am indebted to all for being models professionals, and for taking the first steps to cross John Bruer's "Bridge Too Far" (1997) by symbolically traversing into the newly charted land of Mind, Brain, and Education science when others doubted.

I confess I am nothing but a translator. The brilliant leaders in MBE have individually brought us better insight into how the brain learns and how we must, therefore, change the way we teach. I have humbly tried to bring together their ideas here. Transdisciplinary translation in a global context has been a challenge for me, but the lion's share of the work was already accomplished by the many authors cited here. I like to believe, however, that the whole is greater than the sum of its parts.

In May 2013, I had the pleasure of participating in the "Translating Mind, Brain and Education Across Disciplines, Cultures and Contexts" conference in Ecuador, hosted by the Universidad San Francisco de Quito. This conference brought together 40 of the top professionals in MBE from around the world, educational neuroscience, neuropsychology, and education to work with teachers from 19 different countries in hopes of advancing the field. The energy and enthusiasm of the hundreds of participants indicates that the MBE wave is still swelling. There is a lot to be done, but we should first celebrate where we currently find ourselves. It is my hope that this book will serve to inspire more people to join the paradigm shift in teaching catalyzed by the MBE movement.

I owe thanks to the Universidad San Francisco de Quito in Ecuador for the intellectual freedom to think outside the box. Thank you to Harvard University for allowing me to co-teach a new course on Mind, Brain, Health, and Education with Stephanie Peabody, Bryan Hudson, Leslie Williams, and Julia Volkman, and to learn from our amazing guest speakers: Adele Diamond, who specializes in executive functions; Ellen Langer, who shared her insights on mindfulness; Kathy Hirsh-Pasek who shared her expertise on play, health, and development; Todd Grindal, whose work on stress and learning proved so insightful, and the others who so generously come to motivate general interest in viewing human development, wellness, and learning from their new vantage point.

I am indebted to a wonderful team at the Institute for Teaching and Learning, who despite working in a developing country, lead the world both in technological as well as scientific support of education: Isabel Merino, Claudia Tobar, Isabel Solano, Scarlet Proaño, Nancy Crespo,

Paulina Lozada, Myriam Rodríguez, Lester Lopez, Marco Jarrín, Paulina Rodríguez, María Dolores Idrovo, Mishel Tirira, Mariana Rivera, Monica Montahuano, Paulina Dueñas, and Carlos Luzuriaga.

My deep appreciation goes to Deborah Malmud at Norton for her steadfast, concrete, and motivating editorial guidance, Sophie Hagen and Kathryn Moyer for their organization, and Rachel Keith for copywriting expertise and enthusiasm.

Most of all, I am thankful to my students and colleagues, whom I learn from every day.

While I am indebted to all, any errors are mine alone.

Preface

Teaching is perhaps the most advanced of all human activity—all animals learn, few teach (Blakemore & Frith, 2007). To honor our profession, we teachers must learn how to leverage the information from brain science in our favor. Mind, Brain, and Education (MBE) science offers us what is perhaps the best guide ever seen in the history of education to do this by nurturing our know-how with information from neuroscience and psychology. To play our part as teachers, however, we need to learn how to judge the information before we can apply it, and to define our roles as research-practitioners in this new field.

Historically we have come a long way in learning to maximize the potential of all the kids in our classroom, but there is still far to go. In a perfect world there would be no guesswork or interpretation in education. Experiments would be conducted, results found and confirmed, and we would all know exactly what to do when, with whom, how, and why in every classroom. Further, these findings would be reconfirmed over time with a broader scope of participants and in culturally diverse settings until no doubt remained and we could then say how a specific teaching method yields success with a precise population under exact conditions.

Ideal situations rarely exist in education, however.

MBE must move toward a more perfect methodological design, and this progress can take several paths. An obvious choice would be to try and find experts in all three areas of education, neuroscience, and psychology who want to work together. Metaphorically speaking, these experts resemble perfect trilingual translators. A perfectly balanced trilingual is someone who not only understands and can read others' work, but who also can speak and write in the other languages fluently. Translators "have to somehow represent the integrity, nuance, and specificity of science while honoring the complexity and dynamic system that is the classroom and student/teacher interaction," until the general research-practitioner in MBE can fill this gap (David Daniel, 2013, personal communication). This means that, to be an MBE educator, we must adopt a mind-set that applies scientific rigor while appreciating the individual, complex nature of our students. Teachers, like doctors, must learn to review the evidence, diagnose with care, treat with empathy, and reassess. Also like doctors, a teacher must do this routine dozens of times a day, each time learning from the previous case. Teaching is often called "the hardest job" (Duckworth, Quinn, & Seligman, 2009), both because of the sheer number of our daily encounters (outnumbering most doctors), but also because each individual brings new information to the table, new challenges to our classroom dynamics, and unique combinations of factors that we need to know about in order to maximize his potential as a learner. This is a tall order.

Do these kinds of experts exist? Of course they do! But not on a sufficient scale to grow a society dedicated to improving the teaching-learning process in the short term.

Another way to improve MBE methodology would be to allow people to grow in their distinct fields of expertise (educators, neuroscientists, and psychologists), and then unite them in collaboration. In this case we would be looking for moderately fluent translators who are experts in one language and comfortable in others, but who might not be able to write a technical paper or debate at a sophisticated level outside of their own tongue. In this situation, the translators are not perfect linguists, but rather collaborators who are willing to share new vocabulary when needed, open to creative word choices, and willing to interpret meaning where necessary. This is an ongoing iterative process, which actually improves the shared language used between the equal partners as their research and practice evolve.

Just as it is difficult to find a translation unanimously agreed upon by all readers, we will be hard-pressed (or will have to wait a long time) to find many good translators in MBE. While collaborative efforts should be a goal, we should also consider a third option, which is to use high-quality research in each field that is already available, uniting studies from neuroscience, psychology, and pedagogy that can give us a new take on old problems in education. Why do this? Because high-quality information does already exist, and in order for the field to grow, people need to see advances.

One of my three children is a perfectionist. He knows three languages but waited several years before trying to speak any of them because he didn't want to open his mouth until what came out was perfect. One of my other children is a talker; she used all of her four languages imperfectly for many years, and later improved them all to a fluent level. Both kids are now perfectly balanced multilinguals and you wouldn't know which methodology they used to approach their expertise if I hadn't told you. Neither method is superior, as they both have native-like levels today. The difference is that the talker showed us evidence of progress, while the perfectionist made us doubt anything was happening inside that head of his. There is a space for both talkers and perfectionists in MBE. Transdisciplinary collaboration is the key to thorough MBE research; this book is a weigh station in the path toward the goal of a united front combining specialists from education, neuroscience, and psychology to find answers about how to teach best for the benefit of each learner.

We have educational research that shows that the interventions listed in this book work (Hattie, 2009, 2012). This is a step forward. We also have supporting evidence from neuroscience and psychology that explains *why* and *how* many of these interventions work at a neurological or psychological level, though in most cases the evidence comes from experiments that were not conducted in classrooms. While only well-conducted, peer-reviewed studies are used to support the proven classroom practices shared here, the links between studies from the three fields are engineered based on available data. In a perfect world we wouldn't have to link independent studies, but rather be able to offer carefully controlled scientific experiments done by the three areas simultaneously on the same topic. This is not a perfect world. But we are moving in the right direction.

> *I am convinced that empowering teachers with the appropriate knowledge of the principles of human neuroplasticity and learning will lead to better class-room practices.*
> —Stanislas Dehaene, 2011b, p. 20

Sebastian Seung, author of the best-selling book *Connectome: How the Brain's Wiring Makes Us Who We Are* (2012), explains how the genes we are born with (our genome) are influenced by our environment to make up the unique connections in the brain (our connectome). He asks,

> Do we really have to wait decades before connectomes tell us something about the human brain? Fortunately, no. Our technologies are already powerful enough to see the connections in small chunks of the brain, and even this partial knowledge will be useful. (p. xvi)

Do we really have to wait decades before MBE tells us something about educational practice? Fortunately, no. Giants in the field of educational neuroscience, like Stanislas Dehaene who studies reading and math in the brain, argue against the "bridge too far" notion separating education and neuroscience: As Dehaene writes, "Considerable cognitive neuroscience knowledge is already highly relevant to education" (2011, p. 19).

We have a great deal of evidence in some areas so we can begin to make recommendations to teachers, if and when we remember our first professional rule, which we share with physicians: *Do no harm.* The first thing we teachers must learn to do is evaluate the quality of the evidence before leaping into popular methodologies, trends, or activity books that have no scientific backing and which, indeed, may do harm. This book purposefully goes from the classroom evidence—interventions that positively impact student learning outcomes—to the lab (neuroscience and psychology studies), and extends the invitation to review both classroom and lab findings by uniting efforts in the MBE spirit.

> *It is in the realm of discovery that science becomes a direct partner of imagination.*
> —Hoover, 1984, p. 11

This book is a humble effort to contribute to Mind, Brain, and Education's search for better classroom practices. I believe MBE science seeks to demonstrate how the collective body of evidence from the three parent fields supports educational intervention. The field continues to advance: In years it is still an adolescent, and though it is not yet full-grown, it continues to mature since its birth around 1997. In the past, each of MBE's three parent fields worked on their own and rarely shared their theories with each other. Today, the information-based exchange means that each field researches similar topics or educational questions, but, again, does so with its own methodology. In the future it is hoped that people from the three parent fields can work in a coordinated way to share the task of research design and then execute experiments that will unite MBE even further.

Under the best conditions, we would be able to find professionals from different fields who have the time to work together and can conduct appropriate studies that can be replicated in different contexts. They would then pass the first hurdle by designing elegant experiments involving humans, sometimes hard due to ethical issues (Alderson & Morrow, 2006; Xue, 2013), especially related to children (Morrow & Richards, 1996). They would then be able to resolve the great challenge of confirming the validity of findings in natural contexts (as in classroom settings) versus confined to the lab (Pellegrini, Symons, & Hoch, 2013; Uprichard, 2010). Finally, in the best of all worlds they would not only demonstrate academic rigor in their experiments, but also be able to replicate the study and control for the participants' individual differences (Ary, Jacobs, Razavieh, & Sorensen, 2010). Although daunting, the aforementioned challenges are surmountable.

Finding professionals from neuroscience, psychology, and education who share a common research goal is tricky but not impossible, and good research design can be born of this collaboration. This could occur through a "research school" design, for example, in which regular classrooms convert to lab settings (Dressen & Tillmanns, 2010; Hinton, & Fischer, 2010; Schwartz & Gerlach, 2011a, 2011b), or by specifically devising encounters that facilitate research opportunities among these professionals (Fischer, Goswami, & Geake, 2010). Although not numerous, there are initiatives that manage to apply this admirable research-practice protocol. For example, Donna Coch at Dartmouth's Reading Brains Lab spends a great deal of time helping classroom teachers gain a better understanding of neuroscience and how knowledge of the reading brain can improve learning. Teachers are shown how children's phonemic awareness works in the brain and are introduced to interventions that help develop neural networks key to reading. Teachers get to watch how children who use a computer-assisted intervention attain higher scores on phonemic awareness tests and, as a result, read at a faster rate than their peers (Arendal & Mann, 2000; see also Gabrieli, Christodoulou, O'Loughlin, & Eddy, 2010, for a teacher-oriented discussion on reading and the brain).

Neuroscientists, psychologists, and teachers can work to devise and test learning interventions, but such tests are costly at many levels. Perfectly isolating variables in classroom settings is complex if not impossible, and replicating studies outside of the lab is a nearly futile endeavor. This means we live in an educational world that appreciates scientific rigor (Feuer, Towne, & Shavelson, 2002), but also understands the messiness of the classroom (Kincheloe & Berry, 2007). This is the MBE challenge.

MBE also faces the challenge that scientific experimentation requires a great deal of human and lab resources, not to mention time—several decades, in fact, if we were to adhere to the strictest of protocols. To complicate things, even in elegant experimentation results are subject to the influence of unanticipated factors. While most scientists don't begin experimentation expecting errors, we must humbly accept that these mishaps actually advance science in their own way. While scientific rigor must remain the goal, countries can ill afford to wait for a level of perfection in educational studies before embarking on desperately needed changes in the classroom—they also cannot experiment with children's lives irresponsibly. The solution is to take steps that allow for progress but do not compromise the fundamental goals or standards of MBE.

The practical classroom applications noted here should be considered high-priority recommendations for rigorous MBE experimentation to be conducted as close to the "perfect world" of experimental design as possible. For example, this book shares high-quality evidence supporting the use of "spaced versus massed practice" (spreading out concepts over time versus teaching them all together), which exists separately in the fields of neuroscience, psychology, and education (more details on this in Chapter 4). The next step in the evolving MBE methodology would be to call on neuroscientists, psychologists, and educators to work together to design an experiment in a real classroom setting to reconfirm what has been proven by each field separately and to determine the best way to apply these findings in educational contexts to maximize the potential for learning (Daniel, 2012).

The educational practices suggested here are derived from current evidence and are the best guesses we currently have based on the most modern research at hand, but like doctors whose practice is upgraded yearly by new scientific discoveries, we should also be open to a continual renewal of our labor. The reader should rest assured that the educational recommendations in this book are solid, but that the explanations of why and how each practice works may evolve thanks to advances in technology. For example, improved neuroimaging may tell us a new story tomorrow about variations in the precise neural circuits being used or the exact balance of neurotransmitters implicated in a specific stage of learning. If and when this new information is added, teachers should embrace and celebrate the ways science is refining and reaffirming our knowledge about how the brain learns and how best to teach based on their contributions to pedagogy. A very young scientist friend of mine (she is 11) recently wrote:

> When a good scientist finds evidence that disproves an old theory or understanding, he or she might use the new evidence to draw new conclusions about the topic. In the world today, some people don't update their information just because they are afraid to admit that they may have been wrong. If we want to advance as a society, we can't hold onto our old beliefs just to be right. Instead, re-examining what we once thought to be true can give a new dimension to an accepted idea, which helps us progress. (Nora Yang, age 11, 2013)

To be true educational professionals, we should actively look for new research in cognitive neuroscience, question its worth in the classroom, reflect on our practices, and modify our teaching if merited. Becoming a serious teacher research-practitioner in MBE means becoming a steward of good science while retaining the mystique of our craft: embracing the science in the art of teaching.

The research compiled here should be considered an offering from education to neuroscience as a list of experiments for MBE. We "know" what works in education, we "know" what's proven in the lab, and when we confirm this in collaborative studies in the future, we will "know" this together as the field of MBE.

Introduction

Who dares to teach must never cease to learn.
—John C. Dana

This book aims to send three messages.

First, to a certain extent, **almost everything we do in teaching works**. This phenomenon was identified by John Hattie, who coined the term *visible learning* after completing a 15-year comparison of over 50,000 studies involving more than 240 million students from around the world to determine which factors impact achievement (2012). His subsequent work with Anderman (2013), an international comparative look at student achievement, confirmed the fact that nearly everything we do in school helps a bit, but only a few things have a major impact on learning. Hattie, director of the Education Research Institute at the University of Melbourne, Australia, and honorary professor at the University of Auckland, is "possibly the world's most influential education academic" and "has the ear of governments everywhere" (Evans, 2012, para. 1). Colleagues around the world have praised his work as a masterful piece of educational research; the *Times Educational Supplement* in London even called it "Education's Holy Grail" (Hattie, 2009). Hattie has changed the direction of priorities in education, and teachers as well as policy makers will be talking about him for many years to come.

Hattie identified evidence for 150 influences on learning, which he ranked by "effect sizes," or the relative impact each has on learning. His study included almost every imaginable factor that can influence whether or not a child learns successfully, including socioeconomic status, the size of the school, a child's birth weight, teacher self-efficacy, student self-perception, the role of parents, the use of different teaching methodologies, teacher training programs, early interventions, and the role of feedback. He placed these influences on a comparable scale, which allows educators to make important choices. To many people's surprise, Hattie's analysis shows that the majority of influences are positive overall. Out of 150 different influences, 145 improve student learning; almost everything works! Only summer vacations (the long time between learning moments), welfare policies (which both unfairly lock kids into certain school structures and give them a poor sense of self-esteem), retention (which labels students losers and keeps them from believing in themselves as learners), television (which has a negative influence because of content, but also because it takes time away from more intellectual activities), and mobility (changing schools disrupts a student's focus on her studies) had negative effect sizes. In an extreme interpretation of these findings, this means that by simply sitting in a classroom and getting older over a school year, a student is bound to learn! So, if everything works, shouldn't we just relax? We can't go *that* amiss if 96% of our options work right?

Wrong! Even though almost everything we do in teaching works to an extent, certain actions, activities, methodologies, and policies work *better* than others. As educators, we need to make choices based on which influences have the *greatest* impact for the *most* students and use the *least* amount of resources. Such a selection will lead to better learning for *more* students *most* of the time. As policy makers, we need to invest our resources in the best places possible (Roediger & Pyc, 2012). David Daniel argues that one way to approach this challenge is with an MBE filter: "Policy-makers and educators should insist upon evidence of effectiveness before investing time and resources to 'improve' educational practice" (2012, p. 251).

Second, in order to make better choices in classroom design, **teachers need to know not only what works, but also *why* things work**. As teachers, we're often so enthusiastic and so caring that we're willing to try just about anything to help our students. Consequently, we may indiscriminately choose activities based on fad, despite having little evidence showing that they actually work (Carter & Wheldall, 2008). We need to have more scruples than that. In no other profession are practitioners allowed to experiment in the field without evidence, so why should it be acceptable for teachers to do so? Think of doctors, architects, judges, police officers, soldiers, sales managers, bankers—none are allowed to execute their profession without training and an understanding of the "why" behind each of their selected actions. A doctor gives a certain remedy over another because he has a reason that can be justified to the patient. Judges make decisions based on case precedents. Teachers need to be similarly accountable. Fortunately, guidelines for good teaching have never been more numerous, and learning to teach has never been clearer. Doug Lemov, managing director of Uncommon Schools, has confessed that after observing hundreds of great teachers, he has realized that "what look[s] like natural-born genius [is] often deliberate technique in disguise" (Green, 2010, para. 12)—giving us hope that all teachers can contribute to elaborating the profession in their own way, with guidance.

Third, while intuitively known for years, there is now substantial evidence that **the single greatest factor that impacts student learning is teacher quality**. This means that student learning outcomes are not necessarily reliant on costly or policy-dependent choices for new texts, afterschool programs, or expensive technological adaptations to classrooms; high-quality teachers, rather, make for high-quality learning (Nye, Konstantopoulous, & Hedges, 2004), an investment well worth the money. This book accepts that there are no shortcuts (Esquith, 2003, 2007) or magical answers, but also acknowledges that there are dozens of things each of us can do—starting today—to improve the quality of the teaching profession.

What Is Mind, Brain, and Education Science?

Leslie Hart wrote back in 1983 that designing educational experiences without knowledge of the brain is like designing a glove without knowledge of the hand (or a car without knowledge of engines, or a windmill without knowledge of wind—you get the picture) (Hart, 1999). When educators, cognitive neuroscientists, and psychologists became interested in better understanding how to join forces to develop better teaching interventions, Mind, Brain, and Education (MBE) science was born. Fischer and colleagues argue that "[t]he primary goal of the emerging field of Mind, Brain, and Education is to join biology, cognitive science, development, and education in order to create a sound grounding of education in research" (Fischer, Daniel, et al., 2007, p. 3), and hopefully result in the ability to teach more efficiently and more effectively.

The combination of visions from neuroscience, psychology, and education has been referred to by different names, such as *brain-based education* (Caine & Nummela-Caine, 1997; Nummela-Caine & Caine, 1998), *educational neuroscience* (Ablin, 2008; Connell, 2005; Geake, 2000, 2005; Jacobson, 2000; Varma, McCandliss, & Schwartz, 2008), *educational psychology* (Pressley & McCormick, 1995; Schunk, 1998; Zanker, 2005), *cognitive neuropsychology* (Caramazza & Coltheart, 2006; Coltheart, 2004; A. Martin & Caramazza, 2003); *cognitive neuroscience* (Ansari, 2005; Ansari & Coch, 2006; Atherton, 2002, 2005, 2011; Berninger & Corina, 1998; Byrnes & Fox, 1998; Friederici & Ungerleider, 2005; Katzir & Paré-Blagoev, 2006), *neuroeducation* (Ansari, DeSmedt, & Grabner, 2012; Battro, Fischer, & Léna, 2008; Fischer, Daniel, et al., 2007; Howard-Jones & Fenton, 2011: Sheridan, Zinchenko, & Gardner, 2005), and even *neuroconstructivism* (Karmiloff-Smith, 2009; Westermann et al., 2007). The decision to call this exciting new field Mind, Brain, and Education science came out of a consensus building activity by a panel of experts from the three parent fields back in 2008 (Tokuhama-Espinosa, 2008, 2010, 2011) and is now embraced by practitioners around the globe (see Stein & Fischer, 2011, for a summary of this evolution).

At the end of the 1990s and beginning of the 21st century, national movements in governments and universities in the United States, India, France, Spain, Japan, Italy, Holland, Australia, the United Kingdom, Japan, Germany, France, Argentina, Canada, and Mexico, as well as transnational organizations like the Organisation for Economic Co-operation and Development (OECD) (2002, 2007a, 2007b), advanced the links between brain science and education through a series of meetings, publications, and open-forum debates. Commentaries about this important relationship began to emerge with force in the early 2000s (Ansari, 2005; Ansari & Coch, 2006; Blakemore & Frith, 2007; Byrnes, 2007; Christoff, 2008; Ferrari & Vuletic, 2009; Fischer, 2009; Fischer, Daniel, et al., 2007; Geake, 2005, 2009; Goswami, 2004, 2006; Hinton & Fischer, 2008; Kuhn & Dean, 2004; McNamara, 2006; Meissner, 2006; OECD, 2002, 2007a, 2007b; Pickering & Howard-Jones, 2007; Rose, 2005; Stein & Fischer, 2011; Wolfe, 2001). In 2008, when I completed my doctoral dissertation, I was privileged to count on the feedback of a Delphi panel comprising 28 top professionals in MBE science from eight different countries, almost equally balanced between neuroscientists, educators, and psychologists. This group of experts, which agreed to work together to form consensus and pass judgment on concepts in education, helped define the goals of Mind, Brain, and Education science (see Appendix D for a list of research, practice, and policy goals in MBE agreed upon in 2008). Recommendations for "a first course in Mind, Brain, and Education" for educators have been forthcoming (Blake & Gardner, 2007), but they have steered away from content recommendations and focused more on the *type of knowledge* a teacher practicing MBE should have (see Blake & Gardner, 2007; Immordino-Yang, 2013). This book aims to go beyond offering general knowledge and provide *specific suggestions* about how to make classrooms better.

Complex, but Not Necessarily Complicated
MBE uses evidence gathered equally from the classroom and the laboratory to improve learning outcomes. MBE begins with the premise that problems in education are complex, and therefore that they require responses that can be gleaned from a transdisciplinary perspective

rather than from education alone. If teaching were easy, we wouldn't have the number of challenges we do in our classrooms, nor would there be a global crisis in education (as evidenced by the fact that almost every country on earth is now undertaking some kind of "educational reform") (Robinson, 2010). MBE scientists can be educators, neuroscientists, or psychologists, but they differ in their vocabulary, and the perspective of each parent discipline is strengthened when augmented and legitimized by the other two fields.

MBE knowledge saves time and money in educational planning and helps teachers become more successful in their practice. For problem solving, MBE science is more precise and more efficient than education alone because it improves both diagnosis of what a student needs and identification of how best to teach her. As a result, teaching is more gratifying, personalized, and professional (using evidence-based practice rather than simple gut feelings). Some great teachers are already MBE scientists, not because they have been formally trained, but rather because of their experience and meticulous practice.

It's important to remember, however, that while MBE makes things clearer, it does not make them easier, primarily because this new field is out to celebrate—not lament—the complex ways human beings learn. Instead of giving simplistic answers, MBE asks teachers to consider the many facets of the teaching-learning process and the multitude of influences upon them. For this reason, subfields of MBE study aspects of teaching and learning as diverse as chronobiology (how one's internal time clock influences learning), affect, motivation, nutrition, metacognition, executive functioning, aging, and skills sets (reading and math in the brain), among many others. The human brain, the organ of all our learning, is not simple, so the teaching-learning interface can't be simplistic. However, all teachers have the potential to be MBE scientists with the knowledge now available to them.

Levels of Analysis

It is important to recognize that good teaching practice can come from pedagogy alone. It can also be born of an interdisciplinary view, such as combining psychology with education (educational psychology) or neuroscience with psychology (neuropsychology). However, the transdisciplinary approach espoused in MBE offers a higher probability of success than methodologies born of just one field (Daniel, 2012; Howard-Jones, 2007). This means that a teaching methodology backed by all three parent fields yields a much higher probability of success than methodologies or activities supported by just one or two of the fields. Current research points to clear guidelines for best-practice teaching, which is the main focus of this book.

FIGURE I.1
Principles and Tenets of Mind, Brain, and Education Science

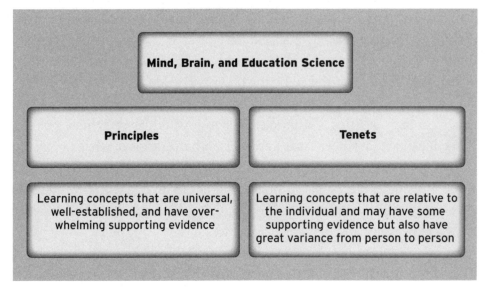

Using Mind, Brain, and Education Science to Structure Learning

Together with the Delphi panel I have categorized education concepts based on recommendations from the OECD's *Understanding the Brain: The Birth of a New Learning Science* (2007b), labeling them as either "well-established concepts," "probably so," "intelligent speculation," or "neuromyths." Concepts in the "well-established" and "probably so" categories helped us to arrive at the main principles and tenets of Mind, Brain, and Education (MBE) science.

Both principles and tenets are vital for learning, but there is one important difference between them (Figure I.1). *Principles* are learning concepts that are important in mostly the same way for all learners across the lifespan. For example, the idea that "all new learning is based on past experience" is a principle. *Tenets*, on the other hand, are relative to each individual. For example, sleep is important for learning, but the amount of sleep needed varies from individual to individual. While both principles and tenets are key to learning how to teach better, individual human variance means we can't prescribe cookie-cutter recommendations to all people in the same way, as we will see in the coming chapters.

Unified, the principles and tenets define *instructional guidelines* of the field (Figure I.2). In the coming chapters, we will look at what has happened in the fast-changing world of MBE science over the past decade and how this points to the most efficient teaching methods possible. Finally, to ground these explanations in reality, we will need to keep the context of each individual learner in mind.

FIGURE I.2
Instructional Guidelines of Mind, Brain, and Education Science

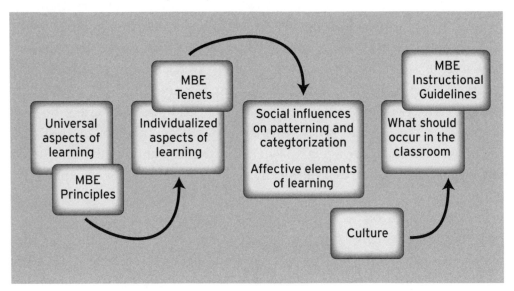

Keeping Things in Perspective

Most positive educational outcomes are the result of a combination of three elements: strong learning communities, great teachers, and the influence of a student's own biology. Almost every important indicator used to measure learning outcomes and success in schools can fit into one of these three categories.

Strong Learning Communities
Some kids are lucky enough to be brought up in strong learning communities—communities with close school-home collaboration, innovative school structures, and firm societal or communal values (Cotton, 2000). A community's support of education improves the quality of an individual's experience in school. Take, for example, the impact of the Harlem Children's Zone program, which approaches education holistically and involves not only schools, but also

other social services that contribute to community building. Or consider Finnish and Japanese home-school-community endeavors to deliver the single, unified message that education is important. These models show that when the school, home, and community all send kids the same communication about the worth of education, they respond positively. The development of shared values, including the importance of education, is vital to providing the right conditions for learning. The community also reflects another factor that influences learning: culture.

The impact of culture on learning is finally getting due attention in MBE. Ansari (2012) notes that it is only recently that the study of brain plasticity has moved from the individual-experience level to a consideration of cross-cultural psychological perspectives. The culture a person grows up in impacts the ways she can learn (Chiao & Ambady, 2010). Advances in cultural neuroscience—defined as "an interdisciplinary field that investigates the relationship between culture (e.g., value and belief systems and practices shared by groups) and human brain functions" (Han et al., 2013, p. 335)—have shown that **a child's environment can actually change gene potentiation and physically reshape her brain**. For example, studies have revealed that number processing in the brains of people who use Arabic numbers differs from number processing in the brains of those who use symbol systems such as Chinese and Japanese (Tang et al., 2006). Neither group is "better" at number processing; they just use slightly different neuronal pathways to perform math and reading. This could mean that these populations should be taught in different ways to take advantage of the brain's natural processing.

There is also evidence that there are cultural differences in neural processing of visual stimuli, such as faces and houses (Goh et al., 2010), as well as significant cultural variances in reactions to other people's emotional states (De Greck et al., 2012). This phenomenon takes on great importance when coupled with the idea that there is no decision without emotion, as we will see in the coming chapters. The general speculation is that "sustained experiences may affect both brain structure and function . . . [and] it is quite reasonable to posit that sustained exposure to a set of cultural experiences and behavioral practices will affect neural structure and function" (Park & Huang, 2010, p. 391). The community a child grows up in shapes not only her values concerning education but also her threshold for stress, her openness to novelty and new learning, her reactions to emotional stimuli in the classroom, and her brain's preparedness for different types of learning.

What can we learn from these studies? Cultural neuroscience is still in its infancy, and we really don't know how subtle differences in neuronal processing interact with societal expectations and with a child's own biology to change how she learns school subjects. But what these studies *do* suggest is that a child brought up in, for example, India, may start her schooling with a potential for certain learning that a child in Bolivia may not have, and vice versa. Culture can influence learning on the biological level, because practices over time by a group of people can predispose their offspring to learn in certain ways. This has numerous implications in school settings across the United States and Europe, in which more children in our classrooms come from what were once considered "minority" groups than from those considered the "majority" group (Memmott, 2012; U.S. Department of Commerce, Census Bureau, 2010). To improve education we need to be aware of how culture can impact learning, but MBE reminds us that there are some aspects of learning that are actually "universal" and work the same for all humans. This means that we should not only be aware of cultural differences in teaching, but also be open to new ideas from abroad that might complement practices in different community settings as they will likely be successful, independent of country of origin.

For example, it came to light that a new math curriculum design in Singapore had excellent results in teaching core math concepts, not only in Singapore but also abroad. After analysis, it was found that the Singapore math model places strong emphasis on problem solving, model drawing, and in-depth understanding of a few essential math skills, which is in sharp contrast to the belabored, wordy explanations of U.S. math texts. The concept that "depth is better than breadth" is a core MBE teaching guideline (Schwartz, Sadler, Sonnert, & Tai, 2009). There is evidence that deep revision of process-based learning is better than superficial review of the same process (Otten, Henson, & Rugg, 2001; Schellenberg, Negishi, & Eggen, 2011). The switch to the Singapore model has yielded favorable results for thousands of students, and the U.S. National Mathematics Advisory Panel has recommend adopting an even greater number of these successful practices as more and more research has come in (National Mathematics Advisory Panel, 2008). This cross-cultural adaptation of teaching methods—which in this case points to a universal "number sense" in all human beings (Dehaene, 2011)—is an example of the types of new methods included in this book that celebrate MBE's not only transdisciplinary, but also intercultural, approach to the teaching-learning process.

Great Teachers

An undisputed point in educational literature is that **the teacher is the single most influential factor in student learning** (see Educational Research Service, 2000; Hattie 2009, 2012; or Marzano, Pickering, & Pollock, 2001, for more details). We also know that that the teacher as a personality and his skills as an instructor override the importance of the subject matter because learning to think can occur in all courses. Most factors in daily educational practices have merely a slight impact on student learning; only high-quality teaching has a profound, long-term effect. Elizabeth Green (2010) reported in the *New York Times* that,

> When researchers ran the numbers in dozens of different studies, every factor under a school's control produced just a tiny impact, except for one: which teacher the student had been assigned to. Some teachers could regularly lift their students' test scores above the average for children of the same race, class and ability level. Others' students [are] left with below-average results year after year. William Sanders, a statistician studying Tennessee teachers with a colleague, found that a student with a weak teacher for three straight years would score, on average, 50 percentile points behind a similar student with a strong teacher for those years. Teachers working in the same building, teaching the same grade produced very different outcomes. And the gaps were huge. Eric Hanushek, a Stanford economist, found that while the top 5 percent of teachers were able to impart a year and a half's worth of learning to students in one school year, as judged by standardized tests, the weakest 5 percent advanced their students only half a year of material each year. (para. 4)

This means that although the home and other community institutions support the educational experience, the greatest hope for cultivating good thinking skills and lifelong learning lies with teachers. But what does a great teacher look like?

Corbett and Wilson (2002) found that, when asked, urban students described six basic qualities of good teachers: "Good teachers push students, maintain order, [are] willing to help, explain until everyone understands, vary classroom activities, and try to understand students," (p.18). Jaime Escalante—whose story was portrayed in the film *Stand and Deliver*—is an example of an outstanding teacher. An immigrant who worked in the poorer parts of East Los Angeles, Escalante managed to elevate the level of his students' performance through sheer hard work and enthusiasm. He communicated to his students the belief that intelligence is fluid, that hard work pays off, and that their brains were malleable and all of them could learn—something they had never heard from a teacher before. Escalante unknowingly applied one of the fundamental rules of MBE practice: Believe in your students' ability to learn. A corresponding, more subtle premise of great teaching is that a student's belief in her own ability to learn plays a great role in her actual level of execution in the learning process (Hattie, 2012). Escalante succeeded because he elevated his students' own belief in their potential to be learners.

Because teaching is a relatively "lonesome" profession in the U.S.—each teacher faces his class without much peer support—most of us appreciate the romantic notion of lone vigilante-style heroes who are forced to go against the general trends in their schools or neighborhoods and manage to change the lives of students along the way. Countless films have hinged on narratives about successful, often unorthodox teachers: Robin Williams's John Keating in *Dead Poets Society*; Sidney Poitier's Mark Thackeray in *To Sir, with Love*; Julia Roberts's Katherine Watson in *Mona Lisa Smile*; Morgan Freeman's Joe Clark in *Lean on Me*; Sandy Dennis's Sylvia Barrett in *Up the Down Staircase*; and Hilary Swank's Erin Gruwell in *Freedom Writers*—to name just a few. Inspirational teachers like Miss Riley (played by Laura Dern) in *October Sky*, Louanne Johnson (Michelle Pfeiffer) in *Dangerous Minds*, Ron Clark (Matthew Perry) in *The Ron Clark Story*, Melvin B. Tolson (Denzel Washington) in *The Great Debaters*, Ken Carter (Samuel L. Jackson) in *Coach Carter*, and William Hundert (Kevin Kline) in *The Emperor's Club* make us cheer as we recognize the inner strength that helps them bring out the potential in their students.

But the aim of this book is to spark a paradigm shift in our conception of the great teacher: **We don't have to do it alone, against the system, to effectively change students' lives.** While there are examples of high-quality teachers who can, without the help of supportive schools or communities, make an impact on student learning, this doesn't have to be the norm. Instead, taking the lead from other successful countries around the world, we can learn as communities to give teachers the strong support they need to provide quality teaching and in turn foster better learning (Senge et al., 2000). To do this, we need to start on an individual level by examining our own attitudes about teaching. We have to believe, as Escalante did, that everyone can learn, given the right circumstances.

Biology

Teachers and their communities undoubtedly influence learning. But learning also hinges on a third factor: biology. In the not-too-distant past, we blamed many learning problems, like ADHD, on behavior or lack of mental discipline. Thankfully, we now understand that some kids are born with physiological differences in their brains that affect the way they take in information (see Levine, 2004, for examples). We now know that a child with dyslexia is not lazy; she has a differently structured brain. Rather than blaming or punishing children for these physiological differences, we now strive to help them learn about plasticity and ways of using their brain most effectively.

But biology goes beyond the brain's wiring. It also relates to the mind-body connection, including all aspects of nutrition, sleep, and exercise. Kids who are poorly nourished at home come to school at a disadvantage through no fault of their own; they have to fill in the gaps despite not being directly responsible for their unpreparedness to learn (Glewwe, Jacoby, & King, 2001; McCabe, 2012; Vance, Roberson, McGuineess, & Fazeli, 2010). Teenagers who are half asleep during classes because of early school start times or because their parents don't enforce bedtime curfews aren't able to learn to their potential and can enter a downward spiral, falling further and further behind in their studies (Menna-Barreo & Wey, 2008; Wolfson & Carskadon, 1998). Children who come from broken homes or live in high-stress environments are also at a disadvantage for learning (Conrad & Wolf, 2010). Violent neighborhoods, parental abuse, and family structures in which kids have to care for younger siblings all contribute to stress and anxiety that make learning difficult (Shonkoff & Phillips, 2000). The environment a student lives in can influence her biology and therefore her potential to learn. But this is a two-way street, our genes determine how areas of our brains are wired and react to the environment as well.

The powerful role of our genetic make-up has received a great deal of popular press lately (e.g., Azar, 2002; Hamer & Copeland, 1999; Wright, 1999). Some of these books claim we can't help but be slave to our genes. However, as Nelkin (1995) wrote in a famous *New York Times* article meant to stave off enthusiasm for blaming one's genes for unwanted behavior, **biology is not destiny**. People can be born with a genetic predisposition toward certain behavior—becoming an alcoholic, having ADHD, getting a stroke later in life, becoming a concert pianist, or mass murderer—but their lifestyles can influence the potentiation of that genetic makeup. Our actions can have more influence than our genes. Learning is a behavior, and behaviors are responses to stimuli in the environment or to internal triggers of memories of external stimuli. They can be conscious or unconscious. Behaviors—including learning—that are repeated over time lead to habituation. This means that learning processes can be modified, which points to a key assumption of this book: **Intelligence is fluid**. The brain is highly plastic and changes daily with experience, even if behavioral changes may take far longer to appear. Just because someone is born with a slightly different kind of brain does not mean she is condemned to a certain type of life; everyone can and does learn. That said, it takes a special teacher to know how to help each student reach his or her potential.

What's to Come?

Part I provides an overview of teaching from an MBE perspective by providing a map for traveling "from the classroom to the lab and back."

Chapter 1 is devoted to explaining the mind frame of a teacher who traverses the "middle way" between the classroom and the lab and confirms hunches in education with hard science. This chapter reviews the fundamental aspects of Mind, Brain, and Education science, including the well-established concepts, principles, tenets, and instructional guidelines, which are based on research conducted with leading experts in this new field around the world. This opening chapter also speaks directly to the challenge of crossing the "bridge too far" between the lab and the classroom and gives examples of brave professionals who are already doing this.

Chapter 2 presents the reader with a summary of the most important influences on student learning outcomes as determined by the most exhaustive study in the history of education. John Hattie's list of influences on student learning outcomes is synthesized into 10 evidence-based categories of key influences on student learning, which the reader is asked to embrace and use as a new framework for thinking about teaching.

With this framework in mind, we turn in *Chapter 3* to global perspectives about the role of formal education. This chapter argues that the purpose of formal education is to develop lifelong thinkers, not just students who pass tests. By thinking within the new MBE framework, we can advance this goal more effectively and more efficiently in terms of time and resources. Some of the most influential teaching models to date are summarized to show how the best ways to think about education have existed for several decades but have not yet been universally applied.

Part II shares 50 classroom influences that impact student learning outcomes as established by evidenced-based research in education, specifically John Hattie's *Visible Learning* (2009, 2012). Each influence has been filtered through research in cognitive neuroscience, psychology, and education, which collectively constitute Mind, Brain, and Education science. Finally, only the most important influences that contribute to better thinking skills have been included in order to reflect the qualities most in demand as established by 21st-century learning goals. By joining MBE, *Visible Learning*, and the great thinking frameworks of our time, this book shares some of the best evidence-based practices known to date.

Chapter 4 explains the filters that can be used to sort the wheat from the chaff in good teaching, and applies a *backward design* approach (Wiggins & McTighe, 2005) to show how the planning, evaluation, and execution of teaching relate to specific MBE best practices. These fundamental filters don't prescribe exact classroom activities, but rather offer teachers a guide for judging the quality of their own actions against clear criteria. We then move to the heart of the matter: what has always worked in classroom and why (**Chapter 5**), and then what *could* work and why, if teachers and administrators could just move beyond their comfort zones (**Chapter 6**).

The MBE + Visible Learning combination yields clear guidelines for a best-practice approach to classroom influences that we as teachers can control. But as good critical thinkers, we need to keep an open mind and accept that science is dynamic and that there are new discoveries in the field each day. The information in this book is the best available to date, but we have to remember to always stay alert to new scientific discoveries that can influence our actions in the classroom and to make careful decisions about how to apply them in the teaching-learning context. Welcome to a new era in teaching.

Suggested Readings and Videos

John Hattie's Visible Learning

Hattie, J. (2009). *Visible learning: A synthesis of over 800 meta-analyses relating to achievement.* London, UK: Routledge.
Hattie, J. (2012). *Visible learning for teachers: Maximizing impact on learning.* New York, NY: Routledge.
Hattie, J., & Anderman, E. M. (2013). *International guide to student achievement.* New York, NY: Routledge.

Excellent Community Education Initiatives

Geoffrey Canada's Harlem Children's Zone
Harlem Children's Zone: www.hcz.org/hcz-home.php
Schorn, D. (Writer), & Bradley, E. (Reporter). (2009, February 11). The Harlem Children's Zone: How one man's vision to revitalize Harlem starts with children [Television broadcast]. In J. Fager (Executive Producer), *60 Minutes.* New York, NY: CBS.
Tough, P. (2008). *Whatever it takes: Geoffrey Canada's quest to change Harlem and America.* Boston, MA: Houghton Mifflin Harcourt.

Vega, I. (Producer), & Rose, C. (Host & Executive Producer). (2008). A conversation with Geoffrey Canada, president and CEO of the Harlem Children's Zone [Video]. In *Charlie Rose*. New York, NY: PBS. Retrieved April 30, 2013, from http://www.charlierose.com/guest/byname/geoffrey_canada

Japan's Community Learning Initiatives

Hess, R. D., & Azuma, H. (1991). Cultural support for schooling: Contrasts between Japan and the United States. *Educational Researcher, 20*(9), 2–9.

Lewis, C. C. (1995). *Educating hearts and minds: Reflections on Japanese preschool and elementary education*. Cambridge, UK: Cambridge University Press.

Shields, J. J. (2010). *Japanese schooling: Patterns of socialization, equality, and political control*. University Park, PA: Penn State University Press.

Suzuki, S., Holloway, S. D., Yamamoto, Y., & Mindnich, J. D. (2009). Parenting self-efficacy and social support in Japan and the United States. *Journal of Family, 30*(11), 1505–1526.

Finland's Community Learning Initiatives

Sahlberg, P. (2007). Education policies for raising student learning: The Finnish approach. *Journal of Education Policy, 22*(2), 147–171.

Sahlberg, P. (2011 Summer). Lessons from Finland. *American Educator*, 34–38.

Titti, K. (2011). Holistic school pedagogy and values: Finnish teachers' and students' perspectives. *International Journal of Educational Research, 50*, 159–165.

Recommended Films About Great Teaching

Abraham, M., Karsch, A., & O'Neill, M. (Producers), & Hoffman, M. (Director). (2002). *The emperor's club* [Motion picture]. Universal Studios, CA: Universal Studios.

Brockway, J., Bukrons, H., Cox, T., Friend, B., Gilad, A., Jackson, P., . . . Randall, J. (Producers), & Haines, R. (Director). (2006). *The Ron Clark story* [Motion picture]. Atlanta, GA: TNT Drama.

Clavell, J. (Producer & Director). (1967). *To Sir, with love* [Motion picture]. Los Angeles, CA: Columbia Pictures.

DeVito, D., Shamberg, M., & Sherm S. (Producers), & LaGravenese, R. (Director). (2007). *Freedom writers* [Motion picture]. Hollywood, CA: Paramount Pictures.

Evans, B. A., & Sceinman, A. (Producers), & Reiner, R. (Director). (1986). *Stand by me* [Motion picture]. Los Angeles, CA: Columbia Pictures.

Gale, D., Robbins, B., & Tollin, M. (Producers), & Carter, T. (Director). (2005). *Coach Carter* [Motion picture]. Hollywood, CA: MTV Films, Tollin&Robbins Productions, Paramount Pictures.

Gordon, C., & Franco, L. J. (Producers), & Johnston, J. (Director). (1999). *October sky* [Motion picture]. Universal City, CA: Universal Pictures.

Haft, S., Junger Witt, P., & Thomas, T. (Producers), & Weir, P. (Director). (1989). *Dead Poets Society* [Motion Picture]. Burbank, CA: Walt Disney Studios, Touchstone Pictures.

Johanson, F. (Producer), & Newell, M. (Director). (2003). *Mona Lisa's smile* [Motion picture]. Hollywood, CA: Revolution Studios.

Mauvernay, N., Perrin, J., Jugnot, G., & Cohn, A. (Producers), & Barratier, C. (Director). (2004). *The chorus* [Motion picture]. France: Pathé.

Mulligan, R. (Producer & Director), & Pakula, A. J. (Producer). (1967). *Up the down staircase* [Motion picture]. Burbank, CA: Warner Brothers.

Simpson, D., & Bruckheimer, J. (Producers), & Smith, J. N. (Director). *Dangerous minds* [Motion picture]. Hollywood, CA: Hollywood Pictures.

Twain, N. (Producer), & Avildsen, J. G. (Director). (1989). *Lean on me* [Motion picture]. Burbank, CA: Warner Brothers.Bender, L. (Producer), & Van Sant, G. (Director). (1997). *Good Will hunting* [Motion picture]. New York, NY: Miramax Films.

Winfrey, O., Roth, J., Black, T., Weinstein, B., & Weinstein, H. (Producers), & Washington, D. (Director). (2007). *The great debaters* [Motion picture]. Chicago, IL: Harpo Productions.

Making Classrooms Better

PART I

From the Classroom to the Lab and Back

CHAPTER **1**

Great Minds Don't Think Alike
The Transdisciplinary Mind, Brain, and Education Approach

Different specialty groups approach learning in different ways. If you are a cognitive neuroscientist in the lab, you will probably focus on genes or the biological roots of learning. If you are a psychologist, you will consider behavioral issues. And if you are a teacher, you will watch the child in front of you as he either clicks with an educational method or rejects it. But if you think like an MBE scientist, you will keep all three levels of analysis in mind when planning learning activities.

A Unified Vision

Jacques Cousteau once said, "However fragmented the world, however intense the national rivalries, it is an inexorable fact that we become more interdependent every day" (1981). While Cousteau was talking about national rivalries in the quote above, his message can be useful to teachers. Like Cousteau, who found opposition from people who believed that humans should determine all choices about how to use resources (including other animals), some professional fields think they have the final say on what should be done about challenges in education. Leave the teaching to the teachers is their motto. Why would we want to complicate things and change the way we have approached challenges in education thus far by involving foreign disciplines?

The answer is that, despite approximately 125 years of good intentions in formal education, we have not yet managed to find the "right" answers to meet all kids' needs. **While other professions have evolved and adapted to their times, education has not advanced at a similar pace**. Figure 1.1 makes this strikingly clear.

FIGURE 1.1
Education Is Behind the Times Compared with Other Social Institutions

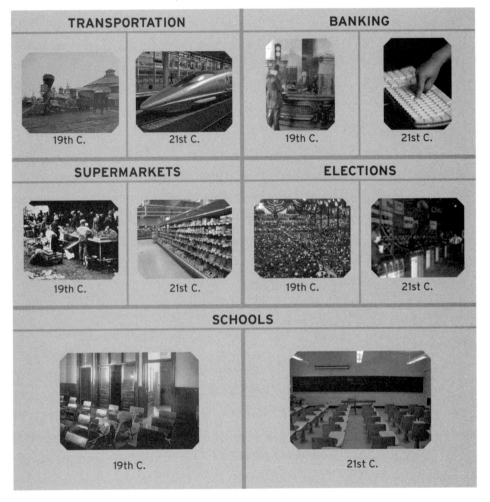

Education has to catch up with other aspects of society, but how? We can continue to attempt educational "reforms," which drag out for years with little significant impact because they are aimed at short-term solutions, or we can take bold steps toward shifting our mindset about education from one-dimensional thinking to the multiple lens of MBE.

We know that separate visions about problems in education have yielded fragmented solutions. Without a unified vision, it is hard to advance. When talking about the challenges of differentiation in the classroom, for example, you will get very distinct responses from a neuroscientist, a psychologist, and an educator (Imbeau & Tomlinson, 2010; Levy, 2008).

Additionally, it is clear that when just one type of educational specialist tries to deal with a child's problem on her own, she may miss something because she is simply not looking for it. But once these professionals unite, they can develop a far more comprehensive solution that considers the whole child, not just his biology, his behavior, or his school marks (Figure 1.2). It is clear that "the way we diagnose our students' condition will determine the kind of remedy we offer" (Palmer, 1998, p. 41).

FIGURE 1.2
Disciplines and Subdisciplines in Mind, Brain, and Education Science

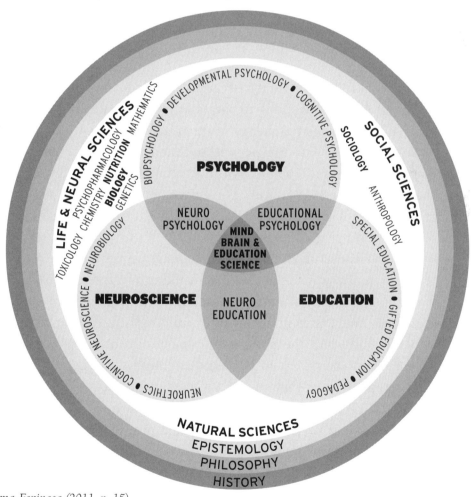

Tokuhama-Espinosa (2011, p. 15).

For example, suppose Alex's math grades suddenly drop drastically in the sixth grade. The school administrator looks within his world and sees that there was a change in the schedule and consequently a change in teachers and timetables. He is sure Alex hasn't adjusted to the earlier-morning math classes or to the teacher. As there is nothing he can really do about this, he leaves Alex to deal with the problem on his own.

A neurologist has a look at Alex's case and, on the mother's recommendation, gathers a history that indicates that Alex has always had concentration problems that have gone undiagnosed. The neurologist prescribes medication for ADD to treat Alex's overlooked attention problem.

The psychologist meets with Alex and finds that what is "really" at the root of the problem is early adolescence settling in, combined with his parents' worsening marital discord. She recommends giving Alex unconditional support along with space and time to ride out the wave of change.

All three specialists have reasons for the decisions they came to, but none is working in concert with the others. A person working in the MBE model would consider *all* the information—the factors affecting Alex's physiology, psychology, and school outcomes. As David Perkins of Harvard's Project Zero likes to note, **without the whole picture there is no whole child** (2010b). Some educators are so obsessed with teaching the child's brain that they miss problems of the heart or weariness in the body. Some neurologists are so focused on the child's biology that they miss psychological symptoms. Psychologists may be so keen to find mental triggers that they miss simple physiological catalysts.

I once knew a woman who spent 20 years suffering from a depressive state that would come and go. She went to numerous psychologists, but none could find a cure. Finally she decided, on her own, to keep a journal of when her depressive episodes took place. There was no correlation between these occurrences and events in her life or encounters with certain people, disproving the psychologists' best guesses about the root cause. Then one day she saw it: Every time she ate wheat bread, she went into a depressive state that lasted several days. The psychologists had been so sure her problem was mental that they never considered a physiological trigger (see Daynes, 1956, for further explanation of wheat sensitivity). An MBE approach would have led to this discovery much sooner, probably sparing the woman decades of depressive incidents.

Similar undiagnosed learning problems are experienced daily in all classrooms around the world. Many excellent teachers instinctually try to integrate different perspectives when they consider the root causes of a child's learning challenges. This book implores these teachers to formalize their practice while hoping to encourage others who may not think holistically to consider this approach. Let's look at another school example.

Angel began kindergarten when he was five years old and started first grade without incident the following year. During kindergarten he appeared to play happily, loved to draw, and enjoyed imaginary games with plastic zoo animals in which he narrated continually. He didn't do well in sports requiring gross motor skills, like soccer, but he enjoyed taking the scooter in endless circles around the yard. When he started first grade, his mother wanted to be sure he was adjusting to the new school setting and took the time to drop him off personally and ask how things were going.

After the first month, the teacher began reporting problems. Angel didn't socialize much. He was deeply introverted and appeared to have limited vocabulary. He couldn't follow simple written directions well. In terms of language, socioemotional development, and gross motor coordination, he seemed to lag behind the majority. Angel's mother became alarmed. Could her son be mentally slower than the other kids? She recalled her poor prenatal diet as a teenage mother and the long and difficult delivery, during which, according to her doctors, Angel had perhaps been briefly deprived of oxygen. She remembered her poor living arrangements in Angel's first years—could he have been exposed to lead or asbestos? Angel's grandmother took a different view. She was sure that Angel's problems were due to the lack of attention his deadbeat father paid to him.

The classroom teacher, however, had another idea. She said although these signs might be indicators of learning problems or psychological issues as the mother and grandmother suggested, it would be wise to rule out other possible causes first. Like eyesight. She suggested that before they go to the school psychologist to see why Angel didn't interact much with the other kids, or to a physical therapist to improve his gross motor skills, they simply have his vision tested. On doing this, they found that Angel was nearly blind in one eye and could see only when objects were presented up close (hence his inability to read written instructions and gauge depth perception with the soccer ball). He couldn't perceive the facial expressions of people unless they were very close to him, and therefore he had awkward social encounters, explaining his poor social skills. Angel's life was changed with the simple acquisition of a pair of glasses.

Knowingly or not, Angel's teacher was following the MBE model: She considered the potential physiological, mental, and pedagogical roots of Angel's problem before jumping to conclusions. And she designed thoughtful and organized stages of intervention before "scaling up" to different levels (Figure 1.3). By looking at the big picture, she spared Angel months of unnecessary treatments that would have led to his being labeled "slow" or "awkward" (Figure 1.4). She literally saved not only his academic future, but his social future as well.

FIGURE 1.3
Scaling Up Interventions Gradually

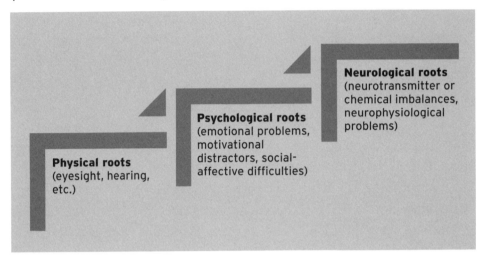

FIGURE 1.4
Results of a Bad Diagnosis

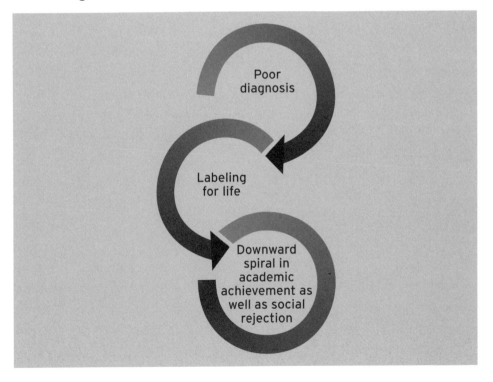

Kids with problems like Angel's are not the only ones who need attention; MBE educators view *all* their students as a priority from those with learning problems to the gifted. The transdisciplinary approach espoused by MBE science (Figure 1.5) offers a higher probability of broad success than methodologies derived from just one or two fields. MBE practitioners know that although good teaching practice can come from pedagogy alone, or be born of a combination of psychology and education ("educational psychology") or neuroscience and psychology ("neuropsychology"), the most effective teachers incorporate information from all of the parent fields to devise the best teaching and learning experiences possible for all students.

FIGURE 1.5
Mind, Brain, and Education Science: A Transdisciplinary Field

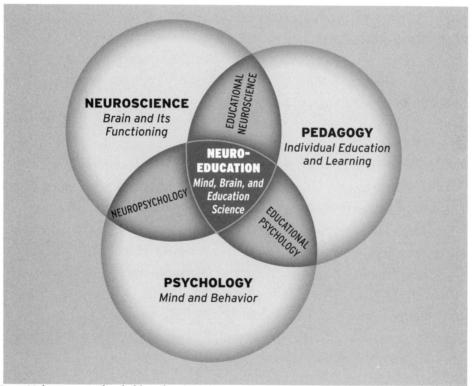

Credit: Dana Nakagawa, Author holds rights (2008).

Catching Up With the Times

Some teachers think they are successful and need not change their methodologies despite the lack of innovation in their practice for decades. MBE educators humbly recognize that the world has changed in the past few decades: Kids are more tech savvy than they were before, and consequently what captures their attention is different than it has been in years past.

Recognizing that attention and its partner, memory, are fundamental to learning, an MBE educator modifies her teaching practices to fit the times—perhaps by using the "flipped" classroom, for example. Developed by visionaries like Eric Mazur of Harvard (1991), Salman Khan of MIT (2012), and Presidential Award for Excellence for Math and Science Teaching recipients Jonathan Bergmann and Aaron Sams (2012), the flipped classroom is a structure in which what normally happens in schools occurs in the home and vice versa. Instead of boring, cookie-cutter deliveries in class where the teacher presumes that all of her students are at the same starting point with the new information, the flipped classroom asks students to learn basic concepts on their own at home through a series of videos or other support materials and then come to class with specific questions about anything they didn't understand (see Noer, 2012, and Tomaszewski, 2012, for more on the flipped classroom).

For example, let's say Madison's class is studying addition (or exponents, or calculus, or irregular verbs, the names of presidents, historical dates, the periodic table, or any other concept taught in schools). In a flipped setting, the teacher asks the students to go home and learn the concept by watching several short videos and then doing the practice questions that follow each video. Madison makes it through all of the assigned videos and answers almost all of the accompanying questions correctly; she seems ready to be evaluated for mastery concepts and move on to the next task, which will apply this basic knowledge. But Kevin, Madison's classmate, makes it through only one of the videos and can answer only about half of the questions correctly. When Madison and Kevin come to class the next day, the teacher can attend to their specific needs. Madison no longer has to sit and be bored—she can move on to more complex concepts. And Kevin won't begin a downward spiral of failure because the class has moved on without him—he can get the remedial help he needs.

From an MBE perspective, there are three main benefits to the flipped classroom. First, it allows for **differentiated instruction**. Each student learns at his or her own pace, and the teacher's role is to fill in conceptual gaps in a very personalized way. This changes the focus of class time from simply "covering" material to mastery learning. As all new learning passes through the filter of past experiences and different kids will have different amounts of previous exposure to prerequisite concepts, flipping is beneficial because it provides just the right amount of practice for each person.

Second, the flipped classroom takes advantage of the **flexible use of technology**. One of the reasons Madison learned so quickly is that she replayed the first video several times and looked at its supplementary material, which gave her a strong basis from which to advance to the second video, and so on. A kid can't replay the teacher's classroom exchanges. Students become more autonomous in their learning when appropriate tools are provided and they choose the steps.

The third benefit of the flipped classroom is that it allows different people to learn at different paces and therefore **improves efficiency of class time use**. Watching videos at home allows students to replay the parts that are hard for them and skip over parts that are easier. Both "faster" and "slower" kids can come to class the next day and use the teacher to help fill in the gaps in a much more differentiated manner and with a better use of contact time.

The flipped classroom, discussed in more depth in Chapter 6, is only one of several teaching methodologies that take into account the way the modern brain wants to learn.

Teacher Training in the Context of Mind, Brain, and Education Science

We have begun moving in the right direction: More and more teacher training programs are promoting MBE ideas, and many teacher certification programs are incorporating crucial knowledge of the brain in the designs they teach. In the past decade alone, Johns Hopkins, Harvard, Dartmouth, the University of Texas at Arlington, Bristol, and UPenn have added study programs in this field. In 2000, it was rare to see graduate work in education that focused on MBE themes, but this has changed in the last decade, as Figure 1.6 shows. In 2011, Zachary Stein and Kurt Fischer of the Graduate Schools of Education at Harvard proudly announced that after a decade of productive advances, the MBE movement was well under way and that the "training of a new generation of educational researchers and practitioners ha[d] begun" (p. 57).

In 2012, Harvard University expanded the MBE vision to include health and devised a course in MBHE (Mind, Brain, Health, and Education) science. This expanded view acknowledges the important role of physical well-being in learning. Others have suggested that even more elements could be integrated into MBE, such as morality of values. The important takeaway from these developments is that transdisciplinary thinking is being prized over individual visions or perceptions of problems in society.

But there is still a long way to go. Although newly qualified teachers receive more and more MBE information, many teachers who have been in the classroom for years have little exposure to it. To reach all teachers, we need to create a better framework within which to conduct best-practice activities.

FIGURE 1.6
Growth in the Mind, Brain, and Education Field Over the Past Decade

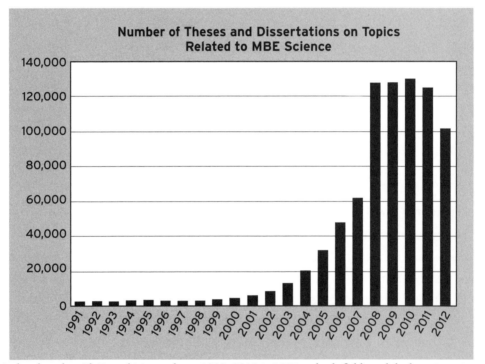

Souce: Author, based on Ph.D. and Master theses 1990–2012 in MBE and sub-fields, and the learning sciences.

Stein and Fischer (2011) suggest thinking about MBE in terms of models that are quality-oriented and interdisciplinary and that marry theory and research with practice. They believe that a key to making MBE more attractive is to offer pragmatic activities and usable knowledge, not just lab experiments with little connection to real students. Fischer and colleagues share this type of information in the *Usable Knowledge* digital newsletter from the Harvard Graduate

School of Education (http://www.uknow.gse.harvard.edu). They remind us that **teacher education is a lifelong process** and takes place not only within classrooms, but also throughout society. Fischer and Stein suggest that, to make a real difference, education must become the center of debate in not only educational circles among teachers, but also among scientists, lawmakers, philosophers, parents, and other stakeholders (2011).

MBE goals have only recently been agreed upon by some members of the field (see Appendix D). The application of evidence-based information framed by MBE concepts is a wonderful objective, but a word of caution is merited here. Scientific research into human learning has yielded clear guidelines about how to teach so that students learn better, but **not everything from the lab yields results worth applying in the classroom**. A little knowledge can be a dangerous thing. Overly broad generalizations, the application of animal studies to humans, and stretching conclusions beyond their intended scope have led to some misguided gestures in the classroom. Teachers need to learn to be critical consumers of "brain-based" information.

Far too many neuromyths continue to be repeated in educator circles (see Table 1.1 for a list of neuromyths still prevalent today). Results of a recent study showed that teachers believed 49% of the neuromyths presented in the survey, "particularly myths related to commercialized educational programs" (Dekker, Lee, Howard-Jones, & Jolles, 2002, para. 1). For example, there are myths about the fixed nature of intelligence, which are born of the misconception that genes determine whether a person excels or not in educational settings. There are other myths about basic brain structure and function based on early brain imaging techniques. These techniques made it appear that people used far fewer areas of their brains. Current, more advanced methods now demonstrate far more elaborate neural networks than could have been imagined a decade ago. Quick-fix teaching methods can also be blamed for other myths, such as the popular idea of teaching to learning styles—as if the human brain preferred one sensory mode to another, or "right brain learners" deserved more attention in the classroom.

Some myths stem from misunderstandings about how the environment influences learning, like the assertions that one's first three years of life or socioeconomic status determine one's future. Some focus on precise mechanisms of the brain, such as misplaced faith in multitasking (Rosen, 2008; also see Deprez et al., 2013, for examples of experiments in this area). Some relate to sensationalist half-truths from the popular press, like the idea that learning creates new brain cells (not true: new synapses, yes, new brain cells, no) or that children are "sponges" and can learn anything if taught before a certain age. Other myths mix philosophical discussions with neuroscience, such as the idea that the soul can be studied through brain scans or spirituality can be measured with an EEG.

We are also brought up with social customs that influence myths about the brain, such as the idea that decisions should be made "with a cool head" and without the influence of emotions—an assertion that has been proven to go against the basic physiology of sensory input in the brain. Beliefs about gender and race have also sparked many myths. The debate still runs strong as to whether boys and girls have different brains (see Fine, 2011, and Gurian & Stevens, 2010, for a sampling), but the harmful effects of insisting on gender-based strengths and deficits to students are clear. Finally, and unfortunately, there are still far too many commercial ventures that take advantage of our love for everything "neuro" and the promise of a better brain. It is human nature to try and get as much with as little as possible. We would all love to be smarter or even raise "baby Einsteins" by playing music or doing a few exercises. Marketing specialists are far more advanced in their trade than we educators; it is up to us to learn to separate the wheat from the chaff, avoid the myths, and apply the high-quality information in neuroscience instead of fads. For MBE practice to really take hold in society, we need to improve "neuroscience literacy" education among teachers in training as well as in teacher in-service programs.

TABLE 1.1
Neuromyths Still Prevalent Now

MYTHS ABOUT INTELLIGENCE
- Mental capacity is hereditary and cannot be changed by the environment or experience.
- Intelligence is fixed: You can't change the brain.

MYTHS ABOUT BRAIN ARCHITECTURE
- Most people use about 10% of their brains.
- The left and right hemispheres of the brain are separate systems for learning. Hemispheric dominance can help explain individual differences among learners. Some people are more "right brained"; others are more "left brained."
- Our brain acts like a video camera; we store and make a memory of everything we see.
- Your brain will shrink if you don't drink six to eight glasses of water a day.
- Alcohol kills brain cells; drug use makes holes in your brain.
- Brain parts work in isolation from one another.

MYTHS ABOUT TEACHING AND LEARNING
- Individuals learn better when they receive information in their preferred learning styles.
- The theory of multiple intelligences is validated by neuroscience research.
- Forget music, the arts, PE—spend more time studying!
- Use lots of the same kinds of math problems (drill and kill).
- High-stakes tests are an accurate measure of what a student knows.

- Learning occurs only in the classroom.

MYTHS ABOUT DEVELOPMENT AND THE ENVIRONMENT

- Human infants are born with a "blank slate," and they will learn if knowledge is simply provided.
- Everything important about the brain is determined by the age of three.
- Violent video games have no effect on behavior.
- Using the Internet makes you smarter/dumber.
- Environments rich in stimuli improve the brains of preschool children.
- Vaccines cause autism.
- Learning is independent of the learner's history.
- Learning problems associated with developmental differences in brain function cannot be remediated by education.
- Individuals are not responsible for behavior associated with a developmental difference in brain function.
- Teens are irresponsible and "act out" because the prefrontal cortex doesn't develop until the mid-20s.

MYTHS ABOUT BRAIN ACTIVITY

- People can multitask.
- When you sleep, your brain shuts down.
- People who are "brain dead" are still conscious.

MYTHS ABOUT BRAIN PLASTICITY

- The brain is plastic for certain kinds of information only during specific "critical periods,"; the first three years of a child's life being decisive for later development and success in life.
- Neurons are never replaced (you can't grow new brain cells).
- Brain damage is always permanent.
- Neurogenesis optimizes learning.
- Neural plasticity is due to good pedagogy.
- Learning creates new brain cells.

MYTHS ABOUT MEMORY

- Memory is like an objective recording of a situation, and reality exists in an abstract form for all to perceive.
- The brain has unlimited capacity for memory.
- Memorization is unnecessary for complex mental processing.
- The brain remembers everything it has ever experienced; forgetting is simply an absence of recall ability.

MYTHS ABOUT THE MIND-BRAIN CONNECTION

- The brain and mind are unconnected.
- The mind is the result of the action of the spirit, or of the soul, on the brain.
- Intuition is a "special sense" that cannot be explained by the brain.

MYTHS ABOUT EMOTIONS AND LEARNING

- Learning can be isolated from the social/emotional context.
- Reasoning and decision making can be divorced from emotion and feeling, and doing so improves the quality of thought one engages in.

MYTHS ABOUT BILINGUALISM

- Language is located in the "left brain," spatial abilities in the "right brain."
- Children must acquire their native language before learning a second language. If they don't, neither language will be fully acquired.
- Children are sponges and learn foreign languages effortlessly.

MYTHS ABOUT GENDER AND RACE

- Differences between the male and female brain anatomy have been scientifically proven to reflect differences in behavior and learning potential.
- Gender differences outweigh individual differences when it comes to learning abilities.
- There are brain differences between races.

MYTHS ABOUT NUTRITION AND THE BRAIN-LEARNING DYNAMIC

- Children are less attentive after consuming sugary drinks or snacks.
- It has been scientifically proven that fatty acid supplements (omega-3 and omega-6) have a positive effect on academic achievement.

MYTHS RELATED TO COMMERCIAL VENTURES

- Practicing simple body movements used to integrate all areas of the brain is an effective way to enhance young children's learning potential.
- Listening to classical music makes you smarter.
- Short bouts of coordination of motor-perception skills can improve literacy skills.

Source: Based on Dekker, Howard-Jones, & Jolles, 2012; Geake, 2008; Rodriguez, 2006; Valtin, 2002; Waterhouse, 2006; Weisberg, Keil, Goodstein, Rawson, & Gray, 2008.

Do No Harm

Subscribing to neuromyths goes against the first rule of educators: *Do no harm* (Tokuhama-Espinosa, 2011). Telling girls that they just don't have the right kind of brain to do science does harm. Suggesting that a child and teacher have "styles" that don't coincide causes harm. Telling a teenager that there is a critical period for learning a foreign language and he has passed it does harm. Teachers need to become better at filtering good information from bad and avoiding harmful neuromyths that limit a student's potential to learn.

To help dispel myths and promote good science by teachers, a number of conferences share findings from the lab with teachers. The International Mind, Brain, and Education Society encounter (see www.imbes.org); the Learning and the Brain conference (see www.learningandthebrain.com); meetings of the American Educational Research Association's special interest group Brain, Neurosciences and Education (see www.aera-brain-education.org/AnnualMeeting.aspx); and initiatives of the Society for Neuroscience (see www.sfn.org) are just some of the most prestigious of these gatherings. Other conferences have occasionally attempted to integrate the brain and teaching, such as meetings of the Association for Supervision and Curriculum Development (see www.ascd.org/conferences) as well as multiple individual initiatives by enthusiastic teachers around the globe. There are a host of movements outside the United States that also try to share high-quality information with teachers, such as that of the Centre for Educational Neuroscience in the UK (see http://cen.squarevale.com/wordpress) and the International Brain Research Organization (see www.ibro.org). These organizations offer teachers the opportunity to better their practice by broadening and elevating the quality of information used in our classrooms. Given what seem to be multiple entry points into MBE, it is only a matter of time before best practice in the field becomes more widespread.

Teachers have not yet learned to champion their own learning. There *are* opportunities for high-quality encounters in which teachers are given equal footing, and we need to step up to the plate and become more active members of these communities. I recall my own decision to do a doctorate that would spill into cognitive neuroscience and psychology—it was scary and intimidating at first. There were new words to learn and new mentalities to adopt. But after getting over the initial fear, I realized that this was not some exclusive club whose doors are open only to arrogant scientists. MBE is a community seeking better teaching practices, and in general, the main players are very humble and sincerely excited that teachers are now more active members in the movement. As teachers, we can take what is known about how the brain learns (their area of expertise) and actually apply it in the classroom (our area of expertise). By wearing the MBE hat, we can finally begin to elevate our status in society to respectable professional, something that is long overdue (Esch et al., 2005). **By making teaching as much a science as an art, we can change the way society views the teaching profession**.

How can we promote more productive exchanges between neuroscientists, psychologists, and teachers? Order, form, and content are all important to consider.

Order
Unfortunately, because teacher conferences are generally structured around who can give the lectures rather than around specific teacher needs, information is rarely presented in an orderly fashion. Some conferences are driven by specific topics, but presentations usually cover a broad range of themes, from music and memory to discipline and space distribution to body-mind connections and the importance of sleep for learning, or whatever other topic is hot at the

moment. At most teacher conferences, there is no orderly way to go about receiving training in educational neuroscience, MBE or otherwise. Haphazard delivery of information about the brain and learning is also seen in some popular books, in which a bit of information on motivation is smattered with a dab of information about the amygdala and then blended with snippets of chemistry. This leads to mystification more than improved practice. **When teachers attend MBE events, they need to keep a critical eye on what is being delivered, if it is evidence-based, and whether it's of real use to them in their particular classroom setting.** Not all information is useful to all teachers at all times, and not all teachers are prepared for the depth of information being presented. Despite this, many teachers still flock to hear the word of neuroscientists without first evaluating its relevance to their own teaching. Why does this happen?

Form

Teachers have an unquestioning trust in scientists. But we need to open our eyes and accept that, in Stein and Fischer's words, "it is clear that the standard conception in which scientists hand over their results from on high to educators in the trenches is not working" (Stein & Fischer, 2011, p. 59). **Not enough teachers have learned to think like MBE scientists**. The MBE approach supports an equal balance between neuroscience, psychology, and education, meaning teaches have to move beyond their areas of immediate comfort and learn to interpret studies in other fields. Teachers need to be more proactive in setting the agendas for these types of encounters. Active participation in groups like the International Mind, Brain, and Education Society, for example, raises the voices of teachers and helps shape information into a form that can be shared among all groups.

Content

Although the information being offered by neuroscientists is generally reliable and of very high quality, and although teachers work honestly and sincerely to apply the correct information, the random order in which concepts are learned prevents their proper application and use. I once attended a teacher conference in which a group of well-meaning teachers told me they did "brain-based things" in their school. "What, exactly?" I asked innocently. They chimed off the list of themes being presented at the conference: multiple intelligences, emotions and learning, the importance of the learning environment. Unfortunately, teachers often attend these conferences and learn a little about attention and memory, a bit about emotions and learning, and a tad about dyslexia and ADHD, but they are rarely given a macro vision of the tools of the trade or an orderly arrangement of the information. The knowledge that can be shared by neuroscientists is undeniable, but we have not yet structured this exchange in a way that is methodically sound and invites reflection on the part of teachers.

Crossing the "Bridge Too Far": From the Classroom to the Lab and Back

Educational problems are complex. The solution? "Transdisciplinarity is a perspective on knowledge creation that integrates disciplines at the level of a particular issues. It is an approach ideally suited for finding complex solutions to complex problems" (Samuels, 2009, p. 46). It was once thought that linking the lab to the classroom was an elusive endeavor, but recent dynamics have changed and our views have evolved. John Bruer's article "Education and the Brain: A Bridge Too Far" (1997) has been the starting point for the discussion about MBE for years (Ansari & Coch, 2006; Aubrey, 2000; Darling-Hammond & Bransford, 2012; Geake, 2009; Howard-Jones, 2010; Marzano, 2007; Mayer & Alexander, 2011; McGregor, 2007; Smidt, 2006). The "bridge" in Bruer's article referred to the idea that neuroscience and education were too far apart as sciences to be linked, with only "cognition" in common, but this opinion has recently begun to be refuted. Some believe the gap is being filled because of improved study methods and technology, while others such as myself believe that the people behind the science are themselves helping close the gap.

The People

Individuals committed to the Mind, Brain, and Education movement have published articles to unite the field and selflessly taken on jobs to promote it. David Daniel from James Madison University, managing editor of the journal *Mind, Brain, and Education*, is one such person (see Daniel, 2012). A psychologist, Daniel is also a master teacher and has been one of the leaders of the new field, reaching out across the aisle to join together different visions about problems in education. Other MBE proponents, such as Daniel Ansari of the Numerical Cognition Laboratory at the University of Western Ontario, are neuroscientists who have extended an open hand to teachers and worked closely with them to develop strong partnerships to improve our understanding of children and numeracy. Daniel Ansari is an active member of IMBES and as a German working in Canada, he is deeply committed not only to bridging the fields but also to bringing together different world perspectives of MBE. Doris Alvarez, a teacher, runs the Educator Network in San Diego, whose primary purpose is to bring neuroscientists closer to education. She also runs the Preuss School on the University of California at San Diego campus and focuses on integrating technology into education with an eye toward MBE. Adele Diamond, whose research centers on executive functions, runs the Developmental Cognitive Neuroscience Lab at the University of British Columbia, and her research focuses on executive functions. Diamond spends a great amount of time sharing her information with teachers in order to improve classroom practice. Pat Wolf, a former teacher, has devoted her life to improving teachers' understandings about the brain. Wolf wrote some of the first books on the topic for teachers starting back in the 1980s, and her summer workshops for educational leaders in Napa, California, have become legendary for elevating knowledge in the MBE field. Donna Coch at Dartmouth leads research on early reading and the brain and works tirelessly in her Reading Brains Lab to bring information to the public. Mary Helen Immordino-Yang of the Rossier School of Education at the University of Southern California is a teacher and affective neuroscientist. She generously shares her knowledge through open-source videos aimed at teachers to elevate their understanding of the brain and learning. Kurt Fischer at Harvard has spent much of his professional life forging the foundations of a professional society dedicated to bringing neuroscience, psychology, and education together, as has Jelle Jolles in Holland, Hideaki Koizumi in Japan, Stanislas Dehaene in France, Paul Howard-Jones in the UK, and many, many others. Others, such as Nora Newcombe of Temple University, Ralph Schumacher of the MINT project in Switzerland, Elsbeth Stern at the Swiss Federal Institute of Technology in Zurich, Sarah-Jayne Blakemore and Uta Frith of the University College of London have published work showing exactly how specific aspects of learning well documented in neuroscience can be applied in classrooms to make a difference in learning outcomes. This might seem like a short list, but it's growing, and quality counts more than quantity and the initial stages of a change process: "A small group of thoughtful people could change the world. Indeed, it's the only thing that ever has" (Mead, as cited in Sommers & Dineen, 1984, p. 158).

Daniel, Ansari, Alvarez, Diamond, Wolf, Coch, Immordino-Yang, Fischer, Jolles, Koizumi, Dehaene, and Howard-Jones are wonderful professionals, but perhaps their most important characteristic is that they are extremely good people. They all have a sincere interest in sharing information to advance the understanding of how the brain learns so that we can all teach better. Their intellectual generosity is one of the characteristic traits of MBE: Most are willing to share for the common good. A second common trait is that each of these professionals invests in his or her students and colleagues. Each of them believes in change that takes place one person at a time. Kurt helped Mary Helen, who helped me—all with selfless disregard and with an eye on the target, inching toward better teacher practice.

Bruer (1997) spoke of a "bridge too far" because he was metaphorically dividing the academic fields of neuroscience and education, not people. If Bruer were to rethink the bridge, I am sure he would agree that people have begun to cross it. From an engineering perspective, we don't have to worry about a bridge too far, but rather whether or not it is wide, broad, and strong enough to handle all the people who are starting to march across it. In fact, Bruer himself is a great contributor, not only because he has been a catalyst for discussion, but also because he has provided an exceptional overview of the maturation of the field over time (Bruer, 2005, 2009, 2010; Hirsh-Pasek & Bruer, 2007). As president of the James S. McDonnell Foundation, Bruer helped start the Latin American School for Education, Cognitive and Neural Sciences, which has an eight-year mandate to run intensive programs to respond to the need for more scientifically based educational interventions. Despite early cautious speculation, it seems Bruer himself can be considered one of the great contributors to the growth of MBE over the past decade.

The divide between neuroscience and education (and the divide between psychology and education) will always exist—a field is a field is a field. However, some people are bringing their visions together, and that's what's important. While many professionals who have contributed to MBE remain loyal to their "own" field (e.g., they were trained as psychologists and still call themselves a "psychologist" when anyone asks), about half of those mentioned above would identify themselves as Mind, Brain, and Education scientists, even though the term is still hard for many to grasp. But I like to quote Shakespeare on this one: "What's in a name? that which we call a rose / By any other name would smell as sweet" (1597, Act II, Scene II).

The Science

A lot has changed between 1997 and 2013, when the bridge turned Sweet 16. While still irrational and adolescent, the field is no longer babyish, and because it has had good nurturing in its early years, it is growing big and strong. For instance, advances in technology over the past 16 years mean that we now can take more than a quick peek into working, healthy, learning human brains. We are able to capture more refined glimpses into the human brain that were not available when Bruer wrote his treatise a dozen and a half years ago.

For example, thanks to the excellent work done in the laboratory to identify the different circuits in the brain, we can understand the various neural networks (16 at last count) involved in the process of reading a simple sentence (see Farstrup, 2002; OECD, 2014; Tokuhama-Espinosa, 2011; Tokuhama-Espinosa & Rivera, 2013). Knowing this helps us design teaching activities that address each pathway individually to ensure that our students can read better, faster, and more efficiently than before. Authors like Arendal and Mann (*Fast ForWord Reading: Why It Works*, 2000); Bach, Richardson, Brandeis, Martin, and Brem ("Print-Specific Multimodal Brain Activation in Kindergarten Improves Prediction of Reading Skills in Second Grade," 2011); Dehaene (*Reading in the Brain*, 2009); Devlin, Jamison, Gonnerman, and Matthews ("The Role of the Posterior Fusiform Gyrus in Reading," 2006); and Fischer, Bernstein, and Immordino-Yang (*Mind, Brain, and Education in Reading Disorders*, 2007) should be thanked for sharing such valuable information with teachers. Each of their contributions has added a piece to the puzzle of how best to teach reading. This means that we are finally beginning to reach a critical mass of information, strong enough to allow us to suggest concrete interventions.

We have also learned more and more about the dyslexic brain, which ironically tells us a great deal about how "normal" brains read (see Lyon, Shaywitz, & Shaywitz, 2003; Shaywitz et al., 2004; Ziegler & Goswami, 2005). Improved neuroimaging techniques and studies with greater numbers of participants mean that the information being generated in the lab is more and more reliable and generalizable to greater populations. This means there is not just a single study that says something about the importance of recognizing symbol-sound relationships when learning to read, but rather dozens on the topic, giving us more confidence in specific recommendations.

Moving from reading to math, we can see similar trends in evidence-based interventions. Today we know much more about the basics of number sense in the brain than we did a decade ago. Studies by Ansari ("Effects of Development and Enculturation on Number Representation in the Brain," 2008); De Smedt, Verschaffel, and Ghesquiere ("The Predictive Value of Numerical Magnitude Comparison for Individual Differences in Mathematics Achievement," 2009); Lee and colleagues ("Strategic Differences in Algebraic Problem Solving: Neuroanatomical Correlates," 2007); Zago and colleagues ("Neural Correlates of Simple and Complex Mental Calculation," 2011); and Zamarian, Ischebeck, and Delazer ("Neuroscience of Learning Arithmetic: Evidence From Brain Imaging Studies," 2009) are just a few of the many contributions from neuroscience that have changed the way teachers can now approach math instruction to improve their practice. Understanding the many different neural pathways in the brain for math skills (relating symbols to sounds, mentally visualizing the number line, estimating quantity, understanding order of operations, etc.), as well as comprehending that they are distinct mechanisms in the brain, gives us the ability to plan teaching and learning activities that address each sub-element of math more efficiently.

Improvements in education aren't found only in subject-specific areas, however. Take executive functions, for example. Better scientific measurement tools and new technology are helping us understand executive functions, which play a major role in learning across subject areas and are influenced by a variety of habituated reactions learned over the life span. We now are able to perform brain scans of people as they improve their executive functions by doing exercises to boost their working memory (e.g., McCabe, Roediger, McDaniel, Balota, & Hambrick, 2010), increase inhibitory skills (e.g., Munakata, Herd, Chatham, & Depue, 2011), and improve mental flexibility (e.g., Meltzer, 2011), all sub-elements of executive functions. Other studies measure how executive functions are improved as people learn a foreign language. Great pioneers in this field include Ellen Bialystok (Bialystok, 2011a; Bialystok & Feng, 2009; Bialystok & Viswanathan, 2009; Luk, de Sa, & Bialystok, 2011; Pouin-Dubois, Blayne, Coutya, & Bialystok, 2011), Andrew Meltzoff (Carlson & Meltzoff, 2008), and J. Bruce Morton (2007, 2010), whose work, along with that of others (e.g., Rodriguez-Fornells, DeDiego Balaguer, & Münte, 2006), has established the link between foreign languages and executive functions. Both science and education have advanced enough over the past few decades that we can begin to "speak each other's language," advance our communication, and cross Bruer's bridge.

A sub-area of executive functions is self-regulation. Self-regulation and it neural substraits have been studied by neuroscientists for some time (Tops, Boksem, Luu, & Tucker, 2010). Self-regulation is considered to be directly related to inhibitory control and other executive functions in the brain (Berger, 2011), and is a fundamental element in school success (Morrison, Ponitz & McClelland, 2010). According to neuroscientists, self-regulation is something learned early in development (Rothbart, Sheese, Rueda & Posner, 2011), that should be habituated over the life span (Costa & Kallick, 2009), and can be improved upon through simple biofeedback exercises (Zotev, Krueger, Phillips, Alvarez, Simmons, Bellgowan, P., ... & Bodurka, 2011). This means that while better learned early in life, self-regulation can be improved upon throughout the life span. One of the primary indicators for young learners relates and school readiness to self-regulation (Ursache, Blair & Raver, 2012), which is also one of the key factors in long-term academic success (Zimmerman & Schunk, 2013).

Another area in which significant advances in MBE have been made over the past decade comes from the field of emotions and affective neuroscience. We know that affect plays a huge role in how, why, and when a person can learn; how we feel about a learning situation changes how well we can learn something new (Lee & Siegle, 2012; Savion & Glisczinski, 2012; Pekrun, Goetz, Titz, & Perry, 2002; Pekrun, Goetz, Frenzel, Barchfeld, & Perry, 2011; Van Overwalle, 2009; Vul, Harris, Winkielman, & Pashler, 2009). Before, it was speculated that emotive or psychological aspects of learning were unreliable measures of how to teach, but with the help of technology we can now see how the brain reacts to uncomfortable (threatening, stressful or anxious) situations and actually becomes incapable of new learning (Lovinger, 2010; Puig & Miller, 2012; Stagg, Bachtiar, & Johansen-Berg, 2011) or how the right learning environment can facilitate the release of the correct neurotransmitters to improve the probability of learning (Plotnik & Kouyoumdjian, 2013). The bridge between education and neuroscience has become shorter, linking aspects of learning in a way that was once unheard of. While all of the neuroscientific studies mentioned here took place in labs, not classrooms, due to ethical and technological constraints, the lab findings support the evidence from the classroom and should be weighed carefully into the decision-making equation about how to approach better teaching.

As more and more people from the fields of neuroscience, psychology, and education cross the bridge to the middle ground of an MBE perspective on classroom challenges, policymakers are beginning to open their eyes to the potential of this collaboration. This research is beginning to take hold in regular classrooms, and governments around the world are taking notice of contributions from the lab to the classroom. For example, the Costa Rican government is beginning to revamp its early reading and math programs to apply findings from neuroscience (see Tokuhama-Espinosa & Rivera, 2013), and in the United States, the Center for the Developing Child at Harvard (2013) is developing policy initiatives that apply MBE principles and envision child development from a holistic perspective (for another good reference on this topic, see Bear & Minke, 2006).

A Final Analogy: Connections Through People, Connections Through Synapses
If the bridge still seems too far, let's think of complex systems and, in particular, how synapses are formed in the reading brain. Anyone who has taught a child to read realizes that it often takes weeks and sometimes months of effort. And when the child finally does read, it's as if everything clicks at once and appears magically effortless. The behind-the-scenes work is phenomenally complex, however, as any good teacher knows and as neuroscientists can confirm. Each teaching moment is accompanied by important, albeit microscopic, changes in the brain. I liken the crossing of the bridge to forging the synapses needed to create just the right neural network for reading. Think of a complex system of educators, neuroscientists, and psycholo-

gists as if each were a neuron firing off in his or her own space. Sometimes it takes a long time before they connect. When the child finally reads, everything looks "obvious," but we shouldn't forget the tremendous amount of background work that had to happen first. Some read out loud to the child, some bought him books, some fingered the words over the page and hung pictures of the alphabet around the room, and still others made decisions to snuggle at bedtime with a book as opposed to watching TV. These resources, decisions, and actions all resulted in the child learning to read. In a similar way, getting MBE to "read" smoothly is like getting those synapses to fire together.

MBE Concepts, Principles, Tenets, and Guidelines

One way to approach the MBE challenge is to go from the classroom to the lab and back by recognizing what works in real learning contexts, explaining why it works from the lab evidence, and then replicating it in the classroom again. Another more complex method, as mentioned in the preface, would be to design elegant experiments with MBE experts who can manage the classroom-lab-classroom-lab dialogue. Both bring the art of teaching closer to the science of teaching, paving the road for a "middle way." With its emphasis on cooperation among the disciplines of neuroscience, psychology, and education, the MBE model provides an ideal framework for traveling down a transdisciplinary path to improved education. Much of the core knowledge needed by people who wear the MBE hat is embodied in its principles, tenets, and instructional guidelines.

As discussed briefly in the Introduction, MBE *principles* tend to be the same for all brains regardless of cultural influence, age, race, or gender—such as that all new learning takes place against the backdrop of past experiences. These principles are built off of MBE *concepts*, which are the ideas that were categorized as "well-established" by the Delphi panel of experts. MBE *tenets* are true for all brains but have wide variance from person to person—such as sleep, which is important for learning but whose quantity varies depending on the individual. Many of these tenets are ideas assigned to the "probably so" category by the Delphi panel as comparative experimentation is difficult, if not impossible, to undertake. Finally, MBE *instructional guidelines*, which are based on the principles and tenets, are what we use to structure our class practice.

Let's take a closer look at the concepts, principles, tenets, and instructional guidelines of MBE (see Table 1.2).

TABLE 1.2

The Guiding Principles, Tenets, and Instructional Guidelines of Mind, Brain, and Education Science

PRINCIPLES THAT GREAT TEACHERS FOLLOW

1. Great teachers know that each brain is unique and uniquely organized.
2. Great teachers know that all brains are not equally good at everything.
3. Great teachers know that the brain is a complex, dynamic system and is changed daily by experiences.
4. Great teachers know that learning is a constructivist process, and that the ability to learn continues through developmental stages as an individual matures.
5. Great teachers know that the search for meaning is innate in human nature.
6. Great teachers know that brains have a high degree of plasticity and develop throughout the lifespan.
7. Great teachers know that MBE science principles apply to all ages.
8. Great teachers know that learning is based in part on the brain's ability to self-correct.
9. Great teachers know that the search for meaning occurs through pattern recognition.
10. Great teachers know that brains seek novelty.
11. Great teachers know that emotions are critical to detecting patterns, to decision-making, and to learning.
12. Great teachers know that learning is enhanced by challenge and inhibited by threat.
13. Great teachers know that human learning involves both focused attention and peripheral perception.
14. Great teachers know that the brain conceptually processes parts and wholes simultaneously.
15. Great teachers know that the brain depends on interactions with other people to make sense of social situations.
16. Great teachers know that feedback is important to learning.
17. Great teachers know that learning relies on memory and attention.
18. Great teachers know that memory systems differ in input and recall.
19. Great teachers know that the brain remembers best when facts and skills are embedded in natural contexts.
20. Great teachers know that learning involves conscious and unconscious processes.
21. Great teachers know that learning engages the entire physiology (the body influences the brain, and the brain controls the body).

TENETS

1. Motivation
2. Stress
3. Anxiety
4. Depression
5. Tones of voice
6. Facial expressions
7. Movement and exercise
8. Humor (laughter)
9. Nutrition
10. Sleep
11. Cognitive preferences
12. Differentiation

INSTRUCTIONAL GUIDELINES

1. Good learning environments are made, not found.
2. Good lessons take into account both sense (logical order) and meaning (personal relevance).
3. Teaching to different memory systems enhances recall.
4. Well-managed classes take advantage of natural human attention spans.
5. Good classroom activities take advantage of the social nature of learning.
6. Good teachers understand the mind-body connection (sleep, nutrition, exercise).
7. Good teachers understand how to manage different students (orchestrated immersion).
8. Skills are retained better when learned through active processes.
9. Explicit teaching of metacognitive skills aids higher-order thinking across subjects.
10. Learning can and does take place throughout the lifespan.

Source: Tokuhama-Espinosa, T. (2011), p. 206.

Principles that Great Teachers Follow

Principle 1. Each brain is unique and uniquely organized. Human brains are as unique as human faces. Our faces all have the same parts—eyes, ears, nose, mouth—but none of us has exactly the same features as someone else. The same can be said of our brains. Just as we share the same face parts, we all generally share the same brain parts (similar location of lobes, etc.) whose functions operate similarly but whose exact appearance is unique at microscopic level, due to individual experiences. This means that we can generalize about the basic nature of learning mechanisms which will be similar for all individuals, but we must remember that there will also likely be variances among learners that will prevent us from running lessons which always resonate with all learners at all levels all of the time. All learning passes through the filter of our past experiences (for studies in this area, see Greenough, Black, & Wallace, 1987, on experience and development; see McClelland, McNaughton, & O'Reilly, 1995 on ongoing hippocampal-dependent learning; Squire, 1992a, 1992b; Tyler, Alonso, Bramham, & Pozzo-Miller, 2002), which changes the brain. Because no two individuals' past experiences are identical, no two brains are identical (Devlin & Poldrack, 2007). Therefore, while most of us will learn the same thing in a similar way, we may vary the pace at which we learn or the cues that best help us link our prior knowledge to new learning.

Principle 2. All brains are not good at everything; context and ability influence learning; brains are not equal. The classic discussion in psychology about nature versus nurture cannot be escaped in MBE. Many an idealist would like to believe that we, the wise teacher, can successfully mold students into anything we want as in a *My Fair Lady* transformation. However, factors such as poor nutrition during gestation or early infancy can limit a teacher's magical transformations of a child. The intelligence of the student's parents can have an impact on his potential, as can their views on education (Hattie, 2009). The values of the community he lives in can shape him.

While no one knows how much of our intelligence is due to our genes, there is more and more evidence that we react to "nature" via our "nurture" (Caspi & Moffit, 2006). A key idea in MBE is that the environment can actually change our biology. For example, someone born with a tendency for shyness (Arbelle et al., 2003; Battaglia et al., 2005; Rasmus, Wang, Varnell, Osterag, & Cooper, 2011; Schmidt, Fox, Hu, & Hamer, 2002) may actually never exhibit shyness if brought up in an environment that celebrates and rewards extroverted behavior. Likewise, someone born with a talent for musical genius, may never exhibit such behavior if his environment deprives him of the proper stimulus (access to a piano, for example) (Lee, 1906). It is debatable, however, whether the physiology causes the genius or the genius changes brain physiology. In any case, it is clear that humans are not born with blank slates to be written on, but rather with potentials that can either be stimulated or repressed by the environment.

People are born on an uneven playing field, and some kids get the short end of the stick, whether due to poor prenatal care, genes, early life traumas such as neglect or abuse, toxic stress in their surroundings, or other causes. It's nearly impossible for the brain not to learn barring extreme cases of neuroparalysis, as this is fundamental to its survival (Doidge, 2007). Although we can guarantee that all kids will learn, we can't say that everyone will learn at the same pace and reach the same level within the same time frame. This knowledge poses a great challenge to the way we currently structure formal education, which is based on age rather than on preparedness for learning, something we'll talk about more in Best Classroom Practice 45.

Principle 3. The brain is a complex, dynamic system and is changed daily by experience is a concept proven in rats forty years ago (Rosenzweig, Bennett, & Diamond, 1972), but also now evident in humans today (Greenough, Black, & Wallace, 1987; Hedman, van Haren, Schnack, Kahn, & Hulshoff Pol, 2012; Pascual-Leone, Amedi, Fregni, & Merabet, 2005). The main differences that can be found in people's brains are due to the unique experiences we each have in our daily lives that change depending on our biology as well as our culture (Li, 2003), and which can even be influenced by physical activity (Huttenlocher, 2009; Kramer & Erickson, 2007). New learning is a function of the brain's ability to be molded and altered, and this plasticity occurs as a result of the formation of new synapses and connections between different areas, which occur throughout the lifespan (Freitas et al., 2011). Since these changes occur at a microscopic level, most of them don't immediately result in changes in behavior. This means there are microscopic physiological changes in the brain due to daily experiences, like classroom lessons, before people actually change the way they act or demonstrate learning. It can often take multiple repetitions of the same type of learning before there is actually behavioral evidence that learning has taken place.

Principle 4. Learning is both a constructivist as well as developmental process (Quartz & Sejnowski, 1997; Wadsworth, 1996). People learn based on the building blocks of past experience (constructivism), but learning is also regulated by different developmental stages— cognitive, emotional, social, physical—that limit how we can react to the world around us at different moments in our lives. This means that there is an important distinction between "ages" and "stages" that influence how we learn (more on this in Chapter 6). A teacher's art is based partially on being able to adjust for both the student's age and stage of development as well as his past experiences. Leveraging constructivist activities appropriately designed for each student's cognitive level can significantly improve instruction (Nie & Lau, 2010).

Principle 5. The search for meaning is innate in human nature. As mentioned before, it is impossible for the brain not to learn. Newborns are naturally curious, and new learning is a survival mechanism (Lorch & Hellal, 2010). This should give teachers hope; if learning is a natural state, then it should be easy to develop the right classroom settings. However, we know that not everything we want kids to learn is of interest to them, nor is everything useful for their survival; therefore, the innate nature of learning isn't a guarantee that students will do what we ask in class (Meltzoff, Kuhl, Movellan, & Sejnowski, 2009). When a person wants to learn something, there are no limits to what he will do, which is why the innate drive to learn is linked to human invention and creativity (Robinson, 2011). In the classroom context, we need to use more methodologies that capitalize on this aspect of human nature.

Principle 6. The brain is highly plastic and learns throughout the lifespan. The brain is highly malleable; although its plasticity is more prevalent in childhood, it exists into old age (Kempermann, Gast & Gage, 2002; Lövdén, Bodammer, Kün, Kaufmann, Schütze, Tempelmann, Heine, Düzel, Scmiedek & Lindenberger, 2010; Rosenzweig & Bennett, 1996). Popular wisdom tends to view the brain in old age as fragile because of the onset of many neurodegenerative diseases, but the brain can and does learn "until death do us part." Continued learning is necessary if we want to remain fit mentally. For example, the natural decline of the brain in old age can be staved off for as many as four to five years when the brain learns a foreign language (Bialystok, 2009; Bialystok, Craik, & Luk, 2012; Craik, Bialystok, & Freedman, 2010; Luo, Craik, Moreno, & Bialystok, 2012; Lavin, Thompson, & Ungerleider, 2010). One problem we face in society is that we think of old age as a time to relax and refrain from activity, despite the overwhelming evidence that remaining active (physically and mentally) benefits the brain. We somehow believe we are rewarding the older generation by telling them they don't have to help in the kitchen or that they should allow someone else to do their grocery shopping for them—when the reality is that both the body and the mind need the exercise (see DeWeerdt, 2011; Mowszowski, Batchelor, & Naismith, 2010).

Principle 7. Mind, Brain, and Education principles apply to all ages. Mind, Brain, and Education science considers the individual across the lifespan. While school-age learning is of great importance to the field, practitioners in MBE appreciate the fact that studies consider the span of human development, prenatally to old age (Tokuhama-Espinosa, 2008). As more and more countries experience the growth of aging populations due in great part to advances in medicine, there is a call in MBE to balance how well we keep the body with how well we nurture the brain and mind into old age (see Grady, 2012; Richards & Hatch, 2011; Williams, Higgs, & Katz, 2012). There is a rapidly growing field of geriatric neurology that focuses on not only physical, but also mental fitness into old age and learning (Coffey, Cummings, Lovell & Parlson, 1994; Das, 2005)

Principle 8. Learning is based in part on the brain's ability to self-correct (learn from experience through analysis of data and self-reflection): The brain connects new information to old (Greenough & Black, 2013; May, 2011). All learning is conducted against the backdrop of past experiences (Nelson, Thomas, & de Haan, 2012). Since Aristotle's *The Republic*, we know that information is received through the senses and compared with memories before it is evaluated for new learning. We also know that this basic physiology of learning is the same for all learners. This means that both the teacher and the students themselves need to take advantage of the students' past knowledge to capitalize on learning moments. Obviously, the student has greater access to his own memories, which is why asking oneself, "What do I already know about this topic?" should become a habit during early school experiences (Mills, Legare, Grant, & Landrum, 2011). As teachers, we may know our own subject matter inside and out, but if we don't know our students, we will never fulfill their potential to learn because we aren't taking advantage of the foundation of the past in helping them to construct new knowledge.

The brain's ability to self-correct means that the brain is constantly comparing the past with new information. The brain is very efficient. It wants to use what it already knows to build ideas. Normally the brain doesn't find "reinventing the wheel" beneficial, and it always tries to connect similar concepts, comparing old information with new. This has great implications for how we teach. For example, if I help a student realize that he already knows how to add, I can teach him to subtract by comparing what is known (addition) to what I want him to know (subtraction). By making the similarities between the past (known) and the present (new or unknown) explicit to students, I can facilitate learning. However, as a teacher I also need to realize that I am biased by my own personal experiences, which color the way I "know" the information. Our own personal biases, interests, and history with the information influence the way we teach.

Principle 9 and 10. The brain seeks patterns as well as novelty. Learning is based on the brain's ability to see what is different by comparing recognizable patterns (in numbers, behaviors, landscapes, and so on) with things that stand out as different (novelty) (see Balderston, Schultz, & Helmstetter, 2011; Biederman & Vessel, 2006; Beitman, 2009; Berns, Cohen, & Mintun, 1997; Weierich, Wright, Negreira, Dickerson, & Barrett, 2010). Detecting novelty, or things that are different from what is expected, is one of the key ways humans learn about their world as well as prepare for threats or other things that might be "out of place". However, because each human has different past experiences, what we identify as a pattern and what we see as novel differ between individuals.

We know that the brain processes different symbolic representations of the same concept in different ways, and the more ways a child has been exposed to that same concept, the easier it is for him to retrieve and use it in meaningful contexts. According to Gardner (2008), "individuals who can generate several representations of the same idea or concept are far more likely to come up with potent syntheses than those who are limited to a single, often attenuated representation of that idea" (p. 69). For example, Dehaene (2009) noted that mental representations for "three," "3," "III," and ". . ." are in slightly (though sometimes overlapping) areas of the brain. This means that if the teacher exposes the child to as many different conceptual representations of the concept *three* as possible, the child will be more likely to recall and use *three* in an appropriate way, as well as integrate this into his known patterns for the use of three in different contexts. Patterns are not only recognizable, but also generalizable.

"The more you know, the more you can know" is a debatable concept but has merit when discussed related to patterns and novelty: The more patterns you can see, and the more efficient you are at detecting novelty, the greater the pool of connections in your brain, and therefore the greater your potential to link ideas. For example, if I know what a good school generally looks like (I can see patterns based on my past knowledge of having visited thousands of schools), I can quickly detect what's out of sync (novel), be it good or bad, and help others see this. The number of schools I've visited and the total patterns I've seen have colored my vision of "good schools" related to what tends to work and what tends to fail. In the classroom context, this can be seen as a child recognizes the pattern in a life cycle, for example, whether it be in the class pet, a plant, or a person who passes away. If the child experiences the life cycle enough times in or out of school, he can generalize his understanding of the patterns that it should follow as well as identify novel situations when they arise. In an English literature class, this can be exemplified by genres of writing. Patterns are developed if a student is exposed to many different plays (or novels or poems), for example. A student will learn the basic format a play takes (its pattern), and can anticipate what a "good" one looks like. He can also tell, based on novelty, what something that breaks the pattern looks like, as in a "bad" or "outstanding" play.

The patterns one establishes outside of school also have an impact on learning in school. Students base their knowledge on patterns and novelty in their own lives. One of the reasons that children from families of high socioeconomic status do better in school from the start is because they have already begun to establish a wealth of patterns through the many stories read to them in their preschool years, the puzzles they have pieced together with their parents, and the dialogue they have been engaged in. Students from low socioeconomic backgrounds may not have had as many stories read to them, put together as many puzzles, or engaged in as many rich conversations.

Principle 11. Emotions are critical to detecting patterns, to decision-making, and to learning. An important connection to patterning and novelty detection is through emotional content. Everything that can be remembered has some emotional link to it and we construct patterns after repeated experiences and outcomes, even if the decision seems mundane or routine (Andrade & Ariely, 2009). As mentioned above, we learn through our senses. We hear, feel, see, smell, or taste our world, and this sensory input passes from our ears, fingertips, eyes, nose, or mouth to our brain. Senses are perceived and progress up the spinal cord to the two important parts of the brain related to memory processing, first the amygdala and, after a momentary stop in the frontal lobes, to the hippocampus (Freeman, 1991). This filtered review of the past is an evolutionary design. The brain is out to preserve itself, and as the brain is housed in the body, it does everything possible to protect the body. For example, if I see a lion coming and my memory tells me that the last time this occurred, someone from the village was eaten, I do my best to avoid being eaten by running away. In a similar fashion, if I remember that the last time I was in a classroom the teacher allowed me to be ridiculed and bullied by my peers, I also try to run away to avoid the mental torture. We often try to regulate our emotional responses to stimuli. The act of emotional regulation also has an influence on decision-making (for a non-school example, see Heilman, Crisan, Houser, Miclea, & Miu, 2010. For a school example, see Fried, 2011; Kim & Pekrun, 2014). These instinctual mechanisms and their influence on how students behave in class are discussed further in Chapter 6 and are based on the fundamental roles that emotions play in new learning.

Principle 12. Learning is enhanced by challenge and inhibited by threat. Emotions are wide ranging and can be pleasurable, horrific, stressful, fearful, exciting, enjoyable, or anything in between. We know, however, that when a person is threatened, the combination of neurotransmitters present in the brain will prevent other chemicals from successfully creating the needed synapses for new learning (Crestani et al., 1999; LeDoux, 1995; LeDoux & Phelps, 2008). On the other hand, manageable challenges enhance the probability of learning because they generate a favorable combination of neurotransmitters (Blascovich, Mendes, Hunter & Salomon, 1999; LeDoux, 1995; LeDoux & Phelps, 2008). While this principle sounds straightforward, the individual nature of learning means that what one person might consider threatening is what another might consider a manageable challenge. This makes it very hard for the teacher to choose appropriate activities that suit the group, as different people will be at different stages of their learning because of different past experiences. Responses to this challenge are discussed in chapters 4 through 6. It should be noted that fear can also motivate learning; however, this is not considered best practice in education for obvious reasons.

Principle 13 and 17. Learning requires highly functioning attention systems. Human learning involves focused attention as well as peripheral perception. To many people's surprise—especially that of teachers frustrated by kids who are "off in the clouds"—the brain is *always paying attention* (Baars, 1998; Peterson & Posner, 2012). It just may not be paying attention to what the teacher *wants* it to be paying attention to! A kid staring out the window is, indeed, paying attention—to whatever is outside the window. There are at least three ways attention systems can be disturbed in a normal brain. Sometimes attention problems are caused by chemical imbalances (Faraone & Biederman, 1998). Other times the physical network or attentional circuitry in the brain is faulty—parts that should be connected are not. This can be caused by congenital defects (you are born with them) (Brookes, Xu, Chen, Zhou, Neale, Lowe, et al., 2006), or they can be acquired later on as a result of damage. For example, traumatic brain injury happens as a result of a blow to the head, as in a sports or car accident, and is a major cause of death and disability worldwide, not to mention long-term attention problems (Yeates et al., 2005). Finally, some attention problems can be attributed to poor habituation to behavior models (this will be explained further in Chapter 4). In addition to these three possible problem areas, there are at least three different attentional networks in the brain: the alerting system, the sustaining system, and the executive function system (Raz & Buhle, 2006). If any of the three main attentional networks is not in sync with the others, learning can be impaired (Fan et al., 2009; Fan, McCandliss, Fossella, & Posner, 2005; Raz & Buhle, 2006). Studies of attention networks related to the registration of new learning are just recently coming to light. Michael Posner and Mary K. Rothbart's "Attention to Learning of School Subjects" (in press) offers explanations of "a mechanism for how attention influences learning" and points to promising suggestions for learning in school setting (personal communication with Michael Posner, October 14, 2013).

Humans know about their world thanks to their senses, and all senses are working at all times. Inhibitory controls in the brain try to keep perception systems focused on core stimuli, but this doesn't work 100 percent of the time. For example, right now you are reading, but a sudden movement in the periphery of your visual field, a slightly louder sound than usual, or a pungent odor can divert your attention from the page. This kind of peripheral perception helps the body survive—that pungent odor may have distracted you from your reading, but noticing it was what made you take the pot off the stovetop before the whole kitchen burned down. To a child with attention problems, the formula on the board may not be as important to his brain as the facial expressions of the teacher, the loud noise in the hall, or the pretty girl sitting behind him. A teacher's job is to help the student choose the right focus by explicitly calling attention to what he considers important ("Now pay attention to this formula, because it's going to be important in solving the upcoming problems"). Because each person's brain is unique, teachers can't presume that all students' attention systems are working in sync; what calls one student's attention may not attract another's.

Principle 14. The brain conceptually processes parts and wholes simultaneously. This means that there is not necessarily a sequential, structured, orderly processing of information going into the brain—rather, the brain works hard to piece puzzles together as it goes along, based on its past experiences and motivations (Tononi, Sporns & Edelman, 1994; Tononi, Edelman & Sporns, 1998). Some new pieces of information will come into play and then get in line to await a call back, while other pieces will be identified as relating to already known concepts and be thrown into the mix immediately to complete a data group.

For example, anyone who has taught a child to read understands what an "aha!" moment looks like—pieces that were previously disconnected fall into place. What happened previous to the "aha!" moment? The brain inched its way toward making new connections. To learn, the brain processed all the various parts of reading (symbol-sound connections, semantic meaning, context, order of text on the page, rules of grammar, etc.) as well as the whole (the conceptual idea of reading) simultaneously to give birth to the moment of new knowledge.

Principle 15. *The brain is a social organ*. The brain depends on interactions from other people to make sense of social situations. Students can, and often do, achieve learning without a teacher. Linking ideas is a sign of intelligence, and many children master this on their own. In fact, this type of mastery learning conducted in autonomous settings—in which a student "owns" the new knowledge—should be the goal of all teachers. When a teacher hears, "I get it; it's just like a cocoon, but only a little different!" from a first-grader as he observes the change of a pollywog to a frog or a flower to a fruit, she knows that the student has mastered the competencies of that particular learning encounter or dominated a core mental schema. Although this student may have come to this discovery "on his own," it is likely that he has developed a habit of mind related to thinking processes that previous teachers helped him to master. An appreciation of the fact that there are no two identical brains is fundamental to applying MBE in the classroom.

Humans will generally choose to learn in groups as opposed to on their own (Paulus, 2000). This changes, of course, depending on the stimuli, the learner's previous knowledge, his relationship with the instructor, and his motivation for the task. But most of us learn better when we bounce ideas off of one another. Some people insist they are loners in their learning, but this reminds me of the people who swear they never dream. We all dream, whether we acknowledge it or not, and it is likewise human nature to understand ourselves and judge our own knowledge based on what others around us think and do. The now-famous *theory of mind* concept relates to the idea that we know ourselves best when we compare our actions with those of others (Blakemore & Decety, 2001; Decety & Lamm, 2007; Decety & Sommerville, 2003). We not only gain information by listening, watching, and interacting with other people, we learn about ourselves when we compare our own actions and thoughts with those of others.

Principle 16. *Feedback is important to learning*. A principle closely related to the social nature of learning is that feedback is vital to education. It is human nature to want to be better, and it is natural to want guidance from an authority figure (for a student example see Nihart, Lersch, Sellers, & Mieczkowski, 2005). By learning what others think about our conduct and actions, we measure ourselves against our social group (Hattie, 1999). Feedback helps us compare ourselves and our actions with expectations of peers as well as people in positions of authority (Nicol & Macdarlane-Dick, 2006). We will look more closely at feedback in chapter 4.

Principle 17 and 18. Learning requires highly functioning memory systems. Different memory systems (short, working, long term, emotional, spatial, rote, and so on) receive and process information in different ways and can be retrieved through different neural pathways (Arnold, 2013; Squire, Knowlton, & Gazzaniga, 1995), as well as via different combinations of neurotransmitters (Lynch, 1998; Squire & Kandel, 2008). This means that the ways memories are connected in the brain as well as the chemicals that trigger retrieval vary slightly among types of memories. Without memory we wouldn't be able to know what, how, or why different types of information are important, nor relate them to new experiences to construct learning. Learning is optimal only when all of our memory systems are working well.

Memory is complex and comprises several different and often overlapping systems. For example, it is vital that teachers understand the importance of long-term memory for learning (for a great explanation see Ormrod & Davis, 2004). Long-term declarative memory usually passes through short-term and working memory before it reaches a nesting spot, which serves as a jumping-off point for new connections in the brain. (Some terms for certain kinds of memory—such as *auditory memory*—refer more to where recall structures are located in the cortex than to how the information got there in the first place.)

Information gets into the brain through different pathways depending on sensory input. When we listen to a new song played by a live musician with the intention of remembering it, it enters our brain through the auditory pathways, is "heard" in the brain, and can be remembered by retracing this auditory network in the cortex. However, when we remember the way the musician looked as he played, we are triggering slightly different neural pathways and a memory system linked more to the visual (occipital) cortex. The learning objective *as interpreted by the learner* determines which memory systems will be activated. For example, a professional musician will use different neural pathways to process a song than a non-professional musician (Ohnishi et al., 2001). Why? Because the professional is paying attention to the sequential order of notes, intonation, pitch, appropriate spacing between sounds, and so forth, whereas the amateur may be focusing only on the lyrics. Great teachers know that memory systems differ in input and recall, and they take advantage of this information by teaching several different modalities to improve the chance of recall. Additionally, great teachers understand the idea of "use it or lose it," The Hebbian synapse model (Hebb, 1949) proposes that things we learn are not always remembered; only the things that are constantly in use stay in mind. This is why those of us who studied French in high school usually can't string two words of it together today (unless, of course, we use French in our daily lives). When knowledge retrieval of a concept is applied frequently it is accessible, but when it goes unused, it is forgotten. The brain is very efficient and doesn't waste space; unused connections are released to make way for new connections. Synapses and subsequent "connectomes" or neural circuits (Seung, 2013) are the evidence of new learning, but when the learning experience is not reinforced, the dendritic connections weaken and the memories are lost, and without memory, there is no learning.

Principle 19. The brain remembers best when facts and skills are embedded in contexts that are authentic for the learner (Frymier & Shulman, 1995; Hollins, 2008). This means that students who see how classroom information relates to their real life are able to remember that information better than students who cannot link the information to an authentic context. For example, if we teach a student fractions by baking cookies, an experience in which he can see, feel, smell, weigh, and conceptualize each measurement as it relates to an ingredient, it is likely that he will remember the relative size of each fraction better than filling in a simple worksheet because the information is transferred into a real-life experience. That is, the student who can apply classroom learning to out-of-class contexts will remember the information better than a student who only has a textbook example. For this reason, simulations, role-plays, and other real-life exercises that apply problem-based learning activities are excellent teaching devices, and they will be discussed further in Chapters 4 through 6.

Principle 20. Learning involves conscious and unconscious processes. Remember how the brain is always paying attention? Well, this explains, in part, why and how learning is dependent on both conscious and unconscious processes. The brain unconsciously pays attention to stimuli in the periphery as well as to primary targets. This means that sensory perception of stimuli occurs in both overt and conscious ways, as well as in more covert and unconscious ways (Mandler, 1989). A second way that unconscious processes are involved in learning has to do with long-term memory consolidation during REM sleep (Stickgold, 2005), an "unconscious" state. We know that a good night's sleep (or power nap) is necessary for the consolidation of long-term memories, without which there is no learning due to a combination of neurotransmitters released during the REM stage of sleep (where most dreams occur) that does not occur at any other time. It is important to remember that we can't learn new information in our sleep, but we can review old information and consolidate firm memories by dreaming (Stickgold, Hobson, Fosse, & Fosse, 2001).

Principle 21. Learning engages the entire physiology. The body influences the brain, and the brain controls the body. This means that if we give the body what it needs, there is a higher likelihood that the brain will be able to learn efficiently. We know, for example, that sleep influences both memory and attention, two fundamental elements in learning. When the body is at the deepest stages of sleep, it rests and as a result, the brain can pay better attention the next morning. We also know that the dream stage (notably different as far as brain activity is concerned [see Hobson & Pace-Schott, 2002]) influences learning due to the consolidation of memory that occurs in REM sleep (Stickgold, 2005). This means that both attention and memory are aided by sleep and dreaming. The mind-body connection also relates to exercise. We know that a well-oxygenated brain can pay better attention than a brain deprived of oxygen (Erikson et al., 2011). We also know that exercise can release endorphins, which facilitate neuroconnections (Dishman & O'Connor, 2009). Children who don't have their basic nutritional needs met can't learn: Their brains don't have the necessary "fuel" to drive the complex processes needed to pay attention, remember, relate past information with new, and so on (Glewwe, Jacoby, & King, 2001; Levinger, 1992; Worobey, Tepper, & Kanarek, 2006). While there is no such thing as a perfect "diet for your brain," the rule of thumb is that what's good for your heart is good for your brain: a balance of grains, protein, and fruits and vegetables, and avoidance of too many processed sugars and fats (Restak, 2009). When thinking about the mind-body balance, it is important to remember that there are general human parameters for sleep, exercise, and nutrition, but not all people need exactly the same things to learn best.

The Tenets of MBE

Tenets are highly personalized aspects of learning. For example, we all know that **motivation** plays a huge role in learning, but what motivates one person might not motivate another. We also know that **stress**, **anxiety**, and **depression** can influence learning, but what triggers these states in one person does not necessarily trigger them in others. All humans react to *facial expressions* and *tones of voice* instantly and almost unconsciously; however, an individual's history and past experiences influence his interpretation of these stimuli. Oxygenation through *movement*, *exercise*, and **laughter** can improve learning environments, but at different levels for different individuals. **Nutrition** and **sleep** are also important to learning, and while there are basic parameters in all humans, there is also great variance in what is considered "normal." Eight hours of sleep a night is "average," but some sleep only four or five hours and others need twelve. Everyone needs to eat, but some people are happy with two or three meals a day while others prefer eight or nine smaller servings.

While the concept of learning styles has been rejected in MBE science as an efficient way to design classes (Pashler, McDaniel, Rohrer, & Bjork, 2008), the belief that people can express *cognitive preferences* for learning modalities is accepted. Past experience with the subject at hand, the learner's relationship with his teacher, the methodology being used, and the learner's level of motivation for the subject influence his cognitive preferences.

The Instructional Guidelines of MBE

The neuromyths tell us what *not* to do or believe in classroom settings, and the well-established concepts, principles, and tenets from Mind, Brain, and Education point clearly to what we should do. Although the instructional guidelines are listed concisely in Table 1.2 (Tokuhama-Espinosa, 2010, 2011), they are interwoven with and explained more fully in the Best Classroom Practices included in Chapters 4 through 6.

"Proven" in Education but Not in Neuroscience?

This brings us to ideas in education that don't yet have the backing of neuroscience but for which there is evidence in education—for example, differentiation. Differentiation basically means giving each person what he or she needs to succeed and is considered best practice in modern teaching circles. Because not everyone will learn things at the same pace, educators need to apply differentiation (Sousa & Tomlinson, 2010). Roe and Egbert have shown that differentiation means recognizing that different people have different abilities in different areas as well as different past experiences upon which they can learn new information that influences the speed with which they learn (2010; also see Imbeau & Tomlinson, 2010). Because all new learning occurs against the backdrop of past knowledge (Argote, 2012; Kaplan & Murphy, 2000; Princeton University, 2013; Shapiro, 2004; Svinicki, 1993; Tobias, 1994; von Krogh, Ichijo, & Nonaka, 2000), differentiating for this becomes fundamental in a teacher's job description. The result of successful differentiation is inclusion. Inclusion means accepting that there is a continuum of human potential that includes "outliers" on both ends, special needs and gifted. In any classroom representative of an "average" population, a teacher can expect between 5 and 7% of the students to have special needs and learning deficits, while another 5 to 7% will have some form of advanced knowledge. That is, roughly 10 to 14% of the kids in our classrooms are *not* going to be "average" (Armstrong, 2012; Bender, 2012). Classroom objectives stay the same for everyone, but differentiation allows the teacher to modify activities or evaluation tools, thus permitting a focus on mastery learning instead of on "covering the text" within a specified time. Accommodations to meet differentiation needs can take the form of adjustments in activities, time, or place (Levine, 2002; Sousa & Tomlinson, 2010) and simplifying the conditions under which objectives are reached. For example, a student with attention problems can be moved to the front of the room where there are fewer distractions. Similarly, a student with time management issues can be given more time on a test if the objective does not require a timely response. After all, we know that timed tests are part of our educational culture, but why? The reason is because we have only a certain amount of time in class to carry out our evaluations, not because the skill we seek to measure is necessarily time sensitive. Why should a person write a time-bound, in-class essay in 45 minutes, if in real life we know that writing can take much longer, depending on the theme and depth required? (To appreciate this complexity, see Dehaene, Cohen, Sigman, & Vinckier, 2005, for an explanation of the neural code for written words.)

In 2008, the concept of differentiation was categorized as "intelligent speculation" by the Delphi panel because it was too difficult to measure, meaning it was all but rejected as best practice in the classroom. Because of the uniqueness of each individual brain, the effectiveness of differentiation is, by its very nature, impossible to prove (Tokuhama-Espinosa, 2008). This means that although we all might value differentiation as part of the art of teaching, there is little scientific data supporting it. It is in this gray area of education that we can begin to bridge the gap between the cleanliness of the lab, where most variables can be controlled for, and the "messiness" of the classroom.

Differentiation is a core element of the modern classroom, but it is all but rejected by neuroscience. How do we square that circle? Thanks to our more sophisticated understanding of the contributions of MBE, we can now disaggregate learning challenges and respond to them with scientific backing piece by piece. Let's consider someone with clearly diagnosed ADHD, their need for differentiation, and what MBE would add to the conversation. In 2004 Alicia Callejas, Juan Lupianez, and Pío Tuleda (2004) (also see Fan, McCandliss, Fossella, &

Posner, 2005; Posner, Sheese, Oldludas, & Tang, 2006; Raz & Buhle, 2006) identified three attentional networks, but few teachers know they exist and can be at the root of some students' attentional problems (Fan et al., 2009). Posner helped us understand that kids with ADHD can have trouble with their attentional "sustaining" networks while their "alerting" networks are on overdrive, calling their brain's attention to everything around it. We also suspect that, in kids with attention problems, the executive function networks are not as well tuned as we'd like them to be, meaning that these individuals have trouble choosing the right thing to pay attention to. By incorporating what Posner knows about the brain and attentional network functioning with what teachers know about the success of differentiation, we can improve teaching by accommodating individual needs to increase the probability of learning. In a second example, Posner suggests that the Attention Network Test (Fan, Wu, Fossella, & Posner, 2001) shows differences between "normal" individuals through scores that correlate to connectivity of certain white matter pathways (Niogi & McCandliss, 2009). This means that there are measureable "individual differences in distinct components of attention [which] are linked to anatomical variations in distinct white matter tracts" (Michael Posner, personal communication, October 14, 2013).

This example means we are reaching a point where we might be able to move the concept of differentiation of the intelligent speculation category into one of greater evidence. To an extent, Posner and his colleagues have given teachers justifiable cause to apply differential techniques. This means that we are finally reaching a point, both in educational and neuroscience research, where we can make concrete recommendations about how to approach concepts like differentiation in the modern classroom.

As a science, education is based on evidence. As an art, it is a uniquely human endeavor. Although some would say that other animals also teach, Blakemore and Frith argue that when a lioness takes her cubs out to hunt even though it would be far easier for her to hunt on her own (and much safer for the cubs), or when a bird parent slowly increases the time it stays away from the nest so that the fledglings can learn to fly in a safe, gradual way, these are survival mechanisms, not teaching moments. While survival mechanisms do require a type of long-term memory, they are unrelated to the long-term explicit (declarative) memory tracks employed in school contexts. Human teaching is in a class by itself (Battro, 2010).

Next we turn to a discussion of how MBE can be intertwined with Hattie's *Visible Learning* to arrive at the latest "edition" of brain-based learning and yield success amid the messiness of the modern classroom.

Suggested Readings

"A Bridge Too Far" Commentaries

Ansari, D., & Coch, D. (2006). Bridges over troubled waters: Education and neuroscience. *Trends in Cognitive Sciences, 10*(4), 146–151.

Ansari, D., Coch, D., & DeSmedt, B. (2011). Connecting education and cognitive neuroscience: Where will the journey take us? *Educational Philosophy and Theory, 43*(1), 37–42.

Bruer, J. T. (1997). Education and the brain: A bridge too far. *Educational Researcher, 26*(8), 4–16.

Bruer, J. T. (2009). Mapping cognitive neuroscience: Two-dimensional perspectives on twenty years of cognitive neuroscience research (pp. 1221–1234). In M. S. Gazzaniga (Ed.), *The cognitive neurosciences* (4th ed.). Cambridge, MA: MIT Press.

Bruer, J. T. (2010). Can we talk? How the cognitive neuroscience of attention emerged from neurobiology and psychology, 1980–2005. *Scientometrics, 83*(3), 751–764.

Della Sala, S., & Anderson, M. (2012). *Neuroscience in education: The good, the bad and the ugly.* New York, NY: Oxford University Press.

Fischer, K. W. (2009). Mind, brain, and education: Building a scientific groundwork for learning and teaching. *Mind, Brain, and Education, 3*(1), 3–16.

Fischer, K. W., Goswami, U., & Geake, J. (2010). The future of educational neuroscience. *Mind, Brain, and Education, 4*(2), 68–80.

Geake, J. (2005, August). Educational neuroscience and neuroscientific education: In search of a mutual middle way. *Research Intelligence, 92,* 10–13.

Goswami, U. (2006). Neuroscience and education: From research to practice. *Nature Reviews Neuroscience, 7*(5), 406–413.

Hirsh-Pasek, K., & Bruer, J. T. (2007). The brain/education barrier [Editorial]. *Science, 317*(5843), 1293.

Howard-Jones, P. A. (2007). *Neuroscience and education: Issues and opportunities.* London, UK: Teaching and Learning Research Programme.

Howard-Jones, P. A. (2010). *Introducing neuroeducational research: Neuroscience, education and the brain from contexts to practice.* New York, NY: Taylor & Francis.

McNamara, D. S. (2006). Bringing cognitive science into education and back again: The value of interdisciplinary research. *Cognitive Science, 30,* 605–608.

Newcombe, N. S. (2002). Biology is to medicine as psychology is to education: True or false? *New Directions for Teaching and Learning, 2002*(89), 9–18.

Newcombe, N. A. (2013). Educating to use evidence in thinking about education. *Mind, Brain, and Education, 7*(2), 147–150.

Samuels, B. M. (2009). Can differences between education and neuroscience be overcome by Mind, Brain, and Education? *Mind, Brain, and Education, 3*(1), 45–53.

Varma, S., McCandliss, B., & Schwartz, D. (2008, April). Scientific and pragmatic challenges for bridging education and neuroscience. *Educational Researcher, 37*(3), 140–152.

Differentiation

Bender, W. M., & Waller, L. B. (2011). *The teaching revolution: RTI, technology, and differentiation transformation teaching for the 21st century.* Thousand Oaks, CA: Corwin.

Cash, R. M. (2010). *Advancing differentiation: Thinking and learning for the 21st century.* Minneapolis, MN: Free Spirit Publishing.

Diller, D. (2007). *Making the most of small groups: Differentiation for all.* Portland, ME: Stenhouse.

Kerry, T., & Kerry, C.A: (1997). Differentiation: Teachers' views of the usefulness of recommended strategies in helping the more able pupils in primary and secondary classrooms. *Educational Studies, 23*(3), 439–457.

Latz, A. O., Neumeister, K. L. S., Adams, C. M., & Pierce, R. L. (2008). Peer coaching to improve classroom differentiation: Perspectives from project CLUE. *Roeper Review, 31*(1), 27–39.

Lee, C., & Picanco, K. E. (2013). Accommodating diversity by analyzing practices of teaching (ADAPT). *Teacher Education and Special Education, 36*(2), 132–144. doi: 10.1177/0888406413483327

Roe, M. F., & Egbert, J. (2010). Four faces of differentiation: Their attributes and potential. *Childhood Education, 87*(2), 94–97. doi: 10.1080/00094056.2011.10521452

Sousa, D. A., & Tomlinson, C. A. (2010). *Differentiation and the brain: How neuroscience supports the learner-friendly classroom.* Bloomington, IN: Solution Tree.

Tobin, R., & McInnes, A. (2008). Accommodating differences: Variations in differentiated literacy instruction in grade 2/3 classrooms. *Literacy, 42*(1), 3–9.

Tobin, R., & Trippet, C. D. (2013). Possibilities and potential barriers: Learning to plan for differentiated instruction in elementary science. *International Journal of Science and Mathematics Education.* doi: 10.1007/s10763-013-9414-z

Tomlinson, C. A., & Edison, C. A. (2003). *Differentiation in practice: Grades 5–9: A resource guide for differentiating curriculum.* Alexandria, VA: ASCD.

Tomlinson, C. A., & Strickland, C. A. (2005). *Differentiation in practice: A resource guide for differentiating curriculum, Grades 9–12.* Alexandria, VA: ASCD.

Valiande, S., & Tarman, B. (2011). *Differentiated teaching and constructive learning approach by the implication of ICT in mixed ability classrooms.* Ahi Evran Üniversitesi Eðitim Fakültesi Dergisi, Cilt 12, Sayý 1, Nisan, Sayfa 169–184.

Van Hover, S., Hicks, D., & Washington, E. (2011 Winter). Multiple paths to testable content? Differentiation in high-stakes testing context. *Social Studies Research and Practice, 6*(3), 34–51.

VanTassel-Baska, J., & Stambaugh, T. (2005). Challenges and possibilities for serving gifted learners in the regular classroom. *Theory Into Practice, 44*(3), 211–217.

Westwood, P. (2001). Differentiation as a strategy for inclusive classroom practice: Some difficulties identified. *Australian Journal of Learning Disabilities, 6*(1), 5–11.

Wormeli, R. (2007). *Differentiation: From planning to practice, Grades 6–12.* Portland, ME: Stenhouse.

Wu, E. H. (2013). The path leading to differentiation: An interview with Carol Tomlinson. *Journal of Advanced Academics, 24*(2), 125–133. doi: 10.1177/1932202X13483472

Executive Functions, Self-Regulation, and Metacognition

Anderson, P. (2002). Assessment and development of executive function (EF) during childhood. *Child Neuropsychology, 8*(2), 71–82.

Barkley, R. A. (2012). *Executive functions: What they are, how the work, and why they evolved.* New York, NY: Guilford Press.

Berger, A., Kofman, O., Livneh, U., & Henik, A. (2007). Multidisciplinary perspectives on attention and the development of self-regulation. *Progress in Neurobiology, 82*(5), 256–286.

Best, J. R., & Miller, P. H. (2010). A developmental perspective on executive function. *Child Development, 81*(6), 1641–1660.

Best, J. R., Miller, P. H., & Naglieri, J. A. (2011). Relations between executive function and academic achievement from ages 5 to 17 in a large, representative national sample. *Learning and Individual Difference, 21*(4), 327–336.

Carlson, S. M., Moses, L. J., & Breton, C. (2002). How specific is the relation between executive function and theory of mind? Contributions of inhibitory control and working memory. *Infant and Child Development, 11*(2), 73–92.

Cooper-Kahn, J., & Dietzel, L. (2008). *Late, lost, and unprepared: A parents' guide to helping children with executive functioning.* Bethesda, MD: Woodbine House.

Dawson, P., & Guare, R. (2010). *Executive skills in children and adolescents: A practice guide to assessment and intervention* (2nd ed.). New York, NY: Guilford Press.

Deco, G., & Rolls, E. T. (2005). Attention, short-term memory, and action selection: A unifying theory. *Progress in Neurobiology, 76*(4), 236–256.

Denckla, M. (2005, April). *Paying attention to the brain and executive function: How learning and memory are impaired by the syndrome called ADHD.* Paper presented at the Learning and the Brain Conference, Harvard University, Cambridge, MA.

Diamond, A. (2012). Activities and programs that improve children's executive functions. *Current Directions in Psychological Science, 21*(5), 335–341.

Diamond, A., & Lee, K. (2011). Interventions shown to aid executive function development in children 4 to 12 years old. *Science, 333*(6045), 956–964.

Diamond, A., Barnett, W. S., Thomas, J., & Munro, S. (2007). Preschool program improves cognitive control. *Science, 318*(5855), 1387–1388.

Engle, R. W. (2002). Working memory capacity as executive attention. *Current Directions in Psychological Science, 11*(1), 19–23.

Frith, C. D. (2012). The role of metacognition in human social interactions. *Philosophical Transactions of the Royal Society Biological Sciences, 367*(1599), 2213–2223.

Garon, N., Bryson, S. E., & Sith, I. M. (2008). Executive function in preschoolers: A review using an integrative framework. *Psychological Bulletin, 134*(1), 31–60.

Hofer, B. K., & Sinatra, G. M. (2010). Epistemology, metacognition, and self-regulation: Musings on an emerging field. *Metacognition and Learning, 5*(1), 113–120.

Holmboe, K., & Johnson, M. H. (2005). Educating executive attention. *Proceedings of the National Academy of Sciences of the United States of America, 102*(41), 14479–14480.

Kacker, D. J., Dunlosky, J., & Graesser, A. C. (2009). *Handbook of metacognition in education.* New York, NY: Routledge.

Livingston, J. A. (1997). *Metacognition: An overview.* Retrieved from http://www.josemnazevedo.uac.pt/pessoal/textos/Metacognition.pdf

Logam, J. M., Castel, A. D., Haber, S., & Biehman, E. J. (2012). Metacognition and the spacing effect: The role of repetition, feedback, and instruction on judgment of learning for massed and spaced rehearsal. *Metacognition and Learning, 7*(3), 175–195.

McCabe, D. P., Roediger, H. L., III, McDaniel, M. A., Balota, D. A., & Hambirck, D. Z. (2010). The relationship between working memory capacity and executive functioning: Evidence for a common executive attention construct. *Neuropsychology, 24*(2), 222–243.

McCabe, J. (2011). Metacognitive awareness of learning strategies in undergraduates. *Memory and Cognition, 39*(3), 462–476.

McCaig, R. G., Dixon, M., Keramatian, K., Liu, I., & Christoff, K. (2010). Improved modulation of rostrolateral prefrontal cortex using real-time fMRI training and meta-cognitive awareness. *NeuroImage, 55*(3), 1298–1305.

Moore, C. M., & Egeth H. (1997). Perception without attention: Evidence of grouping under conditions of inattention. *Journal of Experimental Psychology: Human Perception and Performance, 23,* 339–352.

Mundy, P., & Newell, L. (2007). Attention, joint attention, and social cognition. *Current Directions in Psychological Science, 16*(5), 269–274.

Peña, A., Kayashima, M., Mizoguchi, R., & Dominguez, R. (2011). Improving students' metacognitive skills within intelligent educational systems: A review. *Foundations of Augmented Cognition, 6780,* 442–451.

Pennequin, V., Sorel, O., & Moainguy, M. (2010). Metacognition, executive functions and aging: The effect of training in the use of metacognitive skills to solve mathematical word problems. *Journal of Adult Development, 17*(3), 168–178.

Posner, M. I. (2011). *Cognitive neuroscience of attention.* New York, NY: Guilford Press.

Salatas Waters, H., & Schneider, W. (Eds.). (2009). *Metacognition, strategy use and instruction.* New York, NY: Guilford Press.

Son, L. K., & Simon, D. A. (2012). Distributed learning: Data, metacognition, and educational implications. *Educational Psychology Review, 24*(3), 379–399.

Stillman, G., & Mevarech, Z. (2010). Metacognition research in mathematics education: From hot topic to mature field. *ZDM, 42*(2), 145–148.

Willcutt, E. G., Doyle A. E., Nigg, J. T., Faraone, S. V., & Pennington, B. F. (2005). Validity of the executive function theory of attention deficit/hyperactivity disorder: A meta-analytic review. *Biological Psychiatry, 57*(11), 1336–1346.

Yeager, M., & Yeager, D. (2013). *Executive function and child development.* New York, NY: W. W. Norton.

Zalazo, P. D., & Carlson, S. M. (2012). Hot and cool executive function in childhood and adolescence: Development and plasticity. *Child Development Perspectives, 6*(4), 354–360.

Mind, Brain, and Education Science

Battro, A., Fischer, K. W., & Léna, P. J. (Eds). (2008). *The educated brain: Essays in neuroeducation.* Cambridge, UK: Cambridge University Press.

Blakemore, S., & Frith, U. (2007). *The learning brain: Lessons for education.* Malden, MA: Blackwell.

Bransford, J., Brown, A. L., & Cocking, R. R. (2008). Mind and brain. In *The Jossey-Bass reader on the brain and learning* (pp. 89–108). San Francisco, CA: Wiley.

Bransford, J., Brown, A. L., & Cocking, R. R. (Eds.). (2003). *How people learn: Brain, mind, experience and school.* Washington, DC: National Academy Press.

Byrnes, J. (2001). *Minds, brains, and learning: Understanding the psychological and educational relevance of neuroscientific research.* New York, NY: Guilford Press.

Byrnes, J. P. (2007). *Cognitive development and learning in instructional contexts* (3rd ed.). Boston, MA: Allyn & Bacon.

Byrnes, J. (2010). Some ways in which neuroscientific research can be relevant to education. In D. Coch, K.W. Fischer, and G. Dawson, *Human behavior, learning, and the developing brain: Typical development* (pp. 30–49). New York, NY: Guilford Press.

Coch, D., Dawson, G., & Fischer, K. W. (Eds.). (2007). *Human behavior, learning, and the developing brain: Atypical development.* New York, NY: Guilford Press.

Coch, D., Fischer, K. W., & Dawson, G. (Eds.). (2007). *Human behavior, learning, and the developing brain: Typical development.* New York, NY: Guilford Press.

Diamond, A. (2010). The evidence base for improving school outcomes by addressing the whole child and by addressing skills and attitudes, not just content. *Early Education and Development, 21,* 780–793.

Fischer, K. W. (2007). Dynamic cycles of cognitive and brain development: Measuring growth in mind, brain, and education. In A. M. Battro & K. W. Fischer (Eds.), *The educated brain.* Cambridge, UK: Cambridge University Press. Retrieved January 28, 2008, from http://gseweb.harvard.edu/~ddl/publication.htm

Fischer, K. W. (2007). *Mind, brain, and education: Analyzing human learning and development* [Podcast]. Inaugural launch of the journal Mind, Brain, and Education, April 2, 2007. Cambridge, MA: Harvard University.

Fischer, K. W. (2009). Mind, brain, and education: Building a scientific groundwork for learning and teaching. *Mind, Brain, and Education, 3*(1), 3–16.

Fischer, K. W., Daniel, D. B., Immordino-Yang, M. H., Stern, E., Battro, A., & Koizumi, H. (Eds.). (2007). Why mind, brain, and education? Why now? *Mind, Brain, and Education, 1*(1), 1–2.

Geake, J. (2009). *The brain at school: Educational neuroscience in the classroom.* England: Open University Press.

Goswami, U. (2004). Neuroscience and education. *British Journal of Educational Psychology, 74,* 1–4.

Goswami, U. (2005). The brain in the classroom? The state of the art. *Developmental Science, 8*(6), 468–469.

Goswami, U. (2005). Neuroscience and education: The brain in the classroom [Target article with commentaries]. *Psychology of Education Review, 29*(2).

Goswami, U. (2006). Neuroscience and education: From research to practice. *Nature Reviews Neuroscience, 7*(5), 406–413.

Goswami, U. (2007). *Cognitive development: The learning brain.* London, UK: Taylor & Francis.

Goswami, U. (2008). Neuroscience and education. In *The Jossey-Bass reader on the brain and learning* (pp. 33–50). San Francisco, CA: Wiley.

Hart, L. (1999). *Human brain and human learning* (5th ed.). Kent, WA: Books for Educators.

Howard-Jones, P. (2007). *Neuroscience and education: Issues and opportunities* (Commentary by the Teacher and Learning Research Programme). London: TLRP. Retrieved January 14, 2008, from http://www.tlrp.org/pub/commentaries.html

Howard-Jones, P., & Pickering, S. (2006). *Perception of the role of neuroscience in education: Summary report for the DFES Innovation Unit.* Retrieved January 14, 2008, from http://www.bristol.ac.uk/education/research/networks/nenet

Larrison, A. (2013). *Mind, Brain and Education as a framework for curricular reform.* Unpublished doctoral dissertation, University of California, San Diego.

Levine, M. (2000). *A mind at a time.* New York, NY: Simon & Schuster.

Newcombe, N. A. (2013). Educating to use evidence in thinking about education. *Mind, Brain, and Education, 7*(2), 147–150.

Tokuhama-Espinosa, T. (2010). *Mind, brain, and education science: The new brain-based teaching.* New York, NY: Teachers College Press.

Tokuhama-Espinosa, T. (2011). *Mind, brain, and education science: A comprehensive guide to the new brain-based teaching.* New York, NY: W.W. Norton.

Transdisciplinary Fields

Johnson, J. M., & Littlefield, M. M. (Eds.). (2012). *Neuroscientific turn: Transdisciplinarity in the age of the brain.* Ann Arbor: University of Michigan Press.

Koizumi, H. (1999). A practical approach to trans-disciplinary studies for the 21st century. *Journal of Seizon and Life Sciences, 9,* 5–24.

Samuels, B. M. (2009). Can differences between education and neuroscience be overcome by Mind, Brain, and Education? *Mind, Brain, and Education, 3*(1), 45–53.

CHAPTER 2

"Brain-Based Learning 2.0" and the Messiness of the Classroom
What Really Influences Student Achievement?

If a doctor, lawyer, or dentist had 40 people in his office at one time, all of whom had different needs, and some of whom didn't want to be there and were causing trouble, and the doctor, lawyer, or dentist, without assistance, had to treat them all with professional excellence for nine months, then he might have some conception of the classroom teacher's job.

—Donald Quinn

Teachers have one of the most challenging jobs in society: They must, on a daily basis, make dozens of life-impacting choices. Of the thousands of theories about what influences learning, how can we be sure we're including the most important in the execution of our practice? One way we can do this is by looking to the few highly qualified, tried-and-true sources in educational research. As mentioned in the Introduction, John Hattie's *Visible Learning for Teachers* (2012) is a meta-analysis of more than 900 studies investigating what impacts student achievement. *Visible Learning* evidence tells us there are several superior methods that aren't practiced enough in the classroom, and then there are some "disasters" that should be avoided at all costs. Hattie's work also confirms the value of certain interventions that all great teachers know almost instinctively, such as the fundamental role that feedback plays in learning (e.g., see Nicol & Macdarlane-Dick, 2006).

By combining *Visible Learning* with Mind, Brain, and Education science, we can determine the scientifically substantiated art of teaching. No longer must we resign ourselves to trying what our neighboring classroom teacher did last year because it worked for her kids, applying what was the flavor of the month professional development theme, or buying the popular book because it has an attractive cover; now each of us can plan an effective, personalized, professional development program and make our classroom better.

10 Categories of Teacher Influence on Student Learning

After plotting out the effect sizes for 150 different factors that influence student learning, Hattie made a startling discovery: Almost all of them have a positive effect on learning. While it is helpful for teachers to be aware of the effects of all of these factors on student performance, some factors, such as birth weight and school size, are obviously outside a teacher's control. If we narrow down Hattie's list (Appendix B) to things within teachers' realm of influence, then we have a manageable list of just 47 classroom practices to consider (Appendix C). I have categorized these into 10 main areas of teacher influence: (1) students' self-efficacy and self-concept, (2) teacher credibility, (3) students' attitude toward interventions, (4) the use of constructivist designs, (5) evaluation and assessment practices, (6) teacher self-reflection in practice, (7) the use of appropriate methodologies, (8) communication, (9) group learning, and (10) classroom management. Each category and its four to five subelements from Hattie's work are described below.

1. Student Self-Efficacy and Self-Concept

We know that there are students who believe firmly in themselves, and that this has an impact on their general success in the classroom (Riding & Rayner, 2001). For example, on the first day of a new school year, Emily walks into the classroom and knows she is going to succeed. She has no reason to doubt her abilities—after all, her past teachers have told her she's smart, she's always gotten decent grades, and her friends often call her for help. Sitting next to Emily is Sofia. Sofia dreads school because she has frequently been ridiculed for being slower than the others. Teachers rarely give her praise, and she (incorrectly) presumes she is at the bottom of the class. While Emily looks forward to the new school year, Sofia wishes she could run away and hide from an environment she has never felt comfortable in. There is no difference in these two students' IQs; there is only a difference in their perception of themselves as learners.

Self-efficacy is the way self-perception influences what a person believes is within her power to achieve and has a direct impact on her motivation (Schunk & Mullen, 2012). **What a student thinks of her own ability to learn influences her actual ability to perform in school** (Hattie, 2012). Her self-efficacy influences her choice of activities, her effort, her persistence, and her achievement (Bandura, 1997). Schunk and Pajares note that "compared with students who doubt their capabilities to learn or to perform well, those with high self-efficacy participate more readily, work harder, persist longer, show greater interest in learning, and achieve at higher levels" (2009, p. 35; also see Bandura, 1997).

A student's self-reported grades, self-expectations, and level of self-efficacy appear to stem from her self-concept (Hattie, 2012). While self-efficacy and self-concept differ slightly in their definitions—self-efficacy is more connected to self-confidence, whereas self-concept is how one sees oneself descriptively—they both have a tremendous impact on learning outcomes. Feedback from significant adults in a student's life (e.g., teachers or parents) influences both her self-efficacy and her self-concept (Konold, Miller, & Konold, 2004). As we will see in the section on emotions and learning, teachers have a huge potential to improve students' self-images, which in turn has a great influence on the quality and quantity of learning.

For instance, the way a teacher chooses to identify or label his students, consciously or unconsciously, has an impact on their self-concept and thus their attitudes toward learning (Hattie, 2012). Teachers who make a point of saying they have "special ed kids" or "the accelerated group" do harm because the labels they apply to learners become self-fulfilling prophecies. Telling students they are in the "learning needs group" or even identifying them as "gifted," "bilingual," or having "ADHD" or "dyslexia" boxes them into a level of expectations. When a teacher conscientiously decides *not* to label students, he takes a big step toward getting kids to believe in their own potential to learn.

2. Teacher Credibility

"Teacher credibility" refers to students' level of confidence in their professor's capacity to teach and their belief that they will actually learn something from him (Hare, 2007; McGlone & Anderson, 1973). A teacher's credibility is highly influenced by the degree of confidence and self-efficacy he displays as well as by his ability to make his students feel he knows something they don't (Finn et al., 2009). When a teacher is able to make his students feel inspired by the fact that he is bringing them the gift of knowledge, then he has high credibility (Haskins, 2000).

For example, when I was in grade school, one of my teachers, Ms. Houston, was interested in everything we asked and cared that we got the right answers—together, as a team. I remember her answering almost all of our queries with, "Well, I don't know; what a *great* question! Let's figure that out together, shall we?" She made us all feel that we were on a genuine quest to figure out the world, and that she could lead us successfully to that knowledge, which we students all believed she possessed. Ms. Houston's genuine marveling at the world was in stark contrast to the attitude of another teacher I had in middle school, who was quite pompous and, judging by the responses she gave, also quite ignorant of her own field. She reacted as if she knew everything, despite seeming to be quite in the dark about some questions. I remember an incredulous classmate challenging her at the start of the class by asking, "Why is *Romeo and Juliet* such an important work? Isn't is just a simple love story?" Instead of offering an explanation or, better yet, reframing the question and bouncing it back to the student, she went into a long discourse on how we, as teenagers, would never really appreciate *Romero and Juliet* until we were older—at which point we began whispering to one another, "Then why even read it?" She lost us before we had even begun. When she couldn't handle some of our questions as the school year progressed, she would feign an answer, digging herself deeper into the pit of our disrespect. She lost all credibility in our eyes.

Some teachers put on airs when they're afraid. Academic arrogance is not limited to my school experience; I've been to seminars and conferences where the workshop leader was asked something he or she couldn't respond to, and instead of displaying intellectual humility and just saying, "Good question, but I don't know," he or she went on to fabricate a response that most of the participants clearly identified as false. Instead of becoming credible sources of information and making us feel that there was something we could learn from their course, these leaders made us feel that we were wasting our time. This happens far too often in learning contexts, classrooms, professional development days, or otherwise.

Teacher credibility and teacher quality, as evaluated by the students, go hand and hand. Teacher *credibility* has to do with whether or not students believe their teacher is a valid source of information (Beatty & Behnke, 1980), while teacher *quality* has more to do with how well students feel they learned. It is ironic to note that **post-evaluation of a teacher's ability to teach is less important than students' original beliefs about the teacher's credibility** (Hattie, 2009). This implies that students can actually prepare themselves for a good or bad learning experience and create a self-fulfilling prophecy: "This teacher looks great; I am going to learn" versus "This teacher looks terrible; I'm not going to get anything out of this class."

Teacher and student self-efficacy are closely related (Schwarzer & Hallum, 2008). **If a teacher believes in his own skills, he transmits this belief outward, and his students believe they will learn**. Unfortunately, the opposite is also true. If a teacher has a low level of self-efficacy and is not confident in his own skills, he will transmit this low self-expectation outward, and his students will doubt their ability to learn from him. I once had a teacher—let's call him Mr. Mathews—who could have been a great teacher if he hadn't been so nervous around us. In fact, when any of us approached him one on one, he was a near genius and very insightful. Unfortunately, however, he would walk into the classroom with downcast eyes, and he'd often ask for confirmations about what page we should be on or what we'd previously learned, as if he doubted we'd really paid attention in his last class. He didn't believe in himself as a successful teacher, and therefore he wasn't successful in our eyes either.

It is clear that teacher credibility serves as an indicator for student learning: **Higher levels of teacher self-efficacy lead to actual academic gains.** In Guo, Plasta, Justice, and Kaderavek's (2010) study, for instance:

> Teachers' self-efficacy and classroom quality served as significant and positive predictors of children's gains . . . [and their] results also showed a significant interaction among teachers' self-efficacy, classroom quality, and vocabulary gains: for children of teachers with higher levels of self-efficacy, higher levels of classroom quality (emotional support) were associated with higher vocabulary gains. (p.1094)

Others have shown that formative preservice (e.g., Tuchman & Isaacs, 2011) as well as ongoing training (e.g., Ross, 1992) experiences have a positive impact on teacher self-efficacy, which means that the demonstration of self-efficacy is a "teachable" skill that should be developed further in teacher education programs. That is, people like Mr. Mathews can learn to carry themselves with more confidence, which will lead to more classroom success, which will in turn create an upward spiral in teaching ability. One method to do this is "microteaching," which involves analysis of videos of one's teaching in the company of a guide or master teacher who identifies areas for improvement in both pedagogy and manner of communication (Fernandez, 2010; Kallenbach & Gall, 1969). The master teacher helps the novice identify simple body or facial movements that can be modified to give the impression of greater self-confidence (Kilic, 2010).

Unfortunately, it has also been found that **teacher self-efficacy persists at a steady level unless it is explicitly improved upon.** That is, teachers who have low self-efficacy (or high levels of self-doubt) at the start of their teaching career remain at a low level, independent of other variables such as improved educational opportunities, unless they are given specific guidance early in their careers (Settlage, Southerland, Smith, & Cegile, 2009). Work by Klassen and colleagues (2009) has also demonstrated that "teachers' self-efficacy is a valid construct across culturally diverse settings and . . . [is related to] teachers' job satisfaction" (p. 67). Studies of teachers in countries as diverse as Canada, Cyprus, Korea, Singapore, and the United States have shown similar findings: Teacher self-efficacy affects student learning and should be explicitly taught as part of a teacher's education.

Finally, it is important to note that the work environment can shape teacher self-efficacy. In Kelm and McIntosh's (2012) study, schoolwide positive behavior support significantly boosted teacher self-efficacy; that is, when teachers felt that they worked in a positive environment, they also felt a great sense of self-efficacy, and as a result, their students learned more. This has implications for administrators, who have a lot to do with the general institutional climate. If there is high tolerance (and even celebration) of teacher errors on the part of the administrators, then the teachers in turn tend to have high tolerance for student errors and encourage kids in their attempts to come up with the right answers, giving more space in class for exploration and, eventually, learning. Part of learning is daring to participate in class discussions, to question, and to doubt (Harton, Richardson, Barreras, Rockloff, & Latane, 2002). To dare to become involved, both students and teachers need to have a strong sense of self-efficacy.

3. Student Attitude Toward Interventions

A student's attitude toward the help she receives is a good indicator of her potential to learn. If a student is corrected and sees this adjustment as helpful and reacts well to it, it is likely that she will learn from her mistakes and from the assistance she receives (Hattie, 2009). However, if she has a negative attitude toward being corrected, she will likely block her own ability to learn. **How a student reacts to a teacher's attempts to help her learn has a huge impact on the student-teacher relationship** (Mercer & DeRosier, 2010). Good relationships help learning; bad relationships impede learning—it's as simple as that.

It's easy to see this in the classes we teach on a daily basis. For example, let's say that Ms. Diane has just returned to her students the graded outline she assigned for an upcoming essay, and she finds that different students react in distinct ways to her comments, even when the observations are almost identical. For instance, she has written the comment "I'd like to see more examples" on both Jack's and Ethan's papers. Jack looks Ms. Diane up and down with disgust and crumples the paper as he puts it in his bag. Ethan says, "OK, can I take the examples from the same book, or do I need to look for more sources?" Jack's attitude toward the feedback is argumentative and defiant, whereas Ethan's attitude is welcoming. While Jack thinks Ms. Diane is out to get him, Ethan senses that she is out to help him. Who will likely improve on the next draft? Where do these attitudes come from? Can they be changed?

It could well be that Jack and Ms. Diane don't have "chemistry" and just don't get along as human beings (see Adolphs, 2003, for a discussion of how human relationships are influenced by biochemical exchanges). This would mean that Jack's reaction is to the person, not to the feedback. A successful outcome is dependent on Ms. Diane's ability to make the issue about the paper and the feedback, rather than about her and Jack. Jack's learning is at stake. So long as he harbors negative feelings and blocks out offers of help, he won't learn—not only because his psychological orientation prevents it, but also because learning in this setting is neurologically impossible. When a student feels he is under attack, he becomes stressed, and high-stress situations evoke neurotransmitters that are not conducive to learning. Bangasser and Shors (2010) have shown how different types of stressors impede or enhance memory, and since memory is vital to learning, stress can either improve or deteriorate the likelihood of success, depending on the person and situation. If Jack's attitude is a reflection of negative stress, his learning will be impaired. If Ms. Diane can adequately manage the level of stress in her interaction with Jack, then the stress can be helpful, but if she allows Jack's attitude to spiral into the negative, it will impede his learning.

The open attitude with which a student may react to help is very dependent on the relationship cultivated between teacher and student. However, openness to criticism is also nurtured in the home, the broader school culture, and the wider community. Fisher and Frey's book on response to intervention (*Enhancing R[esponse] T[o] I[ntervention]: How to Ensure Success With Effective Classroom Instruction and Intervention*, 2010) entreats both families and schools to work together to inculcate in their kids a positive attitude toward feedback.

As mentioned earlier, the community within which a student lives has a strong impact on what she learns. Just as individuals vary widely in their openness to criticism, some societies are more open to hearing how they can improve, while others have yet to develop a culture of evaluation; some cultures see criticisms as a way to help while others classify corrections as a type of punishment. For example, the culture in Hawaii fosters a very open attitude toward criticism. You can often hear people in educational settings responding to one another's criticisms with "Oh, thanks, I hadn't thought of it that way; next time I'll remember to consider that." This is in stark contrast to the response in settings where the concept of evaluation is outright rejected, since it is presumed to be a reason to reprimand someone. Teacher unions in several South American countries went on strike for several months between 2010 and 2013, each refusing to accept their government's decision to evaluate the quality of the teachers in order to design professional development interventions. The perception (based on history) was that teacher evaluation is a way to punish (i.e., fire) teachers, not help them. Educational reforms are occurring in almost every country on earth; everyone is trying to improve education. The heart of good learning relies heavily on the quality of many elements, not the least of which is the teacher himself. But this means evaluation, and evaluation often induces fear. Sometimes the fear of hearing about what needs to improve is so great that teachers prefer to be fired over being evaluated. But what kind of message does this send to students? If we as teachers refuse to work under the "threat" of constructive criticism, how can we expect our students to respond positively and not give up when we offer them help and redirection? By confronting the fear of criticism that is natural to all of us and choosing to embrace evaluation, teachers can set a strong example for their students that will go a long way toward cultivating a classroom environment where students feel comfortable and are free to learn and grow. A culture open to evaluation that is receptive to continual feedback helps learning environments flourish.

One of the ways teachers can help individual students become more open to feedback is by focusing more on formative evaluation processes than on summative ones, as we will see in Part II of this book. Other helpful interventions—such as offering acceleration programs, which allow students to work faster than the norm, or second- or third-chance programs, which permit students to redo their work several times until they master basic skills—enhance students' levels of concentration, persistence, and engagement, which increases their motivation and improves their general attitude toward learning interventions (Hattie, 2009). Some of the best teachers design their classroom activities to foster mastery by encouraging students to compete against themselves to reach a certain level of competency, not against one another or to pass a certain test. These classes structure learning in a way that permits students to pace themselves and aim toward authentic learning, rather than trying to figure out their place in the pack.

4. Constructivism

Constructivism means building off of what someone already knows to create new knowledge; an individual's past is the key to her gaining new understanding. Constructivism is applicable to all people—teachers as well as students—in their continual formation throughout the lifespan (Martin & Loomis, 2006). Jean Piaget, a Swiss biopsychologist who believed that certain developmental stages lend themselves to the brain's readiness for new types of learning and that all new learning is constructed on the foundations of previous knowledge, promoted the fundamentals of constructivism (1950). Class designs that apply Piagetian concepts of constructivism—for example, by using spaced versus massed practice structures, pursuing mastery learning over product or process dominance, and incorporating early interventions—can positively influence learning (Hattie, 2012). Learning strategies based on constructivist ideas build off of different levels of thinking, depending on where the individual student begins (for concrete examples, see Mayer, 1996).

Suppose, for instance, that an experienced math teacher named Mr. Peters has to teach basic statistics to his class. He knows that to do statistics well, you need a strong foundation on which to build the new math concepts, so his students will need to brush up on their previous skills before starting statistics. Therefore, before he starts explaining statistics, he writes an email to the class (Table 2.1) to confirm his students' prior knowledge (Jantzen, Steinberg, & Scott Kelso, 2004).

TABLE 2.1
Mr. Peters' Email to His Statistics Class

Dear Class,

This Monday we start Statistics. Statistics is very useful in life, in everything from keeping track of basketball scoring data to measuring intelligence. We can use statistics to study the collection, organization, analysis, interpretation, and presentation of all kinds of data in real life as well as to conduct surveys and experiments.

To do statistics well, you need to be able to do arithmetic with exponents, fractions, percentages, and so forth. Since math skills can deteriorate over time if you haven't practiced them in a while, I suggest you conduct a basic review before starting class Monday. One of the reasons some students don't do well in statistics is not because statistics itself is hard, but rather because they have a weakness in a prerequisite. Please be sure you review the following, either by viewing the attached videos or by completing the following practice questions:

A. Integer arithmetic
   1. Evaluate: a. $4 + 3 \times 7 - 8$ b. $(-3)5 - 2(4 + 7)$
   2. Evaluate: a. $(-3)(-7) + 6(-2) + (-8)5$ b. $(-2) [(-2)(-2)(-2) - 2]$
   3. See video: https://www.khanacademy.org/math/arithmetic/absolute-value/adding_subtracting_negatives /v/adding-integers-with-different-signs
B. Exponents and radicals
   1. Evaluate: 5^3
   2. Evaluate: $(x^3)(x^4)$
   3. See video: https://www.khanacademy.org/math/arithmetic/exponents-radicals/world-of-exponents/v/ level-1-exponents

C. Fractions and decimals
   1. Evaluate: a.   1/4 + 3/8   b.   3/5 – 1/3   c.   3/10 + 5/6   d.   5/8 – 3/4
   2. An urn contains 42 red balls, 12 blue balls, and 21 green balls. What proportion of the balls in the urn are red?
   3. See video: https://www.khanacademy.org/math/arithmetic/decimals/decimal_to_fraction/v/converting-fractions-to-decimals

D. Percentages
   1. Express as a percentage: a.   0.25   b.   0.002   c.   28/35   d.   5.4
   2. If 3 students form 15% of a class, how large is the class?
   3. See video: https://www.khanacademy.org/math/arithmetic/decimals/percent_tutorial/v/describing-the-meaning-of-percent

E. Evaluating algebraic expressions
   1. Evaluate $4 \times 2y - 3xy2$ for: a. $x = -2, y = 3$ b. $x = -1, y = -2$
   2. Given $n = 3$, $x1 = 5$, $x2 = -4$, $x3 = 8$, $x = 3$, $s \neq 0$, and $s2 = [(x1 - x)2 + (x2 - x)2 + (x3 - x)2]/(n - 1)$, approximate s.
   3. See video: https://www.khanacademy.org/math/algebra/systems-of-eq-and-ineq

F. Order relations
   1. The **median** of a list is the number in the middle when the list is ordered. Find the median of:
       a.   8, –3, 7, –11, 5   b.   –1, –2, –3, 4, 5
   2. See video: https://www.khanacademy.org/math/algebra/algebra-functions/relationships_functions/v/functional-relationships-1

G. Equations of lines
   1. Graph the linear equation $y = -2x + 8$
   2. See video: https://www.khanacademy.org/math/algebra/linear-equations-and-inequalitie/graphing_solutions2/v/algebra--graphing-lines-1

H. Linear equations in one variable
   1. Solve exactly: a. $5x - 7 = 8$ b. $4 - x = 9$ c. $3x + 5 = 7x - 1$
   2. See video: https://www.khanacademy.org/math/algebra/linear-equations-and-inequalitie/equation-of-a-line/v/linear-equations-in-standard-form

I. Applications of linear equations
   1. Jo has 23 coins. She has twice as many nickels as pennies and three more dimes than pennies. How many of each type of coin does she have?
   2. See video: https://www.khanacademy.org/math/algebra/solving-linear-equations-and-inequalities

J. Systems of equations in two variables.
   1. Alice spent 6 minutes on each factoring problem and 3 minutes on each evaluation problem. She spent a total of 42 minutes on 9 problems. How much time did she spend on factoring?
   2. See video: https://www.khanacademy.org/math/trigonometry/systems_eq_ineq

If you can do these types of questions, then Statistics is going to be a breeze! See you Monday!
Mr. Peters

Piaget's original concept of constructivism has now been applied to all types of development—affective, social, cognitive, and intellectual—through which humans progress as they age (Liu & Chen, 2010). Constructivism is linked directly to what the brain is able to manage at different stages of growth but it depends more on past experience than on an individual's maturity. I like to call this the "ages and stages" way of thinking about a student's preparedness: Most children will take their first steps around a year old (age), and most of them must learn to walk before they can run (stages). The age serves as a benchmark, allowing us to say when most kids will reach a particular developmental milestone, but the stages tell us that process-dependent learning needs to occur in a specific order in a constructivist design. This means that even though a child's brain is ready at a specific age to learn, for example, abstract concepts, if his past knowledge doesn't include the prerequisites necessary, he can't advance to this stage, no matter how old he is. (We will look at ages and stages in more depth in Classroom Practice 45.) This means that **the developmental steps someone has progressed through are actually much more important than how old she is when she learns a given skill**. Thus, to get to deep learning, the teacher has to be prepared to approach the student at both her current intellectual level developmentally, as well as at her starting point constructively.

A good example of constructivist principles comes from adult learning programs. If you didn't learn to read when you were small—maybe four, five, six, or seven years old—you can still learn to read when you are 10, 17, 27, 57, or 70. The constructivist steps you take and the order of skills you learn are far more important than your age. Did you first learn that symbols relate to sounds, and that each letter is a symbol? Did you then learn that each symbol has a distinct sound, but that when it's combined with other letters, that sound can change? Did you learn that words are the combination of letter symbols, and that sentences are made up of combined words? If any step is taken out of order, learning to read will be a hardship, but taking all the steps in the right order facilitates the learning process. (For an excellent description of the child versus adult literacy process, see Dehaene, 2013.)

According to Allan D. Warren (1989),

John B. Carroll inaugurated a fundamental change in thinking about the characteristics of instruction in 1963 when he argued for the idea that student aptitudes are reflective of an individual's learning rate . . . [and that] instruction should focus more on the time required for different students to learn the same material. (p. 1)

Gap analysis is key: We need to know from where our students are starting, where we want them to arrive, and teach to the gap in between. Hattie (2009) believes that teachers are successful to the degree that they can move students from single to multiple ideas, then relate and extend these ideas that students can construct and reconstruct knowledge. It is not the knowledge or ideas, but the learner's construction of the knowledge and ideas that it critical (Hattie, 2009).

Teachers need to wear the hat of a good diagnostic professional. The old model of preparing lessons and simply delivering them to everyone in the same way needs to be replaced by the steps of diagnoses, design, teaching in a differentiated manner, and evaluation in a continual, repetitive cycle.

A Special Word About Math and Science

All good math teachers know that you can't teach algebra if a student hasn't yet mastered the concepts of symbol systems, variables, function order, and so forth. Each of these concepts builds off of the last. This is why so many people have trouble with math and think it's "the hardest subject" to learn (Williams, 2011, p. 213): If one concept or another is missing in an individual's repertoire of knowledge, then the structure on which her knowledge is built is weak. This weakness leads to misunderstandings or misconceptions in an ever-spiraling downward turn. If Jun misses out on a single concept at just one stage of math, he can be lost in math from that point forward in his education. Unlike literature or history class, in which a particular genre of writing (English poetry or 20th-century prose) or a particular event (the Battle of Gettysburg or World War I) can be missed and recovered, math and other sciences depend heavily on previously learned concepts, formulas, and theorems.

Thus, problems in math are accumulated: When one concept is misunderstood, then another and another follows. If a child doesn't manage to fully understand core concepts, such as number lines, it will be very hard for her to understand negative numbers and other concepts that come (constructively) later. If a kid doesn't get symbol systems, she won't be able to grasp variables, and so on. We know that developmentally, a child has a sense of "quantity" even in her preverbal years, but it takes until she's around seven or eight years old before she can formulate a mental number line (Ansari & Karmiloff-Smith, 2002; Dehaene, 1997; Göbel, Shaki, & Fischer, 2012; Izard & Dehaene, 2008; Jordan, Kaplan, Locuniak, & Ramineni, 2007; McCrink, Dehaene, & Dehaene-Lambertz, 2007; Virarouge, Hubbard, Dehaene, & Sackur, 2010) or manage a mental time line (Bonato, Zorzi, & Umilta, 2012). Without a sense of quantity or a mental number line, a student can't grasp addition, or subtraction, or multiplication or division, all of which in turn precede the ability to perform basic algebraic functions. All of this means that we can have 10th graders who can't do algebra, not because they aren't mentally ready for higher-order concepts but because they have gaps in their knowledge base, and we can have 11-year-olds who whiz through basic algebra because they had early exposure to fundamental prerequisites. So while some aspects of learning are based on developmental stages of preparedness, others respond to constructivism (i.e., accumulating the building blocks necessary for constructing a foundation for higher-order concepts). To inculcate deep thinking in our students, we need "deep teaching" that identifies both the ages and stages at which a student starts a learning process.

5. Evaluation and Assessment Practices

The purpose of evaluation is to serve as a teaching tool. If assessments are embedded in classroom activities and occur frequently, then students learn better because they are continually comparing what they thought they knew with what they actually know, and then filling in their own gaps of understanding. Approaching assessment in this manner has been shown to improve learning (Crisp, 2012). In settings in which evaluation occurs only at the end of a teaching endeavor, learning opportunities are lost. In other words, formative assessment, in which there is ongoing feedback about a student's progress, has been shown to significantly outperform summative assessment, in which a single, final grade is given at the end of a unit.

A great deal of literature over the past decade has advocated formative assessment as a way of improving the chances of creating lifelong learners who understand how to think better (e.g., Absolum, Gray, & Mutchmor, 2010; Bennet, 2011; Black & Wiliam, 2009); Dunn & Mulvenon, 2009; Ritchhart, Church, & Morrison, 2011; Sadler, 1998). Formative assessment is mainly seen in mastery learning contexts in which the goal is *learning* as opposed to a final *grade* (Koedinger, McLaughlin, & Heffernan, 2010; Torrance & Pryor, 1998). Black and Wiliam (2010) claim that formative assessment is one of the main keys to the "black box" of the teacher-learner exchange, which often determines educational outcomes. According to Cauley and McMillan (2010), "formative assessment can have a powerful impact on student motivation and achievement" (p. 1) and should be used with greater frequency. Collins has shown that despite overwhelming evidence in favor of formative (versus summative) assessment, "linking assessment to everyday classroom instruction requires a shift in both thinking and practice" (2011, p. 1), which explains why its use is not as prevalent as desired.

For example, a school that one of my children attended required that teachers give at least five assessments per school year. Some teachers did the bare minimum, meaning that they gave their students an assessment every two months or so. Needless to say, this was not enough to help the students understand how to improve, and, since almost all of the evaluations were multiple-choice tests, it was nearly impossible to identify which aspects of learning needed betterment. In many cases, these exams were returned with no feedback, just red marks here and there. The exams had to be signed by the parents and returned to the school, meaning that there was no time for students to review their tests to use them to fill in gaps of knowledge identified in the results. This was a frustrating situation for the students, who didn't know where to begin to improve their learning processes.

With just slightly more planning, evaluations can be used as formative teaching instruments. For example, for a course I am currently teaching, my colleagues and I have designed an evaluation scheme that has proven to have a beneficial impact on student learning:

1. First, students are given a description of the unit in which there are prerequsites (e.g., "This unit presumes a knowledge of basic anatomy. If you want to review basic anatomy before continuing, use the following resources....").
2. Then there is a nongraded pretest, which helps students understand just what types of information they will be expected to learn during the unit.
3. A list of guiding questions is then provided, which students answer in discussion groups throughout the unit, which averages about a week long. Again, there is no grade, but a lot of feedback is offered, allowing students to make sure they share the same focus as the class objectives.
4. To ensure that core concepts are not missed, the teaching team poses additional questions as they see fit to fill in any gaps in knowledge.
5. Students are assigned readings and videos related to the unit and asked to cite references from these and additional sources during class discussion.
6. Near the end of the unit, students are asked to fill out a "Unit Reflection Form" by identifying three things they didn't know before the unit began, two things that were so interesting they would share them with someone else, and one thing they would change to improve their practice. The reflection form also asks them to list the major authors and concepts they have identified within the unit. These Reflection Forms are used to build up material for their final papers.

7. At the end of the unit, students are asked what questions they think will be on the end-of-unit test, forcing them to reflect even further about the core concepts that were covered.
8. Finally, students are given a post-unit quiz, which is graded.
9. If they missed anything or somehow failed to demonstrate mastery of all of the core concepts of the unit, they are given the chance to submit further documentation of their understanding either in written or oral form, and their grade can be amended.

The goal of this scheme is to place more emphasis on learning and less emphasis on grading and move the responsibility for learning on to the student and off of teacher subjectivity.

In teaching online courses at my university, my colleagues and I try to encourage professors to develop ongoing embedded assessment in which the learning activities students undertake are also the graded activities (or evidence of learning outcomes). That is, there is no separation between the activity and the grading. For example, we encourage debates, research projects, problem-based learning, and small-group case study development, because these are all activities as well as evaluation tools. In Chapter 4 we will look more closely at evaluation, assessment, and feedback practices.

Formative evaluation and feedback go hand in hand with other important self-evaluation techniques. Teaching explicit metacognitive skills, self-verbalization and self-questioning processes, study skills, and problem solving steps are all integral parts of helping students become better learners (Hattie, 2012). Given the right feedback and formative assessment, students should be able to rely on their emerging metacognitive skills to improve their learning outcomes. Having strong metacognitive skills doesn't mean that you always have the right answer, but it does mean that you know how to improve upon the answer you have. Metacognition, or "thinking about thinking," involves self-verbalization and self-questioning (the voice inside our head that helps us articulate or rethink problems and self-regulate) (Hofer & Sinatra, 2010), which in turn can be connected to the development of improved study skills. Some people know they study better when they read things out loud to themselves, while others prefer to work in groups and hear their ideas confirmed in social contexts. Both guided reflection and feedback from others encourage the development of personal study skills (Carruthers, 2009; Harmon-Jones & Winkielman, 2007).

6. Teacher Self-Reflection in Practice

> *To teach is to learn twice.*
> —Joseph Joubert

A teacher's day is full of myriad activities and emotions. At the end of the workday, teachers often feel so overwhelmed that the only thing they want to do is to stop thinking. This is not the most effective way to approach professional development; continual reflection yields better results (O'Donnell, Reeve, & Smith, 2012). The guidelines of the National Board for Professional Teaching Standards (NBPTS) for evaluating teachers are an excellent starting point for reflection about best teacher practices. One of their five core propositions is that "teachers think systematically about their practice and learn from experience" (NBPTS, 2002, p. 4). While not explicitly stated in the NBPTS standards, it can be presumed that one of the reasons that learning from experience is so valued is because **modeling the behavior we hope to cultivate in our students requires that we be open to self-improvement ourselves**. The old sayings are true and worth exemplifying: "If at first you don't succeed, try, try again." "It doesn't matter how many times you fall, but how many times you pick yourself back up again." Teachers who take the time to consider what they did right, what they did wrong, and what they want to do differently the next day are those who grow in their practice (Table 2.2). No one is perfect, but teachers who seek perfection are better than those who are complacent.

I once supervised a student thesis on reflective teaching in language arts classes, in which the author claimed that the simplistic habit of reflection ("Think about what you did and how to do it better next time") is deceptively difficult to cultivate (Wong, 2008). Teachers need to *learn* how to reflect, he insisted. The original concept of professional self-reflection, a term coined by Donald Schön (*The Reflective Practitioner*, 1983; *Educating the Reflective Practitioner*, 1987), was meant to be a pause in the daily routine to take stock of progress, problems, possibilities, processes, and products. O'Donnell and colleagues (2012) echo the importance of reflection to guide teacher action.

A teacher's ability to self-improve across his professional lifespan is associated with high-quality professional development sessions (Cubukcu, 2010; Fernandez, 2010). There has been a great deal of literature about teacher reflective practice over the past two decades (Dana & Yendol-Hoppey, 2008), especially through the use of technologies such as blogging, digital journals, video accounts, and other multimodal methods (Kajder & Parkes, 2012) not only

TABLE 2.2
A Teacher's Reflective Journal

UNIT:			
Objectives (competencies)	**How will I evaluate this?**	**What will I do** (how will I teach; what activities will I employ)	**Did it work? Why or why not?**

pen-and-paper journaling. The microteaching technique, in which a teacher reviews his own moves at a micro level through videotaping, has been around since the late 1960s but is currently enjoying a revival (Kallenbach & Gall, 1969; Kilic, 2010; Kpanja, 2001).

According to the UK government, **reflection is recognized as a core characteristic of the best teachers**:

> The most distinctive of these very good teachers is that their practice is the result of careful reflection . . . They themselves learn lessons each time they teach, evaluating what they do and using these self-critical evaluations to adjust what they do next time. (Office for Standards in Education of the UK, 2004, p. 10)

A teacher who embraces reflective practices is usually one who is more empowered, according to (Ghaye, 2010) especially if this reflection is undertaken in groups (Dana & Yendol-Hoppey, 2008). Similarly, Ng and Tan (2009) argue that **reflective practice is successful on an individual level but even more powerful in community settings**. That is, learning communities that take the time to reflect together about institutional as well as personal goals, as suggested by Senge and colleagues (2000), can provide a structure that fosters teacher improvement. Some of the most effective teaching cultures (e.g., Japan and Finland) employ the use of reflective group learning.

Ghaye (2001, 2010) reminds us that reflection on practice generally relates to thinking about problems that have occurred in the class setting, but **it is equally important to reflect on strengths and successes**, because these are natural sources of self-efficacy building. Taggart and Wilson (2005) make the case that reflection takes place on at least three distinct levels: (a) a dialectical (moral or ethical) level, (b) a contextual level, and (c) a technical level. For example, let's say I had a bad day. I blew up at the class and lost patience with a group of talkative kids, whom I accused of not paying attention. Taggart would ask me to reflect dialectically: I acted poorly on an ethical and professional level by yelling. Contextually, I probably employed an unsuccessful methodology, given the group's needs, which is why they began to chat in the first place. And on a technical level, it is likely that I asked the group to do something it wasn't prepared to carry out, either because the students didn't have the necessary skills or because the task didn't meet their personal needs.

How should I improve? First, I should rectify my professional and ethical status by apologizing to the group for my behavior. I should reassess the group's needs in relation to the objectives I have identified (Why didn't my activity work? When did I lose their attention? How can I regain both their trust, after yelling at them, and their interest, after missing the mark the first time around?). In the simplest of reflections, I can ask the students themselves for the answers to these questions, but as sophistication settles in, I should be able to come up with the answers on my own.

7. Appropriate Methodologies

A teacher's choice of classroom activities and methodologies influences student learning outcomes. I have witnessed successful activities without the achievement of class objectives, and the achievement of class objectives without good activities, but the greatest likelihood of success comes when clear objectives are paired with activities that promote their fulfillment. An appropriate methodology is one that responds to the learning objective while taking into account the student's developmental level (age) and background (stage and constructivist readiness). Teaching methodologies include the following strategies, either singly or in combination (although the choices are not limited to this brief list):

- General teaching strategies
  - Explanation
  - Elaboration
  - Modeling
  - Demonstration
  - Encouragement of student questioning
  - Reminders about procedures
- Direct instruction
- Worked examples
- Student-centered teaching
- Small-group learning
  - Discussion
  - Research
  - Peer teaching
  - Peer evaluation
- Writing programs (i.e., writing as a form of metacognitive development)
- Exposing students to reading

- ○ Reading to students
- ○ Having students read with others
- ○ Interpretation of subject-specific texts
- Behavioral organizers
  - ○ Nonlinguistic representations
  - ○ Concept mapping

Activities should not be chosen on the basis of their popularity or because they generally yield good results, but rather because they match the objectives of the class and the students' needs (Wiggins & McTighe, 2005). **Not all methodologies serve all objectives, nor do they resonate with all learners**. Great teachers know how to determine what is most appropriate in which circumstances and adjust their practice. For example, if a teacher's goal is to evaluate whether students master a certain process or structure, sharing a worked example (an example of a good product) is a perfect choice of activities because it satisfies the human brain's need to understand patterns (Beitman, 2009). That is, if I show a student what a great essay looks like (or how a science lab notebook should appear, or how a play should be written, or how a math problem should be laid out) and tell her, "If your work looks something like this, you're on the right track," then I instill in her a sense of confidence because she knows what is expected of her and she develops a mental pattern of "good" work in her area.

On the other hand, if my objective is to explain the relationship between concepts, then I won't necessarily choose a worked example, but rather a conceptual map. A mind map links ideas and offers a visual connection between concepts, which is ideal for showing the relationships between them. Similarly, if my objective is to measure my students' level of understanding or competence in a skill, such as applying a math or science formula, I might consider an activity focused on individual work so I can see what each student already knows on his or her own. While small-group activities in general have a positive impact on learning, it would be inappropriate in this instance because it isn't compatible with my objective (to see who has mastered the skill).

I once observed a young teacher as she reviewed several vocabulary words with her foreign language class, using the words one by one in various sentences. She clearly articulated a model sentence, then asked the students for another based on the pattern. She then gave her students a worksheet and asked them to fill in the blanks in the sentences given. At the end of the class, I asked the teacher the objective of the session, and she said it was for the students to correctly pronounce the appropriate vocabulary from the list. In this case, the activity was inconsistent with the objective of the class, which appeared to be vocabulary or sentence building, not pronunciation. As pronunciation can't be measured through written work, a worksheet was the wrong evaluation tool.

I went to another class and watched a vigorous debate about animal testing for medicines. At the end of the class, the teacher told me that she was measuring intellectual empathy, teamwork, and communication skills. She explained that her choice of topic for the debate was coincidental and served the secondary objective of showing that not all animal testing is legitimate for human products. Debate was an excellent choice of activity, as it coincided perfectly with both her primary and secondary objectives.

Great teachers understand the power of artful questioning to draw out reflections on the part of students. However, like any activity, questioning shouldn't be used all the time in every class, but rather only in those classes in which the objective is best achieved through its use. In fact, asking questions at the wrong moment can actually lead to confusion. Because of a phenomenon called "primacy-recency," the brain remembers best what happens first, second best what happens last, and everything in the middle is kind of blurred (Bradski, Carpenter, & Grossberg, 1994). This means that if I choose to use questioning at the wrong moment, I might instill a strong memory for an erroneous concept. For example, I could start a class by saying, "In the chapter you read last night, there was a very important date related to World War I. Which date was it?" and then call on Lani, who may give the wrong answer ("Uh, around 1860?"). As this is the first question of the class, it is likely that a high percentage of the students will remember Lani's incorrect answer the next day, despite any corrections I might give afterward. Questioning is powerful, but it should be used with questions that call for reflection, not for fact-based knowledge.

Similarly, there has been a lot of discussion about the importance of "discovery learning" in which students are encouraged to explore on their own. This is appropriate at certain moments when the objective is to get students to review their own perceptions of concepts based on past knowledge. However, not all learning is based on discovery, and some learning calls for more explicit teaching formats. For example, if I want students to learn a new math formula, direct instruction may be more compatible with the objective than discovery learning.

Methodology alone is not enough, however; communication plays a key role in guaranteeing the success of any methodology by stating precise objectives. I once observed a young, enthusiastic teacher use the day's newspaper as a prop for her class. She asked the students to identify all the sales they could find in the ads. The session morphed into a discussion about brand names and guarantees. At the end of the class, I asked the teacher what the objective of the lesson had been, and she told me it was to understand how to calculate interest rates. Good idea; bad execution. As the objective was not shared with the group, and as the teacher was inexperienced in classroom management, the course followed the students' whims instead of the teacher's aim and veered into no-man's-land. Had the teacher managed the class better and shared her objective, it is likely that her methodology would have been successful. This turns us to the importance of communication.

8. Communication

The quality of communication is connected to student learning outcomes. Teacher clarity, classroom discussion, concrete goal setting, and teacher expectations are all associated with successful practice (Asseily, 2012; Cruickshank, 1985; Cruickshank, Kennedy, Bush, & Myers, 1979; Hattie, 2012; McCroskey, 1992; L. R. Smith, 1985). The ability of the teacher to communicate well with individual students and with the class has a great impact on student learning (Cruickshank & Kennedy, 1986).

A group of students once complained to me about a teacher, saying he wasn't explicit enough in his directions. I asked what he had said, and they replied that when they had asked what would be on an upcoming test, he had told them, "Everything!" This is an example of how lack of clarity on the teacher's part can lead to anxiety on the students' end. Instead of focusing their energies on studying for the exam, the students were spending their time guessing at what the teacher might consider important enough to put on the exam. Unless the class objective is to learn how to be prepared for uncertainty in life, this is not a useful learning tactic. The students' time would have been better spent thoroughly reviewing important topics.

In other cases I have seen exhausted teachers complain that their students just don't follow instructions. These teachers claim to have articulated expectations dozens of times but report that the students don't come through. While it may be possible for entire groups of students to be lost and confused despite exemplary teaching, it should be a red flag to teachers if the majority of the class doesn't understand the instructions. If most of the students don't understand, it's more likely that the instructions aren't clear than that the students are all ignorant. Levy, Wubbels, and Brekelmans (1992) remind us that teacher and student perceptions about successful communication may differ widely. A teacher may perceive himself to be absolutely clear about an assignment, for example, but what really counts is whether the students share that opinion. That is, the key is what students comprehend, not what the teacher believes he transmits. One way to verify what students are taking in is to ask them to rephrase the instructions, forcing them to communicate with one another based on their perceptions and not rely solely on the teacher's words. I often stop in the middle of class, turn to a student randomly, and ask, "What did I just say?" or "what do you think that means?" to see if he or she can synthesize the ideas in words that might be better understood by the rest of the class.

In *Functions of Language in the Classroom*, Cazden, Vera, and Hymes (1972) began some of the most serious research on student-teacher communication patterns by considering sociological, psychological, linguistic, and anthropological perspectives, which helped advance an understanding of the importance that verbal and nonverbal communication have in classroom success (also see McCroskey, Sallinen, Fayer, Richmond, & Barraclough, 1996; Plax, Kearney, McCroskey, & Richmond, 1986). Cazden (2001) continued to expand on this research into the current millennium and found that **teachers who send clear messages—verbally, with their body language, through written communication, and by asking other students to paraphrase—are more successful than those who use just one mode of communicating the same message**. This might sound logical, but it is not executed with enough frequency in our classrooms.

Some of the most recent studies show that there is a distinct positive relationship between "teacher immediacy and clarity, and student emotional and cognitive interest and engagement" (Mazer, 2013, p. 86), indicating that McCroskey and colleague's model is still considered a good guide for teachers. However, communication is not as straightforward as one might imagine. Several subelements that fall within the communications category are related to student-teacher relations. For example, Andersen, Norton, and Nussbaum (1981) noted that teachers who were perceived by students as having more interpersonal solidarity (i.e., who were more open and friendly) were also perceived as being more effective, although in reality this was not the case. Even though positive perceptions elicit a great attitude toward the instructor, **there is no clear relationship between communicative style and cognitive learning**. That is, teachers with an open demeanor don't necessarily have smarter students. This means that teachers' communication styles—whether they are friendly or firm, approachable or otherwise—doesn't make one teacher better than another, since different students look for different types of guidance in their teachers. Students who are looking for a friend in their teachers prefer outgoing teachers, but they don't necessarily perform better because of this affinity.

Levy, Wubbels and Brekelmans (1997) also found that culture has a great influence on students' perceptions of their teachers' communication styles (see also Ligorio, 2010; Tomasello, 1999). Openness can be perceived as aggressiveness in some cultures, and humility can be mistaken for uncertainty, depending on the society. Independent of individual student perceptions, there is a clear link between students' affect toward their teacher, course content, learning outcomes and motivation levels.

What seems to be most strongly linked to student achievement in the realm of communication, however, is teacher clarity (Hattie, 2012; Land, 1979; Land & Smith, 1979). Is the teacher successful in sending a clear message about classroom goals and expectations, or is the message garbled or confusing? Was appropriate vocabulary used to transmit the message, given the age group? Was there enough discussion available to alleviate doubts and guarantee a precise understanding of teacher expectations? While most teachers enter a classroom with clear objectives in mind, this doesn't necessarily mean that the objectives have been communicated successfully to the students. **Clearly expressed goals are the key to ensuring success** and are highly related to teacher communication

9. *Learning in Groups*

Humans are social creatures, and if given the choice, the vast majority of us would choose to learn in groups where we can bounce ideas off of one another (Frith, 2012). There are few people who would choose to learn in isolation; the brain is a social organ, and much of what we learn about the world is due to our witnessing the different ways people interpret the same event. Thus, in many ways, students' academic success is related to their interaction with one another. Methodologies that incorporate student interaction, such as reciprocal teaching, cooperative versus individualistic or competitive learning activities, and appropriately managed peer tutoring and other peer influences can all have a positive impact on learning (Hattie, 2012).

Reciprocal teaching has the highest yield of all cooperative learning endeavors, primarily because there is a shared advantage: Both parties take turns teaching and learning (Carter, 1997; Palincsar, 1986). To incorporate more reciprocal teaching into my own classes, I changed one of my activities from an individual project to a group project. Whereas I used to ask my students to plan, research, and write a paper, I now ask the class to produce a journal. I achieve the same learning goals, plus I now have the added element of teamwork. The students are happier and inspire one another to achieve, and I am more pleased with their results. Covisibility motivates students who might otherwise turn in less-than-perfect work to perfect their submissions because they know their peers will see them.

It is in our human nature—one of our survival instincts—to prefer to win rather than to lose. This is because humans would prefer to have a reward than to be punished, and "[i]n humans, winning and losing situations can be considered as reward and punishment experiences" (Zalla et al., 2000, p. 1764). This can work either in favor of or against certain classroom activities. Competitive learning processes can yield high results; however, cooperative learning yields even better results (Johnson, Maruyama, Johnson, Nelson, & Skon, 1981). Like decisions about any other kind of learning methodology or classroom activity, the choice of whether to use a competitive, individualistic, or cooperative learning activity is determined by the objective.

The most positive element of cooperative activities involves the belief that "1 + 1 = 3," or that if one person shares her idea with another, then the result is something better than what the two individuals could have generated on their own. The success of most group work, however, depends largely on the way a teacher manages his classroom, which we turn to next.

10. Classroom Management

Today's classrooms are different than they used to be, and though it may sound cliché, there is a lot of truth to the idea that there are a greater variety of brains in our classrooms than ever before. Kids who never would have been given the opportunity to study are now crowding our schools, and seated alongside a student who has special needs because he's gifted is another kid who spends the majority of his day in front of a video screen and can't pay attention to the simplest instructions. **Because of the great variety of students in our classrooms, we need to rethink classroom management skills.**

Without good classroom management, and the control of unwanted disruptions and distractions, instruction is hampered; and without instruction, there is no learning (Hattie, 2009). A teacher can have all the credentials in the world, know his subject, plan a good lesson, and still have abysmal results if he doesn't know how to manage a class well (Fink, 2003). The art of classroom management is all about engaging students in a way that focuses their attention and energy toward the task at hand. One kid can distract the entire group, and if the teacher isn't adept at understanding the motives behind her actions, his reaction can make things worse. I have watched some teachers all but flee the class when faced with an anti-leader, who really only wants to be acknowledged and to help. Teachers need to be taught how to read the real motives of students in order to manage their own reactions well. There is long-standing evidence that precise teacher intervention allowing for more time-on-task in classroom settings leads to better learning (Bloom, 1974b). Teachers who have their fingers on the pulse of classroom activities develop "a form of synchrony or flow" that betters human interaction (Kent, 2013, p.13) and learning. What may appear to be good teacher intuition is now recognized as "teaching as a physiological phenomenon of brain activity" in which the human interaction of teaching moments are in synch (Yano, 2013, p.19).

Some inexperienced teachers make the big mistake of thinking "the class" is against them or that "the class is unmanageable" instead of understanding that the group is made up of individuals. Managing a class well begins with understanding each person's motivations for acting the way he or she does. Having said that, it is clear that masses act differently than individuals and are more than the sum of their parts. Understanding both individual motivators and triggers that get the class as a whole moving in the right or wrong direction is a fundamental aspect of good teaching.

Cultural norms can influence teachers' expectations of their students as well as students' expectations of teachers. I recall that when I was a child, my mother arranged Japanese lessons for my sisters and me. Fuji-San was a mild mannered, soft-spoken Japanese university student who came to our house a few times a week. My sisters and I loved the attention, and as four-, six- and seven-year olds, we thought the entire encounter was a game, like when our mother helped us with homework. My mother would always have infinite patience with us and go along with our imaginary friends and situations, and we expected Fuji-San to do the same. Usually he let us go off on tangents, and he would let the vocabulary lesson follow our lead. But once we hid in the closet, hoping to get Fuji-San to play with us. He had no idea how to react to this, and instead of coaxing us out or playing along, he simply left. I heard my mother apologizing profusely as he walked out. He had no idea how to manage such "undisciplined children." Whereas my sisters and I had every intention of learning (we liked the classes), we just expected something else of the teacher, and he of us. Fuji-San misunderstood our motivations—we didn't mean to be disrespectful and just thought we were playing—but he had other expectations. In this case, the students and the teacher were not on the same page as far as understanding one another's motives, resulting in zero classroom management on the part of the teacher and the sacrifice of any new learning.

Classroom behavior (how group dynamics are played out) is clearly related to classroom cohesion and climate (how well the group trusts itself and supports its members). Both behavior and cohesion are related to classroom management (how well the teacher maintains a high level of engagement of the group) and the ability of the teacher to reduce any tensions in the classroom. While behavior, cohesion, management, and tension regulation are not the same concepts, they are often found to be influenced by the same factors, and all of them impact student learning outcomes (Hattie, 2012). For example, a teacher's management style can have an impact on classroom behavior, cohesion, and climate as well as the engagement level of class members.

Most teachers these days understand that the term *discipline* comes from the Latin word for "teach." Management in a classroom setting means making all of the opportunities and challenges in a class setting work to one's advantage though the engagement of students. *The Highly Engaged Classroom* by Marzano and Pickering (2010) stresses **the importance of reducing the need to discipline by first creating a positive learning environment**. *Successful Classroom Management* (Eyster & Martin, 2010) is another recent title that emphasizes the use of praise to prevent problems in the classroom, thus reducing the need to "manage" problems at all.

There are many different angles to classroom management. Two divergent views are that management implies "care" versus "behavioral modification" (Nie & Lau, 2009). One large-scale study found that "caring" models of classroom management are a predictor of greater student satisfaction with school, whereas behavioral control is a significant predictor of negative classroom misbehavior. It is not surprising that the *Journal of Positive Behavior Interventions* suggests several reasons why **effective classroom managements are clearly those that seek to reinforce positive behavior rather than punish poor behavior**. Many argue that good relationships are at the heart of low-disciplinary-incidence classrooms (e.g., Beatty-O'Ferral, Green, & Hanna, 2010).

This takes us to the most important aspect of classroom management: Classroom management is really not about the classroom at all, but about the individual. Freiberg and Lamb (2009) convincingly argue that 50 years of research have shown that when teachers try to manage classrooms instead of students, they are ineffective. This is like a businessperson managing "the office" as opposed to the individual personalities she works with. Freiberg and Lamb note that person-centered, prosocial classroom management yields better results: "Person-centered classrooms facilitate higher achievement, and have more positive learning environments with stronger teacher-student relationships than teacher-centered or traditional classrooms" (p. 99). They suggest that there are four social dynamics teachers should be aware of: "(a) social-emotional emphasis, (b) school connectedness, (c) positive school and classroom climate, and (d) student self-discipline" (p. 99). Thus, according to Freiberg and Lamb, there are four corresponding keys to good classroom management: (a) making an emotional link to the subject matter, (b) helping students feel like a part of a learning community, (c) ensuring respect in the classroom, and (d) helping students learn how to self-regulate. This model of teachers' pedagogical knowledge is based on the social environment of the student and the belief that when a learner feels she belongs to something greater than herself (her classroom, her school), she will find a better social-emotional balance and have better self-discipline, thus reducing the need to "manage" any bad behavior (Gaustad, 1992).

The confidence of new teachers in handling groups of students can be boosted with in-service training. However, actual classroom management skills are harder to develop in professional development settings and rely more on real-life experience. Just as medical doctors can't fully grasp what their profession will be like until they're in the field treating patients on their own, teachers can never really understand what it's like to successfully manage a classroom until they've done it. This phenomenon gives rise to the ongoing discussion about the importance of on-site training in teacher formation (see Kaufman & Moss, 2010; Wong, 2002) and the role that practicums play in guaranteeing new-teacher success.

Moving On

This categorization of Hattie's findings into 10 subgroups give credence to the classroom interventions suggested in Part II of this book. However, before moving on to the 50 applications of MBE science, we turn to Chapter 3, which visits some of the best 20th-century models of education as a means of clarifying the role of school learning in the 21st century to be sure this book's objectives are clearly articulated.

Suggested Readings

Student Self-Efficacy

Bandura, A. (1997). *Self–efficacy: The exercise of control.* New York, NY: Freeman.

Joët, G., Usher, E. L., & Bressoux, P. (2011, August). Sources of self-efficacy: An investigation of elementary school students in France. *Journal of Educational Psychology, 103*(3), 649–663. doi: 10.1037/a0024048

Konlod, K. E., Miller, S. P., & Konold, K. B. (2004). Using teacher feedback to enhance student learning. *Teaching Exceptional Children, 36*(6), 64–69.

Riding, R. J., & Rayner, S. (2001). *Self-perception: International perspectives on individual differences.* Westport, CT: Greenwood.

Schunk, D. H., & Mullen, C. A. (2012). Self-efficacy as an engaged learner. In S. L. Christenson, A. L. Reschly, & C. Wylie (Eds.), *Handbook of research or student engagement* (pp. 219–235). New York, NY: Springer.

Schunk, D. H., & Pajares, F. (2002). The development of academic self-efficacy. In. A. Wigfield & J. Eccles (Eds.), *Development of achievement motivation.* San Diego, CA: Academic Press.

Schunk D. H., & Pajares, F. (2009). Self-efficacy theory. In K. R. Wentzel & A. Wigfield (Eds.), *Handbook of motivation in school* (pp. 35–54). New York, NY: Taylor & Francis.

Wentzel, K. R., & Wigfield A. (Eds.). (2009). *Handbook of motivation in school.* New York, NY: Taylor & Francis.

Teacher Credibility and Self-Efficacy

Beatty, M. J., & Behnke, R. R. (1980). Teacher credibility as a function of verbal content and paralinguistic cues. *Communication Quarterly, 28*(1), 55–59. doi: 10.1080/01463378009369358

Finn, A. N., Schrodt, P., Witt, P. L., Elledge, N., Jernberg, K. A., & Larson, L. M. (2009). A meta-analytical review of teacher credibility and its association with teacher behaviors and student outcomes. *Communication Education, 58*(4), 516–537. doi 10.1080/03634520903131154

Guo, Y., Plasta, S. B., Justice, L. M., & Kaderavek, J. N. (2010). Relations among preschool teachers' self-efficacy, classroom quality, and children's language and literacy gains. *Teaching and Teacher Education, 26*(4), 1094–1103. doi: 10.1016/j.tate.2009.11.005

Hare, W. (2007). Credibility and credulity: Monitoring teachers for trustworthiness. *Journal of Philosophy of Education, 41*(2). doi: 10.1111/j.1467-9752.2007.00557.x

Haskins, W. (2000, March 3). Ethos and pedagogical communication: Suggestions for enhancing credibility in the classroom. *Current Issues in Education* [Online], 3(4). Available at http://cie.ed.asu.edu/volume3/number4/

Schwarzer, R., & Hallum, S. (2008). Perceived teacher self-efficacy as a predictor of job stress and burnout: Mediation analyses. *Applied Psychology: An International Review, 57,* 152–171 (Special Issue: Health and Well-Being). doi: 10.1111/j.1464-0597.2008.00359.x

Settlage, J., Southerland, S. A., Smith, L., & Ceglie, R. (2009). Constructing a doubt–free teaching self: Self-efficacy, teacher identity, and science instruction within diverse settings. *Journal of Research in Science Teaching, 46*(1), 102–125.

Tuchman, E., & Isaacs, J. (2011). The influence of formal and informal formative pre-service experiences on teacher self-efficacy. *Educational Psychology, 31*(4), 413-433.

Witt, P. L., & Kerssen-Griep, J. (2011). Instructional feedback I: The interaction of facework and immediacy on students' perceptions of instructor credibility. *Communication Education, 60,* 75–94.

Attitudes Toward Academic Interventions

Cochran, J. L., McCallum, R. S., & Bell, S. M. (2010). Three A's: How do attributions, attitudes, and aptitudes contribute to foreign language learning? *Foreign Language Annals, 43*(4), 566–582.

Cote, J. E., & Levine, C. G. (2000). Attitude versus aptitude: Is intelligence or motivation more important for positive higher-educational outcomes? *Journal of Adolescent Research, 15*(1), 58–80. doi: 10.1177/0743558400151004

Fisher, D., & Frey, N. (2010). *Enhancing RTI: How to ensure success with effective classroom instruction and intervention.* Alexandria, VA: ASCD.

Guskey, T. R., & Jung, L. A. (2011). Response-to-intervention and mastery learning: Tracing roots and seeking common ground. *Journal of Educational Strategies, Issues and Ideas, 84*(6), 249–255. doi: 10.1080/00098655.2011.590551

Hwang, A., & Arbaugh, J. B. (2009). Seeking feedback in blended learning: Competitive versus cooperative student attitudes and their links to learning outcome. *Journal of Computer Assisted Learning, 25*(3), 280–293. doi: 10.1111/j.1365-2729.2009.00311.x

Kassim, N. L. A., Daud, N. M., & Daud, N. S. M. (2013). Interaction between writing apprehension, motivation, attitude and writing performance: A structural equation modeling approach. *World Applied Sciences Journal, 21*, 102–108. doi: 10.5829/idosi.wasj.2013.21.sltl.2143

Mekheiemer, M. A. A. (2012). Assessing aptitude and attitude development in a translation skills course. *CALICO Journal, 29*(2), 321–340.

Mercer, S. H., & DeRosier, M. E. (2010). A prospective investigation of teacher preference and children's perceptions of the student-teacher relationship. *Psychology in the Schools, 47*(2), 184–192.

Peterson, P. L. (1977). Interactive effects of student anxiety, achievement orientation, and teacher behavior on student achievement and attitude. *Journal of Educational Psychology, 69*(6), 779–792.

Rao, D. B. (2003). *Scientific attitude vis-à-vis scientific aptitude.* New Delhi, India: Discovery.

Rhodewalt, F., Morf, C., Hazlett, S., & Fairfield, M. (1991). Self-handicapping: The role of discounting and augmentation in the preservation of self-esteem. *Journal of Personality and Social Psychology, 61*(1), 122–131.

Sternberg, L.C., Varua, M. E., & Yong, J. (2012). Attitude, secondary schools and student success in a tertiary mathematics unit. *Journal of Modern Accounting and Auditing, 8*(4), 480–487.

Constructivist Designs

Ansari, D., & Karmiloff-Smith, A. (2002). Atypical trajectories of number development: A neuroconstructivist perspective. *Trends in Cognitive Sciences, 6*(12), 511–516.

Jantzen, K. J., Steinberg, F. L., & Scott Kelso, J. A. (2004). Brain networks underlying human timing behavior are influenced by prior context. *Proceedings of the National Academy of Sciences of the United States of America, 101*(17), 6815–6820.

Karmiloff-Smith, A. (2009). Nativism versus neuroconstructivism: Rethinking the study of developmental disorders. *Developmental Psychology, 45*(1), 56–63.

Martin, D. J., & Loomis, K. S. (2006). *Building teachers: A constructivist approach to introducing education.* Independence, KY: Wadsworth/Cengage.

Mayer, R. E. (1996). Learning strategies for making sense out of expository text: The SOI Model for guiding three cognitive processes in knowledge construction. *Educational Psychology Review, 8*(4) 357–371.

Mayer, R. E., & Alexander, P. A. (Eds.). (2011). *Handbook of research on learning and instruction.* New York, NY: Routledge.

Piaget, J. (1950). *The psychology of intelligence.* New York, NY: Routledge.

Rivet, A. E., & Krajcik, J. S. (2008). Contextualizing instruction: Leveraging students' prior knowledge and experiences to foster understanding of middle school science. *Journal of Research in Science Teaching, 45*(1), 79–100.

Swanson, H. L. (2011). The influence of working memory growth on reading and math performance in children with math and/or reading disabilities. In P. Barrouillet & V. Gaillard (Eds.), *Cognitive development and working memory: A dialogue between neo-Piagetian and cognitive approaches* (pp. 203–231). Hove, England, UK: Psychology Press.

Westermann, G., Mareschal, D., Johnson, M., Sirois, S., Spratling, M., & Thomas, M. (2007). Neuroconstructivism. *Developmental Science, 10*(19), 75–83.

Evaluation and Assessment Best Practices

Bennett, R. E. (2011). Formative assessment: A critical review. *Assessment in Education: Principles, Policy & Practice, 18*(1), 5–25. doi.org/10.1080/0969594X.2010.513678

Black, P., & Wiliam, D. (2009). Developing the theory of formative assessment. *Educational Assessment, Evaluation, and Accountability, 21*, 5–31.

Black, P., & Wiliam, D. (2010). Inside the black box: Raising standards through classroom assessment: Formative assessment is an essential component of classroom work an can raise student achievement. *Phi Delta Kappan, 92*(1), 81–90.

Cauley, K., & McMillan, J. (2010). Formative assessment techniques to support student motivation and achievement. *The Clearing House, 83*(1), 1–6.

Crisp, G. T. (2012). *Integrative assessment: Reframing assessment practice for current and future learning.* Philadelphia, PA: Routledge.

Hofer, B. K., & Sinatra, G. M. (2010). Epistemology, metacognition, and self-regulation: Musings on an emerging field. *Metacognition and Learning, 5*(1), 113–120. doi: 10.1007/s11409-009-9051-7

Koedinger, K., McLaughlin, E. A., & Heffernan, N. T. (2010). *A quasi-experimental evaluation of an on-line formative assessment and tutoring system.* Amityville, NY: Baywood. doi: 10.2190/EC.43.4.d

Nicol, D. J., & Macdarlane-Dick, D. (2006). Formative assessment and self-regulation learning: A model and seven principles of good feedback practice. *Studies in Higher Education, 31*(2), 199–218. doi: 10.1080/03075070600572090

Sadler, R. D. (1998). Formative assessment: Revisiting the territory. *Assessment in Education: Principle, Policy & Practice, 5*(1), 77–84. doi: 10.1080/0969595980050104

Torrance, H., & Pryor, J. (1998). *Investigating formative assessment: Teaching, learning and assessment in the classroom.* Florence, KY: Taylor & Francis.

Trees, A. R., Kerssen-Griep, J., & Hess, J. A. (2009). Earning influence by communicating respect: Facework's contributions to effective instructional feedback. *Communication Education, 58,* 397–416.

Wiliam, D. (2011). *Embedded, formative assessment.* Bloomington, IN: Solution Tree.

Teacher Self-Reflection

Ferraro, J. M. (2000). Reflective practice and professional development. *Teacher and Teacher Education.* Retrieved from http://www.ericdigests.org/2001-3/reflective.htm

Jay, J. K., & Johnson, K. L. (2002). Capturing complexity: A typology of reflective practice for teacher education. *Teacher and Teacher Education, 18*(1), 73–85. doi: 10.1016/S0742-051X(01)00051-8

Larrivee, B. (2000). Transforming teaching practice: Becoming the critically reflective teacher. *Reflective Practice: International and Multidisciplinary Perspectives, 1*(3), 293–307. doi:10.1080/713693162

Loughran, J. J. (2002). Effective reflective practice: In search of meaning in learning about teaching. *Journal of Teacher Education, 53*(1), 33–43.

Moon, J. (2004). *A handbook of reflective and experiential learning: Theory and practice.* London, UK: Routledge.

O'Donnell, A., Reeve, J., & Smith, J. (2012). *Educational psychology: Reflection for action* (3rd ed.). Hoboken, NJ: Wiley.

Schön, D. (1983). *The reflective practitioner.* New York, NY: Basic Books.

Schön, D. (1987). *Educating the reflective practitioner.* San Francisco, CA: Jossey-Bass.

Sutherland, K. A. (2013). The importance of critical reflection in and on academic development. *International Journal for Academic Development, 18*(2), 111–113. doi: 10.1080/1360144X.2013.802074

Van Manen, M. (1995). On the epistemology of reflective practice. *Teachers and Teaching: Theory and Practice, 1*(1), 33–50. doi: 10.1080/1354060950010104

York-Barr, J., Sommers, W. A., Ghere, G. S., & Montie, J. K. (2001). *Reflective practice to improve schools.* Thousand Oaks, CA: Corwin.

Yost, D. S., Sentner, S. M., & Forlenza-Bailey, A. (2000). An examination of the construct of critical reflection: Implications for teacher education programming in the 21st century. *Journal of Teacher Education, 51*(1), 39–49.

Zwozak-Myers, P. (2012). *The teacher's reflective practice handbook: Becoming an extended professional through capturing evidence-informed practice.* New York, NY: Routledge.

Teacher Communication and Clarity

Asseily, A. (2012). The power of language: How small shifts in language create big shifts in relationships and behavior. In M. Shuayb (Ed.), *Rethinking education for social cohesion: International case studies* (pp. 220–231). New York, NY: Palgrave Macmillan.

Cruickshank, D. R. (1985). Applying research on teacher clarity. *Journal of Teacher Education, 36*(2), 44–48.

Cruickshank, D. R., Kennedy, J. J., Bush, A., & Myers, B. (1979). Clear teaching: What is it? *British Journal of Teacher Education, 5*(1), 27–33.

Cruikshank, D. R., & Kennedy, J. J. (1986). Teacher clarity. *Teaching and Teacher Education, 2*, 43–67.

Kerssen-Griep, J. (2001). Teacher communication activities relevant to student motivation: Classroom facework and instructional communication competence. *Communication Education, 50*, 256–273.

Classroom Management and Engagement

Brekelmans, M., Wubbels, T., & den Brok, P. (2002). Teacher experience and the teacher-student relationship in the classroom environment. In S. C. Goh & M. S. Khine (Eds.), *Studies in educational learning environments: An international perspective* (pp. 73–99). Singapore: World Scientific.

Choi, I., & Lee, K. (2009). Designing and implementing a case-based learning environment for enhancing ill-structured problem-solving: Classroom management problems for prospective teachers. *Educational Technology Research and Development, 57*(1), 99–129.

Christenson, S. L., Reschly, A. L., & Wylie, C. (Eds). *Handbook of research on student engagement.* New York, NY: Springer.

Eyster, R. H., & Martin, C. (2010). *Successful classroom management: Real-world, time-tested techniques for the most important skills set every teacher needs.* Naperville, IL: Sourcebooks.

Marzano, R. J., Marzano, J. S., & Pickering, D. J. (2003). *Classroom management that works: Research-based strategies for every teacher.* Alexandria, VA: ASCD.

Marzano, R. J., & Pickering, D. J. (2011). *The highly engaged classroom.* Bloomington, IL: Marzano Research Laboratory.

Ritchhart, R., Church, M., & Morrison, K. (2011). *Making thinking visible: How to promote engagement, understanding, and independence for all learners.* San Francisco, CA: Jossey-Bass.

Valerios, K. (2012). Intrinsic motivation in the classroom. *Journal of Student Engagement: Education Matters, 2*(1), 30–35.

About Math and Science (Challenges)

Berch, D. B., & Mazzocco, M. M. M. (Eds.) (2007). *Why is math so hard for some children? The nature and origins of mathematical learning difficulties and disabilities.* Baltimore, MD: Paul Brooke.

Crawford, A. (2007). Learning to teach science as inquiry in the rough and tumble of practice. *Journal of Research in Science Teaching, 44*(4), 613–642. doi: 10.1002/tea.20157

Dehaene, S. (2011). *The number sense: How the mind creates mathematics* (Rev. and updated ed.). New York, NY: Oxford University Press.

De Smedt, B., Ansari, D., Grabner, R. H., Hannula, M. M. Schneider, M., & Verschaffel, L. (2010). Cognitive neuroscience meets mathematics education. *Educational Research Review, 5*(1), 97–105.

Hiebert, J., Stigler, J. W., Jacobs, J. K., Givvin, K. B., Garnier, H., Smother, M., et al. (2005). Mathematics teaching in the United States today (and tomorrow): Results from the TIMSS 1999 video study. *Educational Evaluation and Policy Analysis, 27*(2), 111–132.

Johnstone, A. H. (1991). Why is science difficult to learn? Things are seldom what they seem. *Journal of Computer Assisted Learning, 7*(2), 75–83.

Kang, N.-H. (2008). Learning to teach science: Personal epistemologies, teaching goals, and practices of teaching. *Teaching and Teacher Education, 24*(2), 478–498. doi: 10.1016/j.tate.2007.01.002

Lowery, N. V. (2002). Construction of teacher knowledge in context: Preparing elementary teachers to teach mathematics and science. *School Science and Mathematics, 102*(2), 68–83. doi: 10.1111/j.1949-8594.2002.tb17896.x

Lozano, M. (2005). *Programas y experiencias en popularización de la ciencia y la tecnología.* Bogotá, Colombia: Andrés Bello.

Millar, R. (1991). Why is science hard to learn? *Journal of Computer Associated Learning, 7*(2), 66–74. doi: 10.1111/j.1365-2729.1991.tb00229.x

Miranda, L. (2010). On trends and rhythms in scientific and technological knowledge evolution: A quantitative analysis. *International Journal of Technology Intelligence and Planning, 6*(1), 76–109.

National Mathematics Advisory Panel. (2008). *Foundations for success: The final report of the National Mathematics Advisory Panel.* Washington, DC: U.S. Department of Education.

Ryve, A. (2011). Discourse research in mathematics education: A critical evaluation of 108 journal articles. *Journal of Research in Mathematics Education, 42*(2), 167–199.

Sjoberg, S., & Schreiner, C. (2008). *Young people, science and technology attitudes, values and interest and possible recruitment.* Brussels: ROSE.

Steele, J. R., & Ambady, N. (2006). "Math is hard!" The effect of gender priming on women's attitudes. *Journal of Experimental Social Psychology, 42*(4), 428–436. doi: 10.1016/j.jesp.2005.06.003

Thomson Reuters. (2011). *National science indicators.* Retrieved January 12, 2011, from http://thomson-reuters.com/products_services/science/science_products/a-z/national_science_indicators/

Titus, G. (2008). *U.S. competitiveness in science and technology.* Pittsburgh, PA: RAND.

Williams, J. (2011). Looking back, looking forward: Valuing post-compulsory mathematics education. *Research in Mathematics Education, 13*(2), 213–222. doi: 10.1080/14794802.2011.585831

Yanowitz, K. L. (2010). Using analogies to improve elementary school students' inferential reasoning about scientific concepts. *School Science and Mathematics, 101*(3), 133–142. doi: 10.1111/j.1949-8594.2001.tb18016.x

CHAPTER 3

Why Do We Teach?
Models of Education that Create Usable Knowledge

Our progress as a nation can be no swifter than our progress in education. The human mind is our fundamental resource.
—John F. Kennedy

Pretest yourself: Do you think, given what we know about evidence-based best practices today, that teachers should spend more time (a) giving feedback, (b) setting challenging goals, (c) fighting for smaller class sizes, or (d) separating boys and girls during instruction time?

According to Hattie's research (2009, 2012), the first two interventions are far more powerful than the second two. While smaller class sizes and single-sex schools may seem an attractive solution to the challenge of improving learning, giving feedback and setting challenging goals have effect sizes almost double those of class size and splitting boys and girls during instruction. The reasons for this can be described by psychological theories of motivation that are now confirmed in neuroscience.

Teachers work hard. Despite their relatively short workday, it is estimated that good teachers spend the same amount of time planning and grading as they do in front of the class, resulting in a work schedule that is far longer than that of most other professions: perhaps more than 50 to 60 hours a week (Kennedy, 2010; Strauss & Alexander, 2012). Because time is always of the essence in schools, we as teachers need to be clear about which teaching interventions have the most impact and devote our energies toward those activities rather than tasks that result in only minor gains. And to do that, we need to clearly understand our role and the reasons we teach at all.

The Actors and Locations of Learning

There are a lot of stakeholders in education. The individual child, his parents, the teachers, the school administrators, the school board, and society at large all want the student to succeed. We know, however, that teaching and learning are not always as successful as everyone would like, and different actors tend to blame one another. As teachers, it's important that we understand not only what others can be expected to contribute to a student's academic achievement, but also what we are responsible for as professionals.

We all know that **children come to our schools with a lot of baggage**. Those of poorer socioeconomic status (SES) have challenges that richer children don't; low-SES kids tend to be exposed to far fewer intellectual stimuli than high-SES kids. Kids with books in their homes come to school with a leg up on pre-reading skills, widening the disparity between the "haves" and the "have-nots" even before their first day of formal classes. The evidence for the influence of home reading on literacy is overwhelming (e.g., L. Baker & Scher, 2002; L. Baker, Scher, & Mackler, 1997; L. Baker & Wigfield, 1999; Coley, 2002; Duncan et al., 2007; Guthrie et al., 2007; Purves & Elley, 1994; Whitehurst & Lonigan, 2001). But which has more impact on student achievement, the home or the school (the parents or the teachers)?

According to Hattie, the teacher (as a personality) and teaching (how subjects are taught) have greater impact on student achievement than the home or school environment (2009). Teachers are often heard grumbling in the classroom about the poor "raw material" they have been given to work with. "If only the kids came from better homes . . . ," "If only their parents would be more involved . . . ," "If only the neighborhood was better . . . "—*then* they would be able to be better teachers because the students would be able to learn. It behooves us to accept that we as teachers have a far greater impact on student achievement than what happens in the home. While good home and school environments are important and definitely help, their influence is not as weighty as that of teachers and teaching, given the time spent at school and the intellectual quality of the interactions that occur. Many teachers reject the idea that their role is greater than that of parents (this is an awesome responsibility), but when they are told *why* this is so, they embrace their role accordingly. While it sounds counterintuitive, the amount of time a mother spends with her kids has a significant impact in its absence but not its presence; if a mother is not around or available, adolescent risky behavior is increased (Milkie, Nomaguchi, & Denny, 2012). Teachers actually have a greater impact on student learning outcomes than parents because their main objective with students is to help them learn, whereas parents have several different objectives, such as well-being, nutrition, and safety, and concentrate a smaller portion of their efforts on their kids' academic achievement.

As mentioned in the Introduction, the community and society as a whole do have an important role to play in shaping the way a learner thinks about education. A student's attitude toward schooling influences his learning outcomes. However, in terms of positive influences on academic achievement, nothing is more important than the quality of the teacher and her level of teaching expertise (Green, 2010). Rather than measuring the quality of a teacher by what her best students can do—they will generally do well in school independent of or despite us—we should judge a teacher's quality based on how far she can pull up her worst students (Hattie, 2012). A child who has a poor teacher will attain about two and a half years' worth less of learning across his lifespan than a child with a good teacher (Sanders & Rivers, 1996). So, given all of the stakeholders in education and the various actors that influence the teaching-learning process, teachers would do well to accept that, after the student's own self-perception as a learner, their role has the greatest impact on achievement.

This brings us to a vital question: Just what are we trying to get students to achieve?

The Goals of Great Teaching

Formal education has managed to reach an average level unthought-of a century ago. The presumption that everyone in the neighborhood can and should be able to read is only four or five generations old. Basic math and literacy knowledge are now more the rule than the exception, something the Founding Forefathers would have thought enviable as they dreamed of a more perfect union shouldered by a highly educated workforce. Today, education is no longer just for the elite; it's regarded as everyone's right, as declared in 1990 during the World Declaration on Education for All. We have come a long way, but it's not enough. Not all classroom experiences yield the expected academic and social norms of achievement, and some of the best and brightest students either opt out of the system or fail to reach their potential because our classroom experiences are dull or deaden the innate drive to learn. We teachers can do better.

Thinking About Teaching and Teaching to Think

> *The world as we have created it is a process of our thinking. It cannot be*
> *changed without changing our thinking.*
> —Albert Einstein

There is a lot of talk these days about the need to develop "deep" thinkers for societal and individual growth, although what exactly this means is somewhat undefined (Chart & Kendall-Taylor, 2008). The 21st-century models indicate that teachers must go beyond teaching superficial levels of understanding and help learners reach a more profound level of knowledge about subjects that transcend the classroom and impact real life (Commission on the Future of Higher Education, 2006; Niemi, 2009). Business leaders tell us that without deep thinking, classroom experiences consist of simple memory exercises that constitute superficial jabs at knowledge. This structure can't yield graduates who are able to compete for jobs internationally, care for their communities, think creatively and critically about their world, or learn across the lifespan.

Few would argue against cultivating deeper thinking skills; however, articulating and visualizing what should actually be taking place in the classroom is more complex. But let's take a stab at it. What does ideal, progressive, 21st-century education look like? We can imagine a school system that cultivates **creative**, **problem-solving** individuals who work in **collaborative** and **innovative** environments, guided by **ethical** standards. In this system, *how* **to think carries more weight than a score on any particular topic or subject matter.** Students are **digitally literate**, use **communication** tools efficiently, and maintain a level of **flexibility** by taking advantage of **cross-cultural** and **interdisciplinary** approaches to problems. They are **productive** while remaining **accountable**, and they take **responsibility** for their actions. Their effective **management of information** and their **use of technology** stimulate their great **curiosity**, which in turn inspires them to seek yet more knowledge as **life-long learners**. This definition of 21st-century skills is derived from the work of various authors on the topic (e.g., Binkley, Erstad, Herman, Raizen, & Ripley, 2010; European Parliament, 2007; European Parliament, 2007; Gardner, 2008; Jerald, 2009; Metiri Group, 2003; Mishra & Kereluik, 2011; Organisation for Economic Co-operation and Development, 2005; Partnership for 21st Century Skills, 2007; Trilling & Fadel, 2009; Zhao, 2012). If we combine these various academic visions of 21st-century skills, it's easy to appreciate the InfoSemantics interpretation of Bloom's taxonomy (Figure 3.1). From this perspective, curriculum choices (what to teach) are less important than **being open to new ideas**, the ability to **manage complexity**, **knowing**

FIGURE 3.1
Performance Verbs for Learning Outcomes

Performance Verbs for Learning Objectives							
		Behavioral Verbs				Weighing	Delivery formats
Level 1 Knowledge	Recall or remember previously learned information without necessarily understanding, using, or changing it.	Count Identify **Match** Quote Recognize **Select** View	Define Indicate **Name** Read Record Select Write	Draw **Label** **Outline** Recall Repeat **Tabulate**	Enumerate **List** Point Recite Reproduce Trace	1	Drill & Practice; Online self-study; Traditional Classroom
	>>>Novice Level						
Level 2 Comprehension	Understands the meaning and interpretation of instructions and problems to the point of explaining a problem in own words.	**Associate** Communicate Estimate Exrapolate Infer Restate	Compare Describe Explain Generalize **Interpolate** Summerize	Contrast Discuss Express Give examples Paraphrase Trace	Convert **Distinguish** Extend Interpret Predict	2	Presentation followed by practice; Online self-study Traditional Classroom
Level 3 Application	Applies knowledge and concepts learned to solve new, concrete or abstract problems in the work place.	Administer Chart Control Inform Operate Report **Transfer**	Apply **Collect** Demonstrate Execute Instruct Present Show	Calculate **Complete** Deploy **Find** **Modify** Produce **Solve** Use	Change Compute Determine Implement Navigate Relate Teach Utilize	3	Presentation followed by practice; Online self-study Traditional Classroom
Level 4 Analysis	Breaks problems, materials, or concepts into component parts to understand structural relationships and abstract organizational principles.	Analyze Correlate **Distinguish** **Isolate** **Organize** **Separate**	**Break Down** Diagram Examine Illustrate Outline Subdivide	**Categorize** **Deconstruct** Focus Infer **Prioritize** Translate	**Classify** **Differentiate** **Group** **Order** Resolve Transform	5	Case Study or other Problem-Solving session, followed by discussion and debrief; Traditional Classroom or Live Virtual Classroom
Level 5 Synthesis	Combines components or elements together in structures or patterns to create new concepts, meanings, objects, or wholes.	Adapt **Combine** Create Facilitate **Integrate** Personalize Produce **Reorganize** **Structure**	**Arrange** Compile Design Formulate Model Plan Propose **Restructure** **Substitute**	**Assemble** **Compose** Develop Generate Modify Predict **Prearrange** Revise Write	**Build** **Construct** Devise Incorporate Negotiate Prepare **Reconstruct** Rewrite	7	Case Study or other Problem-Solving session, followed by discussion and debrief; Traditional Classroom or Live Virtual Classroom
Level 6 Evaluation	Uses definite criteria to make assessments and/or value judgments to choose between different applications of concepts, ideas, methods or materials to achieve a given purpose.	Appraise Contrast Determine **Grade** Measure Test	Approve Criticize Defend Interpret **Rank** Recommend	Assess Critique Discriminate Judge **Rate** Support	Compare Decide Evaluate Justify Select	10	Complex problem-solving sessions using case studies, role plays etc; Traditional Classroom or Live Virtual Classroom
					>>>Expert Level		

Note: All learning behaviors must be observable and measurable. Do not use vague, nebulous or immeasurable verbs in learning objective statements.
Note: Verbs in bold black text suggest drop and drag activities.

Used with permission from Infosemantics Pty Ltd (infosemantics.com.au)

how to use tools, the ability to **work with heterogeneous groups**, being **tech savvy**, being an **autonomous** learner, and being **empathetic** intellectually. In other words, which courses or subject areas we teach doesn't matter nearly as much as teaching kids *how* to think in general.

While it can be argued that curriculum choices are important to the extent that they reflect market demands for skills sets and cultural values (Altonji, Blom, & Meghir, 2012), the merit of subject-based curricula in a knowledge-based society has to be questioned (Young, 2010). Independent of whether school should be structured around subjects or something else, we all agree on the need for better thinkers.

Cultivating Good Thinking Over Time
Thanks to plasticity, the brain adapts to what it does most (Butz, Wörgötter & van Ooyen, 2009). If I mindlessly memorize facts, then my rote memory pathways will be refined. However, if I am constantly challenged to analyze and empathize with views unlike my own, then my brain should be able to adapt to the habit of critical thinking.

Benjamin Bloom suggested the concept of mastery learning back in the 1960s with the goal of elevating the general objectives in every class from simple knowledge to greater skill and attitude development (Bloom, 1968). More than a decade ago, Fink (2003) echoed Bloom's call to educators to move away from "covering material" to improving results on specific learning outcomes, a viewpoint that is very much appreciated today and incorporated into all of the 21st-century models presented here. Current thinking in MBE also reinforces this perspective: How I am taught shapes my brain as much as or more than what I am taught. Habituated processes automate certain actions, including thinking skills (Costa & Kallick, 2009).

For example, if a student is constantly challenged by his teacher to see other viewpoints and to entertain the least likely scenario, the probability that he will eventually be able to do this on his own without a teacher's guidance is higher than if he has never been coached in these habits. Similarly, if a student is constantly reminded that working with others instead of against them tends to yield greater results, then he will eventually habitually think this way on his own. In like manner, learners who are continually encouraged to never give up and persevere in finding the best answers, even if they're not the easiest, will eventually develop the habit of doing this on their own. One of the reasons that the Japanese are superior in math learning outcomes is that teachers consistently ask their students to think about what they already know about the problem at hand and to review all resources that could possibly help them solve the problem. This kind of habituated revision of past knowledge ("What do I already know that can help me resolve this?") serves the learner not only in school, but throughout his life. Whenever the learner is faced with a new problem, he knows the steps to take to resolve it because he has become habituated to the process of retrieval over many years of practice.

Thinking about thinking, or metacognition, is a core aspect of deep learning. Despite calls across several decades for the development of improved metacognition (A. L. Brown, 1975, 1978, 1980, 1987; Dunlosky & Metcalfe, 2009), the availability of stimulating activities (Pang, 2010), and the backing of school systems around the world (Longworth, 2013; Pellegrino & Hilton, 2012), it is evident that not enough teachers work on boosting their students' general thinking and metacognitive skills (Hutchinson, 2004). The 21st-century learner requires a special kind of teacher who can cultivate these skills.

Some teachers are naturally successful in getting their students to think deeply about the subject at hand and potentiate their ability to link surface and deep levels of understanding to arrive at truly higher-level learning experiences. Unfortunately, there is also a clamor from teachers who feel that the time they could be using to teach more deeply is being relegated to preparing for and administering mandatory testing (Kelly, 2013a; 2013b). Thus, even when test scores are high, administrators should be wary of becoming complacent and continually ask themselves, "Which is really more important in the long run, not just during the school years: our students' test scores, or their ability to think?"

What's Worth Learning?

> *Next in importance to freedom and justice is popular education, without which neither freedom nor justice can be permanently maintained.*
> —James A. Garfield

David Perkins likes to ask, "What's worth learning?" in school (2010a) in the context of contemporary times. Perkins believes we spend far too much time talking about what method or activity to use as opposed to first clearly establishing what should be learned (see, e.g., Figure 3.2). **If we establish that the objective of our learning endeavors is deeper thinking as opposed to memorization of superficial knowledge, then choosing appropriate methodologies becomes far easier, as the activity should match the learning objective.** Some activities stimulate deep thinking; others don't. Taking notes of "Googleable" information is only desirable if our objective is improved penmanship. Activities such as debate and project-based learning are more desirable if we seek deeper thinking.

Perkins suggests that we need to "educate for the unknown" with a welcoming attitude toward what might be or what may emerge in life, rather than living in a fantasy world in which the isolated instruction of different subjects in silos will somehow magically help us in the world in which we live today. Subject-specific instructional vacuums, in which topics are covered stripped of their natural contexts, deprives the learner of authentic experiences. Even well-executed in-class exercises don't often transfer out of the classroom, leaving both students and teacher bewildered about the true objectives of learning.

FIGURE 3.2
The Goals of Formal Education

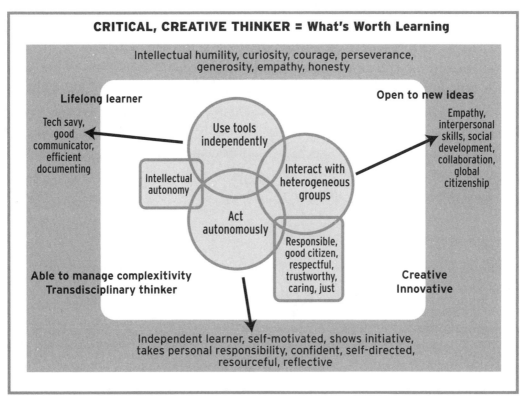

Source: Author.

I once had a medical student who took my education class as an elective course. Throughout the semester he became more and more aware of the unbalanced system in which he was captive. On the one hand, he had some teachers who required him to read like crazy and prepare for problem-based learning encounters in class, which made him feel alive and challenged. He had to link knowledge and applications from the past to new situations, which demanded a creative and agile response. Other teachers, however, presented him with a battery of multiple-choice questions, for which he could often find reasonable explanations for *a*, *b*, *c*, and *d* (the smarter you are, the less effective standardized tests are at reaching your level of understanding, because you can find a way to justify all the answers). As teachers, we have to stop sending mixed messages to our students about the importance of thinking skills.

To do this, we have to embrace higher-level thinking skills as our ultimate classroom objective and conduct classroom activities that reach that goal. Some authors argue that, while it may not be easy to do, we can rework state-mandated tests to serve as critical thinking activities. Stuart Yeh recommends constructing "tests worth teaching to . . . that emphasize critical thinking" (2001). The trap of standardized tests is what Howard Gardner, one of the leading educators of our time, calls the passage of society from an environment that nurtures "universal" men and women to "specialized black out" (2008, p. 74), in which we reward very limited types of knowledge and narrow thinking in daily classroom practice. If we as teachers don't rethink the way we teach and evaluate, we'll send students the message that specialized, limited, single-answer thinking is the key to success. But there are very few problems in life that have just one answer (which can be "found at the back of the book, but don't look!" as Sir Ken Robinson likes to say. For a tragic-comic view of the ironic state of education, readers are encouraged to watch Robinson's video *Changing Education Paradigms* [2010]). Deeper, higher, broader, and more profound reflection in all subject areas is needed.

Gardner (2008) notes that for the first three decades of a person's life, a person spends more time in school than in any other societal institution, which places a great deal of pressure on the teacher as a key facilitator in forming the type of society we seek by cultivating basic thinking regimes. Most habits of mind are cultivated in school settings. It would be criminal to convince a generation of students that the importance of school—and therefore, of life—is to pass tests. Twenty-first century skills lists can be varied, but one thing stands out: The world needs more people who think deeply, connect ideas, and construct knowledge in new ways. Thus, we teachers need to foster better habits of mind that result in more of what Ritchhardt, Church, and Morrison (2011) refer to as "visible thinking," or observable evidence of deeper, more connected reasoning.

Dozens of new contributions have been made to MBE since *Mind, Brain, and Education Science* was published (Tokuhama-Espinosa, 2011), and this book summarizes the best of these additions to the field. To offer a backdrop against which to consider the new findings, it's important to recognize existing models that are highly effective in focusing attention on quality student learning by striving to cultivate deep thinkers. Many of the great educational frameworks of our times celebrate the ultimate goal of teaching as the enhancement of thinking skills: Critical thinking (Paul, 1992; Paul & Elder, 2001), "Six Facets of Understanding" (Wiggins & McTighe, 2005), significant learning (Fink, 2003), best practice (Zemelman, Daniels, & Hyde, 2005), "Five Minds for the Future" (Gardner, 2008), habits of mind (Costa & Kallick, 2000, 2009); Bloom's "LOTS vs. HOTS" scale (Anderson & Krathwohl, 2001; Bloom, Engelhart, Furst, Hill, & Krathwohl, 1956), theory of mind (Baron-Cohen, 1991; Buckner & Carroll, 2007; Siegel, 2001; Torey, 2009), "Nine Instructional Strategies" (Marzano, Pickering, & Pollock, 2001), and "Teaching the Digital Generation" (McCain & Jukes, 2008). We will briefly review some of these key contributions in the remaining part of this chapter.

Strong Teaching Models

The object of education is to prepare the young to educate themselves throughout their lives.
—Robert M. Hutchins

Albert Einstein's reflection that "Education is what remains after one has forgotten what one learned in school," is not a slight to teachers, but rather a way of emphasizing that life-long learning is a habituated set of practices rather than a list of specific formulas or grammatical rules. Teachers are vital in teaching learning habits to think better. To go beyond superficial learning and foster deep thinking, we need to connect fundamental and less tangible concepts into an authentic context for the student. Over the past 50 years there has been a movement to broaden student-teacher interactions and thereby heighten social and cognitive processes by going beyond the "surgical delivery model" (the "classic" childbirth position is comfortable for the doctor but illogical for the patient), in which methodologies are chosen for the convenience of teachers and schools rather than for the well-being of the student. There are a number of great "deep thinking" frameworks, a few of which are shared below and whose main characteristics are then cross-referenced to suggested a new framework for thinking: MBE + Visible Learning.

Beyond Bloom's Taxonomy: LOTS and HOTS
One of the oldest "modern" frameworks for thinking in formal education is Benjamin Bloom's taxonomy, which is familiar to most teachers. Bloom and his colleagues (1956) developed descriptors for affective, psychomotor, and cognitive domains that soon morphed into a simple

hierarchy of solely cognitive functions, which was not their intention, leading to a classification of lower-order thinking skills (LOTS) versus higher-order thinking skills (HOTS). Two of Bloom's students and coauthors of the 1956 publication tried to bring this hierarchy into the more practical realm by attaching specific verbs to items in the list (Anderson & Krathwohl, 2001), which revived interest in Bloom's taxonomy at the beginning of the century (Figure 3.3).

FIGURE 3.3
Bloom's Taxonomy Now and Then

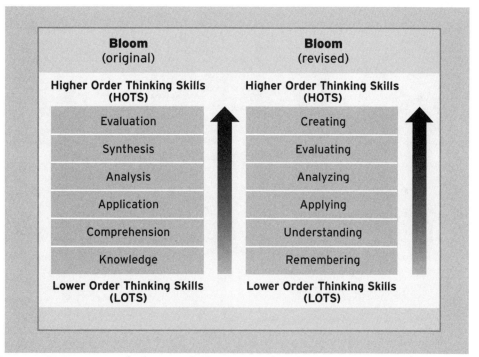

Bloom, Benjamin S., Taxonomy of Educational Objective, *Book 1, Cognitive Domain, 1ˢᵗ Edition, © 1984, p.18. Reprinted by permission of Pearson Education, Inc., Upper Saddle River, NJ.*

Suppose Ms. Green and Ms. Potts both teach third-grade science, and on a particular day in March they both claim to be teaching the same class objective: categorization of animals. In Ms. Green's class, the students are given an example and then asked to complete a worksheet by drawing a line from each animal to its category (Figure 3.4).

On the other hand, in Ms. Potts's class, the students are shown pictures of different types of animals and then asked to practice categorizing together as she asks them questions. Which animals have heads? What about tails? Which have two feet? Four feet? Which of them move

FIGURE 3.4
Ms. Green's Categorization Game

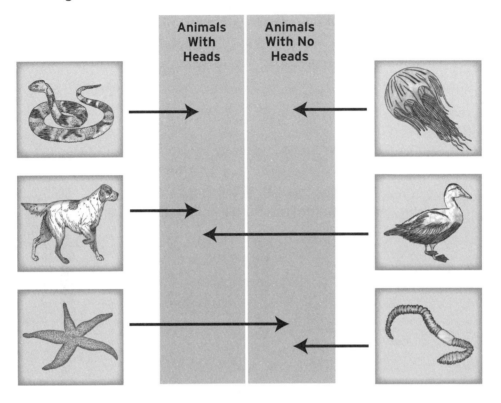

FIGURE 3.5
Ms. Potts' Categorization Game

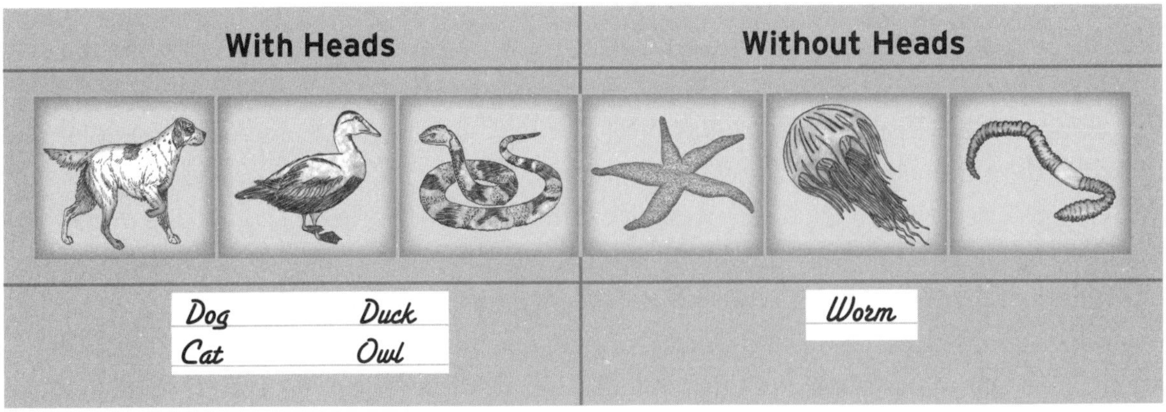

by walking? Flying? Swimming? Slithering? Which animals have they seen in real life? Where? What do they think animals with no heads can eat? How do animals without heads get nutrition? The children shout out their animals, and Ms. Potts confirms or corrects their answers as needed. She then shows them how to draw a diagram of their categorization, put cutouts of different animals into the correct category box, and then write out the names of the animals.

To put Ms. Green's and Ms. Potts's classes into perspective, let's compare each of their methodologies to some of the criteria suggested by the Teaching as Leadership website (2011):

1. "Teach skills through real-world contents" (p. 56). Teachers can facilitate learning by framing new ideas in authentic contexts for students, using examples from their daily lives. In Ms. Potts's class there was time devoted to discussion about where the animals live, what they eat, and how they get nutrition and whether the children had ever seen the animals in real life before. In Ms. Green's class, students simply memorized categories (with or without heads) so there was little contextualization of the information outside of the activity itself.

2. "Vary the content in which students use a newly taught skill" (p. 57). The key to transfer is the application of concepts in a variety of settings. This means that instead of simply handing out worksheets, teachers should consider a variety of contexts, such as games, simulations, case studies, and problem-based learning. Ms. Potts was slightly better at this, as she made a game out of the classification process, motivating the students' involvement.

3. "Throughout . . . instruction, take every opportunity to emphasize the building blocks of higher-order thinking" (p. 57). Remember that basic concepts must be learned and memorized before moving ahead in constructivist design. Teachers who take a constructivist approach and scaffold lessons to different developmental levels will be more successful. Ms. Potts explicitly taught categorization skills before asking her students to categorize on their own and called attention to this process so that the students were able to do this later, on their own. She took the time to build background knowledge by showing the children how to classify, then arranged the items along the dimension of body parts. In the future she can build off this lesson by asking students to make hypotheses about the categories (for example, do all animals without heads live in the water or underground? Is a head necessary for certain nutritional needs?). She can then ask the children to draw inferences about the information (Can we say that all farm animals have heads? Why or why not?). From there, she can scale up the lesson even further and ask her students to analyze the animals on the basis of their components (What are the characteristics of animals with heads? Do they all have four legs?). She can then ask them to solve problems and encourage them to think about the thinking strategies they are using. For example, she can ask them to complete this sentence: "All animals need nutrition to live, but only animals with heads can...."

As we compare classrooms that emphasize LOTS versus those that incorporate HOTS, however, it's important to remember that **integration of all of the levels results in better thinking, and different levels of thinking require different teaching techniques**. Unfortunately, some members of the learning community took Bloom and his colleagues' ideas to imply that some levels are "better" than others and showed Bloom's taxonomy as climbing from simple understanding through comprehension, application, and synthesis and finally up to evaluation and creation of something new. Most educational models now shy away from a simplistic hierarchy model and embrace the idea that both LOTS and HOTS are important in the learning process. The danger occurs when classroom time is dominated by lower-level skills, detracting from the time needed to develop HOTS. The children in Ms. Green's class will reach a lower level of thinking on the LOTS-HOTS scale than Ms. Potts's class, not only because of the amount of exposure to the concept they are given (discussion, cut-out classification, writing names of the animals), but also because of the depth of thinking required. Which teacher's students will achieve the class objective? Gareth Surgey (2012) has shared some ideas about how to meet objectives at each level of Bloom's Taxonomy (Figure 3.6). While many still think of Bloom's work as a hierarchy, the modern vision is more circular or iterative in practice as it is clear that each level is of equal importance. (Another model that should be considered is Structured Observed Learning Outcomes [SOLO] by Biggs and Collis [1982] which seeks to remedy some of the LOTS vs. HOTS controversies rethinking the process of evaluating outcomes in a slightly different way.)

Something Benjamin Bloom could not have known back in the 1950s and 60s was that there are distinct neural mechanisms underlying each level of thinking, linking his taxonomy to modern MBE concepts. Remembering a word (Paller & Gross, 1998), understanding the meaning of the word something (Jackendoff, 2002; Pulvermüller, Shtyrov, & Ilmoniemi, 2005), applying the word in a proper sentence (Jackendoff, 2002), analyzing the word's meaning and usage (Mills et al., 2004), evaluating the best choice of words (Brookshire & Nicholas, 1993), and creating the context for the right use of the word (Butterworth, 1975; Patterson, Nestor, & Rogers, 2007) use distinct though sometimes overlapping connectomes in the brain. The brain is trained through different neural circuitry to remember, understand, analyze, synthesize or create, with some levels serving as building blocks for others, and all need to be reinforced through good teaching.

FIGURE 3.6

How to Meet Objectives at Each Level of Bloom's Taxonomy, According to Surgey (2012)

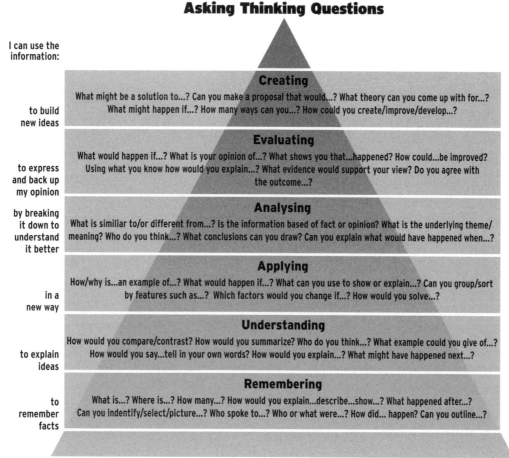

Asking Thinking Questions

I can use the information:

Creating
What might be a solution to...? Can you make a proposal that would...? What theory can you come up with for...? What might happen if...? How many ways can you...? How could you create/improve/develop...?

to build new ideas

Evaluating
What would happen if...? What is your opinion of...? What shows you that...happened? How could...be improved? Using what you know how would you explain...? What evidence would support your view? Do you agree with the outcome...?

to express and back up my opinion

Analysing
What is similiar to/or different from...? Is the information based of fact or opinion? What is the underlying theme/meaning? Who do you think...? What conclusions can you draw? Can you explain what would have happened when...?

by breaking it down to understand it better

Applying
How/why is...an example of...? What would happen if...? What can you use to show or explain...? Can you group/sort by features such as...? Which factors would you change if...? How would you solve...?

in a new way

Understanding
How would you compare/contrast? How would you summarize? Who do you think...? What example could you give of...? How would you say...tell in your own words? How would you explain...? What might have happened next...?

to explain ideas

Remembering
What is...? Where is...? How many...? How would you explain...describe...show...? What happened after...? Can you indentify/select/picture...? Who spoke to...? Who or what were...? How did... happen? Can you outline...?

to remember facts

Used with permission of Gareth Surgey © 2012, Creative Commons.

Fink's Significant Learning

L. Dee Fink (2003) defines learning in terms of observable changes in behavior. That is, he sees learning as being integrated and constituting a continuum of growth over the lifespan. Fink's taxonomy is a successor to Bloom's in that he has, after more than 50 years, reintegrated the affective elements, which have long been overshadowed by the cognitive elements of Bloom and his colleague's original ideas. The first three elements of Fink's taxonomy seem nearly the same as Bloom's first five levels: **Foundational knowledge** is the combination of knowledge and comprehension (understanding and remembering information and ideas); **application** is, well, application (skills, critical, creative and practical thinking skills, managing projects); and **integration** is analysis and synthesis (connecting ideas, disciplines, people, realms of life). Fink's "new" contribution appears in the second three elements, which venture into the unique social-emotional-personal realm: **learning how to learn** (becoming a better student, inquiring about a subject, becoming a self-directed learner, applying metacognitive skills), **caring** (developing new feelings, interests, and values), and the **human dimension** (learning about oneself and others).

Significant learning takes many forms and usually starts with a hook. A hook I used recently in class had to do with sleep. In a neuropsychology course I taught, we discussed the mind-body relationship and the impact that sleep has on learning. After I explained the mechanisms of sleep and their role in attention and memory, the students shared personal applications of this knowledge, such as how their sleep patterns had been changed by external forces, or how being particularly tired had affected their studies. The energy in the room crept higher and higher as the students commiserated about the impact lack of sleep had had on their memory and attention. Andrés became excited and shared how this information was going to *change his life*, then devised an experiment for the class. Several students volunteered to participate by taking power naps at various assigned intervals during the following weeks to determine the impact on their learning. Many students were never the same after this class.

This is, hopefully, an example of significant learning. If a teacher helps a student gain **foundational knowledge** about a topic (sleep, in this case), then she can facilitate his **application** of that same knowledge to different types of problems in real life by evoking his deep personal interest (his **caring**) and inspiring him to **seek his own learning** on the subject. And if the student is able to mentally **integrate** the new subject material with his other knowledge and experiences (e.g., see how lack of sleep has actually impacted all aspects of his life, including his learning in other classes), this allows him to experience the **human dimension** of the subject by seeing its authenticity in his own life (e.g., by considering how power napping might help improve his attention and memory both in class and in life in general). Fink reminds us that any single type of learning is good, but that the significance of the learning experience is much greater when all six kinds of learning occur (Figure 3.7).

FIGURE 3.7
Fink's Significant Learning

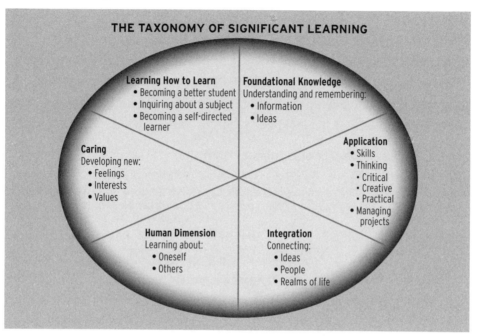

The important role of emotions in the learning process becomes even clearer when we consider classroom studies (e.g., Kovalik, 1998) and new discoveries in Mind, Brain, and Education science, such as Mary Helen Immordino-Yang's findings on social affect, which show that how we feel influences how well we can learn (see, e.g., Immordino-Yang & Damasio, 2007). To Fink, **caring and the human dimension are the human face of learning interactions.** They're also what students remember most about their classes often years later. The human dimension happens when a teacher takes a personal interest in a student or encourages a passion for a particular topic, or when a teacher asks a student why he's distracted and then listens to his story with genuine concern. The caring element is evident in the sincere interest a sincere teacher shows in the learner's development (Teven & McCroskey, 1997).

Similar to Fink's taxonomy is Wiggins and McTighe's "Six Facets of Understanding" in that there is the presumption that all six aspects of learning work simultaneously, are equally important, and nurture one another.

Wiggins and McTighe's Six Facets of Understanding
Wiggins and McTighe's "Six Facets of Understanding," which structure the *Understanding by Design* (2005) framework, are **explanation**, **interpretation**, **application**, the ability to **shift perspective**, **empathy**, and **self-assessment** (Figure 3.8). Like the thinking models just described, this model moves away from a purely hierarchical mindset and gives equal importance to each element, all of which are considered crucial to deeper thinking and learning.

FIGURE 3.8
Wiggins and McTighe's Six Facets of Understanding

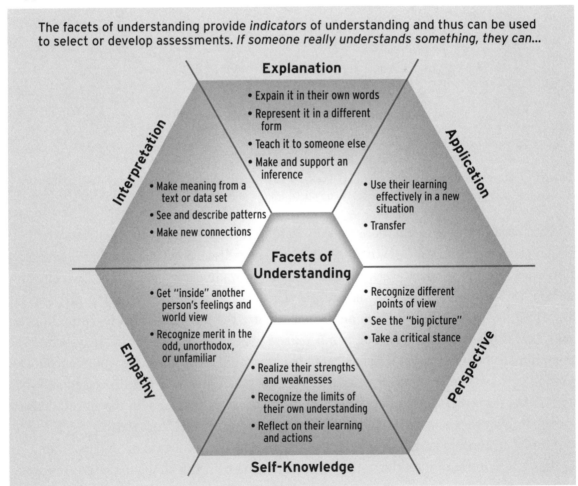

The facets of understanding provide *indicators* of understanding and thus can be used to select or develop assessments. *If someone really understands something, they can...*

Explanation
- Expain it in their own words
- Represent it in a different form
- Teach it to someone else
- Make and support an inference

Interpretation
- Make meaning from a text or data set
- See and describe patterns
- Make new connections

Application
- Use their learning effectively in a new situation
- Transfer

Facets of Understanding

Empathy
- Get "inside" another person's feelings and world view
- Recognize merit in the odd, unorthodox, or unfamiliar

Perspective
- Recognize different points of view
- See the "big picture"
- Take a critical stance

Self-Knowledge
- Realize their strengths and weaknesses
- Recognize the limits of their own understanding
- Reflect on their learning and actions

Wiggins and McTighe (2011)

Wiggins and McTighe suggest that teachers who incorporate all six facets in their teaching-learning design are more successful than those who use only one or a few (or none) of the facets. Let's look at Mr. Daniels, a 10th-grade chemistry teacher. Mr. Daniels begins by insisting that students do the lion's share of the work: His mantra is "Never work harder than your students" (Jackson, 2009). He feels that students must learn to **explain** and "provide thorough and justifiable accounts of phenomena, facts, and data" (Wiggins & McTighe, 1998, p.1). So when he asks them about elements on the periodic table, he is not seeking a memorized answer, but rather a justification for each element's placement.

To keep his students engaged, Mr. Daniels uses the Bryn Mawr Serendip website's "Periodic Table of Comic Books" (Holler & Selegue, 2012) to help students relate each chemical element to a story. They must then learn to **interpret** what they are learning about the periodic table by "tell[ing] meaningful stories, offer[ing] apt translations, [and] provid[ing] a revealing historical or personal dimension to ideas and events[,] mak[ing] [the subject] personal or accessible through images, anecdotes, analogies, and models" (Wiggins & McTighe, 1998, p. 1). This means that students in Mr. Daniels's chemistry class not only learn where the elements came from, but also begin to appreciate where they come into play in their own lives. Simultaneously, they learn to **apply** and "effectively use and adapt what they know in diverse contexts" (Wiggins & McTighe, 1998, p. 1). For example, a particular student may know that oxygen is something needed to sustain life, but Mr. Daniels invites her to expand her understanding by reading the comic books or taking advantage of videos and extra readings.

At the same time, Mr. Daniels's students must be able to **shift perspective** by "see[ing] and hear[ing] points of view through critical eyes and ears" and "see[ing] the big picture" (Wiggins & McTighe, 1998, p.1). Even as they are learning about the action of oxygen in various contexts, they are discovering how oxygen is similar to and different from other elements and investigating its role in relation to other elements. This process is not complete unless they also learn to **empathize**—that is, to "find value in what others might find odd, alien, or implausible" and "perceive sensitively on the basis of prior indirect experience" (Wiggins & McTighe, 1998, p.1). Perhaps Mr. Daniels's students learn to appreciate how the depletion of oxygen sources in the ocean is affecting other life on earth. This global process should then lead to a **bettered self-knowledge** in which students "perceive the personal style, prejudices, projections, and habits of mind that both shape and impede our own understanding" and become "aware of what they do not understand and why understanding is so hard" (Wiggins

& McTighe, 1998, p. 1). What Mr. Daniels knows, either instinctively or through training, is that each of the different facets of understanding relates to different neural circuits in the brain and needs to be developed over time.

While Mr. Daniels's example seems to exemplify a step-by-step process with a clear beginning and end, Wiggins and McTighe argue that the learning process can begin with any one of the facets; the key is including them all in the learning design. One way that Wiggins and McTighe suggest remembering to include each of the six facets is to think of performance verbs associated with each phase (Table 3.2). Teachers can use these verbs to ensure they are giving equal attention to each facet.

TABLE 3.1
Performance Verbs Associated With the Six Facets of Understanding

Explanation	Interpretation	Application	Perspective	Empathy	Self-knowledge
demonstrate	create analogies	adapt	analyze	assume role of	be aware of
derive	critique	build	argue	be like	realize
describe	document	create	compare	be open to	recognize
design	evaluate	debug	contrast	believe	reflect
exhibit	illustrate	decide	criticize	consider	self-assess
express	judge	design	infer	imagine	
induce	make sense of	exhibit		relate	
instruct	make meaning of	invent		role-play	
justify	provide metaphors	perform			
model	read between the lines	produce			
predict	represent	propose			
prove	tell a story	solve			
show	translate	test			
synthesize		use			
teach					

Source: Adapted from Understanding by Design Professional Development Workbook *(p. 23), by Grant Wiggins and Jay McTighe, Alexandria, VA: ASCD. © 2004 by ASCD. Adapted with permission. Learn more about ASCD at www.ascd.org.*

Costa and Kallick's Habits of Mind

Costa and Kallick (2000, 2009) describe the habits of mind theory they developed in the 1980s as a way to stimulate reflection by rehearsing certain questions until they become automatic. Costa and Kallick believe that if students cultivate a habitual questioning of their actions, they will better prepared to meet new learning challenges not only in school, but also in life. For example, let's say that Rachel is in the fifth grade. In history class she is faced with learning about the development and significance of the U.S. Constitution. According to her state's standards (see, e.g., State of California, 2011), she will have to understand how the 13 autonomous states defeated British rule and how they eventually needed to modify the Articles of Confederation. She will need to learn about the key people who brought together the representatives at the Constitutional Convention in Philadelphia in 1787 and understand how hard it was for them to agree on the new rules of the nation.

Costa and Kallick hope that Rachel's teachers are astute enough to capitalize on her developing habits of mind to help her think about how to learn this information. They create a mock convention to help Rachel resolve the following questions (based on Costa & Kallick, 2000, pp. 13–14):

Rachel Thinks: *How can I learn from this? What are my resources? How can I draw on my past successes with problems like this? What do I already know about the problem? What resources do I have available or need to generate?*

Rachel Answers: We made up rules for our class at the beginning of the year. Maybe it's just the same thing on a bigger scale?

Rachel Thinks: *How can I approach this problem flexibly? How might I look at the situation in another way? How can I draw on my repertoire of problem solving strategies? How can I look at this problem from a fresh perspective?*

Rachel Answers: When I disagree with someone, my mom always tells us to find "a middle way" and compromise. Instead of being pigheaded, what can I compromise on?

Rachel Thinks: *How can I illuminate this problem to make it clearer? More precise? Do I need to check my data sources? How might I break this problem down into its component parts and develop a strategy for understanding and accomplishing each step?*

Rachel Answers: We're being asked to write a new Constitution for a new nation. That's a big job! What are the smaller parts? My teacher always said to think about who, what, when, where, why, and how. How can I dividide this job into these pieces to make it more manageable?

Rachel Thinks: *What do I know or not know? What questions do I need to ask? What strategies are in my mind now? What am I aware of in terms of my own beliefs, values, and goals in regard to this problem? What feelings or emotions am I aware of that might be blocking or enhancing my progress?*

Rachel Answers: I know I don't know what this should look like when we're finished. Maybe if we find a constitution that was already written by another country, we could use that as a model?

Rachel Thinks: *How does this problem affect others? How can we solve it together, and what can I learn from others that would help me become a better problem solver?*

Rachel Answers: Will the British hate us afterwards? What new problems will this cause? What can we tell them that will make them stay friends with us, even after we split?

If repeated over time, these types of questions become automatic and, eventually, "habits of mind." Teachers need to know how to stimulate this type of reflection in their students. The activities that motivate students to use these habits have clear neuroscientific underpinnings, which many teachers may not yet understand. For example, the neural networks involved in strengthening executive functions are exercised by the type of self-questioning activities exemplified above and should be enhanced throughout the lifespan (see Diamond, 2012).

If successful, Costa and Kallick's model would yield a society in which we all were continually:

1. Persisting
2. Thinking and communicating with clarity and precision
3. Managing impulsivity
4. Gathering data through all our senses
5. Listening with understanding and empathy
6. Creating, imagining, innovating
7. Thinking flexibly
8. Responding with wonderment and awe
9. Thinking about thinking (metacognition)
10. Taking responsible risks
11. Striving for accuracy
12. Finding humor
13. Questioning and posing problems

14. Thinking interdependently
15. Applying past knowledge to new situations
16. Remaining open to continuous learning

These characteristics are typical of good problem solvers as well as deep thinkers and result not only in good school learners, but also in good citizens overall.

Premack and Woodruff's Theory of Mind

A key element of teaching is grounded in the Oracle of Delphi's advice to Socrates to "know thyself." In modern terms, this can be equated with self-knowledge that allows us to locate ourselves on the scale of social norms. (*Am I behaving as the group would expect? Do my actions preserve or disturb the social expectations of my peers?*) Knowing who I am, what I value, and how I fit in (or not) within the social scheme of things is essential to self-knowledge. Self-knowledge plays chicken-or-egg with theory of mind, which suggests that in order to understand oneself, one has to understand the "Other" (but to understand the Other, one needs to know oneself). The Other does not have to be one's best friend or family members, or even one's peers or teachers; these days, the Other can be social media.

Let's say that it's Saturday night and 15-year-old Pedro contemplates whether he should go to a party he's been invited to or stay at home, do some exercise, read a bit for school, and watch a movie. He flips on his computer to see if the Facebook invitation has been updated and comes across a video recommended by a friend on the volleyball team. It's a short motivational video featuring footage of all the best athletes over the past year, and it's narrated by an energetic, strong-willed believer in the power of pushing yourself to your own limits. It talks about how one person who thought he had reached his own personal best pushed beyond it. It acknowledges that things might take longer than one would expect, or be harder than one believes they should be, but highlights how the payoff is worth it. It talks of short-term decisions that have long-term repercussions and recommends postponing gratification in order to obtain "real" rewards in life, not just a quick thrill (Cohen et al., 2009). Pedro decides to stay in, watch a movie, and exercise rather than going out partying. The power of social media has overwhelmed the power of his real friends.

Many teenagers find themselves trapped between how they would choose to act on their own and what others (parents, peers, teachers) ask of them. Nowadays social media play an equally strong role in changing self-perception. Pedro decided that his "peers" were actually the athletes who sacrificed going to parties for better treatment of their bodies and who sought fulfillment of long-term goals over short-term satisfaction. By appreciating the mindsets of the other athletes—the one who talked of taking 12 years to get a GED, and the one who said he'd gotten up at 4 a.m. to train for years, and the coach who told how he'd pushed a football player into the water and let him know that he'd be ready to play when he wanted to win as much as he wanted to breathe—he decided this was the group against which he wanted to measure himself in terms of personal growth.

Theory of mind tries to elaborate and define the individual in the context of the people and society in which he lives. Humans have the capacity to attribute mental states to others by interpreting what others feel and think. The theory of mind, which rests on the belief that learning is highly dependent on contact with others as well as the emotions one feels when with those "others," is a deep-thinking model that has guided modern reflection in classroom settings and beyond.

Premack and Woodruff (1978) introduced the concept of theory of mind in the 1970s. It was defined clearly in humans by Baron-Cohen (1991), Dennett (1992), Meltzoff (1995), and Gagliardi in the 1990s (Gagliardi et al., 1995), and has recently been made popular by Daniel Siegel (2001, 2012), Steven Pinker (1997, 2002), Jaime Pineda (2008), and Uta Frith and Cris Frith (2003). Work by Iacoboni, Molnar-Szakacs, Gallese, Buccino, and Mazziotta (2005) and Rizzolatti and Craighero (2004) helped bring the mirror neuron system into the theory of mind discussion by suggesting that an individual "mirrors" the behavior of others.

The idea of the "social brain," or social cognition, has been around for several decades, starting with Michael Gazzaniga's classic book *The Social Brain* (1985), but only in recent years has it become viewed as one of the keys to education. Why? Theory of mind, which may at first seems purely individualistic, is actually the key to understanding human survival (Gazzaniga, 1985). Gazzaniga makes it clear that "when you get up in the morning . . . You think about status. You think about where you are in relation to your peers" (Waytz, 2009, para. 2). Given the importance of social cognition to self-knowledge, it's surprising that it isn't more widely studied and appreciated by teacher practitioners.

Theory of mind is rooted in a great deal of neurological studies that have taken place over the past decade (Ochsner et al., 2004; Pelphrey, Morris, & McCarthy, 2004; Samson, Apperly, Chiavarino, & Humphreys, 2004; Saxe, 2004; Saxe & Powell, 2006; Scholz, Triantafyllou, Whitfield-Gabrieli, Brown, & Saxe, 2009; Schultz, 2003), and reminds us that in order to survive, we need to not only know how to manage ourselves well, but be aware of and respond to the social expectations of others (Mundy & Newell, 2007). For example, if my social network reacts in shock to my actions, I have the ability to be conscious of their reaction. For the good of the group I can modify my actions, and eventually I should learn to anticipate their reactions based on an "adaptive function" in my brain (Heatherton, 2011). This is a self-regulatory component in the human brain that allows me to moderate my actions to respond to others. This adaptive function helps me not only fit into school, but life in general.

The theory of mind complements the models previously mentioned and highlights the importance of integrating knowledge of social cognition into education. Since much of what a student learns is based on what his peers consider worth learning, teachers must be highly aware of the social dynamics they create when planning learning activities in the classroom.

Gardner's Five Minds for the Future
Howard Gardner (2008) has called for a more thoughtful approach to the minds we cultivate in society and illuminated the need for teachers and parents alike to escape the easy answers and delve into a more reflective practice. Gardner asks us to acknowledge that it is our collective responsibility to cultivate five different mindsets throughout each learner's life. Each of these five "minds" is explained below.

The Disciplined Mind. The disciplined mind implies a mastery of a subject area (discipline), indicating a professional level of expertise. Such a discipline is developed over the lifespan and implies a deep and thorough understanding of one's field. Society needs more disciplined minds, argues Gardner, because we now have too many people who know a little about a lot of things, but society would be better served by people who know a lot about a few things in depth. Our formal education models do not respond well to allowing students to go deeply into subjects; they are often rushed through the curriculum with only cursory glances at topics. A good example of a disciplined mind might be a medical doctor who not only studies her profession, refines her work through practice, and reflects upon her actions, but also continues to improve through continual study. A physician is usually someone who never stops learning about her own profession, and who can eventually reach a level of expertise that earns her recognition by her peers as someone truly versed in her discipline of choice.

The Synthesizing Mind. This synthesizing mind integrates schema from a variety of disciplines and experiences and reintegrates them into a new whole, which can result in a new way of thinking about something. This means uniting ideas that were once unconnected into a new vision. This mind is one that has analyzed various situations and which then unifies all of those previous reviews into a single new idea. Synthesizing information successfully usually results in an interdisciplinary perspective on information as well. To be able to synthesize, a person will have had to develop the habits of perseverance and be thorough in the consideration of pertinent information in order to evaluate its utility in new contexts. One of my children was in the ninth grade and on the National Model United Nations team, and he was named head of a committee charged with considering child labor laws. After researching several illustrations of child labor, including child beggars visible to him on the streets of Ecuador (analyzing various representations of the same concept), he decided to focus on the most extreme of cases: blood diamond miners in Africa. While the visibility of something real in one's own environment (children asking for handouts on the street corners of Quito) is harsh, he felt that the gut-wrenching reality of children in the mining pits of several African nations under even worse living conditions would be more startling and get more attention from his peers. He was betting that he could get laws passed by using the shock factor to shake people out of complacency. To reach this level of thinking, he had to do copious research, integrate a variety of ideas, and see parallels between concepts not necessarily visible to all. This same exercise might not have been possible a year earlier, given the level of maturity he was working from. He might have simply found the first example of child labor he came across and used that, but with his new maturity, he was able to link ideas previously unrelated in his mind. A synthesizing mind develops over the life span and often reflects a maturity about the topic at hand.

The Creating Mind. Gardner considers creativity to be, in part, the ability to clarify and identify new problems, which means the power to question one's world and think outside the box. You can't think outside the box until you understand the box itself, however. This means that, to reach the level of creativity, you must have mastered one or several disciplines. There is a fine balance between pursuing creativity and steeping yourself in the core knowledge of your field so that you can create something new out of it, between exploring the world for yourself and maintaining a reality check on existing contributions. For example, I direct many undergraduate theses at my university, and it never fails to amaze me how many students think they've discovered something new simply because they don't know enough about their own field. I have students who, for lack of research, think they came up with constructivism, multiple intelligences theory, or cooperative learning. The fact that they reached these ideas is a marvel, but the fact that they didn't know about them before they came up with their "own" idea shows a lack of understanding of their discipline. I have to maintain a delicate balance between helping them realize they are not original and applauding their creative energies. This emphasizes the point that true creativity can only come after mastery of one or more disciplines. It is not easy to be creative, which is why it is valued as one of the most important skills a person can develop in school and considered one of the highest mental functions.

The Respectful Mind. There is only one rule common to the six major religions: respect (the

Golden Rule). The respectful mind implies accepting that different people may act or value different things, which is not illogical or wrong—it is simply different. Accepting diversity as a fact of modern society implies developing a tolerance for structures that may differ from one social group to another. Respect is the first step in cultivating empathy. I think I was privileged with a childhood environment in which people made a point of not judging based on race or gender. In fact, I wasn't conscious of how blissfully ignorant I was of race issues until I left Berkeley and went to Boston and heard Jewish, black, Irish, and Polish jokes with a frequency I'd never experienced before. Upon moving to South America after finishing college, I found that the typical insult for a stupid person was to call him or her a variety of names, all of which meant you were Indian. I also had no idea that the incidence of violence toward women could be so high; it never occurred to me that one human being could abuse another in this way. My ignorance cost me insight. I was truly shocked to hear kids in Peru talk about "El Chino" (the Chinese man), which was the common nickname for Alberto Fujimori, the ex-president when we lived in Peru. Fujimori was Japanese and I corrected my kids, to which they replied, "Isn't that the same?" I nearly died. My father (a Japanese American) would have, too, had he heard them.

Sensitivity and respect for people of different races begin with exposure. I never appreciated the rich cultural mix I grew up with in the Bay Area until I left it. How does one cultivate a respectful mind when there is no daily exposure to people of different backgrounds? It is, after all, the brain's job to look for patterns and novelty; people who look different are a novelty, and it's only natural to fear what we don't know. Teachers as well as the family have a responsibility to foster respectful attitudes within class settings and to serve as models of respectful behavior.

The Ethical Mind. Having an ethical mind means being able to fulfill one's responsibilities in society, both as a worker as well as a citizen (Gardner, 2012). This often means thinking of consequences over the long term; being ethical involves planning actions over time that have positive consequences not just the promise of immediate reward. Professional ethics is a hot topic right now, as is the subject of teaching values in schools. I find Lawrence Kohlberg's studies on stages of moral development to be helpful in understanding that one's ability to react to different ethical challenges goes hand in hand with age and maturity as well as with experience (1973). In one case, which Kohlberg labeled the Heinz dilemma, a woman is about to die from cancer (Kohlberg, 1981). The only druggist who can sell the medicine guaranteeing a cure is doing so at 10 times the real cost of the medicine, and the woman's husband, Heinz, can't afford it. He manages to gather together half of what he needs by begging his friends and neighbors for help, but the druggist refuses to sell it to him for that price. Heinz breaks into the druggist's store and steals the drug. Should Heinz have broken in and stolen the drug? Why or why not?

Kohlberg sought to study the ways individuals justified their answers. If someone has a clear moral compass and reasons at the highest stage of Kohlberg's scale (Stage 6), she could say that Heinz should steal the medicine because an individual's life is more important than money. Or, equally morally, she could say that Heinz shouldn't steal because other people who also need the medicine will now no longer have access to it legally. In any case, both answers display a far more ethical response than those lower on Kohlberg's scale, which one would justify for reasons of obedience, self-interest, conformity, law and order, or even human rights. The two responses at the highest stages of Kohlberg's scale respond to the concept of universal human ethics. Someone with an ethical mind would not simply be obedient, show self-interest, conform, obey the law blindly, or guide himself with human rights, but would go beyond these stages to consider universal human ethical boundaries when making the decision (Kohlberg, 1971).

The five minds model (Figure 3.9) presumes that fundamental learning (understanding, comprehension, application) already exists and that proper formation should yield minds that are disciplined, synthesizing, creative, respectful, and ethical. Gardner is hopeful that schools can contribute to this formation because it will benefit not only the individual, but also society (2008).

FIGURE 3.9
Gardner's Five Minds for the Future

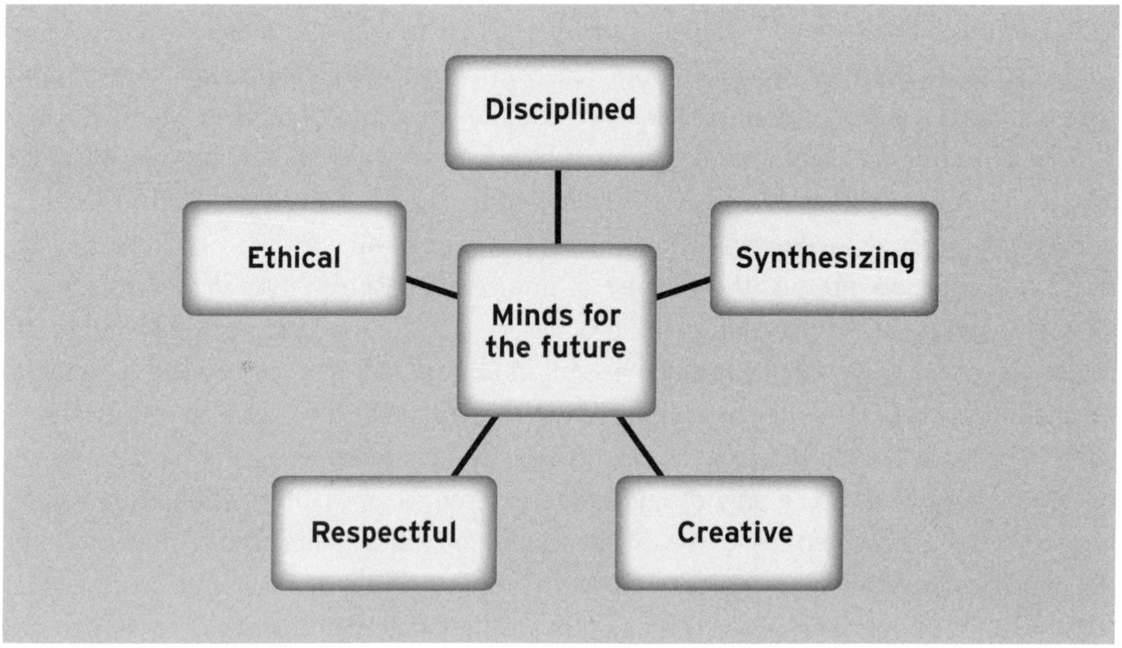

Source: Based on Gardner, 2009.

Unlike the other taxonomies or hierarchies of thinking, Gardner's five minds are *the end result of these thinking models.* That is, after executing Wiggins and McTighe's six facets or Bloom's taxonomy, one would be prepared to shape an ethical, disciplined, respectful, creative, and/or synthesizing mind if other life conditions were also available. If society continues on without developing more people who embrace these characteristics, we may end up with the opposite: minds that are unethical, disrespectful, undisciplined, superficial (unable to synthesize), and conformist (noncreative). A person who is able to embody the characteristics of the five minds is a treasure to society. This is someone who has reached a level of expertise in his area of formation, displays perseverance and synthesizes new ideas in detail, thinks outside the box, displays respect and a high degree of emotional intelligence, and in all cases maintains a high degree of professional ethics.

Where the Thinking Models Point Us

According to the aforementioned great thinking models, cumulatively speaking, we are looking for individuals who:

1. Understand
2. Compare and contrast
3. Apply
4. Evaluate
5. Analyze
6. Synthesize
7. Create
8. Are flexible
9. Exhaustively review data
10. Infer
11. Are fair-minded
12. Make relevant links
13. Interpret
14. Judge
15. Display metacognition
16. Empathize

17. Are ethical
18. Persevere
19. Listen critically
20. Communicate clearly
21. Clarify information
22. Manage impulsivity
23. Take responsible risks
24. Apply theory to practice
25. Show a questioning mind
26. Wonder
27. Are lifelong learners
28. Understand cause and effect
29. Are precise
30. Trust in reasoning
31. Display integrity
32. Are autonomous
33. Show respect
34. Care
35. Reflect
36. Are humorous
37. Think interdependently

So, how do we go about cultivating such thinkers? To cultivate, stimulate, motivate, and inspire the type of thinking we desire in our classrooms, we as teachers must model that kind of thinking themselves. Teachers can't instill practices in students that they themselves are incapable of understanding. In Ecuador, an attempt was made to measure student learning of content knowledge, but it was found that in the majority of cases, teachers knew just one point's worth (5%) more of knowledge than the students themselves. Whereas students scored a failing 10/20 on the test, teachers scored a failing 11/20 on the same test (PREAL, 2010). It is illogical, irresponsible, and impossible to evaluate students against criteria teachers themselves can't meet. This places a huge burden on those of us in the teaching profession to consider which of these characteristics we already embrace and which we need to improve upon personally in order to live up to the expectations of our field.

A good teacher is one who makes himself progressively unnecessary.
—Thomas Carruthers

You can't get apples from a pear tree. The way teachers are trained and how they are taught to think about their own learning can have an inspiring or a devastating effect on what they then do in the classroom. Hattie notes that an average high school graduate will have had between 30 and 50 teachers over the course of his academic life, but when asked, most of us can remember only three to five of our teachers. Something is wrong with a profession that leaves so few marks on students' lives. Sadly, few teachers have had teachers in their own lives who inspired them to reflect on their own level of thinking, and most of us teach as we were taught. On a positive note, great teaching skills can be learned, and we can all become a special memory in the lives of our students.

Teachers must model the high level of thinking they expect from their students, as this doesn't spontaneously occur. While it is impossible for the brain not to learn, it doesn't naturally think at a deeper level and must be taught to do so. For example, it's clear that "until students can name a process they cannot control it" (Ritchhart, Church, & Morrison, 2011, p. 29), meaning that naming, noticing, and categorizing processes is vital to being able to learning and control them. I've encountered many teachers who've been told to apply processes without being able to name or understand them first. That is, they execute activities in class but don't know why they do so. This leads to a memory-based structure that a student can learn to get around, resulting in a situation in which he might appear to do well (for example, he executes the process correctly and gets a high score on the test), but in which he does not really learn because he cannot apply the same process outside of class. Students can train and extend their working memory to a point where they can keep answers in mind just long enough to spew out their responses on paper, but when they are retested a few days later on the same material they have no recall. All of this is to say that if teachers don't have the correct training, they'll never be able to help students think deeply and for the long term. Some teacher training programs are more successful than others in developing these skills.

What Deep Thinking Looks Like in the Classroom

The book *The Teaching Gap* (Stigler & Hiebert, 2009), which emphasizes that deep reflection is fundamental to developing lifelong learners, explains that such thinking is practiced with less frequency in American classrooms than in the classrooms of various countries around the world. The result is an ever-growing "teaching gap" between classroom objectives and what is actually accomplished, as well as between what we do in the United States and what schools do in other successful countries. *The Teaching Gap* highlights how American classes have the goal of deep thinking just as other countries do, but other factors get in the way, such as student disruptiveness and PA announcements, which are rarely if ever encountered in Japanese, Finish, Korean, German or Singaporean classrooms. It seems that the teaching profession is taken far more seriously than it is in the United States and is highly respected; teaching is considered almost a sacred act in some places, and classes are almost never disturbed when in progress.

The Teaching Gap (Stigler & Hiebert, 2009; see also Hiebert et al., 2005) includes an explanation of 1995 video documentation undertaken to find out how high-scoring countries like Japan and Germany managed to inculcate a deeper level of thinking in their students compared to countries that scored in the middle of the pack, such as the United States. It appears that American teachers spend a great deal of time writing examples on the board. This isn't necessarily bad, but when a lot of time is spent demonstrating, less time is available for real, reflection-based problem solving by the students themselves. Comparative videos of Japanese and American eighth-grade classrooms showed that the Japanese teachers spent a significant amount of time encouraging students to exercise flexible, divergent thinking, whereas the American classrooms revolved around student practice and formula rehearsal. Teachers in Japan and Germany—the two countries at the top of the math and science scoreboard—gave far more time to student-focused problem solving, whereas U.S. teachers emphasized drill and memorization. While Japanese students were being challenged to solve real problems, the Americans were doing worksheets.

A final, major difference is classroom activities. It is typical to see a Japanese teacher enter the classroom and pose a problem. She then might say, "Get into groups of three. Use anything you've learned over the past two weeks to solve this problem." In the United States, almost all seatwork time (95.8%) is spent drilling recently learned concepts. While drilling happens in Japan as well, only about 40% of the time is used for recently learned concepts; 44% of the time is spent thinking and 15% in real-life application through recall of past learning. Both the Germans and Americans spent the lion's share of class time (89.4% and 95.8%, respectively) practicing concepts, while the Japanese spend a great deal of their time (44.1%) prodding students to invent or think on their own (Stigler & Hiebert, 2009).

The Japanese example gives us a hint as to what really works in classrooms and why. John Hattie (2009, 2012) says that it has become clear that certain activities have a greater impact on student learning outcomes because they push students "upward" in their thinking from superficial knowledge to deep understanding, combining these levels to enable them to construct individual learning. There are many ways to nurture the intellect. In Part II we will consider how and why some classroom activities have worked for decades—and some for centuries.

Is There an Ideal Teaching Model?

There is a great chasm between appreciation of the brain as the most complex organ on earth and the belief that anyone can teach (Figure 3.10).

FIGURE 3.10
An Ideal Model?

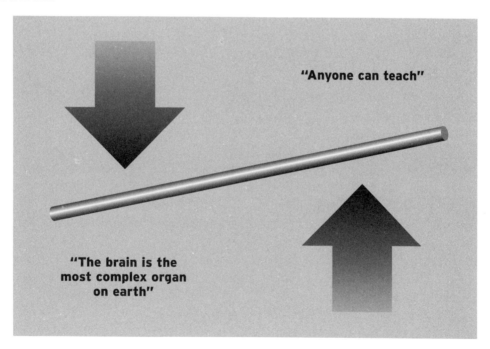

Teaching is hard, and great teaching requires a deeper understanding of the brain, the mind, and the dynamics of social learning environments to reach the higher levels of thinking and cultivate a love of learning. It is no wonder that many well-meaning teachers seek out any device possible to improve their practice.

If we analyze the characteristics of teachers who have been given prizes for their efforts by both government and private bodies, we can see patterns emerge (see Darling-Hammond & Bransford, 2012). Award-winning teachers are **humane** and **care** about their students. They **believe** in their students and in their ability to learn. They **stretch** their students, pushing them to be more than they themselves think they can be. They know what they're doing and have **deep knowledge** about their subject. They push their students to **think deeply and profoundly about themselves and their beliefs** regarding the topic so as to **construct their own learning**. This is not to say that there is a formula for good teaching, but the characteristics we equate with good teaching are all "learnable" traits; there is no mystery here, we can all learn to teach better. Activities that develop deep thinking skills allow students to interact with one another in dynamic ways, planting the seeds of lifelong learners.

We now turn to a list of specific activities, methodologies, and actions in class that, according to MBE science evidence, have the biggest impact on student learning outcomes.

Suggested Readings

Great Thinking Frameworks of the 20th and 21st Centuries
Anderson, L. W., & Krathwohl, D. R. (Eds.) (2001). *A taxonomy for learning, teaching, and assessing: A revision of Bloom's taxonomy of educational objectives.* New York, NY: Longman.
Baron-Cohen, S. (1991). Precursors to a theory of mind: Understanding attention in others. In A. Whiten (Ed.), *Natural theories of mind: Evolution, development, and simulation of everyday mindreading* (pp. 233–251). Cambridge, MA: Basil Blackwell.
Bellanca, J., & Brandt, R. (2010). *21st century skills: Rethinking how students learn.* Solution Tree Press.
Binkley, M., Erstad, O., Herman, J., Raizen, S., Ripley, M., & Rumble, M. (2010). *Defining 21st century skills* (Draft white paper 1). Melbourne, Australia: University of Melbourne.
Bloom, B. S. (Ed.), Engelhart, M. D., Furst, E. J., Hill, W. H., & Krathwohl, D. R. (1956). *Taxonomy of educational objectives: Handbook I: Cognitive domain.* New York, NY: David McKay.
Costa, A., & Kallick, B. (2009). *Learning and leading with habits of mind.* Alexandria, VA: ASCD.
Darling-Hammond, L., & Bransford, J. (2012). *Preparing teachers for a changing world: What teachers should learn and be.* Hoboken, NJ: Wiley.

Duron, R., Limbach, B., & Waugh, W. (2006). Critical thinking framework for any discipline. *International Journal of Teaching and Learning in Higher Education, 17*(2), 160–166.

Fink, L. D. (2003). *Creating significant learning experiences.* San Francisco, CA: Jossey-Bass.

Gardner, H. (2008). *Five minds for the future.* Boston, MA: Harvard Business Press.

Greenfield, S. (2008). *ID: The quest for identity in the 21st century.* UK: Hodder & Stoughton.

Hays-Jacobs, H. (2010). *Curriculum 21: Essential education for a changing world.* Alexandria, VA: ACSD.

Howard-Jones, P. A. (2009). Neuroscience, learning and technology (14–19). *Learning, 16*(17), 18.

Jerald, C. D. (2009). *Defining a 21st century education.* Retrieved October 29, 2010, from http://www.centerforpubliceducation.org/atf/cf/%7B00a4f2e8-f5da-4421-aa25-3919c06b542b%7D/21ST%20CENTURY[1].JERALD.PDF

Jukes, I., McCain, T., & Crockett, L. (2012). Education and role of the educator in the future. *Phi Delta Kappan, 94*(4), 15–21.

Marzano, R. J., Pickering, D. J., & Pollock, J. E. (2001). *Classroom instruction that works: Research-based strategies for increasing achievement.* Alexandria, VA: ASCD.

McCain, T., & Jukes, I. (2008). *Teaching the digital generation.* Thousand Oaks, CA: Corwin.

Metiri Group. (2003). *enGauge 21st century skills for 21st century learners.* Retrieved October 29, 2010, from http://www.metiri.com/21/Metiri-NCREL21stSkills.pdf

Mishra, P., & Kereluik, K. (2011). *What 21st century learning? A review and a synthesis.* Michigan State University. Paper submitted to the 2011 SITE Conference.

Partnership for 21st Century Skills. (2007). *Framework for 21st century learning.* Retrieved October 29, 2010, from http://www.p21.org/documents/P21_Framework_Definitions.pdf

Paul, R. (1990). Critical thinking: What, why and how. In J. A. Binker (Ed.), *Critical thinking: What every person needs to survive in a rapidly changing word* (pp. 1–25). Rohnert Park, CA: Sonoma State University, Center for Critical Thinking and Moral Critique.

Paul, R. (1992). Critical thinking: What, why and how. *New Directions for Community Colleges, 77,* 3–24. doi: 10.1002/cc.36819927703

Paul, R., & Elder, L. (2001). *Critical thinking: Tools for taking charge of the learning in your life* (2nd ed.). New York, NY: Prentice Hall.

Paul, R., & Elder, L. (2010). *The miniature guide to critical thinking concepts and tools.* Dillon Beach: Foundation for Critical Thinking Press. Retrieved from http://louisville.edu/ideastoaction/about/criticalthinking/framework

Siegel, D. (2012). *The developing mind: how relationships and the brain interact to shape who we are.* New York, NY: Guilford Press.

Smidt, S. (2006). *The developing child in the 21st century: A global perspective on child development.* New York, NY: Routledge.

Torey, Z. (2009). *The crucible of consciences: An integrated theory of mind and brain.* Cambridge, MA: MIT Press.

Trilling, B., & Fadel, C. (2009). *21st century skills: Learning for life in our times.* San Francisco, CA: Jossey-Bass.

Wiggins, G., & McTighe, J. (2005). Six facets of understanding. In *Understanding by design* (pp. 82–104). Alexandria, VA: ASCD.

Zemelman, S., Daniels, H., & Hyde, A. (2005). *Best practice: New standards for teaching and learning in America's schools* (3rd ed.). New Hampshire: Heinemann.

PART II

----

50 Best Classroom Practices
Using Mind, Brain, and Education Science

CHAPTER 4

Filters

Electing the Best Planning, Evaluation, and Activities

> *A good teacher is a master of simplification and an enemy of simplism.*
> —Louis Berman

Choosing the best methodologies can be a challenge, especially for open-minded teachers who are willing to look at everything available. Understanding what really works can be confusing, and colleagues' testimonies can be compelling even when there is no scientific evidence supporting the methodology they are endorsing.

Teachers need to be aware that some methodologies are high on fad and low on fact (Rabipour & Raz, 2012). They come in and out of fashion, offering a quick fix "to all our teaching needs." Brain Gym, Baby Mozart, drinking water every few minutes, boy-friendly classrooms, and right-brained learning all sound enticing and easy to apply, but they have little or no evidence behind them. Sadly, most quick fixes are myths as seen in Table 1.1. There are no shortcuts in good teaching.

Most great teachers know that finding the "right" methodology or activity takes time and often a lot of trial-and-error experimentation. They understand that the messiness of the classroom, the complexity of each child, and the density and intricacy of levels of learning mean that there are no easy answers. Of course, as we saw in the previous chapters, John Hattie determined that almost everything works to a certain extent. **While *good* activities abound, however, *great* activities are far and few between.** What's more, not all methodologies work for all kids; **different activities resonate with different kids in different ways.** The goal of this chapter is to help identify what has always worked for the majority. This will be followed by evidence from MBE science to help teachers decide where they should invest their time and energy.

This chapter came out of an experience I had at the Ecuadorian university where I teach. Maria, a humble public school teacher in Quito, sought me out for some advice. Despite being in her early 40s, Maria was just finishing her first university degree and had been asked to complete a mini-thesis on any method, activity, action, or intervention she had learned about during her studies that she felt affected student learning. She came to talk to me because she felt sure there must be a much longer list of possible topics than she had been exposed to in her studies. "I want to know what you do in the United States," she said, because, while doing an Internet search for different methodologies, she had stumbled across "the use of drama to enhance language use," "mind maps," and "making school newspapers." She assured me she had never been introduced to these concepts in her university studies, nor did any of her professors know about them.

This made me realize that in the United States we have been lucky enough to reach a basic level of teacher formation that ensures that educators are exposed to a variety of activities and methodologies before going into the classroom. This is not true in all countries. When Maria came to me, I realized that although I'd been exposed to several classes on various methodologies, no one had told me how to separate the "good" information from the "bad" using clear measures of comparison, nor how to choose interventions based on clear objectives. I sat down with Maria and shared with her what I had never seen written. The filters I shared with her that day have evolved into the best classroom practices I outline in the next few chapters.

Some educational practices have worked for dozens, hundreds, or even thousands of years and have a great deal of supporting evidence behind them (we'll look at these in Chapter 5). They have stood the test of time because they get to the core of what real educational objectives should be about: deep, connected thinking that leads to a lifelong love of learning. Other approaches to the teaching-learning process can be divided into the three main stages of educational design: (1) planning lessons, (2) evaluation, and (3) methodologies and activities. For readers well acquainted with Wiggins and McTighe's *Understanding by Design* format (1998, 2005), this "backward" design structure will be familiar: Begin with the end in mind (identify the objectives through clear planning), decide on what evidence will be accepted as an indicator of achieving the objectives (evaluation), and then plan what to do in class (methodologies and activities) (Figure 4.1). Designing learning moments using backward design permits clear evidence of student learning outcomes and is highly encouraged at both macro as well as micro levels of assessment (Darling-Hammond, 2006; Graff, 2011).

FIGURE 4.1
Backward Design Steps

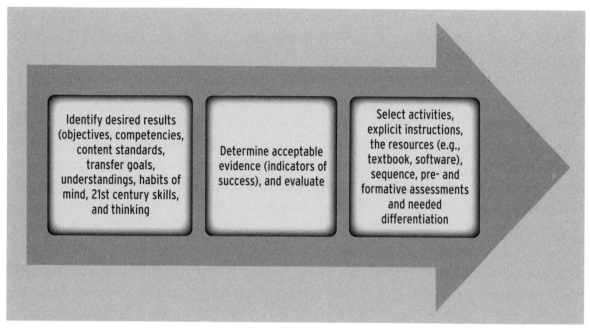

Identify desired results
(objectives, competencies,
content standards,
transfer goals,
understandings, habits of
mind, 21st century skills,
and thinking

Determine acceptable
evidence (indicators of
success), and evaluate

Select activities,
explicit instructions,
the resources (e.g.,
textbook, software),
sequence, pre- and
formative assessments
and needed
differentiation

Source: Adapted from Understanding by Design *(p. 9), by Grant Wiggins and Jay McTighe, Alexandria, VA: ASCD. © 1998 by ASCD. Adapted with permission. Learn more about ASCD at www.ascd.org.*

Planning Lessons

Planning is a key element in creating significant learning experiences. Without good planning, there is no guaranteeing high-quantity or high-quality learning. Random classroom activities may be enjoyable and lead to some type of learning, but we can be sure of success only when we plan well.

The dynamic duo of attention and memory is the key to planning success: We know that both **memory and attention are vital to learning** (Chun & Turk-Browne, 2007; Fougnie, 2008; Ormrod & Davis, 2004; Norman, 1968). Can you learn something if you can't remember it? No, because learning implies being able to transmit and transfer new ideas into different contexts (which can't be done without memory). Can you learn without paying attention? No, because attention is what permits topic salience and determines the relative worth of information; without that hierarchy, there is no orderly connection of ideas, and therefore no new learning. To learn something new, you have to pay attention to it as well as remember it.

Some methodologies are more attention grabbing than others. For example, for most people, pure lecture delivery of information is less memorable than interactive group work, discussion, or debate (see Michael, 2006, for a general review on the benefits of active learning). When we use memory and attention as filters for planning activities, our students learn better. If you plan to enhance memory and attention, you can guarantee that learning will occur for the majority of students in your classroom.

Best Classroom Practice 1. Plan Activities That Grab Attention
Mel Levine (2002) posited that there are eight neurodevelopmental constructs in the brain, among which memory and attention are core (the other six are temporal-sequential ordering, spatial ordering, language, neuromotor functions, social cognition, and higher-order cognition). Levine, a pediatric neurologist, called attention to the fact that there are several overlapping neural circuits related to attention in the brain, all of which can influence learning outcomes. Among the circuits identified are those triggered by autonomic (involuntary) reactions to senses, hormonal circuits, emotional circuits, and executive function circuits (those related to working memory, cognitive flexibility, and inhibitory control). He divided the role of attention into three types of "control" structures: mental energy control (which decides one's level of alertness, the balance between sleep and wakefulness, and consistency in achievement), processing control (which decides what's important, as in saliency, and is responsible for detail processing), and production control (which determines orders and steps and is responsible for self-monitoring). Each of these control structures is really a different neuronal network (see Posner, 2011, for an excellent explanation of this concept). This means that information is processed in the brain differently through the saliency control system, for example, than it would be through the sustained attention system in the brain. This is important to know, because teachers need to plan activities that help them strengthen all of the different networks associated with each learning task. Just getting the kids' attention on entering class (alerting system) isn't enough; we have to both sustain that attention and get the executive functions to assign importance to it.

The brain is able to focus better and pay more attention to what's important when it knows what to look for. As noted earlier, studies in MBE show that **it is impossible for the brain not to pay attention; it is always paying attention to something** (Koenig, 2010). Just because Isabel isn't looking you in the eye doesn't mean she isn't listening, nor does the fact that she *is* looking at you and nodding mean she's really paying attention to what you're saying. This follows the important MBE principle that **human learning involves both focused atten-**

tion and peripheral perception. The main teaching takeaway here is that it's difficult for many students to know what exactly is important.

A wonderful video from Daniel J. Simons and Christopher Chabris (1999) provides a test of selective attention. The video begins by asking viewers to count the number of passes made between basketball players dressed in white. It then cuts to a small group of players, some wearing white and some wearing black, passing basketballs to one another. After a few moments, a person dressed in a black gorilla suit walks through the scene and pounds his chest. Around half the people who watch this video don't see the gorilla because they're so focused on counting the passes. This video accompanied an article by the same authors in which they looked at over a hundred years of studies related to the brain's tendency to not see things right in front of it when attention has been called to something different (Simons & Chabris, 1999). **If a student is not sure of the learning objective, she may pay attention to irrelevant aspects of the activity and therefore fail to learn.** Over a century ago, Rezsö Bálint, an Austro-Hungarian psychiatrist and neurologist, wrote:

> It is a well-known phenomenon that we do not notice anything happening in our surroundings while being absorbed in the inspection of something [else]; focusing our attention on a certain object may happen to such an extent that we cannot perceive other objects placed in the peripheral parts of our visual field. (Bálint, 1907, translated in Husain & Stein, 1988, p. 91, as cited in Simons & Chabris, 1999, p. 1059)

You often hear parents and teachers lamenting the lack of attention their kids pay to something the they think is important. Strangely enough, if you ask the kid, she often responds that she *was* paying attention. How can this be explained? By the fact that what the kid considered to be important (worth knowing) wasn't the same as what the parent or teacher expected to be the focus of attention.

Students can be guided by deliberate practice to focus on specific competencies (knowledge, skills, and attitudes). This helps them hone in on shared learning goals. According to the Carnegie Mellon Eberly Center for Teaching Excellence (2013), **setting clear learning objectives allows learners to know what they need to do and thus become more autonomous.** The Eberly Center also promotes the idea that "clearly articulated learning objectives will help our students to learn new material in such a way that they can flexibly and appropriately use it in a variety of contexts, both in the short term and down the road" (Carnegie Mellon University

Eberly Center for Teacher Excellence, 2013, p. 2; see also Betts, 2004). Clear, shared learning objectives and explicit goals are fundamental to new learning as we saw in the previous summary of Hattie's findings (2009, 2012) in Chapter 2. **Because learners often lack the instinct to intuit the desired focus of the class's attention, teachers must explicitly call attention to the important parts of the class.** Telling students to "pay attention; this is really important" is not cheating; it is being clear.

Problems with attention can stem from the inability to fall asleep at night, resulting in constant sleepiness in class as well as inconsistent work performance (Mitru, Millrood, & Mateika, 2002; Mindell & Owens, 2009; Wolfson & Carskadon, 2003). Attention problems also result from the inability to determine saliency. This is evident in students who, when asked to identify key parts of a study, underline everything, for example. Attention problems can also manifest themselves as the inability to identify key characters, concepts, or level of importance of information; the tendency to wait until the last minute to complete assignments; and the inability to keep oneself on task (Levine, 2002). Other problems relate to staying "on task" despite distractions in the classroom—the cute boy in the corner or the open window with street noises creeping in—and this appears to be directly connected to successful executive-function activities.

Michael Posner is a leader on attention studies and has probably published more on this topic than 99% of the people in the field. He and his colleagues have spent dozens of years documenting the cognitive neuroscience of attention. Posner speaks of attention more as "an organ system" than a single circuit, because he views the specialized networks needed for different types of attention to be adaptive (Posner & Fan, 2007). Posner and Rothbart (1998) have described three attention systems crucial for learning: the orienting system, the alerting system, and the executive-function systems. The *orienting system* allows an individual to place herself in time or space relative to others or the target stimulus. The *alerting system* allows an individual to know when to keep her guard up against perceived threats or to stay on the lookout for rewarding situations. The *executive functioning systems* are particularly vital to learning, as they help a person decide what's "important" and deserving of the brain's focus. The value of active learning can be explained by the fact that it's impossible for a student not to pay attention when she's the center of attention. Posner's research on attention has evolved over the decades to focus on executive functions and how they regulate attention in the context of learning.

These attention systems coincide with Immordino-Yang's findings about attention-driven affect. Immordino-Yang (2011; see also Saxbe, Yang, Borofsky, & Immordino-Yang, 2012) found that an individual's attention span for a given stimulus is directly related to the type and level of affect experienced. This means that when we're interested in or enjoy a particular situation, we'll be motivated to continue the activity and will learn faster and with less resistance than we would if we'd been faced with an unpleasant activity that caused us to feel ill at ease, bored, scared, frustrated, or threatened. One's attention level is based on the affect accompanying the situation: Better affect equals better attention and better learning (Pekrun, Goetz, Frenzel, Barchfeld, & Perry, 2011). Immordino-Yang's and Posner's work substantiate the importance of attention in learning outcomes. This gives support to the fourth MBE instructional guideline: **Well-managed classes take advantage of natural human attention spans**.

Best Classroom Practice 2. Plan Activities That Stimulate Memory

> *By viewing the old we learn the new.*
> —Chinese proverb

Attention forms a twosome with memory. Levine (2002) divides memory into varying neuronal circuits, including short-term memory (which relates to recoding information into intelligible terms), emotional memory, and active working memory (keeping ideas in mind, as well as short- and medium-term planning and linking short- and long-term memories to complete the process) (Baddeley, 2003). All of these are distinct but related to long-term memory (which implies memory consolidation and ease of access for memory retrieval), important for demonstrable learning. As indicated in the MBE principles, memory circuits are related and sometimes overlapping but distinct. This means that, as teachers, **we need to understand each circuit in order to devise instructional moments that take advantage of each** to maximize the potential of learning. Important breakthroughs in neuroscience indicate that there are multiple neural pathways for different types of memory circuits (e.g., short, working, long, semantic, declarative, and emotional) (Baddeley, Eyseneck, & Anderson, 2009; Eichenbaum, 2011; Radvansky, 2010; Squire & Kandel, 2008).

All learning occurs through sensory perception (Jarvis, 2012). Research indicates that after we see, feel, hear, smell, touch, or taste something, this perception enters the brain. It stops first at the amygdala (to check for threats) then, after a momentary stop in the frontal lobes, it enters the hippocampus (to confirm information stored in declarative memory)—two areas that are important in new memory processing (Freeman, 1991). Research indicates that memory is fallible, however, and not everything that is perceived by the brain ends up becoming a memory. Breakdowns may occur between the moment new information is presented and put into temporary storage, where it could be lost and never reach long-term memory storage (Baddeley et al., 2009). However, research has also shown that working memory training can enhance learning (Engle, 2002), indicating that teaching practices exploiting this feature of working memory may facilitate retention (Barrouillet & Gaillard, 2011). Research also supports the idea that new information is better retrained when it is related to real-life contexts because both the attentional networks are well focused on the task as well as taking advantage of associative memory networks (Meltzoff, Kuhl, Movellan, & Sejnowski, 2009).

All new learning passes through the filter of prior experiences (Lewis & Williams, 1994; Tokuhama-Espinosa, 2008), which helps the brain work efficiently. As the brain is primed to detect patterns (for an example see Vandenberghe et al., 1996) as well as novelty (see Knight, 1996), sensory perception is first reviewed in the brain through the filter of memory. If the brain recognizes some type of pattern already in memory, it compares the new and the old to determine what information might be missing for new learning, which is why association works well in schools. If there is nothing recognizable, the brain detects novelty. Novelty detection highlights similarities and differences of known concepts, also permitting new learning. Research shows that the brain actually craves novelty (Biederman & Vessel, 2006), which explains why some students become easily bored in class when the same things occur every day.

Different social contexts create different types of learning motivators. Drach-Zahavy and Erez explain that "[challenge] is experienced when there is an opportunity for self-growth with available coping strategies, whereas threat is experienced when the situation is perceived as leading to failure with no available strategies to cope with it" (2002, p. 667). We know that learning is enhanced by challenge but repressed by threat (Tokuhama-Espinosa, 2011), and that different students will perceive the same class setting as challenging or as threatening, depending on their past experiences. Due to the differences in students' past experiences, they will react differently to emotional stimuli, which then can influence their learning (Immordino-Yang & Faeth, 2010).

One common problem associated with short-term memory is the inability to remember small pieces of information (less than 7 "bits") in the immediate term (shorter than 5 minutes). This can be seen in the inability to identify what's important in a lecture, for example, or in difficulty reformatting information into meaningful chunks (related to past experience) (McLaren, 2009). Links to emotional memory can lead to overassociation or underassociation with feelings, as well as to difficulty in retaining information (key ideas) for a minimum sustained period of time.

People with memory problems show an inability to determine what belongs in long- or short-term planning. In a typical class there are some students who plan well and others who don't. If we assign an essay that's due in two weeks, for example, we can observe how some of the students will take the time to pace themselves and manage to turn in everything on time, and others who will mismanage their planning and inevitably miss the deadline. The inability to link short- and long-term planning relates to the incapacity to link short- and long-term memories. More obvious problems with memory relate to a difficulty in consolidating information (via repetition, sleep, review) (Stickgold, 2005) or the inability to easily retrieve information that has been stored in long-term memory (Schacter, 2002).

Numerous studies on the neural networks for memory are currently being conducted in MBE. Since 1987 with his *Memory and the Brain*, Larry Squire has been a driving force in efforts to define memory pathways (Squire, 1987, 1992a, 1992b; Squire & Kandel, 2008). Other leaders in the memory research field whose findings have confirmed the vital role of memory in learning include Kandel (2007) and Klingberg (2008, 2012). One of the most important insights about memory (like other network systems in the brain) is that **both the neural circuitry as well as chemical makeup (that is, the entire physiology) in the brain play fundamental roles in proper memory functioning**.

Neurotransmitters in the brain serve to "seal the deal" or confirm learning moments, according to Yamada and Nabeshima (2003): "Activity-dependent changes in synaptic strength are considered mechanisms underlying learning and memory, [and] brain-derived neurotrophic factor (BDNF) plays an important role in activity-dependent synaptic plasticity such as long-term potentiation" (p. 267). This means that memory processes are mediated by chemicals and depend on specific neurotransmitters. These neurotransmitters become active depending on emotional states. For example, Tan and his colleagues (2007) showed that the ability to focus on specific elements, ideas, and concepts (related to both attention and memory) is tied to "dopaminergic and glutamatergic systems, [which] are critical components responsible for prefrontal signal-to-noise tuning in working memory" (p. 12536). They found that the "signal-to-noise" component is an individual's ability to block out extra distracters and focus on the main element. This means that much of memory is dependent on attention mechanisms, and, thus, on the relationship between the two.

Preferences

Along with memory and attention networks come preferences: Our brain chooses to pay attention and remember different things for different reasons. It is presumed that different types of methodologies create different types of neuronal networks in the brain (for a good example of how this happens, see Giard and Peronnet's [1999] study on multi-modal processing in the human brain or Amedi and colleagues' [2005] explanation of cross-modal perception). That is, learning through visual representations strengthens a slightly different pathway than learning through discussion or by teaching someone else, which can be influenced by individual preferences as well as past memories (see supporting evidence for this idea in Calvert, 2001; C. Frith, Perry, & Lumer, 1999; M. H. Johnson, 2003; Patterson, Nestor, & Rogers, 2007).

When we use a variety of methods to learn something, we are putting the same information in our brain in slightly different neural pathways. This means that locating the information for later retrieval will be easier, because there are now a variety of ways to reach it. Consider this analogy: Let's say I desperately want to be able to find my socks first thing in the morning but never remember which drawer they're in. If I want to make sure I can always find a pair of socks, I would be wise to put a pair in each drawer. This way, regardless of which drawer I open, I find the socks. One of the greatest contributions of Gardner's "multiple intelligences" theory is that it reminds educators that they need to teach in a variety of ways in order to keep attention and facilitate recall. Gardner acknowledges that multiple intelligences theory is not supported by neuroscience (Tokuhama-Espinosa, 2008), but the multiple-input aspect of his theory suggests that recall is enhanced because of the numerous neural pathways employed.

Best Classroom Practice 3. Plan to Use Spaced Versus Massed Learning Moments

Memory is enhanced by spacing the introduction of concepts (separating learning moments by long or short periods of time and large or small amounts of content) as opposed to massing them together (Enikö et al., 2012; Grote, 1995; Izawa, 1971; Murphy & Miller, 1956; Roediger & Butler, 2010; Seabrook & Brown, 2005; Son, 2004). The idea of spaced versus massed learning was first discussed in the late 1930s and 1940s (Cain & De Veri, 1939; Dore & Hilgard, 1938; Garrett, 1940; Tsao, 1948) and studied in depth in the 1960s. Despite over 60 years of undisputable proof in education and psychology (Izawa, 1971; Litke, 2011; Tsao, 1948; Xue et al., 2011) and the positive results this method produces (Wahlheim, Dunlosky, & Jacoby,

2011), spaced versus massed practice is not as widely applied as one would expect and is just beginning to be studied in cognitive neuroscience (see Benjamin & Craik, 2001; Commins, Cunningham, Harvey, & Walsh, 2003; Enikö et al., 2012; Naqib, Farah, Pack, & Sossin, 2011; Sisti, Glass, & Shors, 2007), though this is well established in animal neuroscience. While this is sufficiently evident in education and psychology, there is now additional evidence in neuroscience (Cohen & Ranganath, 2007; Xue et al., 2011). Many teachers know instinctively that spacing learning moments rather than lumping them together is beneficial (as shown in Carpenter, Cepeda, Rohrer, Kang & Pashler, 2012), yet many teachers have difficulty applying this concept because it requires extra planning time. "The spacing effect would appear to have considerable potential for improving classroom learning, yet there is no evidence of its widespread application" (Dempster, 1988, p. 627). In addition, much of spacing has to do with student choices, not the teacher's. Many students don't prioritize their time well (Pyc & Dunlosky, 2010), don't allocate enough time for learning tasks, and end up trying to cram learning moments into small amounts of time rather than spreading them out as recommended. However, teachers can help by designing lessons that enhance the probability of better spacing.

In poorly designed classes, we teach (or "cover") subject areas in a vacuum and never return to most of them, or at least not until the final exam! Some teachers are culpable of "covering Chapter 2 algebra" or "World War II" or "Shakespeare" or "volcanoes" and never returning to the subject again. Far too few teachers take the time to coordinate with other subject-area teachers in a way that would reinforce conceptual learning over time. Teachers who plan to revisit a concept several times over the course of the year ensure that memory networks are reinforced over time. The failure to revisit concepts over the course of the year means that we don't take advantage of spaced learning (Cain & De Veri, 1939; Callan & Schweighofer, 2010). If we were to teach the concepts in Chapter 2 algebra and then revisit them explicitly several times over the student's educational career (as we progress through Chapters 3, 4, and beyond into subsequent grades), we could guarantee learning because those neural networks would be reinforced over time. As discussed earlier, one of the reasons Japanese math and science teachers are so effective is because they continually return to learned concepts, which places past knowledge in new contexts. **When teachers fail to reinforce concepts, various memory pathways are weakened, and without memory, there is no ability to retrieve the concept or to demonstrate real new learning**.

Some talk about "spiraling up" activities, in which instructors return to concepts over and over, each time getting closer to a precise and complete understanding. This relates to the idea inherent in MBE principles that the search for meaning occurs through pattern recognition (i.e., the brain's continual comparison between what it senses and what it already knows). **Revisiting ideas and concepts solidifies understanding.** This also relates to the MBE principle, "Use it or lose it," which is based on the idea that learning requires constant review, rehearsal, and reuse of information or it will be lost. This explains why you can't remember the quadratic formula or periodic table you learned 20 years ago in high school unless you've been exposed to it regularly over the years.

Introducing, explicitly teaching, and then reinforcing a learning concept by revisiting it in new contexts is known as *transfer*, and this is perhaps one of the greatest goals in education (Darling-Hammond, 2006; Halpern, 1998; Tuomi-Gröhn, 2007). This means that in the planning stage, a teacher must not only identify clear objectives or competencies (knowledge, skills, or attitudes), but he must also plan how he will continually reinforce them throughout the school year to strengthen pathways for retrieval of that information in the brain.

For example, let's say that at the planning stage, a teacher identifies that "understanding the causes of war" is a key learning competency for his history class for the year. He will then find ways to return to the causes of war throughout all the lessons, whether "covering" the Civil War, the Korean War, or the War in Afghanistan. Although independent triggers for war might differ among these situations, the global, overarching ideas will eventually emerge. Similarly, great teachers use the tactic of revisiting core knowledge by asking students to remind themselves of what they already know about a topic before moving into it. Remember Rachel's fifth-grade class on the development of the U.S. Constitution (Chapter 3)? The habits of mind she formed helped her to think about her existing knowledge on the topic, which gave her a strong anchor to guide her thinking. Some teachers decide on essential questions (Wiggins & McTighe, 2005) that the class will continually return to throughout the learning period to confirm that everyone shares the same focus throughout the year. When the Japanese teachers mentioned in Chapter 3 said, "Use anything you've learned over the past two weeks to solve this problem," they were helping their students apply a structure that forced them to recall (reinforce neural pathways for) what they'd learned in the recent past and see the same information in the new context of a different problem (transfer).

Acceptance and understanding of spaced versus massed learning is relatively new in neuroscience, though its proof in animals has been around for years (Sisti, Glass, & Shors, 2007). Pashler, Cepeda, Lindsey, Vul, and Mozer (2009) found that "appropriate spacing of study can double retention on educationally relevant time scales" (p. 1321). Many teachers know that several exposures to explicit teaching and learning opportunities are needed—usually over several days—before students learn, which is now evident in neuroscientific studies that show a correlation between reinforced neural pathways and learning (Callan & Schweighofer, 2010; van Turennout, Bielamowicz, & Martin, 2003). Ease of recall depends on the number of rehearsals, and the strength of the connections relate to the spaced way in which the concept was reinforced.

So, test yourself: If you have five hours to study physics this week, are you better off spending all five hours on the same day or spreading out your studies to an hour a day for five days? As most school learning is dependent on long-term declarative memory, **there is no doubt that spreading out learning over time is more beneficial than cramming**. Slow and steady wins the long-term memory race (Roediger, Finn, & Weinstein, 2012); sprints result in short-term memory gains that don't last over time (Cain & De Veri, 1939; Callan & Schweighofer, 2010). Donovan and Radosevich (1999) concluded that students in spaced-concept conditions performed higher than those in massed-concept conditions. Concept spacing enhanced both acquisition and retention of new information.

Choices about spaced versus massed learning occur at policy levels as well as classroom levels as well. One year my son came home with a school schedule indicating that six hours of math would be taught Monday, Tuesday, and Wednesday and no math would be taught Thursday or Friday. The explanation? The administration wanted to experiment with block scheduling (two-hour blocks), but the teacher was divided between middle and high school and thus needed to "group" his hours. Although block scheduling isn't a bad idea, it can achieve success only if the spacing between blocks is relatively even—for example, a Monday-Wednesday-Friday schedule. (A Monday-Tuesday-Wednesday schedule could also work if the teacher gave homework over the Thursday-Friday gap, but he didn't.) As a consequence, this class didn't take advantage of spaced learning concepts, and learning was so impaired that 87% of the students had to hire outside tutors to keep up with the work.

Another important concept related to spaced versus massed learning is that the appropriate length of spacing is determined by the complexity and challenge of the task. Some studies have suggested that stronger effects are found for relatively brief rest periods for simple tasks, and for longer rest periods (24 hours or more) for more complex tasks (see Hattie, 2009, for several examples). In other words, **the harder the learning task, the more time and space needed between learning moments**. For example, simple addition can be learned over a relatively short period of time with only brief interludes between learning moments. However, calculus concepts need to be learned over a longer period of time, with greater amounts of time between learning moments. Interestingly, this actually fits the way our schools normally work—primary school math classes tend to be daily experiences, whereas university math studies are usually twice-a-week encounters.

Hattie (2009) showed that "a common denominator to many of the effective practices . . . such as direct instruction, peer-tutoring, mastery learning, and feedback . . . [is] the frequency of different opportunities rather than merely spending 'more' time on task" (p. 185). This means that conscientiously planning spaced learning activities will improve learning conditions in classrooms. Before Hattie published his work, Robert Marzano, a lifelong educational researcher, documented the benefit of what most teachers already embrace either consciously or unconsciously as good practice: repetition, variation, and depth of thought, all of which are reflective of spaced learning concepts. In his book *Classroom Instruction That Works*, Marzano (2001) highlighted the effectiveness of providing enough repetition to reinforce neuronal mechanisms related to memory, varying the way information is communicated, and aiding students to reach a depth of thought. These three important aspects of learning are supported by MBE information and are explained below.

Best Classroom Practice 4. Plan to Incorporate Repetition
The value of using many forms of repetition to teach the same idea is supported by MBE science. Even when the same form of repetition (e.g., visual or auditory) is always used, the act of repeating, itself, helps move a word or concept from working memory to long-term memory, where real learning occurs (Jacoby, 1978). In other words, **repeating a concept or idea, silently or aloud, over a long period of time helps future recall of the concept**.

Allan Pavio of the University of Western Ontario suggested one of the first widely accepted models of memory structures in the 1970s (Pavio, 1976). This model suggested that **both mental imagery and verbal encoding assist memory** (and therefore learning). Pavio believed (he was later proved correct) that verbal associations and visual imagery are conducted within two different neural networks and thus complement each other when unified (Pavio, 1971, 1990). This means that seeing something written *and* hearing it reinforces learning because they are distinct neural pathways that reinforce the same concept or schema. Baddeley and Hitch introduced a related idea called the *phonological loop* in 1974 (Figure 4.2). The phonological loop is how we hear information as we read it in both linguistic and mathematical conceptual structures (for an example, see Plaza & Cohen, 2003). That model has since been modified to also include a "visuospatial sketchpad" (which holds information about what we see) and an "episodic buffer" (which links visual, spatial, and verbal information). All three are processed via the central executive functions (which is very similar to Pavio's original idea). According to Baddeley, Gathercole, and Papagno (1998):

> The phonological store acts as an "inner ear," remembering speech sounds in their temporal order, whilst the articulatory process acts as an "inner voice" and repeats the series of words (or other speech elements) on a loop to prevent them from decaying. (p. 158)

Lending support to this idea, researchers such as Parrila, Kirby, and McQuarrie, (2004) and Plaza and Cohen (2003) have shown that being able to hear is key to the speed and accuracy with which one can read.

FIGURE 4.2
Baddeley's Phonological Loop

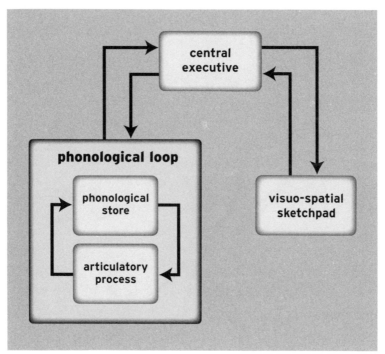

© Kurzon, 2007.

Swanson (2011) has shown that working memory is closely related to phonological knowledge upon which reading and math skills are based (see also Plaza & Cohen, 2003) and enhanced by repetition. Balata, Douche, and Logan's meta-analysis of studies on spaced retrieval of information demonstrates that **when we try to remember new information, we repeat it over and over, either out loud or in our heads**. This practice rehearses different neuronal networks, allowing for faster retrieval. Strengthening these networks actually results in an enhanced myelin sheath between neurons, which is why retrieval is faster. As teachers, we should plan activities in such a way that we reinforce both the phonological loop and visual sketchpad by spacing concepts over time to ensure sufficient repetition occurs.

Best Classroom Practice 5. Take Advantage of Variation and Transdisciplinarity
Varying the way a concept or idea is rehearsed also helps recall. Saying something to ourselves over and over is effective, but saying it over and over *and* writing it down is even more effective. And it's even *more* effective to say it, write it, and then make a mind map of it. Better still is saying it, writing it, making a mind map, and then teaching it to someone else, and so on (Figure 4.3). Forms (written and spoken) and modes (as in different senses) are both ways of varying input in the brain.

FIGURE 4.3
Sample Mind Map

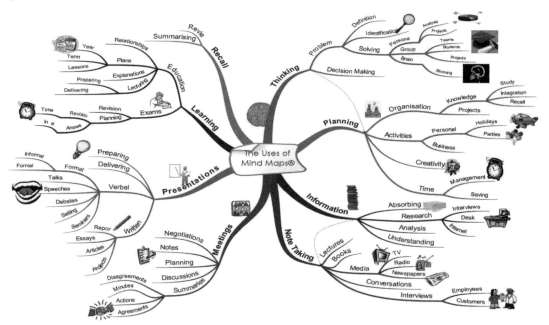

Lewis, 2008 Use of Mind Maps. Used with permission of Sian Lewis at Illumine Training

The greater variety of ways we can input information into our heads, the easier the recall will be. Classes that rely on a simplistic delivery of information by a teacher or on copying notes will not be as successful as classes that find ways to space information over time in a variety of ways. Students who discuss class content (talk), review their notes (read), rewrite and summarize, read, and watch videos on the topic will put the same information in their brains in slightly different neural pathways, allowing for more efficient recall. Research shows that if the same concept can be taught in a variety of ways, there is a greater likelihood of recall as well as of transfer (Bevan & Dukes, 1967; O'Donnell, Dansereau, & Hall, 2002). Variation can be achieved through different modes, methods, or contexts. For example, learning through visual representations strengthens a slightly different pathway than learning through discussion or by teaching someone else, which can be influenced by individual preferences as well as past memories (see supporting evidence for this idea in Calvert, 2001; C. Frith, Perry, & Lumer, 1999; M. H. Johnson, 2003; Patterson, Nestor, & Rogers, 2007). In other words, varying the way we rehearse a concept or idea helps us remember it.

When we consider ways to incorporate variation and link ideas in our classrooms, we also need to consider depth. Depth implies going from simple ideas to more and more complex ideas related to the same topic. As mentioned earlier, bringing learning to different levels of thinking leads to better thinking overall. This means that as we introduce the core elements of a new learning idea or concept and then build on them by going deeper into increasingly complex concepts, we can expect our students' understanding to flourish. New network studies have helped establish the third MBE instructional guideline: **Teaching to different memory systems reinforces different neuronal networks and thus enhances recall** (Squire, 1992a, 1992b; Squire & Kandel, 2008).

There is evidence that most exchanges in classrooms are linguistic and orally conveyed, which challenges students who don't pick up on these auditory cues as well as they should. According to the Northwest Regional Educational Laboratory (2005), "**All the senses come into play in learning**. In most classrooms, however, reading and lectures dominate instruction, engaging students through the "linguistic mode" (para. 1). The current thinking is that when students are exposed to linguistic as well as nonlinguistic representations of the same concepts, there is a higher probability of true learning because different memory systems for that concept are enhanced. Several authors have established the effectiveness of nonlinguistic representations (Athappilly, Smidchens, & Kofel, 1983; Brabec, Fisher, & Pitler, 2004; Padak, 2002; Pavio, 1990). One way to incorporate nonlinguistic representations is to structure concepts by filling out graphic organizers (e.g., descriptive, time/sequence, process/cause-effect, episode, generalization/principle, concept pattern). Multiple organizers can be used for the same topic. Students can also be asked to compose or view pictures or pictographs, form mental pictures, create or observe models, or perform kinesthetic tasks. Classrooms that are planned around these activities can help consolidate core concepts about any school topic. Linguistic prowess has been rewarded in educational systems for over 60 years, which means that kids who lack the vocabulary to explain themselves well via words have been left behind. The use of mind maps allows kids who traditionally haven't been successful learners to fluidly articulate concepts without words.

Depending on the subject and students' motivation for learning, relationship with the teacher, and past knowledge, some kids will find visual representations easier to understand than linguistic representations. A child who is strong in visual representations needs to be explicitly taught the accompanying vocabulary, and a child who is linguistically fluent should learn to improve her visual representations. The more students use both forms in the classroom, the more opportunity they will have to achieve because they will create distinct neural networks for the same mental schema, allowing for better recall. Once kids understand the utility of both visual and linguistic expression, they can become proficient in both of them and have more than one means of expression at their disposal in all learning situations.

Variation is enhanced when there is also significance and a connection to the learner's real world experiences. Teaching the same concept through different disciplines reinforces the variety of ways a concept is remembered, or transferred to long-term memory (and therefore retrievable) (Bernsen, 1994), but transdisciplinarity requires planning and cooperation among teachers. For example, if all the fifth-grade teachers can work together and choose thematic learning units, they will reinforce one another. Let's say they choose "arches" (or "time" or "color" or any number of ideas). The art, science, math, history, and literature teachers can all approach "arches" from different perspectives, and in doing so they reinforce one another's learning outcomes. Further, by making curriculum choices in which a variety of ways of thinking are prized (math as much as art, chemistry as much as history), we improve the likelihood of cultivating interdisciplinary thinkers who are able to show intellectual empathy and approach problems with greater success. If more classes could be planned in an interdisciplinary way, learning would be improved.

One of the most fascinating discoveries in modern neuroscience occurred when Miriam Diamond took a slice of Einstein's brain with the hypothesis that his brilliance was due to a greater number of neurons—only to find that she was wrong (Diamond, Scheibel, Murphy, & Harvey, 1985; Lepore, 2001). Einstein didn't have more cells—he had more connections between them. There was far more white matter in Einstein's brain than in that of the average person; Einstein connected more dots than others. By knowing lots of different things from philosophy to physics, Einstein was able to link ideas that had never before been connected. The variety of ways he interpreted the same concepts was part of his brilliance.

One of the best ways we can foster a transdisciplinary mindset is by noticing and appreciating the links our students forge on their own and praising them for the creativity they display. I've watched small kids spend hours and hours building Lego structures that are not very complex or much beyond what the picture on the box has shown them. But I've also seen kids of the same age take the same Lego pieces and devise marvelous structures that required a seemingly boundless imagination. What happened in the lives of these two types of kids that led one to explore and experiment, and the other to simply reproduce a given model with no imagination? Kids with creative minds link ideas together, and they have been rewarded for this in simple but meaningful ways. When a parent says, "Wow! That looks great! You sure are smart [creative, resourceful, etc.]!" the child begins to realize that she can reproduce the good feeling that accompanies praise through her own actions. If she keeps creating new things, her parents keep praising her.

Conversely, the kid who builds the same structure he saw on the box probably has a parent, teacher, or group of friends who never praised him for ingenuity. Instead of looking at the strange concoction of Legos and saying, "Cool! How does it work?" they likely said something like, "What's that supposed to be?" This sends several messages to the child. First, it tells him that his effort has failed. "What is it supposed to be?" means that it isn't what it was supposed to be. Second, there is no reward for creativity. The child thinks to himself that it would be better to do something easily recognizable by others and at least get a pat on the head rather than risk indifference or, worse yet, ridicule. The lack of interest shown by parents and teachers toward efforts at creativity quickly dampens the fires of experimentation. The study of creativity and neuroscience are relatively young, but they are powerful in evidence-backed information (see Abraham, 2013; Abraham et al., 2012; Andersen, 2005; Dietrich, 2004; Fink, Benedek, Grabner, Staudt, & Neubauer, 2007; Jauk, Benedek, & Neubauer, 2012; Sawyer, 2011; Shen, Liu, & Chen, 2010). These studies confirm the different neural circuits combine to show divergent thinking. Like Einstein, creative kids are linking ideas that might not normally be connected,

Of course, simply exposing children to a lot of different ideas does not make genius; kids need to be trained in *how* to think about information. That said, you can't make links between two ways of thinking if you don't have one or the other. For example, if a child has been taught core concepts in music and math, it's easier for her to understand the idea of wholes and quarters because she has both mathematical and musical understandings of those ideas. However, if a child has learned the music without the math (or the math without the music), her learning is truncated because it is not linked to something else. Thus, **the ability to generate complex ideas needs to be nurtured throughout the lifespan** through multiple experiences. The more ideas someone has, the more connections between ideas she can have. One plus one equals three: There is one concept, and there is a second concept; if they are linked, the resulting conceptual understanding is greater than the sum of its parts.

Best Classroom Practice 6. Plan Authentic Lessons
One of the most time-consuming aspects of learning relates to planning activities that connect with each individual learner. We are trained in teacher education schools to make sense of the material—put it in a logical order and structure lessons within a specific time frame—but we are often not guided in how to give the material meaning to the individual students in our classroom. Making a lesson authentic to learners is a difficult task because it presumes knowledge of students' past experiences. To plan an authentic lesson, a teacher must know her audience well. Authenticity can be judged at a cultural level as well as at an individual level. That is, there are some things that each culture knows and doesn't know that can be the starting point for creating authentic lessons, and there are things that individuals know or don't know that also contribute to authenticity.

For example, at a cultural level, many textbooks make it clear that context matters in learning. When my family and I lived in Peru, my children were given English textbooks for the English classes they received. These were expensive, highly prized books from Europe, and the school was very proud to have them. Unfortunately, the examples used to teach vocabulary were also very European and often out of context in South America. I recall a beautifully illustrated chapter on "weather" terms that showed lots of pictures of snowstorms, warm jackets, and umbrellas and explained the distinctions between rain, sleet, hail, and so on. My children had the privilege of already speaking English and having lived in Europe, so they found the text intriguing and useful. However, 90% of their classmates had lived in Lima their entire life, where the rainfall is less than a quarter inch a year. Some of the children managed to memorize the vocabulary blindly, with no link to real-life concepts; however, many were completely confused by the need to differentiate types of precipitation that they never experienced. Lack of context dooms students to a lower level of comprehension. Research shows that students who learn information in real-life contexts do so more efficiently than students who have to make inferences about context (Agarwal, Bain, & Chamberlain, 2012; Horz, 2012). There is evidence that teachers who use examples that are close to the students' contexts and as authentic as possible are more successful (Gordon, 1998; Lombardi, 2007; Reeves & Herrington, 2010). Authenticity means things are "real" in the students' worldview.

In another example, I recall a creative third-grade teacher who wanted her students to identify shapes and forms in their homes. One day she asked them to go home and count the number of angles in their kitchen, and the next day one little girl came back saying "zero." The teacher presumed the child didn't understand the assignment or simply hadn't done it. When she asked the parents why their daughter refused to do the homework, they explained that they lived in a dome and had purposefully built their home without any angles! Without understanding the child's home context, it's impossible to devise authentic learning experiences. (The teacher would have been better off giving the children cutouts of different size angles and asking them to walk around the classroom and count how many they could fit into different places.)

To make lessons authentic, teachers must devote enough time to planning that recognizes cultural contexts and individuals' past experiences. A teacher who takes the time to integrate into his lessons examples and course materials that allow his students to contextualize the utility of the concepts being learned will have more successful learners.

Evaluation

Evaluation, assessment, and feedback are some of the most important yet most controversial aspects of student learning. "Learning" implies that you didn't know something before; if you weren't previously ignorant of the knowledge you have acquired, it doesn't count as learning. An assessment or diagnosis of what a student knows, what she is able to do, or her attitude toward the subject or concept is important because it allows us to compare that current state with our "ideal" state or objective and then determine what's missing. As mentioned earlier, gap analysis is the key.

Hattie (2012) asks us to flip our mentality about evaluation on its head. We as teachers should think of student learning outcomes as being related to teaching results, not only to learning results. This means that each time we evaluate a student, we should actually be evaluating our own success with that student. **When students fail, it is *our* failure.** If we own the learning process, Hattie claims, we begin to change our perspective of evaluation practices. Gone are the days when teachers could throw up their hands and say, "I taught well; it was my student's fault he didn't learn!" Although there is evidence that some students need more time, more resources, or a different approach than others, there are very few "unteachable" cases; far more frequent is a teacher's inability to identify the student's needs. The now-popular concept of differentiation in education was foreign just a generation ago; before, students who didn't adapt to the teacher failed. Modern education reverses this way of thinking: Today's teacher must know each student well enough to identify his or her needs. **Treating everyone fairly doesn't mean giving each person the same thing; it means giving each learner what he needs to succeed** (Tomlinson & Edison, 2003; Tomlinson & Strickland, 2005).

This is not to say that each student requires a personalized methodology or class activity. However, it behooves teachers to accept that when a student fails, the first place to look for improvement is at themselves. **Teachers need to realize that they are paid not to teach, but rather to guarantee student learning**. This is a hard pill to swallow for many teachers (and it gets harder the higher in educational practices that you go!), mainly because many feel that learning is a matter of personal responsibility on the part of the student.

Let's liken this to mechanics. I have a personal responsibility to make sure that my car is running safely for my own benefit as well as for the benefit of other drivers on the road with me. But I don't know anything about how my car works, or what is needed to make it run smoothly. Fortunately, my local mechanic *does* know. He can guide me and tell me what I need to do to ensure safe functioning of the car. That, at a minimum, is what we hope of teachers. Another quick analogy: I love my dentist—not because she's particularly good at cleaning my teeth, but because she reminds me when I'm overdue for a checkup and offers me preventative advice. We expect almost all practitioners not only to treat problems but also to seek to prevent them; why should we expect less from teachers?

In regard to the evaluation process, teachers need to realize that part of learning is understanding (and not just recognizing) one's mistakes, teachers and students alike. Philosophically, I believe that the role of evaluation in classrooms is to serve as a teaching aid. Evaluation should not be used to rank, ridicule, or reprimand a student, but rather to identify her learning needs. This, unfortunately goes against some of the ways evaluation is being used today. Standardized testing is being used to rank not only students but also states and schools districts;

many are reprimanded and ridiculed for not reaching the expected level. It's hard to maintain the original concept of "evaluate" (to estimate the value of) a student's competency in a subject matter without feeling the pressure of national standards breathing down your neck. However, I believe that individual teachers have to embrace the belief that the process of assessing a student to determine her starting point, evaluating her against the objectives of the class, and then offering her quality feedback on how to improve her class performance, is for the sole purpose of improving her learning. Easy to say, but hard to put into practice? Some concrete suggestions on how to do this follow.

Best Classroom Practice 7. Implement Formative Evaluation
Summative evaluation tools are those that appraise learning through a single product, normally a test or a presentation that assesses domination of certain knowledge or a particular skill. *Formative evaluation* tends to measure improvement in processes and individual progress in relation to global competencies in a subject area (R. A. Smith, 2001; Wiliam, 2011). Formative evaluation involves qualitative feedback on the details of content and performance, whereas summative evaluation focuses on educational outcomes (K. G. Brown & Gerhardt, 2006; Perrenoud, 1998). Both are very important in formal education, but when it comes to improving student learning outcomes, there is no doubt that **thoughtful, embedded, formative assessment is superior to grading practices based solely on a final number** (Yorke, 2003). Although snap grading techniques like pop quizzes can give a teacher some insight regarding students' level of recall and even help students identify areas in need of improvement, they are not indicators for deep thinking and should be used sparingly. If we seek evidence of real learning, activities that provide application in context (such as problem-based learning, discussed later) are more recommendable. Formative feedback is corrective and gives space for growth. This goes in both directions: students to teachers and teachers to students. **The classrooms that employ formative assessment in the best possible ways are those in which both teacher and student learn from continual, conscientious, quality feedback**, an important principle in MBE. Evidence of the success of embedded assessment can be found at all education levels, from kindergarten through university (e.g., Absolum, Gray, & Mutchmor, 2010; Nicol & Macdarlane-Dick, 2006; Yorke, 2003). Formative assessment is mainly seen in mastery learning contexts in which the goal is learning as opposed to a final grade (Koedinger, McLaughlin, & Heffernan, 2010; Torrance & Pryor, 1998). Formative, embedded assessment is the same as feedback for mastery, but is

integrated into classroom activities (Heritage, 2010; Wiliam, 2011). This type of evaluation improves the chances of creating lifelong learners who understand how to think better (e.g., Absolum, Gray, & Mutchmor, 2010; Bennett, 2011; Black & Wiliam, 2009; Dunn & Mulvenon, 2009; Sadler, 1998). Formative assessment means that evaluation and activity are one and the same: Classroom activities actually lead to assessment of some kind. For example, debate, class projects, research, case studies, and Problem Based Learning can be activities as well as grading tools (Brown & Gerhardt, 2006). These will all be discussed in the following chapters in more detail.

I have yet to find a serious politician, let alone educator, who really believes we are serving students in the best way possible when we simply teach to the test (see S. Gallagher, 2008, for a good argument on this topic). Evaluation structures that view standardized testing as the ultimate measure of education have been criticized sufficiently by others more prepared than I, so I'll just say this: **If the true objective of teaching goes beyond passing the standardized test and improving thinking skills, our evaluation tools have to do the same.** Teaching to the test leaves deficits in student learning, and because of the poor foundation students are receiving, they aren't aware of what they're missing. The standardized testing movement has left a generational gap in skills needed for lifelong learning and warped the real purpose of school, changing the focus from thinking to passing exams.

MBE principle 6 is that brains are highly plastic and develop throughout the lifespan, which means they can continually adapt and restructure connections based on new experiences. Since learning is based in part on the brain's ability to self-correct (see MBE principle 8), teachers should take advantage of the important role that feedback plays in helping students understand what they don't know and teach to those weaknesses. Learning doesn't happen when we already know (or think we know) something, only when we realize we don't know it. Providing the space for this type of growth is fundamental to a deeper understanding of the subject and to the individual himself.

If there was one lesson about evaluation that should be emphasized far more in modern education, it would be **the need to celebrate errors** because they are evidence of thinking (albeit incorrectly). To really be able to do this, however, we need to remember that "good learning environments are made, not found" (MBE instructional guideline 1). It's up to teachers to help students feel happy about making mistakes by telling them that it shows they're making an effort to fill in their gaps in knowledge. We know that most people can and do want to learn ("The search for meaning is innate in human nature" [MBE principle 1]), but many feel discouraged from doing so in the classroom. Students learn best in classroom environments that not only tolerate but celebrate attempts at learning, which often look like mistakes.

Best Classroom Practice 8. Use Product, Process, and Progress Evaluations
Evaluation can be conducted on a variety of levels, but in education we tend to measure a final product (a test, a project presentation, etc.) ignoring that there are other ways to judge student learning. MBE evidence indicates that motivation is important in learning (Berridge, 2004; Daw & Shohamy, 2008; Harmon-Jones & van Honk, 2012). Breaking evaluation schemes down into "products," "processes," and "progress" measures, as suggested by Guskey (1996, 2001, 2011), helps students understand where they need to improve, keeps motivation high for learning even if they receive low grades, and shows them that the teacher takes a personal interest in their stages of learning.

A "product" is what most teachers typically evaluate: a test, a final project, a pop quiz, an essay—in other words, a task or product in a single defining moment. Product evaluations are usually summative. A "process" evaluation breaks down the steps a student took to arrive at the product. A process evaluation can indicate that a student reached her product the wrong way (for example, by downloading an essay from the Internet as opposed to writing it herself). Did she use Wikipedia instead of primary sources? Did just one student complete the group project? Did the student use quality sources to do his research and then compare his findings with those of others, or did he simply present his work? A "progress" evaluation is the hardest to administer, because it requires the teacher to know where the student began and where she is now so that he can chart her growth in learning. Product, process, and progress evaluations should be an ongoing part of a teacher's interaction with his students.

One way to increase the use of process evaluations is to consider embedded assessment. As noted in Best Classroom Practice 7, some of the greatest impacts on learning occur through formative, embedded assessment. "Embedded" means that the teacher doesn't need to call out to students that "there's a test coming up!"; rather, the assessment occurs within the context of everyday activities (Wiliam, 2011). **This means that there is no separate space or time for evaluation; instead, it occurs all the time through the class activities**. Evaluation activities that are seamlessly integrated into the classroom fabric serve several objectives. First, they occur frequently and are therefore a better measure of where the student actually stands. Second, because they happen so often, teachers have more space to make adjustments to their own instruction, hopefully curtailing nosedives into failure territory. Third, they don't come with the burden of stress that often accompanies summative assessment. Fourth, they often allow teachers to spend more time concentrating on the actual teaching rather than on the grading.

One of my children once waited over a month for the teacher to get around to returning a major test because it took so long for her to correct (one student had been absent for the exam, and the teacher felt she had to make an entirely new set of questions to ensure he didn't cheat and therefore did not give anyone back the test until the late student was also graded). In the meantime, a new theme that relied heavily on the information from the tested material was introduced, but because the students didn't know where they had erred, they began to do the second theme incorrectly. This is a frequent problem with math and science subjects that rely heavily on prior knowledge (Bransford et al., 2006; Rivet & Krajcik, 2008). It's impossible to build on a weak foundation, as explained in the section on constructivism.

Frequent, embedded assessment can take several forms. Teachers can use an observation rubric for class discussions and monitor the level of quality responses on a daily basis. They can ask for group work in which completion of certain tasks is required. They can ask the students to correct one another's work, then help them do the correcting and monitor areas of frequent error. The possibilities are numerous (for more examples, see Black, Harrison, Lee, Marshall, & William, 2004).

Since all brains are not equally good at everything (MBE principle 2), it's important to manage learning at the level of the individual, not at the level of state standards or even classrooms. As Wiggins and McTighe (2011) note, feedback should serve as "a continual improvement approach to student achievement and teacher craft. The results of our designs—student performance—inform needed adjustments in curriculum as well as instruction so that student learning is maximized" (pp. 1–2). That is, **every time we evaluate student-learning outcomes, we need to accept that we are actually measuring our own success as teachers and our ability to integrate the different personalities and needs in our classrooms**. "Good teachers understand how to manage different students" and their individual needs (MBE instructional guideline 7).

Best Classroom Practice 9. Test to Improve Learning
While summative evaluations should not make up the lion's share of evaluation techniques, it might seem ironic to note that frequent testing may lead to improved learning (Glass, Ingate, & Sinha, 2013; Pyc & Rawson, 2009; Roediger & Karpicke, 2006). This is easier to understand when it is clear that it is not the testing *per se* that enhances learning, but rather the forced

retrieval of information (Karpicke & Blunt, 2011; Keresztes, Kaiser, Kovács, & Racsmány, 2013) that occurs when practicing for a test due to elaborated mechanisms for linking information cues to targets (Pyc & Rawson, 2010). Review practice reinforces learning pathways and much of test preparation is review. When we prepare for a test, we review our notes, reread passages, talk about what was learned, and rehearse processes to enhance recall. All of these activities improve the likelihood of correct memory retrieval during a test because they reinforce key neural networks that actually change the brain structure itself (Karpicke & Blunt, 2011). By practicing or studying for a test, we are reinforcing the circuitry for recall, which is, in essence, learning (Zatorre, Fields, & Johansen-Berg, 2012). Teachers who incorporate frequent testing (graded or not) can enhance learning if and when errors are identified and gaps in knowledge are filled in subsequent learning moments.

Best Classroom Practice 10. Develop Shared, Explicit Learning Objectives
Shared, explicit learning objectives keep everyone on the same page and improve the chances of success. Wiggins and McTighe (2005) have suggested an idea borrowed from business: Begin with the end in mind. Where do we want to be at the end of the lesson? By clearly identifying where you want to go, you ensure smooth sailing toward your target, mastery learning.

This means that before we undertake activities or decide on evaluation methods, we should state our objectives clearly, expressing them as the educational competencies (knowledge, skills, and attitudes) (Rychen & Salganik, 2000) we want our students to attain. MBE instructional guideline 2 states that "good lessons take into account both sense (logical order) and meaning (personal relevance)." Students will find it difficult to adhere to learning objectives they don't share or that they aren't privy to. For example, many claim that evaluation criteria in art classes are too subjective. To avoid unclear messages, the teacher can show a complete worked example of what is expected, then ask students to develop the rubric for grading that same piece. By developing the rubric together, each criterion for grading is clarified by and for the whole group. This forces students to reflect on what they've just seen as it compares to their own work. Do colors matter? How do materials change the end product? What is the importance of proportion? How about style? Once shared criteria for grading have been developed, the teacher can reiterate all the elements that will be graded. This process takes longer than a normal lesson would, but the clarity gained eliminates all shades of gray when it comes to grading and actually saves time in the overall teaching-learning process.

FIGURE 4.4
Student Motivation Is Linked to Teacher Clarity

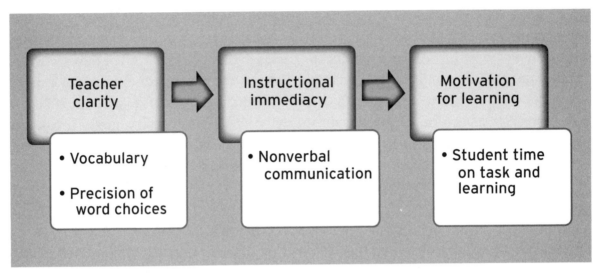

According to the research, much of discovery learning is either an inefficient use of time or misguided because there is no clear "north" in terms of learning goals (see Kirschner, Sweller, & Clark, 2006 for a more detailed explanation). The principal of minimal effort (Kingsley, 1949) means that humans will do the least possible to get the most possible. Students will expend the just amount of energy on tasks that is necessary and no more. Guided discovery is slightly better than pure discovery, but Hattie (2007) believes they both leave open too many possibilities for erroneous learning, in which students presume X is the goal when it is really Y. This often happens when classroom activities are too advanced or too slow for the learner because the teacher hasn't taken the time to know his students well. Most of what students "discover" in inquiry-based learning is wrong. If you observe a group of students in a simulation, the process of hypothesis building might be excellent, but most of the content information they exchange is likely to be incorrect (Hattie, 2009). The teacher's role is essential in clarifying content delivery and structuring quality learning experiences. Passion and being a catalyst for change outweigh a reliance on discovery learning anytime.

Clearly stating objectives provides students with unmistakable direction for their learning (Marzano, 2009) and increases the likelihood that teachers will achieve their learning goals. **Goals shouldn't be too specific; they should be adaptable to students' own objec-**

tives so that there is alignment between teachers' and students' class goals. This means that while the specific competency (knowledge, skill, or attitude) should be spelled out for each person, we should allow flexibility in how the student demonstrates her mastery of that competency.

For example, by the second grade, children in the New York State public school system should know about the digestive and excretory systems (State of New York, 2011). The State suggests some texts (*What Happens to a Hamburger*; *The Digestive System*, p. 46), but it doesn't dictate exactly how the teacher should teach the unit. Some students might show great interest in this topic because they have a new baby brother and have watched how he eats and goes to the bathroom. Others might have seen the excretory process in their pets. Yet others might be lucky enough to have dolls that "go." If the teacher lets the students know they all need to be able to understand the digestive and excretory systems (identify processes, relevant bodily parts, etc.), then it shouldn't matter if the students choose to demonstrate that understanding by explaining how these systems work in humans, in dolls, or in animals, for example. So long as the goal is achieved, the teacher should allow enough flexibility for the students to align their own interests to the learning task.

To ensure that the objectives are shared and explicit, great teachers check for comprehension of the "rules of the game" before they begin. Many prepared teachers start a unit by saying what they plan to do, then write the instructions on the board. Others follow up these two steps with a final check by asking one of the students to articulate the task at hand (i.e., say what the teacher said in his or her own words; just because the teacher says it doesn't mean the students heard it).

Anita Archer and Charles A. Hughes (2010) believe that explicit instruction is the key to effective and efficient teaching due to the shared objectives they provide. **It is in human nature to enjoy success; no one likes failure**. Humans are good at modeling behavior, and when they are given a clear model and opportunities to practice, they are able to replicate what they observe. However, true learning is not only a matter of copying a model; it involves deeper understanding, which is why offering clear learning objectives is crucial.

How can clear learning objectives be developed in all classrooms? The "SMART" acronym (**s**pecific, **m**easureable, **a**ttainable, **r**elevant, and **t**argeted) is an excellent guide used by many classroom teachers. Like many a contribution to pedagogy, SMART was devised in the business world to measure outcomes and then imported into the educational setting (Doran, 1981; also see P. J. Meyer, 2003). SMART goals have the following characteristics:

Specific: SMART objectives are limited in scope. "The students should know all the important theories" is not as specific as "The students should know the Pythagorean theorem."

Measurable: SMART goals break down intangible concepts into observable objectives. "Critical thinking" is not as measurable as the level of intellectual curiosity (or intellectual perseverance, intellectual integrity, etc.) displayed based on the total number of deep questions asked.

Attainable: SMART goals can be accomplished by the target audience within the scheduled time and under the specified conditions. A teacher who sets too many goals or goals that are too high is not as successful as one who sets staged goals appropriate to the students' ages and knowledge level, given the time available to cover the information.

Relevant: SMART goals are results oriented. A teacher who demands strong writing skills in an acting class or requires oral ability in a sports class may have some kind of reasoning behind his request; however, it is likely that these are secondary or even irrelevant objectives. Oral skills are probably more appropriate in an acting class, while physical coordination, speed, agility are relevant in a sports class.

Targeted: SMART goals are tailored to the learner and to the desired level of learning. Teachers whose learning objectives are gauged to the personal learning needs of each student are more successful. Whereas global goals for the group are important and necessary, targeting these goals to the specific learner and her needs is even more so. Not everyone will be at the same stage of subject knowledge at the same time, and teachers must differentiate to appropriately evaluate each student.

By using SMART objectives (or other guides), teachers push themselves to develop shared, explicit criteria by which students can plan their own study activities to match learning goals. Their planning and effort can be further encouraged with ongoing feedback.

Best Classroom Practice 11. Strive for Clarity and Immediacy
The ability of a teacher to communicate clearly is one of the cornerstones of good teaching as we saw in Chapter 2 (Cheseboro, 2002, 2003; Mottet, Richmond, & McCroskey, 2006). Teacher clarity ensures that the students understand the focus of the lesson as well as the path toward successful learning—in other words, there is no guessing about what is acceptable as "good work" (Simonds, 2007). Clarity of speech is fundamental to ensuring that students have good examples and appropriate guided practice, and that they understand how and why assessment will occur (Cheseboro & McCroskey, 1998, 2000, 2001). Several articles in the *Journal of Effective Teaching* testify to the importance of teacher clarity in enhancing the prob-

ability of learning. Several relatively recent journal articles identifying the characteristics of effective teachers note that the best combination is instructional immediacy and clarity accompanied by a humanistic view of students (Ginsberg, 2007; Ripski, LoCasale-Crouch, & Decker, 2011; Teven & Hanson, 2004).

Two leaders in the area of instructional communication are Joseph L. Cheseboro and James C. McCroskey, both of Western Virginia University. Their work, collectively and individually, has spanned several decades, refined several tools in the field, and sparked a boom in publications in the 1980s (see Brophy & Good, 1986; Civikly, 1992; Cruickshank & Kennedy, 1986; Rosenshine & Stevens, 1986). Their Teacher Clarity Short Inventory (TCSI) has been a guide for decades in establishing the parameters of good communication between teacher and student.

According to Cheseboro and McCroskey, a teacher's verbal clarity can be broken down into several subareas, such as fluency, precision, and class structure (as in course organization, including transitions within in class activities). Parameters of a teacher's nonverbal communication include the time spent covering a topic, speaking pace, body movement, and instructional immediacy (Cheseboro & McCroskey, 1998). Not all of these important aspects of communication may be at the forefront of every teacher's mind. For example, something as subtle as tone of voice can change how a student perceives the teacher's meaning (S. A. Myers, 1995; S. A. Myers & Knox, 2000), and if a student believes the instructor is being aggressive (even though the actual words are not aggressive), her learning is reduced (S. A. Myers & Rocca, 2001; Schrodt, 2003; Schultz, 2003). Rocca (2007) defines instructional immediacy as the ability to bridge the gap between the instructor and the learner through nonverbal signals:

> Instructional immediacy is behavior that brings the instructor and the students closer together in terms of perceived distance. Non-verbal immediacy includes behaviors such as smiling, gesturing, eye contact and having relaxed body language. Verbal immediacy refers to calling the students by name, using humor and encouraging student input and discussion. (Rocca, 2007, slide 1)

According to McCroskey and his colleagues (1996; see also Hurt, Scott, & McCroskey, 1978), communication immediacy has legitimacy across cultural boundaries and is appreciated around the world.

While it may seem like stating the obvious, it is evident that a teacher's lack of clarity reduces achievement and increased clarity improves it. A study conducted by L. R. Smith (1984; see also Land, 1979) found that uncertain and unprepared teachers (e.g., those who paused too much, looked at their notes often, said "uh" frequency, or gave other signals of self-doubt) were significantly less effective than teachers who did not display this uncertainty. **The brain's ability to perceive and judge human faces and voices quickly and almost unconsciously means that a student loses confidence in the teacher when he is not clear** (Engell, Haxby, & Todorov, 2007). Bluffing also has highly negative effects on learning outcomes. Teachers who don't know answers but pretend they do and are caught in the act have far lower credibility and much less success than teachers who are purposeful and don't bluff (S. A. Myers, 2004).

Pogue and Ahyun found that instructional immediacy improves students' affect and reduces their level of apprehension (2006; see also Andrew, Cobb, & Giampierto, 2005). At the same time, the use of precise vocabulary improves learning outcomes because it facilitates the explicit communication of goals. In Pogue and Ahyun's study, teachers were shown to influence their students in both positive and negative ways based on their level of clarity. In the best case, teacher clarity can reduce student anxiety and improve learning outcomes (Rodger, Murray, & Cummings, 2007). Teacher clarity, relevance, caring, and verbal aggressiveness have been shown to impact student responses to learning, for better or for worse, especially their receptiveness to new information (see Zigarovich & Myers, 2011). When students perceived their teachers to be clear, relevant, and caring, the impacts were positive; when they perceived a teacher to be aggressive, they shut down and their learning was impaired as seen in MBE principle 12, "Learning is enhanced by challenge and inhibited by threat". The connection between teacher clarity and instructional immediacy seems to provide a formula for motivation (Figure 4.4). A student's motivation for learning is increased when a teacher uses precise words and clear vocabulary and conveys nonverbal messages of encouragement (Crow & Small, 2011).

In an almost counterintuitive finding, recent research in teacher communication has shown that teacher clarity and instructional immediacy can be developed outside traditional face-to-face, teacher-to-student models with the assistance of computers. Sullivan, Hunt, and Lippert (2004) found evidence that psychological closeness can be fostered via computer-mediated communication. As an online instructor myself in some classes, I can see how some students consider the "anonymity" and democratic division of work in online environments to foster confidence and closeness. This means that some components of traditional communication models can be modified. More important than eye contact and soothing tones of voices may be the actual words used and their context. It may seem surprising to some, but online teachers can achieve equal clarity without eye contact because precision, clarity and concern can often be equal or superior in online contexts (see Borup, Graham, & Velasquez, 2013; Lee, Srinivasan, Trail, Lewis, & Lopez, 2011).

Best Classroom Practice 12. Provide Feedback for Mastery Learning
It is now very apparent that feedback that delivers formative evaluation plays a huge role in learning. When we learn what others think about our thinking (what a teacher thinks about how well we resolved a problem, for example), our own thinking processes are changed and refined through that feedback (Popham, 2013). **Feedback triggers the confirmation, negation, new adaptation, or modification of our mental schema, or mindsets**. Feedback on what things we did correctly or incorrectly or ideas about how to improve processes are a key part of learning. Reactions to the ways we express thoughts and suggestions on how we could express them more clearly are excellent learning moments.

There are still old-fashioned teachers who believe teaching is like aiming at small prey. They shoot toward their learning goals and that's it: hit or miss. Teachers who have benefited from MBE know teaching is more like a tennis match with a volley here, then a return (feedback) followed by a new volley (teaching), and so on. Feedback serves as a type of "checks and balances" to individual thought processes in which someone or something outside the learner has a say on the quality of her work. Neuroscientist Chris Frith (2007) identifies this give-and-take with the outside world as a key way of stimulating all of us to find out more about ourselves and others. It is hard to know ourselves without such an exchange as seen in the information about Theory of Mind in Chapter 3.

Depending on our relationship with the person giving the feedback or the signal received, feedback volleys can be a powerful model of learning. **Small comments by people in authority (e.g., teachers) can have an amazing impact on the way we think about ourselves as learners as well as the thinking processes we develop throughout our lifetime**. Depending on who we are and how we see our status in life, different people have an extraordinary influence over our beliefs about the world and about ourselves. Weisberg, Keil, Goodstein, Rawson, and Gray (2008) found that the allure of graphs, charts, and brain images convinced adults of illogical findings; they "judged that explanations with logically irrelevant neuroscience information [to be] more satisfying than explanations without" because they were delivered by authority figures. Farah and Hook (2013) also found that "brain images are inordinately influential" because they represent authoritative information. These two examples show how people tend to be swayed by information they perceive to be generated by experts, especially in teacher-student settings. On a positive note, Whitebread and colleagues found that authority figures can help shape metacognitive habits of mind in young learners (Whitebread, Coltman, et al., 2009). Starting early in life (3–5 years old), Whitebread shows how authority figures who encourage us to develop habits of mind about our own thinking and help us refine our metacognitive processes, help us become more autonomous learners. Giordano (2004) showed how we as teachers often don't realize the weight our comments carry with students who can make life-altering decisions based on short conversations with us. Teachers who accept their authoritative role and guide students in explicitly developing better thinking skills have an impact over the student's lifetime.

This idea is aligned with a key instructional guideline (number 9) in MBE: "Explicit teaching of metacognitive skills aids higher-order thinking across subjects." Well-designed, constructive feedback—the goal of which is to guide without causing harm—is one of the single most impactful ways teachers influence learning outcomes, because the checks and balances to our own thought processes refine our mental schema of the world and improves metacognition skills. Humans are social beings and we continually learn, unconsciously or consciously, from one another (Bargh & Williams, 2006; C. D. Frith & Frith, 2012). Another MBE instructional guideline (number 5) reminds us that **"good classroom activities take advantage of the social nature of learning,"** and feedback takes advantage of the natural exchange between teacher and student as a social as well as academic exercise.

Stanford University psychologist Carol Dweck celebrates this concept in *Mindset* (2007), in which she explains how achievement in both personal as well as academic settings is influenced by the subtle messages we pass on to students in the simple comments we make about their work. Teachers must learn how to apply conscientious, purposeful identification of the right moments to promote authentic esteem-building and give feedback that nurtures growth. However, feedback is a powerful tool only when it is sincere and based on evidence. When students perceive praise to be "canned" or rehearsed, it has little effect on their learning, and in fact can raise questions about the teacher's credibility in their eyes. A *Los Angeles Times* article called attention to the inefficiency of offering "praise" to students in hopes that raising self-esteem would lead to better learning (Colvin, 1999). The article points out that time would be better spent teaching the subject basics than offering false celebrations of attempts at learning. Telling a kid he is "doing great!" when he really has a lot to improve on or giving the whole class stickers for their "good work!" doesn't help the student or accelerate the learning processes (for more on this phenomena, see Decker, 1997). There are some who strongly believe that learning should be its own reward. Daniel T. Willingham gives weight to this claim in the *American Educator* (2007–2008) and points out that students who work for external rewards never really gain an intrinsic satisfaction with the love of learning.

The debate on whether school motivators are better driven by carrots or sticks is still hot. Two main pairs of motivators in psychology are positive-negative and intrinsic-extrinsic (Isen & Reeve, 2005; Vallerand et al., 1993), though they can interact, as in measuring the influence of extrinsic rewards on intrinsic motivation (see Deci, Koestner, & Ryan, 1999). People can and do learn in all four combinations (positive-intrinsic, positive-extrinsic, negative-intrinsic, negative-extrinsic), but long-term use and application of new knowledge is enhanced when the learner chooses (positive) to learn for himself rather than having learning forces (negative) on him from the outside (extrinsic) (Isen & Reeve, 2005), though there are variants across the lifespan (Lepper, Corpus, & Iyengar, 2005). Rewards for learning can motivate when the learner believes he deserves the prize. Sanctions can also force learning moments but as they may be connected to negative emotions, there may be a psychological conflict in the learner, reducing the likelihood of use or application of the learned information in the future (Deci, Vallerand, Pelletier, & Ryan, 1991). That is, unless the learner considers the sanction a reward (see Kim, Shimojo, & O'Doherty, 2006), positive-intrinsic motivators are more effective in learning than negative, extrinsic motivators. Normally, sanctions can increase the level of stress one feels, leading to a combination of neurotransmitters that reduces the probability of new synaptic creation for long-term memory (Chen et al., 2010; Joëls, Pu, Wiegert, Oitzl & Krugers, 2006; Lupiens, McEwen, Gunnar, & Heim, 2009; Schwabe & Wolf, 2012), though studies now show there are great human variances (Bangasser & Shors, 2010).

Crow and Small (2011) try to find a happy compromise by convincing teachers that **intrinsic motivators work best**. However, it is incumbent on external forces, often the teacher, to cultivate this belief in students through the feedback process. Some argue that the ultimate goal of all our efforts at motivation is to develop autonomously motivated students who can push themselves toward learning goals (R. E. Johnson, Chang, & Lord, 2006). This is taken as a given in modern classrooms, in which we now accept that "motivation plays a significant role in a student's learning and development. It is part of teachers' pedagogy to develop in students the desire for new knowledge and understandings, known as intrinsic motivation" (Valerio, 2012, p.30). **Feedback, then, takes on a new twist and grows beyond evaluations to being an instructional tool** that hopefully catalyzes intrinsic motivation to improve.

When used to teach, feedback is completed at different "levels," all of which are important. Feedback is developed though personal interactions (Frymier & Wanzer, 2006; Frymier & Weser, 2001) but achieved in written as well as face-to-to-face formats. This brings us to the importance of teacher-student relationships, which we will look at more closely in Best Classroom Practice 13.

Mastery Goals. There's a difference between giving feedback to achieve "mastery goals" and giving it to meet "performance goals," in which the objective of teaching moves from producing indicators of real learning (mastery) to competitive and artificial representations of learning (performance measurements, such as grades and test scores). Unfortunately, as teachers **we often place too much emphasis on the right answer and not on the processes that go into reaching the right answers**. I have watched more than one teacher finish a teaching unit, pass back the evaluation from that section, and move on without taking the time to help students fill in their gaps in learning. **Some of the best teaching moments happen right alongside evaluation moments:** when a student realizes she got something wrong, but perhaps doesn't know why it's wrong. Because the student both recognizes the gap herself and feels the need to fill in that gap, this would be one of the best times to teach, but we as teachers often move on to the next topic. Teacher feedback must help the learner distinguish between the goal and her current understanding, with the end goal being to help her regulate her own learning (Pintrich, 1995).

Should one compete against oneself or others? Mastery learning goals eliminate unnecessary and unhelpful competition against others and returns the focus to individual learning. Barrett (2008) writes of competitive classrooms in which students measure their own worth by comparing their grades to those of others in the group, as opposed to measuring their individual gains and true learning through mastery goal achievement. Barrett believes in eliminating the "winners" and "losers" in a classroom and allowing students to compete against themselves. This is often difficult in settings where extrinsic rewards (teacher- or state-driven grades) are accepted as success standards.

Benjamin Bloom began the discussion about the importance of mastery learning in the late 1960s (1968, 1971a, 1974).

Bloom believed that a far better approach would be for teachers to use their classroom assessments as learning tools, and then to follow those assessments with a feedback and corrective procedure. In other words, instead of using assessments only as evaluation devices that mark the end of each unit, Bloom recommended using them as part of the instructional process to identify individual learning difficulties (feedback) and to pre-scribe remediation procedures (correctives). (Guskey, 2009, para. 7)

As the discussion about "teaching to the test" versus actual learning processes has become the focus of hot debate, the use of mastery learning objectives has become popular once again. It is generally accepted that mastery (allowing individuals to reach clear learning objectives at their own pace) is far superior to performance goal objectives (the display of how well a student does on a test) for long-term, transferable learning.

Best Classroom Practice 13. Nurture Teacher-Student Relationships
A core MBE principle (number 11) is that "Emotions are critical to detecting patterns, to deci-sion-making, and to learning." If the student doesn't have positive, affective connections to her teacher, her learning is compromised. Positive student-teacher relationships aren't easy to cultivate, however intuitive it may seem to develop them (H. A. Davis, 2003). Much of the student-teacher relationship is grounded in feedback exchanges about the learner's processes.

In MBE, we find that the ways in which we receive feedback are deeply ingrained in both our psyche and our neural mechanisms. For example, a professor might think he's delivering the right feedback in the word he chooses, but fails to understand that his face, tone of voice and body language are sending another message. **The brain is wired to warn us of threats perceived either through facial expressions or tones of voice** (Winston, Strange, O'Doherty & Dolan, 2005); however, the perception of threats is not always completely accurate. Ambady and Rosenthal (1994) found that a teacher has just half a minute to establish credibility with learners before they judge whether or not he is competent based on body languages. This means that establishing good relationships and getting off on the right foot are time-sensitive ventures in teaching (Becker, Davis, Neal, & Grover, 1990). Although first impressions can be changed, it takes more time to repair a poorly established relationship than to start a new one.

Perry, VanderKamp, Mercer, and Nordby (2002) argue that **the personal link between student and teacher is very important in fostering effort on the part of the student.** In their study of young children (kindergarten through third grade), they considered what teachers say and do to improve metacognitive reflection, intrinsic motivation, and strategic behavior. They found that when teachers explicitly encouraged students' efforts, they made a positive difference in the students' self-regulation of their behavior. That is, the students worked to please the teachers. A teacher's guidance is fundamental to students' development of metacognitive skills via the nurturing elements of formative evaluation and feedback that work over the life span (Fuchs & Fuchs, 1993).

Different teachers approach student relationships in different ways. Hattie (2003) has identified a great difference between teachers who are "expert" and those who are "experienced" in managing how they think about learning, and this is communicated, willingly or not to their students (Kerrins & Cushing, 1998). Experts know how to adjust and adapt to challenges in the class—the need for differentiation, disturbance, finding the right methodologies—while "experienced" teachers work solely based on their own contact with teaching experiences (they tend to teach the way they were taught). Hattie found that teachers in the expert category can adjust to individual learning situations and are flexible in their approach, which contributes to stronger bonds in their relationships with students. Expert teachers have their finger of the pulse of all of their students and adjust their practice accordingly.

Fostering student effort is often seen as an individual teacher's role, but authors such as Tschannen-Moran and Barr (2004) remind us that "collective teacher efficacy" is equivalent to a positive school learning environment and relationships between groups of teachers and students (see also Goldman, Botkin, Tokugana & Kuklinski, 1997) and improves student learning (see also Tschannen-Moran & Woolfolk-Hoy, 2001; Tschannen-Moran, Woolfolk-Hoy, & Hoy, 1998). Collective teacher efficacy is accomplished by groups of teachers who, either by policy decree or by their own initiative, make "an educational difference to their students over and above the educational impact of their homes and communities" (p. 189) by developing coherent self-regulatory learning models via the rehearsal of formative evaluation and feedback. Tschannen-Moran and Barr found that **the collective fostering of student effort actually led to better achievement than individual praise**. That is, effective formative feedback can have benefits both when it is conducted individually and when it is carried out by groups because both nurture relationships. The quality of student-teacher relationships, either in pairs or institutionally, has a great impact on student learning.

Best Classroom Practice 14. Believe in the Role of Plasticity and in Your Students
Hattie believes that **aside from the student herself, the teacher is the actor with the most influence over student learning outcomes** (2012). Specifically, the teacher is responsible for

students doing better or worse than expected, and Hattie notes that a powerful indicator of student learning is whether the teacher believes intelligence is changeable or malleable, not fixed, everyone can and will learn, and that his students can progress. A teacher's preconceived notions of these elements, even before he meets a student for the first time, influence the learner's success rate.

However, as Hattie points out, many teachers aren't even aware of their own biases toward their students or about learning processes. Many teachers don't consciously reflect on their beliefs about teaching (what they envision the role of the teacher to be), learning (whether intelligence is fluid or fixed due to genes), evaluation (whether it's an end-of-process event or an ongoing teaching tool, as in formative assessment), and the student (whether their learning potential is rigidly determined by factors such as their genes and socioeconomic status, or whether all students can learn). **Students excel when teachers believe their intelligence is ever changing and that their potential can be elevated by the right adjustments to individual needs**. Learning occurs when teachers and students both believe that everyone can learn.

But all teachers think their students can learn, or they wouldn't be in the teaching business, right? Wrong. Hattie establishes the worrisome fact that many teachers have preconceived notions about students. Early and often unfounded judgments of students and their abilities have a profound impact on learning potential. **Students who think their teachers think they can learn, do learn. Students who believe, erroneously or not, that their teachers think their intelligence is inflexible will not even try, and therefore complete a self-fulfilling prophecy.** Likewise, if a teacher has the preconceived notion that intelligence is fixed and that a student is trapped by the brain potential she is born with, then he is unlikely to seek out creative methods of teaching because he already presumes that nothing can change. Without attempts to design good classroom experiences, the probability of learning is highly reduced.

One of the most encouraging findings in neuroscience today has to do with plasticity. Perhaps the most articulate writer on this subject is Norman Doidge, whose book *The Brain That Changes Itself* (2007) opens the door of possibility when it comes to new learning. After interviewing neuroscientists around the world, he summarized their research as follows:

[These neuroscientists have shown] that children are not always stuck with the mental abilities they are born with; that the damaged brain can often reorganize itself so that when one part fails, another can often substitute; that if brain cells die, they can at times be replaced; that many "circuits" and even basic reflexes that we think are hardwired are not. One of these scientists even showed that thinking, learning, and acting can turn our genes on or off, thus shaping our brain anatomy and our behavior—surely one of the most extraordinary discoveries of the twentieth century. (Doidge, 2008, p. xv)

Thus, great teachers realize that the brain changes daily with experience and that new learning is always possible (for a neurological explanation of this phenomenon, see Draganski et al., 2004, and Maguire et al., 2000). Education on the fundamental mechanisms of new learning in the brain, including neuroplasticity and the precise combination of neurotransmitters necessary to form synapses, should be a part of all teachers' continual professional development.

Because excellent teachers have such faith in human nature and the abilities of their students, they believe that teaching involves going beyond instruction, or a purely motivational role, and into planning clear learning goals and achieving them. **Good teaching is active and passionate and leaves nothing to chance**. Hattie makes the distinction between teachers who think of themselves as "facilitators" versus those who consider themselves "activators." Facilitators choose instructional strategies that are not dependent on good teaching (inductive teaching, simulations, problem-based learning), while activators deliberately choose instructional strategies that require goal setting, explicit instruction, feedback, reciprocal teaching methods, and strong teaching skills). Hattie compared the "active teacher," who is "passionate for their subject and for learning" and serves as a change agent, to "a facilitative inquiry or discovery based provider of engaging activities" (2007, slide 29). In general, activators have better results than facilitators.

Great teachers plan learning activities around the learner's constructivist stage, believing that, with the right planning, everyone can learn to his or her potential; intelligence is fluid. We now turn to some recommendations in learning activities that are supported both by *Visible Learning* and MBE.

Instructional Designs: Methods, Techniques, Strategies, Actions, and Activities

Teaching is about the combination of techniques, strategies, actions, and activities a teacher applies to develop his unique instructional design in classroom settings. While often used interchangeably, a "teaching method" is different from a "technique," "strategy," "action," or "activity" (Figure 4.5).

For clarity, this section defines *methods* as general practices or frameworks for instructional practice. For example, the "Socratic method" is a means of instruction that can be combined with the *technique* of using certain types of questions that require a specific response ("What makes you say that?"). Within the Socratic method might be the *strategy* of using student-centered dialogue, and this might call for turn-taking *action* in small group *activities*, which are processes designed to facilitate students' movement toward common learning goals (R. E. Mayer, 2008).

FIGURE 4.5
Terms for Instructional Practices

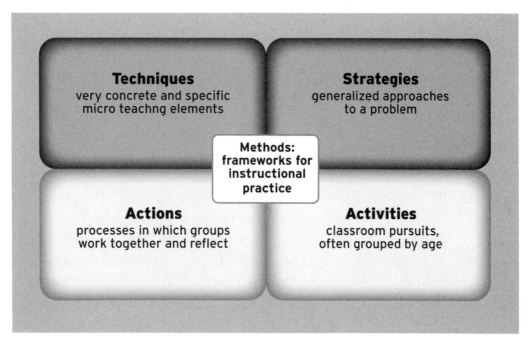

For many of us, teaching is focused innately on what we do in the classroom in terms of the methodologies we apply or the techniques and strategies that we use to execute actions or activities. There are more books written on classroom activities than on any other teaching focus (see Beesley & Apthorp 2010 for a recent example of this genre). If you conduct a quick Amazon or general Internet search, you can find hundreds of thousands of books on teaching activities and relatively few related to deep thinking skills, improving learning outcomes, planning, or evaluation. This is helpful and dangerous at the same time. With so many books out on teaching methods and activities, teachers are sometimes overwhelmed by the offerings. So many books tell us what to do, but few explain *why*.

The next two Best Classroom Practices (15 and 16) provide filters that can help teachers choose support materials that will best help them reach their classroom goals. The additional filters detailed in Best Classroom Practices 17 through 23 are based on Marzano, Pickering, and Pollock's work *Classroom Instruction That Works* (2001) and constitute specific strategies to help kids develop good thinking habits. (Only seven of Marzano and colleagues' nine strategies are covered in this chapter; cooperative learning and nonlinguistic representations will be discussed separately.) These strategies are simple at first blush, but they get to the core of thinking skills, and any activity that employs them is better than an activity that does not. While Marzano's work has evolved over the years (1988, 2003, 2011), it retains its original evidence-based focus. Marzano's website (http://www.marzanoresearch.com) offers further material on the concepts he has embraced over the years.

Best Classroom Practice 15. Foster Metacognition and Mindfulness

> *We cannot teach people anything; we can only help them discover it within themselves.*
> —Galileo Galilei

If we as teachers hope to contribute to lifelong learning, then we must choose classroom methodologies, actions, and activities that improve thinking. These methodologies should be accompanied by specific teaching techniques that maximize the classroom time on task in as profound a way as possible. Learning to be more conscious of our own thinking—the how and why of our ideas—is called metacognition (Borkowski, Carr, Rellinger, & Pressley, 2013; Hacker, Dunlosky, & Graesser, 2009). As noted earlier, stimulating students' critical thinking and metacognition are the perhaps greatest of goals in modern education and a teacher's greatest challenge (Desautel, 2009; Hacker, Dunlosky & Graesser, 2009; Larkin, 2010; Leat & Lin, 2003). Higher order cognition is a prized skill in almost every society imaginable and often equated with metacognitive skills and critical thinking (Voss, Perkins, & Segal, 2012). There is evidence in neuroscience that shows how metacognitive skills are developed in the brain and how they can be stimulated with training and rehearsal (e.g., Fleming & Dolan, 2012). While a great deal of the research on metacognitive activities in the brain is based on deficits, such as when someone loses these skills after an accident or trauma (see Choiu, Carlson, Arnett, Costntino, & Hillary, 2011; Fleming, Weil, Ngy, Dolan, & Rees, 2010; Ownsworth, Quinn,

Fleming, Kendall, & Shum, 2010), others are focused on how metacognition works in the brain (Fleming, Dolan, & Frith, 2012) and how specific types of training improves it (Dekker, Krabbendam, Gemmink, De Groot, & Jolles, 2012; Fleming et al., 2010; Middlebrooks & Sommer, 2012). Many studies on metacognitive abilities and the brain point to similar areas for decision making as for metacognition (e.g., Fleming, Huijgen, & Dolan, 2012), which could mean that activities that rehearse decision making are beneficial in developing some aspects of higher order thinking.

Metacognition as a theory of learning was proposed centuries ago but in the modern era has been celebrated with the launching of the journal *Metacognition and Learning* (2005). It is based on the idea that better knowledge, understanding, and regulation of one's own cognitive activities will improve learning processes (A. L. Brown, 1975, 1978, 1987; Flavell, 1982, 1987). In other words, understanding why we think about things in a particular way helps us learn better (Azevedo, 2005; Schellenberg, Negishi, & Eggen, 2011), a principle established in cognitive neuroscience (Shimamura, 2000). This occurs through training, incentives, feedback, and helping students predict their own learning outcomes (Miller & Geraci, 2011).

Why is training in metacognitive skills important in overall thinking ability? Because through metacognitive practices we learn how to consciously follow self-proposed steps tailor-made to our own thinking processes, creating a cycle of improved thinking across our lifespan. Thus, **metacognition is fundamental to lifelong learning and is highly individual**. Despite the brain's desire to learn, however, metacognitive skills don't come naturally and must be consciously cultivated. Knowing how you know something requires guidance by a skilled teacher who helps you understand yourself better. A great teacher doesn't just say, "Great answer!" which merely boosts your self-esteem, but rather adds, "*How* did you get that?" which helps you think about your own thinking process. This is perhaps one of the most powerful influences in learning across the life span, because once that habit is cultivated, it comes naturally to the learner in every new learning situation she faces. "It seems problem number ten was hard for a lot of people. Mariana, you got it right; how did you go about resolving the problem?" Such questions stimulate the learner to develop the habits of mind that precede metacognition. One of the most powerful self-insights is the understanding of how to facilitate this type of learning for oneself and use it across the lifespan.

It is important to recognize the neural elements associated with this type of learning. The brain can't help but learn—it is its *raison d'être*—but it is not automated to think about how it thinks. According to Bollich, Johannet, and Vazire (2011), **there are "two main avenues for learning about the self: looking inward (e.g., introspection) and looking outward (e.g., feedback)"** (p. 312), but both avenues have to be modeled or taught explicitly to be successful. Some students learn about themselves by making mental connections after mindful reflection (see Vazire & Wilson, 2012, for a more detailed look at this important concept). Self-reflection is different from metacognition, but also important in learning.

Mindfulness, Ellen Langer tells us (1990), is becoming conscious of the what and why of our actions. The "wellness" movement in North America is stimulating more and more schools to adopt mindfulness programs for their students (Anspaugh, Hamrick, & Rosato, 2010; Department of Healthy and Inclusive Communities of Canada, 2012; Lawson, 2013; Pilzer, 2007). These programs teach students to concentrate on their breathing and to be more conscious of the world around them (the breeze, the cold floor, the feel of the pencil, the taste of a piece of fruit, etc.), as well as to meditate and be more aware of their own bodies, the people around them, and how their actions cause reactions in others and how certain stimuli create different reactions in themselves.

According to Hooker and Fodor, "Mindfulness training emphasizes focused attention to internal and external experiences in the present moment of time, without judgment" (2008, p. 75). Teaching mindfulness to children means helping students understand the balance between their bodies and minds and their internal and external worlds, and has been shown to have positive effects on concentration in schools as well as address general behavioral problems (Berkovich-Ohana, Glicksohn, & Goldstein, 2011; Hooker & Fodor, 2008; van der Oord, Bögels, & Pejinenburg, 2012). Biegel and Brown (2010) have studied the Mindful Schools movement in California and report that "mindfulness can be used to increase the space between a stimulus and one's response to it, enabling improved decision-making ability and shifts in long standing behavior" (p. 1). Helping students develop mindfulness has shown positive results in general learning outcomes, including testing, social skills improvement, attention, and motivation (Biegel & Brown, 2010). This points to the idea that learning communities that foster mindfulness produce better academic outcomes.

Becoming mindful of one's actions is vital to becoming a good teacher as well as to becoming a successful student. A teacher who has mastered regular, mindful reflection on his practice is a better teacher than one who acts without caring about or understanding the implications of his actions. A supportive learning environment, in which all learners—teachers included—

help one another to improve their thinking and content skills, is key to facilitating this process (Lin, 2001). Project Zero researchers remind us that "children grow into the intellectual life of those around them" (Vygotsky, 1978, p. 88, as cited in Ritchhart, Church, & Morrison, 2011, p. 28). Mindful instruction helps students develop their own self-reflection skills, which in turn improve learning. In other words, once a teacher has mastered his own mindfulness and metacognitive skills, he can begin to guide others in the same process. A teacher can improve his metacognition by habitually searching his own past for connections and continually engaging higher-order thinking.

Metacognition is actually one of the easiest skills to teach, but it must usually be taught explicitly. "Today we're going to think about how we think" wouldn't be a bad way to start a lesson emphasizing metacognition. However, **teaching metacognitive skills can often be embedded in other activities and doesn't take up much classroom time**. The key to inculcating good metacognitive skills, according to Kuhn (2000), is to focus on the development of students' own awareness rather than on specific steps or procedures for improving these skills. Hennessey (1999) suggests that a key element in developing good metacognitive skills is helping students to reason, understand concepts, and make their beliefs more "visible" to themselves and others. A great teacher is able to facilitate the retrieval of past knowledge, help identify patterns, and point out novelties to improve student learning.

This year my older son was asked keep a journal for math class and note what he thought about the class each day. W. Baker and Czarnocha have reviewed the utility of writing in math and state that:

> The ability to express one's mathematical thoughts in writing and computational proficiency can be viewed as reflecting different aspects of an individual's understanding of mathematics. Computational proficiency is the primary means used by educators to assess students' understanding of mathematics, and thus in the mathematics classroom cognitive development is measured for the most part through students' ability to apply their procedural knowledge in a problem solving environment. In contrast, in written mathematics one's thoughts are not so much involved with the application of procedural knowledge as with reflection upon the concepts and procedures themselves. (2002, p. 1)

Writing about math forced my son to be more conscious and mindful of his own mental processes. What did he like or understand? What was he confused by or fail to understand? What was easy and what was hard? How could what he was learning be used in other settings? Why were some concepts more difficult than others? When was something hard? Who else had good suggestions about how to do a problem that were different from his own approach?

Activities that stimulate metacognition do one of two things: they either enhance knowledge about cognition, or they enhance monitoring of cognition (Flavell, 1979; Schneider, 2008, 2010). Metacognitive activities fall into six general categories: (a) knowledge about oneself as a learner and factors affecting cognition; (b) awareness and management of cognition, including knowledge about strategies; (c) knowledge about why and when to use a given strategy; (d) identification and selection of appropriate strategies and allocation of resources; (e) attending to and being aware of comprehension and task performance; and (f) assessing the processes and products of one's learning and revisiting and revising learning (Lai, 2011, p.7). When my son kept a journal in math class, he was achieving all of these types of metacognition-boosting activities.

Teachers should be aware of specific activities and strategies that facilitate metacognitive development. For example, "explicit attention to declarative, procedural, and conditional knowledge about reading strategies" was found to be helpful in guiding third and fifth graders (Cross & Paris, 1988, as cited in Lai, 2011, p. 20). It has also been found that self-motivational strategies, cognitive strategies, planning, self-evaluation, and problem-solving strategies enhance metacognition (Eshel & Kohavi, 2003; Hofer & Sinatra, 2010; Lai, 2011; Schunk & Zimmerman, 1994). It is interesting to note that brain studies have shown that self-assessment and self-understanding use similar neural networks as assessment of others (Legrand & Ruby, 2009), which lends support to the theory of mind concept that we know ourselves by knowing others.

Others have elaborated on the work of Arthur Costa by developing practical means of monitoring metacognitive development in classrooms. For example, the Tahoma School District in Washington has developed a performance checklist to help kids assess their own metacognitive skills (Figure 4.6). The Educational Resource Information Center (U.S. Department of Education, 2004) suggests that teachers should explicitly work on Blakey and Spence's *Strategies for Developing Metacognitive Behaviors* (1990) with the students in their classes (Table 4.1).

FIGURE 4.6
Performance Checklist: Metacognition

Name _____   Date _____

Performance Checklist

Attribute: *Metacognition*
Puts into words his/her own thinking; self-reflects

Observable Indicators	Often	Sometimes	Not Yet
What it looks like:			
Thoughtful expressions			
Writes personal reflections using phrases like "I think," "I feel," "I believe," "I like"			
Keeps a journal or learning log			
Demonstrates perseverance			
What it sounds like:			
Describes own thinking:			
• Selects best idea			
• Gives reasons for responses			
• Articulates a plan of action			
• Plans, monitors, and adjusts			
Self-generates questions about learning			
Self-evaluates, keeping a criterion in mind			
Can identify what information, materials, or skills are needed to perform a task			
Can label behaviors and skills that are being used			
Notes:			

Adapted from a checklist by Arthur L. Costa (2000).

TABLE 4.1
Strategies for Developing Metacognitive Behaviors

1. *Identifying "what you know" and "what you don't know."* At the beginning of a research activity students need to make conscious decisions about their knowledge. Initially students write "What I already know about..." and "What I want to learn about...." As students research the topic, they will verify, clarify and expand, or replace with more accurate information, each of their initial statements.

2. *Talking about thinking.* Talking about thinking is important because students need a thinking vocabulary. During planning and problem-solving situations, teachers should think aloud so that students can follow demonstrated thinking processes. Modeling and discussion develop the vocabulary students need for thinking and talking about their own thinking. Labeling thinking processes when students use them is also important for student recognition of thinking skills. Paired problem-solving is another useful strategy. One student talks through a problem, describing his thinking processes. His partner listens and asks questions to help clarify thinking. Similarly, in reciprocal teaching (Palinscar, Ogle, Jones, Carr, & Ransom, 1986), small groups of students take turns playing teacher, asking questions, and clarifying and summarizing the material being studied.

3. *Keeping a thinking journal.* Another means of developing metacognition is through the use of a journal or learning log. This is a diary in which students reflect upon their thinking, make note of their awareness of ambiguities and inconsistencies, and comment on how they have dealt with difficulties. This journal is a diary of process.

4. *Planning and self-regulation.* Students must assume increasing responsibility for planning and regulating their learning. It is difficult for learners to become self-directed when learning is planned and monitored by someone else. Students can be taught to make plans for learning activities including estimating time requirements, organizing materials, and scheduling procedures necessary to complete an activity. The resource center's flexibility and access to a variety of materials allows the student to do just this. Criteria for evaluation must be developed with students so they learn to think and ask questions of themselves as they proceed through a learning activity.

5. *Debriefing the thinking process.* Closure activities focus student discussion on thinking processes to develop awareness of strategies that can be applied to other learning situations. A three step method is useful. First, the teacher guides students to review the activity, gathering data on thinking processes and feelings. Then, the group classifies related ideas, identifying thinking strategies used. Finally, they evaluate their success, discarding inappropriate strategies, identifying those valuable for future use, and seeking promising alternative approaches.

6. *Self-evaluation.* Guided self-evaluation experiences can be introduced through individual conferences and checklists focusing on thinking processes. Gradually self-evaluation will be applied more independently. As students recognize that learning activities in different disciplines are similar, they will begin to transfer learning strategies to new situations.

Source: Blakey and Spence (1990). Used with permission from the Teacher Librarian: The Journal for School Library Professionals.

The most logical way to measure metacognitive awareness is through the Metacognitive Awareness Inventory (Scrhaw & Dennison, 1994), or in the case of children, through the Junior Metacognitive Awareness Inventory (Sperling, Howard, Miller, & Murphy, 2002), which comprises 18 items on a five-point Likert scale. It's not surprising that students' scores on the Junior Metacognitive Awareness Inventory correlate with general cognitive gains; that is, the higher they score on the Inventory, the better they generally do at school. The 18 items are as follows:

1. I am a good judge of how well I understand something.
2. I can motivate myself to learn when I need to.
3. I try to use strategies that have worked in the past.
4. I know what the teacher expects me to learn.
5. I learn best when I already know something about the topic.
6. I draw pictures or diagrams to help me understand while learning.
7. I ask myself if I learned as much as I could have once I finish a task.
8. I ask myself if I have considered all options when solving a problem.
9. I think about what I really need to learn before I begin a task.
10. I ask myself questions about how well I am learning while I am learning something new.
11. I focus on the meaning and significance of new information.
12. I learn more when I am interested in the topic.
13. I use my intellectual strengths to compensate for my weaknesses.
14. I use different learning strategies depending on the situation.
15. I ask myself periodically if I am meeting my goals.
16. I find myself using helpful learning strategies automatically.
17. I ask myself if there was an easier way to do things after I finish a task.
18. I set specific goals before I begin a task. (Sperling, Howard, Miller & Murphy, 2002, pp. 58–59)*

Lai's literature review of metacognition (2011) notes that metacognitive abilities can and should be developed in children as young as preschool age. Children as young as three exhibit metacognitive abilities when thinking about problem solving (Whitebread, Bringham, Grau, Pino Pasternak, & Sangster, 2007; Whitebread et al., 2009), and children four or five years of

* Reprinted from Contemporary Educational Psychology, Volume 27, Issue 1, Sperling, R.A., Howard, B.C., Miller, L., Murphy, C. "Measures of Children's Knowledge and Regulation of Cognition," © 2002, with permission from Elsevier.

age can theorize about their own thinking processes (Schraw & Moshman, 1995). The development of metacognitive skills benefits overall learning in all fields.

Best Classroom Practice 16. Employ Zemelman and Colleagues' Best Practice Filter When Selecting Activities
In the third edition of *Best Practice* (2005), Zemelman, Daniels, and Hyde considered successful classroom activities and then sorted them by similar characteristics. They found 13 characteristics common to activities that have the most impact in classrooms. As explained under Best Classroom Practices 1 and 2, learning is dependent on memory and attention, and activities that meet Zemelman and colleagues' best practice criteria are more likely to produce effective learning experiences because they are memorable or grab the attention of the learner. Each criterion can be associated with one or more of the MBE concepts, principles, tenets, and instructional guidelines, as seen in Figure 4.7 and Table 4.2. Each of the best practice characteristics is described briefly below, and its relation to either to either memory or attention is highlighted.

FIGURE 4.7
Zemelman and Colleagues' Best Practice Activities and Associated MBE Principles, Tenets, and Instructional Guidelines

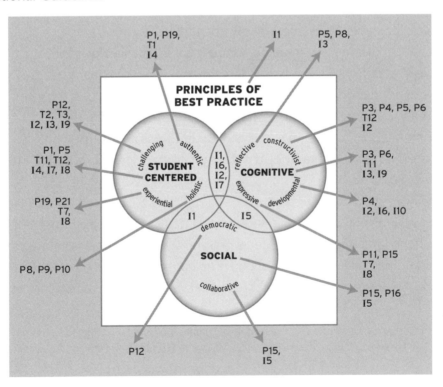

TABLE 4.2
MBE Intersections With Zemelman and Colleagues' Best Practice

		STUDENT-CENTERED	challenging	authentic	active	holistic	COGNITIVE	constructivist	reflective	expressive	developmental	SOCIAL	democratic	collaborative
Principles	Principle 1: Each brain is unique and uniquely organized.			X										
	Principle 2: All brains are not equally good at everything.		X											
	Principle 3: The brain is a complex, dynamic system and is changed daily by experiences.				X									
	Principle 4: Learning is a constructivist process, and the ability to learn goes through developmental stages as an individual matures.							X						
	Principle 5: The search for meaning is innate in human nature.								X					
	Principle 6: Brains have a high degree of plasticity and develop throughout the lifespan.										X			
	Principle 7: Neuroeducation principles apply to all ages.										X			
	Principle 8: Learning is based in part on the brain's ability to self-correct (learn from experience through analysis of data and self-reflection).							X						
	Principle 9: The search for meaning occurs through pattern recognition (i.e., the brain's continual comparison between what it senses and what it already knows).							X						
	Principle 10: Brains seek novelty.							X						
	Principle 11: Emotions are critical to detecting patterns, to decision-making and to learning.							X				X		
	Principle 12: Learning is enhanced by challenge and inhibited by threat.													X
	Principle 13: Human learning involves both focused attention and peripheral perception (various attentional networks)					X								

		STUDENT-CENTERED	challenging	authentic	active	holistic	COGNITIVE	constructivist	reflective	expressive	developmental	SOCIAL	democratic	collaborative
	Principle 14: The brain conceptually processes parts and wholes simultaneously.					X								
	Principle 15: The brain depends on interactions from other people to make sense of social situations.											X		
	Principle 16: Feedback is important to learning.											X		
	Principle 17: Learning relies on memory and attention.								X					
	Principle 18: Different memory systems (short term, working, long term, emotional, spatial, rote) receive and process information in different ways, and can be retrieved through different neural pathways.					X								
	Principle 19: The brain remembers best when facts and skills are embedded in natural (authentic) contexts.	X		X	X									
	Principle 20: Learning involves conscious and unconscious processes.							X						
	Principle 21: Learning engages the entire physiology (the body influences the brain and the brain controls the body).					X				X				
Tenets														
	Tenet 1: Motivation	X					X					X		
	Tenet 2: Stress		X											
	Tenet 3: Anxiety		X											
	Tenet 4: Depression		X											
	Tenet 5: Voices											X		
	Tenet 6: Faces											X		
	Tenet 7: Movement				X									
	Tenet 8: Humor											X		
	Tenet 9: Nutrition	X												

		STUDENT-CENTERED	challenging	authentic	active	holistic	COGNITIVE	constructivist	reflective	expressive	developmental	SOCIAL	democratic	collaborative
	Tenet 10: Sleep	X												
	Tenet 11: Cognitive preferences	X												
	Tenet 12: Differentiation							X						
Instructional Guidelines	Instructional Guideline 1: Good learning environments are made, not found.	X	X	X	X	X	X	X	X	X	X	X	X	X
	Instructional Guideline 2: Good lessons take into account both sense (logical order) and meaning (personal relevance).							X						
	Instructional Guideline 3: Teaching to different memory systems enhances recall.	X					X							
	Instructional Guideline 4: Well-managed classes take advantage of natural human attention spans.			X								X		
	Instructional Guideline 5: Good classroom activities take advantage of the social nature of learning.						X					X		
	Instructional Guideline 6: Good teachers understand the mind-body connection (sleep, nutrition, exercise).										X			
	Instructional Guideline 7: Good teachers understand how to manage different students (orchestrated immersion).	X					X						X	
	Instructional Guideline 8: Skills are retained better when learned through active processes.				X									
	Instructional Guideline 9: Explicit teaching of metacognitive skills aids higher order thinking across subjects.						X							
	Instructional Guideline 10: Learning can and does take place throughout the lifespan.										X			

Source: Zemelman, Daniel & Hyde, 2005, p. 12, combined with the Principles and Instructional Guidelines in MBE (Tokuhama-Espinosa, 2011).

Student centered: The brain is always paying attention to the world around it, but when activities are focused away from the student it can be difficult for her to identify the most important or salient information and sustain her concentration. On the flip side, it is impossible for students not to pay attention when activities are centered on them. Teacher lecturing is on the opposite end of the spectrum from student-centered work. Some believe student-centered learning works due to the focus of attentional networks and motivational factors (Doyle, 2011).

Active: Classroom activities that are student-centered are also normally active as opposed to passive. Passive activities are boring and easy to forget, while activities that require the learner to move in some way—intellectually or physically—are more memorable. Recent studies document how children's active writing activities help the brain learn more efficiently than passive observation to learn letters, for example (see Kersey & James, 2013). Changing seating, acting out a scene (by reading aloud, for instance), constructing a product of some kind, and discussion are all examples of active activities. When students do more than just "receive" and have to produce something, their learning is more effective. It's also easier to pay attention when the environment is more dynamic. Think of the difference between a speaker who walks among participants versus one who stands at a podium. Activity-dependent neuroplasticity has been studied for the past decade and indicates that memory systems are reliant on movement (Butz, Wörgötter, & Ooyen, 2009; Knaepen, Goekint, Heyman, & Meeusen, 2010; Hariri et al., 2003; Rothman & Mattson, 2013).

Holistic: Activities that are interdisciplinary and bridge learning across domains are easier to remember because they take advantage of connections between different types of learning and therefore different memory circuits. Thematic curricula, in which topics are approached from a variety of subject areas to form interconnected experiences, are an excellent way to incorporate holistic learning. For example, using the theme of "measurement" (history, math, poetry, health), "Egypt" (art, literacy, civics), or "climate" (science, literature, physical education) across the curriculum allows the student to approach conceptual development and deeper learning via a variety of disciplines, which is far more memorable than learning isolated concepts. As Robert Marzano suggests, reviewing information across disciplines can create the repetition necessary to improve memory (2007). One of the reasons interdisciplinarity improves learning is that it creates more space for authenticity (Crowley, Schunn, & Okada, 2001) and on a cognitive level makes the way mental schema are transparent (Derry, Schunn, & Gernsbacher, 2009; DuRussel & Derry, 2005).

Authentic: Authentic learning experiences are those that are "real" for the learner primarily because he can relate the new information to past experiences. As all new learning passes through the filter of what we already know, making explicit connections to our knowledge base aids learning (Schacter, 1996). Thus, authentic activities are those that allow a student to make her own observations, by which she links what she already knows about the world, to her past experience in some other way. For example, instead of teaching the concept of the water cycle in a vacuum, the teacher can cover a cup with plastic wrap (familiar, everyday items) and let her students watch (with their own eyes) how the water evaporates and condenses, then falls back into the cup. Meaningful exchanges are more motivational to the learner and keep learners on task longer, primarily because they stimulate a learner-focused interaction in a social context (Meyers & Nulty, 2009).

Expressive: There are both receptive skills and expressive skills associated with all learning. For example, in language arts, reading and listening are more passive than the expressive skills of writing and talking. Allowing students to share their views, opinions, ideas, and visions creatively through written or visual means provides them with an experience more memorable than passive reception of new information. There are distinct neural pathways used for expressive learning. For example, (active) writing triggers more neural pathways than (passive) reading (Lamb, 1999). Similarly, music perception is more passive and a different neural pathway from music production (Zatorre, Chen, & Penhune, 2007). Expressive learning is connected to heightened attention, important for learning.

Reflective: Just as white space on a busy piece of text permits the eye to really focus on what it needs to see, activities that allow for "empty space" in the learning timetable facilitate a better self-understanding of what is truly known and what is not understood. Journal entries, one-minute essays, and other "time-outs" from the intense bombardment of new information allow students to take stock of what they have and have not assimilated into their own knowledge base (Wood Daudelin, 1997). Asking students to think about their answers or what they appear to understand after a lesson consolidates and bolsters their knowledge (Ghaye, 2010). The act of articulation (in written form or orally) moves reflection beyond superficial learning to deep learning and improves the quality of true understanding. Reflective practice gives the brain time to return to things that are known, ruminate, and sometimes reinforce those pathways, as well as reassess choices by comparing what was thought to occur and what did occur. The neuroscience of decision-making is closely related to reflective practice (Capelo & Dias, 2009; Cohen & Ranganath, 2007; Hare, Camerer, & Rangel, 2009). Decisions offer a hierarchy of thoughts and ideas, and reflective practice helps us learn by ordering our understanding of learned concepts.

Social: By their very nature, activities that involve interaction with others tend to be expressive and serve to anchor memories in a multilayered fashion, allowing for quicker recall. Students learn a great deal from one another and can take advantage of the viewpoints shared in group contexts to construct a broader appreciation of topics. In addition, since students' language is different from teachers' language, social activities reinforce learning concepts because they are explained differently between peers as opposed to between teachers and students. The role of social cognition in learning is an area of great interest in the field of education (Pineda, 2008). Its importance justifies using more activities that motivate interaction between individuals due to heightened attention (Mundy & Newell, 2007).

Collaborative: Class activities that are collaborative, in which members work toward a similar goal, are more memorable than activities without defined goals. Setting clear objectives and working with others to achieve them is one of the most memorable ways of structuring learning, and therefore one of the most effective. Collaborative activities are even more beneficial when learners' progress toward goals is shared with them so that each of them feels he or she is advancing toward the common objective (Kirschner, Paas, & Kirschner, 2009). Shared goals are also more memorable than goals set individually. Working with others (teamwork) generates a different type of satisfaction and therefore enhances student motivation (Saleh, Lazonder, & Jong, 2007). Collaborative activities differ from purely social contact in that they push participants to share a common goal and are related to different neural networks in the brain (see Woolley et al., 2007). Social collaboration in cognitive neuroscience is a new field, but growing quickly as the study of "neural, hormonal, cellular, and genetic mechanisms underlying social behavior" offers hard evidence to support collaborative learning activities in class settings (Cacioppo, Berntson, & Decety, 2010, p. 675; also see Decety & Baston, 2007; De Hann & Grunnar, 2009).

Democratic: Class activities that enforce the idea that each member has not only a right but also a responsibility to contribute are more memorable, and they are also better attention-getters because each of the participants must at some point be the center of attention. A balanced distribution of power is fundamental in creating class climates conducive to learning (Mitchell, Bradshaw, & Leaf, 2010), which can be achieved through balanced discussion (Brookfield & Preskill, 2012). In a classroom setting, this fair allocation of work is the responsibility of the teacher. Whereas an individual can choose to be collaborative on her own, only the teacher can structure experiences that are democratic. Equality is a slippery concept, but humans like to feel that they have the same worth as the next guy. Teachers who manage to make all students feel of equal importance raise the probability of lower-achiever participation (Ackley, Colter, Marsh, & Sisco, 2003). Democratic classrooms tend to be more participatory and active, placing the student at the center of attention.

Cognitive: Entertaining activities are enjoyable, but cognitive activities have a real impact on learning outcomes as they elevate conceptual knowledge about the world from surface to deep thinking (which is, after all, the focus of school learning). While it is presumed that most activities in class settings are cognitive, one of the travesties of some learning institutions is the low level of thinking required by both teacher and learner. Activities that raise cognitive effort from simple comprehension to actual use of information—or, even better, to analysis or even synthesis of concepts—are more significant and therefore more memorable than activities that require only lower-level understanding (Bloom, 1968). Cognitive activities work all levels of thinking, solidifying multiple neural pathways and thus refining memory and facilitating learning.

Developmental: Activities that are developmentally appropriate are better remembered because they respond to the learner's cognitive, emotional and physical ability levels. In other words, to be effective, learning goals must be geared toward the physical and mental achievement levels possible for the learners. We don't ask Johnnie to run before he can walk or walk before his brain has figured out how to manage balance. Developmentally appropriate activities are those that a learner can achieve with a reasonable amount of effort, when his organism is ready for the challenge (Bee & Boyd, 2011; Copple, 2010; Kostelnik, Soderman, & Whiren, 2010). Sending 15-year olds on a scavenger hunt for answers on a certain topic instead of having them sit through an end-of-chapter test is a wonderful idea, but asking five-year-olds to do the same would yield different results. This is why teachers need to vet age-appropriate activities as opposed to generic, broad-range "activity books" that promise to reach all levels. Just as developmental processes impact preparedness for learning, neuroplasticity can also be influenced by the environment (Huttenlocher, 2009). Developmental cognitive neuroscience studies many aspects of learning, including the development of perceptual abilities (being able to see, touch, hear, and sense the world), language, and memory, all of which have a profound effect on school achievement (Fan et al., 2011; Johnson, 2010). Neurobiological changes are also regulated by development (hormones), which influences learning over the lifespan (Mustard, 2010).

Constructivist: As noted in Chapter 2, constructivist classroom designs are perhaps the most important but least applied activities because not all teachers know their students well enough to gauge levels of intervention for all the students in their classes. Since constructivist activities build off of the learner's own past knowledge of the world, the teacher has to know her well enough to take advantage of her past experiences and assemble new conceptual, factual, and hypothetical knowledge about the topic at hand. Thus, to successfully apply constructivist strategies (as in Hattie's Piagetian programs) (Piaget, 1950), teachers must take the time to delve into their students' past experiences. When you build a house, beautiful walls and fixtures mean nothing if they're structured on a weak foundation. To solidify the construction, as a teacher you have to fill in the gaps; to fill in the gaps, you need to know where they are; and to know where they are, you need to know your students well. Jeanne Ormrod (2000) investigated the concepts of "meaningful learning" and "elaboration" in the context of university instruction and showed that "learning is easier and retention is better when learners can relate new information to things learners already know" (p. 1). "Neuroconstructivism" is activity-dependent structural changes that occur in the brain (Karmiloff-Smith, 2012). In *Human Behavior, Learning, and the Developing Brain* (Coch, Fischer, & Dawson, 2010), Sidney Segalowitz explores the role of neuroscience in contemporary theories of human development, including constructivism. In this chapter he considers "the building blocks of constructivism" in the brain (p. 20) and concludes that they are different level systems (learning takes place at the level of a person, while brain construction takes place at the level of cells) but work in the same way.

Challenging: Humans live by the "Goldilocks principle": No one likes things that are too easy or too hard. When learning objectives are appropriately gauged to the learner's needs—in the Vygotskian sense of being just a little bit harder than what she is already able to achieve on her own and just beyond the zone of proximal development (Daniels, 2010)—then she feels that they are within her grasp and approaches tasks with a "can do" attitude. For example, let's say I someday would like to run a marathon. I won't run the whole 26 miles on the first day, but rather pace myself so that little by little I'll reach my goal. Facing big challenges in smaller pieces helps achieve learning. The development of resiliency toward letdowns is vital for success in school and in life (Henderson & Milstein, 2003) and is built up by meeting challenges little by little. Some argue that the drive to do anything—including learning—rests in the human desire to be autonomous, master areas of expertise, and give purpose to our lives (Pinker, 2009). Challenging activities call attention to themselves and are more memorable as well as give the learner a sense of achievement. Evidence from *The Neuroscience of Learning: Beyond the Hebbian Synapse* (Gallistel & Matzel, 2013) shows that we not only learn through reinforcement experiences, but also when challenges are scaled upward.

These 13 characteristics are good descriptors and can serve as excellent filters for choosing classroom activities. Most of you reading this book can probably think of dozens of activities that fit one or more of these 13 criteria, but it gets harder to think of activities that meet several criteria. How do you choose which activities are best? If you're faced with deciding between a pop quiz and a debate, the choice is clear—the pop quiz doesn't meet any of the 13 criteria, while the debate meets almost every one. However, there are other less obvious choices. For example, which would be better if our objective is to learn a math formula: asking kids to learn a song about the math formula or having them act out a play on the same concepts? Table 4.3 shows how Zemelman and colleagues' 13 characteristics serve as a clear filter.

TABLE 4.3
Singing About Math vs. Acting Out a Play About Formulas

	Sing about math	Act out a play about formulas
Student-centered	X	X
Challenging		X
Authentic		X
Active	X	X
Holistic		
Cognitive		
Constructivist		
Reflective		
Expressive	X	X
Developmental		X
Social	X	X
Democratic		X
Collaborative		X

It's clear that writing and acting out a play about a concept would be much more power-ful an experience than singing a song about the same ideas. We would do well to be cautious, however: As Farrington (2011) reminds us, **simply adding on new methodologies doesn't guarantee learning.** More is not necessarily better; it's the careful selection of activities and methodologies that's important. To be sure that we choose the best classroom activities pos-sible, there are additional filters that we can apply. Robert Marzano, Debra Pickering and Ellen Pollock's nine instructional strategies (2001), seven of which form the basis of the next Best Classroom Practices, can be employed to help kids develop the basic habits of good thinkers.

Best Classroom Practice 17. Develop Students' Ability to Identify Similarities and Differences
Marzano and colleagues suggest that "presenting students with explicit guidance in identifying similarities and differences enhances students' understanding of and ability to use knowledge" (Marzano, Pickering, & Pollock, 2001, p. 15). One of the first intellectual habits we try to develop in our schools (and one that we prize all the way through doctoral work) is the ability to iden-tify similarities and differences. In the earliest years we focus on the physical: What is similar between a pineapple and an apple? What is different? How are pine and oak trees similar? How are they different? Is there evidence that the causes of the American Revolution and the causes of the French Revolution were similar or different? Later, as students progress and develop, we ask them to identify similarities and differences between and among intangible concepts like freedom, justice, and citizenship. How were the values of social responsibility similar and differ-ent between Anne Frank and Adolf Hitler, as evidenced by their actions? How are Shakespeare's writings similar to and different from those of Cervantes? In what ways can we say religions are the same, and in what ways can we say they are different? Do all humans need culture, or is it inevitable? Labeling and categorizing use distinct neural correlates from other aspects of learning (Martin, Wiggs, Ungerielder, & Haxby, 1996) and need to be reinforced independently.

There is evidence in MBE science (principles 9 and 10) that the brain looks for both patterns and novelty: The brain learns by comparing past experiences with similarities (pat-terns) and differences (novelty) in new information. It is most likely that the brain's "need" to look for patterns as well as identify novel aspects comes from survival mechanisms for deal-ing with situations in which novelty often meant danger. There is evidence that novelty also helps reinforce new neural pathways in the brain (see Otmakhova, Duzel, Deutch & Lisman, 2013). Teachers need to take advantage of this basic brain instinct to help students learn better. Ongoing classroom activities that encourage the refinement of this mental habit help students automatically consider similarities and differences in all situations, elevating the way they are able to think about both physical and intangible concepts. This skill is useful in adapting to the second of Marzano and colleagues' strategies, which is to learn to summarize and take notes.

Best Classroom Practice 18. Develop Students' Summarizing and Note Taking Ability
Summarizing and note taking are skills that force students to make judgments and choices about the information they are receiving: "[S]tudents must delete some information, substitute some information, and keep some information" (Marzano, Pickering, & Pollock, 2001, p. 30). Different levels of thinking require different skills, and the ability to synthesize and summarize requires far more neural circuits than simple memorization. When we ask students to paraphrase what others have said, we are exercising their summary skills. Note taking, which requires higher-order thinking than simple copying, brings this to yet another level. Copying notes from the board does little more than improve penmanship and perhaps give space for superficial reflection; deep reflection requires deep understanding. A great challenge in many classrooms is that teachers presume students have learned note taking skills at some other earlier stage of their education, and rarely do teachers take the time to explicitly teach these skills. However, **note taking needs constant refinement.** It can be modeled, done simplistically, and then developed to a sophisticated level over the education of a student.

Learning to express oneself in written form requires a much more complex set of skills than repetition in oral form. Summarizing and note taking require reviewing all forms of the same information and one's mental thesaurus to find analogical relations between past and present information. Note taking thus reinforces memory networks and improves recall of information. Summarizing information requires the simultaneous retrieval of information in various memory pathways (Otten, Henson, & Rugg, 2001), self-reflection (Johnson et al., 2002), different levels of consciousness (Raichle, 1998), as well as subjective choice (Kable & Glimcher, 2007). **Brain scans of people writing confirm that reexpressing and synthesizing demand a great amount of brain "real estate" and integrate many areas simultaneously** (motor intention and imagery; lexical access and word identification; semantic and episodic memory retrieval; phonology; orthography; grammar, etc.) (Dehaene, 2009).

Best Classroom Practice 19. Reinforce Effort and Provide Recognition
Though it sounds intuitive, it is good to remind ourselves that "reinforcing effort can help teach students one of the most valuable lessons they can learn—the harder you try, the more

successful you are" (Marzano, Pickering, & Pollock, 2001, p. 59). The interesting thing about reinforcement is that while the psychological dimensions of motivation are well understood by teachers, few teachers are aware of the neuropsychological underpinnings that also support reinforcement and effort recognition. Encouragement provides a "feel good" aspect to learning, which is the psychological interpretation of a neurological fact. "Feeling good" in the brain is due to a combination of neurotransmitters that give a sense of pleasure (see Houck, Davis, & Beiser, 1995 for a more detailed explanation of this concept). We know that humans and other mammals will do almost anything to feel good. Rats will even self-administer cocaine until they die (as will some human addicts). When a teacher offers sincere praise to a student and recognizes her efforts, he initiates a virtuous circle. The student feels good and wants to continue this feeling; therefore, she makes more effort and spends more time on task, and as a result she does better and better. This motivational cycle is known as the *dopaminergic loop* in neuroscience (see Morita, Morishima, Sakai, & Kawaguchi, 2013). Thus, the mental connection a student forms between effort and achievement is key to her continued success: "It was hard, but the time invested paid off because I learned more and got a good grade as a result." Teachers who reinforce student effort and attempts at learning (independent of the student's success) aid the learning process.

Best Classroom Practice 20. Provide Purposeful Homework and Practice
Retrieval of information from memory systems in the brain depends on the strengths of neural networks (for initial studies in this area related to retrieval time compared with number of exposures, see Dosher, 1984, and Ratcliff, 1978). Synapses between groups and neurons in the brain reinforce the myelin sheath, which determines the speed with which information can be retrieved (Eichenbaum & Cohen, 2001). Homework, which provides students with the opportunity to extend their learning outside the classroom and which is commented upon (via feedback mechanisms) offers the repetition needed to strengthen neural networks, making recall and thereby learning possible.

However, only when homework is meaningful will it serve a purpose and inspire students to complete it. Homework is controversial, but the bottom line is that **"good" homework helps and "busywork" disguised as homework does not work** (Hattie, 2009; Marzano & Pickering, 2007). The key for teachers is to use homework to complement instructional practice. As we will see when we discuss the flipped classroom, there are great benefits to having students learn definitions, concepts, and other material requiring simple memorization at home and using class time to focus on the individual needs of students (Lim & Morris, 2009). It has been shown that when homework is supervised by either teachers (Huang & Cho, 2009) or family members (Wingard & Forsberg, 2009), and when its purpose and connection to school learning are clear to students (VanVoorhis, 2011), it plays a key role in improving learning outcomes. Teachers should explain the purpose of homework, give feedback and use its content in class activities (Marzano & Pickering, 2007).

Best Classroom Practice 21. Prepare Students to Set Personal Objectives and Give Themselves Feedback

As we saw earlier, clear goal setting is a fundamental aspect of learning. It has been known for decades that productivity and satisfaction in organizational settings, schools as well as businesses, is based on feedback from others as well as clear goal setting between parties (Kim & Hammer, 1976). The development of these skills in classroom contexts is the first step in habituating students to this action, although the home influence is also important. Initially it's the teacher's responsibility to set clear goals and provide feedback as the student progresses toward them, but the real role of the teacher is to eventually ensure that the student learns to execute these skills on her own (Zimmerman & Schunk, 2013). Part of being an autonomous learner is knowing how to determine your own targets, set a path toward achieving those goals, and find ways to self-assess. Autonomous learners don't wait for others to judge their actions or the success of their endeavors. The ability to give yourself a mental pep talk means you understand what it means to set goals and generate feedback to reach your own objectives (Mynard & Navarro, 2010).

Assessment of one's learning progress can and should be developed on various levels: peer-to-peer, learner-to-advisor, and internal dialogue, according to Mynard and Navarro (2010). Ligorio (2010), who agrees with this idea, has analyzed how teachers can foster an internal as well as communal identity in their students that motivates learning. Thus, after successfully modeling how to determine learning objectives, teachers need to guide their students through the development of ways to construct internal dialogue so that they continually self-improve. Students who become habituated to this objective-setting cycle will become strong, lifelong learners.

Best Classroom Practice 22. Teach Students to Generate and Test Hypotheses

Students should learn to assess information and come up with hypotheses about how the world works. Students should be pushed to make predictions and generate hypotheses that they can explain to others (Marzano, Pickering, & Pollock, 2001). The daily fare of learners is to test thesis proposals and modify hypothesis, improve upon theories, and try again. The only way to learn is to recognize mistakes and methodologically seek new possible answers. The National Science Foundation suggests a **basic "discovery cycle" or "cycle of innovation"** in the K–12 curriculum that can be applied to all thinking (see Figure 4.8).

FIGURE 4.8
Cycle of Innovation

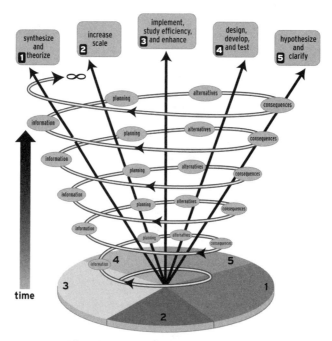

National Science Foundation. Retrieved from http://www.nsf.gov/pubs/2011/nsf11546/nsf11546.htm

From the developmental perspective, small children start by understanding "if-then" scenarios (e.g., "If I leave an ice cube on the table, then it will turn from a solid into a liquid") and hopefully develop a hypothesis testing mentality throughout their schooling. Students need to cultivate inquisitiveness as well as the generation of "if" questions and the tools to test them. Marzano's research shows that organizing students into cooperative groups yields a positive effect on overall learning and fosters improved habituation to hypothesis proposition and testing.

One of the challenges to completing a good learning cycle in classrooms is time. Time limits prevent many teachers from giving children opportunities to develop their own hypotheses and reassess their ideas about the world. However, Marzano, Pickering, and Pollock call on teachers to realize that this is a life skill that must be learned in school and that in the long run, a teacher is better off giving time to this reflective activity than he is rushing to "cover the material" (2001; see also Dana & Yendol-Hoppey, 2008). Dougherty, Thomas, and Lange (2010) argue that **students have increased motivation for activities that allow them to generate their own hypothesis and test them.** As we will see in the next chapter, techniques such as the 5Es create the space needed for hypothesis making and testing.

Best Classroom Practice 23. Use Cues and Triggers

Cues are great ways to trigger past knowledge, while questions instigate reflection. Teachers who use cues, questions, or academic hints in their daily practice are giving students a pattern for the way they should approach self-questioning in the future. Students need to heed the inscription on the temple of the Oracle of Delphi and "know thyself" to self-start their thinking. Part of autonomous learning is discovering what types of things work best for you that might not work for someone else. One of the reason hints are even more successful than direct questioning is that the learner is able to believe she found the answer herself (Bowden, 1997).

However, we need to remember that **not all interventions work for all students**. Each individual's unique past shapes the way he or she takes in information, and therefore some types of cues and questions serve as successful triggers for some people but not for others (see Hammer, 1995, for a good example of how this played out in a physics class). A simple cue that works well as a starting place is "What do you already know about this topic?" As we saw in the discussion on Costa and Kallick's habits of mind in Chapter 3, becoming habituated to these kinds of questions allows students a starting point for self-reflection.

Schacter (2002) talks about the sins of memory and what can serve as a trigger to recall, including cues. Cues can be used to create key steps to remember something, but are fragile and can "fail to trigger recall of appropriate actions when people are preoccupied with attention-consuming matter" (Schacter, 2002, p. 55). Cues can take the form of images, words, signs, digital sequences, or any number of other symbolic combinations. Ironically, unwanted memories can be triggered by cues as easily as those explicitly created by the learner to enhance recall; "seemingly lost information can be recovered by cues or hints that remind us of how we initially encoded the experience" (Schacter, 2002, p. 33). This means that only well thought-out cues should be used.

Summary

In this chapter we applied a backward design structure to order our thinking about what happens in a successful MBE classroom. From there, we considered important filters that can be applied at the planning, evaluating, and instructional design stages. Under planning, we saw how we should choose activities that focus on stimulating memory and attention. We also talked about the importance of planning activities that take advantage of spaced versus massed practice and retrieval, that are transdisciplinary, and take into account the students' contexts. Under evaluation, we were reminded to emphasize formative evaluation practices and to always provide explicit objectives for our students. We also embraced the perception that teaching is a dynamic process and that intelligence is fluid and ever changing. Under instructional design, we were reminded to apply methods, techniques, strategies, actions, and activities than enhance metacognitive skills that meet Zemelman and colleagues' *Best Practice* recommendations, and that follow Marzano and colleagues' instructional strategies for fostering in our students the thinking habits of lifelong learners. (See Table 4.4.)

These first three of the 23 Best Classroom Practices serve as a basic guide for learning.

TABLE 4.4
Summary of Best Classroom Practices 1–22

Planning	Design activities that stimulate: Memory and attention	Design activities that take advantage of: Spaced versus massed practice and retrieval				Design activities that are: Transdisciplinary and in context
		Repetition	Variation	Significance	Depth	Authenticity
Evaluation	Emphasize: Formative evaluation practices	Always provide: Shared, explicit learning objectives				Embrace the perception that: Teaching is dynamic and intelligence is fluid
	Product / Process / Progress	Teacher clarity	Communication immediacy	Feedback	Student-teacher relationship	
Activities	Apply methods, techniques, strategies, actions, and activities that enhance: Metacognitive skills	Apply methods, techniques, strategies, actions, and activities that have characteristics similar to: Zemelman et al.'s Best Practice guidelines				Apply methods, techniques, strategies, actions, and activities that incorporate: Marzano et al.'s instructional strategies

In the next chapter we will move beyond the basic filters described in this chapter to more specific methodologies and actual classroom practices. In the first instance we will consider best classroom practices that have always worked and explain why. This is followed by other classroom best practices that are equally influential but which have yet to be implemented in full force.

Suggested Readings

Memory and Attention

Berkovich-Ohana, A., Glicksohn, J., & Goldstein, A. (2011). Mindfulness-induced changes in gamma band activity: Implications for the default mode network, self-reference and attention. *Clinical Neurophysiology, 123*(4), 700–710.

Bressler, S. L., & Menon, V. (2010). Large-scale brain networks in cognition: Emerging methods and principles. *Trends in Cognitive Neuroscience, 14*(6), 277–290.

Callejas, A., Lupianez, J., & Tuleda, P. (2004). The three attentional networks: On their independence and interactions. *Brain and Cognition, 54*, 225–227.

Colombo, J. (2002). Infant attention grows up: The emergence of a developmental cognitive neuroscience perspective. *Current Directions in Psychological Science, 11*(6), 196–200.

Fan, J., Gu, X., Guise, K. G., Liu, X., Fossella, J., Wang, H., & Posner, M. I. (2009). Testing the behavioral interaction and integration of attentional networks. *Brain and Cognition, 70*(2), 209–220.

Fan, J., McCandliss, B. D., Fossella, J. I., & Posner, M. I. (2005). The activation of attentional networks. *NeuroImage, 26*, 471–479.

Fernandez-Duque, D., & Posner, M. I. (2010). Brain imaging of attentional networks in normal and pathological states. *Journal of Clinical and Experimental Neuropsychology, 23*(1), 74–93. doi: 10.1076/jcen.23.1.74.1217

Fossella, J., Posner, M. I., Fan, J., Swanson, J. M., & Pfaff, D. M. (2002). Attentional phenotypes for the analysis of higher mental function. *Scientific World Journal, 2*, 217–223.

Grossberg, S. (2010). The link between brain learning, attention, and consciousness. In A. Carsetti (Ed.), Causality, meaningful complexity and embodied cognition. *Theory and Decision Library, 48*, 3–45.

Kandel, E. (2007). *In search of memory: The emergence of a new science of mind.* New York, NY: W.W. Norton.

Klingberg, T. (2012). *The learning brain: Memory and brain development in children.* New York, NY: Oxford University Press.

Kok, A., Ridderinkhof, K. R., & Ullsperger, M. (2006). The control of attention and actions: Current research and future developments. *Brain Research, 1105*(1), 1–6.

Kyndt, E., Cascallar, E., & Dochy, F. (2012). Individual differences in working memory capacity and attention, and their relationship with students' approached to learning. *Higher Education,* *64*(3), 285–297.

Lawrence, N., Ross, T. J., Hoffmann, R., Garavan, H., & Stein, E. A. (2003). Multiple neuronal networks mediate sustained attention. *Journal of Cognitive Neuroscience, 15*(7), 1028–1038.

McCabe, D. P., Roediger, H. L., III, McDaniel, M. A., Balota, D. A., & Hambirck, D. Z. (2010). The relationship between working memory capacity and executive functioning: Evidence for a common executive attention construct. *Neuropsychology, 24*(2), 222–243.

Mundy, P., & Newell, L. (2007). Attention, joint attention, and social cognition. *Current Directions in Psychological Science, 16*(5), 269–274.

Pashler, H., Johnsyon, J. C., & Ruthruff, E. (2001). Attention and performance. *Annual Review of Psychology, 52*(1), 629–651.

Posner, M. (Ed.). (2011). *Cognitive neuroscience of attention* (2nd ed.) New York, NY: Guilford Press.

Posner, M. I., Rothbart, M. K., & Rueda, M. R. (2008). Brain mechanisms and learning of high level skills. In A. M. Battro, K. W. Fischer, & P. J. Lena (Eds.), *The educated brain* (pp. 151–165). Cambridge, UK: Cambridge University Press.

Posner, M. I., Sheese, B. E., Oldludas, Y., & Tang, Y. Y. (2006). Analyzing and shaping human attentional networks. *Neural Networks, 19,* 1422–1429. doi:10.1016/j.neunet.2006.08.004

Posner, M., & Rothbart, M. K. (2007). Research on attention networks as a model for the integration of psychological science. *Annual Review of Psychology, 58*(1), 1–23.

Raz, A., & Buhle, J. (2006 May). Typologies of attentional networks. *Nature Reviews Neuroscience, 7,* 367–379. doi:10.1038/nrn190

Rueda, M., Fan, J., McCandliss, B. D., Halparin, J., Gruber, D., Lercari, L. P., et al. (2004). Development of attention during childhood. *Neuropsychologia, 42,* 1029–1040.

Saito, S. (2001). The phonological loop and memory for rhythms: An individual differences approach. *Memory, 9*(4–6), 313–322.

Simons, D. J., & Chabris, C. F. (1999). Gorilla in our midst: Sustained inattentional blindness for dynamic events. *Perception, 28,* 1059–1074.

Squire, L., & Kandel, E. (2008). *Memory: From mind to molecules.* New York: W. H. Freeman.

Wolf, O. T. (2010). Effects of stress on learning and memory. In C. D. Conrad (Ed.), *The Handbooks of stress: Neuropsychological effects on the brain.* Oxford, UK: Wiley-Blackwell. doi: 10.1002/9781118083222.ch27

Spaced vs. Massed Learning

Balota, D. A., & Duchek, J. M., & Logan, J. M. (2007). Is expanded retrieval practice a superior form of spaced retrieval? A critical review of the extant literature (pp. 83–105). In J. S. Nairne, *The foundations of remembering: Essays in honor of Henry L. Roediger, III* (Psychology Press Festschrift Series). New York, NY: Psychology Press.

Bonato, M., Zorzi, M., & Umilta., C. (2012). When time is space: Evidence for a mental time line. *Neuroscience and Behavioural Reviews, 36*(10), 2257–2273. doi.org/10.1016/j.neubiorev.2012.08.007

Cain, L. F., & De Veri, R. (1939). The effect of spaced learning on the curve of retention. *Journal of Experimental Psychology, 25*(2), 209–214. doi: 10.1037/h0054640

Enikö, A., Kramár, E. A., Babayan, A. H., Gavin, C. F., Cox, C. D., Jafari, M., . . . Lynch, G. (2012). Synaptic evidence for the efficacy of spaced learning. *PNAS, 109,* 5121–5126.

Garrett, H. E. (1940). Variability in learning under massed and spaced practice. *Journal of Experimental Psychology, 26*(6), 547–567. doi: 10.1037/h0061166

Grote, M. G. (1995). Distributed versus massed practice in high school physics. *School Science and Mathematics, 95*(2), 97–101.

Izawa, C. (1971). Massed and spaced practice in paired-associated learning: List versus item distribution. *Journal of Experimental Psychology, 89*(1), 10–21. doi: 10.1037/h0031177

Janiszewski, C., Noel, H., & Sawyer, A. G. (2003 June). A meta-analysis of the spacing effect in verbal learning: Implications for research on advertising repetition and consumer memory. *Journal of Consumer Research, 30*(1), 138–149.

Litke, M. D. (2011). *Predicted levels of learning for massed and spaced practice: Do people appreciate the benefits of spacing.* Unpublished master's thesis, Villanova University, Villanova, PA. AAT 1497680

Naqib, F., Farah, C. A., Pack, C. C., & Sossin, W. S. (2011). The rates of protein synthesis and degradation account for the differential response of neurons to spaced and massed training protocols. *PLoS Computational Biology, 7*(12), e1002324. doi:10.1371/journal.pcbi.1002324

Pyc, M. A., & Dunlosky, J. (2010). Toward an understanding of students' allocation of study time: Why do they decide to mass or space their practice? *Memory and Cognition, 38*(4), 431–440. doi:10.3758/MC.38.4.431

Seabrook, R., & Brown, G. D. A. (2005). Distributed and massed practice: From laboratory to classroom. *Applied Cognitive Psychology, 19*(1), 107–122. doi: 10.1002/acp.1066

Tsao, J. C. (1948). Studies in spaced and massed learning: II. Meaningfulness of material and distribution of practice. *Quarterly Journal of Experimental Psychology, 1*(2), 79–84. doi:10.1080/17470214808416748

Xue, G., Mei, L., Chen, C., Lu, Z.-L., Poldrack, R., & Dong, Q. (2011). Spaced learning enhances subsequent recognition memory by reducing neural repetition suppression. *Journal of Cognitive Neuroscience, 23*(7), 1624–1633. doi:10.1162/jocn.2010.21532

Repetition and Learning

Cook, T. W. (1944, January). Repetition and learning: I. Stimulus and response. *Psychological Review, 51*(1), 25–36. doi: 10.1037/h0058927

Jacoby, L. L. (1978). On interpreting the effects of repetition: Solving a problem versus remembering a solution. *Journal of Verbal Learning and Verbal Behavior, 17,* 649–668.

Monaghan, P., & Rowson, C. (2008). The effect of repetition and similarity on sequence learning. *Memory and Cognition, 36*(8), 1509–1514. doi: 10.3758/MC.36.8.1509

Pavio, A. (1976). Coding distinctions and repetition effects in memory. In G. H. Bower (Ed.), *Psychology of learning and motivation* (pp. 179–212). Academic Press.

Trow, W. C. (1928, January). Recall vs. repetition in the learning of rote and meaningful material. *American Journal of Psychology, 40*(1), 112–116.

Wogan, M., & Waters, R. H. (2959). The role of repetition in learning. *American Journal of Psychology, 72,* 612–613.

Xue, G., Mei, L., Chen, C., Lu, Z.-L., Poldrack, R., & Dong, Q. (2011). Spaced learning enhances subsequent recognition memory by reducing neural repetition suppression. *Journal of Cognitive Neuroscience, 23*(7), 1624–1633. doi:10.1162/jocn.2010.21532

Authentic Learning

Ambrose, S. A., Bridges, M. W., DiPietro, M., Lovett, M. C., & Norman, M. K. (2010). *How learning works: Seven research-based principles for smart teaching.* San Francisco, CA: Jossey-Bass.

Fink, L. D. (2013). *Creating significant learning experiences: An integrated approach to designing college courses.* San Francisco, CA: Jossey-Bass.

Fink, L. D., & Knight Fink, A. (Eds.). (2009). *Designing courses for significant learning: Voices of learning experience: New Directions for teaching.* San Francisco, CA: Jossey-Bass.

Meltzoff, A. N., Kuhl, P. K., Movellan, J., & Sejnowski, T. J. (2009, July 17). Foundations for a new science of learning. *Science, 325*(5938), 284–288. doi: 10.1126/science.1175626

Meyer, N. M., & Nulty, D. D. (2009). How to use (five) curriculum design principles to align authentic learning environments, assessment, students' approaches to thinking and learning outcomes. *Assessment and Evaluation in Higher Education, 34*(5), 565–577. doi: 10.1080/02602930802226502

Motschnig, R., & Cornelius-White, J. H. D. (2012). Experiential/significant learning. *Encyclopedia of the Sciences of Learning,* 1219–1223.

Evaluation

Brown, K. G., & Gerhardt, M. W. (2006). Formative evaluation: An integrative practice model and case study. *Personnel Psychology, 55*(4), 951–983.

Butler, S. M., & McMunn, N. D. (2006). *A teacher's guide to classroom assessment: Understanding and using assessment to improve student learning.* San Francisco, CA: Jossey-Bass.

Fisher, D., & Frey, N. (2007). *Checking for understanding: Formative assessment techniques for your classroom.* Alexandria, VA: ASCD.

Fuchs, L. S., & Fuchs, D. (1993). Formative evaluation of academic progress: How much growth can we expect? *School Psychology Review, 22*(1), 1–30.

Nicol, D. J., & Macdarlane-Dick, D. (2006). Formative assessment and self-regulation learning: A model and seven principles of good feedback practice. *Studies in Higher Education, 31*(2), 199–218. doi: 10.1080/03075070600572090

Perrenoud, P. (1998). From formative evaluation to a controlled regulation of learning processes: Towards a wider conceptual field. *Assessment in Education: Principles, Policy and Practice, 5*(1), 85–102. doi: 10.1080/0969595980050105

Popham, W. J. (2013). *Classroom assessment: What teachers need to know* (7th ed.). Boston, MA: Pearson.

Sadler, R. D. (1998). Formative assessment: Revisiting the territory. *Assessment in Education: Principle, Policy and Practice, 5*(1), 77–84. doi: 10.1080/0969595980050104

Smith, R. A. (2001, Winter). Formative evaluation and the scholarship of teaching and learning. *New Directions for Teaching and Learning, 88*, 51–62.

Torrance, H., & Pryor, J. (1998). Investigating formative assessment: Teaching, learning and assessment in the classroom. Florence, KY: Taylor & Francis.

Wiliam, D. (2011). *Embedded, formative assessment*. Bloomington, IN: Solution Tree.

Yorke, M. (2003). Formative assessment in higher education: Moves towards theory and the enhancement of pedagogic practice. *Higher Education, 45*(4), 477–501.

Mastery Learning

Arlin, M. (1984). Time, equality, and mastery learning. *Review of Educational Research, 54*(1), 65–86. doi: 10.3102/00346543054001065

Block, J. H. (1972). Student learning and the setting of mastery performance standards. *Educational Horizons, 50*(4), 183–191.

Bloom, B. S. (1968). Learning for mastery. *Evaluation Comment, 1*(2), 1–12.

Bloom, B. S. (1971). Mastery learning. In J. H. Block (Ed.), *Mastery learning: Theory and practice* (pp. 47–63). New York, NY: Holt, Rinehart & Winston.

Bloom, B. S. (1974). An introduction to mastery learning theory. In J. H. Block (Ed.), *Schools, society and mastery learning* (pp. 3–14). New York, NY: Holt, Rinehart & Winston.

Daniel, L. M., Stupisky, R. H., Pekrun, R., Haynes, T. L., Perry, R. P., & Newall, N. E. (2009). A longitudinal analysis of achievement goals: From affective antecedents to emotional effects and achievement outcomes. *Journal of Educational Psychology, 101*(4), 948–963.

Guskey, T. R. (1996). *Implementing mastery learning* (2nd ed.). Independence, KY: Cengage Learning.

Guskey, T. R., & Jung, L. A. (2011). Response-to-intervention and mastery learning: Tracing roots and seeking common ground. *Journal of Educational Strategies, Issues and Ideas, 84*(6), 249–255. doi: 10.1080/00098655.2011.590551

Kulik, C.-L. C., Kulik, J. A., & Bangert-Drowns, R. L. (1990). Effectiveness of mastery learning programs: A meta-analysis. *Review of Educational Research, 60*(2), 265–299.

Lai, E. R. (2011). *Metacognition: A literature review* (Research report prepared for Pearson). New York, NY: Pearson.

Levine, D. U. (1985). *Improving student achievement through mastery learning programs.* San Francisco, CA: Jossey-Bass.

Morgan, K. (2011). *Mastery learning in the science classroom.* Arlington, VA: National Science Teachers Association Press.

Patrick, H., Kaplan, A., & Ryan, A. M. (2011). Positive classroom motivational environments: Convergence between mastery goal structure and classroom social climate. *Journal of Educational Psychology, 103*(2), 367–382.

Slavin, R. E. (1987). Mastery learning reconsidered. *Review of Educational Research, 57*(2), 175–213.

Student-Teacher Relationships

Blacher, J., Baker, B. L., & Eisenhower, A. S. (2009, September). Student–teacher relationship stability across early school years for children with intellectual disability or typical development. *American Journal on Intellectual and Developmental Disabilities, 114*(5), 322–339. doi: http://dx.doi.org/10.1352/1944-7558-114.5.322

Carroll, R. G. (2012). It's all about the teacher-student relationship. *Advances in Physiology Education, 36*(4), 233. doi: 10.1152/advan.00127.2012

Crosnoe, R., Johnson, M. K., & Elder, G. H. (2004). Intergenerational bonding in school: The behavioral and contextual correlates of student-teacher relationship. *Sociology of Education, 77*(1), 60–81. doi: 10.1177/003804070407700103

Eisenhower, A. S., Baker, B. L., & Blacher, J. (2007). Early student-teacher relationships of children with and without intellectual disability: Contributions of behavioral, social, and self-regulatory competence. *Journal of School Psychology, 45*(4), 363–383.

Hamre, B. K., & Pianta, R. C. (2006). Student-teacher relationships. In G. G. Bear & K. M. Minke (Eds.), (2006). *Children's needs: III. Development, prevention, and intervention,* (pp. 59–71). Washington, DC: National Association of School Psychologists.

Myers, S. S., & Pianta, R. C. (2008). Developmental commentary: Individual and contextual influences on student teacher relationships and children's early problem behaviors. *Journal of Clinical Child and Adolescent Psychology, 37*(3), 600–608.

Roorda, D. L., Koomen, H. M. Y., Split, J. L., & Oort, F. J. (2011). The influence of affective teacher-student relationships on students' school engagement and achievement: A meta-analysis. *Review of Educational Research, 81*(4), 493–529. doi: 10.3102/0034654311421793

Rudasill, K. M., Reio, T. G., Stipanovic, N., & Taylor, J. E. (2010). A longitudinal study of student teacher relationship quality, difficult temperament, and risky behavior from childhood to early adolescence. *Journal of School Psychology, 48*(5), 389–412. doi: 10.1016/j.jsp.2010.05.001

CHAPTER 5

What Has Always Worked and Why
What Traditionally Happens in Great Classrooms

This chapter considers specific teaching methods and activities that can be conducted in almost any classroom, independent of subject area. Some are aimed at slightly older students (middle school and above), while others can reach across all age groups. This review is meant to identify, based on MBE criteria, methods that have always worked in classrooms and why they work. We begin with a look at the Socratic method. Next, we consider cooperative and reciprocal methods of teaching as well as the use of tools such as concept mapping. We close with a consideration of the importance of analogies in building mental schemas about intangible concepts, such as those found in science and math.

Ancient Methods in a Modern World

Best Classroom Practice 24. Use the Socratic Method
A teacher's role is to participate in others' quests for knowledge. **The oldest known teaching method still used today is the Socratic method** (Reich, 2003). This method was first documented around 450 B.C., although it has probably been used throughout human history. One of Socrates's ideas was that the survival of the species is dependent on learning about oneself as well as on learning how to learn.

Despite being the most commonly applied method of teaching, the Socratic method is not "teaching" in the conventional sense of the word (Reich, 2003). **The Socratic method**

has survived the test of time mainly because it is student centered, based on the art of questioning, and fundamentally constructivist in design. This means it takes advantage of several MBE principles and is also supported by Hattie's research (2009, 2012). The Socratic method comprises class discussions, questioning, and debate, all of which are noted to yield high results and have a strong positive impact in classroom settings.

Socrates believed that education is a lifelong mission and a means of self-improvement, and the goal of employing the Socratic method is to reach a very deep level of thinking rather than superficial memorization. **Socratic dialogue is meant to help students discover their own "ignorance" or gaps in knowing through constant questioning.** Questions to which the teacher doesn't already know the answer are even more powerful in "creating a classroom culture that feels intellectually engaging" (Ritchhart, Church, & Morrison, 2011, p.31). The best questions aren't knowledge based but rather constructive, based on the learner's understanding. The teacher's role is that of a "midwife" who helps the student give birth to his own ideas—ideas that have always been inside him but that he himself might not yet realize. The teacher doesn't aim to answer questions, but rather to respond to each question with another question (Molenaar, van Boxtel, & Sleegers, 2011). The objective of the Socratic method is to provide space for reflection about what one knows and what one does not yet know, after which the teacher helps the student fill in his own gaps. The purpose of this reflection, as Maxwell states, is "to induce a person to realize a particular fact or to cause a person to rethink an idea" (2009, para. 1).

To manage Socratic dialogue, a teacher must thoroughly dominate the topic. It could be that many teachers shy away from the Socratic method because it takes an incredibly high degree of understanding the subject matter. To ensure deep intellectual reflection, Socratic teachers must become skilled in stimulating dynamic conversation that captures student attention. The ability to form questions rather than offer answers is the hallmark of a true Socratic teacher.

Socratic Class Preparation. To use the Socratic method well, there are several ways to prepare for class. According to award-winning Stanford professor Rob Reich, students need to approach the Socratic class with clear conversational guidelines. Students should know one another's names and understand that their active participation is key to success; monosyllabic answers need to be milked for more profound thinking. While the Socratic method allows many ways to determine terms, concepts, and ideas based on the objectives of the class, one common strategy is to use a controversial topic. For example, moral dilemmas (certainly kill five people or possibly kill 500 by choosing to drive one direction or another; break one CD on purpose or break 100 by accident), controversial questions (Should uniforms be obligatory in school? Should drugs be legal?), or tough reflection (Should educational policy be focused on quantity—getting everyone into school – or on high-quality education for a few?) are all great ways to start. A guiding recommendation is to tell students to make sure their comments are based on concepts or principles and not first-person narratives to ensure that they are thinking globally and not merely solving academic problems.

A professor who isn't comfortable with silence won't be successful with the Socratic method. Once a question is asked, the brain need time to think and find the right reaction. This harkens back to the importance of reflection to improve the level of thinking. On average, teachers wait one to two seconds before they launch into rhetorical replies; Reich (2003) recommends at least 10 seconds. Teachers have to learn to be more at ease with cognitive dissonance, which Ian Jukes likes to call "planned discomfort" (e.g., Jukes, McCain, & Crockett, 2012). This pause gives students time to look into their own heads and find reflections of a higher level than those that can be generated in shorter reaction times. Reich recommends avoiding cold calling of students and suggests preparing students ahead of time with framed questions and giving them time to reflect. Since most people are more comfortable addressing a single peer than they are a large group, one strategy is to circulate the question among pairs before bringing the conversation to the larger group.

Socrates left no writings whatsoever, so we can presume he didn't track his dialogues with notes. While taking notes is not part of the original Socratic methodology, many teachers find it beneficial to use visuals, such as a note on the chalk-, SMART-, or whiteboard, to help students keep track of their own thinking and the development of the ideas.

Facilitating Dialogue. While many teachers are good at asking a single question, a great Socratic teacher knows how to extend an exchange on a given topic into a true dialogue. Follow-up questions are one of the keys to successful Socratic dialogue development. Reich recommends that teachers stop thinking about teaching in the traditional sense of giving answers and be open to leaving uncertainty at the end of a conversation. This means that a teacher needs to be secure with unsure situations, be confident enough to say "I don't know," and, even better, defer the answering of all questions to her students. Reich suggests that while a teacher should choose questions carefully, she should also be open to new angles or different takes on concepts being discussed. Creative, "wild" ideas should be welcome, but the teacher must also be able to redirect ideas and stay within broad parameters to ensure that each student is slowly but surely advancing toward a better conceptualization of the topic at hand. To develop this art of questioning, the Foundation for Critical Thinking (2011) suggests the following guidelines: Teachers engaged in a Socratic dialogue should:

- Respond to all answers with a further question (that calls upon the respondent to develop his thinking in a fuller and deeper way)
- Seek to understand—wherever possible—the foundations for what is said or believed and follow the implications of those foundations with further questioning
- Treat all assertions as a connecting point to further thoughts
- Treat all thoughts as if they are in need of development
- Recognize that any single thought can exist fully only in a network of connected thoughts; thus, stimulate students—through questions—to pursue those connections
- Recognize that all questions presuppose prior questions and that all thinking presupposes prior thinking; thus, when raising questions, be open to the questions they presuppose

One of the hardest jobs of a teacher managing Socratic dialogue is to know her students well enough that she can pose developmentally and constructively appropriate questions for them. **A key reason the Socratic method works is because questioning, along with the reflection that ensues, drives thinking**.

> The goal of critical thinking is to establish a disciplined "executive" level of thinking to our thinking, a powerful inner voice of reason, to monitor, assess, and re-constitute—in a more rational direction—our thinking, feeling, and action. Socratic discussion cultivates that inner voice by providing a public model for it. (Foundation for Critical Thinking, 2011, para.11)

The Foundation of Thought. The Foundation for Critical Thinking (2011) further suggests that all thoughts reflect an agenda, which means that you can't fully understand any of your own or others' thoughts without first understanding the agenda behind them. And, as we saw in earlier chapters, understanding the other is key to understanding ourselves. Regardless of what a student might express in terms of words, we may not be able to understand the real meaning behind his thinking until we understand his agenda. For example, a student who says, "But abortion is right, isn't it?" may be attempting to sort out his own person belief system, or he may be declaring his allegiance to another classmate's beliefs.

Thoughts are also the reflection of an information base, constructed by past knowledge and experiences. For example, a student may make a comment that sounds racist to others (e.g., "That's how Asians are") but do so in total innocence, as his own personal experience may have limited his understanding or his vocabulary. Our expression of thoughts is also a reflection of the way we construct meaning; because we have limited information with which to create that meaning, inference (a dangerous thing on its own) is highly necessary. To determine how to manage a student's assertions or questions, teachers need to understand whether the student's ideas are based on his experience or based on inference. Thus, when teachers are faced with a declaration about a concept that seems erroneous, an excellent reply is, "What makes you say that?" (Ritchhart et al., 2011, p. 35). This question serves to ground the student's perceptions.

Thoughts rely on assumptions, which need to be clarified to reach deep understanding. Deep thoughts are based on a series of concepts. Unless the concepts are clear to all learners, the likelihood of confusion is high. Asking students to synthesize or rephrase others' ideas allows space to confirm that everyone comprehends the underlying concepts and is on the same page. As the Foundation for Critical Thinking (2011) explains, thoughts rest upon other thoughts like building blocks; if one of the underlying thoughts is misunderstood, then it is almost certain that what a student is trying to convey will be misconstrued. Thoughts also take place within a framework, which may be culture-, gender-, or age-dependent, and this needs to be transparent to the individual interpreting them (Tomasello, 1999).

All thoughts are an answer to a question, independent of whether a question has been asked or not; that is, the question may be implicit or explicit. Many students struggle because they eventually find out that the answers they're looking for don't correspond with the questions they originally posed, forcing them to come up with a new or additional question. The clarity of the question is fundamental in understanding the mindset of others.

The context of thoughts is also important in a Socratic dialogue. Participants must "recognize that all thought has three possible functions: to express a subjective preference, to establish an objective fact (within a well-defined system), or to come up with the best of competing answers (generated by competing systems)" (Foundation for Critical Thinking, 2011, para. 16). If the thought system or context in question is not understood, the precise meaning will be lost or misconstrued. For example, let's take the thought "The Socratic method is the best teaching method possible." If the purpose of the thought is to express a subjective preference, the speaker probably feels the statement to be true in his case and is giving a personal opinion. If the purpose of the thought is to establish a fact, perhaps the speaker believes he has evidence to establish that the Socratic method is the best methodology in the context of the current educational system. And if the purpose of the thought is to come up with the best of competing answers, the speaker may be trying to convey that, compared with certain other methodologies, the Socratic method is better. This means that each participant in a Socratic dialogue has to make certain he is clear about the intentions of the others (a practice that helps him, eventually, to know himself better). While Socrates was unaware of the role of mirror neurons, newer studies by Iacoboni, Molnar-Szakacs, Gallese, Buccino, and Mazziotta (2005) show how the brain grasps the intentions of the others through the mirror neuron system. Refining our understanding of others' thought processes is a sophisticated level of thinking and requires practice.

The Structure of Socratic Dialogue. There is an art to selecting questions. Questions that have a single answer are generally deadening, whereas questions that are open-ended lead to a greater number of possible answers. Excellent teacher guidance and prodding are required to steer everyone in the right direction (Molder & Potter, 2005). Although the conversation focuses on individuals, the teacher's task is to ensure that all students move forward in their own way, but harmoniously, and that no one's thinking stays too far behind that of the others.

A conversation applying the Socratic method could look like this:

Teacher: Let's discuss the relationship between the brain and the mind. Does one dominate over the other? Can one survive without the other? Can anyone argue that one creates the other?

Student 1: They are the same.

Teacher: The mind and the brain are the same? How do you know that?

Student 2: They are not the same! One is physical; the brain is physical.

Teacher: And the mind? Is the mind something physical? And if it isn't physical, how do we know it exists?

Student 3: They depend on each other?

Teacher: What does that mean?

Student 3: They need each other to survive.

Teacher: OK. But how?

Student 1: Like I said, they are the same!

Teacher: In what way are they the same and in what way do they appear to depend on each other for existence? Robert?

Student 4: Well, I never thought about it before.

Teacher: Then let's think about it like this: Can the brain survive without the mind? Can the mind survive without the brain?

Student 5: The mind is in the brain.

Teacher: Explain. What do you mean? The brain gives birth to the mind?

Student 5: I guess.

Teacher: Think about their jobs. What does the mind do? And what does the brain do?

Student 5: The brain thinks.

Teacher: So the mind doesn't think?

Students 1, 2, 5: No!

Student 5: The mind has the thoughts!

Teacher: And the brain does not have thoughts?

Student 5: But the brain's function is to allow the mind to think thoughts. Like the sewer system helps the water flow, but it isn't the water itself.

Teacher: Great analogy. Can anyone think of another analogy for the mind and the brain?

And so on. This pattern of questioning and clarification is fundamental to Socratic dialogue. Richard Paul, and Elders, two of the most prolific writers on critical thinking and the use of Socratic dialogue, recommend questions such as the folowing (see Paul, 2012, and Paul & Elders, 2007, for more detailed examples):[1]

- What do you mean by _____?
- Could you give me an example?
- What is your main point?
- Would this be an example: _____?
- How does _____ relate to _____?
- Could you explain that further?
- Could you put that another way?
- Would you say more about that?
- Is your basic point _____ or _____?
- Why do you say that?
- What do you think is the main issue here?
- Let me see if I understand you; do you mean _____ or _____?
- How does this relate to our discussion (problem, issue)?
- What do you think John meant by his remark?

1 Critical Thinking: What Every Person Needs to Survive in a Rapidly Changing World, *4th Edition, Richard Paul,* © 2012. *Used with permission from the Foundation for Critical Thinking (FCT), www.criticalthinking.org.*

- What did you take John to mean?
- Jane, would you summarize in your own words what Richard has said? . . .
- Robert, is that what you meant? (Paul & Elders, 2007)[1]

Paul and Elders then suggest that when a student begins to make unsubstantiated declarations, he be called into check with questions that probe assumptions:

What are you assuming?
- What is Karen assuming?
- What could we assume instead?
- You seem to be assuming _____. Do I understand you correctly?
- All of your reasoning depends on the idea that _____, correct?
- Why have you based your reasoning on _____ rather than _____? You seem to be assuming _____.
- How would you justify taking this for granted? Is it always the case?
- Why do you think the assumption holds here?
- Why would someone make this assumption? (Paul & Elders, 2007)[1]

These authors then recommend asking the following types of questions when you're faced with a barrage of opinions and no evidence:

What would be an example?
- Are these reasons adequate?
- How do you know?
- Why did you say that?
- Why do you think that is true?
- What led you to that belief?
- Do you have any evidence for that?
- How does that apply to this case?
- What difference does that make?
- What would change your mind?
- What are your reasons for saying that?
- What other information do we need?
- Could you explain your reasons to us?

1 Critical Thinking: What Every Person Needs to Survive in a Rapidly Changing World, *4th Edition, Richard Paul,* © *2012. Used with permission from the Foundation for Critical Thinking (FCT), www.criticalthinking.org.*

- But is that good evidence to believe that?
- Is there reason to doubt that evidence?
- Who is in a position to know if that is so?
- What would you say to someone who said _____?
- Can someone else give evidence to support that response?
- By what reasoning did you come to that conclusion?
- How could we find out whether that is true?

To help students understand that there is value but not absolute "truth" in their logic, Paul and Elders (2007)[1] recommend asking the following:

- You seem to be approaching this issue from a different perspective. Why have you chosen this rather than that perspective?
- How would other groups/types of people respond? Why?
- What would influence them?
- How could you answer the objection that would make?
- What might someone who believed _____ think?
- Can/did anyone see this another way?
- What would someone who disagrees say?
- What is an alternative?
- How are Ken's and Roxanne's ideas alike? Different?

When overseeing a Socratic dialogue about what should happen in a given situation, Paul and Elders (2007) suggest leading the conversation with the following types of questions to help students understand the consequences of the actions they propose:

- What are you implying by that?
- When you say _____, are you implying _____?
- But if that happened, what else would happen as a result? Why? What effect would that have?
- Would that necessarily happen or only probably happen?
- What is an alternative?
- If this and this are the case, then what else must also be true? If we say that this is unethical, how about that?

1 Critical Thinking: What Every Person Needs to Survive in a Rapidly Changing World, *4th Edition, Richard Paul,* © 2012. *Used with permission from the Foundation for Critical Thinking (FCT), www.criticalthinking.org.*

Finally, these authors believe that it is highly beneficial to have students question their own questioning, and he provides the following prompts:

- How can we find out?
- Is this the same issue as _____?
- What does this question assume?
- How would _____ put the issue?
- Would _____ put the question differently?
- Why is this question important?
- How could someone settle this question?
- Can we break this question down at all?
- Is the question clear?
- Do we understand it?
- Is this question easy or hard to answer? Why?
- Does this question ask us to evaluate something?
- Do we all agree that this is the question?
- To answer this question, what questions would we have to answer first? I'm not sure I understand how you are interpreting the main question . . . (Paul & Elders, 2007)[1]

What Does a Socratic Class Look Like? A truly Socratic classroom is dominated by student discussion, not teacher lecture points, and is grounded in real-life examples and experiences. Socratic environments are free of formality and deference to the teacher. They have a clearly democratic air, despite the obvious role the teacher plays in guiding the discussion and forming questions most appropriate for each student. The teacher needs to be aware, however, that intellectual risks can be taken only when students feel they are in a safe environment in which their opinions will be respected and in which they can be honest about their own personal and intellectual reflections. There is no room for hypocritical thinking in Socratic dialogue. Neither should the Socratic method be used to "break down" a student; rather, it should push him toward a level of reflection and deeper thinking that wouldn't be possible without the guidance of the teacher. In a good Socratic dialogue, the individual with the best argument, the most evidence, and the deepest reflection can slowly guide the group toward his way of thinking.

The physical layout of a Socratic class is one that allows all students to see one another

1 Critical Thinking: What Every Person Needs to Survive in a Rapidly Changing World, *4th Edition, Richard Paul,* © *2012. Used with permission from the Foundation for Critical Thinking (FCT), www.criticalthinking.org.*

easily. The likelihood that a student will respond to the comment of another student is far greater when he can see him. **Desks bolted to the floor in stiff rows don't allow the flexibility of space management needed to create a truly Socratic interaction.** Although many imagine Socrates surrounded by a handful of devoted students, it is possible for Socratic dialogue to occur in large groups as well if the teacher arranges the classroom to accommodate everyone and deftly orchestrates the exchange.

Best Classroom Practice 25. Cultivate the Art of Questioning

> *Good teaching is more a giving of right questions than a giving of right answers.*
> —Josef Albers

Humans are naturally curious, which explains how the species has survived. Innovation and self-improvement are actually our trademark characteristics (Loflin, 1978). The question that all three-year-olds master (and that we all should hope to sustain into old age) is "Why?" Questions that begin with *who*, *what*, *when*, and *where* are finite and closed, generally leading to rote answers that don't require deep thinking skills (as in "Where [or when] was the Gettysburg Address delivered?"), but *how* and *why* questions give pause for reflection because they're open to interpretation and require argumentation ("How was the Gettysburg Address delivered?"; "Why was the Gettysburg Address delivered?").

Using questioning as a teaching technique has at least 90 years of documentation (Dillon, 1983; Gould, 1923; Grossier, 1964; Moses, 2006; Role, 2007; Walsh & Sattes, 2004). We know that for most people, it is harder coming up with good questions than providing a good answer. This means that getting students to develop their own questions about topics is a better mental workout than simply posing questions in class (Franke et al., 2009; Olivera, 2010). Questions elevate the level of discussion and require students to review what they already know and become more precise in reflecting on what they do and do not yet know (Rothstein & Santana, 2011), all of which require the contributions of working and long-term memory (Arnold, 2013; Binder & Desai, 2011; Eichenbaum & Fortin, 2009; Hynie & Klenerová, 2010). While Socrates knew the value of questioning thousands of years ago, many school accreditation bodies today fail to recognize the importance of developing habits of mind that lead an individual to reflect upon his world in a deeper way to attain more profound understanding. Standardized tests based on simple *what* questions dominate the educational landscape and attest to the lower-level, rote thinking going on in schools. On the other hand, when someone asks *why*, he is seeking meaning, not simplistic lists of memorized concepts. Why aren't more *why* questions on standardized tests? Because they can't be answered within a multiple-choice format, which is the most cost-effective evaluation instrument available. It seems it costs too much to test deep thinking.

The human brain needs to search for meaning, and schools should find ways to reward students for pursuing higher-level learning through questioning. To prepare students for modern expectations, teachers need to spend more time developing skills that allow students to answer *how* and *why* questions easily. For instance, artful questioning can prompt students to think more deeply about the material being taught and thus help stimulate recall of all types of factual information, from math formulas to prose (Frase & Schwartz, 1975). This is not to say that learning purely factual data is unimportant, but it doesn't require the same level of thinking. **Great teachers instill the habit of asking *why* (or *how*) after every fact is delivered**. This practice constitutes the difference between someone who can use an algebraic formula because he knows the steps and a person who knows *why* it's appropriate to use the formula in certain instances (and not in others) and can explain *how* it's used.

Small-Group Learning

The next activities have been grouped together because they all involve small-group interaction and all work toward a specific goal. Problem-based learning, cooperative learning, reciprocal teaching, and case studies all enjoy support from Hattie's research in both implicit and explicit forms. All four methodologies require students to approach novel situations and compare them with what is already known, which takes advantage of the fact that the search for meaning occurs through recognizing patterns and embedding facts in real situations. They are treated here as separate best practice elements because they serve to meet different learning objectives and should be used with different competencies in mind.

Small group learning activities permit the instructor to design learning activities that make sense, are significant to the learner, and allow space for the learner to self-correct as he learns from experience. This dovetails with the idea that emotions are critical to detecting patterns, to decision-making, and to learning; if students are more comfortable doing cooperative learning activities, they will produce higher-quality work. These activities also work because shared goals create memorable and challenging experiences.

One clear advantage of cooperative methodologies is the ability to address learning anxieties. Math anxiety, for example, is well-established (see Geist, 2010), and it's clear that once fear memories take hold, they can be difficult to extinguish (C.-H. Lin, Yeh, Lu, & Gean, 2003). Student roles in problem-based learning, cooperative learning, reciprocal teaching, and case studies can be adjusted in such a way as to create high levels of personal differentiated learning thus lower levels of student anxiety (Beck & Mostow, 2008), which can lead to improved motivation (see Kerry, 2002).

Best Classroom Practice 26. Incorporate Problem-Based Learning
Problem-based learning, alongside project-based learning and learning-through-design models, is one of the main inquiry-based methods of teaching (Dumont, Istance, & Benavides, 2010). Problem-based learning (PBL) focuses on real situations (problems) that have yet to be resolved (Choi & Lee, 2009). Fink (2003) believes that problem-based learning is a powerful tool and agrees with Hattie (2012) that when students are guided in their thinking, PBL is a superior method of teaching. However, Hattie (2012) has also criticized problem-based learning because students often are not given appropriate tools with which to approach a solution and are not well guided in developing their own thought processes. If foundational information is complete, problem-based learning can elevate thinking and inspire better learning outcomes.

Problem-based learning works because learning takes place in an authentic context that students can relate to, which easily leads to transfer. *Transfer* is in part, the ability to view and use information in a variety of settings. "To know is not enough" (*Non Satis Scire*, AERA conference theme, 2012); application takes knowledge beyond the classroom and places it in real life, turning it into "usable knowledge." When students are faced with a real-life problem as found in PBL structures instead of a problem set in a textbook, they are more motivated to seek the correct answers. For example, which of the following would be a better classroom activity: (a) responding to questions at the back of the text or (b) using anything you've learned in the past week to resolve a real-life problem? **Most students will opt for the real-life problem, as it makes their learning more authentic.** Textbook problems are symbolic, whereas PBL uses words to describe situations that are often more illustrative. For example, a textbook question might simply ask, "3 − 2 = ?" whereas a problem-based learning question might read, "If you have three cupcakes and give two of them away to your friends, how many cupcakes do you have left?"

Students can be challenged with real-life tasks that vary in scope and scale. For example, some teachers may choose to focus on local problems, others may concentrate on national dilemmas, and yet others may have a global perspective. If you're teaching a unit on conservation, for example, PBL themes can range from the use of plastic bottles in school (a local problem) to capturing sharks for their fins (a national issue in Ecuador) to the destruction of the world's rain forests (a global concern).

Torp and Sage (1998) have identified key steps and characteristics of successful PBL structures, including the following:

1. Educators present the problematic situation first, and it serves as the organizing center and context for learning.
2. The problematic situation has common characteristics:
   ◦ It is ill-structured and messy.
   ◦ It often changes with the addition of new information.
   ◦ It is not solved easily or with a specific formula.
   ◦ It does not result in one right answer.

[For example, the teacher can enter the room and happily announce, "We have a problem!" then explain that too much trash is being produced in town and that there is no more space to drop trash pickups. This problem is ill structured (there isn't a lot of data); if more data are added, then the problem can change; there is no pat formula; and there is no such thing as a single right answer.]

3. Students are active problem-solvers and learners; teachers are cognitive and meta-cognitive coaches.
4. Learners share information but personally and individually construct knowledge. Discussion and challenge expose and test thinking.
5. Assessment is an authentic companion to the problem and process.
6. A PBL unit is not necessarily interdisciplinary, but it is always integrative.

PBL research happens individually, but solutions are found at the group level. This means that problem-based learning can be considered a type of cooperative learning, and vice versa (Figure 5.1). While PBL can be undertaken by a single student at the research level, its effectiveness is far greater in group contexts during the solution-finding stage. Benefits of problem-based learning in groups include reduced fatigue (Czabanowske, Moust, Meijer, Schröder-Bäck, & Roebertsen, 2012), as the work is distributed and student motivation is higher.

FIGURE 5.1
Problem-Based Learning and Cooperative Learning

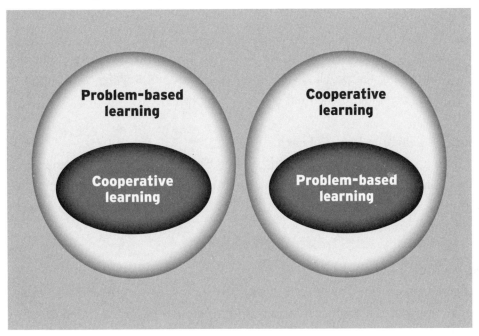

The Illinois Mathematics and Science Academy (2011) thoroughly supports the use of PBL in teaching math and science. Torp and Sage describe some of the major benefits of PBL (1998, pp. 23–25):

Increases Motivation
PBL engages students in learning through the attraction or pull of problem dissonance or tension. They take on more and delve deeper as they make a personal investment in the outcome of their inquiry (p.23).

Makes Learning Relevant to the Real World
PBL offers students an obvious answer to their questions:
"Why do we need to learn this information?"
"What connection does school work have to the real world?" (p.23)

Promotes Higher Order Thinking

Coupled with cognitive coaching strategies, the ill-structured problem scenario calls upon critical and creative thinking by suspending the guessing game of:

"What's the answer that the teacher wants me to find?"

Students gather information significant to the problem and assess its credibility and validity. In bringing the problem to acceptable closure with evidence to support decisions, students meet high benchmarks of thinking (p.24).

Encourages Learning How to Learn

PBL promotes metacognition and self-regulated learning as students generate strategies for defining problems, gathering information, analyzing data, building and testing hypotheses, comparing strategies with those of other students and mentors, and sharing methods and conclusions (p.24).

Requires Authenticity

PBL engages student learning in ways that are similar to real world situations and assesses learning in ways that demonstrate understanding and not mere replication (p. 25).

One might ask, if problem-based learning is such an effective means of teaching, why isn't it used more frequently? (Strobel & van Barneveld, 2009). PBL is well known in medical school circles and has been a chosen methodology in fields such as law and business as well. PBL is also a good strategy to use in teacher education programs. For example, Etherington (2011) found that a "PBL course had a positive impact on . . . pre-service teachers' motivation to teach science ideas within a real world context" (p. 36). Why, then, isn't PBL more widely applied in primary, middle, and high school settings?

One reason may be that **PBL is useful only when examples can be found that are commonly understood by all of the students.** While examples in law (someone is on trial for a specific crime), medicine (someone is ill with *X* disease), and business (there is a specific rival in the marketplace) are easy to find, there is often less information common to all the kids in a school class, making the selection of problems more difficult. It takes time and imagination to find the right problems for some topics, but the benefits are well worth the investment.

Best Classroom Practice 27. Incorporate Cooperative Learning
Cooperative learning occurs when two or more learners work toward a collaborative solution to a challenging situation. Marzano (2009) notes that organizing students into cooperative groups yields a positive effect on overall learning. **Cooperative learning is based on the human need for social exchange, goal setting, and relationship acquisition**.

For example, let's say that in Mr. Thomas's seventh-grade art class, one of the goals is to identify, understand, and appreciate the different genres of art used to express civil unrest in the 1960s. These artistic genres can range from graffiti to poems and songs, from paintings and drawings to movies, from sculptures to plays, or to anything else the students can justify as "art." During the first class on the topic, Mr. Thomas asks his students how they can express their feelings (shouting, crying, laughing hysterically, etc.), then asks them to refine their thinking and consider how they can express their feelings through the arts (songs, poems, drawings, plays, etc.). After listing the different modes on the board, he asks more specifically how people can express their feelings about topics of racial equality and women's rights (protest songs, angry graffiti, catchy bumper stickers, trash sculptures, etc.).

Once these ideas have been shared as a group, Mr. Thomas organizes small groups of two to five students and has them plan a research project. He asks them to get together and decide on one of the two topics (racial equality or women's rights), then plan how they will identify different artistic genres that helped express people's feelings about the topic. The students go and do their initial research to see what was actually done in the 1960s and then come back and join the larger group. They talk about examples they found as well as the challenges they are having in finding information. Mr. Thomas encourages them to share sources and help one another. The students then go out and continue their research in the library, on their computers, or by asking older adults about their firsthand memories. After they spend several days gathering evidence, Mr. Thomas explains how he would like to see their results shared with the group: They can either do a Prezi, a PowerPoint, a short video, a song, a podcast, a poster, or a skit, and everyone has to play a role in the oral presentation to the class. Mr. Thomas's class activity embodies the best elements of cooperative learning because he models how the students should listen to one another, then has them work together toward a common goal and finally celebrate their findings with the entire class.

Cooperative learning relies heavily on both the ability to express ideas and the ability to listen to others. "The pedagogy of listening" from the Reggio Emilio school of thinking

(Giudici, Rinaldi, & Krechevsky, 2001, as cited in Ritchhart et al., 2011, p. 37) begins with the teacher modeling listening by hearing what students have to say and using their dialogue as a jumping-off point for further instruction, then progresses to where the children themselves are able to model this listening. This listening stage not only conveys respect for others, but also allows participants in a conversation to better understand the level of thinking at which their partner is working. This means that cooperative learning activities have added benefits, such as the development of empathy and an appreciation of others' viewpoints. **A group's capacity for working together is far less dependent on the academic prowess of its members than it is on participants' "ability to listen and respond to one another's ideas"** (Barron, 2003, as cited in Ritchhart et al., 2011, p. 37). Cooperative learning also offers an avenue for age-appropriate exchanges of information as a means of explaining terms in alternative forms or vocabulary that might not be so clear when a teacher uses textbook vocabulary. Kid-to-kid conversations often lead to a clarity that eludes teacher-to-kid or text-to-student interaction.

While cooperative learning activities may seem like a way to place the burden of learning on the student, really successful structures require a great deal of forethought as well as in-class guidance on the part of the teacher.

Best Classroom Practice 28. Incorporate Reciprocal Teaching
Peer teaching, or reciprocal teaching, occurs when two or more people teach one another (Rosenshine & Meister, 1994). Reciprocal teaching can be done between a teacher and a student, between two students, or even between two teachers, usually for the mutually beneficial outcome of learning on both sides, but without the goal of a shared outcome (even though the two learners can have two different objectives). The idea is that each takes turns leading and following. For example, when a student and his teacher take turns reading to one another, they are teaching reciprocally: One reads a page of a book and explains it to the other, and then the other learner does the same (Doolittle, Hicks, Trilett, Nichols, & Young, 2006; Slater & Horstman, 2002; Spörer, Brunstein, & Kieschke, 2009; Sticklin, 2011; Williams, 2010). One of the benefits of this methodology is that students' concentration is expanded as they are forced to persist in their learning, since reciprocal teaching generally focuses on a single page of text (or step of a math problem, science concept, art idea, etc.) at a time.

In reciprocal teaching, four specific steps are followed to enhance comprehension: (a) questioning, (b) clarifying, (c) summarizing, and (d) predicting. These steps are conducted interchangeably by student and teacher (Pilonieta & Medina, 2009). For example, suppose that Ms. Ashton is a first-grade teacher modeling best-practice reciprocal teaching with her student, Greg, by keeping up a running commentary that will hopefully help him develop the habit of reflection:

> Do you think the wolf will be able to blow down the house? [prediction]. I think the Big Bad Wolf is very mean and plans to eat the pigs if he can [interpretation and labeling of emotional states of others]. After going to the first pig's straw house and blowing it down and chasing him out, he did the same to the second pig's wood house [review of facts]. Now he's at the brick house where all three pigs are hiding. I wonder what will happen now? [summation of past events and current situation; anticipation of next steps]. Brick is much stronger than straw and wood, so maybe he won't be able to blow it down so easily [facts to support predictions] . . .

Reciprocal teaching demands the articulation of presumptions, doubts, and projections, leading to higher-order thinking. In the event that Greg responds to any of these prompts in an incorrect fashion, Ms. Ashton can correct him, in a friendly conversational tone, reducing the anxiety he might ordinarily have with being corrected in front of his peers. When two students are teaching one another and conflicts arise, the teacher should be present to offer guidance and help them develop argumentative skills without allowing them to fight about the "right" answer.

The success of reciprocal teaching can be explained in part by Vygotsky's belief that oral language and cognitive process development are inextricably linked. Reciprocal teaching relies on the learner's articulation of his own ideas about reading as he "teaches," which enhances his own understanding of the work at hand. According to this "scaffolding and apprenticeship" (Vygotsky, 1978) or "cognitive apprenticeship" model (Collins, Brown, & Newman, 1989), the learner continually revisits his own thinking about the learning process and thus develops better metacognitive skills (X. Lin, 2001). This process also reinforces the learner's belief that teaching is one of the best ways to learn something new. Students involved in reciprocal teaching are forced to think about why they believe the things they do and articulate these beliefs as they teach them to their partner. Schneider (2008, 2010), a leading thinker on the development of metacognitive skills, connects the reciprocal teaching process to the theory of mind concept which is that we know ourselves based on our comparisons with others.

MBE evidence in favor of reciprocal teaching is just beginning to emerge in force. One crucial benefit of reciprocal teaching has to do with thinking about how and what we know, or introspection. Some neuroscientists seek to understand introspection by understanding its physical traits. Fleming and colleagues, for example, have found that the neuroanatomical basis for personal introspection varies widely between individuals according to the level of introspection reached, and that this type of reflection is highly beneficial in developing thinking skills, as reflected in brain changes (Fleming, Weil, Nagy, Dolan, & Rees, 2010). They also note that "introspective ability is correlated with gray matter volume in the anterior prefrontal cortex, a region that shows marked evolutionary development in humans" (Fleming, Dolan, & Frith, 2012, as cited in Ritchhart et al., 2011, p. 37). This means that **"bouncing" ideas around between learners in the reciprocal model actually increases gray matter in the brain** (Tate, 2010). During reciprocal teaching, the learner constantly compares his beliefs or predictions with reality and compares subjective perceptions with facts. This introspection defines the learner's beliefs through a constant barrage of external and internal realities and leads to a clarification of his own mental schema of the world.

The way that small children slowly but surely come to know themselves and others has been a core focus of developmental psychologists for decades. Piaget (1950), unknowingly a champion of MBE core concepts, predicted how children pass through internally focused, egotistical visions of their world as they come to understand concrete operational structures. This mental transformation occurs through a continual evaluation and reevaluation against experiences in the external world, such as those that take place in the learner's mind during reciprocal teaching.

Thus, reciprocal teaching is a fabulous classroom tool, but it's only as good as the ability of the partners to articulate their learning goals. This means that teacher-supervised interactions or scaffolded partnerships, in which one learner has slightly more vocabulary and knowledge on the subject than the other, are best. Reciprocal teaching is also more successful when no external stress is brought into the picture by negative class relations between partners. Stress hormones block natural plasticity and memory building (Krugers, Hoogenraad, & Groc, 2010), so partnerships should be as acceptable as possible to each party. This brings up an added benefit of reciprocal teaching: Since it is generally conducted in pairs, the anxiety that often occurs in larger classroom settings is reduced.

Best Classroom Practice 29. Incorporate Case Studies

Case studies are written summaries or syntheses of real-life situations. They differ from problem-based learning in that they examine problems that have already reached some kind of a conclusion. For example, a problem-based learning activity could focus on how to reduce the pollution level arising from car emissions (something not yet resolved), whereas a case study could investigate how methane-based fuels have been marketed in Brazil with mixed results (something that has already happened). Although case studies are generally cooperative classroom activities, case studies are now being widely conducted in virtual settings to complement face-to-face work (see Choi & Lee, 2009; Lim & Morris, 2009).

Case studies require each participant to take on the viewpoint of a specific actor and think of key points of the case from that perspective only. For example, in the methane fuels case, one person could be Brazil's minister of energy, another could be a farmer who has been forced to plant sugarcane instead of corn, another could be a consumer who has been asked to switch fuel sources, and yet another could be a car manufacturer who has to decide what types of cars to make in the future. The students must then appropriately identify strategies to resolve the case from the viewpoint of the person they represent. The students must consider both the pros and cons and all possible opinions for resolution, and then recommend (present) an analysis of possible solutions.

For case studies to work, students need to be prepared. They must first read the case very carefully and ask themselves, "In general, what is this case about? What do I need to know to be able to analyze it correctly?" They then should reread the entire case carefully, underlining key facts and taking notes from the perspective they have been assigned. By providing an opportunity to take on the guise of someone else, case studies build intellectual empathy and help students think more critically about situations (Sergiovanni, 1994).

For case studies to work, the teacher needs to be fully prepared as well. She must begin with clear objectives for the class (what knowledge, skills, and attitudes are expected of the students?) and choose appropriate cases to achieve her chosen objectives. To be truly successful, she needs to anticipate student interpretations and prepare questioning tactics that will lead to resolution of the problem. As discussion ensues, her role is to keep a clear register of who said what, identifying key conflicts and differences of opinion, and make this record visible to all (e.g., noting points on a whiteboard where each party can see disagreements). To maximize the potential of the case study, she must ensure that the investigation goes further than superficial diagnosis of the problem and seeks solutions. She needs to help keep the conversation and debate on task, weaving different opinions together and summarizing effectively so that closure can be reached.

Thus, to recap, overseeing a case study involves the following steps:

1. Identify (justify) the objectives of the class
2. Choose an appropriate case
3. Learn the details of the case
4. Anticipate basic arguments and potential conflicts
5. Initiate student discussion and exploration
6. Take advantage of student arguments to improve deep analysis of the case
7. Take good notes and track the development of the discussion
8. Continually remind group of the main objectives and offer summary comments

Traditionally, case studies have been successful in medicine, law, and business, but they have only recently been incorporated into K–12 learning. In its simplest form, **a case study can probe a children's storybook**: Think of *Goldilocks and the Three Bears* or *Little Red Riding Hood*. Students in kindergarten can be asked to envision the situation from the perspective of Baby Bear or the Big Bad Wolf in order to begin cultivating intellectual empathy for others. Older children can participate in case studies of decisions that have affected them personally, such as historical choices about battles in war, decisions related to environmental problems, or policy decisions that have changed laws pertaining to women's rights, the black vote, or child labor. **Successful case studies result in better problem solving and collaboration skills** (Capelo & Dias, 2009).

It is important to remember that **not all subjects lend themselves to the case study method**. For example, decisions that have been made about the use of pesticides on certain crops, the location of nuclear power plants, abortion, trade, how to market a product, and whether or not to drop the atomic bomb or expand the space program all lend themselves to case studies, but other important topics such as algebra and black holes do not. Not every method is good for every class or for every age, and while case studies are an excellent method for exploring the social sciences and humanities, they don't always lend themselves to teaching hard sciences. There are some best practice activities, however, that can be applied to all students and all ages, such as analogies, which we turn to next.

Methods for Teaching All Subjects and All Ages

Best Classroom Practice 30. Harness the Power of Analogies

> *To know how to suggest is the art of teaching.*
> —Henri-Frédéric Amiel

Kauchak and Eggan (1998) suggest that **the introduction of new content should always be done within a familiar frame of reference.** When direct links to past knowledge are not available, **the use of analogies is key**: "The closer the fit of the analogy, the more learning is facilitated" (Kauchak & Eggan, 1998, pp. 295–296). Ever since human communication has existed, analogies have been used to help learners connect with unknown concepts by offering "parallel" ideas (Harrison & Croll, 2007). Aesop's fables, Bible teachings, and almost all forms of teaching before the written word were passed down through stories, a special type of analogy (see Hulshof & Verloop, 2002, for concrete examples of analogy use in language teaching).

Analogies work because the brain is consistently comparing what it already knows with new experiences to find patterns and novelty, which places concepts into known mental schemata (McDaniel & Donnelly, 1996; Richland, Zur, & Holyoak, 2007). Being able to piece together knowledge from past experiences is a fundamental aspect of all new learning and vitally important in developing thinking skills. Using teamwork to develop analogies and other metacognitive facilitators enhances the probability of learning (Hooper, Sales, & Rysavy, 1994; T., Johnson, Archibald, & Tenenbaum, 2010). According to researchers, analogies are a particularly powerful way to teach because they take advantage of relational reasoning processes in the frontal cortex (Knowlton, Morrison, Hummel, & Holyoak, 2012; Krawczyk, McClelland, & Donovan, 2011; Krawczyk, McClelland, Donovan, Tillman, & Maguire, 2010) by paralleling something known to the student with new knowledge. Recent neuroscientific studies show that analogies are key to "relational knowledge" understanding and lead to higher-order cognitive ability (Halford, Wilson, & Phillips, 2010). Many modern intelligence tests are based on an individual's ability to create analogies. One of my favorite parts of the old SAT tests was the analogies section, which can also be found on the Miller Analogies Test for graduate school entrance.

An interesting aspect of analogies is the self-verbalization involved. "Captain:ship:: coach:_____ " can be thought of as "A captain is to a ship [a captain runs a ship; a captain leads a ship] as a coach is to a team [a coach runs a team; a coach leads a team]." This inner

FIGURE 5.2
Analogy Examples

Measurement	Parts to wholes	Cause and effect
Kilogram: Pound :: Liter: ?	Hard drive: Computer :: Engine: ?	Fatigue: Yawning :: Fright: ?
Shape and Proportion 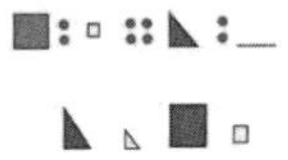	**Profession and tools:** Photographer: Camera :: Mason: ?	**Person to situation** Teacher: School :: Pilot: ?
Forms and Orientation 	**Synonyms** Slender: Think :: Obese: ?	**Geography** Washington: DC :: San Francisco: ?
Agent and Action Brain: Thinking :: ? : Typing	**Proportion and Form** 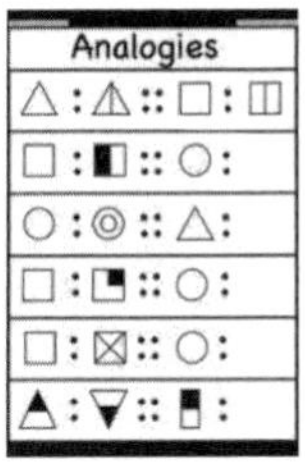	**Relationships** Geologist: Rocks :: Astronomer: ?
Category Orange: Fruit :: Pecan: ?	**Part to whole** Chapter: Book :: Scenes: ?	**Type and sub-type** Basil: Herb :: Oak: ?
Measurement 	**Degree** Admire: Idolize :: Loath: ?	**Form and Relationships** 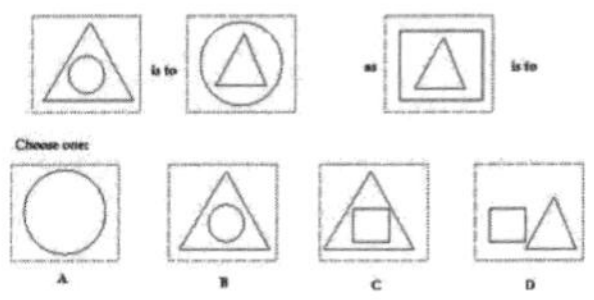

speech and "talking to ourselves" is fundamental not only in improving our relational thinking, but also in shaping our view of the world. Rehearsing the many ways different concepts (verbs, historical moment, formulas, etc.) are connected expands our vision of those concepts in our surroundings. Analogies allow us to articulate how one thing is associated with another, and as we build these associations and a network of interconnections forms in our mind, we begin to see how everything is related to everything else through expanded mental schema.

Analogies are used in many different formats. Back in the 1960s, Mary Hesse (1966) suggested that models and analogies be the main mode of conveying scientific concepts, and in 1989, Spiro, Feltovich, Coulson, and Anderson recommended that complex concepts always be framed as analogies for better learning. Harrison and Coll (2007) have demonstrated that the use of analogies to teach middle and secondary school science can be very successful, and Richland and colleagues (2007) have shown the superior utility of analogies in teaching math. In 1991, Duit reiterated the utility of analogies and described them as a valuable tool for teaching difficult concepts in science while in 2002, Hulshof and Verloop showed the benefits of using analogies in language teaching, showing their utility beyond science concepts. The benefit of broad use of analogies as a key learning tool has substantial evidence behind it (Bingham & Kahl, 2012; Glynn, Duit, & Thiele, 2012; Yanowitz, 2010) in all subject areas.

Because the brain remembers best when facts and skills are embedded in natural or authentic contexts (MBE principle 19), **analogies facilitate connection to and therefore comprehension of previously unknown concepts**. In MBE, we know that the search for meaning occurs through pattern recognition and the brain's continual comparison between what it senses and what it already knows (principles 10 and 11). The structure of analogies facilitates this comparison, making it a natural effort for the brain. However, analogies work because they play off the idea that each brain is unique and uniquely organized (principle 1), requiring that teachers know their students well enough to use their past experiences to construct analogies related to each learner's known concepts.

Analogies help students develop learning habits that lead to improved metacognition and problem solving (see, e.g., Dixon, 2010). It is clear that "embedding analogy in a text improves accurate inferencing," especially if combined with the highlighting of key words (McDaniel & Donnelly, 1996, p. 508). Creating analogies is also an excellent means of motivating students (Burleson, 2005). Analogies are not included in Hattie's list, but related concepts are. The process of analogy development is based on self-verbalization and self-questioning; an analogy can be considered a version of a worked example in which a correct structure is offered as a model for future structure, and analogies can also be deemed a type of simulation.

What happens when analogies are hard to come by? A teacher who has never had experiences similar to those of a given student will be hard pressed to help that student link new ideas to old, which is why teaching in context is so vital. Luckily, concrete experiences aren't the only way to take advantage of past knowledge, and this is where empathy comes in. If a teacher is adept enough to empathize with her students and with realities she might not have any personal connection to, she can be effective in creating analogies for which she has no direct experience. Most experienced teachers note how students appreciate personal narratives. When a teacher draws connections between her own past and the learner's present, she increases the learner's confidence in her understanding of his reality and the validity of her observations. For example, a teacher might say, "I've never been hunting, but I have been fishing and I bet those moments of silence and the patience you need are the same," or "I'm no cook, but I love my garden, and I can see how putting the right ingredients into helping my roses grow is something like baking a good cake."

Schooler, Fallshore, and Fiore (1995) indicate that "insight" (the "aha!" moments that occur when learners link past and present ideas) relies in part on analogies: "Insight involves . . . features [such] as creativity, including examining all factors that could be causing a problem, searching for a new way to state the problem, finding alternative approaches, persevering, taking risks, applying broad knowledge, and recognizing analogies" (as cited in King, Goodson, & Rohani, p. 16). This means that links between ideas are often possible thanks to creating analogies or thinking through analogies, especially in subject areas where concepts can be intangible (Hesse, 1966). To construct analogies, however, teachers have to have a great amount of mental resources, and they need to know what students already know in order to make connections.

Orgill and Thomas (2007) show how analogies can be incorporated at each state of the 5Es model, which is explained next.

Best Classroom Practice 31. Implement the 5Es: Engage, Explore, Explain, Elaborate, Evaluate
Anyone could teach if teaching objectives were always predictable; however, they aren't. The 5Es design is a wonderful structure that helps teachers anticipate some of the unpredictable aspects of teaching and reach their learning goals.

At the turn of the 20th century, German philosopher Johann Friedrich Hebart proposed that there are two main foundations of teaching: interest and conceptual understanding (Bybee et al., 2006; English, 2013). Hebart believed that learning depends on a student's personal interest in the subject at hand. To better engage learners, he suggested that teachers take advantage of two types of student interest, the first generated by direct experiences and the second by social interactions. John Dewey's reflections on the same subject in education led to the publication *How We Think* (1910/1971) and pointed to the general applications of the scientific method that is still used today to approach learning problems. According to Dewey, **a primary function of formal education is to generate dissonance through reflection**. This "discomfort" arises from the incoherency between what we know or believe and what we are faced with, which challenges our general mental schema of the world we live in.

Both Hebart and Dewey identified at least three basic stages in a successful learning cycle, including exploration, invention, and discovery (English, 2013). These stages were confirmed by later reviews of more contemporary models (e.g., Karplus & Their, 1967; Renner, Abraham, & Birnie, 1985), which finally resulted in the establishment of the 5Es model suggested by the National Science Foundation after the Science Curriculum Improvement Study (SCIS) took on the task of putting the U.S. back on the top of science education following the launch of Sputnik in 1957. The Biological Science Curriculum Study (BSCS) published the historical development of the 5Es (Eisenkraft, 2012) and recommended a slight modification of Herbert and Dewey's original ideas. In 2011, the National Science Teachers Association published a modified version to expand on the BSCS model, which included seven "Es" (Eisenkraft, 2012). (See Table 5.1 for a summary of the progression of the model.) Each of the five stages of the 5Es guide students toward a better understanding and deeper exploration of the subject at hand and is explained below.

TABLE 5.1
Progression of the 5Es Model

SCIS Model (Hebart & Dewey, 1910)	BSCS 5Es Instructional Model (1960s)	7Es (Eisenkraft, 2012)
		Elicit prior knowledge (new phase)
	Engagement (new phase)	Engagement
Exploration	Exploration (adapted from SCIS)	Exploration
Invention (term production)	Explanation (adapted from SCIS)	Explanation
Discovery (concept application)	Elaboration (adapted from SCIS)	Elaboration
	Evaluation (new phase)	Evaluation
		Extend (practice transference) (new phase)

Stage 1: Engage. Each class should begin with an event that captures students' attention. This awakens any natural curiosity they might have about the topic and helps them make links with past knowledge, as well as calling attention to the class focus. For example, instead of starting a physics class with a list of proofs, drop an apple and a feather and ask which will hit the ground faster. Instead of beginning a genetics class by handing out a list of chromosomes, show a picture of a two-headed snake and ask, "What happened?" If you're teaching a social studies class, you could start off with a folk or rap song about a social issue and ask students to focus on the words the author uses to express his or her feelings about the injustice being described. The objective of stage 1 is to hook students and get their attention.

Stage 2: Explore. Next, students should do an activity or have a discussion that allows them to explore a new concept or skill related to the engaging prop in E1 (Harton, Richardson, Barreras, Rockloff, & Latane, 2002). Students can be asked to look for solutions to problems or explain a phenomenon in their own words: "What do you know about apples and feathers that explains how fast they fall?" "Why did the snake end up with two heads?" "How did the words in the song make you feel?" This stage permits students to gather a group of shared experiences and work together to find a solution.

Stage 3: Explain. Students should now be asked to articulate their ideas as clearly as possible and explain them to the group. Forcing students to clarify their meanings and be more precise with their words will encourage refinement of their ideas and push them to become more accurate in their beliefs relating to the ideas shared. Ask each student to explain how he thinks Newton came up with the law of gravity, what he thinks happened to the snake, or why the artist wrote the song the way she did.

Stage 4: Elaborate. Only after students have explained the concept on their own should the teacher elaborate by using the correct terminology (stages 1, 2, and 3 are entirely student-centered; only at stage 4 does the teacher come into the picture as a supporting figure). Remember: Elaborations or additions to the students' knowledge should come after they've had their own experience! Be sure to allow students to discuss their ideas and give them guidance to help them deepen their understanding and apply what they've learned to new situations. Here is where you can explain how radical Newton was for his times, the concept of genetic mutations, or expound on the issues of injustice expressed in the song.

Stage 5: Evaluate. The final unit of the class should have two objectives. First, students should develop a clear understanding of what parts of the lesson they do and don't comprehend. This self-evaluation is key in allowing them to develop criteria for what is and is not important about the topic at hand and identify gaps in their own knowledge. Second, the

"Evaluate" stage serves to assess whether key concepts and skills have been learned. Teachers can use this moment to consider the next lesson and what aspects of the lesson need to be retaught or reinforced in order to proceed.

Some newer versions of the 5Es go even further and add two additional stages as bookends. Some models suggest adding "Elicit prior understandings" before the other five and "Extend" at the end (Eisenkraft, 2012).

Why do the 5Es work? **They work because they offer the right balance between discovery learning and explicit instruction.** Yes, it's good for students to be able to find things out on their own, but we also know that a high percentage of the information exchanged between students is incorrect (Hattie 2009); students can mislead each other because they haven't really mastered the concepts at hand. The 5Es provide space for explicit instruction (in the elaboration phase), in which the teacher can confirm that everyone is on the same page in regard to vocabulary, definitions, and core concepts. Unlike other explicit teaching models, however, the 5Es are dominated by student-centered, not teacher-centered, activity. This ensures that student attention is high; it's impossible not to pay attention when you're the center of attention. The 5Es are also more memorable than other teaching methods, meaning that both attention and memory are high, leading to long-term learning.

A review of the effectiveness of the 7Es version of the 5Es model in science classes demonstrated learning outcomes superior to those of "traditional" lecture models, including increased mastery of the subject matter, more sophisticated scientific reasoning, and greater interest in science. The 5Es method may also yield benefits in development of teamwork skills (Bybee et al., 2006). The utility of the 5Es in science classes is well established, and this instructional model has provided the general structure of informal learning (as in children's museums, for example) for the past three decades. It is only recently, however, that use of the 5Es model has been encouraged in teacher training programs, and into all subject areas at all ages.

Summary

Certain teaching practices have been successful in classrooms for centuries. The Socratic method, PBL, cooperative learning, case studies, reciprocal teaching, and the use of analogies have withstood the test of time and the 5Es have been around since Dewey's time a century ago. It is safe to say that if teachers consistently apply just a few of these ideas in their classrooms, their students' learning will improve. However, there are other methods and activities that are not so intuitive that could have equal or even greater influence on student learning. In the next chapter we turn to methodologies supported by both MBE and Visible Learning that could be implemented more frequently to produce better learning in our classrooms.

Suggested Readings

The Socratic Method

Browne, M. N., & Keeley, S. M. (2006). *Asking the right questions: A guide to critical thinking* (8th ed.). New York, NY: Prentice Hall.

Copeland, M. (2005). *Socratic circles: Fostering critical and creative thinking in middle and high school.* Portland, ME: Stenhouse.

Foundation for Critical Thinking. (2011). *The role of Socratic questioning in thinking, teaching, and learning.* Retrieved April 30, 2013, from http://www.criticalthinking.org/pages/the-role-of-socratic-questioning-in-thinking-teaching-learning/522

Garilkoy, R. (2011). *The Socratic method: Teaching by asking instead of telling.* Retrieved from http://www.sophia.ac.jp/syllabus/2012/09/09_AIBE3450/The%20Socratic%20Method.pdf

Kreeft, P., & Doughtery, T. (Eds.). (2010). *Socratic logic: A logic text using Socratic method, Platonic questions, and Aristotelian principles* (3rd ed.). St. Augustine's Press.

Lam, F. (2011). *The Socratic method as an approach to learning and its benefits.* Unpublished thesis, Carnegie Mellon University.

Maxwell, K. J. (2009). *The Socratic temperament.* Retrieved July 4, 2012, from http://www.socraticmethod.net/the_socratic_temperament.htm

Overholser, J. C. (1993). Elements of the Socratic method: I. Systematic questioning. *Psychotherapy: Theory, Research, Practice, Training, 30*(1), 67–74. doi: 10.1037/0033-3204.30.1.67

Paul, R., & Elder, L. (2007). *The thinker's guide to the art of Socratic questioning.* Tomales, CA: Foundation for Critical Thinking.

Peterson, E. (2009). Teaching to think: Applying the Socratic method outside of the law school setting. *Journal of College Teaching and Learning, 6*(5), 83–88.

Reich, R. (2003, Fall). The Socratic method: What it is and how to use it in the classroom. *Speaking of Teaching, 13*(1), 1–4.

Questioning

Alro, H., & Johnsen-Hoines, M. (2012). Inquiry—without posing questions. *Mathematics Enthusiast, 9*(3), 253–270.

Flage, D. (2003). *The art of questioning: An introduction to critical thinking.* New York, NY: Pearson.

Girling Fitch, J. (2012). *The art of questioning.* Ulan Press.

McTighe, J., & Wiggins, G. (2013). *Essential questions: Opening doors to student understanding.* Alexandria, VA: ASCD.

Rothstein, D., & Santana, L. (2011). *Make just one change: Teach students to ask their own questions.* Cambridge, MA: Harvard Education Press.

Walsh, J. A., & Sattes, B. D. (2004). *Quality questioning: Research-based practice to engage every learner.* Thousand Oaks, CA: Corwin.

Zwiers, J., & Crawford, M. (2011). *Academic conversations: Classroom talk that fosters critical thinking and content understandings.* Portland, ME: Stenhouse.

Problem-Based Learning

Barekkm, J. F. (2006). *Problem-based learning: An inquiry approach* (2nd ed.). Thousand Oaks, CA: Corwin.

Ferreira, M. M., & Trudel, A. R. (2012). The impact of problem based learning (PBL) on student attitudes towards science, problem-solving skills, and sense of community in the classroom. *Journal of Classroom Interaction, 47*(1), 23–30.

Gallagher, S. A., & Gallagher, J. J. (2013). Using problem-based learning to explore unseen academic potential. *Interdisciplinary Journal of Problem-based Learning, 7*(1).

Hmelo-Silver, C. E. (2012). International perspectives on problem-based learning: Contexts, cultures, challenges, and adaptation. *Interdisciplinary Journal of Problem-based Learning, 6*(1), 10–15.

Ronis, D. L. (2007). *Problem-based learning for math and science: Integrating inquiry and the Internet.* Thousand Oaks, CA: Corwin.

Cooperative Learning

Ashman, A., & Gilles, R. (2003). *Cooperative learning: The social and intellectual outcomes of learning in groups.* London, UK: Routledge.

Gillies, R. M., Ashman, A., & Terwel, R. M. (Eds.). (2010). *The teacher's role in implementing cooperative learning in the classroom.* New York, NY: Springer.

Hsiung, C.-M. (2012). The effectiveness of cooperative learning. *Journal of Engineering Education, 101*(1), 119–137.

Laal, M., & Ghodsi, S. M. (2012). Benefits of collaborative learning. *Procedia: Social and Behavioral Sciences 31,* 486–490.

Sears, D. A., & Pai, H. H. (2012). Effects of cooperative versus individual study on learning and motivation after reward-removal. *Journal of Experimental Education, 80*(3), 246–262.

Case Studies

Freeman Herreid, C., Schiller, N. A., & Herreid, K. F. (2012). *Science stories: Using case studies to teach critical thinking.* Arlington, VA: National Science Teachers Association.

Lehrer, R., & Chazan, D. (Eds.). (1998). *Designing learning environments for developing understanding of geometry and space.* London, UK: Routledge.

Llewellyn, D. J. (2004). *Teaching high school science through inquiry: A case study approach.* Thousand Oaks, CA: Corwin.

Maasz, J., & O'Donoghue, J. (2011). (Eds.). *Real-world problems for secondary school mathematics students: Case studies.* Rotterdam, The Netherlands: Sense Publishers.

Reciprocal Teaching

Ahmadi, M. R. (2013). Goals of reciprocal teaching strategy instruction. *International Journal of Language Learning and Applied Linguistics World, 2*(1), 21–88.

Ahmadi, M. R., & Ismail, H. N. (2012). *Reciprocal teaching strategy as an important fact of improving reading comprehension.* Creative Commons, MacroThink. doi: 10.5296/jse.v2i4.2584

Ghorbani, M. R., Gangeraj, A. A., & Alavi, S. Z. (2013). Reciprocal teaching of comprehension strategies improves EFL learners' writing ability. *Current Issues in Education, 16*(1). Retrieved from http://cie.asu.edu/ojs/index.php/cieatasu/article/viewArticle/1046

Pilonieta, P., & Medina, A. (2011). Reciprocal teaching for the primary grades: "We can do it, too!" *Reading Teacher, 63*(2), 120–129. doi: 10.1598/RT.63.2.3

Stricklin, K. (2011). Hands-on reciprocal teaching: A compression technique. *Reading Teacher, 64*(8), 620–625.

Williams, J. (2010). Taking on the role of questioner: Revisiting reciprocal teaching. *Reading Teacher, 64*(4), 278–281. doi: 10.1598/RT.64.4.6

Analogies

Bingham, C., & Kahl, S. (2012, July). The process of schema emergence: Assimilation, deconstruction, utilization and the plurality of analogies. *Academy of Management Journal.* doi:10.5465/amj.2010.0723

Gentner, D., & Colhoun, J. (2010). Analogical processes in human thinking and learning. *Towards a Theory of Thinking on Thinking,* 35–48.

Glynn, S. M., Duit, R., & Thiele, R. B. (2012). Teaching science with analogies: A strategy for constructing knowledge. In S. M. Glynn & R. Duit (Ed.), *Learning science in the schools* (pp. 247–296). New York, NY: Routledge.

Harrison, A. G., & Coll, R. K. (2007). *Using analogies in middle and secondary science classrooms: The FAR guide.* Thousand Oaks, CA: Corwin.

Hofstadter, D., & Sander, E. (2013). *Surfaces and essences: Analogy as the fuel and fire of thinking.* New York, NY: Basic Books.

Holyoak, K. J., & Morrison, R. (2012). *The Oxford handbook of thinking and reasoning.* New York, NY: Oxford University Press.

Hulshof, H., & Verloop, N. (2002). *The use of analogies in language teaching: Representing the content of teachers' practical knowledge. Journal of Curriculum Studies,* 34(1), 77–90. doi: 10.1080/00220270110037177

Jee, B. D., Uttal, D. H., Gentner, D., Manduca, C., Shipley, T. F., Tikoff, B., . . . Sageman, B. (2010). Commentary: Analogical thinking in geoscience education. *Journal of Geoscience Education,* 58(1), 2–13.

Richland, L. E., Zur, P., & Holyoak, K. J. (2007). Cognitive supports for analogies in the mathematics classroom. *Science, 316,* 1128–1129.

Sarina, V., & Namukasa, I. K. (2010). Nonmath analogies in teaching mathematics. *Procedia: Social and Behavioral Sciences,* 2(2), 5738–5743.

Yanowitz, K. L. (2010). Using analogies to improve elementary school students' inferential reasoning about scientific concepts. *School Science and Mathematics,* 101(3), 133–142. doi: 10.1111/j.1949-8594.2001.tb18016.x

The 5Es

Bybee, R. W., Taylor, J. A., Gardner, A., Van Scotter, P., Carlson Powell, J., Westbrook, A., & Landes, N. (2006). *The BSCS 5E instructional model: Origins and effectiveness. A Report prepared for the Office of Science Education and the National Institutes of Health.* Colorado Springs, CO: BSCS.

Cramer, K. B. (2012). *Impact of constructivism via the biological sciences curriculum study (BSCS) 5E model on student science achievement and attitude. A professional development submitted in partial fulfillment of a Master of Science degree.* Unpublished document, Montana State University.

Eisenkraft, A. (2012). *Expanding the 5E Model: A proposed 7E model emphasizes "transfer of learning" and the importance of eliciting prior understanding.* Arkansas Department of Education: National Science Teachers Association. Retrieved from pbworks.com

Orgill, M. K., & Thomas, M. (2007). *Analogies and the 5E model.* National Science Teachers Association.

Tanner, K. D. (2010). Order matters: Using the 5E model to align teaching with how people learn. *American Society for Cell Biology, Life Sciences Education,* 9(3), 159–164. doi: 10.1187/cbe.10-06-0082

Tural, G., Akdeniz, A. R., & Alev, N. (2010). Effect of 5E teaching model on student teachers' understanding of weightlessness. *Journal of Science Education and Technology, 19,* 470–488.

CHAPTER 6

What *Could* Work in the Classroom and Why
Getting Teachers (and Administrators) out of Their Comfort Zones

This chapter calls on teachers to consider attempting methodologies that they may not have tried before but have considerable evidence behind them. These methods and activities are often applied less frequently than those outlined in Chapter 5 but could have just as much or more impact on student learning if teachers, and in some cases administrators, were to get out of their comfort zones and risk trying something new.

A Teacher's List of Habits

Just as students have a list of habits of mind that need development (remember Costa and Kallick, 2000, 2009) teachers have their own list of habits that they must perfect across their careers. Teachers must remember to:

1. Improve student self-efficacy
2. See learning as fluid
3. Appreciate the role of affect in learning
4. Take the lead in social cognition
5. Award perseverance and celebrate error
6. Be passionate!
7. Never work harder than their students
8. Design engaging classrooms

9. Motivate
10. Manage
11. Use thinking routines

Developing each of these 11 habits will improve a teacher's likelihood of designing significant and empowering classroom experiences. Each forms one of the following 11 Best Classroom Practices.

Best Classroom Practice 32. Improve Student Self-Efficacy

If a student thinks she can learn, she will. There is now no doubt that a student's own self-efficacy as a learner has an influence on how well how she actually does in school. According to Hattie's research (2009), a student's self-reported grades are the greatest indicator of improved learning. In many ways, this is a self-fulfilling prophecy: "If I think I can learn, I will; if I believe I am incapable of learning, I will fail." As Hattie points out, a child's willingness to invest in learning, openness to experiences, and the general reputation she can build as a "learner" are keys to success (2009), and this self-efficacy is prejudiced by the way the teacher makes the child feel. Why, then, don't all teachers make it their first act to instill a sense of self-confidence in their students?

As Hattie tells us, some teachers believe that their students are limited in their potential because of poor genes, low socioeconomic status, or other negative preexisting conditions. Since they don't believe the student can learn, they teach in such a way that the student does not learn: a vicious circle. A student believes she is a learner when she has experienced a pattern of successes in learning environments. When she's been told, "You're quick!" "You're smart!" "You have talent!" and "You're clever!" many times in her formative years, these affirmations also become a self-fulfilling prophecy. "I can learn; I am a learner; I can figure this out!" is the best thing a child can tell herself. However, many children don't feel this level of empowerment, and worse yet, they may not believe the people who encourage them because the words aren't accompanied by actions worthy of praise.

If most of us know all of this from our life experiences, why do so many of us teachers fail to build up our students' self-perceptions as learners? As I correct papers and write feedback to my students, I realize that two things challenge me as I try to balance out my comments. First, after correcting the same mistakes over and over, I'm almost angry at having to reteach items that I'm sure I taught (well) before. I'm annoyed that I have to spend time on concepts that were supposedly taught weeks ago. Why did they fail to learn in the first place? How did I fail to teach this right the first time? This frustration leads me to leave feedback that is less than gentle (e.g., "I recommend you review the previous feedback and go over the support documents in the classroom" instead of "You've made a lot of progress. To continue improving, I recommend that you reread previous feedback and reread the documents related to this assignment"). Second, I find it easier to note the mistakes ("Citations are not in APA format") than to try to motivate the student ("I know you're smart and will be able to learn this if you spend a bit more time reviewing exercises similar to number 3").

Positive feedback works only when it's sincere and based on praiseworthy deeds. Self-esteem is evident in risk-takers, and risk-takers are born of secure environments and high self-efficacy. How can we promote this virtuous cycle in the classroom? One way is to create a climate in which students believe that it's okay to make errors ("I can always try again; I am not my failures but rather my successes"). In the U.S. there is the belief that "if I try hard [meaning if I persevere], "it doesn't matter if I'm behind [America loves underdogs], and if I pick myself up at least one time more than the times I fall, I will be a success." When a learner meets with success, she develops a positive self-image, and this colors all of her future learning endeavors. Teachers can influence this element by building up students' self-esteem and helping them believe they all have the potential to learn.

I have always believed that early literary experiences have not only greatly influenced my own personal beliefs about learning, but also probably shaped many a country's thinking about learning. Despite the existence of such a great variety of cultures around the globe, there appear to be some universal values, many of which are apparent in the children's literature of all countries. In the U.S., "I think I can, I think I can" (from *The Little Engine That Could*) and Dr. Seuss's *Oh, the Thinks You Can Think!* and *Oh, the Places You'll Go!* are mantras of learning potential that have shaped generations. *Mike Mulligan and His Steam Shovel*, Curious George's curiosity, and *The Story of Babar* were key in determining my generation's mentality about learning: Be curious, try new things, invent, put things together in a different way than others have put them together before, dream, use tools flexibly, and feed your imagination.

Books can be a fabulous influence, but books alone often cannot foster a "can do" attitude; there are myriad factors in an individual's life that come into play when shaping the fragile self-image of small children. Children form an image of themselves as learners partly based on inspiration from literary characters, but they also learn from the real people who surround them. Did the child have models in her life that showed her the rewards of being smart, or were the prizes in her environment given to lazy people who cheated and beat the system? Was *The Little Engine That Could* read to her at bedtime, or did she sit in front of the TV watching shows celebrating low achievers? As Costa and Kallick (2009) note, the habits of mind form early. If a child sees that learning is rewarded (you can advance to a higher-paying job; you are praised by your parents or peers; you simply feel good because people acknowledge your intelligence), then her brain craves that good feeling repeatedly.

It is possible to feel addicted to praise. The dopaminergic loop, which has to do with feel-good sensations, defines motivation in the brain (Reeve & Reeve, 2001). It is possible to self-medicate with praise and feel good about oneself without input from others. Learners who manage to encourage themselves, who believe in themselves, and see themselves as able individuals are those who achieve because it is a reward in itself.

Both parents and teachers shape a child's self-image by their comments and actions. While the role models a child is exposed to prior to entering school are powerful, **children spend more of their waking moments in school than they do in their own homes, and as a consequence receive more influence from teachers and schools than they do from their parents and home related to academic success criteria**. However, when asked what has the greatest impact on student learning, teachers inevitably say that "parents" have a bigger influence on student learning outcomes. One of the reasons we as teachers think that the home has a greater influence on learning than we do is because the learning models tells us that a child's self-efficacy develops early. However, we now know that "self-concept is a structural product of reflective activity, but it is also susceptible to change as the individual encounters new roles, situations, and life transitions" (Demo, 1992, p. 303), many of which occur in school settings. When viewed from a sociological perspective, this information can be devastating. For instance, telling a certain racial group that they will likely not go to college, or telling girls they're not as capable of doing math or science, often turns into a self-fulfilling prophecy. I once knew a teacher who told his entire class that there are some groups that are cut out for math and others that are not, and unfortunately, this group was not. The result? *An entire class that failed.*

I firmly believe in the power of one: one teacher, one student at a time. An important battle is won for each student empowered to believe she is a learner. Levine (2002) used to preach that **our job as teachers is to help students find success every day so that they develop a perception of themselves as learners.** With each little battle won, self-confidence improves. While students can drive their own self-efficacy if they have strong personalities, most rely on teacher guidance to develop this positive inner vision.

Best Classroom Practice 33: Maintain High Expectations
This leads to a very important conclusion: **Learners respond to expectations**. When teachers and parents let kids know they expect a lot from them, the kids react positively. In 1984 C. Pat-

rick Proctor wrote an interesting article from the perspective of the Department of Education in which he showed that students who were asked to reach high levels of achievement did so, and those for whom expectations were lower did not. That is, the students performed to the level of their teacher's expectations, high or low (Good, 1987; Good & Brophy, 1997; Rubie-Davies, 2010). **This tells us, both as parents and as teachers, that while we should be realistic, we should also ask the kids in our lives to stretch just a bit higher than they think they can reach**. We have "known" this for years in education, but knowing this information is different from actually using it to modify behavioral and improve learning outcomes.

Good (1987) echoes Proctor's findings and highlights how teachers often convey expectations without clearly understanding their own impact on student learning. Many teachers don't even realize how they are communicating low expectations to their students. For instance, a noteworthy finding of Hattie's work is that failing a grade is a strong indicator for future failure, primarily because the student loses faith in her own ability to learn because her teachers— those "in the know"—have deemed her unable to learn. On the other hand, the joy of learning is a great motivator, and people who love learning have often had at least one teacher in their lives who has given them confidence in their ability to learn and pushed them to achieve more than they believed they were capable of.

Independent of the level of expected achievement (low, middle, or high) of a group, teachers should aim high (Rist, 1970). The higher the expectations, the higher the achievement (Good, 1987; Good & Brophy, 1997). If the teacher aims low or middle, students will only push themselves low or middle level. As demonstrated in the classic experiment conducted by Rosenthal and Jacobson in 1968, the "Pygmalion effect" implies that teachers can influence performance based on expectations transmitted to students. In this classic experiment teachers were told that a certain group of kids showed great promise academically. In reality there was no difference between the students. At the end of the year the students for whom the teachers had higher expectations did significantly better than the students about whom the teachers had no prior judgments. Several studies over the past 45 years have given credence to this fundamental aspect of teacher education: Students will live up (or down) to expectations (see Clifford & Walster, 1973; Cooper, 1979; Cooper & Tom, 1984; Eden, 1990; Feldman & Prohaska, 1979; Jussim, 1989; Rosenthal, 1994, 2002; Rosenthal & Jacobson, 1966, 1968).

Teachers often unconsciously have different expectations for different students (related to race, gender, socio-economic status and even physical attractiveness [see Clifford & Walster, 1973]), contributing to the self-fulfilling prophecy of failure for many (Graham, 1991), or unintentional raising of IQs with "exceptional ability" for others (Rosenthal & Jacobson, 1968).

Teachers often gravely underestimate student potential based on their personal pre-conceptions, consequently expect less of students, and as a result, have students who produce less, in some cases over their lifespan. In a dramatic study, Alvidrez and Weinstein demonstrated that expectations in kindergarten had an effect on students' high school SAT scores and grade point averages, indicating the long-term effects of expectations based on external factors such as socio-economic status, gender, and race on learning (Alvidrez & Weinstein, 1999).

Do high expectations always yield high results? Hattie (2009) notes that "parents can have a major effect in terms of the encouragement and expectations that they transmit to their children" (p. 61), and he found that parent aspirations are among the most important factors in student achievement. Hong and Ho (2005) found that "the higher the hopes and expectations of parents with respect to the educational attainment of their child, the higher the student's own educational expectations and, ultimately, the greater the student's academic achievement" (as cited in Hattie, 2009, p. 69). The balance of studies indicate that when parents display sincere interest, high expectations, and clear academic aspirations for their children, their children are more likely than not to comply and achieve at high levels. When aspirations are low, students rarely stretch themselves and are unlikely to achieve. Low expectations from parents and students lead to student apathy and lack of effort, while high expectations can lead to better results than originally projected.

Remember that communicating high expectations is part of goal clarity. Students generally live up to the expectations of the teacher: **If the teacher communicates low expectations, the students perform at a low level; the higher the expectations, the higher the student achievement.**

Best Classroom Practice 34. See Learning as Fluid

As we know from studies in MBE, it is actually impossible for the brain not to learn. Intelligence is fluid, not fixed, though this has been debated for fifty years (Cattell, 1963; Kane & Engel, 2002; Sternberg, 1981). It is only recently that the general neural correlates for fluid intelligence have started to be identified (Gray, Chabris, & Braver, 2003), and its links to other functions, such as working memory (Burgess, Gray, Conway & Braver, 2011) and executive functions (Roca et al., 2010) been clarified. Teachers who believe that their students are locked into a level of intelligence that is fixed are less effective than teachers how believe that intelligence in fluid and ever-changing (Geake, 2011). The human potential to learn exists throughout the lifespan (barring neurodegenerative diseases or accidents); a normal human can and does learn because intelligence is fluid. Teachers with the right mentality know that all students can learn, as it is the brain's natural state. This means that although expert teachers understand that the home situation can have an influence on learning, they accept that their own influence is generally greater, and no matter what a child has been given in terms of biology, it can be improved upon by good pedagogy. Expert teachers believe that learning as well as intelligence levels can be influenced by their actions and is not fixed by external structures, such as a child's race or socioeconomic status. Teachers who mentally condemn learners from certain neighborhoods or ethnic backgrounds are unable to teach successfully. These limited-minded individuals should not be allowed anywhere near students because, as we just saw, a teacher's lack of confidence in her students will cause them to doubt themselves as well. An expert teacher takes advantage of her students' pasts to contextualize new information when designing authentic learning experiences, but she understands that their past doesn't define who they are.

This leads to a second important point: **Expert teachers do not label their students**. When something is repeated over and over, it becomes true in the mind. Daniel Schacter (2002) writes about "the seven sins of memory" and notes that due to the "sin" of suggestibility, we can be talked into believing something is true, despite our own personal memory of the information (that is, we can own a memory that is constructed by others). Hattie (2009, 2012) notes that avoiding the labeling trap boosts student achievement. There should be no "smart kids" or "dumb kids," no "free lunch kids" or "special needs kids." Calling someone "learning disabled," "ADD," or "dyslexic" isn't helpful, and only places impediments in the path of learning (Levine, 2002). Understanding a child's strengths and weaknesses is vital to structuring proper learning experiences, but this doesn't mean kids have to be sorted into categories that change the way they perceive themselves. Great teachers embrace the fact that intelligence is ever changing and fluid.

Best Classroom Practice 35: Appreciate the Role of Affect in Learning
There is strong evidence in neuroscientific research and in psychology that affect influences learning (Durlak, Weissberg, Dymnicki, Taylor, & Schellinger, 2011; Kim & Pekrun, 2014; Pekrun, Goetz, Frenzel, Barchfeld, & Perry, 2011). Another key belief that teachers should embrace is that emotions are critical to learning. The exact relation? **There is no decision without emotion, and there is no learning without decision-making; therefore, there is no learning without emotion.** Since one's self is defined by one's reactions to the environment and the people in it, Mary Helen Immordino-Yang and Antonio Damasio (2007) asks us to consider whether "I feel, therefore I am" is a more accurate statement than the centuries-old "I think, therefore I am" perspective. Daniel Goleman (2005) has pushed the emotional intel-

ligence movement to the point where many now accept it as an attribute of any well-educated person. According to the editors of *The Nature of Learning*, "emotions are the primary gatekeepers to learning" (Dumont, Istance, & Benavides, 2010, p.4), and Kovalik (1998) places this information in the school context. Affective states can influence the encoding of information, (though whether one is happy or sad does not seem to influence retrieval of information). That is, learning new information is influenced more by emotional states than retrieval of the same information (Storbeck & Clore, 2011). Teachers who cause students to experience high anxiety lower the probability of learning as compared with students who feel calm or happy or consider the learning experience pleasurable (D'Mello, 2012). Despite these references, the role of affect in learning has yet to be incorporated into most teacher education programs.

How well do we recognize our own emotions and those of others? How well do we manage the emotional states of others and ourselves? Emotional abilities and social functioning are closely related (Brackett, Rivers, Shiffman, Lerner, & Salovey, 2006). Being able to manage one's own feelings and clearly understand their origins is important in decision-making, which is a decision in and of itself. A quote attributed to Aristotle (384–322 B.C.) in *Ética a Nicómaco* captures how difficult it is to control and direct emotions: "Anyone can get angry, that is simple. But to get angry with the right person in the right degree and the right moment, with just reason and delivered in the right way, that, most certainly, is not easy."

MBE principle 12—learning is enhanced by challenge and inhibited by threat—highlights the importance of emotions. While this statement seem fairly obvious, it is clear that the level of challenge or threat felt by one person relative to another is difficult to measure, making this a hard concept to nail down. If we agree that we cannot precisely measure the level of threat someone perceives (after all, even though we can measure heart rates, sweating, etc., we don't know if the person "feels" the same emotion we presume she is feeling), there are still clear indicators that she is experiencing a threatening situation. For example, when someone is threatened, adrenaline is released, telling the brain that the individual must flee from the situation and protect herself. This, of course, isn't possible in a classroom situation, where there is nowhere to run to and nowhere to hide.

Challenge is also difficult to measure precisely, but it may be slightly easier to quantify than threat, as self-reported levels of challenge are relatively accurate ("I feel challenged by this situation"; "I don't feel challenged by this situation"). It is curious to note that people would rather face a challenge they think they can overcome than do what's easiest for them. Humans enjoy living up to a test (Brophy, 2010; Dweck, 2006). Thus, successful classroom situations are usually those in which students feel they are continually being offered challenges and meeting them successfully.

Immordino-Yang and Faeth (2010) call our attention to several core ideas about affect and learning. First, "emotion guides cognitive learning" (Immordino-Yang & Faeth, 2010, p. 70; see also Moran, Macrae, Heatherton, Wyland, & Kelly, 2006); second, "emotional contributions to learning can be conscious or nonconscious" (p. 71); third, "emotional learning shapes future behavior" (p. 73); fourth, "emotion is most effective at facilitating the development of knowledge when it is relevant to the task at hand" (p. 73); and fifth, "without emotion, learning is impaired" (p. 74). (See Figure 6.1)

FIGURE 6.1
The Intersection Between Emotion and Cognition

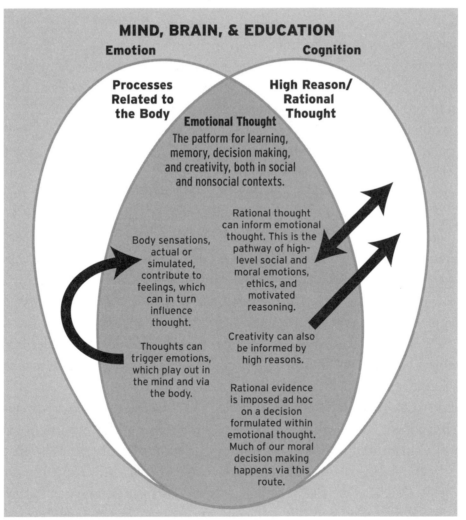

Source: Reprinted from Mind, Brain, and Education, *Mary Helen Immordino-Yang and Antonio Damasio, "We Feel, Therefore We Learn: The Relevance of Affective and Social Neuroscience to Education," pp. 3-10, March 12, 2007, with permission from John Wiley & Sons. © 2007 International Mind, Brain, and Education Society and Blackwell Publishing, Inc.*

The message from social and affective neuroscience is clear: no longer can we think of learning as separate from or disrupted by emotion, and no longer can we focus solely at the level of the individual student in analyzing effective strategies for classroom instruction. Students and teachers socially interact and learn from one another in ways that cannot be done justice by examining only the "cold" cognitive aspects of academic skills. (Immordino-Yang & Faeth, p. 67)

In *The Role of Emotion and Skilled Intuition in Learning* Immordino-Yang and Faeth (2010) also suggests at least three strategies to integrate emotions into the learning arena. First, they suggest fostering emotional connection to the subject matter. **Establishment of relevant emotional connections to what is being learned is key to remembering that information**. Second, they suggest that teachers encourage students to **develop smart academic intuitions**: "From a neuroscientific perspective, intuition can be understood as the incorporation of the nonconscious emotional signals into knowledge acquisition" (2011, p. 78). This means that students should be taught how to understand their conscious emotional responses to their own learning and how to take advantage of them. Finally, they suggest that **teachers should be more conscious of actively managing the social and emotional climate of the classroom**. Feelings about the class environment should not be left to chance.

Both positive and negative actions result from the emotional relationships between students and teachers. Davis and Dupper (2008) blame the increasingly high number of student dropouts, especially due to poor student-teacher relations, and Hamre and Piata (2006) point out that the effects of student-teacher relationships can extend beyond academic achievement and into the realm of a student's general well-being. Magg (2008) appreciates the role of affect in student learning but also understands how frequently students challenge teachers' patience levels:

Students with challenging behaviors are very deft at engaging teachers in power struggles as a way to either feel empowered, obtain attention, or escape an unpleasant task. The more frustrated that teachers permit themselves to get, the less capable they are of responding in a therapeutic, productive fashion to students' challenging behaviors. (p. 52)

Magg showed how rational-emotive therapy might help teachers work with disagreeable students. He found that "emotionally controlled teachers have greater access to behaviors in their repertoire for responding effectively to students' challenging behaviors" (p.52)

In summary, good student-teacher relationships "are fundamental to [students'] success in school, and as such, these relationships should be explicitly targeted in school-based prevention and intervention efforts" (Hamre & Pianta, 2006, p. 59). The quality of the relationship, in turn, is based on the affective perception of each of the parties. It is important to understand that **affect in the teacher-student relationship may or may not be perceived by both parties the same way**. That is, a teacher may think he has a great relationship with his entire class, but one of the students may think the teacher doesn't like her. **The student's perception of the relationship is more powerful than the actual relationship**. Teachers thus need to habitually incorporate positive affective signals into their exchanges with students to enhance the probability of learning.

Best Classroom Practice 36. Take the Lead in Social Contagion
Social cognition (understanding others) plays a large part in how and what we choose to learn (Campbell-Meiklejohn, Bach, Roepstorff, Dolan, & Frith, 2010), as well as how information is processed in our brains (Immordino-Yang, 2011; Nummenmaa, Glerean, & Sams, 2012). Teachers communicate to their students verbally and nonverbally, but they are often conscious only of the message sent and not the message received. Unfortunately, I have witnessed many crash-and-burn scenarios during teacher observations. A young, bright, motivated teacher may walk into a classroom, and suddenly the self-confident presence that I knew from her previous exchanges as a student teacher disappears as she takes on her new role as the lead in determining classroom ambience. She sees the sea of (what she perceives to be) aggressive teenage faces staring back at her, and instead of summoning her energy and revealing her passion for her subject, she cowers and begins the class badly. She sees the students smirk, loses even more confidence, and fumbles the introduction. The students have lost all confidence that she is capable of teaching them anything, and they begin to chat among themselves. The teacher becomes desperate and shouts at the group to get their attention. They look back at her condescendingly. The few kids who actually love the subject still hope that the teacher will recover and teach them something, but they soon begin to realize that it's already too late.

The complex mirror neuron system in the brain appears to be triggered when the brain perceives, then acts on, an understanding of "the Other" (Pineda, 2008). When the teacher came in and saw aggressive faces, her natural reaction was to flee; no smart brain would leave its body in this vulnerable state. When the students smirked and started chatting, the teacher's natural reaction was to be offended. But teachers should know better. Mirror neurons go both ways. If the teacher had taken the role of leader, guide, instructor, and mentor (instead of a meek, shadowy presence), the students' mirror neuron system would have allowed them to begin to reflect her physiology instead of the other way around, and she would have had a very different class. If she had entered with confidence, greeted the group, engaged her students in what she felt was a fascinating topic, and then began allowing them to explore ideas for themselves, all the while transmitting her passion for her subject, then she would have been the one to spread the contagious feeling of high motivation to them, rather than allowing the demotivated group to bring her down, and as a result, the rest of the group down as well (Radel, Sarrazin, Legrain, & Wild, 2010).

Best Classroom Practice 37. Award Perseverance and Celebrate Error

Americans don't usually come out on top in international standardized tests (we generally settle near the middle), but we do rank number one in terms of self-esteem (Guggenheim, 2010). How is self-perception molded, and is this a reflection of the entrepreneurial, risk-taking mentality of inventors in the U.S.?

I recall observing the NBA playoffs in 2012. The Miami Heat lost a home game. As the players filed into the locker room, the microphone caught the voice of a young boy, cheering for his team: "You guys did great! You'll get 'em next time! Hang in there, man; you know you're the best!" Despite the fact that they were losing the series, there was an amazing sound of celebration. Do American school kids have a high level of self-efficacy and hope because of *what* they are taught or because of *how* they are taught? Is the idea that "you're great," even if the score (or the final grade) doesn't evidence greatness, one of the reasons we end up being great in the end?

But very few people make it to the NBA, and not very many show the resilience required to pick themselves up after defeats in school, and almost none do so without the support of at least one special teacher (or coach) who in the best cases gives them hope that they can learn and in the worst case doesn't damage the self-image they do have (Henderson & Milstein, 2003).

Some people are open to the world. They welcome new experiences and enjoy the challenges of life. But there is a special subgroup of this crowd who welcome error because it helps them learn. To them, "Every problem is an opportunity." They are not fearful of constructive criticism, but embrace it. We learn about the world through our senses, which means that our learning is dependent on new experiences. Thus, **people who have a great degree of open-**

ness to experiences learn faster than those who don't: If I can handle facing the error, I can learn faster. If I shun correction, I stunt my own growth. A key idea in MBE is that all new learning is based on the ability to self-correct (Principle 8). People who expect that trial and error will eventually beget success try more, err more, and therefore are more successful. Those who are open to new experiences learn faster than those who refuse to experiment. While none of this should come as a surprise, it raises the question of why some people have a greater degree of openness to new experiences and error than others.

Children who are reared in environments where experimentation is welcomed and error is greeted with praise (for the child's intentions, if not her success) are kids who learn fast. They make a lot of mistakes, but they learn from them. Children who are brought up in families or schools that praise only excellent work or obvious successes and fail to recognize good tries do not dare to err and thus do not learn as much as fast. "Dare to err" should be a mantra in education. Learning environments that give the brain space to err and correct itself foster the greatest mental progress. Thus, one of the most powerful ways that school administrators impact student learning outcomes is by encouraging students and teachers to show initiative. Humans tend to learn from their mistakes; in fact, it is the only way learning is evident (if you didn't know something before and got it wrong on a test, the evidence of your learning is that you subsequently got it right).

One of the topics that comes up without fail at the beginning of each school year at my university is the fact that many first-year students don't dare to participate in class discussion. They withhold commentary despite having strong opinions. The unfortunate reality is that many students in our school system aren't open to new ideas because they've been punished for having them in formal school settings. If they had been raised in an environment that was open and receptive to new ideas, few of them would hesitate to raise their hands and express their viewpoint because they would have the assurance that others would also be open, that their comments would be welcomed by the teacher, and that intellectual freedom would be protected.

I grew up in an environment that encouraged experimentation with ideas (Berkeley, California, in the 1960s). We were never punished for thinking outside of the box; in fact, it was expected that we do so. Why does openness flourish in some settings and not in others? Because **being open to new ideas requires a mind frame that takes fear out of the equation.** If learning was appreciated as a collection of corrected errors, maybe we would be more open to new ideas because we either had been rewarded for having these ideas or, at the least, had not been punished for sharing them. The brain is out to preserve the body and will tell the individual to flee from threat. If a student is ridiculed for having a new idea, she quickly learns that experimenting is a threat and will learn to repress this desire. However, if error is not only tolerated but rather encouraged, she will be open to the ideas of others and feel free to express them herself.

Openness to new experiences is a habit cultivated over time, and it is shaped, little by little, by each of the learner's encounters with those around her (see Costa and Kallick, 2009, for a suggested regime of such habituation). If the people in the learner's life are open, her openness flourishes. Thus, it is interesting to note that while a school might limit openness to new or divergent ideas, out-of-school experiences can change the learner as well. Summer camps and other informal learning experiences, such as guided visits to children's museums, encourage openness to new ideas and can be an amazing source of new learning. Hattie (2012) considers the structure of the Outward Bound programs to be exemplary: The new skills are modeled, then experienced; corrections are made, attention is high and focused, and the learner is fully engaged and can't wait to repeat the experience. Hattie wonders why all learning experiences can't be as engaging as Outward Bound.

The concept of brain plasticity (MBE principles 3 and 6) tells us that **the brain adapts to what it does most:** If the brain is in contact primarily with tolerance of error and openness, it remains open. However, if it has been punished for being open—as in being told, "Don't be ridiculous!" or "Why would you every think *that*?"—then it learns to retreat from such negative confrontation and learning is stunted. Thus, while singular experiences can be powerful, it is usually the pattern of successes or failings that shapes the individual over her lifetime.

Students aren't the only ones who need to learn to be open to new experiences and welcome their mistakes. A teacher's attitude toward his own continual formation—and thus his own openness to new ideas—is fundamental in creating the space he needs to stay up to date with processes. School settings that motivate teachers to try new things, confess their errors, and then rectify them are true learning institutions. Intellectual humility is a desired quality in academic practice, and being able to accept error and improve oneself is a key trait of high-quality teachers.

Best Classroom Practice 38. Motivate
Why do some kids stay on the fringe and show no motivation for classroom activities? School isn't for everyone, apparently, or at least our schools haven't found a recipe for assuring all

kids get what they need to stay motivated. Dan Willingham, author of *Why Don't Students Like School?* (2010), looks at this question from a cognitive scientist's angle and makes the case that the way school is structured, and the way teachers teach, is not compatible with how the brain wants to learn.

A few years back there was a study undertaken in Europe to understand why students weren't going into science and technology careers (Eurostat, 2009). What was it about these subjects that kept kids from studying them? The answers were surprising. The students actually showed a high interest in scientific topics. When asked what issues they felt passionate about, many students listed global warming, the disappearance of species due to human encroachment, and alternative energy sources—all scientific topics. However, when they were asked what topics they enjoyed in school, science and math bottomed out as their least favorite. Why? It can be deduced that while science itself was motivating, the way we teach often does not match students' interests. Teachers rushed through textbook definitions of concepts whereas students wanted real life, authentic world impacting drama; a rush of another kind.

Motivation hinges on a few of the key concepts outlined in other Best Classroom Practices, as shown in Hattie's studies. Constructivist activities help sustain focus on learning tasks. No one likes to do things that are too easy or too hard; we seek learning experiences that are just slightly beyond our reach. Classroom interventions that are active, social, collaborative, and authentic lead to better memory and more sustained attention. As noted earlier, intrinsic motivation can have many sources, but dull or uninspiring textbooks are not among them.

Motivation is a tenet of MBE because it influences all learners, but no one in exactly the same way. When students do not exhibit high motivation, they either do not initiate or discontinue learning tasks because they do not perceive a reward for their efforts (Pierce, Cameron, Banko, & So, 2003). People spend time and energy doing things they think are important. When students think something is worth learning, they invest time in the process, and the more time they spend, the more likely they are to actually learn the new competency. People may assign importance to new learning based on value judgments, while others work for more immediate rewards (doing *X* gets me *Y*). For example, my daughter was highly motivated to learn to drive, as she believed it would lead to more independence and give her more prestige with her peers. She didn't enjoy the driving teacher or the driver's ed classes, but she was thoroughly determined to learn because she believed the payoff was well worth the investment.

The individual nature of motivation makes it hard to nail down exactly what should happen in a classroom (Walker & Plomin, 2005). However, certain global practices seem apparent in all highly motivated classes. Anderman, Andrzejewski, and Allen (2011) tried to determine how teachers can increase student motivation and learning in their classrooms and "suggested a model that consists of three core themes: supporting understanding, building and maintaining rapport, and managing the classroom" (p. 969). That is, part of a student's motivation comes from simple best practice planning, teaching, and managing. Earlier studies note that classes that provide regular, formative feedback and espouse mastery learning goals rather than simply "teaching to the test" produce more highly motivated students (Ames, 1992; Ames & Archer, 1988). None of these ideas should come as a surprise as they commonly occur in great classrooms and are all part of teacher training programs. This means that just by doing our job well (the basics of teaching), we can enhance motivation.

Best Classroom Practice 39. Never Work Harder Than Your Students
Robyn Jackson considers several core principles of teaching in her book *Never Work Harder Than Your Students* (2009). The brain is a complex organ and full of surprises. For example, the law of minimal effort applies to almost everything we do. That is, **human beings usually choose to do the minimum to get by** (Kingsley, 1949). This is efficient and logical: Extra effort can be detrimental to one's existence, and energy should be saved for when we really need it. Just as neuroconnections are lost when they go unused—see the Hebbian synapse (Hebb, 1949), "use it or lose it"—due to the brain's efficiency, some students save up their energy for use on "more important" things.

When my son was three, he attended the German School of Geneva. His classmates were primarily German, but there were a handful of native French speakers, one English-Spanish speaker (my son), and a Hungarian. After circle time in the morning, the teacher would gently ask the students to get up and grab the materials needed for the next activity. All of the German-speaking students would jump up and dutifully get their materials. Then she would look kindly at the French students and repeat the instructions in French. The French students would jump up and grab their materials. Then she would look at Gabriel and repeat the instruction in English, and he would go get his materials. The little Hungarian girl would look back and forth anxiously between her classmates and her teacher, but because the teacher knew no Hungarian, she would imitate her classmates by jumping up and looking for her materials. At the end of three months I asked the teacher how the students were coming along, especially in language skills. She brightly responded that this was a wonderful group and that they were all very cooperative and learning so much.

"And the nonnative speakers?" I asked.

"Well, they are all learning German pretty quickly, but the Hungarian girl is just amazing; she's learned nearly double the vocabulary of the other nonnative speakers and is actually speaking!"

"Hmm, I wonder why that could be?" I asked her.

The teacher's brow furrowed in reflection, and then suddenly her face lit up. She understood at that moment that because she always repeated the instructions in each child's native language, they didn't learn as quickly because the brain is so efficient. "Why stretch myself?" the children were probably telling themselves. "If I wait just a few minutes and put on my lost-puppy-dog face, the teacher will say it in my language": the law of minimal effort.

In the classroom setting, many students don't exert more effort because their energy is better spent doing other things. It takes energy to learn, and students parcel it out sparsely in order to survive. An observer might say that these students aren't motivated, but they are actually conserving their energy and lying in wait for something that deserves their attention. Thus, instead of being discouraged, teachers should take control of the situation and spiral up the energy. For instance, this might mean refraining from giving students the answers to questions and instead formulate questions that force them to find their own answers. Some students become frustrated when the teacher withholds information in this way. What they fail to recognize in that learning is born of this frustration or cognitive dissonance. This doesn't mean that teachers should exert minimal force, but rather they should create learning moments that push students and their efforts upwards.

Best Classroom Practice 40. Be Passionate!
Imagine a beginning course in education: "Teacher Passion 101." Could you pass this class? If you aren't passionate about what you're doing, you should really look for another career; the **teaching profession can't afford apathy or fear.** However, passion is not a tangible or easily structured concept, which is why it has evaded the core curricula in teacher colleges: "Resorting to obedience to teach passion just isn't going to work" (Godin, 2012, p. 48). We have to find the innate drive within us to execute teaching well.

The passion with which a teacher approaches the profession is more important than all other factors combined; passionate people are the reason teaching works (Hattie, 2009). This is not to say that someone with passion and no skills can a run a classroom, but rather that someone with all of the content knowledge, techniques, methodologies, and activities in the world won't be successful unless he is also passionate. **Without passion, there is no motivation, and without motivation (positive or negative, intrinsic or extrinsic), there is no learning.**

> The key component of passion for the teacher and for the learner appears to be the sheer thrill of being a learner or teacher, the absorption that accompanies the process of teaching and learning, the sensations of being involved in the activity of teaching and learning, and the willingness to be involved in deliberate practice to attain understanding. (Hattie, 2012, p.16)

People who love what they are doing are contagious and inspirational. We know that people can't help but take their cues from others in terms of emotions (Radel, Sarrazin, Legrain, & Wild, 2010). The brain's mirror neuron system allows us to read others and to a certain extent, their intentions, which is how society functions; without empathy for others we would live in a chaotic, self-centered world, and this is not the brain's natural state. When a teacher enters the room alive with a passion for his work, the students feel this energy and are infected by it, and they, too, become lovers of the knowledge being shared. A teacher who enters the room and announces his own boredom with the subject at hand also transmits a powerful message: There is no passion here; go back to sleep.

If we accept that passion is a key ingredient in teaching, we then have to ask ourselves, can passion be taught? We all know that "naturals" are people who seem to instinctively know what to do in a variety of situations. A natural teacher is expected to transmit his passion without guidance, but what about the not-so-natural teacher who has recently been recruited? Can she learn to be passionate? I suppose this can be likened to learning to love someone after an arranged marriage. Impossible, no. Difficult, yes. **Great teachers are passionate, and instinctually so; others can try to cultivate a passion for their work, but not all do so successfully.** Parker J. Palmer's book *The Courage to Teach* (2007) has inspired thousands to enter the profession (and probably also discouraged hundreds from doing so). Parker also suggests that teachers be guided by "wisdom of the heart" as opposed to textbook treatments. Internal wisdom and passion don't seem necessarily aligned with Mind, Brain, and Education science until we link these two ideas to their role in motivation, which has been established in evidence-based settings (Karsdrop, Hasenbring, & Lorenz, 2012; Lang & Davis, 2006; Lang, Bradley, & Cuthbert, 1998; Pierce et al., 2003; Radel et al., 2010; Richard, Castro, DiFelice-antonio, Robinson, & Berridge, 2012; Schunk & Zimmerman, 1994). We know that passion goes a long way in inspiring new learners, but part of being passionate is authenticity: You can't fake it.

In *Stop Stealing Dreams* (2012), author Seth Godin asks, "What is school for?" only to find that the current answer crushes creativity and that education is at the mercy of high-stakes testing (something few are passionate about!). Passion is what keeps a great teacher coming back year after year, even if he is discouraged because he hasn't met with all the success he had hoped for. The key to good schooling is in finding out "how to create a workplace culture that attracts the most talented teachers, fosters a culture of ownership, freedom and accountability, and then relentlessly transfers this passion to their students," (Godin, 2012, p. 8). The key to turning schools around and helping them react to the needs of the 21st century is to reduce fear and enflame passion: "Our chaotic world is open to the work of passionate individuals, intent on carving their own paths" (Godin, 2012, p. 35).

Best Classroom Practice 41. Design Engaging Classrooms
As classes let out in today's schools, students are often heard ruminating about the value of what they just supposedly learned: "When will I ever use *that* in real life?" When students don't see how the new knowledge or skill will benefit them in the real world, they won't spend time on it and they are more likely to create distractions (Nelson, Lynn, & Glenn, 1999).

As mentioned under Best Classroom Practice 31 on the 5Es, the first stage in a classroom activity can be "engagement," or a "hook" that draws students to the subject matter, perhaps by way of surprise or awe. This can happen by showing a map of the world in which the lingua franca is German and asking what the world look like today had Hitler won World War II asking what would the world look like without arches or how CSI (crime scene investigator) techniques work in real life. **An engaged classroom is like a suspense film, keeping students hooked throughout the entire class period.**

One of the greatest challenges in education today relates to the fact that times are changing; skills sets identified as worthy of 21st-century curricula are different from those we have traditionally taught. Curricula that are multidisciplinary and based on real-life problems yield not only greater learner interest but also more applicable life skills for the world we live in. The reasons for this may seem obvious, but Posner (2011) has shown that the anatomy, circuitry, development, and genetics of the brain make way for three attentional systems: alertness, orienting to sensory events, and voluntary control of thoughts, or executive functions. All three attentional networks are busy when a class is engaging; all three are deactivated when the brain is bored (Callejas, Lupianez, & Tuleda, 2004). **Your brain pays attention to different things at different times for different reasons.** Your brain is drawn to elements that help sustain your focus. When the situation is not engaging, sustained focus is dropped.

However, what's worth learning changes based on the perceptions of the individual as well as on her belief systems, which are far more complex than curriculum plans or lists of standards. That is, students decide on different priorities for learning based on their own value system, which they compare to what's occurring in class. **The difference between what's happening in class and what's important in real life is sometimes a formula for "boredom."**

Different students care about different topics for different reasons. For example, some students may have been exposed to an example of how waste produced in society is reaching a breaking point and decide that overconsumption is the priority for new learning. Others may have heard how humanity won't survive unless we treat one another with more respect and therefore believe that the main role of schooling should be the cultivation of empathy and preparation for carrying out charitable acts. Another student may have seen a report on the news indicating that child slavery is still prominent in some parts of the world and decide that her personal mission in life is to help eradicate this injustice. Yet another may have received a Tweet about the plight of whales or sharks and decide to give his energy to this important topic. These intriguing problems make typical school subjects look mundane in comparison. Almost no one will have received instant messaging about the importance of the quadratic formula or how to memorize the periodic table. How can a teacher compete with the real-life interests of the student?

If you can't beat them, join them. **Teachers need to be more aware of ways that their school subjects can be integrated with (not replace) the students' natural interests.** There are some interests that we all share, although the variety and spectrum of our preferences sometimes makes us forget they are similar. For example, we all have heroes. We all value freedom. We all value respect. We all like vacations, and we all have favorite foods, favorite music, and favorite entertainment. By using universals, teachers can celebrate great individual variances but also approach topics in an engaging way for students.

For example, a physics teacher can ask which superhero is the best. *Superman? Batman? Flash? Iron Man? Spiderman? Cat Woman? Wonder Woman?* Once students have shouted out their favorite, he can ask students to calculate just how their superpowers can be real. How can Superman fly? At what speed is Flash running so that he goes around the world in a few frames of the comic book? How far does Wonder Woman's whip reach?

Or, instead of heroes, we can think of vacations. Planning a vacation involves much more math than one would imagine. Here's our budget; where can we go? What is the cost of gas, hotels, airfare? What if the goal is to go to as many places as possible? Or as far away as possible? Or to experience as much gastronomical variety as possible?

Or how about musical tastes? How many kinds of music are there? Will we ever run out of new genres of music? For thousands of years good teachers have used what students already know and like to teach. We need to adapt this wisdom to our times.

We all know how easy it is to get the self-motivated kids going (they would survive without us and often learn in spite of us). The true test of teaching comes when marginalized kids need to be cajoled into class discussion or pushed into class projects. A great teacher knows how to maintain a high level of engagement by the majority of the class, across most topics, most of the time. Engagement is closely related to but distinct from motivation, and is heavily dependent on attention. **People who are highly engaged in their own learning learn best.** The structure of the memory and attention systems of the brain means that "time flies when you're having fun." To be engaged is to be "in the zone," "mindful," and clearly focused on a goal (see Csikszentmihalyi, 1997, for more on "flow"). When a student is engaged in learning, her entire being is in sync with the experience.

In *The Highly Engaged Classroom* (2010), Marzano and colleagues recommend a thoughtfully planned classroom with space to adjust for individual needs through tactics like "initiating friendly controversy," "presenting unusual information," "connecting to students' lives and ambitions," and using "effective pacing" to precisely stimulate memory and attention mechanisms. While many great teachers already implement these strategies by instinct, Marzano, Pickering, and Hefelbower (2010) recommendations make engagement "teachable" for those of us who haven't managed to engage all of our learners.

Best Classroom Practice 42. Manage

Great teachers know that, even if you have oodles of content knowledge and a firm handle on teaching methodologies, you won't succeed if you have poor class management skills. Here we take a broad view and consider a good classroom manager to be someone who expertly manages the socioemotional ambience of the group and encourages student experimentation and even error. For instance, **effective classroom management often entails stifling negative disturbances.** According to Hattie (2009), a teacher's ability to perceive and take action on potential problems has a significant impact on learning for the entire group. A single student can have a detrimental effect on the class's learning as a whole, so being able to contain negative behavior is a must.

Teachers face two broad categories of problems in managing their classrooms: Logistical problems (the total number of students or the different levels of ability in a single classroom), and discipline problems or distractions (class clowns, bullies, laziness, etc.).

Logistical Problems. Logistical problems primarily have to do with class size. My sister is a substitute teacher in California and tells me she is often faced with classes of 40 or more students. However, Hattie has shown that class size has less impact on overall student learning than a great many other factors; the issue is not really the total number of students in the classroom, nor their different needs, but rather the skill with which the teacher manages the group. **Class size has less of an impact on student learning than effective management of behavior.**

What do expert teachers do to manage large classes? They apply the oldest war tactic in history: Divide and conquer. One way to "divide" is to move the furniture in your classroom around until you've structured seating for smaller groups, which are easier to handle. You can create thematic divisions by setting up "corners" or "centers"; this can be as simple as putting a few pillows in a corner and calling it the "Reading Corner." Another popular structure is "islands," or groups of three to six individual desks or tables joined together. With older students, the use of circles or semicircles helps create a more unified atmosphere without the obvious physical divisions.

Why is it so important to divide in this way? The answer is simple: Faces.

MBE science provides us a simple yet very human bit of information: **When we can see one another's faces, we're more likely to respond to someone else's comments** (Winston, Strange, O'Doherty, & Dolan, 2005). While lecture-style formats, with students in rows, are good at directing attention to the professor, circles or divisions in which people can see one another are helpful in stimulating student exchange and social engagement. When this energy is well focused, extended student learning occurs.

This might seem counterintuitive in unruly classes: Why would you want to encourage more talking between students if you're trying to better "manage" the class? A teacher might think that when students are in rows, it's easier to pinpoint "troublemakers," but such an arrangement treats the group as a mass. A teacher who looks at "the mass" and asks, "Any questions?" is unlikely to get an affirmative answer. However, a teacher who circulates among islands or small groups of students will probably be bombarded with queries. Usually, the more questions asked, the higher the level of discussion, and we would do well to remember that **good classroom management doesn't result in silence; it results in learning.**

Another way to manage large classes, especially those that include students with many different learning needs, is through cooperative teaching. Cooperative teaching involves two or more teachers with different skills sets who coordinate their efforts in the classroom to manage heterogeneous groups (Bauwens & Hourcade, 1995). Cooperative teaching can take a variety of forms. For example, teachers can experiment with alternate leadership, in which one teacher presents the main information and the other monitors and helps; the teachers then change roles. Another structure involves parallel teaching, in which the teachers plan the class together and then divide the students into two heterogeneous groups according to skill level. The class subject is then taught using the same materials, but with different techniques. Finally, team teaching is the classic cooperative structure in which both teachers instruct the class simultaneously. They both run activities for the large group and intervene whenever there's a need. Many administrators think that cooperative teaching is a waste of resources, since two teachers instruct a single group, but this has been disproven (Morocco & Mata, 2002). When "co-teaching" and "co-teacher" are redefined, the structure becomes more appealing. Two classes can be taught together, for example, and "co-teachers" might be a teacher and an assistant, a teacher and a student, or a teacher and a parent.

There are a variety of classroom management problems that can be handled by changing the types of activities that normally constitute course design. These activities usually focus on harnessing the energies of small groups of students to meet collaborative learning goals and include peer teaching, peer correction of homework, small-group discussion, collaborative writing of a script, debate, group mind maps, shared responses to essential questions, research projects (in jigsaw fashion) (Aronson, 1978), and "one-minute paper" discussions (Angelo, 1991).

Distractions. The second category of classroom management problems relates to distractions. "Distracters" are students whose actions call attention away from planned activities and learning goals and to themselves.

It's important to remember that *discipline* **comes from the Latin word for "instruct."** Although we haven't used this word correctly for decades, to discipline does not mean to punish, but rather to teach. Discipline is a positive process that guides students toward better self-control and leads to a better learning situation for all not just the individual, but the entire group (Brass & Haggard, 2007; Rachlin, 2004). Discipline, like all types of learning, is based on changes in the brain (Figner et al., 2010; Hare, Camerer, & Rangel, 2009).

To better understand discipline, we need to first reflect on our own particular triggers as teachers. What *actions* do we punish as teachers? For many teachers, triggers are things like tardiness or absences, forgotten homework, attention seeking, plagiarism and lying, displays of lack of respect (students who bother others, use bad words, challenge the teacher's directions, etc.), and low achievement. To better deal with these distracters, we need to first understand the true motivation behind the behavior. Are students truly absent or do they forget homework for reasons other than the obvious? We also need to understand why we as teachers punish, understand the options that exist to avoid public humiliation in class, and then rethink our own strategies about how to react by anticipating difficult situations.

Why do students misbehave? Unfortunately, MBE and basic psychology tell us that **negative attention is better than none at all** (Maag, 2001). Sometimes a misbehaving child is a discouraged individual, according to Nelson, Lynn, and Glenn (1999). Students may misbehave in order to get attention from peers. When students cause problems in class, often we react quickly, and punish students without thinking. Punishment (physical or verbal) is the easiest reaction to undesirable behavior. It is motivated by emotion and doesn't require much thought (LeDoux, 1998). It normally makes us feel better, temporarily—after which there is a horrible feeling of guilt. And although it teaches the student to take steps to avoid punishment, it doesn't necessarily get her to change her behavior (Brophy, 2010).

MBE teachers need to consider the true motivations behind students' perceived misbehavior. The class clown, the anti-leader, and the whiny, lazy student may appear different in the way they act, but they often have the similar goal of getting our individual attention in ways they don't normally receive it in school (Nelson et al., 1999). In many cases, students are just looking for a way to shine in class and get recognition from their peers and authority figures. Engaging activities and help focusing on positive learning goals can channel energy in the right direction and reduce classroom disturbances ("busy hands stay out of trouble").

Best Classroom Practice 43. Use Thinking Routines
Most teachers want to stimulate better thinking in their students and see it as their job to inculcate more sophisticated processes than simple, direct instruction. There are a number of ways to do this, and one of them is by habituating students to short classroom patterns

that hone in on ways of thinking to improve understanding. Ritchhart, Church and Morrison (2011) propose 21 "thinking routines" that support understanding. These quick and easily applied classroom tools improve thinking in class settings, but they have not yet reached all teachers. A sampling of these excellent ideas are described here, and readers are encouraged to read Ritchhart and colleagues' book *Making Thinking Visible* (2011) for greater detail. It is important to note that all of the structures below operate well in group settings; that is, they benefit from group discovery and peer observations and are supported by MBE principle (number 15) that the brain is a social organ. While each of the routines suggested by Ritchhart and colleagues (2011) is a powerful tool in and of itself, an even better culture of thinking can be created by using the routines together (Ritchhart, 2006). When teachers incorporate these types of thinking processes in their classes, kids learn to habituate them over the course of their lives.

Interpretation and Articulation

Ritchhart and colleagues' thinking routines serve different objectives. For example, See-Think-Wonder is meant to emphasize description, interpretation, and inference of the world around us as well as articulation of events, phenomena, schema, and concepts. This thinking routine emphasizes the idea that observation is fundamental to thinking and interpreting. The ability of a student to pay attention to detail and the subtleties of a visual image allows her to posit why the author of the piece chose to interpret his image in the way he did. In studying literature, students are often asked to identify salient messages, and the same goes for visual imagery as well: What are the really important details in this drawing (photo, painting, advertisement)? (See Ritchhart et al., 2011, pp. 55–63 for a full explanation of this routine.)

Guiding Inquiry

Patterns of thinking developed through the Think-Puzzle-Explore routine get students involved in activating prior knowledge, wondering, and planning in order to help them develop a hypothesis-generating mentality. According to Doughtery, Thomas, and Lange (2010), helping students learn to conjecture, judge probability, and test hypotheses is key to self-motivation in learning. This routine provides for inquiry in which a student is asked to state not what she knows, but rather what she *thinks* she knows about a topic as the starting point. Students observe a phenomenon (a floating piece of wood, a painting by DaVinci, a math problem) and are asked, "What do you think you know about this?" And then, in a reduced version of Socratic reasoning, they are asked, "What puzzles you about this?" Exploration is then undertaken to investigate unknowns. (See Ritchhart et al., 2011, pp. 71–77 for a full explanation of this routine.)

Decision-Making

Other thinking routines is to help students develop patterns of a variety of processes that can be used to reach decisions.

Compass Points is a tool that solicits the group's ideas and reactions to a proposal, plan, or possible decision. The north, south, east, and west directions on a compass serve as a mnemonic for remembering steps to take when making a decision: E = excitements; W = worries; N = needs; and S = stance, steps, or suggestions. The idea is that students view the same decision from a variety of decision-making angles before embarking on them. Some people see change as exciting, while others find it worrisome. This thinking pattern forces students to develop the habit of mind of evaluating circumstances in a more balanced manner. The teacher labels four pieces of butcher paper with each of the compass points, places them in different corners of the room, and asks students to contribute to each page. The group then reviews each compass point and considers everyone's comments in depth. Finally, a group consensus is sought and "suggestions for moving forward" are developed. Different types of groups can do this exercise (e.g., parents and students or teachers and administrators), and their answers can be compared. (See Ritchhart et al., 2011, pp. 93–100 for a full explanation of this routine.)

Synthesizing and Summarizing

Other tools in this series focus on the learner's ability to synthesize information and find the most salient aspects of a topic. Headlines is a routine that asks students to identify the most important aspects of something they've read or viewed and then offer either concise renditions or metaphors to help others understand the same idea.

Headlines. At the end of a learning process, students are asked to synthesize their perceptions of what went on in a short, snappy summary, much like a headline. This exercise serves to determine if the whole class is on the same page as well as to force synthesis and clarification of ideas. Students are then asked to explain their headline further, and these clarifications are incorporated. (See Ritchhart et al., 2011, pp. 111–118 for a full explanation of this routine.)

Understanding One's Own Understanding

Yet other tools focus on helping the learner better understand her own biases and perceptions. ***Generate-Sort-Connect-Elaborate in Concept Maps*** encourages an "uncoverage" process and the organization of prior knowledge to identify connections with old and new, and highlights the thinking steps involved in making an effective concept map. Most teachers understand conceptual mapping, but the stages of thinking involved might not be as clear. When students are asked to simply brainstorm ideas and list concepts, they are using a different kind of thinking than when they are asked to categorize, unite, or order like ideas (sorting). This is also different from being able to link like concepts and connect ideas, which in turn is different from elaborating after reflection and adding on more concepts. Concept mapping helps students gain insight into their own mental schemata, as in how they order their conceptual world. Once concept maps are developed and shared, students can be encouraged to try to join their maps with those of others, and in doing so, come to the realization that the way they order their world is different from how others do so. (See Ritchhart et al., 2011, pp. 125–131 for a full explanation of this routine.)

Metacognition

Some of the classroom pattern structures presented by Ritchhart and colleagues go to the heart of thinking about thinking and developing reflective skills. For example, "I Used to Think . . . Now I Think . . . " teaches students intellectual humility.

This habituated thinking practice can be used to help learners reflect on how their thinking has shifted and changed over time. This routine is used at the end of a class session to allow students time to reflect and help them clarify for themselves the evolution of their own thoughts on the unit. By sharing individually or in small groups what they *used* to think, and what they *now* think, students document their own progress in building on new concepts to broaden their knowledge base. (See Ritchhart et al., 2011, pp. 154–161 for a full explanation of this routine.)

Empathy

Ritchhart and colleagues also suggest thinking routines that encourage intellectual empathy, or the ability to understand others' viewpoints. While the previously mentioned tools are internally focused and require personal reflection, structures in this group are designed to aid the slightly more developed student in adopting the perspectives of others.

Step Inside is useful in helping students gain historical perspective, it can also be used in any context where the development of empathy is treasured. This thinking tool might be based off of a well-known community problem (crime in a neighborhood, the controversial construction of a new mall in a green space, trash collection schedules) or an academic or global challenge (climate change, population explosions, space or ocean exploration), which helps students hone in on issues they are passionate about and teaches them problem solving skills. Students are asked to adopt the perspective of a relevant character and ask themselves what they observe or notice that might be different from what someone else can see. What does this person care about? What does this person wonder about? Students may also be asked to answer these questions from the perspective of something that is typically considered inanimate—the rainforest, for example, or a stoplight, or even an iPod as it shuffles music. (See Ritchhart et al., 2011, pp. 178–184 for a full explanation of this routine.)

Limiting One's Own Presumptions

Society is, unfortunately, full of examples in which decisions are made for the wrong reason or based on incorrect logic. There are often promises of X (e.g., happiness, well-being) through Y (e.g., opening a bank account for your kid or joining a gym), which are not always fulfilled. In this final category of thinking routines, Ritchhart, Morrison, and Church encourage deeper reflection about the roots of these claims through thinking tools that help develop better decision-making skills.

Claim-Support-Question is very apropos when viewing the false claims that riddle the American commercial landscape, the claim-support-question routine is designed to help students develop the habit of identifying the promises being offered by advertisements and other communications. In this setting, students are asked to identify support or evidence for a given claim. From there, they can raise questions about the claim and explain why they might doubt it. (There are few claims that have no truth behind them, meaning the real work is in judging the quality of the evidence, not the quantity.) Students usually find that certain patterns emerge based on the characteristics of the claims, and this allows them to become more critical consumers of information. This routine can and should be extended beyond commercial claims and be applied to the situations of everyday life. There are hundreds of scientific claims, math theories, and other presumptions that have yet to be proven; by bringing these to the forefront of student awareness, teachers allow students to develop better insights about motivators and perspectives and to judge claims in a more refined way based on evidence. (See Ritchhart et al., 2011, pp. 191–198 for a full explanation of this routine.)

Best Classroom Practice 44: Keep Abreast of Technology and Flip the Classroom
There are many examples of how technology is being used to make formal educational opportunities more attractive as well as more effective for students. The International Mind, Brain,

and Education Society called for papers in 2012 to consider "what can be learned from neuro-science research to enhance science, technology, engineering, and mathematics (STEM) education" and explore "(1) uses of new technologies to help people teach and learn more effectively, (2) uses of individual laptops to help children learn, (3) creation of new tools for learning and assessment, and (4) techniques that image brain structure and activity" (Battro & Fischer, 2012, pp. 49–50) to explore some of these challenges.

There is also some evidence that technology changes the brain (Howard-Jones, Ott, van Leeuwen, & de Smedt, 2011), as do all experiences, but little direct evidence of how this occurs in a classroom (for some promising areas of research, see Laffey, Schmidt, & Galyen, 2013; Long, 2013; Low, Jin, & Sweller, 2011; Schrader & Bastiaens, 2012; Torrente, Del Blanco, Marchiori, Moreno-Ger, & Fernández-Manjón, 2010). This means that brains today have possibly been rewired in a distinct way from brains of previous generations due to the new and ever-changing array of technologies found in society but we are unsure of all the positive and negative implications of this. Technology changes the brain not only for children, but also for adults, and the results range from neutral to generally positive. A study by Patricia Tun and Margie Lachman (2010) "sought to understand the association between computer use and cognition across adulthood" and found that adults between the ages of 32 and 84 (n=2,671) "who used the computer frequently scored significantly higher" on cognitive tests.

While it is logical to presume that rapid texting, video games, and filming techniques with brisk movement that integrate ever-rapid changes of scenes demand that attention networks reprioritize routes for processing, the precise way this happens is still unknown. The information that does exist indicates that the brain changes with experience, and that kids these days spend a good deal of time on computers and gaming, at least some of which can be leveraged for better teaching (for examples see Annetta & Minogue, 2011; Cheng & Annetta, 2012; Gratch & Kelly, 2009). The problem with judging whether or not "technology" is good or bad is similar to trying to judge whether or not "books" or "television" are bad; it depends on the content. Kurt Squire considers how appropriate gaming can serve highly academic purposes and enhance cognition (2011) indicating the most positive of these results.

Brains bathed in technology are wired distinctly from those with no contact with technology. Some studies show that the brain's need for novelty is better satisfied with these quick changes, more so than that achieved by a static teacher who stands at the front of the room and lectures in a monotone voice (Barceló, Periañez & Knight, 2002; Huang, Belliveau, Tengshe, & Ahveninen, 2012). Howard-Jones, Ott, van Leeuwen, and De Smedt (2011) have been researching a variety of technologically based interventions, including computer-mediated communication and the use of computer games in classroom settings, as well as how to enhance creativity by taking advantage of what we know about the brain and learning and combining it with technology. Specific learning interventions that unify efforts from neuroscience, psychology, and education include Fast ForWord (Arendal & Mann, 2000), the Number Race (Wilson, Revkin, Cohen, Cohen, & Dehaene, 2006), and RAVE-O (SEDL, 2009; Wolf, Miller, & Donnelly, 2000), which focus on basic reading and math interventions.

There are myriad approaches that link technology and learning by trying to document neural networks in the brain. What parts of the brain join forces when a person pays attention, does math, or writes a sonnet? These studies investigate how technology has influenced the "standard" networks in the brain, which are now adapting to a high-tech, globalized era. There has been substantial evidence for over a decade that the brain via the power of the mind can control technology—as when a person can move a cursor on a screen just by thinking it so—but how does technology change the brain? Gary Small has spent several years documenting how activities like Google searches change the brain and actually stimulate more connections between regions (Small, Moody, Siddhartha, & Bookheimer, 2009). Other researchers, such as Abramson and colleagues (2009), have found that everyday activities using electronic devices, such as texting on a cell phone, influence both the speed and accuracy with which one reacts to cognitive tasks. "Overall, mobile phone use [is] associated with faster and less accurate responding to higher level cognitive tasks" (p. 678). It is yet unknown, however, what the long-term consequences of this are for our typical classroom settings

It is clear that humans process language differently in the brain depending on whether or not is it spoken, read on a screen or in a book, for example: "By far the most common experimental finding is that silent reading from screen is significantly slower than reading from paper" (Dillion, 1992, p. 1300). Reading is also distinct depending on whether it is conducted out loud or silently and by looking at someone when hearing speech, or only hearing their voice (Hall, Fussell, & Summerfield , 2005), but it has not been determined if videos have the same effects on the brain as live speech. The way advances in technology have changed communication has made many wonder whether the quality of human interactions is declining, but the general outlook appears to be quite positive. At the American Educational Research Association meeting in 2012, there was a lot of talk about "expanding literacies" (see Daley, 2003; Simon, 2007) based on early childhood exposure to the media. It was found that most uses of interactive technology in the classroom enhanced student ability in subjects ranging from social studies to math to language acquisition, but that not all attempts at technology integration were successful. That is, what was done right had positive impacts in the classroom.

A word of caution is in order: The brain adapts to what it does most. Thus, if an individual plays high-speed video games that continually demand quick but simple responses, it will not be as adept at managing other behaviors that require longer periods of concentration or more precise responses. I have maintained a rule in my home since my children were small. For every hour on any screen (TV, computer, video game), they give back an hour of reading. Since reading requires sustained attention, the goal is to balance out the demands of quick changes in focus required by screen action.

Flip the Classroom. One example of technology use that takes advantage of what we know about the brain and learning is the flipped classroom. To use this methodology, a teacher must ask himself one question: What is the best use of my face-to-face time with my students? And then, with that in mind, he "flips" most everything else. What would normally happen in a classroom (teaching the subject) is done at home by watching videos and reflecting on content through exercises, and what usually takes place at home (reviewing what you don't know) is done in the classroom along with other inquiry-based learning activities with the teacher. Flipped teaching uses both face-to-face and technology-based support (mainly videos) to review core course content, allowing the teacher to spend more time attending to individual students' learning needs rather than teaching a general lesson with hopes of reaching all, but in reality, missing (too) many.

When designed correctly, the flipped classroom is:

> A means to INCREASE interaction and personalized contact time between students and teachers; an environment where students take responsibility for their own learning; a classroom where the teacher is not the "sage on the stage," but [rather] the "guide on the side"; a blending of direct instruction with constructivist learning; a classroom where students who are absent due to illness or extra-curricular activities such as athletics or field-trips, don't get left behind; a class where content is permanently archived for review or remediation; a class where all students are engaged in their learning; a place where all students can get a personalized education. (Bergmann, Ovemyer, & Willie, 2011)

The attractiveness of new technologies makes at-home learning experiences more engaging for many students. There are literally thousands of sources of technology-supported material available on the Internet, especially in video format. Some of the better known sources include Khan Academy and MOOCs (massive open online courses), which provide very high quality conceptual videos about core concepts in education (Tomaszewski, 2012). Following Stanford University's wild success in offering open online courses (over 100,000 students registered for some), other universities began offering their classes as well through Coursera: University of Pennsylvania, Princeton University, the University of Michigan. This was followed by MIT's launch of MITx, and Harvard followed with edX. They were soon joined by UC Berkeley, the University of Texas system, Wellesley College, and Georgetown University. The first MOOCs for high school were started in 2012, and the first Spanish MOOCs began in 2012 as well. Though there are criticisms and many as-of-yet unanswered queries about the role of MOOCs in formal education (Norton, 2013; Schwartz, 2013), the strong pedagogical underpinnings behind these technological interactions is sound (see Williams, 2013).

The concept of the flipped classroom has taken off over the past few years, thanks to the work of dedicated, award-winning teachers. Some identify Eric Mazur of Harvard University's Physics Department as one of the first to use computer-aided instruction in the 1990s to allow more time for "coaching" as opposed to "lecturing" in class. His 1991 article "Can We Teach Computers to Teach" explored the possibility of using support material for core concepts to free up time in class for student-centered questions and to maintain higher levels of attention. Jonathan Bergmann and Aaron Sams, both recipients of the Presidential Award for Excellence in Math and Science Teaching, made the concept popular with their book *Flip Your Classroom: Reach Every Student in Every Class Every Day* (2012), and Salman Khan's suggested paradigm shift in teaching (2012) has garnered thousands of new converts each year.

In 2013, Jerry Ovemyer created the Flipped Learning Network for devoted teachers to share their experiences and videos with one another; over 10,000 members joined in its first week of operation. During the first flipped class conference in Woodland Park, Colorado, in 2011, all of the aforementioned flipped classroom backers strongly emphasized that contrary to some critics' beliefs, flipped classrooms are highly structured (students do not work without structure nor at their own pace), students do a great deal of group work (they do not work in isolation), and in-class, face-to-face contact is fundamental (students don't spend the entire class staring at computer screens; flipped classrooms are not just online videos).

The International Society for Technology and Education heartily backs the flipped classroom concept and sees it as one way of equalizing the playing field (Bergmann & Sams, 2012). According to one study, when flipped learning was implemented, "teachers reported benefits for all students, and in particular AP and Special Needs students"; 67% of students had improved test scores; and 80% of students had improved attitudes about learning. This means that technology can be used to create more personalized lesson plans for students (Dede & Richards, 2012), if and when they are well designed.

It is curious to analyze the success of the flipped classroom thinking like a Mind, Brain, and Education scientist. The flipped classroom works because it takes into account the fact that each brain is unique and uniquely organized (MBE principle 1). The structure of the flipped classroom permits teachers to meet each student's needs in an individual way. The flipped classroom also addresses the fact that not all brains are equally good at all things, and therefore different students will need more rehearsal of different concepts; flipping allows students to review as many times as necessary on an individual basis. Similarly, some students will want to hear the information while others will want to reread and underline ideas; flipping provides these options. Brains seek novelty (MBE principle 10), and offering information in a variety of formats aids memory systems. Feedback is vital to learning, and the flipped classroom creates more time and space for student-to-teacher interactions. The format of the flipped classroom also means that there is a great deal more practice of concepts as opposed to simple theoretical exchanges. The flipped classroom reduces anxiety because questioning can occur in non-threatening ways (via email or one-on-one) as opposed to in large classroom settings in front of many peers. The flipped classroom also permits better classroom design and management. On the whole, the flipped classroom takes advantage of technology to improve learning experiences and is compatible with many MBE principles.

The choice to flip or not to flip is often undertaken by individuals, but sometimes administrators adapt policies to do so. We now turn to school policy choices that have existed for many years, but for which there is little evidence supporting their sustained existence in the 21st century.

School Design Choices That Impact Student Learning

We must recognize that the current education system has been set up to prepare students perfectly for a world that no longer exists.
—Jukes, McCain, and Crockett (2012, p. 19)

We now turn to changes in teaching that are within our grasp, but which most of us have not acted upon. If you could make adjustments in your classroom that would have a guaranteed impact on your students' learning, you would apply these changes in an instant, wouldn't you? How about if they meant going against the administration? Would you be willing to fight to change certain policies in your schools if you knew they benefited student learning?

Not only should society's focus turn to *learning* as opposed to *teaching* (Niemi, 2009), but we also have to change a lot of what we've become used to in formal education. According to Jukes, McCain, and Crockett, almost everything in the teaching-learning dyad has changed in the past few decades. "Learning is both virtual and physical" (2012, p. 20) and not confined to the four walls of a classroom. Learning needs to be customized for the learner, not the teacher. Learning is nonlinear and collaborative and will be facilitated by multimedia modalities, so classes can no longer be one dimensional. Most of all they believe learning is focused on the whole mind, not compartmentalized, and based on real-life problem-solving, meaning it is necessarily holistic in nature (see Noddings, 2005, for examples). This means dividing curricula into separate subjects is no longer considered optimal and interdisciplinarity is more highly prized.

Who are the change agents in education? A teacher's reflective practice has a great deal to do with not only personal but also institutional and societal growth (Douglas, 2009; Rogers, 2002). Ian Jukes talks of the "committed sardine" movement in which single individuals can make a change. Jukes suggests that most teachers know what needs to be done to help cultivate deeper thinkers, but many fail to do because no one else is doing it. This academic inertia can be attributed to mindlessness. Mindfulness means "paying attention in a particular way: on purpose, in the present moment, and non-judgmentally" according to Jon Kabat-Zinn (1994, p. 4). Mindlessness means going about things in the same anesthetized manner simply because of precedent. **Ironically, many of the things we do mindlessly in classrooms are precisely the things that, if changed, would make our schools better learning environments.** MBE gives us a new kind of evidence that might give some of us the courage to go against the mindlessness around us. Hopefully, most of the information in this section will strike you as obvious. Deep down, we know what needs to be done.

Best Classroom Practice 45. Pay Attention to Ages and Stages
Modern education is conscious of the "ages versus stages" divide: School systems tend to divide students by age, despite the fact that many are at different stages of development (Chaudhari & Kadam, 2012; Heo & Squires, 2012). Not all students are ready to do the same thing in a given discipline at the same age, and often times students who seem hopelessly lost in a topic early on in the school year end up excelling and even passing up the early starters in the group by the end (Sawyer, Chittleborough, Mittinty, & Lynch, 2013; Welsh, Nix, Blair, Bierman, &

Nelson, 2010). A fundamental truth that many teachers fail to understand is that different kids are ready for different things at different times because of their age, their past experiences, and their biology (Doherty, 2007; Hertzman & Boyce, 2010). There is no exact age at which we should teach algebraic formulas, for instance (some countries teach pre-algebra in 5th or 6th grade, others in 8th, some not until 9th or 10th grade). Age divisions for classroom distribution were introduced when Horace Mann suggested modeling U. S. education on the Prussian system in 1843 (Mondale, 2001). Before that, we used to group everyone together and allow each to advance at his or her own pace, similar to what was done in Socratic classrooms 2500 years ago. What we have lost in this historical development of public education is the ability to respond to individual learning stages.

Teachers are reminded to be mindful of variances that are natural in human development. School readiness can be influenced by a myriad of family and environmental factors (Obradović, Bush, Stamperdahl, Adler, & Boyce, 2010; Whitebread & Bingham, 2011). Some kids have matured enough to be prepared to read at age three, while others need to wait until age six, seven, eight, or beyond to do so fluidly. The maturity of neural circuits is dependent both on the genes one is born with and the past experiences of the individual (Kolb, Forgie, Gibb, Gorny, & Rowntree, 1998). An example of environmental influences can be seen in children from homes in which parents read to them, who read earlier and faster than those who have had not had comparable experiences (Reese, Sparks, & Leyva, 2010).

The practicality and logistics of designing schooling experiences based on stages rather than ages is far more complicated to structure than age-based school design, but is potentially highly beneficial: Student learning can be optimized, motivation is heightened, and learning is accelerated when students can approach topics they are ready for. Montessori-style education, in which multiple age groups are joined by design to maximize individual learning by responding to each student's appropriate learning level, is an example of successful age-stage balancing. Teachers should ask themselves what would happen if teachers had the flexibility to allow students to group by stages of mastery learning of concepts, rather than age groupings.

Best Classroom Practice 46. Improve Nutrition
Approximately 20% of the body's energy is used by the brain (Magistretti & Allaman, 2013) but not all calories are created equal, and not all of them help students' brains learn in the best way possible. Thanks to some specific policy measures to improve nutrition in U.S. schools,

many are beginning to ban empty calories in cafeterias. The body and the brain mutually impact each other (what is eaten by the body influences the brain's ability to learn and the brain in turn makes choices about what to put into the body). MBE science tells us that nutrition impacts learning (Principle 21; Figure 6.2). If school cafeterias were to offer healthier choices, teachers would have better prepared students in their classrooms. Nutrition influences student learning and varies greatly between students. While good eating habits can rarely be regulated by teachers, teachers should be aware of their importance. Though there are many studies that attempt to prescribe "brain food," there is no consensus on the perfect diet (Benton, 2010; Joseph, Cole, Head, & Ingram, 2009; Lieberman, 2003; La Rue et al., 1997; Rosales, Reznick, & Zeisel, 2009). While there is no specific "diet for the brain," a general rule of thumb is that what is good for the heart is good for the brain (Restak, 2009). Dictating the proper eating regime is not part of the school's role; however, educating students and their parents about the importance of good nutrition for good school performance is part of a teacher's role and the collective voice of teachers can possibly change cafeteria offerings.

FIGURE 6.2
You Are What You Eat

© www.CartoonStock.com

Best Classroom Practice 47. Get Students Out of Rows

The study of physical ergonomics looks at how humans use their space to achieve processes; there are some physical designs more conducive to achieving certain tasks than others (International Ergonomics Society, 2013). There is a lot to be said about classroom space and our use of it to maximize learning.

Is there a difference between "front row kids" and "back row kids"? What would happen if our rows changed to semi-circles (Figure 6.3)? If we know that kids in the back perform worse than kids in the front (because we pay less attention to them, not because they are necessarily any less bright), why don't we do something about this? If we know that seating students in a way in which they can see one another stimulates greater exchange (Marx, Fuhrer, & Hartig, 1999; Rosenfield, Lambert, & Black, 1985), why do we insist on rows if the activity calls for discussion? While not all classes call for discussion, those that do are better off seating students in semi-circles than in rows (Wannarka & Ruhl, 2008). Humans thrive on interaction. When a person can see another person, the probability of interaction between those two people increases, and when interaction increases, learning increases.

FIGURE 6.3
Which Classroom Layout Is Better for Discussion?

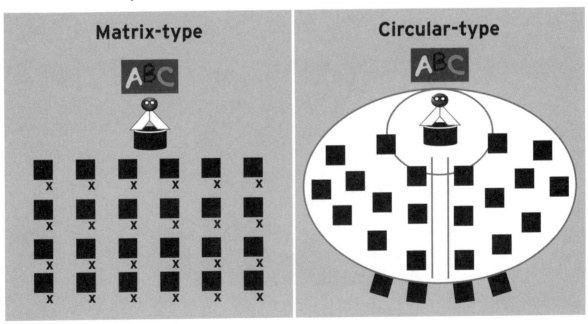

The physical design of a learning space can impact the quality and quantity of exchange between students and the teacher. People respond to comments made by others they can see; that is, students are more likely to react to each other if they can see their faces rather than their backs (Winston, Strange, O'Doherty, & Dolan, 2004). It was once believed that educators, not unlike religious leaders, military heads, and entertainers had to be center stage in order to successfully execute their roles. We now know that learning is a highly social endeavor and that all learners learn from one another, not just from the teacher (Jones, Somerville, & Casey, 2011). Seating students in rows is an unfavorable structure for interaction and dialogue; class structures that permit learners to see one another and encourage dialogue stimulate more cross-germination of ideas and greater exchange. Whereas rows only permit learners to see the teacher, semi-circles, theater-style rooms, or moveable islands allow for greater dialogue between learners (McCroskey & McVetta, 1978; Rosenfield, Lambert, & Black, 1985).

Best Classroom Practice 48. Begin Year-Round Schooling
The current academic calendar was designed for an agriculturally based society in the 1900s, not a service, technology, and knowledge-based society at the opening of the 21st century. Summer vacations were designed to allow children to help with the harvest. Less than 1% of the population in the United States claims farming as an occupation, and only about 2% actually live on farms. And this is a world phenomenon: A smaller and smaller percentage of the world's population engages in agricultural activities. In other words, there is a very low likelihood that our students are needed during summer to help on the farm.

Of all the major influences on learning that were measured by John Hattie in 2012 (n=150), all but five showed some positive learning outcomes, to differing degrees. Everything from sitting in class (maturing) to specific teacher interventions such as frequent feedback helps learners. One of the five negative influences was summer vacation. The gap between learning moments (June to August in the Western hemisphere) detracts from the strengthening of memory pathways and, as many teachers can attest, this results in spending the first month of class reviewing the previous year's work just to establish the foundations to begin new work. A year-round calendar would service learning needs far better than the current school calendar (Cooper, 2004). In a year-round calendar, students have the same amount of school days but they are more evenly distributed across the 12 months with four to six weeks of school then a small break, and four two-to-three-week breaks spread throughout the calendar (see Figure

6.4). Some states in the U.S. have experimented with this format and found it popular with students, parents, teachers, and administrators alike (Cooper, Valentine, Charlton, & Melson, 2003; Palmer & Bemis, 1999).

The greatest benefit of year-round schooling is the improved learning continuity, especially for the most needy: A multitude of studies have established that summer learning loss exists and occurs disproportionately for minorities and disadvantaged students (Alexander, Entwisle, & Linda, 2007; Burkam et al., 2003; California Department of Education, 2007; Cooper, Valentine, Charlton, & Melson, 2003; Downey, Hippel, & Broh, 2004). However, there are also other non-academic benefits, including less teacher and student burn-out. Additionally, there are savings for families (Cooper, 2004; Kneese & Ballinger, 2009) who do not have to pay to keep students entertained during the summer months.

Spacing learning activities in small increments aids learning, but large gaps (as in several months) lead to forgetfulness on account of the brain's tendency to "use it or lose it" (Hebb, 1949). Forgetting that occurs over the summer break retards the learning process. Schools using year-round calendars report positive results: Students don't forget, learning advances more quickly, and fewer students and teachers experience burnout, among other benefits.

FIGURE 6.4
Year-Round Schooling

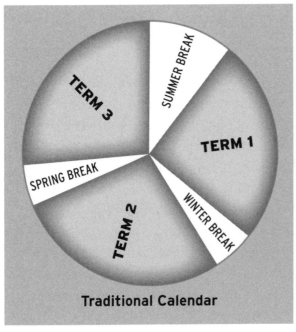 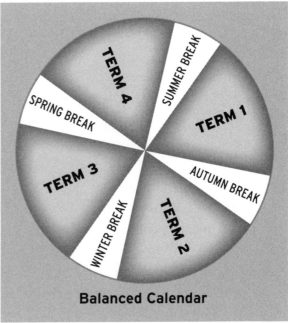

Best Classroom Practice 49. Change The School Day

We know that early school start times may not be conducive to learning. Studies in chronobiology or the study of how different body rhythms are impacted by sleep-wake patterns, show that many students, especially teenagers, experience changes in hormonal balances and prefer later school day starts as they tend to go to bed later (Menna-Barreto & Wey, 2008; Wolfson & Carskadon, 1998). We know that a slightly later school day improves not only learning outcomes, but also student attitudes toward school (for great examples of research in this area, see Azevedo et al., 2008; F.M. Fischer et al., 2008; Golombek & Cardinali, 2008; Menna-Barreto & Wey, 2008; Miller, Shattuck, Matsangas, & Dyche, 2008; Valdez, Reilly, & Waterhouse, 2008). Some authors have gone so far as to suggest that early school starts or testing procedures actually punish late risers. Callan (1995) suggests that there are potential negative effects for many students on the SAT (Scholastic Aptitude [Assessment] Test), and Cardinali (2008) explains how one's biological clock can influence optimal learning times, especially in the teen years when changes in hormonal balance changes sleep patterns. In many countries, school days are arranged for the convenience of parents' workdays but go against what we know about students' brains. Knowing that even a small delay (less than an hour) in school start times can have a positive effect on learning outcomes, why don't we have the courage to defend what is better for the learner?

Best Classroom Practice 50. Stop Using Tests as Indicators of Higher Thinking

We have progressively adapted more extreme testing measures, in many cases presuming that test results are a reflection of teacher efficacy or student learning outcomes. Is this correct? Daniel Koretz at Harvard University notes that "accountability systems based only on test scores are too simple" (2008) and can only offer a limited amount of information to policy makers, a sentiment echoed by many leaders in education (see Baker et al., 2010). The overwhelming faith placed in testing to gauge everything from teacher quality to budgets to whether or not a student advances to the next level of education is daunting. There are at least four main arguments against high stakes testing.

First, in educational research you are told to choose the evaluation tools that can best measure your objectives. If, at the beginning of this book we argued for higher order thinking and the development of life-long lovers of learning as the ultimate objectives of education, are multiple-choice tests the correct assessment tool? The ability to think deeply is actually contrary to many standardized testing practices, which are conducted with little critical thinking (see K. Gallagher, 2010, for a great explanation of *"Why I Will Not Teach to the Test"*). In this book, we tried to argue that *how* to think is often more important than what to think. Teaching to the test, especially a standardized test where the student is required only to choose the best answer among a few prewritten options, may help an administrator measure a student's minimal core knowledge, but it does nothing to promote or measure his success as a deep thinker.

Second, we also showed how an integrated transdisciplinary mentality about the world is needed to resolve problems faced in daily life. Teaching subjects in silos of information with little contact with other disciplines does not help students develop the thinking skills necessary for real life. Worse yet, our testing system treats subjects in separate ways and tests by subject area, forging a divide between integrated reasoning and subject-specific mastery. Only some subject areas lend themselves to multiple-choice formats to measure content knowledge, and only superficially at that. Do we care only about math, reading, writing, and science? What about the arts and stimulating creativity? Real metacognitive and critical thinking skills are "messy"; we have yet to develop sophisticated enough tools to measure the expanses of human ingenuity. Curt Bonk (2011) shows how multiple-choice standardized tests look ridiculous in light of goals for higher-order thinking. David Perkins (1992, 2010a, 2010b) agrees, and he forces teachers to consider how to respond to the wake-up call for change by progressing beyond our fragmented, boxy, subject-area teaching and moving toward "making learning whole." **We haven't managed to match our evaluation systems to the types of skills we hope to cultivate in society.**

Third, many argue that the valuable time used to prepare, take, and grade tests should be used for other activities that promote higher-order thinking and prepare students for lifelong learning. Should we be teaching to the test or teaching life skills? What do we know and believe about the application of "21st-century skills" development, and how do our classes respond to "real learning goals," such as developing habits of mind (Costa & Kallick, 2009; Greenfield, 2008)?

Fourth, we have seen throughout this book that learning is influenced by a myriad of factors, not the least of which is teacher quality. However, equating teacher quality to student test scores is not logical as there is no control for other variables. Children in rural communities may score lower not because their teacher is bad or they themselves are not smart, but rather because they miss more school days, have poor nutritional habits, work more often after school than urban kids, have access to fewer informal learning experiences or technology, and so forth. No one controls for these variables when applying the state exam, so no one will really know what causes one child to do better than another.

High-stakes testing tries to get a lot of information out of a lot of people in a small amount of time with relatively few resources (multiple-choice tests are the cheapest to produce and the easiest to grade). This sounds economically sound, but it ignores the ultimate goal of our educational endeavor: to foster learning. One of the important ideas in MBE is to celebrate, not lament, the complexity of the human brain. Learning is not simple; measuring true learning outcomes cannot be simple either.

An alternative to high stakes testing is to monitor learning outcomes over time and to document interventions with outcomes. This would offer a much more coherent measure of a school's worth. Why isn't it applied more frequently? Because the least costly tool is education is a multiple-choice test. Long-term studies can't compare. But, you get what you pay for.

We argued for several classroom practices that look at learning across its continuum (both ages and stages), through distinct forms (product, process, progress), and especially in formative designs. Formative evaluation, the opposite of summative high stakes testing, focuses on nurturing each individual student along her own path toward success in such a way that she develops her own habits of self-regulation and reflects on how she knows what she knows (and what she needs to know to be a better learner). While high stakes testing may be a reality in current society, it should be accepted for what it really is: a macro look at a micro-level process. State test scores are one of many indicators that policy makers can use to guide their thinking, but if we are true to our teaching profession, we need to be more broadly concerned with each individual's biology, experiences, and community rather than what an imperfect assessment tool says about a group.

Summary

In this chapter we looked at aspects of learning that can greatly influence student mastery of concepts but that are applied less frequently in our classrooms than desired in the best of worlds. First, we focused on a list of 11 habits that teachers can cultivate to improve their teaching. We then considered how to integrate appropriate technologies into the classroom while differentiating both instruction and evaluation and detailed the use of the flipped classroom as a way of doing this. The final section proposed broad-scale changes that schools need to make if they really seek to improve student learning. These practices are not necessarily in the hands of teachers, and are perhaps an unfair gauntlet to lay down here at the end of this book. However, reflection about their influences on learning on the part of teachers is necessary because teachers' collective voices can turn the tide of opinions on many of these policy issues.

We are all part of a system that gives clear indicators for new paths to improvement. We can apply tools from Mind, Brian, and Education science, find ways of applying thorough studies in *Visible Learning* (Hattie, 2009, 2012), and anticipate trends in pedagogy. All of these activities tell us, however, that one of the reasons our profession has not been successful at reaching its goals is perhaps not because teachers in the classroom are not fulfilling their end of the bargain, but rather because some of society's expectations about the role of schools are not in sync with what we know about how the brain learns best. We have to work to improve classrooms at all levels: We have a personal responsibility as teachers to give our students the best education possible, and there are policy decisions that would have a great impact as well. Effort in both arenas is needed to meet the challenges ahead.

Suggested Readings

Student Self-Efficacy

Bresó, E., Schaufeli, W. B., & Salanova, M. (2011). Can a self-efficacy-based intervention decrease burnout, increase engagement, and enhance performance? A quasi-experimental study. *Higher Education, 61,* 339–355.

Chester, M., Buntine, A., Hammond, K., & Atkinson, L. (2011). Podcasting in education: Student attitudes, behavior and self-efficacy. *Educational Technology and Society, 14*(2), 236–247.

Huang, D., Seth, L., Hodson, C., LaTorre, D., Obregon, N., & Rivera, G. (2010). *Preparing students for the 21st century: Exploring the effect of afterschool participation on students' collaboration skills, oral communication skills, and self-efficacy.* Los Angeles, LA: National Center for Research on Evaluation, Standards, and Student Testing.

Schunk, D. H., & Mullen, C. A. (2012). Self-efficacy as an engaged learner. In *Handbook of research on student engagement* (pp. 219–235). Retrieved from http://link.springer.com/chapter/10.1007/978-1-4614-2018-7_10

Walker, N. J. (2003). The cultivation of student self-efficacy in reading and writing. *Reading and Writing Quarterly, 19*(2), 175–187.

Zimmerman, B. J., Bandura, A., & Martinez-Pons, M. (1992). Self-motivation for academic attainment: The role of self efficacy beliefs and personal goal setting. *American Educational Research Journal, 29*(3), 663–676.

Thinking of Learning as Fluid

Gentile, J. R., & Lalley, J. P. (2003). *Standards and mastery learning: Aligning teaching and assessment so all children can learn.* Thousand Oaks, CA: Corwin.

Glasser, W., & Mamary, A. (2006). *Every student can succeed: Finally a book that explains how to reach and teach every student in your school.* Black Forest Press.

Levine, M. (2002). *A mind at a time.* Simon & Schuster.

Shanker, S. (2011). *The contribution of teacher beliefs and student motivation on the academic lives of different learners.* Retrieved from https://repositories.tdl.org/tdl-ir/handle/2152/ETD-UT-2010-12-2321

Tough, P. (2012). *How children succeed: Grit, curiosity and the hidden power of character.* Boston, MA: Houghton Mifflin Harcourt.

Turner, J. C., Christensen, A., & Meyer, D. K. (2009). Teachers' beliefs about student learning and motivation. *International Handbook of Research on Teachers and Teaching, 21,* 361–371.

Affect, Emotions, and Learning

Brackett, M. A., Rivers, S. E., Shiffman, S., Lerner, N., & Salovey, P. (2006). Relating emotional abilities to social functioning: A comparison of self-report and performance measures of emotional intelligence. *Journal of Personality and Social Psychology, 91*(4), 780–795.

Broderick, P. C. (2013). *Learning to breathe: A mindfulness curriculum for adolescents to cultivate emotion regulation, attention, and performance.* Oakland, CA: New Harbinger.

Ekman, P. (2007). *Emotions revealed: Recognizing faces and feelings to improve communication and emotional life* (2nd ed.). New York, NY: Holt Paperbacks.

Glover, G., & Mackey, S. C. (2004). Reflecting upon feelings: An fMRI study of neural systems supporting the attribution of emotion to self and other. *Journal of Cognitive Neuroscience, 16*(10), 1746–1772. doi:10.1162/0898929042947829

Goetz, T., Pekrun, R., Hall, N., & Haag, L. (2010). Academic emotions from a social-cognitive perspective: Antecedents and domain specific students' affect in the context of Latin Instruction. *British Journal of Educational Psychology, 76*(2), 289–308. 10.1348/000709905X42860

Immordino-Yang, M. H., & Damasio, A. R. (2007). We feel, therefore we learn: The relevance of affective and social neuroscience to education. *Mind, Brain, and Education, 1*(1), 3–10.

Immordino-Yang, M. H. (2011). Implications of affective and social neuroscience for educational theory. *Educational Philosophy and Theory, 43*(1), 98–103. doi: 10.1111/j.1469-5812.2010.00713.x

Maag, J. (2008). Rational-emotive therapy to help teachers control their emotions and behavior when dealing with disagreeable students. *Intervention in School and Clinic, 44,* 52–57.

Moran, J. M., Macrae, C. N., Heatherton, T. F., Wyland, C. L., & Kelley, W. M. (2006). Neuroanatomical evidence for distinct cognitive and affective components of self. *Journal of Cognitive Neuroscience, 18*(9), 1586–1594. doi:10.1162/jocn.2006.18.9.1586

Ochsner, K. N., Knierim, K., Ludlow, D. H., Hanelin, J., Ramachandran, T., Glover, G. & Mackey, S. C. (2004). Reflecting upon feelings: An fMRI study of neural systems supporting the attribution of emotion to self and other. *Journal of Cognitive Neuroscience, 16*(10), 1746–1772. doi:10.1162/0898929042947829

Pekrun, R., Goetz, T., Titz, W., & Perry R. (2002). Academic emotions in students' self-regulated learning and achievement: A program of qualitative and quantitative research. *Educational Psychologist, 37*(2), 91–105. doi:10.1207/S15326985EP3702_4

Saxbe, D. E., Yang, X.-F., Borofsky, L. A., & Immordino-Yang, M. H. (2012). The embodiment of emotion: Language use during the feeling of social emotions predicts cortical somatosensory activity. *Social Cognitive and Affective Neuroscience.* doi: 10.1093/scan/nss075

Perseverance

Boone, R. Y. (2011). *The effects of effort-based and ability-based reinforcement cues on student perseverance.* Unpublished doctoral dissertation, Liberty University, School of Education, Lynchburg, VA.

Hawkins, V. J. (2009). Barriers to implementing differentiation: Lack of confidence, efficacy and perseverance. *NERA Journal, 44*(2), 11–113.

Marshakk, J. M. (2009). *Keep going: The art of perseverance.* New York, NY: Sterling Ethos.

Wheatley, M., Salaam, A., & Bash, B. (2010). *Perseverance.* San Francisco, CA: Berrett-Koehler.

Teacher Passion

Boonshaft, P. L. (2010). *Teaching with passion, purpose and promise.* Des Moines, IA: Meredith.

Crosswell, L. J., & Elliott, R. G. (2004, November 28 through December 2). *Committed teachers, passionate teachers: The dimension of passion associated with teacher commitment and engagement.* AARE Conference, Melbourne, Australia.

Day, C. (2004). *A passion for teaching.* London: Routledge.

Goldstein, L. S. (2002). *Commitment, community, and passion: Dimensions of a care-centered approach to teach education.* Lanham, MD: Rowman & Littlefield.

Maiers, A., & Sandvold, A. (2010). *The passion-driven classroom: A framework for teaching and learning.* Larchmont, NY: Eye on Education.

Mirochnik, E., & Sherman, D. C. (Eds.). *Passion and pedagogy: Relation, creation, and transformation in teaching.* Pieterlen, Switzerland: Peter Lang.

Neumann, A. (2006). Professing passion: Emotion in the scholarship of professors at research universities. *American Educational Research Journal 43*(3), 381–424.

Nilson, L. B. (2010). *Teaching at its best: A research-based resource for college instructors.* San Francisco, CA: Jossey-Bass.

Palmer, P. J. (2007). *The courage to teach: Exploring the inner landscape of a teacher's life.* San Francisco, CA: Jossey-Bass.

Posner, R. (2009). *Lives of passion, school of hope: How one public school ignites a lifelong love of learning.* Boulder, CO: Sentient.

Smith, R. L., Skarbek, D., & Hurst, J. (Eds.) (2005). *The passion of teaching: Disposition in the schools.* Lanham, MD: Rowman & Littlefield.

Motivation

Ames, C. (1992). Classrooms: Goals, structures, and student motivation (APA Centennial Feature). *Journal of Educational Psychology, 84*(3), 261–271.

Ames, C., & Archer, J. (1988). Achievement goals in the classroom: Students' learning strategies and motivation processes. *Journal of Educational Psychology, 80*(3), 260–267.

Anderman, L. H., Andrzejewski, C. E., & Allen, J. (2011). Ho do teachers support students' motivation and learning in their classrooms? *Teachers College Record, 113*(5), 969–1003.

Burleson, W. (2005). Developing creativity, motivation, and self-actualization with learning systems. *International Journal of Human-Computer Studies, 63,* 436–451.

Crow, S., & Small, R. V. (2011, February). Developing the motivation within: Using praise and rewards effectively. *School Library Monthly, 27*(5), 5–7.

Cushman, K. (2012). *Fires in the mind: What kids can tell us about motivation and mastery.* San Francisco, CA: Jossey-Bass.

Ferlazzo, L. (2011). *Helping students motivate themselves: Practical answers to classroom challenges.* Larchmont, NY: Eye on Education.

Frymier, A. B., & Shulman, G. M. (1995). What's in it for me: Increasing content relevance to enhance students' motivation. *Communication Education, 44*(1), 40–50.

Lavoie, R. (2008). *The motivation breakthrough: 6 secrets to turning on the tuned-out child.* New York, NY: Simon & Schuster/Touchstone.

Mendler, A. (2009). *Motivating students who don't care: Successful techniques for educators.* Bloomington, IN: Solution Tree.

Shanker, S. (2011). *The contribution of teacher beliefs and student motivation on the academic lives of different learners.* Retrieved from https://repositories.tdl.org/tdl-ir/handle/2152/ETD-UT-2010-12-2321

Valerios, K. (2012). Intrinsic motivation in the classroom. *Journal of Student Engagement: Education Matters, 2*(1), 30–35.

Technology

Battro, A., & Fischer, K. (2012). Mind, brain and education in the digital era. *Mind, Brain, and Education, 6*(1), 49–50.

Berninger, V. W., & Winn, W. D. (2006). Implications of advancements in brain research and technology for writing development, writing instruction, and educational evolution (pp. 96–114). In C. A. MacArthur, S. Graham, & J. Fitzgerald (Eds.), *Handbook of writing research.* New York, NY: Guilford Press.

Blake, R. J., & Kramsch, C. (2013). *Brave new digital classroom: Technology and foreign language learning* (2nd ed.). Washington, DC: Georgetown University Press.

Chester, M., Buntine, A., Hammond, K., & Atkinson, L. (2011). Podcasting in education: Student attitudes, behavior and self-efficacy. *Educational Technology and Society, 14*(2), 236–247.

Howard-Jones, P. A. (2009). Neuroscience, learning and technology. *Learning, 16*(17), 18.

Howard-Jones, P. A., Ott, M., van Leeuwen, T., & de Smedt, B. (2012). *Neuroscience, technology and learning: Areas and issues for interdisciplinary progress.* Workshop.

Khan, S. (2012). *The one world school house.* London: Hodder & Stoughton.

Koehler, M., & Mishra, P. (2009). What is Technological Pedagogical Content Knowledge (TPACK)? *Contemporary Issues in Technology and Teacher Education, 9*(1), 60–70. Retrieved from http://www.editlib.org/p/29544

Lim, D. H., & Morris, M. L. (2009). Learner and instructional factors influencing learning outcomes within a blended learning environment. *Educational Technology and Society, 12*(4), 282–293.

Pitler, H., Hubbell, E. R., & Kuhn, M. (2012). *Using technology with classroom instruction that works* (2nd ed.). Alexandria, VA: ASCD.

Richardson, W. (2010). *Blogs, wikis, podcasts, and other powerful web tools for classrooms.* Thousand Oaks, CA: Corwin.

Schrum, L., & Levin, B. B. (2009). *Leading 21st–century schools: Harnessing technology for engagement and achievement.* Thousand Oaks, CA: Corwin.

Smith, G., & Throne, S. (2007). *Differentiating instruction with technology in K–5 classrooms.* Washington, DC: International Society for Technology in Education

Tapscott, D. (2008). *Grown up digital: How the next generation is changing your world.* New York, NY: McGraw-Hill.

Thomas, M. (2011). *Deconstructing digital natives: Young people, technology, and the new literacies.* London, UK: Routledge.

The Flipped Classroom

Bender, W. N., & Waller, L. B. (2012). *Cool tech tools for lower tech teachers: 20 tactics for every classroom.* Thousand Oaks, CA: Corwin.

Bergmann, J., & Sams, A. (2012). *Flip your classroom: Reach every student in every class every day.* Washington, DC: International Society for Technology in Education.

Bergmann, J., Overmyer, J., & Willie, B. (2011, July). The flipped class: What it is and what it is not. *Daily Riff.* Retrieved January 6, 2012, from http://www.thedailyriff.com/articles/the-flipped-class-conversation-689.php

Gerstein, J. (2012). *The flipped classroom: The full picture* [Kindle version]. Amazon Digital Services.

Quinn, P. (2013). *Instructional strategies that work.* Milwaukee, WI: Julian John.

Sweet, C., Carpenter, R., Blythe, H., & Apostel, S. (2013). *Teaching applied creative thinking: A new pedagogy for the 21st century.* Stillwater, OK: New Forums Press.

Tomaszewski, J. (2012). *Khan Academy part of "flipped" classroom trend.* Meriden, CT: Education World. Retrieved from http://www.educationworld.com/a_curr/vodcast-sites-enable-flipped-classroom.shtml

Conclusion

"If you change the way you look at things, the things you look at change"
—Wayne Dyer

Education has a wonderful opportunity to change for the better, thanks to Mind, Brain, and Education science.

In the past, the main arguments against joining neuroscience and education were based on insufficient studies in real classrooms. This challenge remains. However, this book has tried to approach the goal of unification from a different angle: from the classroom to the lab and back. By showing what works in classrooms and suggesting which evidence in neuroscience explains their success, it is hoped that this book has helped to bridge the gap, or at least inch us closer together. As mentioned at the start of this book, I am merely a translator. Hattie (2009, 2012) has shown us what works in the classroom, MBE has shown us what works in the lab, and their union results in a list of classroom best practices. After I wrote my first books on Mind, Brain, and Education science (2010, 2011), someone said to me, "Great, but just *how* can we put this into practice?" This book has tried to respond to that request by offering specific actions that teachers can undertake to make their classrooms better.

We teachers need to live by the chant "Apply, but understand *why*." Exemplary teachers have always known how to nurture students, make the most of classroom time, and produce fabulous results in the course of their careers. Hopefully this book has given them confirmation, as well as explanations as to *why* these approaches work. I hope that beginning teachers have been assured of the strength of their gut instincts when it comes to interactions with their classes. And those of us in the middle should have learned how to navigate brain-based promises in a better way and select the most evidence-based practices to maximize our time and resources. If each of us, in our own classrooms, can understand why our art works so well, then we have made significant strides on behalf of the teaching profession.

There is so much to be learned from the past—in order to know where to head we need to know where we came from—but we can't keep teaching based on last century's information. Technology is unfolding a whole new story about how humans learn, and we need to take advantage of this information to shape our classrooms in the 21st century. This doesn't mean throwing the baby out with the bathwater, however. As noted previously, there are dozens of excellent interventions which have been practiced for years; MBE is all about unifying what we know from the past, celebrating what works, and reexamining it through the lenses of cognitive neuroscience, psychology, and pedagogy to explain why these interventions are successful.

A lesson from the past: Two and a half decades ago, the American Academy of Sciences (1990) listed simple principles of teaching and learning that are well worth rethinking today in light of MBE:

Principles of Learning

- Learning is not necessarily an outcome of teaching.
- Students' existing knowledge base influences their learning.
- Learning usually progresses from the concrete to the abstract.
- People learn most effectively through practice.
- Effective learning requires feedback.
- Expectations affect performance.

Principles of Teaching

- Teaching should be consistent with the nature of inquiry.
  - Start with questions.
  - Engage students actively.
  - Concentrate on the collection and use of evidence.
  - Provide historical perspectives.
  - Insist on clear expression.
  - Use a team approach.
  - Do not separate knowing from finding out.
  - De-emphasize the memorization of technical vocabulary.

- [Science] teaching should reflect [scientific] values.
  ○ Welcome curiosity.
  ○ Reward creativity.
  ○ Encourage healthy questioning.
  ○ Avoid dogmatism.
  ○ Promote aesthetic responses.
- All teaching should aim to counteract learning anxieties.
  ○ Build on success.
  ○ Provide abundant experience in using tools.
  ○ Support the roles of girls and minorities in science and mathematics.
  ○ Emphasize group learning.
- [Science] teaching should extend beyond the school.
- Teaching should take its time.

Thinking like an MBE scientist means reviewing the old studies, evaluating all the new evidence, and drawing conclusions about best practices in our classrooms. The two and a half decades since this list was generated have allowed technology and our understanding of the brain to catch up with some of the great thinkers of the past. All of these points from the American Academy of Sciences have been emphasized in this book, but they are now paired with specific learning activities backed by neuroscience. We can now explain why these principles for teaching and learning have substance, and in doing so, also delineate effective classroom actions that really make a difference in learning outcomes.

In this book we saw how biology, cognitive neuroscience, society, and genetics all influence and are influenced by good teaching and good teachers. We celebrated the fact that the teacher is the single most influential factor when it comes to improving learning outcomes, and we focused on specific interventions that can be applied in a variety of classroom settings. Finally, we considered some new ideas that should be applied if we sincerely hope to make progress in better education for all.

Some final reminders. If we remember that intelligence is fluid and that everyone can learn, we will be better teachers. If we keep in mind the importance of memory and attention as we conduct our classes, we are sure to get better results. Likewise, integrating activities that take into consideration spaced versus massed practice will surely improve learning outcomes. If we find ways to elevate the level of thinking in class through reflective activities that stir internal questioning, we are bound to develop students' metacognitive skills and produce the deep thinkers that society deserves. Great teachers know that taking advantage of interdisciplinary teaching, variation, and strategies that celebrate the teacher-student relationship will yield good results, as will reinforcement of learning concepts through authentic experiences. The complete list of the 50 classroom best practices is indicated below:

1. Plan Activities That Grab Attention
2. Plan Activities Stimulate Memory
3. Plan to Use Spaced Versus Massed Learning Moments
4. Plan to Incorporate Repetition
5. Take Advantage of Variation, Transdisciplinarity, and Creativity
6. Plan Authentic Lessons
7. Implement Formative Evaluation
8. Use Product, Process, and Progress Evaluations
9. Testing to Improve Learning
10. Develop Shared, Explicit Learning Objectives
11. Strive for Clarity and Immediacy
12. Provide Feedback for Mastery Learning
13. Nurture Teacher-Student Relationships
14. Believe in Your Students and in Your Role as a Teacher
15. Practice and Foster Metacognition and Mindfulness
16. Employ Zemelman and Colleagues' Best Practice Filter When Selecting Activities
17. Develop Students' Ability to Identify Similarities and Differences
18. Develop Students' Summarizing and Note Taking Ability
19. Reinforce Effort and Provide Recognition
20. Provide Purposeful Homework and Practice
21. Prepare Students to Set Personal Objectives and Give Themselves Feedback
22. Teach Students to Generate and Test Hypotheses
23. Use Cues
24. Use the Socratic Method
25. Cultivate the Art of Questioning
26. Incorporate Problem-Based Learning
27. Incorporate Cooperative Learning

28. Incorporate Reciprocal Teaching
29. Incorporate Case Studies
30. Harness the Power of Analogies
31. Implement the 5Es: Engage, Explore, Explain, Elaborate, and Evaluate
32. Improve Student Self-Efficacy
33. See Learning as Fluid
34. Appreciate the Role of Affect in Learning
35. Understand the Other
36. Award Perseverance and Celebrate Error
37. Be Passionate!
38. Never Work Harder Than Your Students
39. Design Engaging Classrooms
40. Motivate
41. Manage
42. Use Thinking Routines
43. Keep Abreast of Technology
44. Flip the Classroom
45. Adjust Teaching to Match Ages and Stages
46. Educate About the Role of Good Nutrition
47. Get Students out of Rows
48. Begin Year-Round Schooling
49. Change Class Times
50. Stop Using Tests as Indicators of Higher Thinking

Progress is impossible without change, and those who cannot change their minds cannot change anything.
—George Bernard Shaw

From the start, this book had three main messages to convey. First, nearly every teaching intervention works, which means we have to be more critical in our selection of methodologies and choose what works for the majority of students, most of the time to get the best results. Second, most characteristics of great teaching can be taught. A paradigm shift in teacher education is needed both in new as well as continual professional development programs. And third, we teachers need to know *why* some things work better than others in the classroom. Our professional reputation depends on improved documentation of our practice. When we understand why we choose certain classroom interventions and can articulate our knowledge to others, we elevate the status of our practice. This book examined more than 1,200 of the most influential studies undertaken during the cognitive revolution and suggested how to incorporate their findings into our professional practice. We also saw how neuromyths continue to prevail and potentially contaminate best practice in classrooms; to improve our practice we must not only avoid the myths, but learn to substantiate our practice with evidence.

We are in a new era. Technology, especially that applied through educational neuroscience, has given us a new way to look at our practice and improve our profession. To many of us—especially those of us who remember the good old days of chalkboards—this is a daunting task. It is challenging to think about the teaching-learning process through this new lens, because to do so we must openly acknowledge—even celebrate—the complexity of the human brain. But the results are worth it. The students are worth it.

A teacher affects eternity; he can never tell where his influence stops.
—Henry Adams

Members of the Original Delphi Panel on Mind, Brain, and Education Science

	Achievements
Daniel Ansari	Professor of psychology and education, University of Western Ontario. Research chair in developmental cognitive neuroscience, London and Canada. President-elect of IMBES.
Michael Atherton	Former head of the American Educational Research Association Special Interest Group on the Brain and Learning.
Antonio Battro	Coauthor of *The Educated Brain: Essays in Neuroeducation* (2008). Named the second president of the International Mind, Brain, and Education Society in 2008. CEO of One Laptop per Child.
Virginia Berninger	Professor of educational psychology, University of Washington. Research affiliate, Center on Human Development and Disability, Seattle, Washington.
Jane Bernstein	Senior associate in psychology/neuropsychology at Children's Hospital, Boston. Faculty member of the Department of Psychiatry at Harvard Medical School and faculty fellow of the Mind/Brain/Behavior Initiative of Harvard University.
Sarah Jayne Blakemore	Coauthor of *The Learning Brain: Lessons for Education* (2005). Research fellow at the Institute of Cognitive Neuroscience, London.

John T. Bruer	Author of the "Education and the Brain: A Bridge Too Far" (1997) as well as the book *The Myth of the First Three Years* (1999). Established the McDonnell–Pew Program in Cognitive Neuroscience in collaboration with the Pew Charitable Trusts. Founded the program Cognitive Studies for Educational Practice. President of the James S. McDonnell Foundation, Saint Louis, Missouri.
Donna Coch	Founding board member of the International Mind, Brain, and Education Society. Associate professor in the Department of Education at Dartmouth College as well as researcher in the Reading Brains Lab of Dartmouth College, Hanover, New Hampshire.
David Daniel	Managing editor of the *Mind, Brain, and Education* journal. Founding member of the International Mind, Brain, and Education Society. Professor of psychology at James Madison University.
Stanislas Dehaene	Coauthor of the computer program *The Number Race*. Renowned author of *Reading in the Brain* (2009). Chairman of the Experimental Cognitive Psychology Department and Director of the Cognitive Neuroimaging Unit at the Collège de France, Saclay and Paris, France.
Bruno Della Chiesa	Coordinator, coauthor, and editor of *Understanding the Brain: The Birth of a Learning Science* (2007). Visiting lecturer, Harvard Graduate School of Education. Senior analyst and project manager of OECD's Centre for Educational Research and Innovation.
Marian Diamond	Head of Integrative Biology at the University of California at Berkeley, California.
Kurt Fischer	Founder and chair of the Mind, Brain and Education Program at Harvard University's Graduate School of Education. First president of the International Mind, Brain, and Education Society (2007) and editor of the *Mind, Brain, and Education* journal.
Howard Gardner	Author of *Theory of Multiple Intelligences* (1983) and more recently *Five Minds for the Future* (2007) and the Good Works Project. John H. and Elisabeth A. Hobbs Professor of Cognition and Education at the Harvard Graduate School of Education and director of Project Zero.

John Geake	Professor of learning and teaching in the School of Education at the University of New England, Armidale, New South Wales, Australia.
Usha Goswami	Author of *Cognitive Development: The Learning Brain* (2008). Director of the Centre for Neuroscience in Education at the University of Cambridge.
Paul Howard-Jones	Author of *Introducing Neuroeducational Research* (2009). Member of the UK's Royal Society Working Group on Neuroscience and Education. Coordinator of the NeuroEducational Research Network at the Graduate School of Education, University of Bristol, UK.
Mary Helen Immordino-Yang	Assistant professor of psychology at the Brain and Creativity Institute and assistant professor of education at the Rossier School of Education at the University of Southern California.
Eric Jensen	Renowned speaker on brain-based education.
Jelle Jolles	Director of the Amsterdam Centre for Brain & Learning. Full professor of Brain, Behavior, & Education at VU University Amsterdam and director of the Centre for Brain & Learning Amsterdam.
Hideaki Koizumi	Inventor of optical tomography neuroimaging. Founding board member of the International Mind, Brain, and Education Society. Visiting professor, Research Center for Advanced Science and Technology, University of Tokyo. Lead researcher in neuroimaging for Hitachi, Tokyo, Japan.
Renate Nummela-Caine	One of the first educators to publish in the area of brain-based education. Renowned speaker on brain-based education. Professor emeritus of education at California State University, San Bernardino.
Michael Posner	Author of more than 200 articles on cognitive neuroscience. Adjunct professor at the Weill Medical College in New York (Sackler Institute) and emeritus professor of psychology at the University of Oregon.
Marc Schwartz	Director of the Mind, Brain, and Education Program at the University of Texas and associate researcher in the Science Education Department at the Harvard-Smithsonian Center for Astrophysics.

Rita Smilkstein	Internationally known speaker and author on brain-compatible teaching, whose book *We're Born to Learn* (2003) won the Delta Kappa Gamma Society International's Educator's Book of the Year Award.
David Sousa	One of the most widely published educational authors on the brain and learning. World-renowned speaker on brain-based education and former adjunct professor at Rutgers and Seton Hall universities.
Judy Willis	Best known for her books, including *Brain-Friendly Strategies for the Inclusion Classroom* (2007).
Patricia Wolfe	Author of *Brain Matters: Translating Research Into Classroom Practice* (2010) and coauthor of *Building the Reading Brain PreK–3* (2004). World-renowned teacher trainer on the brain.

John Hattie's *Visible Learning*
150 Influences That Impact Student Learning Outcomes

Ranking (based on effect size)	Domain	Effect size	Measure (intervention, methodology, condition, activity)
1	Student	1.44	Self-reported grades/Student self-expectations/Self-efficacy
2	Student	1.28	Piagetian (constructivist) programs
3	Student	1.07	Response to intervention (attitude)
4	Teacher	0.90	Teacher credibility
4	Teaching	0.90	Formative evaluation
6	Teacher	0.88	Microteaching
7	Teaching	0.82	Classroom discussion
8	Teaching	0.77	Comprehensive interventions for students with learning disabilities
9	Teacher	0.75	Teacher clarity
10	Teaching	0.75	Feedback
11	Teaching	0.74	Reciprocal teaching
12	Teacher	0.72	Teacher-student relationships
13	Teaching	0.71	Spaced vs. mass practice
14	Teaching	0.69	Metacognitive practices
15	School	0.68	Acceleration
16	School	0.68	Classroom behavior
17	Curricula	0.67	Vocabulary program
18	Curricula	0.67	Repeated reading programs
19	Curricula	0.65	Creativity programs on achievement

Ranking (based on effect size)	Domain	Effect size	Measure (intervention, methodology, condition, activity)
20	Student	0.65	Prior achievement
21	Teaching	0.64	Self-verbalization and self-questioning
22	Teaching	0.63	Study skills
23	Teaching	0.62	Teaching strategies (explanation, elaboration, modeling, demonstration, reminders of procedures, etc.)
24	Teaching	0.61	Problem solving teaching
25	Teacher	0.61	Not labeling students
26	Curricula	0.60	Comprehension programs
27	Teaching	0.60	Concept mapping
28	Teaching	0.59	Cooperative vs. individualistic learning
29	Teaching	0.59	Direct instruction
30	Curricula	0.58	Tactile stimulation programs
31	Teaching	0.58	Mastery learning
32	Curricula	0.57	Worked examples
33	Teaching	0.55	Visual perception programs
34	Teaching	0.55	Peer tutoring
35	Teaching	0.54	Cooperative vs. competitive learning
36	Curricula	0.54	Phonics instruction
37	Teaching	0.54	Student-centered teaching
38	School	0.53	Classroom cohesion and climate
39	Student	0.53	Preterm birth weight
40	Teaching	0.53	Keller's Master Learning
41	School	0.53	Peer influence
42	School	0.52	Classroom management
43	School	0.52	Outdoor/adventure programs
44	Curricula	0.52	Home environment
45	Home	0.52	Socioeconomic status
46	Teaching	0.52	Interactive video methods
47	Teacher	0.51	Professional development
48	Teaching	0.50	Goals
49	Curricula	0.51	Play programs
50	Curricula	0.50	Second-/third-chance programs

Ranking (based on effect size)	Domain	Effect size	Measure (intervention, methodology, condition, activity)
51	Home	0.49	Parental involvement
52	School	0.49	Small-group learning
53	Teaching	0.48	Questioning
54	Student	0.48	Concentration/persistence/engagement
55	School	0.48	School effects
56	Student	0.48	Motivation
57	Teacher	0.48	Quality of teaching as rated by students
58	Student	0.47	Early intervention
59	Student	0.47	Self-concept (cognitive appraisals: descriptions of pride, worth, confidence)
60	Student	0.45	Preschool programs
61	Curricula	0.44	Writing programs
62	Teacher	0.43	Teacher expectations
63	School	0.43	School size
64	Curricula	0.42	Science programs
65	Teaching	0.42	Cooperative learning
66	Curricula	0.42	Exposure to reading
67	Teaching	0.41	Behavioral organizers/adjunct question
68	Curricula	0.40	Mathematics programs
69	Student	0.40	Reducing anxiety
70	Curricula	0.39	Social skills programs
71	Curricula	0.39	Integrated curricula programs
72	School	0.39	Enrichment
73	School	0.39	Principals/school leaders
74	Curricula	0.38	Career interventions
75	Teaching	0.38	Time on task
76	School	0.38	Psychotherapy programs
77	Teaching	0.37	Computer-assisted instruction
78	Teaching	0.37	Adjunct aids
79	Curricula	0.37	Bilingual programs
80	Curricula	0.35	Drama/arts programs
81	Student	0.35	Creativity related to achievement

Ranking (based on effect size)	Domain	Effect size	Measure (intervention, methodology, condition, activity)
82	Student	0.35	Attitude to mathematics/science
83	Teaching	0.34	Frequency/effects of testing
84	School	0.34	Decreasing disruptive behavior
85	Teaching	0.34	Various teaching on creativity
86	Teaching	0.33	Simulations
87	Teaching	0.33	Inductive teaching
88	Student	0.32	Ethnicity
89	Teacher	0.32	Teacher effects
90	Student	0.32	Drugs
91	Teaching	0.31	Inquiry-based teaching
92	School	0.31	Systems accountability
93	School	0.30	Ability grouping for gifted students
94	Teaching	0.29	Homework
95	Home	0.29	Home visiting
96	Student	0.28	Exercise/relaxation
97	School	0.28	Desegregation
98	Teaching	0.27	Teaching test-taking and coaching
99	Curricula	0.27	Use of calculators
100	Teaching	0.26	Volunteer tutors
101	Student	0.25	Lack of illness
102	School	0.24	Mainstreaming
103	Curricula	0.24	Values/moral education programs
104	Teaching	0.24	Competitive vs. individualistic learning
105	Teaching	0.23	Programmed instruction
106	School	0.23	Summer school
107	School	0.23	Finances
108	School	0.23	Religious schools
109	Teaching	0.22	Individualized instruction
110	Teaching	0.22	Visual/audiovisual methods
111	Teaching	0.22	Comprehensive teaching reforms
112	Teacher	0.22	Teacher verbal ability
113	School	0.21	Class size

Ranking (based on effect size)	Domain	Effect size	Measure (intervention, methodology, condition, activity)
114	School	0.20	Charter school
115	Teaching	0.19	Aptitude/treatment interactions
116	Curricula	0.19	Extracurricular programs
117	Teaching	0.19	Learning hierarchies
118	Teaching	0.19	Co-/team teaching
119	Student	0.18	Personality
120	School	0.18	Within-class grouping
121	Teaching	0.18	Special college programs
122	Home	0.18	Family structure
123	School	0.18	School counseling effects
124	Teaching	0.18	Web-based learning
125	Teaching	0.17	Matching style of learning
126	Teaching	0.16	Teacher immediacy
127	Teaching	0.16	Home-school programs
128	Teaching	0.15	Problem-based learning
129	Curricula	0.15	Sentence-combing programs
130	Teaching	0.15	Mentoring
131	School	0.12	Ability grouping
132	Student	0.12	Diet
133	Student	0.12	Gender
134	Teacher	0.12	Teacher education
135	Teaching	0.11	Distance education
136	Teacher	0.09	Teacher subject matter knowledge
137	School	0.09	Changing school calendars/timetables
138	School	0.09	Out-of-school curricular experiences
139	Curricula	0.08	Perceptual motor programs
140	Curricula	0.06	Whole language
141	School	0.05	Ethnic diversity of students
142	School	0.05	College halls of residence
143	School	0.04	Multi-grade/multi-age classes
144	Teaching	0.04	Student control over learning
145	School	0.01	Open vs. traditional

Ranking (based on effect size)	Domain	Effect size	Measure (intervention, methodology, condition, activity)
146	School	-0.02	Summer vacation
147	Home	-0.12	Welfare policies
148	School	-0.13	Retention
149	Home	-0.18	Television
150	School	-0.34	Mobility

Source: Based on John Hattie (2009; 2012).

47 Interventions Mentioned by Hattie That Are Interpreted To Be Within the Teacher's Realm of Influence

	Ranking (based on effect size)	Domain	Effect size	Measure (intervention, methodology, condition, activity)	Category
1	1	Student	1.44	Self-reported grades/Student self-expectations/Self-efficacy	Student self-efficacy
2	2	Student	1.28	Piagetian (constructivist) programs	Reinforcement learning
3	3	Student	1.07	Response to intervention (attitude)	Knowing students
4	4	Teacher	0.90	Teacher credibility	Teacher as seen by students
5	4	Teaching	0.90	Formative evaluation	Thinking about thinking
6	6	Teacher	0.88	Microteaching	Teacher self-improvement
7	7	Teaching	0.82	Classroom discussion	Clear objectives
8	9	Teacher	0.75	Teacher clarity	Clear objectives
9	10	Teaching	0.75	Feedback	Thinking about thinking
10	11	Teaching	0.74	Reciprocal teaching	Group learning
11	12	Teacher	0.72	Teacher-student relationships	Knowing students
12	13	Teaching	0.71	Spaced vs. mass learning	Reinforcement learning
13	14	Teaching	0.69	Metacognitive practices	Thinking about thinking
14	15	School	0.68	Acceleration	Knowing students
15	16	School	0.68	Classroom behavior	Managing
16	21	Teaching	0.64	Self-verbalization and self-questioning	Thinking about thinking
17	22	Teaching	0.63	Study skills	Thinking about thinking

	Ranking (based on effect size)	Domain	Effect size	Measure (intervention, methodology, condition, activity)	Category
18	23	Teaching	0.62	Teaching strategies (explanation, elaboration, modeling, demonstration, reminders of procedures, etc.)	Activities
19	24	Teaching	0.61	Problem-solving teaching	Thinking about thinking
20	25	Teacher	0.61	Not labeling students	Knowing students
21	27	Teaching	0.60	Concept mapping	Activities
22	28	Teaching	0.59	Cooperative vs. individualistic learning	Group learning
23	29	Teaching	0.59	Direct instruction	Activities
24	31	Teaching	0.58	Mastery learning	Reinforcement learning
25	32	Curricula	0.57	Worked examples	Activities
26	34	Teaching	0.55	Peer tutoring	Group learning
27	35	Teaching	0.54	Cooperative vs. competitive learning	Group learning
28	37	Teaching	0.54	Student-centered teaching	Activities
29	38	School	0.53	Classroom cohesion and climate	Managing
30	41	School	0.53	Peer influence	Group learning
31	42	School	0.52	Classroom management	Managing
32	47	Teacher	0.51	Professional development	Teacher self-improvement
33	48	Teaching	0.50	Goals	Clear objectives
34	50	Curricula	0.50	Second-/third-chance programs	Knowing students
35	52	School	0.49	Small-group learning	Group learning
36	53	Teaching	0.48	Questioning	Activities
37	54	Student	0.48	Concentration/persistence/engagement	Knowing students
38	56	Student	0.48	Motivation	Knowing students
39	57	Teacher	0.48	Quality of teaching as rated by students	Teacher as seen by students
40	58	Student	0.47	Early intervention	Reinforcement learning
41	59	Student	0.47	Self-concept (cognitive appraisals: descriptions of pride, worth, confidence)	Student self-efficacy
42	61	Curricula	0.44	Writing programs	Activities
43	62	Teacher	0.43	Teacher expectations	Clear objectives
44	65	Teaching	0.42	Cooperative learning	Group learning
45	66	Curricula	0.42	Exposure to reading	Activities
46	67	Teaching	0.41	Behavioral organizers/adjunct question	Activities
47	69	Student	0.40	Reducing anxiety	Managing

Source: Grouped by Author. Based on John Hattie's Visible Learning (2009; 2012).

The Goals in Mind, Brain, and Education Science

Goals in the New Discipline

Like all disciplines, the goals of MBE science can be divided into three categories: research, practice, and policy. These goals help put the parameters around what, how, who, when, where, and why studies are conducted, thus serving as basic guidelines for researchers, practitioners, and policy makers. Teachers can use the goals to ensure that they ground their practice in solid principles. Students of MBE science can use these goals to develop new research questions. Leaders in the discipline can use the goals to guide policy decisions. The goals give MBE Educators a "north" by which to guide their work. Goals, however, are meaningless unless they are matched with standards, which are also explained below.

Research Goal

The research goal of the emerging discipline of MBE science is to:

Establish a working understanding of the dynamic relationships between how we learn, how we educate, how the brain constructs new learning, and how the brain organizes and processes information.

HOW?

- Study how brain mechanisms contribute to education and learning.
- Study relationships between human development and the biology of the brain.
- Develop insights into the neuroscientific and cognitive scientific determinants of nor-

mal, successful, and borderline/pathological learning and apply these in the field of education according to evidence-based principles.

- Study context and psychosocial factors (e.g., socioeconomic factors, levels of parental education, intellectually stimulating environments, culture) as they interact with biological influences on learning.
- Study how biopsychological factors (e.g., sleep, nutrition, stress) can modulate learning and the efficiency of teaching.
- Study lifelong learning in the context of the developing teacher, including how teacher self-efficacy impacts student learning, teacher experience contributes to classroom experiences, and information processing in a teachers at different ages.
- Study how student self-regulation, metacognition, and higher-order thinking skills can be best developed by determining how and why certain pedagogical practices are successful.

This research goal and its eight sub-elements make it clear that MBE science considers the entire range of human learning and the consequences of teaching, ranging from neuroanatomical to socioeconomic factors, from normal to pathological development, from infant to adult learning processes, and from the role of the teacher to the role of the student.

Practice Goal
The practice goal of MBE science is to:
Align learning and teaching with how human beings are biologically organized for learning.

HOW?
- Reciprocally connect research with practice on processes of learning and teaching.
- Apply neurobiological principles to the theory and practice of education.
- Study and evaluate how findings from research in neurosciences can be applied to educational practice.
- Apply research findings in cognitive neuroscience to educational practice and theory.
- Use successful classroom experiences as points of departure for continued research in the neurosciences.
- Apply our understanding of the brain to education.

In real-life application, this list of how to implement the practice goal means that teachers use all they can glean from quality information about the brain to devise best-practice instructional methods. From a researcher's perspective this means using what works in classrooms as a point of departure for lab study. On the whole, implementing this list bridges the gap dividing neuroscientific lab studies and the classroom setting.

Policy Goal
The policy goal of the emerging discipline is to:
> Continually encourage the pursuit of neuroscientifically substantiated beliefs founded in educationally-inspired research questions, the results of which have potential application to educational practice.

HOW?
- Inform educational policy and practice with research on the science of learning.
- Improve the efficiency of educational policies, both for normal and for at-risk children, by relying on scientific principles of how the child's brain/mind operates, both for the design and for the evaluation of education strategies.
- Inform neuroscientific research directions through experiences in education.

The points in this list mean that policy decisions in MBE science walk the fine line linking neuroscience, psychology, and education. This balance is achieved in such a way as to approach educational strategies for both normal and at-risk students using the refined multiple-lens of the new discipline.

Source: Tokuhama-Espinosa (2011, pp. 86–88) based on Delphi Panel findings (2008).

References

Ablin, J. L. (2008). Learning as problem design versus problem solving: Making the connection between cognitive neuroscience research and educational practice. *Mind, Brain, and Education, 2*(2), 52–54.

Abraham, A. (2013). The promises and perils of the neuroscience of creativity. *Frontiers in Human Neuroscience, 7,* 246. doi:10.3389/fnhum.2013.00246

Abraham, A., Pieritz, K., Thybusch, K., Rutter, B., Kröger, S., Schweckendiek, J., Stark, R., Windmann, S., & Hermann, C. (2012). Creativity and the brain: Uncovering the neural signature of conceptual expansion. *Neuropsychologia, 50*(8), 1906–1917.

Abramson, M. J., Benke, G. P., Dimitriadis, C., Inyang, I. O., Sim, M. R., Wolfe, R. S., & Croft, R. J. (2009). Mobile telephone use is associated with changes in cognitive functions in young adolescents. *Bioelectricmagnetics, 30*(8), 678–686. doi:10.1002/bem.20534

Absolum, M., Gray, J., & Mutchmor, M. (2010). *Clarity in the classroom: Using formative assessment for building learning-focused relationships.* Winnipeg, Canada: Portage & Main Press.

Ackley, B. C., Colter, D. J., Marsh, B., & Sisco, R. (2003). *Student achievement in democratic classrooms.* Paper presented at the Annual Meeting of the American Educational Research Association (Chicago, IL, April 21–25, 2003).

Adolphs, R. (2003). Cognitive neuroscience of human social behaviour. *Nature Reviews Neuroscience, 4*(3), 165–178.

Agarwal, P. K., Bain, P. M., & Chamberlain, R. W. (2012). The value of applied research: Retrieval practice improves classroom learning and recommendations from a teacher, a principal, and a scientist. *Educational Psychology Review, 24*(3), 437–448.

Ahmadi, M. R. (2013). Goals of reciprocal teaching strategy instruction. *The International Journal of Language Learning and Applied Linguistics World, 2*(1), 21–88.

Ahmadi, M. R., & Ismail, H. N. (2012). *Reciprocal teaching strategy as an important fact of improving reading comprehension.* Creative Commons, MacroThink, doi:10.5296/jse.v2i4.2584

Alderson, P., & Morrow, G. (2006). Ethics, social research and consulting with children and young people. *Children, Youth and Environments, 16*(2).

Alexander, K., Entwisle, D., & Linda, O. (2007). Lasting consequences of the summer learning gap. *American Sociological Review, 72*, 167–180.

Alro, H., & Johnsen-Hoines, M. (2012). Inquiry-without posing questions. *The Mathematics Enthusiast 9*(3), 253–270.

Altonji, J. G., Blom, E., & Meghir, C. (2012). *Heterogeneity in human capital investments: High school curriculum, college major, and careers* (No. w17985). National Bureau of Economic Research.

Alvidrez, J., & Weinstein, R. S. (1999). Early teacher perceptions and later student achievement. *Journal of Educational Psychology, 91*(4). doi:10.1037/0022-0663.91.4.731

Ambady, N., & Rosenthal, R. (1994). Half a minute: Predicting teacher evaluations from thin slices of nonverbal behavior and physical attractiveness. *Journal of Personality and Social Psychology, 64*(3), 431–441.

Ambrose, S. A., Bridges, M. W., DiPietro, M., Lovett, M. C., & Norman, M. K. (2010). *How learning works: Seven research-based principles for smart teaching.* San Francisco, CA: Jossey-Bass.

Amedi, A., Von Kriegstein, K., Van Atteveldt, N. M., Beauchamp, M. S., & Naumer, M. J. (2005). Functional imaging of human crossmodal identification and object recognition. *Experimental Brain Research, 166*(3–4), 559–571.

American Academy of Sciences. (1990). *Effective learning and teaching: Principles of learning.* Retrieved 9 Aug 2013 from http://www.project2061.org/publications/sfaa/online/chap13.htm

American Association for the Advancement of Science. (1990). *Science for all Americans.* New York, NY: Oxford University Press.

American Educational Research Association. (2012). *Expanding literacies strand.* Meeting in Vancouver, Canada (April 13–16).

American Educational Research Association. (2012). *"Non Satis Scire: To Know Is Not Enough" theme of 2012 AERA conference.* Opening speech by Arnetha F. Ball, 2012 AERA President.

Ames, C. (1992). Classrooms: Goals, structures, and student motivation. APA Centennial Feature. *Journal of Educational Psychology, 84*(3), 261–271.

Ames, C., & Archer, J. (1988). Achievement goals in the classroom: Students' learning strategies and motivation processes. *Journal of Educational Psychology, 80*(3), 260–267.

Anderman, L. H., Andrzejewski, C. E., & Allen, J. (2011). How do teachers support students' motivation and learning in their classrooms? *Teachers College Record, 113*(5), 969–1003.

Andersen, J. F., Norton, R. W., & Nussbaum, J. F. (1981). Three investigations exploring relationships between perceived teacher communication behaviors and student learning. *Communication Education, 30*(4), 377–392. doi:10.1080/03634528109378493

Andersen, N. C. (2005). *The creating brain: The neuroscience of genius.* Washington, DC: Dana Press.

Anderson, D., Piscitelli, B., Weier, K., Everett, M., & Tayler, C. (2002). Children's museums experiences: Identifying powerful mediators of learning. *Curator, The Museum Journal, 45*(3), 213–231.

Anderson, L. W., & Krathwohl, D. R. (Eds.) (2001). *A taxonomy for learning, teaching, and assessing: A revision of Bloom's taxonomy of educational objectives.* New York, NY: Longman.

Anderson, P. (2002). Assessment and development of executive function (EF) during childhood. *Child Neuropsychology, 8*(2), 71–82.

Andrade, E. B., & Ariely, D. (2009). The enduring impact of transient emotions on decision making. *Organizational Behavior and Human Decision Processes, 109*(1), 1–8.

Andrew, M., Cobb, C., & Giampierto, P. (2005). Verbal ability and teacher effectiveness. *Journal of Teacher Education, 56*(4), 343–354.

Angelo, T. A. (1991). Introduction and overview: From classroom assessment to classroom research. *New Directions for Teaching and Learning, 1991*(46), 7–15.

Annetta, L., & Minogue, J. (2011). Science teacher training through Serious Educational Games. In M. Koehler & P. Mishra (Eds.), *Proceedings of Society for Information Technology & Teacher Education International Conference 2011* (pp. 2025–2033). Chesapeake, VA: AACE. Retrieved October 21, 2013 from http://www.editlib.org/p/36601.

Ansari, D. (2005). Paving the way towards meaningful interactions between neuroscience and education. *Developmental Science, 8*(6), pp. 466–467.

Ansari, D. (2008). Effects of development and enculturation on number representation in the brain. *Nature Reviews. Neuroscience 9*(4), 278–291.

Ansari, D., & Coch, D. (2006). Bridges over troubled waters: Education and neuroscience. *Trends in Cognitive Sciences, 10*(4), 146–151.

Ansari, D., Coch, D., & DeSmedt, B. (2011). Connecting education and cognitive neuroscience: Where will the journey take us? *Educational Philosophy and Theory, 43*(1), 37–42.

Ansari, D., DeSmedt, B., & Grabner, R. H. (2012). Introduction to the special section on numerical and mathematical processing. *Mind, Brain and Education 6*(3), 117–118.

Ansari, D.,& Karmiloff-Smith, A. (2002). Atypical trajectories of number development: A neuroconstructivist perspective. *Trends in Cognitive Sciences, 6*(12), 511–516.

Anspaugh, D., Hamrick, M., & Rosato, F. (2010). *Wellness: Concepts and applications* (8th ed.). New York, NY: McGraw-Hill Humanities.

Arbelle, S., Benjamin, J., Golin, M., Kremer, I., Belmaker, H., & Epstein, R.P. (2003). Relation of shyness in grade school children to the genotype for the long form of the serotonin transporter promoter region polymorphism. *American Journal of Psychiatry 160*, 671–676. doi:10.1176/appi.ajp.160.4.671

Archer, A., & Hughes, C. A. (2010). *Explicit instruction: Effective and efficient teaching.* New York, NY: Guilford.

Arendal, L., & Mann, V. (2000). *Fast ForWord reading: Why it works.* Berkeley, CA: Scientific Learning Corporation.

Argote, L. (2012). *Organizational learning: Creating, retaining and transferring knowledge.* New York, NY: Springer.

Arlin, M. (1984). Time, equality, and mastery learning. *Review of Educational Research, 54*(1), 65–86. doi:10.3102/00346543054001065

Armstrong, T. (2012). *Neurodiversity in the classroom: Strength-based strategies to help students with special needs succeed in school and life*. Alexandria, VA: ASCD.

Arnold, M. B. (2013). *Memory and the brain*. Florence, KY: Psychology Press.

Aronson, E. (1978). *The jigsaw classroom*. Thousand Oaks, CA: Sage.

Ary, D., Jacobs, L.C., Razavieh, A., & Sorensen, C. (2010). *Introduction to research in education*. Belmont, CA: Wadsworth.

Ashman, A., & Gillies, R. (2003). *Cooperative learning: The social and intellectual outcomes of learning in groups*. London, UK: Routledge.

Asseily, A. (2012). The power of language – How small shifts in language create big shifts in relationships and behavior. In M. Shuayb's *Rethinking education for social cohesion: International case studies* (pp. 220–231). New York, NY: Palgrave Macmillan.

Athappilly, K., Smidchens, U., & Kofel, J. W. (1983). A computer-based meta-analysis of the effects of modern mathematics in comparison with traditional mathematics. *Educational Evaluation and Policy Analysis, 5*(4), 485–493.

Atherton, J. S. (2011). *Teaching and learning: What works and what doesn't*. Retrieved 4 December 2011 from http://www.learningandteaching.info/teaching/what_works.htm

Atherton, M. (2002). *A neurocognitive model for student and educators*. Fairfax, VA: Paper presented at the annual meeting of the Cognitive Science Society.

Atherton, M. (2005). *Applying the neurosciences to educational research: Can cognitive neuroscience bridge the gap? Part I*. Retrieved 5 May 2007 from www.tc.umn.edu/~athe0007/BNEsig/papers/Educationand Neuroscience.pdf

Aubrey, C. (2000). *Early childhood educational research: Issues in methodology and ethics*. New York, NY: Routledge.

Azar, B. (2002). Searching for genes that explain our personalities: Identifying such genes could eliminate the distinction psychologists make between personality and psychopathology. *Monitor on Psychology, 33*(8), 44.

Azevedo, R. (2005). Using hypermedia as a metacognitive tool for enhancing student learning? The role of self-resulted learning. *Educational Psychologist, 40*(4), 199–209. doi:10.1207/s15326985ep4004_2

Azevedo, C. V., Sousa, I., Paul, K., MacLeish, M. Y., Mondejar, M. T., Sarabia, J. A., ... & Madrid, J. A. (2008). Teaching chronobiology and sleep habits in school and university. *Mind, Brain, and Education, 2*(1), 34–47.

Baars, B. J. (1998). Metaphors of consciousness and attention in the brain. *Trends in Neurosciences, 21*(2), 58–62.

Bach, S., Richardson, U., Brandeis, D., Martin, E., & Brem, S. (2011). Print-specific multimodal brain activation in kindergarten improves prediction of reading skills in second grade. *Neuroimage*. Retrieved from http://www.sciencedirect.com/science/article/pii/S1053811911007841

Baddeley, A. D. (2003, October). Working memory: Looking back and looking forward. *Nature Reviews Neuroscience, 4,* 829–839. doi:10.1038/nrn1201. Retrieved 1 Aug 2013 from http://www.nature.com/nrn/journal/v4/n10/fig_tab/nrn1201_F2.html

Baddeley, A., Eyseneck, M. W., & Anderson, M. C. (2009). *Memory.* New York, NY: Psychology Press.

Baddeley, A.D., Gathercole, S., & Papagno, C. (1998 Jan). The phonological loop as a language learning device. *Psychological Review 105*(1), 158–173. doi:10.1037//0033-295X.105.1.158.

Baker, E. L., Barton, P. E., Darling-Hammond, L., Haertel, E., Ladd, H. F., Linn, R. L., ... & Shepard, L. A. (2010). *Problems with the use of student test scores to evaluate teachers* (Vol. 278). Washington, DC: Economic Policy Institute.

Baker, L., & Scher, D. (2002). Beginning readers' motivation for reading in relation to parental beliefs and home reading experiences. *Reading Psychology, 23*(4), 239–269.

Baker, L., Scher, D., & Mackler, K. (1997). Home and family influences on motivations for reading. *Educational Psychologist, 32*(2), 69–82.

Baker, L., & Wigfield, A. (1999). Dimensions of children's motivation for reading and their relations to reading activity and reading achievement. *Reading Research Quarterly, 34*(4), 152–177.

Baker, W., & Czarnocha, B. (2002). *Written meta-cognition and procedural knowledge.* Paper presented to the 2nd international conference on the teaching of mathematics (at the undergraduate level). New York, NY: Wiley.

Balderston, N. L., Schultz, D. H., & Helmstetter, F. J. (2011). The human amygdala plays a stimulus specific role in the detection of novelty. *Neuroimage, 55*(4), 1889–1898.

Balota, D. A., & Duchek, J. M., & Logan, J. M. (2007). Is expanded retrieval practice a superior form of spaced retrieval? A critical review of the extant literature. In James S. Nairne, *The foundations of remembering: Essays in honor of Henry L. Roediger, III* (Psychology Press Festschrift Series) (pp. 83–105). New York, NY: Psychology Press.

Bandura, A. (1997). *Self–efficacy: The exercise of control.* New York, NY: Freeman.

Bangasser, D. A, & Shors, T. J. (2010). Critical brain circuits at the intersection between stress and learning. *Neuroscience Behavioral Review, 34*(8), 1223–1233. doi:10.1016/j.neubiorev.2010.02.002

Barceló, F., Perianez, J. A., & Knight, R. (2002). Think differently: A brain orienting response to task novelty. *NeuroReport, 13*(15), 1887–1892.

Barekkm J. F. (2006). *Problem-based learning: An inquiry approach* (2nd ed.). Thousand Oaks, CA: Corwin.

Bargh, J. A., & Williams, E. L. (2006). The automaticity of social life. *Current Directions in Psychological Science, 15*(1), 1–4. doi:10.1111/j.0963-7214.2006.00395.x

Barkley, R. A. (2012). *Executive functions: What they are, how they work, and why they evolved.* New York, NY: The Guildford Press.

Baron-Cohen, S. (1991). Precursors to a theory of mind: Understanding attention in others. In

A. Whiten (Ed.), *Natural theories of mind: Evolution, development, and simulation of everyday mindreading* (pp. 233–251). Cambridge, MA: Basil Blackwell.

Barrett, R. A. (2008). Motivation in the foreign language classroom by elimination of winners and losers: Mastery goals versus performance goals. In A. Moeller (Ed.), *Turning today's students into tomorrow's stars* (pp. 146–151). Milwaukee, WI: Report for the Central States Conference on the Teaching of Foreign Languages.

Barron, B. (2003). When smart groups fail. *Journal of Learning Sciences, 12*(3), 307–359.

Barrouillet, P., & Gaillard, V. (2011). *Cognitive development and working memory: A dialogue between neo-Piagetian and cognitive approaches.* Hove, UK: Psychology Press.

Basile, B., Bassi, A., Calcagnini, G., Strano, S., Caltagirone, C., Macaluso, E….& Bozzali, M. (2013). Direct stimulation of the autonomic nervous system modulates activity of the brain at rest and when engaged in a cognitive task. *Human Brain Mapping, 34*, 1605–1614. doi:10.1002/hbm.22013

Bassett, D. S., Wymbs, N. F., Porter, M. A., Mucha, P. J., Carlson, J. M., & Grafton, S. T. (2011). Dynamic reconfiguration of human brain networks during learning. *Proceedings of the National Academy of Science of the United States of America, 108*(18), 7641–7646.

Battaglia, N., Ogliari, A., Zanoni, A., Citterio, A. Pozzoli, U., Giorda, R., Maffei, C., & Marino, C. (2005). Influence of the serotonin transporter promoter gene and shyness on children's cerebral responses to facial expression. *JAMA Psychiatry, 62*(1), 85–94. doi:10.1001/archpsyc.62.1.85.

Battro, A. M. (2010). The teaching brain. *Mind, Brain, and Education, 4*(1), 28–33.

Battro, A., Fischer, K. W., & Léna, P. J. (Eds.) (2008). *The educated brain: essays in neuroeducation.* Cambridge, UK: Cambridge University Press.

Battro, A. M., & Fischer, K. W. (2012). Mind, Brain, and Education in the digital era. *Mind, Brain, and Education, 6*(1), 49–50.

Bauwens, J., & Hourcade, J. J. (1995). *Cooperative teaching: Rebuilding the schoolhouse for all students.* Austin, TX: Pro-Ed.

Bear, G. G., & Minke, K. K. M. (Eds.) (2006). *Children's needs III: Development, prevention, and intervention.* Washington, DC: United States National Association of School Psychologists.

Beatty, M. J., & Behnke, R. R. (1980). Teacher credibility as a function of verbal content and paralinguistic cues. *Communication Quarterly, 28*(1), 55–59. doi:10.1080/01463378009369358

Beatty-O'Ferral, M. E., Green, A., & Hanna, F. (2010). Classroom management strategies for difficult students: Promoting change through relationships. *Middle School Journal, 41*(4), 4–11.

Beck, J., & Mostow, J. (2008). How who should practice: Using learning decomposition to evaluate the efficacy to different types of practice for different types of students. *Intelligent Tutoring Systems, 5091*, 353–362. doi:10.1007/978-3-540-69132-7_39

Becker, A. H., Davis, S. F., Neal, L., & Grover, C. A. (1990). Student expectations of course and instructor. *Teaching of Psychology, 17*, 159–162.

Bee, H. L., & Boyd, D. R. (2011). *The developing child* (13th ed.). New York, NY: Pearson.

Beesley, A. D., & Apthorp, H. S. (2010). *Classroom instruction that works* (2nd ed.). Denver, CO: Mid-continent Research for Education and Learning.

Beitman, B. D. (2009). Brains seek patterns in coincidences. *Psychiatric Annals, 39*(5), 255–264.

Bender, W. N. (2012). *Differentiating instruction for students with learning disabilities: New best practices for general and special educators.* Thousand Oaks, CA: Sage.

Bender, W., & Waller, L. B. (2011). *The teaching revolution: RTI: technology, and differentiation transformation teaching for the 21st century.* Thousand Oaks, CA: Corwin.

Bender, W., & Waller, L. B. (2012). *Cool tech tools for lower tech teachers: 20 tactics for every classroom.* Thousand Oaks, CA: Corwin.

Benjamin & Craik. (2001).

Bennett, R. E. (2011). Formative assessment: A critical review. *Assessment in Education: Principles, Policy & Practice, 18*(1), 5–25. http://dx.doi.org/10.1080/0969594X.2010.513678

Benton, D. (2010). The influence of dietary status on the cognitive performance of children. *Molecular Nutrition & Food Research, 54*(4), 457–470.

Berch, D. B., & Mazzocco, M. M. M. (Eds.) (2007). *Why is math so hard for some children: The nature and origins of mathematical learning difficulties and disabilities.* Baltimore, MD: Paul Brooke Publishing.

Berger, A., Kofman, O., Livneh, U., & Henik, A. (2007). Multidisciplinary perspectives on attention and the development of self-regulation. *Progress in Neurobiology, 82*(5), 256–286.

Bergmann, J., Overmyer, J., & Willie, B. (2011 July). The flipped class: What it is and what it is not. *The Daily Riff.* Retrieved 6 Jan 2012 from http://www.thedailyriff.com/articles/the-flipped-class-conversation-689.php

Bergmann, J., & Sams, A. (2012). *Flip your classroom: Reach every student in every class every day.* Washington, DC: International Society for Technology in Education.

Berns, G. S., Cohen, J. D., & Mintun, M. A. (1997). Brain regions responsive to novelty in the absence of awareness. *Science, 276*(5316), 1272–1275.

Bernsen, N. O. (1994). Foundations of multimodal representations: A taxonomy of representational modalities. *Interacting with Computers, 6*(4), 347–371.

Berkovich-Ohana, A., Glicksohn, J., & Goldstein, A. (2011). Mindfulness-induced changes in gamma band activity – Implications for the default mode network, self-reference and attention. *Clinical Neurophysiology, 123*(4), 700–710.

Berninger, V. W., & Corina, D. (1998, Sep). Making cognitive neuroscience educationally relevant: Creating bidirectional collaborations between educational psychology and cognitive neuroscience. *Educational Psychology Review, 10*(3), 343–354.

Berninger, V. W., & Winn, W. D. (2006). Implications of advancements in brain research and technology for writing development, writing instruction, and educational evolution. In C.A. MacArthur, S. Graham & Fitzgerald, J. (Eds.), *Handbook of writing research* (pp.96–114). New York, NY: Guilford.

Berridge, K. C. (2004). Motivation concepts in behavioral neuroscience. *Physiology & Behavior, 81*(2), 179–209.

Berthold, K., & Renkl, A. (2010). How to foster active processing of explanations in instructional communication. *Educational Psychology Review, 22*(1), 25–40.

Best, J. R., & Miller, P. H. (2010). A developmental perspective on executive function. *Child Development, 81*(6), 1641–1660.

Best, J. R., Miller, P. H., & Naglieri, J. A. (2011). Relations between executive function and academic achievement from ages 5 to 17 in a large, representative national sample. *Learning and Individual Difference, 21*(4), 327–336.

Betts, G. (2004). Fostering autonomous learners through levels of differentiation. *Roeper Review, 26*(4), 190–191. doi:10.1080/02783190409554269

Bevan, W., & Dukes, W. F. (1967). Stimulus-variation and recall: The role of belongingness. *The American Journal of Psychology, 80*(2), 309–312.

Bialystok, E. (2009). Effects of bilingualism on cognitive and linguistic performance across the lifespan. In I. Gogolin and U. Neumann (Eds.), *The bilingual controversy* (pp. 53–67). Germany: Springer. doi:10.1007/978-3-531-91596-8_4

Bialystok, E. (2011a). Coordination of executive functions in monolingual and bilingual children. *Journal of Experimental Child Psychology, 110*(3), 461–468. doi:10.1016/j.jecp.2011.05.005

Bialystok, E. (2011b). Reshaping the mind: The benefits of bilingualism. *Canadian Journal of Experimental Psychology/Revue Canadienne de Psychologie Expérimentale, 65*(4), 229–235. doi:10.1037/a0025406

Bialystok, E., Craik, F. I. M., & Luk, G. (2012). Bilingualism: Consequences for mind and brain. *Trends in Cognitive Neuroscience, 16*(4), 240–250. doi:doi.org/10.1016/j.tics.2012.03.001

Bialystok, E., & Feng, X. (2009). Language proficiency and executive control in proactive interference: Evidence form monolingual and bilingual children and adults. *Brain and Language, 109*(2–3), 93–100. doi:10.1016/j.bandl.2008.09.001

Bialystok, E., & Viswanathan, M. (2009). Components of executive control with advantages for bilingual children in two cultures. *Cognition, 112*(3), 494–500. doi:10.1016/j.cognition.2009.06.014. Epub 2009 Jul 16.

Biederman, I., & Vessel, E. (2006). Perceptual pleasure and the brain: A novel theory explains why the brain craves information and seeks it through the senses. *American Scientist, 94*(3), 247–253.

Biegel, G. M., & Brown, K. W. (2010). *Assessing the efficacy of an adapted in-class mindfulness-based training program for school-age children: A pilot study.* White Paper. Available on tinyurl.com/6ftayyx

Biggs, J. B., and Collis, K. (1982). *Evaluating the quality of learning: The SOLO taxonomy.* New York, NY: Academic Press.

Binder, J. R., & Desai, R. H. (2011). The neurobiology of semantic memory. *Trends in Cognitive Sciences, 15*(11), 527–536.

Bingham, C., & Kahl, S. (2012 July). The process of schema emergence: assimilation, deconstruction, utilization and the plurality of analogies. *Academy of Management Journal*. doi:10.5465/amj.2010.0723

Binkley, M., Erstad, O., Herman, J., Raizen, S., & Ripley M. (with Rumble, M.). (2010). *Draft White Paper 1: Defining 21st century skills*. Melbourne, Australia: University of Melbourne.

Bishka, A. (2010). Learning styles fray: Brilliant or batty? *Performance Improvement, 49*(10), 9–13.

Bishop, R., & Glynn, T. (2003). *Culture counts: Changing power relations in education*. New Zealand: Zed Books.

Blacher, J., Baker, B.L., & Eisenhower, A.S. (2009) Student–teacher relationship stability across early school years for children with intellectual disability or typical development. *American Journal on Intellectual and Developmental Disabilities: September 114*(5), 322–339. doi:http://dx.doi.org/10.1352/1944-7558-114.5.322

Blake, P. & Gardner, H. (2007). A first course in Mind, Brain, and Education. *Mind, Brain, and Education, 1*, 61–65.

Black, P., Harrison, C., Lee, C., Marshall, B., & William, D. (2004). Working inside the black box: Assessment for learning in the classroom. *Phi Delta Kappan, 86*(1), 8–21.

Black, P., & Wiliam, D. (2009). Developing the theory of formative assessment. *Educational Assessment, Evaluation, and Accountability, 21*, 5–31.

Black, P., & Wiliam, D. (2010). Inside the black box: Raising standards through classroom assessment: Formative assessment is an essential component of classroom work and can raise student achievement. *Phi Delta Kappan, 92*(1), 81–90.

Blake, R. J., & Kramsch, C. (2013). *Brave new digital classroom: Technology and foreign language learning* (2nd ed.). Washington, DC: Georgetown University Press.

Blakemore, S. J., & Decety, J. (2001). From the perception of action to the understanding of intention. *Nature Reviews Neuroscience, 2*, 561–567.

Blakemore, S. J., & Frith, U. (2005). *The learning brain*. Oxford: Blackwell.

Blakemore, S. J., & Frith, U. (2007). *The learning brain: Lessons for education*. Malden, MA: Blackwell.

Blakey, E., & Spence, S. (1990). Thinking for the future. *Emergency Librarian, 17*(5), May–June 1990, 11–14. Available on http://www.education.com/reference/article/Ref_Dev_Metacognition/

Blascovich, J., Mendes, W. B., Hunter, S. B., & Salomon, K. (1999). Social "facilitation" as challenge and threat. *Journal of Personality and Social Psychology, 77*(1), 68.

Block, J. H. (1972). Student learning and the setting of mastery performance standards. *Educational Horizons, 50*(4), 183–191.

Bloom, B. (1968). Learning for mastery. *Evaluation Comment, 1*(2), 1–12.

Bloom, B. S. (1971a). Mastery learning. In J. H. Block (Ed.), *Mastery learning: Theory and practice* (pp.47–63). New York, NY: Holt, Rinehart & Winston.

Bloom, B. S. (1971b). *Individual differences in school achievement: A vanishing point?* Bloomington, IN: Phi Delta Kappan International.

Bloom, B. S. (1974a). An introduction to mastery learning theory. In J. H. Block (Ed.), *Schools, society and mastery learning* (pp. 3–14). New York, NY: Holt, Rinehart & Winston.

Bloom, B. S. (1974b). Time and learning. *American Psychologist, 29*(9), 682.

Bloom, B. S. (1977). Favorable learning conditions for all. *Teacher, 95*(3), 22–28.

Bloom, B. S. (Ed.), Engelhart, M. D., Furst, E J., Hill, W. H., & Krathwohl, D. R. (1956). *Taxonomy of educational objectives: Handbook I: Cognitive domain.* New York, NY: David McKay.

Bollich, K. L., Johannet, P. M., & Vazire, S. (2011). In search of our true selves: Feedback as a path to self-knowledge. *Frontiers in Psychology, 2,* 312. doi:10.3389/fpsyg.2011.00312

Bonato, M., Zorzi, M., & Umilta., C. (2012). When time is space: Evidence for a mental time line. *Neuroscience and Behavioural Reviews, 36*(10), 2257–2273. doi.org/10.1016/j.neubiorev.2012.08.007

Bonk, C. (2011). *The world is open.* San Francisco, CA: Jossey-Bass.

Boone, R.Y. (2011). *The effects of effort-based and ability-based reinforcement cues on student perseverance.* Dissertation (Ph.D.). Lynchburg, VA: School of Education, Liberty University.

Boonshaft, P. L. (2010). *Teaching with passion, purpose and promise.* Des Moines, IA: Meredith.

Borkowski, J. G., Carr, M., Rellinger, E., & Pressley, M. (2013). Self-regulated cognition: Interdependence of metacognition. *Dimensions of Thinking and Cognitive Instruction, 53.*

Borup, J., Graham, C. R., & Velasquez, A. (2013). Technology-mediated caring: Building relationships between students and instructors in online K–12 learning environments. *Advances in Research on Teaching, 18,* 183–202.

Bowden, E. M. (1997). The effect of reportable and unreportable hints on anagram solution and the Aha! experience. *Consciousness and Cognition, 6*(4), 545–573. http://dx.doi.org/10.1006/ccog.1997.0325

Boyd, R., Richerson, P. J., & Henrich, J. (2011). The cultural niche: Why social learning is essential for human adaptation. *Proceedings of the National Academy of Sciences, 108*(Supplement 2), 10918–10925.

Brabec, K., Fisher, K., & Pitler, H. (2004). *Building better instruction: How technology supports nine research-proven instructional strategies.* Eugene, OR: ISTE.

Brackett, M. A., Rivers, S. E., Shiffman, S., Lerner, N. & Salovey, P. (2006). Relating emotional abilities to social functioning: A comparison of self-report and performance measures of emotional intelligence. *Journal of Personality and Social Psychology, 91*(4), 780–795.

Bradski, G., Carpenter, G. A., & Grossberg, S. (1994). STORE working memory networks for storage and recall of arbitrary temporal sequences. *Biological Cybernetics, 71*(6), 469–480.

Bransford, J., Vye, N., Stevens, R., Kuhl, P., Schwartz, D., Bell, P., Meltzoff, A., Barron, B., Pea, R., Reeves, B., Roschelle, J., & Sabelli, N. (2006). Learning theories and education: Toward a decade of synergy. In P. Alexander & P. Winne (Eds.), *Handbook of educational psychology* (2nd ed.) (pp. 209–244). Mahwah, NJ: Erlbaum.

Bransford, J. D., Barron, B., Pea, R., Meltzoff, A., Kuhl, P., Bell, P., Stevens, R., Schwartz, D., Vye, N., Reeves, B., Roschelle, J. & Sabelli, N. (2006). Foundations and opportunities for an interdisciplinary science of learning. In K. Sawyer (Ed.), *The Cambridge handbook of the learning sciences* (pp. 19–34). New York, NY: Cambridge University Press.

Brass, M., & Haggard, P. (2007). To do or not to do: The neural signature of self-control. *The Journal of Neuroscience, 27*(34), 9141–9145. doi:10.1523/JNEUROSCI.0924-07.2007

BrckaLorez, A., Cole, E., Kinzie, J., & Ribera, A. (2011). *Examining effective faculty practice: Teaching clarity and student engagement*. Paper presented at the annual meeting of the American Educational Research Association in New Orleans, April 2011.

Brekelmans, M., Wubbels, T., & den Brok, P. (2002). Teacher experience and the teacher-student relationship in the classroom environment. In S. C. Goh & M. S. Khine (Eds.), *Studies in educational learning environments: an international perspective* (pp.73–99). Singapore: World Scientific.

Bresó, E., Schaufeli, W. B., & Salanova, M. (2011). Can a self-efficacy-based intervention decrease burnout, increase engagement, and enhance performance? A quasi-experimental study. *Higher Education, 61*, 339–355.

Broderick, P. C. (2013). *Learning to breathe: A mindfulness curriculum for adolescents to cultivate emotion regulation, attention, and performance*. Oakland, CA: New Harbinger Publication.

Brookfield, S. (1995). *Becoming a critically reflective teacher*. San Francisco, CA: Jossey-Bass.

Brookfield, S. D., & Preskill, S. (2012). *Discussion as a way of teaching: Tools and techniques for democratic classrooms*. Hoboken, NJ: John Wiley & Sons.

Brookes, K., Xu, X., Chen, W., Zhou, K., Neale, B., Lowe, N., ... & McGuffin, P. (2006). The analysis of 51 genes in DSM-IV combined type attention deficit hyperactivity disorder: association signals in DRD4, DAT1 and 16 other genes. *Molecular Psychiatry, 11*(10), 934–953.

Brookshire, R. H., & Nicholas, M. E. (1993). Word choice in the connected speech of aphasic and non-brain damaged speakers. *Clinical Aphasiology, 21*, 101–112.

Brophy, J. E. (2010). *Motivating students to learn*. New York, NY: Routledge.

Brophy, J., & Good, T. (1986). Teacher behavior and student achievement. In M. Wittrock (Ed.), *Handbook of research on teaching* (3rd ed.) (pp. 328–375). Washington, DC: American Educational Researchers Association.

Brown, A. L. (1975). The development of memory: Knowing, knowing about knowing, and knowing how to know. In H. W. Reese (Ed.), *Advances in child development and behavior* (Vol. 10). New York, NY: Academic Press.

Brown, A. L. (1978). Knowing when, where, and how to remember: A problem of metacognition. In R. Glaser (Ed.), *Advances in instructional psychology 7* (pp.55–111). New York, NY: Academic Press.

Brown, A. L. (1980). Metacognitive development and reading. In R. S. Spiro, B. B. Bruce, & W. L. Brewer (Eds.), *Theoretical issues in reading comprehension*. Hillsdale, NJ: Erlbaum.

Brown, A. L. (1987). Metacognition, executive control, self-regulation and other more mysterious mechanism. In F.E. Weinert, & R.H. Kluwe (Eds.), *Metacognition, motivation, and understanding* (pp. 65–116). Hillsdale, NJ: Lawrence Erlbaum Associates.

Brown, K. G., & Gerhardt, M. W. (2006). Formative evaluation: An integrative practice model and case study. *Personnel Psychology, 55*(4), 951–983.

Browne, M. N., & Keeley, S. M. (2006). *Asking the right questions: A guide to critical thinking* (8th ed.). New York, NY: Prentice Hall.

Broyd, S. J., Demanuele, C., Debner, S., Helps, S. K., James, C. J. & Sonuga-Barke, E. J. S. (2008). Default-mode brain dysfunction in mental disorder: A systematic review. *Neuroscience and Behavioral Reviews, 33*(3), 279–296.

Bruer, J. T. (1997). Education and the brain: A bridge too far. *Educational Researcher, 26*(8), 4–16.

Bruer, J. T. (2005). Cognitive science: Interdisciplinary and intradisiplinary collaboration. In S. J. Derry, C. D. Schunn & M. A. Gernsbacher (Eds.), *Interdisciplinary collaboration: An emerging cognitive science* (pp. 222–224). New York, NY: Taylor & Francis.

Bruer, J. T. (2008). Building bridges in neuroscience. In A. M. Battro, K. W. Fischer & P. J. Léna (Eds.), *The educated brain* (pp. 43–58). Cambridge, UK: Cambridge University Press.

Bruer, J. T. (2009). Mapping cognitive neuroscience: Two-dimensional perspectives on twenty years of cognitive neuroscience research. In M. S. Gazzaniga (Ed.), *The Cognitive Neurosciences* (4th ed.) (pp. 1221–1234). Cambridge, MA: The MIT Press.

Bruer, J. T. (2010). Can we talk? How the cognitive neuroscience of attention emerged from neurobiology and psychology, 1980–2005. *Scientometrics, 83*(3), 751–764

Bruner, J. S. (2009). *The process of education*. Cambridge, MA: Harvard University Press.

Buckner, R. L., & Carroll, D. C. (2007). Self-projection and the brain. *Trends in Cognitive Sciences, 11*(2), 49–57.

Burgess, G. C., Gray, J. R., Conway, A. R., & Braver, T. S. (2011). Neural mechanisms of interference control underlie the relationship between fluid intelligence and working memory span. *Journal of Experimental Psychology: General, 140*(4), 674.

Burkam, D., Ready, D., Lee, V., & LoGerfo, L. (2003). Social class differences in summer learning between kindergarten and first grade: Model specification and estimation. *Sociology of Education, 77*(1), 1–31.

Burleson, W. (2005). Developing creativity, motivation, and self-actualization with learning systems. *International Journal of Human-Computer Studies, 63*, 436–451.

Butler, S. M., & McMunn, N. D. (2006). *A teacher's guide to classroom assessment: Understanding and using assessment to improve student learning*. San Francisco, CA: Jossey-Bass.

Butterworth, B. (1975). Hesitation and semantic planning in speech. *Journal of Psycholinguistic research, 4*(1), 75–87.

Butz, M., Wörgötter, F., & van Ooyen, A. (2009). Activity-dependent structural plasticity. *Brain Research Reviews, 60*(2), 287–305. doi:http://dx.doi.org/10.1016/j.brainresrev.2008.12.023,

Buzsaki, G. (2006). *Rhythms of the brain*. New York, NY: Oxford University Press.

Bybee, R. W., Taylor, J. A., Gardner, A., Van Scotter, P., Carlson Powell, J., Westbrook, A., & Landes, N. (2006). *The BSCS 5E instructional model: Origins and effectiveness*. A report prepared for the Office of Science Education and the National Institutes of Health. Colorado Springs, CO: BSCS.

Byrnes, J. (2010). Some ways in which neuroscientific research can be relevant to education. In D. Coch, K.W. Fischer, G. Dawson (Eds.), *Human behavior, learning, and the developing brain: typical development* (pp.30–49). New York, NY: Guilford.

Byrnes, J., & Fox, N. A. (1998 Sep). The educational relevance of research in cognitive neuroscience. *Educational Psychology Review, 10,* 297–342.

Cain, L. F., & De Veri, R. (1939). The effect of spaced learning on the curve of retention. *Journal of Experimental Psychology, 25*(2), 209–214. doi:10.1037/h0054640

Caine, G., & Nummela-Caine, R. (1997). *Education on the edge of possibility.* Alexandria, VA: Association for Supervision and Curriculum Development.

California Department of Education. (2007). *Year-round education program guide.* Sacramento, CA: Author. Retrieved 1 Aug 2013 from http://www.cde.ca.gov/ls/fa/yr/guide.asp

Callan, D. E., & Schweighofer, N. (2010). Neural correlates of the spacing effect in explicit verbal semantic encoding support the deficient-processing theory. *Human Brain Mapping, 31,* 645–659. doi:10.1002/hbm.20894

Callan, R. J. (1995). Early morning challenge: The potential effects of chronobiology on taking the scholastic aptitude test. *The Clearing House, 68*(3), 174–176.

Callejas, A., Lupianez, J., & Tuleda, P. (2004). The three attentional networks: On their independence and interactions. *Brain and Cognition, 54,* 225–227.

Calvert, G. A. (2001). Crossmodal processing in the human brain: Insights from functional neuroimaging studies. *Cerebral Cortex, 11*(12), 1110–1123.

Capelo, C., & Dias, J. (2009). A feedback learning and mental models perspective on strategic decision making. *Educational Technology, Research and Development, 57*(5), 629–644.

Caramazza, A., & Coltheart, M. (2006, Feb). Cognitive neuropsychology twenty years on. *Cognitive Neuropsychology, 23*(1), 3–12.

Cardinali, D. P. (2008). Chronoeducation: How the biological clock influences the learning process. In A. Battro, K. Fischer, and P. Lená (Eds.), *The educated brain: Essays in neuroeducation,* (pp. 110–126). Cambridge, UK: Cambridge University Press.

Carlson, S. M., & Meltzoff, A. N. (2008). Bilingual experience and executive functioning in young children. *Developmental Science, 11*(2), 282–298.

Carlson, S. M., Moses, L. J., & Breton, C. (2002). How specific is the relation between executive function and theory of mind? Contributions of inhibitory control and working memory. *Infant and Child Development, 11*(2), 73–92.

Carpenter, S. K., Cepeda, N. J., Rohrer, D., Kang, S. H. K., & Pashler, H. (2012). Using spacing to enhance diverse forms of learning: Review of recent research and implications for instruction. *Educational Psychology Review, 24*(3), 369–378.

Cacioppo, J. T., Berntson, G. G., & Decety, D. (2010). Social neuroscience and its relationship to social psychology. *Social Cognition, 28*(Special Issue), 675–685.

Campbell-Meiklejohn, D. K., Bach, D. R., Roepstorff, A., Dolan, R. J., & Frith, C. D. (2010). How the opinion of others affects our valuation of objects. *Current Biology, 20*(13), 1165–1170.

Carnegie Mellon Eberly Center for Teaching Excellence & Educational Innovation. (2013). *How learning works.* Retrieved 14 Sept 2013 from http://www.cmu.edu/teaching/

Carroll, R.G. (2012). It's all about the teacher-student relationship. *Advances in Physiology Education, 36*(4), 233. doi:10.1152/advan.

Carruthers, P. (2009). How we know our own minds: The relationship between mindreading and metacognition. *Behavioral and Brain Sciences, 32,* 121–138 doi:10.1017/S0140525X 09000545

Carter, C. (1997). Why reciprocal teaching? *Educational Leadership. 54,* 64–68.

Carter, M., & Wheldall, K. (2008). Why can't a teacher be more like a scientist? Science, pseudoscience and the art of teaching. *Australian Journal of Special Education 32*(1), 5–12. doi:10.1080/10300110701845920

Cash, R. M. (2010). *Advancing differentiation: Thinking and learning for the 21st century.* Minneapolis, MN: Free Spirit Publishing.

Caspi, A., & Moffitt, T. E. (2006 July). Gene–environment interactions in psychiatry: joining forces with neuroscience. *Nature Reviews Neuroscience 7,* 583–590. doi:10.1038/nrn1925

Cattell, R. B. (1963). Theory of fluid and crystallized intelligence: A critical experiment. *Journal of Educational Psychology, 54*(1), 1.

Cauley, K., & McMillan, J. (2010). Formative assessment techniques to support student and achievement. *The Clearing House 83*(1), 1–6.

Cazden, C. (2001). *Classroom discourse: The language of teaching and learning* (2nd ed.). Portsmouth, NH: Heinemann.

Cazden, C., Vera, J. P., & Hymes, D. (Eds.) (1972). *Functions of language in the classroom.* New York, NY: Teachers College Press.

Center for the Developing Child at Harvard. (2013). *Resources.* Available on http://developing-child.harvard.edu/

Chaudhari, S., & Kadam, S. (2012). Ages and stages questionnaire–A developmental screening test. *Indian Pediatrics, 49*(6), 440–441.

Chart, H., & Kendall-Taylor, N. (2008). *Reform what? Individualist thinking in education: American cultural models on schooling.* Quincy, MA: The Frame Works Institute of the Nellie Mae Education Foundation and the Lumina Foundation for Education.

Chen, Y., Rex, C. S., Rice, C. J., Dubé, C. M., Gall, C. M., Lynch, G., & Baram, T. Z. (2010). Correlate memory defects and hippocampal dendritic spine loss after acute stress involve corticotropin-releasing hormone signaling. *Proceedings of the National Academy of Science of the United States of America, 107*(29), 13123–12128. doi:10.1073/pnas.1003825107

Cheng, M. T., & Annetta, L. (2012). Students' learning outcomes and learning experiences through playing a Serious Educational Game. *Journal of Biological Education, 46*(4), 203–213.

Cheseboro, J. L. (2002). Teaching clearly. In J. L. Chesebro & J. C. McCroskey (Eds.), *Communication for Teachers* (pp. 93–103). Boston, MA: Allyn and Bacon.

Cheseboro, J. L. (2003). Effect of teacher clarity and nonverbal immediacy on student learning, receiver apprehension, and affect. *Communication Education, 52*(2), 135–147. doi:10.1080/03634520320000085108

Cheseboro, J. L., & McCroskey, J. C. (1998). The development of the teacher clarity short inventory (TCSI) to measure clear teaching in the classroom. *Communication Research Reports, 15*, 262–266.

Cheseboro, J. L., & McCroskey, J. C. (2000). The relationship between students' reports of learning and their actual recall of lecture material: A validity test. *Communication Education, 49*, 297–301.

Cheseboro, J. L., & McCroskey, J.C. (2001). The relationship of teacher clarity and immediacy with student state receiver apprehension, affect, and cognitive learning. *Communication Education, 50*(1), 59–68. doi:10.1080/03634520109379232

Chester, M., Buntine, A., Hammond, K., & Atkinson, L. (2011). Podcasting in education: Student attitudes, behavior and self-efficacy. *Educational Technology and Society, 14*(2), 236–247.

Chiao, J. Y., & Ambady, N. (2010). Cultural neuroscience. In S. Kitayama and D. Cohen (Eds.), *Handbook of cultural psychology*. New York, NY: Guilford.

Choi, I., & Lee, K. (2009). Designing and implementing a case-based learning environment for enhancing ill-structured problem-solving: classroom management problems for prospective teachers. *Educational Technology Research and Development, 57*(1), 99–129.

Chiou, K. S., Carlson, R. A., Arnett, P. A., Cosentino, S. A., & Hillary, F. G. (2011). Metacognitive monitoring in moderate and severe traumatic brain injury. *Journal of the International Neuropsychological Society, 17*(4), 720.

Christenson, S. L., Reschly, A. L. & Wylie, C. (Eds.) (2012). *Handbook of research on student engagement*. New York, NY: Springer.

Christoff, K. (2008). Applying neuroscientific findings to education: The good, the tough and the hopeful. *Mind, Brain, and Education, 2*, 55–58.

Chriuckshank, D. R. & Kennedy, J. J. (1986). Teacher clarity. *Teaching and Teacher Education, 2*(1), 43–67.

Chun, M. M., & Turk-Browne, N. B. (2007). Interactions between attention and memory. *Current Opinion in Neurobiology, 17*(2), 177–184.

Clark, R. C., Nguyen, F., & Sweller, J. (2005). *Efficiency in learning: Evidence-based guidelines to manage cognitive load*. Hoboken, NJ: John Wiley.

Clifford, M. M., & Walster, E. (1973). The effect of physical attractiveness on teacher expectations. *Sociology of Education, 46*(2), 248–258.

Church, A. (2007). Educational origami. *Bloom's and ICT Tools*. Available on http://www.techlearning.com/studies-in-ed-tech/0020/blooms-taxonomy-blooms-digitally/44988

Civikly, J. M. (1992). Clarity - Teachers and students making sense of instruction. *Communication Education, 41*(2), 138–152.

Coch, D., Fischer, K. W. & Dawson, G (2010). *Human behavior, learning, and the developing brain: Typical development.* New York, NY: Guilford.

Cochran, J. L., McCallum, R. S., & Bell, S. M. (2010). Three A's: How do attributions, attitudes, and aptitudes contribute to foreign language learning? *Foreign Language Annals, 43*(4), 566–582.

Coffey, C., Cummings, J. L., Lovell, M. R., & Pearlson, G. D. (1994). *The American Psychiatric Press textbook of geriatric neuropsychiatry.* Arlington, VA: American Psychiatric Association.

Cohen, M., Axmacher, N., Lenartz, D., Elger, C., Sturm, V., & Schlaepfer, T. (2009). Neuroelectric signatures of reward learning and decision-making in the human nucleus accumbens. *Neuropsychopharmacology, 34*(7), 1649–58.

Cohen, M., & Ranganath, C. (2007). Reinforcement learning signals predict future decisions. *Journal of Neuroscience 27*(2), 371–378.

Coley, R., (2002). *An uneven start: Indicators of inequality in school readiness.* Princeton, NJ: Educational Testing Service, Policy Information Center.

Collins, A., Brown, J. S., & Newman, S. (1989). Cognitive apprenticeship: Teaching the craft of reading, writing, and mathematics. In L. Resnick (Ed.), *Knowing, learning and instruction: Essays in honor of Robert Glaserm* (pp.453–494). New York, NY: Taylor & Francis Group.

Coltheart, M. (2004, Feb). Brain imaging, connectionism, and cognitive neuropsychology. *Cognitive Neuropsychology, 21*(1), 21–25.

Colvin, R.L. (1999 Jan 25). Losing faith in the self-esteem movement. *Los Angeles Times.*

Comadena, M. E., Hunt, S. K., & Simonds, C. J. (2007). The effects of teacher clarity, nonverbal immediacy, and caring on student motivation, affective and cognitive learning. *Communication Research Reports, 24*(3), 241–248. doi:10.1080/08824090701446617

Commins, S., Cunningham, L., Harvey, D., & Walsh, D. (2003). Massed but not spaced training impairs spatial memory. *Behavioural Brain Research, 139*(1), 215–223.

Commission on the Future of Higher Education (2006). *Final report—A test of leadership: Charting the future of higher education.* Retrieved September 27, 2008 from http://www.ed.gov/about/bdscomm/list/hiedfuture/reports.html.

Connell, M. (2005). *Foundations of educational neuroscience integrating theory, experiment, and design.* Dissertation (Ed. D.), Harvard Graduate School of Education, Massachusetts. AAT 3207712.

Conrad, C.D., & Wolf, O.T. (2010). Effects of stress on learning and memory. In *The Handbooks of stress: Neuropsychological effects on the brain.* Hoboken, NJ: Wiley Blackwell. doi:10.1002/9781118083222.ch27

Cook, T. W. (1944 Jan). Repetition and learning. I. Stimulus and response. *Psychological Review, 51*(1), 25–36. doi:10.1037/h0058927

Cooper, H. (2004). Year round schooling gives students a boost. *Duke Today.* Durham, NC: Duke

University. Retrieved 1 August 2013 from http://today.duke.edu/2004/08/boost_0804 .html

Cooper, H., Valentine, J., Charlton, K., & Melson, A. (2003). The effects of modified school calendars on student achievement and on school and community attitudes. *Review of Education Research, 73*(1), 1–52.

Cooper, H. M. (1979). Pygmalion grows up: A model for teacher expectation communication and performance influence. *Review of Educational Research, 49*(3), 389–410.

Cooper, H. M., & Tom, D. Y. H. (1984). Teacher expectation research: A review with implications for classroom instruction. *The Elementary School Journal, 85*(1), 76–89.

Cooper, P., & McIntyre, D. (1996). *Effective teaching and learning: teachers' and students' perspectives.* Buckingham: Open University Press.

Cooper-Kahn, J., & Dietzel, L. (2008). *Late, lost, and unprepared: A parents' guide to helping children with executive functioning.* Bethesda, MD: Woobine House.

Cope, J., & Watts, G. (1995). Learning by doing: an exploration of experience, critical incidents and reflection in entrepreneurial learning. *International Journal of Entrepreneurial Behaviour & Research,* 104–124.

Copeland, M. (2005). *Socratic circles: Fostering critical and creative thinking in middle and high school.* Portland, ME: Stenhouse Publishers.

Copple, C. (2010). *Developmentally appropriate practice in early childhood programs servicing children birth through age eight.* Washington, DC: National Association for Education of Young Children.

Corbett, D., & Wilson, B. (2002). What urban students say about good teaching. *Educational Leadership, 60*(1), 18–22.

Cornelius-White, J. (2007). Learner-centered teacher-student relationships are effective: A meta-analysis. *Review of Educational Research, 77*(1), 113–143.

Costa, A., & Kallick, B. (2000). *Habits of mind: A developmental series.* Alexandria, VA: Association for Supervision and Curriculum Development.

Costa, A., & Kallick, B. (2009). *Learning and leading with habits of mind: 16 characteristics for success.* Alexandria, VA: ASCD.

Cote, J. E., & Levine, C. G. (2000). Attitude versus aptitude: Is intelligence or motivation more important for positive higher-educational outcomes? *Journal of Adolescent Research, 15*(1), 58–80. doi:10.1177/0743558400151004

Cotton, K. (2000). *The schooling practices that matter most.* Portland, OR: Northwest Regional Educational Laboratory and Alexandria, VA: ASCD.

Cousteau, J. Y. (1981). *An inventory of life on a water planet.* New York, NY: Knopf Doubleday.

Craik, F. I. M., Bialystok, E., & Freedman, M. (2010). Delaying the onset of Alzheimer disease: Bilingualism as a form of cognitive reserve. *Neurology, 75*(19), 1726–1729.

Cramer, K. B. (2012). *Impact of constructivism via the biological sciences curriculum study (BSCS) 5E model on student science achievement and attitude.* Montana State University. A professional development submitted in partial fulfillment of Master of Science degree. Unpublished document.

Crawford, A. (2007). Learning to teach science as inquiry in the rough and tumble of practice. *Journal of Research in Science Teaching, 44*(4), 613–642. doi:10.1002/tea.20157

Crestani, F., Lorez, M., Baer, K., Essrich, C., Benke, D., Laurent, J. P., ... & Mohler, H. (1999). Decreased GABAA-receptor clustering results in enhanced anxiety and a bias for threat cues. *Nature Neuroscience, 2*(9), 833–839.

Crisp, G.T. (2012). *Integrative assessment: Reframing assessment practice for current and future learning.* Philadelphia, PA: Routledge.

Crosnoe, R., Johnson, M. K., & Elder, G. H. (2004). Intergenerational bonding in school: the behavioral and contextual correlates of student-teacher relationship. *Sociology of Education, 77*(1), 60–81. doi: 10.1177/003804070407700103

Cross, D. R., & Paris, S. G. (1988). Developmental and instructional analyses of children's metacognition and reading comprehension. *Journal of Educational Psychology, 80*(2), 131–142.

Crosswell, L. J., & Elliott, R. G. (2004). *Committed teachers, passionate teachers: The dimension of passion associated with teacher commitment and engagement.* Melbourne, Australia: AARE Conference November 28th–December 2nd.

Crow, S., & Small, R.V. (2011 Feb). Developing the motivation within: Using praise and rewards effectively. *School Library Monthly, 27*(5), 5–7.

Crowley, K., Schunn, C. D., & Okada, T. (2001). *Designing for science: Implications from everyday, classroom, and professional settings.* New York, NY: Taylor & Francis.

Cruickshank, D. R. (1985). Applying research on teacher clarity. *Journal of Teacher Education, 36*(2), 44–48.

Cruickshank, D. R., & Kennedy, J. J. (1986). Teacher clarity. *Teaching & Teacher Education, 2*, 43–67.

Cruickshank, D. R., Kennedy, J. J., Bush, A., & Myers, B. (1979). Clear teaching - What is it. *British Journal of Teacher Education, 5*(1), 27–33.

Csikszentmihalyi, M. (1997). Finding flow: *The psychology of engagement with everyday life.* New York, NY: Basic Books.

Cubukcu, F. (2010). Congruence and dissonance between micro-teaching and macro-teaching. *Procedia - Social and Behavioral Sciences, 2*(2), 326–329. http://dx.doi.org/10.1016/j.sbspro.2010.03.019

Cushman, K. (2012). *Fires in the mind: What kids can tell us about motivation and mastery.* San Francisco, CA: Jossey-Bass.

Czabanowske, K., Moust, J. H. C., Meijer, A. W. M., Schröder-Bäck, P., & Roebertsen, H. (2012). Problem-based learning revisited, introduction of active and self-directed learning to reduce fatigue among students. *Journal of University Teaching and Learning Practice, 9*(1). Retrieved 9 Aug 2013 from http://ro.uow.edu.au/cgi/viewcontent.cgi?article=1266&context=jutlp

Dana, N. F., & Yendol-Hoppey, D. (2008). *The reflective educator's guide: Professional development, coaching inquiry-oriented learning communities* (2nd ed.). Thousand Oaks, CA: Corwin.

Daniel, D. (2012). Promising principles: Translating the science of learning to educational practice. *Journal of Applied Research in Memory and Cognition, 1*(2), 251–253.

Daniel, L. M., Stupisky, R. H., Pekrun, R., Haynes, T. L., Perry, R. P., & Newall, N. E. (2009). A longitudinal analysis of achievement goals: From affective antecedents to emotional effects and achievement outcomes. *Journal of Educational Psychology, 101*(4), 948–963.

Daniels, H. (2010). Vygotsky and psychology. In U. Goswami (Ed.), *The Wiley-Blackwell handbook of childhood cognitive development* (2nd ed.) (pp. 673–696). Oxford, UK: Wiley Blackwell. doi:10.1002/9781444325485.ch26

Darling-Hammond, L. (2006). *Powerful teacher education: Lessons from exemplary programs.* San Francisco, CA: Jossey-Bass.

Darling-Hammond, L., & Bransford, J. (2012). *Preparing teachers for a changing world: What teachers should learn and be.* Hoboken, NJ: John Wiley & Sons.

Das, S. K. (2005). Geriatric neurology-a burgeoning social issue. *Journal of the Indian Medical Association, 103*(3), 131–144.

Daugherty, J., & Mentzer, N. (2008). Analogical reasoning in the engineering design process and technology education applications. *Journal of Technology Education, 19*(2), 7–21.

Davis, H.A. (2003). Conceptualizing the role and influence of student-teacher relationships on children's social and cognitive development. *Educational Psychologist, 38*(4). doi:10.1207/S15326985EP3804_2

Davis, K. S., & Dupper, D. R. (2008). Student-teacher relationships. *Journal of Human Behavior in the Social Environment, 9*(1–2), 179–193. doi:10.1300/J137v09n01_12

Daw, N. D., & Shohamy, D. (2008). The cognitive neuroscience of motivation and learning. *Social Cognition, 26*(5), 593–620.

Dawson, P., & Guare, R. (2010). *Executive skills in children and adolescents: A practice guide to assessment and intervention* (2nd ed.). New York, NY: The Guildford Press.

Day, C. (2004). *A passion for teaching.* London, UK: Routledge.

Daynes, G. (1956). Bread and tears: Naughtiness, depression and fits due to wheat sensitivity. *Proceedings of the Royal Society of Medicine, 49*(7), 391–394.

De Greck, M., Shi, Z., Wang, G., Zuo, X., Wang, X., Northoff, G., & Han, S. (2012). Culture modulated brain activity during empathy with anger. *NeuroImage, 59*(3), 2871–2882.

Decety, J., & Baston, D. (2007). Social neuroscience approached to interpersonal sensitivity. *Social Neuroscience, 2*(3–4), 151–157.

Decety, J., & Lamm, C. (2007). The role of the right temporoparietal junction in social interaction: How low-level computational processes contribute to meta-cognition. *Neuroscientist, 13*(6), 580–593.

Decety, J., & Sommerville, J.A. (2003). Shared representations between self and other: A social cognitive neuroscience view. *Trend in Cognitive Sciences, 7*(12), 527–533. http://dx.doi.org/10.1016/j.tics.2003.10.004

Deci, E., Koestner, R., & Ryan, R. M. (1999). A meta-analytic review of experiments examining the effects of extrinsic rewards on intrinsic motivation. *Psychological Bulletin, 125*(6), 627–668. doi:10.1037/0033-2909.125.6.627

Deci, E. L., Vallerand, R. J., Pelletier, L. G., & Ryan, R. M. (1991). Motivation and education: The self-determination perspective. *Educational Psychologist, 26*(3–4), 325–346.

Decker, J. L. (1997). *Self-styled success from Horatio Alger to Oprah Winfrey.* Minneapolis, MN: University of Minnesota Press.

Deco, G., & Rolls, E. T. (2005). Attention, short-term memory, and action selection: A unifying theory. *Progress in Neurobiology, 76*(4), 236–256.

Dehaene, S. (1997). *The number sense.* London, UK: Oxford University Press.

Dehaene, S. (2009). *Reading in the brain.* London, UK: Penguin Books.

Dehaene, S. (2011a). *The number sense: How the mind creates mathematics* (rev. ed.). New York, NY: Oxford University Press.

Dehaene, S. (2011b). The massive impact of literacy on the brain and its consequences for education. *Human Neuroplasticity and Education.* Pontifical Academy of Sciences, Scripta Varia 17, 201. Retrieved from onwww.pas.va/content/dam/accademia/pdf/sv117/sv117-dehaene.pdf

Dehaene, S., Cohen, L., Sigman, M., & Vinckier, F. (2005). The neural code for written words: A proposal. *Trend in Cognitive Sciences 9*(7), pp. 335–341.

Daley, E. (2003, March–April). Expanding the concept of literacy. *EDUCAUSE*, 33–40. Retrieved 9 Aug 2013 from http://net.educause.edu/ir/library/pdf/erm0322.pdf

Dede, C., & Richards, J. (Eds.) (2012). *Digital teaching platforms: Customizing classroom learning for each student.* New York, NY: Teachers College Press.

Dekker, S., Krabbendam, L., Gemmink, M., De Groot, R., & Jolles, J. (2012). *Implementation of a neuropsychological intervention in secondary school: Targeting executive problems in young adolescent boys.* Poster Session, International Mind, Brain, and Education conference. Retrieved 12 October 2013 from http://dspace.ou.nl/bitstream/1820/4118/1/110330%20Poster%20proposal%20IMBES_BREIN.pdf

Dekker, S., Lee, N.C., Howard-Jones, P., & Jolles, J. (2012 Oct). Neuromyths in education: Prevalence and predictors of misconceptions among teachers. *Frontiers in Educational Psychology.* doi:10.3389/fpsyg.2012.00429

Devlin, J. T., & Poldrack, R. A. (2007). In praise of tedious anatomy. *Neuroimage, 37*(4), 1033–1041.

D'Mello, S. (2012). Monitoring affective trajectories during complex learning. *Encyclopedia of the Sciences of Learning*, 2325–2328.

Demo, D. H. (1992). The self-concept over time: Research issues and directions. *Annual Review of Sociology*, 303–326.

Dempster, F. N. (1988). The spacing effect: A case study in the failure to apply the results of psychological research. *American Psychologist, 43*(8), 627–634. doi:10.1037/0003-066X.43 .8.627

Denckla, M. (2005, April). *Paying attention to the brain and executive function: How learning and memory are impaired by the syndrome called ADHD.* Paper presented at the Learning and the Brain Conference, Harvard University, Cambridge, MA.

Dennett, D. (1992). *Consciousness explained.* Boston, MA: Back Bay Books.

Department of Healthy and Inclusive Communities of Canada. (2012). *Join the wellness movement.* Retrieved 10 Sept 2013 from http://www.wellnessnb.ca/

Deprez, S., Vandenbulcke, M., Peeters, R., Emsell, L., Amant, F., & Sunaert, S. (2013). The functional neuroanatomy of multitasking: Combining dual tasking with a short term memory task. *Neuropsychologia, 51*(11), 2251–2260.

Derry, S. J., Schunn, C. D., & Gernsbacher, M. A. (Eds.) (2009). *Interdisciplinary collaboration: An emerging cognitive science.* Mahwah, NJ: Erlbaum.

Desautel, D. (2009). Becoming a thinking thinker: Metacognition, self-reflection, and classroom practice. *Teachers College Records, 111*(8), http://www.tcrecord.org ID Number: 15504

De Hann, M., & Grunnar, M. R. (2009). *Handbook of developmental social neuroscience.* New York, NY: Guilford.

De Smedt, B., Ansari, D., Grabner, R.H., Hannula, M.M. Schneider, M., & Verschaffel, L. (2010). Cognitive neuroscience meets mathematics education. *Educational Research Review, 5*(1), 97–105.

De Smedt, B., Verschaffel, L., & Ghesquiere, P. (2009). The predictive value of numerical magnitude comparison for individual differences in mathematics achievement. *Journal of Experimental Child Psychology 103*(4), 469–479.

Devlin, J. T., Jamison, H. L., Gonnerman, L. M., & Matthews, P. M. (2006). The role of the posterior fusiform gyrus in reading. *Journal of Cognitive Neuroscience, 18* (6), 911–922.

DeWeerdt, S. (2011). Prevention: Activity is the best medicine. *Nature, 475*(7355), S16–S17.

Dewey, J. (1896). *The university school.* Chicago, IL: University Record, University of Chicago.

Dewey, J. (1929). *Sources of a science of education.* NewYork, NY: Liveright.

Dewey, J. (1971). *How we think.* Chicago, Henry Regnery Company. Originally published in 1910.

Diamond, A. (2010). The evidence base for improving school outcomes by addressing the whole child and by addressing skills and attitudes, not just content. *Early Education and Development, 21,* 780–793.

Diamond, A. (2012). Activities and programs that improve children's executive functions. *Current Directions in Psychological Science, 21*(5), 335–341.

Diamond, A., Barnett, W. S., Thomas, J., & Munro, S. (2007). Preschool program improves cognitive control. *Science, 318*(5855), 1387–1388.

Diamond, A., & Lee, K. (2011). Interventions shown to aid executive function development in children 4 to 12 years old. *Science, 333*(6045), 956–964.

Diamond, M., Scheibel, A. B., Murphy, G. M., & Harvey, T. (1985). On the brain of a scientist: Albert Einstein. *Exploratory Neurology, 88*(1), 198–204.

Dietrich, A. (2004). The cognitive neuroscience of creativity. *Psychonomic Bulletin & Review, 11*(6), 1011–1026.

Diller, D. (2007). *Making the most of small groups: Differentiation for all.* Portland, ME: Stenhouse Publishers.

Dillion, A. (1992). Reading from paper versus screens: A critical review of the empirical literature. *Ergonomics, 35*(10), 1297–1326.

Dillon, J. T. (1983). *Teaching and the art of questioning.* Bloomington, IN: Phi Delta Kappa.

Dishman, R. K., & O'Connor, P. J. (2009). Lessons in exercise neurobiology: The case of endorphins. *Mental Health and Physical Activity, 2*(1), 4–9. doi:http://dx.doi.org/10.1016/j.mhpa.2009.01.002

Dixon, R. (2010). *Experts and novices: Differences in their use of mental representations and metacognition in engineering design.* Dissertation (Ph.D.). Urbana-Champaign, IL: University of Illinois at Urbana-Champaign.

Doherty, G. (2007). *Conception to age six: The foundation to school readiness.* Toronto, Ontario: Learning Partnership. Retrieved 10 Sept 2013 from http://www. thelearningpartnership. ca/policy_research/Early_Years_researchpaper-jan07.pdf

Doidge, N. (2007). *The brain that changes itself: Stories of personal triumph from the frontiers of brain science.* New York, NY: Penguin.

Donovan, J. J., & Radosevich, D. J. (1999). A meta-analysis review of the distribution of practice effect: Now you see it, now you don't. *Journal of Applied Psychology, 84*(5), 795–805. doi:10.1037/0021-9010.84.5.795

Doolittle, P. E., Hicks, D., Triplett, C. F., Nichols, W. D., & Young, C. A. (2006). Reciprocal teaching for reading comprehension in higher education: A strategy for fostering the deeper understanding of texts. *International Journal of Teaching and Learning in Higher Education, 17*(2), 106–118.

Doran, G. T. (1981). There's a S.M.A.R.T. way to write management goals and objectives. *Management Review, 70*(11), 35–36.

Dore, L. R., & Hilgard, E. R. (1938). Spaced practice as a test of Snoddy's two processes in mental growth. *Journal of Experimental Psychology, 23*(4), 359–374. doi:10.1037/h0063101

Dosher, B. A. (1984). Degree of learning and retrieval speed: Study time and multiple exposures. *Journal of Experimental Psychology: Learning, Memory, and Cognition, 10*(4), 541.

Dougherty, M., Thomas, R., & Lange, N. (2010). Toward an integrative theory of hypothesis generation, probability judgment, and hypothesis testing. *Psychology of Learning and Motivation, 52*, 299–342.

Douglas, K. (2009 Oct). Sharpening our focus in measuring classroom instruction. *Educational Researcher, 38*, 518–521. doi:10.3102/0013189X09350881

Downey, D., Hippel, P., & Broh, B. (2004). Are schools the great equalizer? Cognitive inequality during the summer months and the school year. *American Sociological Review, 69*, 613–635.

Doyle. (2011). *Learner-centered teaching: Putting the research on learning into practice.* Sterling, VA: Stylus Publishing, LLC.

Drach-Zahavy, A., & Erez, M. (2002). Challenge versus threat effects on the goal–performance relationship. *Organizational Behavior and Human Decision Processes, 88*(2), 667–682.

Draganski, B., Gaser, C., Busch, V., Schuierer, G., Bogdahn, U., & May, A. (2004). Changes in grey matter induced by training. *Nature, 427*, 311–312.

Dressen, M., & Tillmanns, L. (2010). *Schools as learning communities.* Descrierea CIP a Bibliotecii Naţionale a României The first ten years after Bologna/ed.: Otmar Gassner, 183–199.

Duckworth, A. L., Quinn, P. D., & Seligman, M. E. (2009). Positive predictors of teacher effectiveness. *The Journal of Positive Psychology, 4*(6), 540–547.

Duit, R. (1991). On the role of analogies and metaphors in learning sciences. *Science Education, 75*(6), 649–672. doi:10.1002/sce.3730750606

Dumont, H., Istance, D. & Benavides, F. (Eds.) (2010). *The nature of learning: Using research to inspire practice.* Paris: Author.

Duncan, G. J., Claessens, A., Huston, A. C., Pagani, L. S., Engel, M., Sexton, H., ...& Japel, C. (2007). School readiness and later achievement. *Developmental Psychology, 43*(6), 1428–1446.

Dunlosky, J., & Metcalfe, J. (2009). *Metacognition.* Thousand Oaks, CA: Sage.

Dunn, K. E., & Mulvenon, S. W. (2009). A critical review of research on formative assessment: The limited scientific evidence of the impact of formative assessment in education. *Practical Assessment, Research & Evaluation, 14*(7), 1–11.

Durlak, J. A., Weissberg, R. P., Dymnicki, A. B., Taylor, R. D., & Schellinger, K. B. (2011). The impact of enhancing students' social and emotional learning: A meta-analysis of school-based universal interventions. *Child Development, 82*(1), 405–432.

Duron, R., Limbach, B., & Waugh, W. (2006). Critical thinking framework for any discipline. *International Journal of Teaching and Learning in Higher Education, 17*(2), 160–166.

DuRussel, L. A., & Derry, S. J. (2005). Schema (mis)alignment in interdisciplinary teamwork. In S. J. Derry, C. D. Schunn, & M. A. Gernsbacher (Eds.), *Interdisciplinary collaboration: An emerging cognitive science* (pp.187–222). New York, NY: Taylor & Francis.

Dweck, C. A. (2007). *Mindset: The new psychology of success.* New York, NY: Ballantine Books.

Eberly Center for Teaching Excellence. (n.d.). *The educational value of course-level learning objectives/outcomes.* Retrieved 27 May 2012 from http://www.cmu.edu/teaching/designteach/design/learningobjectives.html

Eden, D. (1990). Pygmalion without interpersonal contrast effects: Whole groups gain from raising manager expectations. *Journal of Applied Psychology, 75*(4), 394–398.

Editor. (2004). Better reading through neuroscience. *Nature Neuroscience 7*(1). doi:10.1038/nn0104-1

Educational Research Service. (2000). *Effective classrooms: Teacher behaviors that produce high student achievement.* Arlington, VA: Author.

Eichenbaum, H. (2011). *The cognitive neuroscience of memory: An introduction.* New York, NY: Oxford University Press.

Eichenbaum, H., & Cohen, N. J. (2001). *From conditioning to conscious recollection: Memory systems of the brain.* New York, NY: Oxford University Press.

Eichenbaum, H., & Fortin, N. J. (2009). The neurobiology of memory based predictions. *Philosophical Transactions of the Royal Society B: Biological Sciences, 364*(1521), 1183–1191.

Eisenhower, A. S., Baker, B. L., & Blacher, J. (2007). Early student-teacher relationships of children with and without intellectual disability: Contributions of behavioral, social, and self-regulatory competence. *Journal of School Psychology, 45*(4), 363–383.

Eisenkraft, A. (2012). *Expanding the 5E Model: A proposed 7E model emphasizes "transfer of learning" and the importance of eliciting prior understanding.* Arkansas Department of Education. National Science Teachers Association. Retrieved from pbworks.com

Ekman, P. (2007). *Emotions revealed: Recognizing faces and feelings to improve communication and emotional life* (2nd ed.). New York, NY: Holt Paperbacks.

Engel de Abreu, P. M. (2011 Jul). Working memory in multilingual children: is there a bilingual effect? *Memory 19*(5), 529–37. doi:10.1080/09658211.2011.590504.

Engell, A. D., Haxby, J. V., & Todorov, A. (2007). Implicit trustworthiness decisions: Automatic coding of face properties in the human amygdala. *Journal of Cognitive Neuroscience, 19*(9), 1508–1519. doi:10.1162/jocn.2007.19.9.1508

Engle, R. W. (2002). Working memory capacity as executive attention. *Current Directions in Psychological Science, 11*(1), 19–23.

English, A. R. (2013). *Discontinuity in learning: Dewey, Hebart and education as transformation.* New York, NY: Oxford University Press.

Enikö, A., Kramár, E. A., Babayan, A. H., Gavin, C. F., Cox, C. D., Jafari, M., …& Lynch, G. (2012). Synaptic evidence for the efficacy of spaced learning. *Proceedings of the National Academy of Sciences 109,* 5121–5126.

Erikson, K., Voss, M., Prakash, R., Basak, C., Szabo, A., Chaddock, L., …& Kramer, A. F. (2011). *Reply to Coen et al.:* Exercise, hippocampal volume. *Proceedings of the National Academy of Sciences, 108*(18), E90. doi:10.1073/pnas.1103059108

Esch, C. E., Chang-Ross, C. M., Guha, R., Humphrey, D. C., Shields, P.M., Tiffany-Morales, J.,…Woodworth, K. R. (2005). *The status of the teaching professions 2005.* Santa Cruz, CA: The Center for the Future of Teaching and Learning.

Eshel, Y., & Kohavi, R. (2003). Perceived classroom control, self-regulated learning strategies, and academic achievement. *Educational Psychology: An International Journal of Experimental Educational Psychology, 23*(3), 249–260. doi:10.1080/0144341032000060093

Esquith, R. (2003). *There are no shortcuts.* New York, NY: Anchor Books.

Esquith, R. (2007). *Teach like your hair's on fire.* New York, NY: Penguin Books.

Etherington, M. B. (2011). Investigative primary science: A problem-based learning approach. *Australian Journal of Teacher Education, 36*(9). doi:10.14221/ajte.2011v36n9.2

European Parliament. (2007). *European reference framework for key competences for lifelong learning.* Lifelong Learning Programme. Luxembourg: Office for Official Publications of the European Communities. Retrieved October 29, 2010, from http://ec.europa.eu/dgs/education_culture/publ/pdf/ll-learning/keycomp_en.pdf

Eurostat. (2009). *Science, technology and innovation in Europe*. Eurostat Statistical Books. Luxembourg: Office for Official Publications of the European Communities.

Eurostat. (2010). *Human resources in science and technology*. Retrieved 9 Aug 2013 from http://appsso.eurostat.ec.europa.eu/nui/setupModifyTableLayout.do

Evans, D. (2012 Sept 14). He's not the messiah…….. but for many policymakers he comes close. *Think, Educate Share Magazine*. London, UK: TES. Available on http://www.tes.co.uk/article.aspx?storycode=6290240

Eyster, R. H., & Martin, C. (2010). *Successful classroom management: Real-world, time-tested techniques for the most important skills set every teacher needs*. Naperville, IL: Sourcebooks.

Falk, J. H., & Dierkin, L. D. (1992). *The museum experience*. India: Howells House/Whalesback Books.

Fan, J., Gu, X., Guise, K. G., Liu, X., Fossella, J., Wang, H., & Posner, M. I. (2009). Testing the behavioral interaction and integration of attentional networks. *Brain and Cognition, 70*(2), 209–220.

Fan, J., McCandliss, B. D., Fossella, J. I., & Posner, M. I. (2005). The activation of attentional networks. *NeuroImage, 26*, 471–479.

Fan, Y., Shi, F., Smith, J. K., Lin, W., Gilmore, J. H., & Shen, D. (2011). Brain anatomical networks in early human brain development. *Neuroimage, 54*(3), 1862–1871.

Fan, J., Wu, Y., Fossella, J. A., & Posner, M. I. (2001). Assessing the heritability of attentional networks. *BMC neuroscience, 2*(1), 14.

Farah, M. J., & Hook, C. J. (2013). The seductive allure of "seductive allure." *Perspectives on Psychological Science, 8*(1), 88–90.

Faraone, S. V., & Biederman, J. (1998). Neurobiology of attention-deficit hyperactivity disorder. *Biological Psychiatry, 44*(10), 951–958.

Farrington, J. (2011). From the research: Myths worth dispelling – seriously, the game is up. *Performance Improvement Quarterly, 24*(2), 105–110.

Farstrup, A.E. (2002). *What research has to say about reading instruction* (3rd ed.). Newark, DE: International Reading Association.

Ferlazzo, L. (2011). *Helping students motivate themselves: Practical answers to classroom challenges*. Larchmont, NY: Eye on Education.

Feldman, R. S., & Prohaska, T. (1979). The student as Pygmalion: Effects of student expectation on the teacher. *Journal of Educational Psychology, 71*(4), 485–493.

Fernandez, M. L. (2010). Investigating how and what prospective teachers learn through microteaching lesson study. *Teaching and Teacher Education, 26*(1), 351–362.

Fernandez-Duque, D., & Posner, M.I. (2010). Brain imaging of attentional networks in normal and pathological states. *Journal of Clinical and Experimental Neuropsychology, 23*(1), 74–93. doi:10.1076/jcen.23.1.74.1217

Ferrari, M., & Vuletic, L. (2009). *The developmental relations between mind, brain, and education: Essays in honor of Robbie Case*. Holanda: Springer.

Ferraro, J. M. (2000). Reflective practice and professional development. *Teacher and Teacher Education*. ERICDigest.org. Available on http://www.ericdigests.org/2001-3/reflective.htm

Ferreira, M. M., & Trudel, A. R. (2012). The impact of problem based learning (PBL) on student attitudes towards science, problem-solving skills, and sense of community in the classroom. *Journal of Classroom Interaction, 47*(1), 23–30.

Fetzer Institute. (2013). *Parker Palmer: Wisdom of the heart*. Retrieved 9 Aug 2013 from http://www.fetzer.org/resources/parker-palmer-wisdom-heart

Feuer, M. J., Towne, L., & Shavelson, R. J. (2002). Scientific culture and educational research. *Educational Researcher, 31*(8), 4–14.

Figner, B., Knoch, D., Johnson, E. J., Krosch, A. R., Lisanby, S. H., Fehr, E., & Weber, E.U. (2010). Lateral prefrontal cortext and self-control in intertemporal choice. *Nature Neuroscience, 13*, 538–539. doi:10.1038/nn.2516

Fine, C. (2011). *Delusions of gender: How our minds, society, and neurosexisms create difference*. New York, NY: Norton.

Fink, A., Benedek, M., Grabner, R. H., Staudt, B., & Neubauer, A. C. (2007). Creativity meets neuroscience: Experimental tasks for the neuroscientific study of creative thinking. *Methods, 42*(1), 68–76. doi:http://dx.doi.org/10.1016/j.ymeth.2006.12.001

Fink, L. D. (2003). *Creating significant learning experiences: An integrated approach to designing college courses*. San Francisco, CA: Jossey-Bass.

Fink, L. D. (2013). *Creating significant learning experiences*. San Francisco, CA: Jossey-Bass.

Fink, L. D., & Knight Fink, A. (Eds.) (2009). *Designing courses for significant learning: Voices of learning experience, new directions for teaching*. San Francisco, CA: Jossey-Bass.

Finn, A. N., Schrodt, P., Witt, P. L., Elledge, N., Jernberg, K. A., & Larson, L. M. (2009). A meta-analytical review of teacher credibility and its association with teacher behaviors and student outcomes. *Communication Education, 58*(4), 516–537. doi:10.1080/03634520903131154

Fischer, F. M., Radosevic-Vidacek, A., Kosec, L. R., Teixeira, C., Moreno, R. C., & Lowden, A. (2008). International and external time conflicts in adolescents: Sleep characteristics and interventions. *Mind, Brain and Education* 2(1), 17–23.

Fischer, K. W. (2009). Mind, Brain, and Education: Building a scientific groundwork for learning and teaching. *Mind, Brain, and Education, 3*(1), 3–16.

Fischer, K. W., Bernstein, J., & Immordino-Yang, M. H. (2007). *Mind, brain, and education in reading disorders*. New York, NY: Cambridge University Press.

Fischer, K. W., Daniel, D. B., Immordino-Yang, M. H., Stern, E., Battro, A., & Koizumi, H. (2007). Why mind, brain, and education? Why now? *Mind, Brain, and Education, 1*(1), 1–2.

Fischer, K. W., Goswami, U., & Geake, J. (2010). The future of educational neuroscience. *Mind, Brain, and Education, 4*(2), 68–80.

Fisher, D., & Frey, N. (2007). *Checking for understanding: Formative assessment techniques for your classroom*. Alexandria, VA: ASCD.

Fisher, D., & Frey, N. (2010). *Enhancing RTI [Response To Intervention]: How to ensure success with effective classroom instruction and intervention*. Alexandria, VA: ASCD.

Flage, D. (2003). *The art of questioning: An introduction to critical thinking*. New York, NY: Pearson.

Flavell, J. H. (1979). Metacognition and cognitive monitoring: A new area of cognitive-developmental inquiry. *American Psychologist, 34*(10), 906–911.

Flavell, J. H. (1982). On cognitive development. *Child Development, 53,* 1–10.

Flavell, J. H. (1987). Speculations about the nature and development of metacognition. In Weinert, F. E., & Kluwe, R. H. (Eds.), *Metacognition, motivation, and understanding*. Hillsdale, NJ: Lawrence Erlbaum Associates.

Fleming, S. M., & Dolan, R. J. (2012). The neural basis of metacognitive ability. *Philosophical Transactions of the Royal Society Biological Sciences, 367*(1594), 1338–1349.

Fleming, S. M., Dolan, R. J., & Frith, C. D. (2012). Metacognition: Computation, biology and function. *Philosophical Transactions of the Royal Society, Biological Science, 367*(1594), 1280–1286.

Fleming, S. M., Huijgen, J., & Dolan, R. J. (2012). Prefrontal contributions to metacognition in perceptual decision making. *Journal of Neuroscience, 32*(18), 6117–6125.

Fleming, S. M., Weil, R. S., Nagy, Z., Dolan, R. J., & Rees, G. (2010). Relating introspective accuracy to individual differences in brain structure. *Science, 329*(5998), 1541–1543. doi:10.1126/science.1191883

Fougnie, D. (2008). The relationship between attention and working memory. *New Research on Short-Term Memory,* 1–45.

Foundation for Critical Thinking. (2011). *The role of Socratic questioning in thinking, teaching, and learning*. Retrieved 30 Apr 2013 from http://www.criticalthinking.org/pages/the-role-of-socratic-questioning-in-thinking-teaching-learning/522

Franke, M. L., Webb, N. M., Chan, A. G., Ing, M., Freund, D., & Battey, D. (2009). Teacher questioning to elicit students' mathematical thinking in elementary school classrooms. *Journal of Teacher Education, 60*(4), 380–392.

Frase, L. T., & Schwartz, B. J. (1975). Effect of question production and answering on prose recall. *Journal of Educational Psychology, 67,* 628–635.

Freeman, W. J. (1991). The brain transforms sensory messages into conscious perceptions almost instantly: Chaotic, collective activity involving millions of neurons seems essential for such rapid cognition. *Scientific American, 264*(2), 78–85.

Freeman Herreid, C., Schiller, N. A. & Herreid, K. F. (2012). *Science stories: Using case studies to teach critical thinking*. Arlington, VA: National Science Teachers Association.

Freiberg, H. J., & Lamb, S. M. (2009). *Dimensions of person-centered classroom management*. New York, NY: Taylor & Francis.

Freitas, C., Perez, J., Knobel, M., Tormos, J. M., Oberman, L., Eldaief, M., ... & Pascual-Leone, A. (2011). Changes in cortical plasticity across the lifespan. *Frontiers in Aging Neuroscience, 3.*

Friederici, A., & Ungerleider, L.G. (2005). Cognitive neuroscience. *Current Opinion in Neurobiology, 15*(2), 131–134.

Fried, L. (2011). Teaching teachers about emotion regulation in the classroom. *Australian Journal of Teacher Education, 36*(3), 2.

Frith, C. D. (2007). *Making up the mind: How the brain creates our mental world.* Hoboken, NJ: John Wiley & Sons.

Frith, C. D. (2012). The role of metacognition in human social interactions. *Philosophical Transactions of the Royal Society Biological Sciences, 367*(1599), 2213–2223.

Frith, C. D., & Frith, U. (2012). Mechanisms of social cognition. *Annual Review of Psychology 63,* 287–313. doi:10.1146/annurev-psych-120710-100449

Frith, C. D., Perry, R., & Lumer, E. (1999). The neural correlates of conscious experience: An experimental framework. *Trends in Cognitive Neuroscience, 3,* 105–114.

Frith, U., & Frith, C. D. (2003). Development and neurophysiology of mentalizing. *Philosophical Transactions R Social Lond B Biological Science 358*(1431), 459–73. doi:10.1098/rstb.2002.1218. PMC 1693139. PMID 12689373

Frymier, A. B., & Houser, M. L. (2000). The teacher-student relationship as an interpersonal relationship. *Communication Education, 49*(3), 207–219.

Frymier, A. B., & Shulman, G. M. (1995). What's in it for me - Increasing content relevance to enhance students' motivation. *Communication Education, 44*(1), 40–50.

Frymier, A. B., & Wanzer, M. B. (2006). Teacher and student affinity-seeking in the classroom. In T. P. Mottet, V. P. Richmond & J. C. McCroskey (Eds.), *Handbook of instructional communication* (pp. 195–211). Boston: Pearson.

Frymier, A. B., & Weser, B. (2001). The role of student predispositions on student expectations for instructor communication behavior. *Communication Education, 50*(4), 314–326.

Fuchs, L.S., & Fuchs, D. (1993). Formative evaluation of academic progress: How much growth can we expect? *School Psychology Review, 22*(1), 1–30.

Gabrieli, J. D. E., Christodoulou, J. A., O'Loughlin, T., & Eddy, M. (2010). The reading brain. In D. Sousa (Ed.), *Mind, Brain, and Education: Neuroscience implications for the classroom.* Bloomington, IN; Solution Tree Press.

Gagliardi, J. L., Kirkpatrick-Steger, K. K., Thomas, J., Allen, G. J., & Blumberg, M. S. (1995). Seeing and knowing: Knowledge attribution versus stimulus control in adult humans (Homo sapiens). *Journal of Comparative Psychology, 109*(2), 107.

Gallagher, K. (2010 Nov 12). Why I will not teach to the test. *Education Week.*

Gallagher, S. (2008). Neural simulation and social cognition. In J. A. Pineda (Ed.), *Mirror neuron systems: The role of mirroring processes in social cognition* (pp. 355–371). Totowa, NJ: Humana Press.

Gallagher, S. A., & Gallagher, J. J. (2013). Using problem-based learning to explore unseen academic potential. *Interdisciplinary Journal of Problem-based Learning, 7*(1).

Gallistel, C. R., & Matzel, L. D. (2013). The neuroscience of learning: Beyond the Hebbian synapse. *Annual Review of Psychology, 64,* 169–200. doi:10.1146/annurev-psych-113011-143807

Gardner, H. (2008). *Five minds for the future.* Boston, MA: Harvard Business Press.

Gardner, H. (2012). *Five minds for the future website* (on Howard Gardner's website). Retrieved 20 Mar 2013 from www.howardgardner.com/five-minds-for-the-future/

Garilkoy, R. (2011). *The Socratic Method: Teaching by asking instead of telling.* Available on http://www.sophia.ac.jp/syllabus/2012/09/09_AIBE3450/The%20Socratic%20Method.pdf

Garon, N., Bryson, S. E., & Sith, I. M. (2008). Executive function in preschoolers: A review using an integrative framework. *Psychological Bulletin, 134*(1), 31–60.

Garrett, H. E. (1940). Variability in learning under massed and spaced practice. *Journal of Experimental Psychology 26*(6), 547–567. doi:10.1037/h0061166

Gaustad, J. (1992). School discipline. *ERIC Digest, 78.* ED350727.

Gazzaniga, M. S. (1985). *The social brain.* New York, NY: Basic Books.

Gazzaniga, M. S. (2011). Who's in charge? Free will and the science of the brain. New York, NY: HarperCollins.

Geake, J. (2000). *The brain at school: Educational neuroscience in the classroom.* Maidenhead, Berkshire: Open University Press.

Geake, J. (2005, Aug). Educational neuroscience and neuroscientific education: In search of a mutual middle way. *Research Intelligence, 92,* 10–13.

Geake, J. (2008). Neuromythologies in education. *Educational Research, 50*(2).

Geake, J. (2009). *The brain at school: Educational neuroscience in the classroom.* Berkshire, UK: Open University Press.

Geake, J. (2011). Position statement on motivations, methodologies, and practical implications of educational neuroscience research: fMRI studies of the neural correlates of creative intelligence. *Educational Philosophy and Theory, 43*(1), 43–47.

Geist, E. (2010). The anti-anxiety curriculum: Combating math anxiety in the classroom. *Journal of Instructional Psychology, 37*(1), 24–31

Gentile, J. R., & Lalley, J. P. (2003). *Standards and mastery learning: Aligning teaching and assessment so all children can learn.* Thousand Oaks, CA: Corwin.

Gentner, D., & Colhoun, J. (2010). Analogical processes in human thinking and learning. In B. Glatzeder, V. Giel, and A. Müller (Eds.), *Towards a theory of thinking on thinking,* (pp. 35–48). New York, NY: Springer.

Gerstein, J. (2012). *The flipped classroom: The full picture.* [Kindle version]. Amazon Digital Services.

Ghaye, T. (2001). Reflection: Principles and practices. *Faster, Higher, Stronger, 10,* 9–11.

Ghaye, T. (2010). *Teaching and learning through reflective practice: A practical guide for positive action* (2nd ed.). New York, NY: Taylor & Francis.

Ghorbani, M. R., Gangeraj, A. A., & Alavi, S. Z. (2013). Reciprocal teaching of comprehension strategies improves EFL learners' writing ability. *Current Issues in Education, 16*(1). Available on http://cie.asu.edu/ojs/index.php/cieatasu/article/viewArticle/1046

Giard, M. H., & Peronnet, F. (1999). Auditory-visual integration during multimodal object recognition in humans: A behavioral and electrophysiological study. *Journal of Cognitive Neuroscience, 11*(5), 473–490.

Gillies, R. M., Ashman, A., & Terwel (Eds.) (2010). *The teacher's role in implementing cooperative learning in the classroom.* New York, NY: Springer.

Ginsberg, S. M. (2007). Shared characteristics of college faculty who are effective communicators. *The Journal of Effective Teaching, 7*(2), 3–20.

Giordano, P. J. (2004). Teaching and learning when we least expect it: The role of critical moments in student development. *Essays from excellence in teaching.* Retrieved 10 Oct 2013 from https://teachpsych.org/Resources/Documents/ebooks/eit2004.pdf#page=21

Girling Fitch, J. (2012). *The art of questioning.* Riverside, CA: Ulan Press.

Giudici, C., Rinaldi, C., & Krechevsky, M. (Eds.) (2001). *Making learning visible: Children as individual and group learners.* Reggio Emilia, Italy: Regio Children.

Glahn, D. C., Winkler, A. M., Kochunov, P., Almasy, L., Duggirala, R., Carless, M. A., ...& Blangero, J. (2009). Genetic control over the resting brain. Proceedings of the *National Academy of Sciences, 107*(3), 1223–1228.

Glass, A. L., Ingate, M., & Sinha, N. (2013). The effect of a final exam on long-term retention. *The Journal of General Psychology, 140*(3), 224–241.

Glasser, W., & Mamary, A. (2006). *Every student can succeed: Finally a book that explains how to reach and teach every student in your school.* Mosheim, TN: Black Forest Press.

Glewwe, P., Jacoby, H. G., & King, E. M. (2001). Early childhood nutrition and academic achievement: A longitudinal analysis. *Journal of Public Economics, 81*(3), 345–368.

Glisczinski, D. J., & Savion, S. M. (2012). I before E precipitates Cs: Rethinking instruction without emotion in light of neuroscientific alternatives. *International Journal of Global Management Studies Professional, 3*(2).

Glover, G., & Mackey, S.C. (2004). Reflecting upon feelings: An fMRI study of neural systems supporting the attribution of emotion to self and other. *Journal of Cognitive Neuroscience, 16*(10), 1746–1772. doi:10.1162/0898929042947829

Glynn, S. M., Duit, R. & Thiele, R. B. (2012). Teaching science with analogies: A strategy for constructing knowledge. In S.M. Glynn and R. Duit's *Learning science in the schools* (pp.247–296). New York, NY: Routledge.

Göbel, S. M., Shaki, S., & Fischer, M. H. (2012). The cultural number line: A review of cultural and linguistic influences on the development of number processing. *Cross-Cultural Psychology, 42*(4), 543–565. doi:10.1177/0022022111406251

Godin, S. (2012). *Stop stealing dreams: What is school for?* Retrieved from http://sethgodin.typepad.com/files/stop-stealing-dreams6print.pdf

Goetz, T., Pekrun, R., Hall, N., & Haag, L. (2010). Academic emotions from a social-cognitive perspective: Antecedents and domain specific students' affect in the context of Latin Instruction. *British Journal of Educational Psychology, 76*(2), 289–308. 10.1348/000709905X42860i

Goh, J. O., Leshikar, E. D., Sutton, B. P., Chow Tan, J., Sim, S.K., Hebrank, A.C., & Park, D.C. (2010). Culture differences in neural processing of faces and houses in the ventral visual cortex. *Social Cognitive and Affective Neuroscience.* doi:10.1093/scan/nsq060.

Goldman, R. K., Botkin, M. J., Tokunaga, H., & Kuklinski, M. (1997). Teacher consultation: Impact on teachers' effectiveness and students' cognitive competence and achievement. *American Journal of Orthopsychiatry, 67*(3), 374–384.

Goldstein, L. S. (2002). *Commitment, community, and passion: Dimensions of a care-centered approach to teach education.* Lanham, MD: Rowman & Littlefield.

Goleman, D. (2005). *Emotional intelligence: Why it can matter more than IQ* (10th anniversary ed.). New York, NY: Bantam.

Golombek, D. A., & Cardinali, D. P. (2008). Mind, brain, education, and biological timing. *Mind, Brain, and Education, 2*(1), 1–6.

Gómez-Pinilla, F., Ying, Z., Roy, R. R., Molteni, R., & Edgerton, V. R. (2002). Voluntary exercise indices a BDNF-mediated mechanisms that promotes neuroplasticity. *Journal of Neurophysiology, 88*(5), 2187–2195.

Good, T. L. (1987). Two decades of research on teacher expectations: Findings and future directions. *Journal of Teacher Education, 38*(4), 32–47. doi:10.1177/002248718703800406

Good, T. L., & Brophy, J. E. (1997). *Looking in classrooms* (7th ed.). New York, NY: Addison Wesley.

Gordon, R. (1998). Balancing real-world problems with real-world results. *Phi Delta Kappan, 79*(5), 390–393.

Gorham, J. (1988). The relationship between verbal teacher immediacy behaviors and student learning. *Communication Education, 37*(1), 40–53. doi:10.1080/03634528809378702

Goswami, U. (2004). Neuroscience and education. *British Journal of Educational Psychology, 74,* 1–14.

Goswami, U. (2006). Neuroscience and education: From research to practice. *Nature Reviews Neuroscience 7*(5), 406–413.

Goswami, U. (Ed.) (2011). *The Wiley-Blackwell handbook of childhood cognitive development.* Oxford, UK: Wiley-Blackwell.

Gould, C. G. (1923). The art of questioning. *The Mathematics Teacher, 16*(1), 52–56.

Graff, N. (2011). "An agonizing way to learn": Backwards design and new teachers. *Teacher Education Quarterly,* 151–168.

Grady, C. (2012). The cognitive neuroscience of ageing. *Nature Reviews Neuroscience, 13*(7), 491–505.

Graham, S. (1991). A review of attribution theory in achievement contexts. *Educational Psychology Review, 3*(1), 5–39.

Gratch, J., & Kelly, J. (2009). A discussion of open source gaming platforms for education. In I.

Gibson et al. (Eds.), *Proceedings of Society for Information Technology & Teacher Education International Conference 2009* (pp. 1470–1473). Chesapeake, VA: AACE. Retrieved October 21, 2013 from http://www.editlib.org/p/30818.

Green, E. (2010 Mar 2). Building a better teacher. *New York Times Magazine.* Retrieved 30 December 2012 from http://www.nytimes.com/2010/03/07/magazine/07Teachers-t.html?pagewanted=all

Greenfield, S. (2008). ID: The quest for identity in the 21st century. UK: Hodder & Stoughton.

Gray, J. R., Chabris, C. F., & Braver, T. S. (2003). Neural mechanisms of general fluid intelligence. *Nature Neuroscience, 6*(3), 316–322.

Greenough, W. T., & Black, J. E. (2013, April). Induction of brain structure by experience: Substrates. In *Developmental behavioral neuroscience: The Minnesota symposia on child psychology* (p. 155). New York, NY: Psychology Press, Taylor & Francis Group.

Greenough, W. T., Black, J. E., & Wallace, C. S. (1987). Experience and brain development. *Child Development*, 539–559.

Grossberg, S. (2010). The link between brain learning, attention, and consciousness. In A. Carsetti (Ed.), Causality, meaningful complexity and embodied cognition. *Theory and Decision Library, 48*, 3–45.

Grossier, P. L. (1964). *How to use the fine art of questioning.* Englewood Cliffs, NJ: Teachers Practical Press.

Grote, M. G. (1995). Distributed versus massed practice in high school physics. *School Science and Mathematic, 95*(2), 97–101.

Guggenheim, D. (2010). *Waiting for "Superman".* Lesley Chilcott (Producer). Davis Guggenheim and Billy Kimball (Writers). Hollywood, CA: Paramount Vintage.

Guo, Y., Plasta, S. B., Justice, L. M., & Kaderavek, J. N. (2010). Relations among preschool teachers' self-efficacy, classroom quality, and children's language and literacy gains. *Teaching and Teacher Education, 26*(4), 1094–1103.

Gurian, M., & Stevens, K. (2010). *Boys and girls learn differently! A guide for teachers and parents.* San Francisco, CA: Jossey-Bass.

Guskey, T. R. (1996) *Implementing mastery learning* (2nd ed.). Independence, KY: Cengage Learning.

Guskey, T. R. (1997). *Implementing mastery learning.* Belmont, CA: Wadsworth Publishing.

Guskey, T. R. (1999). Making standards work. *The School Administrator, 56*(9), 44.

Guskey, T. R. (2001). Helping standards make the grade. *Educational Leadership, 59*(1), 20–27.

Guskey, T. R. (2009). *The development of mastery learning: Misinterpretations of mastery learning; Research results and implications.* The Gale Group. Retrieved 9 Aug 2013 from http://www.education.com/reference/article/mastery-learning/

Guskey, T.R. (2011). Five obstacles to grading reform. *Educational Leadership, 69*(3), 16–21.

Guskey, T. R., & Jung, L. A. (2011). Response-to-intervention and mastery learning: Tracing roots and seeking common ground. *Journal of Educational Strategies, Issues and Ideas, 84*(6), 249–255. doi:10.1080/00098655.2011.590551

Guthrie, J. T., Hoa, A. L. W., Wigfield, A., Tonks, S. M., Humenick, N. M., & Littles, E. (2007). Reading motivation and reading comprehension growth in the later elementary years. *Contemporary Educational Psychology, 32*(3), 282–313.

Hacker, D. J., Dunlosky, & Graesser, A. C. (Eds.) (2009). *Handbook of metacognition in education.* New York, NY: Routledge.

Halford, G. S., Wilson, W. H., & Phillips, S. (2010). Relational knowledge: The foundation of higher cognition. *Trends in Cognitive Sciences, 14*(11), 497–505.

Hall, D. A., Fussell, C., & Summerfield, A. W. (2005). Reading fluent speech from talking faces: Typical brain networks and individual differences. *Journal of Cognitive Neuroscience, 17*(6), 939–953.

Halpern, D. F. (1998). Teaching critical thinking for transfer across domains: Dispositions, skills, structure training, and metacognitive monitoring. *American Psychologist, 53*(4), 449–455.

Hamer, D.H., & Copeland, P. (1999). *Living with our genes: The groundbreaking book about the science of personality, behavior, and genetic destiny.* Flushing, MI: Anchor.

Hammer, D. (1995). Student inquiry in a physics class discussion. *Cognition and Instruction, 13*(3). doi:10.1207/s1532690xci1303_3

Hamre, B.K., & Pianta, R.C. (2006). Student-teacher relationships. In George Bear and Kathleen Mink (Eds.), *Children's needs III: Development, prevention, and intervention* (pp.59–71). Washington, DC: U.S. National Association of School Psychologists.

Han, D., Northoff, G., Vogeley, K., Wexler, B. E., Kitayama, S., & Varnum, M .E. W. (2013 Jan). A cultural neuroscience approach to the biosocial nature of the human brain. *Annual Review of Psychology, 64*, 335–359. doi:10.1146/annurev-psych-071112-054629

Hare, W. (2007). Credibility and credulity: Monitoring teachers for trustworthiness. *Journal of Philosophy of Education, 41*(2). doi:10.1111/j.1467-9752.2007.00557.x

Hare, T. A., Camerer, C. F., & Rangel, A. (2009). Self-control in decision-making involves modulation of the vmPFC valuation system. *Science, 324*(5927), 646–648. doi:10.1126/science.1168450

Hariri, A. R., Goldberg, T. E., Mattay, V. S., Kolachana, B. S., Callicott, J. H., Egan, M. F., & Weinberger, D. R. (2003). Brain-derived neurotrophic factor val66met polymorphism affects human memory-related hippocampal activity and predicts memory performance. *Journal of Neuroscience, 23*(17), 6690–6694.

Harlem Children's Zone. (2012). *Doing whatever it takes to educate children and strengthen the community.* Retrieved 17 Aug 2013 from www.hcz.org/hcz-home.php

Harmon-Jones, E., & van Honk, J. (2012). Introduction to a special issue on the neuroscience of motivation and emotion. *Motivation and Emotion, 36*(1), 1–3.

Harmon-Jones, E. & Winkielman, P. (2007). *Social neuroscience: Integrating biological and psychological explanations of social behavior.* New York, NY: Guilford.

Harrison, A. G., & Coll, R. K. (2007). *Using analogies in middle and secondary science classrooms: The FAR guide.* Thousand Oaks, CA: Corwin.

Hart, L. (1999). *Human brain and human learning* (5th ed.). Kent, WA: Books for Educators. (Original published in 1983).

Harton, H. C., Richardson, D. S., Barreras, R. E., Rockloff, M. J., & Latane, B. (2002). Focused interactive learning: A tool for active class discussion. *Teaching of Psychology, 29*(1), 10–15.

Haskins, W. (2000, Mar 3). Ethos and pedagogical communication: Suggestions for enhancing credibility in the classroom. *Current Issues in Education* [On-line], 3(4). Available: http://cie.ed.asu.edu/volume3/number4/.

Hattie, J. (1992a). Measuring the effects of schooling. *Australian Journal of Education, 36*(1), 5–13.

Hattie, J. (1992b). *What works in special education*. Presentation to the Special Education Conference, May 1992 [On-line; Acrobat file] NZ Available: http://www.education.auckland.ac.nz/webdav/site/education/shared/hattie/docs/special-education.pdf Accessed 15 September 2011

Hattie, J. (1999). Influences on student learning. *Inaugural lecture given on August, 2, 1999*.

Hattie, J. (2001). The assessment of teachers. *Teaching Education, 12*(3), 279–300. doi:10.1080/10476210120096551

Hattie, J. (2003, October). *Teachers make a difference: What is the research evidence?* Paper presented at the Australian Council for Educational Research Annual Conference on Building Teacher Quality, Melbourne.

Hattie, J. (2005). *What is the nature of evidence that makes a difference to learning?* Research Conference, Australian Conference for Educational Research. Available on http://research.acer.edu.au/research_conference_2005/7

Hattie, J. (2007). *Developing potentials for learning: Evidence, assessment, and progress.* Presentation at the EARLI 12th biannual conference, Budapest, Hungary.

Hattie, J. (2009). *Visible learning: A synthesis of over 800 meta-analyses relating to achievement.* London, UK: Routledge.

Hattie, J. (2010 Sept). *Visible learning, Tomorrow's schools, the mindsets that make the difference in education.* University of Auckland: Visible Learning Laboratories.

Hattie, J. (2012). *Visible learning for teachers: Maximizing impact on learning.* London, UK: Routledge.

Hattie, J., & Anderman, E.M. (2013). *International guide to student achievement.* London, UK: Routledge.

Hawkins, V. J. (2009). Barriers to implementing differentiation: Lack of confidence, efficacy and perseverance. *The NERA Journal, 44*(2), 11–113.

Heatherton, T. F. (2011). Neuroscience of self and self-regulation. *Annual Review of Psychology, 62*, 363–390. doi:10.1146/annurev.psych.121208.131616

Hebb, D.O. (1949). *The organization of behavior.* New York, NY: Wiley & Sons.

Hedman, A. M., van Haren, N. E. M., Schnack, H. G., Kahn, R. S., & Hulshoff Pol, H. E. (2012). Human brain changes across the life span: A review of 56 longitudinal magnetic resonance imaging studies. *Human Brain Mapping, 33.* doi: 10.1002/hbm.21334

Heilman, R. M., Crişan, L. G., Houser, D., Miclea, M., & Miu, A. C. (2010). Emotion regulation and decision making under risk and uncertainty. *Emotion, 10*(2), 257.

Henderson, N., & Milstein, M. (2003). *Resiliency in schools: Making it happen for students and educators.* Thousand Oaks, CA: Corwin Press.

Hennessey, M. G. (1999). *Probing the dimensions of metacognition: Implications for conceptual change teaching-learning.* Paper presented at the annual meeting of the National Association for Research in Science Teaching, Boston, MA.

Heo, K. H., & Squires, J. (2012). Cultural adaptation of a parent completed social emotional screening instrument for young children: Ages and stages questionnaire-social emotional. *Early Human Development, 88*(3), 151–158.

Heritage, M. (2010). *Formative assessment and next-generation assessment systems: Are we losing an opportunity?* Washington, DC: National Center for Research on Evaluation, Standards, and Student Testing (CRESST) and the Council of Chief State School Officers (CCSSO).

Hertzman, C., & Boyce, T. (2010). How experience gets under the skin to create gradients in developmental health. *Annual Review of Public Health, 31*, 329–347.

Hess, R. D. (1991). Cultural support for schooling: Contrasts between Japanese and the United States. *Educational Researcher, 20*(9), 2–9.

Hesse, M. B. (1966). *Models and analogies in science.* Notre Dame, IN: University of Notre Dame Press.

Hey, J., Linsey, J., Agogino, A. M., & Wood, K. L. (2008). Analogies and metaphors in creative design. *International Journal of Engineering Education, 24*(2), 283–294

Hiebert, J., Stigler, J. W., Jacobs, J. K., Givvin, K. B., Garnier, H., Smith, M., …Gallimore, R. (2005). Mathematics teaching in the United States today (and tomorrow): Results from the TIMSS 1999 video study. *Educational Evaluation and Policy Analysis 27*(2), 111–132.

Hilchey, M. D, & Klein, R. M. (2011 Aug). Are there bilingual advantages on nonlinguistic interference tasks? Implications for the plasticity of executive control processes. *Psychonomic Bulletin and Review, 18*(4), 625–58. doi:10.3758/s13423-011-0116-7.

Hilgenheger, N. (2000). Johann Friedrich Herbart. Paris: UNESCO, *The Quarterly Review Of Comparative Education, XXIII*(3–4), 649–664. Retrieved 9 Aug 2013 from http://www.ibe.unesco.org/publications/ThinkersPdf/herbarte.pdf

Hinton, C., & Fischer, K. W. (2008). Research schools: Grounding research in educational practice, *Mind, Brain, and Education, 2*(4), 157–160.

Hinton, C., & Fischer, K. W. (2010). Research schools: connecting research and practice at the Ross School. In M. Suarez-Orozco and C. Sattin-Bajaj (Eds.), *Educating the whole child for the whole world: The Ross School model and education for the global era* (pp. 69–79). Berkeley, CA: University of California Press.

Hinton, G. E. (1992). How neural networks learn from experience. *Scientific American, 267*(3), 145–151.

Hirsh-Pasek, K., & Bruer, J. T. (2007). The brain/education barrier [Editorial]. *Science, 317*(5843), 1293.

Hirzy, E. C. (Ed.) (1996). *True needs, true partners: Museums and schools transforming education.* Washington, DC: Institute of Museum Services.

Hmelo-Silver, C. E. (2012). International perspectives on problem-based learning: Contexts, cultures, challenges, and adaptation. *Interdisciplinary Journal of Problem-based Learning, 6*(1), 10–15.

Hobson, J., & Pace-Schott, E. F. (2002, Sep). The cognitive neuroscience of sleep: Neuronal systems, consciousness and learning. *Nature Reviews Neuroscience, 3*(9), 679–693.

Hofer, B. K., & Sinatra, G. M. (2010). Epistemology, metacognition, and self-regulation: musings on an emerging field. *Metacognition and Learning, 5*(1), 113–120. doi:10.1007/s11409-009-9051-7

Hofstadter, D., & Sander, E. (2013). *Surfaces and essences: Analogy as the fuel and fire of thinking.* New York, NY: Basic Books.

Holler, J., & Selegue, J. P. (2012). *The periodic table of comics.* Retrieved 20 Mar 2013 from http://www.uky.edu/Projects/Chemcomics/

Hollins, E. (2008). *Culture in school learning: Revealing the deep meaning.* New York, NY: Routledge.

Holmboe, K., & Johnson, M. H. (2005). Educating executive attention. *Proceedings of the National Academy of Sciences, 102*(41), 14479–14480.

Holyoak, K. J., Morrison, R. (2012). *The Oxford handbook of thinking and reasoning.* New York, NY: Oxford University Press.

Hong, S., & Ho, H. Z. (2005). Direct and indirect longitudinal effects of parental involvement on student achievement: Second-order latent growth modeling across ethnic groups. *Journal of Educational Psychology, 97*(1), 32–42.

Hooker, K. E., & Fodor, I. E. (2008). Teaching mindfulness to children. *Gestalt Review, 12*(1), 75–91.

Hooper, S., Sales, G., & Rysavy, S. D. M. (1994). Generating summaries and analogies alone and in pairs. *Contemporary Educational Psychology, 19*, 53–62.

Horz, H. (2012). Situated prompts in authentic learning environments. In *Encyclopedia of the Sciences of Learning* (pp. 3086–3088). New York, NY: Springer.

Houck, J. C., Davis, J. L., & Beiser, D. G. (1995). *Models of information processing in the basal ganglia.* Cambridge, MA: MIT Press.

Howard-Jones, P. A. (2007). *Neuroscience and education: Issues and opportunities.* London: Teaching and Learning Research Programme.

Howard-Jones, P. A. (2009a). Philosophical exchanges for research at the interface between neuroscience and education. *Journal of Philosophy of Education, 42*(3–4), 361–380. doi:10.1111/j.1467-9752.2008.00649.x

Howard-Jones, P. A. (2009b). Neuroscience, learning and technology (14–19). *Learning, 16*(17), 18.

Howard-Jones, P. A. (2010). *Introducing neuroeducational research: Neuroscience, education and the brain from contexts to practice.* New York, NY: Taylor & Francis.

Howard-Jones, P. A., & Fenton, K. (2011). The need for interdisciplinary dialogue in developing ethical approaches to neuroeducational research. *Neuroethics, 5*(2), 119–134

Howard-Jones, P. A., Ott, M., van Leeuwen, T., & de Smedt, B. (2011). *Neuroscience, technology and learning: Areas and issues for interdisciplinary progress.* White Paper arising from the workshop on: Neuroscience, Technology and Learning: Areas and Issues for Interdisciplinary Progress. Retrieved from http://telearn.archives-ouvertes.fr/docs/00/72/29/61/PDF/ARV2011_White-Paper_NeuroscienceTechnologyandLearning.pdf

Howe, R. (2010). *1001 smartest things teachers ever said.* Guilford, CT: Globe Pequot.

Hsiung, C. M. (2012). The effectiveness of cooperative learning. *Journal of Engineering Education, 101*(1), 119–37.

Huang, D., & Cho, J. (2009). Academic enrichment in high functioning homework afterschool programs. *The Journal of Research in Childhood Education, 23*(3), 382–392.

Huang, S., Belliveau, J. W., Tengshe, C., & Ahveninen, J. (2012). Brain networks of novelty-driven involuntary and cued voluntary auditory attention shifting. *PLoS ONE 7*(8), e44062. doi:10.1371/journal.pone.0044062

Huang, D., Seth, L., Hodson, C., LaTorre, D., Obregon, N., & Rivera, G. (2010). *Preparing students for the 21st century: Exploring the effect of afterschool participation on students' collaboration skills, oral communication skills, and self-efficacy.* Los Angeles, CA: National Center for Research on Evaluation, Standards, and Student Testing.

Hulshof, H., & Verloop, N. (2002). The use of analogies in language teaching: Representing the content of teachers' practical knowledge. *Journal of Curriculum Studies, 34*(1), 77–90. doi:10.1080/00220270110037177

Hurt, T. J., Scott, M. D., & McCroskey, J. C. (1978). *Communication in the classroom.* Reading, MA: Addison-Wesley.

Hutchinson, L. (2004). *Recommended practices for effective teaching in the International Baccalaureate Program: An examination of instructional skills, assessment practices, and teacher-efficacy beliefs of IB teachers.* Unpublished doctoral dissertation, The College of William and Mary, Williamsburg, Virginia.

Huttenlocher, P. R. (2009). *Neural plasticity: The effects of environment on the development of the cerebral cortex.* Cambridge, MA: Harvard University Press.

Hwang, A., & Arbaugh, J. B. (2009). Seeking feedback in blended learning: Competitive versus cooperative student attitudes and their links to learning outcome. *Journal of Computer Assisted Learning, 25*(3), 280–293. doi:10.1111/j.1365-2729.2009.00311.x

Hynie, S., & Klenerová, V. (2010). Neurobiology of memory. *Ceskoslovenská fysiologie/Ústredni ústav biologický* [Czech Physiology and Biology Institute], *59*(2), 44.

Iacoboni, M., Molnar-Szakacs, I., Gallese, V., Buccino, G., & Mazziotta, J. C. (2005). Grasping the intentions of others with one's own mirror neuron system. *PLoS Biology, 3*(3), 529–535.

Illinois Mathematics and Science Academy. (2011). *PBl Network: Collaborative inquiry in action.* Retrieved 9 Aug 2013 from http://pbln.imsa.edu/model/intro/

Imbeau, M. B., & Tomlinson, C. A. (2010). *Leading and managing a differentiated classroom*. Alexandria, VA: ASCD.

Immordino-Yang, M. H. (2011). Implications of affective and social neuroscience for educational theory. *Educational Philosophy and Theory,*, *43*(1), 98–103. doi:10.1111/j.1469-5812.2010.00713.x

Immordino-Yang, M. H., & Damasio, A. R. (2007). We feel, therefore we learn: The relevance of affective and social neuroscience to education. *Mind, Brain, and Education, 1*(1), 3–10.

Immordino-Yang, M. H., & Faeth, M. (2010). The role of emotion and skilled intuition in learning. In D. A. Sousa (Ed.), *Mind, Brain, and Education: Neuroscience implications for the classroom* (pp. 66–81). Bloomington, IN: Solution Tree Press.

InfoSemantics. (n.d.). *Performance verbs for learning objectives*. Retrieved from http://www.infosemantics.com.au/sites/default/files/Blooms_Taxonomy_for_Drag_and_Drop.png

International Ergonomics Society. (2013). *What is ergonomics?* Retrieved from http://www.iea.cc/01_what/What%20is%20Ergonomics.html

Isen, A. M., & Reeve, J. (2005). The influence of positive affect on intrinsic and extrinsic motivation: Facilitating enjoyment of play, responsible work behavior, and self control. *Motivation and Emotion, 29*(4), 295–323.

Izard, V., & Dehaene, S. (2008). Calibrating the mental number line. *Cognition, 106*(2008), 1221–1247.

Izawa, C. (1971). Massed and spaced practice in paired-associated learning: List versus item distribution. *Journal of Experimental Psychology, 89*(1), 10–21. doi:10.1037/h0031177

Jackendoff, R. (2002). *Foundations of language: Brain, meaning, grammar, evolution*. Oxford University Press.

Jackson, R. (2009). *Never work harder than your students*. Alexandria, VA: ASCD.

Jacobson, L. (2000). Demand grows to link neuroscience with education. *Education Week, 19*(28), 5. Retrieved September 9, 2007 from http://www.edweek.org/ew/ewstory.cfm?slug=28brain.h19.

Jacoby, L. L. (1978). On interpreting the effects of repetition: Solving a problem versus remembering a solution. *Journal of Verbal Learning & Verbal Behavior, 17*, 649–668.

Janiszewski, C., Noel, H., & Sawyer, A.G. (2003 June). A Meta-analysis of the spacing effect in verbal learning: Implications for research on advertising repetition and consumer memory. *Journal of Consumer Research 30*(1), 138–149.

Jantzen, K. J., Steinberg, F. L. & Scott Kelso, J. A. (2004). Brain networks underlying human timing behavior are influenced by prior context. *Proceedings of the National Academy of Sciences, 101*(17), 6815–6820.

Jarvis, P. (2012). *Towards a comprehensive theory of human learning*. London, UK: Routledge.

Jauk, E., Benedek, M., & Neubauer, A. C. (2012). Tackling creativity at its roots: Evidence for different patterns of EEG alpha activity related to convergent and divergent modes of task processing. *International Journal of Psychophysiology, 84*(2), 219–225.

Jay, J. K., & Johnson, K. L. (2002). Capturing complexity: a typology of reflective practice for teacher education. *Teacher and Teacher Education, 18*(1), 73–85. http://dx.doi.org/10.1016/S0742-051X(01)00051-8.

Jee, B. D., Uttal, D. H., Gentner, D., Manduca, C., Shipley, T. F., Tikoff, B., ...& Sageman, B. (2010). Commentary: Analogical thinking in geoscience education. *Journal of Geoscience Education, 58*(1), 2–13.

Jerald, C.D. (2009). *Defining a 21st century education.* Retrieved October 29, 2010 from http://www.centerforpubliceducation.org/atf/cf/%7B00a4f2e8-f5da-4421-aa25-3919c06b542b%7D/21ST%20CENTURY[1].JERALD.PDF

Joëls, M., Pu, Z., Wiegert, O., Oitzl, M. S., & Krugers, H. J. (2006). Learning under stress: How does it work?. *Trends in Cognitive Sciences, 10*(4), 152–158.

Joët, G., Usher, E. L., & Bressoux, P. (2011 Aug). Sources of self-efficacy: An investigation of elementary school students in France. *Journal of Educational Psychology, 103*(3), 649–663. doi:10.1037/a0024048

Johnson, C. N., & Wellman, H. M. (1982). Children's developing conceptions of the mind and brain. *Child Development, 53*(1), 222–234.

Johnson, D. W., Maruyama, G., Johnson, R., Nelson, D., & Skon, L. (1981). Effects of cooperative, competitive, and individualistic goal structures on achievement: A meta-analysis. *Psychological Bulletin, 89*(1), 47.

Johnson, M. H. (2003). Functional brain development in infants: Elements of an interactive specialization framework. *Child Development, 71*(1), 75–81. doi:10.1111/1467-8624.00120.

Johnson, M. H. (2010). *Developmental cognitive neuroscience.* Hoboken, NJ: John Wiley & Sons.

Johnson, T., Archibald, T., & Tenenbaum, G. (2010). Individual and team annotation effects on students' reading comprehension, critical thinking, and meta-cognitive skills. *Computers in Human Behaviour, 26,* 1496–1507.

Johnson, S. C., Baxter, L., Wilder, L. S., Pipie, J. G., Heiserman, J. E., & Prigatano, G. P. (2002). Neural correlates of self-reflection. *Brain, 125*(8), 1808–1814. doi:10.1093/brain/awf181

Johnson, R. E., Chang, C. H., & Lord, R. G. (2006). Moving from cognition to behavior: What the research says. *Psychological Bulletin, 132*(3), 381–415. doi:10.1037/0033-2909.132.3.381

Johnstone, A. H. (2008/1991). Why is science difficult to learn? Things are seldom what they seem. *Journal of Computer Assisted Learning, 7*(2), 75–83.

Jones, R. M., Somerville, L. H., & Casey, B. J. (2011). Behavioral and neural properties of social reinforcement learning. *Journal of Neuroscience, 31*(37), 13039–13045.

Jordan, N. C., Kaplan, D., Locuniak, M. N., & Ramineni, C. (2007). Predicting first-grade math achievement from developmental number sense trajectories. *Learning Disabilities Research & Practice, 22*(1), 36–46.

Joseph, J., Cole, G., Head, E., & Ingram, D. (2009). Nutrition, brain aging, and neurodegeneration. *Journal of Neuroscience, 29*(41), 12795–12801.

Jukes, I., McCain, T., & Crockett, L. (2010). Education and role of the educator in the future. *Phi Delta Kappan, 94*(4), 15–21.

Jussim, L. (1989). Teacher expectations: Self-fulfilling prophecies, perceptual biases, and accuracy. *Journal of Personality and Social Psychology, 57*(3), 469–480.

Kabat-Zinn, J. (1994). *Wherever you go, there you are: Mindfulness meditation in everyday life.* New York, NY: Hyperion.

Kable, J. W., & Glimcher, P. W. (2007). The neural correlates of subjective value during intertemporal choice. *Nature Neuroscience, 10,* 1625–1633. doi:doi:10.1038/nn2007

Kacker, D. J., Dunlosky, J., & Graesser, A.C. (2009). *Handbook of metacognition in education.* New York, NY: Routledge.

Kajder, S., & Parkes, K. (2012). Examining preservice teachers' reflective practice within and across multimodal writing environments. *Journal of Technology and Teacher Education, 20*(3), 229–249. Chesapeake, VA: SITE.

Kallenbach, W. W., & Gall, M. D. (1969). Microteaching versus conventional methods in training elementary intern teachers. *The Journal of Educational Research, 63*(3), 136–141.

Kandel, E. (2007). *In search of memory: The emergence of a new science of mind.* New York, NY: Norton.

Kane, M. J., & Engle, R. W. (2002). The role of prefrontal cortex in working-memory capacity, executive attention, and general fluid intelligence: An individual-differences perspective. *Psychonomic Bulletin & Review, 9*(4), 637–671.

Kang, N. H. (2008). Learning to teach science: Personal epistemologies, teaching goals, and practices of teaching. *Teaching and Teacher Education, 24*(2), 478–498. http://dx.doi.org/10.1016/j.tate.2007.01.002

Kaplan, A. S., & Murphy, G. L. (2000). Category learning with minimal prior knowledge. *Learning, Memory and Cognition, 26*(4), 829–846.

Karpicke, J. D., & Blunt, J. R. (2011). Retrieval practice produces more learning than elaborative studying with concept mapping. *Science 331*(6018), 772–775. doi:10.1126/science.1199327

Karmiloff-Smith, A. (2009). Nativism versus neuroconstructivism: Rethinking the study of developmental disorders. *Developmental Psychology, 45*(1), 56–63.

Karplus, R., & Their, H. D. (1967). *A new look at elementary school science.* Chicago, IL: Rand McNally.

Karsdrop, P., Hasenbring, M. I., & Lorenz, J. (2012). Switching attention between pain and other demands: Motivation, behavior and brain mechanisms. *European Journal of Pain Supplements, 5*(S1), 14.

Kassim, N. L. A., Daud, N. M., & Daud, N. S. M. (2013). Interaction between writing apprehension, motivation, attitude and writing performance: A structural equation modeling approach. *World Applied Sciences Journal, 21,* 102–108. doi:10.5829/idosi.wasj.2013.21.sltl.2143

Katzir, T., & Paré-Blagoev, J. (2006). Applying cognitive neuroscience research to education: The case of literacy. *Educational Psychologist, 41*(1), 53–74.

Kauchak, D., & Eggan, P. D. (1998). *Learning and teaching: Research-based methods* (3ʳᵈ ed.). Boston, MA: Allyn and Bacon.

Kaufman, D., & Moss, D. M. (2010). A new look at preservice teachers' conceptions of classroom management and organization: Uncovering complexity and dissonance. *The Teacher Educator, 45,* 118–136. doi:10.1080/08878731003623669

Kelly, M. (2013a). What's at stake? *Netplaces: New Teacher.* Available on http://www.netplaces.com/new-teacher/high-stakes-testing/whats-at-stake.htm

Kelly, M. (2013b). Arguments against high-stakes testing. *Netplaces: New Teacher.* Available on http://www.netplaces.com/new-teacher/high-stakes-testing/arguments-against-high-stakes-testing.htm

Kelm, J. L., & McIntosh, K. (2012). Effects of school-wide positive behavior support on teacher self-efficacy. *Psychology in the Schools, 49*(2), 137–147. doi:10.1002/pits.20624

Kempermann, G., Gast, D., & Gage, F. H. (2002). Neuroplasticity in old age: Sustained fivefold induction of hippocampal neurogenesis by long-term environmental enrichment. *Annals of Neurology, 52*(2), 135–143.

Kennedy, M. M. (2010). Attribution error and the quest for teacher quality. *Educational Researcher, 39,* 591. doi:10.3102/0013189X10390804

Kennedy, J. M. (2008 May 5). *SVG version of Bloom's Taxonomy.* Retrieved 29 Sept 2012 from http://commons.wikimedia.org/wiki/Image:Bloom%27s_Rose.png

Kent, A. (2013). Synchronization as a classroom dynamic: A practitioner's perspective. *Mind, Brain, and Education, 7*(1), 13–18.

Kerrins, J. A., & Cushing, K. S. (1998). *Taking a second look: Expert and novice differences when observing the same classroom teaching segment a second time.* Paper presented at the annual meeting of the American Educational Research Association, San Diego, CA.

Kerry, T. (2002). *Mastering teaching skills series: Learning objectives, task setting and differentiation.* UK: Nelson Thornes.

Kerry, T. & Kerry, C. A. (1997). Differentiation: Teachers' views of the usefulness of recommended strategies in helping the more able pupils in primary and secondary classrooms. *Educational Studies, 23*(3), 439–457.

Kersey, A. J., & James, K. H. (2013). Brain activation patterns resulting from learning letter forms through active self-production and passive observation in young children. *Frontiers in Psychology, 4.*

Kerssen-Griep, J. (2001). Teacher communication activities relevant to student motivation: Classroom facework and instructional communication competence. *Communication Education, 50,* 256–273.

Keresztes, A., Kaiser, D., Kovács, G., & Racsmány, M. (2013). Testing promotes long-term learning via stabilizing activation patterns in a large network of brain areas. *Cerebral Cortex,* bht158.

Khan, S. (2012). *The one world schoolhouse: Education reimagined.* Lebanon, IN: Hachette Book Group Twelve.

Kohlberg, L. (1971). Stages of moral development. *Moral education*, 23–92.

Kim, C., & Pekrun, R. (2014). Emotions and motivation in learning and performance. In *Handbook of research on educational communications and technology* (pp. 65–75). New York, NY: Springer.

Kincheloe, J., & Berry, K. (2007). *Rigour and complexity in educational research*. London, UK: McGraw-Hill International (UK) Limited.

Kilic, A. (2010). Learner-centered micro teaching in teacher education. *International Journal of Instruction, 3*(1), 77–100. Available on http://www.e-iji.net/dosyalar/iji_2010_1_5.pdf

Kim, J. S., & Hammer, W. C. (1976). Effect of performance feedback and goal setting on productivity and satisfaction in an organizational setting. *Journal of Applied Psychology, 61*, 48–57.

Kim, C., & Pekrun, R. (2014). Emotions and motivation in learning and performance. In J. M. Spencer et al. (Eds.), *Handbook of research on educational communications and technology* (pp. 65–75). doi 10.10071978 1-4614-3185-5_6

Kim, H., Shimojo, S., & O'Doherty, J. P. (2006). Is avoiding an averse outcome rewarding? Neural substrates of avoidance learning in the human brain. *PLoS Biology 4*(8), e233. doi:10.1371/journal.pbio.0040233

King, F. J., Goodson, L., & Rohani, F. (n.d.). *Higher order thinking skills: Definition, teaching strategies and assessment*. Vancouver, Canada: Center for Advancement of Learning and Assessment.

Kingsley Z. G. (1949). *Human behavior and the principle of least effort*. Boston, MA: Addison-Wesley Press.

Kirkpatrick Johnson, M. & Elder G.H. (2004). Intergenerational bonding at school: The behavioral and contextual correlated of student-teacher relationships. *Sociology of Education, 77*(1), 60–81.

Kirschner, F., Paas, F., & Kirschner, P. A. (2009). A cognitive load approach to collaborative learning: United brains for complex tasks. *Educational Psychology Review, 21*(1), 31–42.

Kirschner, P. A., Sweller, J., & Clark, R. E. (2006). Why minimal guidance during instruction does not work: An analysis of the failure of constructivist, discovery, problem-based, experiential, and inquiry-based teaching. *Educational Psychologist, 41*(2), 75–86.

Klassen, R. M., Bong, M., Usher, E. L., Chong, W. H., Huan, V. S., Wong, I. Y. F., & Georgiou, T. (2009). Exploring the validity of a teachers' self-efficacy scale in five countries. *Country Educational Psychology, 34*(1), 67–76.

Klingberg, T. (2008). *The overflowing brain: Information overload and the limits of working memory*. New York, NY: Oxford University Press.

Klingberg, T. (2012). *The learning brain: Memory and brain development in children*. New York, NY: Oxford University Press.

Knaepen, K., Goekint, M., Heyman, E. M., & Meeusen, R. (2010). Neuroplasticity—Exercise-induced response of peripheral brain-derived neurotrophic factor. *Sports Medicine, 40*(9), 765–801.

Kneese, C., & Ballinger, C. (2009). *Balancing the school calendar: Perspectives from the public and stakeholders*. Lanham, MD: Rowman & Littlefield Education.

Knight, R. T. (1996). Contribution of human hippocampal region to novelty detection. *Nature, 383*(6597), 256–259.

Knowlton, B. J., Morrison, R. G., Hummel, J. E., & Holyoak, K. J. (2012). A neurocomputational system for relational reasoning. *Trends in Cognitive Sciences, 16*(7), 373–381.

Koedinger, K., McLaughlin, E. A., & Heffernan, N. T. (2010). *A quasi-experimental evaluation of an on-line formative assessment and tutoring system.* Amityville, NY: Baywood Publishing Co., Inc. doi:10.2190/EC.43.4.d

Koehler, M. & Mishra, P. (2009). What is Technological Pedagogical Content Knowledge (TPACK)?. *Contemporary Issues in Technology and Teacher Education, 9*(1), 60–70. AACE. Retrieved from http://www.editlib.org/p/29544.

Koenig, R. (2010). *Learning for keeps: Teaching strategies essential for creating independent learners.* Alexandria, VA: ASCD.

Koretz, D. (2008), *Measuring up: What educational testing really tells us.* Cambridge, MA: Harvard University Press.

Kohlberg, L. (1973). The claim to moral adequacy of a highest stage of moral judgment. *Journal of Philosophy, 70*(18), 630–646. doi:10.2307/2025030

Kohlberg, L. (1981). *Essays on moral development: Vol. 1: The philosophy of moral development.* San Francisco, CA: Harper & Row.

Kolb, B., Forgie, M., Gibb, R., Gorny, G., & Rowntree, S. (1998). Age, experience and the changing brain. *Neuroscience & Biobehavioral Reviews, 22*(2), 143–159.

Konold, K. E., Miller, S. P., & Konold, K. B. (2004). Using teacher feedback to enhance student learning. *Teaching Exceptional Children, 36*(6), 64–69.

Koretz, D. (2008). *Measuring up: What educational testing really tells us.* Cambridge, MA: Harvard University Press.

Kostelnik, M. J., Soderman, A. K., & Whiren, A. P. (2010). *Developmentally appropriate curriculum: Best practices in early childhood education* (5th ed.). New York, NY: Pearson.

Kousaie, S., & Phillips, N. A. (2012). Ageing and bilingualism: absence of a "bilingual advantage" in Stroop interference in a nonimmigrant sample. *Quarterly Journal of Experimental Psychology, 65*(2), 356–69.

Kovalik, S. (1998). How emotions run us, our students, and our classroom. *NASSP Bulletin, 82*(598), 29–37. doi:10.1177/019263659808259805

Kpanja, E. (2001). A study of the effects of video tape recording in microteaching training. *British Journal of Educational Technology, 32*(4), 483–486. doi:10.1111/1467-8535.00215

Knyazev, G. G. (2007). Motivation, emotion, and their inhibitory control mirrored in brain oscillations. *Neuroscience & Behavioral Reviews, 31*(3), 377–395.

Kramer, A. F., & Erickson, K. I. (2007). Capitalizing on cortical plasticity: Influence of physical activity on cognition and brain function. *Trends in Cognitive Sciences, 11*(8), 342–348.

Krawczyk, D. C., McClelland, M., & Donovan, C. M. (2011). A hierarchy for relational reasoning in the prefrontal cortex. *Cortex, 47*(5), 588–597.

Krawczyk, D. C., McClelland, M. M., Donovan, C. M., Tillman, G. D., & Maguire, M. J. (2010). An fMRI investigation of cognitive stages in reasoning by analogy. *Brain Research, 1342*, 63–73.

Kreeft, P., & Doughtery, T. (Eds.) (2010). *Socratic logic: A logic text using Socratic Method, Platonic questions, and Aristotelian principles* (3rd ed.). South Bend, IN: St. Augustine's Press.

Krugers, H. J., Hoogenraad, C. C., & Groc, L. (2010). Stress hormones and AMPA receptor trafficking in synaptic plasticity and memory. *Nature Reviews Neuroscience, 11*, 675–681. doi:10.1038/nrn2913

Kuhn, D. (2000). Metacognitive development. *Current Directions in Psychological Science, 9*(5), 178–181.

Kuhn, D., & Dean, D. (2004). A bridge between cognitive psychology and educational practice. *Theory into Practice, 43*(4), 268–273.

Kulik, C. L. C., Kulik, J. A., & Bangert-Drowns, R.L. (1990). Effectiveness of mastery learning programs: A meta-analysis. *Review of Educational Research, 60*(2), 265–299.

Kyndt, E., Cascallar, E., & Dochy, F. (2012). Individual differences in working memory capacity and attention, and their relationship with students' approached to learning. *Higher Education, 64*(3), 285–297.

Laal, M., & Ghodsi, S. M. (2012). Benefits of collaborative learning. *Procedia Social and Behavioral Sciences 31*, 486–490.

Laffey, J. M., Schmidt, M., & Galyen, K. (2013). Seven virtual gaming and learning environments as experience-tools for learning through problem solving. *Learning, Problem Solving and Mind Tools*, 105.

Lai, E.R. (2011). *Metacognition: A literature review*. Research Report prepared for Pearson. New York, NY: Pearson.

Lam, F. (2011). *The Socratic Method as an approach to learning and its benefits*. (Thesis). Carnegie Mellon University.

Lamar, M. (2006). *Neuroscience and decision making*. Retrieved from http://www. docstoc. com/docs/28616882/Neuroscience-anddecisionmaking/download

Lamb, S. M. (1999). *Pathways of the brain: The neurocognitive basis of language* (Vol. 170). John Benjamins Publishing.

Land, M. L. (1979 Dec). Low-inference variables of teacher clarity: Effects on student concept learning. *Journal of Educational Psychology, 71*(6), 795–799. doi:10.1037/0022-0663.71.6.795

Land, M. L., & Smith, L.R. (1979). Effect of a teacher clarity variable on student achievement. *Journal of Educational Research, 72*(4), 196–197.

Lang, P. J., Bradley, M. M., & Cuthbert, B. N. (1998). Emotion, motivation, and anxiety: Brain mechanisms and psychophysiology. *Biological Psychiatry, 44*(12), 1248–1263.

Lang, P. J., & Davis, M. (2006). Emotion, motivation, and the brain: Reflex foundations in animal and human research. *Progress in Brain Research, 156*, 3–29. doi:http://dx.doi.org/10.1016/S0079-6123(06)56001-7.

Langer, E.J. (1990). *Mindfulness*. South Boston, MA: Da Capo Press.

Langleben D., & Campbell Moriarty, J. (2012). Using brain imaging for lie detection: Where science, law, and policy collide. Duquenesne University School of Law: *Psychology, Public Policy, and Law* Available at: http://works.bepress.com/jane_moriarty/18

Larkin, S. (2010). *Metacognition in young children.* New York, NY: Routledge.

La Rue, A., Koehler, K. M., Wayne, S. J., Chiulli, S. J., Haaland, K. Y., & Garry, P. J. (1997). Nutritional status and cognitive functioning in a normally aging sample: A 6-y reassessment. *American Journal of Clinical Nutrition, 65*(1), 20–29.

Larrison, A. (2013). *Mind, Brain and Education as a framework for curricular reform.* Dissertation (Ph.D.). San Diego, CA: University of California, San Diego.

Larrivee, B. (2000). Transforming teaching practice: Becoming the critically reflective teacher. Reflective Practice*: International and Multidisciplinary Perspectives, 1*(3), 293–307. doi:10.1080/713693162

Latz, A. O., Neumeister, K. L. S., Adams, C. M., & Pierce, R. L. (2008). Peer coaching to improve classroom differentiation: Perspectives fro project CLUE. *Roeper Review, 31*(1), 27–39.

Lavin, T., Thompson, T., & Ungerleider, C. (2010). A systematic review and meta-analysis of the cognitive correlates of bilingualism. *Review of Educational Research, 80*(2), 207–245.

Lavoie, R. (2008). *The motivation breakthrough: 6 secrets to turning on the tuned-out child.* New York, NY: Touchstone, Simon & Schuster.

Lawson, K. (2013). The four pillars of health coaching: Preserving the heart of a movement. *Global Advances in Health and Medicine, 2*(3). Retrieved 1 Aug 2013 from http://www.gahmj.com/doi/abs/10.7453/gahmj.2013.038

Leat, D., & Lin, M. (2003). Developing a pedagogy of metacognition and transfer: Some signposts for the generation and use of knowledge and the creation of research partnerships. *British Educational Research Journal, 29*(3), 383–414. doi: 10.1080/01411920301853

LeDoux, J. E. (1995). Emotion: Clues from the brain. *Annual Review of Psychology, 46*(1), 209–235.

LeDoux, J. (1998). *The emotional brain: The mysterious underpinnings of emotional life.* New York, NY: Simon and Schuster.

LeDoux, J.E., & Phelps, E.A. (2008). Emotional networks in the brain. In M. Lewis, J.M. Haviland-Jones, & L. Feldman Barrett (Eds.), *Handbook of emotions,* (pp.159–179). New York, NY: Guilford.

Lee, C., & Picanco, K.E. (2013). Accommodating diversity by analyzing practices of teaching (ADAPT). *Teacher Education and Special Education, 36*(2), 132–144. doi:10.1177/0888406413483327

Lee, K., Lim, Z. Y., Yeong, S. H., Ng, S. F., Venkatraman, V., & Chee, M. W. (2007). Strategic differences in algebraic problem solving: Neuroanatomical correlates. *Brain Research 1155,* 163–171.

Lee, K. H., & Siegle, G. J. (2012). Common and distinct brain networks underlying explicit emotional evaluation: A meta-analytic study. *Social Cognitive and Affective Neuroscience, 7*(5), 521–534.

Lee, S. J., Srinivasan, S., Trail, T., Lewis, D., & Lopez, S. (2011). Examining the relationship among student perception of support, course satisfaction, and learning outcomes in online learning. *The Internet and Higher Education, 14*(3), 158–163.

Lee, V. (1906). The riddle of music. *Quarterly Review 204,* 207–227.

Legrand, L., & Ruby, P. (2009). What is self-specific? Theoretical investigation and critical review of neuroimaging results. *Psychological Review, 116*(1), 252–282. doi:10.1037/a0014172

Lehrer, R., & Chazan, D. (Eds.) (1998). *Designing learning environments for developing understanding of geometry and space.* London, UK: Routledge.

Lemov, D. (2010). *Teach like a champion: 49 technique that put students on the path to college (K–12).* San Francisco, CA: Jossey-Bass.

Lepore, F. E. (2001). Dissecting genius: Einstein's brain and the search for the neural basis of intellect. *Cerebrum.* The Dana Foundation. Retrieved 9 Aug 2013 from http://www.dana.org/news/cerebrum/detail.aspx?id=3032

Lepper, M. R., Corpus, J. H., & Iyengar, S. S. (2005). Intrinsic and extrinsic motivational orientations in the classroom: Age differences and academic correlates. *Journal of Educational Psychology, 97*(2), 184.

Levine, M. (2002). *A mind at a time.* New York, NY: Simon & Schuster.

Levine, M. (2004). *The myth of laziness.* New York, NY: Simon & Schuster.

Levine, D. U. (1985). *Improving student achievement through mastery learning programs.* San Francisco, CA: Jossey-Bass.

Levinger, B. (1992). Nutrition, health, and learning. *School Nutrition and Health Network, monograph series, 1.*

Levy, J., Wubbels, T., & Brekelmans, M. (1992). Student and teacher characteristics and perceptions of teacher communication style. *Journal of Classroom Interaction, 27*(1), 23–29.

Levy, J., Wubbels, T., & Brekelmans, M. (1997). Language and cultural factors in students' perceptions of teacher communication style. *International Journal of Intercultural Relations, 21*(1), 29–56.

Levy, H. M. (2008). Meeting the needs of all students through differentiated instruction: Helping every child reach and exceed standards. *The Clearing House: A Journal of Educational Strategies, Issues and Ideas, 81*(4), 161–164. doi:http://dx.doi.org/10.1016/S0147-1767(96)00005-3

Lewis, C. C. (1995). *Educating hearts and minds: Reflections on Japanese preschool and elementary education.* Cambridge, UK: Cambridge, University Press.

Lewis, S. (2008). Mind Map created using iMindMap, describing many of the uses of Mind Mapping. *Uses of mind maps.* Illumine Training. Retrieved 4 Apr 2013 from http://www.mindwerx.com/mex/mind-map/software/680/uses-mind-maps

Lewis, L. H., & Williams, C. J. (1994). Experiential learning: Past and present. *New Directions for Adult and Continuing Education, 1994*(62), 5–16.

Li, S. C. (2003). Biocultural orchestration of developmental plasticity across levels: The interplay of biology and culture in shaping the mind and behavior across the life span. *Psychological Bulletin, 129*(2), 171.

Lieberman, H. R. (2003). Nutrition, brain function and cognitive performance. *Appetite, 40*(3), 245–254.

Ligorio, M. B. (2010). Dialogical relationship between identity and learning. *Culture Psychology, 16*(1), 93–107. doi:10.1177/1354067X09353206

Lim, D. H., & Morris, M. L. (2009). Learner and instructional factors influencing learning outcomes within a blended learning environment. *Educational Technology and Society, 12*(4), 282–293.

Lin, C. H., Yeh, S. H., Lu, H. Y., & Gean P. W. (2003). The similarities and diversities of signal pathways leading to consolidation of conditioning and consolidation of extinction of fear memory. *The Journal of Neuroscience, 23*(23), 8310–8317.

Lin, X. (2001). Designing metacognitive activities. *Educational Technology, Research and Development, 49*(2), 23–40.

Litke, M. D. (2011). *Predicted levels of learning for massed and spaced practice: Do people appreciate the benefits of spacing?* Vallanove, PA: Villanova University (MS degree). AAT 1497680.

Liu, C. C., & Chen, J. (2010). Evolution of constructivism. *Contemporary Issues in Education Research, 3*(4). Retrieved 1 Aug 2013 from http://www.cluteonline.com/journals/index.php/CIER/article/view/199/191

Livingston, J. A. (1997). *Metacognition: An overview.* Unpublished document. Retrieved 7 June 2013 from http://www.josemnazevedo.uac.pt/pessoal/textos/Metacognition.pdf

Llewellyn, D. J. (2004). *Teaching high school science through inquiry: A case study approach.* Thousand Oaks: Corwin.

Loflin, M. D. (1978). Discourse and inference in cognitive anthropology. *Discourse and Inference in Cognitive Anthropology: An Approach to Psychic Unity and Enculturation (World Anthropology),* 3–16.

Logam, J. M., Castel, A. D., Haber, S., & Biehman, E. J. (2012). Metacognition and the spacing effect: The role of repetition, feedback, and instruction on judgment of learning for massed and spaced rehearsal. *Metacognition and Learning, 7*(3), 175–195.

Lombardi, M. M. (2007). Authentic learning for the 21st century: An overview. *Educause Learning Initiative, 1*(2007), 1–12.

Long, D. (2013 Aug). Think differently: The game brain [online]. *Independent Education, 2.* Retrieved from http://search.informit.com.au/documentSummary;dn=564339356511979;res=IELHSS> ISSN: 1320-9825

Lorch, M., & Hellal, P. (2010). Darwin's "Natural Science of Babies." *Journal of the History of the Neurosciences, 19*(2), 140–157.

Loughran, J. J. (2002). Effective reflective practice: In search of meaning in learning about teaching. *Journal of Teacher Education, 53*(1), 33–43.

Lövdén, M., Bodammer, N.C., Kühn, S., Kaufmann, J., Schütze, H., Tempelmann, C., ... & Lindenberger, U. (2010). Experience-dependent plasticity of white-matter microstructure extends into old age. *Neuropsychologia, 48*(13), 3878–3883.

Lovinger, D.M. (2010). Neurotransmitter roles in synaptic modulation, plasticity and learning in the dorsal stratum. *Neuropharmacology, 58*(7), 951–961.

Low, R. Jin, P., & Sweller, J. (2011). Learners' cognitive load when using educational technology. *Gaming and Simulations: Concepts, Methodologies, Tools and Applications*. IGI Global. 1787–1806. doi:10.4018/978-1-60960-195-9.ch708

Lowe, P. B., & Kerr, C. M. (2003). Learning by reflection: The effect on educational outcomes. *Journal of Advanced Nursing, 27*(5), 1030–1033.

Lowery, N. V. (2002). Construction of teacher knowledge in context: Preparing elementary teachers to teach mathematics and science. *School Science and Mathematics, 102*(2), 68–83. doi:10.1111/j.1949-8594.2002.tb17896.x

Lozano, M. (2005). *Programas y experiencias en popularización de la ciencia y la tecnología*. Bogotá: Andrés Bello.

Luk, G., de Sa, E., & Bialystok, E. (2011). Is there a relation between onset age of bilingualism and enhancement of cognitive control? *Bilingualism: Language and Cognition, 14*(4), 588–595. doi:http://dx.doi.org/10.1017/S1366728911000010

Luo, L., Craik, F. I., Moreno, S., & Bialystok, E. (2012). Bilingualism interacts with domain in a working memory task: Evidence from aging. *Psychology and Aging*. PMID: 23276212

Lupiens, S. J., McEwen, B. S., Gunnar, M. R., & Heim, C. (2009). Effects of stress throughout the lifespan on the brain, behavior and cognition. *Nature Reviews Neuroscience, 10*, 434–445. doi:10.1038/nrn2639

Lynch, G. (1998). Memory and the brain: unexpected chemistries and a new pharmacology. *Neurobiology of Learning and Memory, 70*(1), 82–100.

Lyon, G. R., Shaywitz, S. E., & Shaywitz, B. A. (2003). Defining dyslexia, comorbidity, teachers' knowledge of language and reading. *Annals of Dyslexia, 53*, 1–14.

Maag, J. (2001). Rewarded by punishment: Reflections on the disuse of positive reinforcement in schools. *Exceptional Children, 67*(2), 173–186.

Maag, J. (2008). Rational-emotive therapy to help teachers control their emotions and behavior when dealing with disagreeable students. *Intervention in School and Clinic, 44*, 52–57.

Mabry, J. B. (1998). *Pedagogical variations in service-learning and student outcomes: How time, contact, and reflection matter*. Michigan Journal of Community Service Learning. Retrieved 1 Aug 2013 from http://eric.ed.gov/?id=EJ582008

Maasz, J., O'Donoghue, J. (Eds.) (2011). *Real-world problems for secondary school mathematics students: Case studies*. Rotterdam, The Netherlands: Sense Publishers.

Magg, J. W. (2008). Rational-emotive therapy to help teachers control their emotions and behavior when dealing with disagreeable students. *Intervention in School ad Clinic*. Retrieved 9 Aug 2013 from http://eric.ed.gov/?id=EJ806359

Magistretti, P. J., & Allaman, I. (2013). Brain energy metabolism. In D.A. Pfaff (Ed.), *Neuroscience in the 21st century* (pp. 1591–1620). New York, NY: Springer.

Maguire, E. A., Gadian, D. S., Johnsrude, I. S., Good, C. D., Ashburner, J., Frackowiak, R. S., &

Frith, C. D. (2000). Navigation related structural change in the hippocampi of taxi drivers. *Proceedings of the National Academy of Sciences,, 97*(8), 4398–4403.

Maiers, A. & Sandvold, A. (2010). *The passion-driven classroom: A framework for teaching and learning.* Larchmont, NY: Eye on Education.

Mandler, G. (1989). Memory: Conscious and unconscious. In *Memory: Interdisciplinary approaches* (pp. 84–106). New York, NY: Springer.

Marshakk, J. M. (2009). *Keep going: The art of perseverance.* New York, NY: Sterling Ethos.

Martin, A., & Caramazza, A. (2003, May). Neuropsychological and neuroimaging perspectives on conceptual knowledge: An introduction. *Cognitive Neuropsychology, 20*(3–6), 195–213.

Martin, A., Wiggs, C. L., Ungerielder, L. G., & Haxby, J. V. (1996). Neural correlates of category-specific knowledge. *Nature, 379.* 649–651.

Martin, D.J., & Loomis, K.S. (2006). *Building teachers: A constructivist approach to introducing education.* Independence, KY: Wadsworth Publishing/Cengage.

Marx, A., Fuhrer, U., & Hartig, T. (1999). Effects of classroom seating arrangements on children's question-asking. *Learning Environments Research, 2*(3), 249–263.

Marzano, R. J. (1988). *Dimensions of thinking: A framework for curriculum and instruction.* Alexandria, VA: Association for Supervision and Curriculum Development.

Marzano, R. J. (2003). *What works in schools: Translating research into action.* Alexandria, VA: ASCD.

Marzano, R. J. (2007). *The art and science of teaching: A comprehensive framework for effective instruction.* Alexandria, VA: Association for Supervision and Curriculum Development.

Marzano, R. J. (2009). *The art and science of teaching: A comprehensive framework for effective instruction* (2nd ed.). Alexandria, VA: Association for Supervision and Curriculum Development.

Marzano, R. J. (2010 May). Representing knowledge nonlinguistically. *Educational Leadership.* Retrieved 9 Aug 2013 from https://www.sheltonschools.org/CAL/InstructionalCoaching/Shared%20Documents/Marzano%20High%20Probability%20Strategies/Representing%20Knowledge%20Nonlinguistically%20-%20Marzano.pdf

Marzano, R. J. (2011). *Effective supervision: Supporting the art and science of teaching.* Alexandria, VA: Association for Supervision and Curriculum Development.

Marzano, R. J., Marzano, J. S., & Pickering, D.J. (2003). *Classroom management that works: Research-based strategies for every teacher.* Alexandria, VA: Association for Supervision and Curriculum Development.

Marzano, R. J., Norford, J. A., Paynter, D.E., Pickering, D.J., & Gaddy, B.B. (2001). *A handbook for classroom instruction that works.* Alexandria, VA: Association for Supervision and Curriculum Development.

Marzano, R. J., & Pickering, D. J. (2007 Mar). The case for and against homework. *Educational Leadership.* Alexandria, VA: Association for Supervision and Curriculum Development. Retrieved 9 Aug 2013 from http://www.ascd.org/publications/educational-leadership/mar07/vol64/num06/The-Case-For-and-Against-Homework.aspx

Marzano, R. J., Pickering, D., & Hefelbower, T. (2010). *The highly engaged classroom*. Alexandria, VA: Association for Supervision and Curriculum Development.

Marzano, R. J., Pickering, D. J., & Pollock, J. E. (2001). *Classroom instruction that works: Research-based strategies for increasing student achievement*. Alexandria, VA: Association for Supervision and Curriculum Development.

Maxwell, K.J. (2009). *The Socratic temperament*. Retrieved 4 July 2012 from http://www.socratic-method.net/the_socratic_temperament.htm

Mayer, R. E. (1996). Learning strategies for making sense out of expository text: The SOI model for guiding three cognitive processes in knowledge construction. *Educational Psychology Review, 8*(4), 357–371.

Model for guiding three cognitive processes in knowledge construction. *Educational Psychology Review 8*(4) 357–371.

May, A. (2011). Experience-dependent structural plasticity in the adult human brain. *Trends in Cognitive Sciences, 15*(10), 475–482.

Mayer, R. E. (2008). *Learning and instruction* (2nd ed.). Upper Saddle River, NJ: Prentice Hall.

Mayer, R. E., & Alexander, P. A. (Eds.) (2011). *Handbook of research on learning and instruction*. New York, NY: Routledge.

Mazer, J. P. (2013). Associations among teacher communication behaviors, student interest, and engagement: A validity test. *Communication Education, 62*(1), 86–96.

Mazur, E. (1991 Jan/Feb). Can we teach computers to teach? *Computers in Physics*, 31–38. Available on: http://mazur.harvard.edu/sentFiles/Mazur_256459.pdf

McCabe, D. P., Roediger, III, H. L., McDaniel, M. A., Balota, D. A., & Hambirck, D. Z. (2010). The relationship between working memory capacity and executive functioning: Evidence for a common executive attention construct. *Neuropsychology, 24*(2), 222–243.

McCabe, J. (2011). Metacognitive awareness of learning strategies in undergraduates. *Memory & Cognition, 39*(3), 462–476.

McCabe, K. (2012). The influences of childhood poverty on life chances: The case of academic performance. *Honors Projects in History and Social Sciences*. Paper 16.

McCaig, R. G., Dixon, M., Keramatian, K., Liu, I., & Christoff, K. (2010). Improved modulation of rostrolateral prefrontal cortex using real-time fMRI training and meta-cognitive awareness. *NeuroImage, 55*(3), 1298–1305. doi:http://dx.doi.org/10.1016/j.neuroimage.2010.12.01.

McCain, T., & Jukes, I. (2008). *Teaching the digital generation*. Thousand Oaks, CA: Corwin..

McClelland, J. L., McNaughton, B. L., & O'Reilly, R. C. (1995). Why there are complementary learning systems in the hippocampus and neocortex: Insights from the successes and failures of connectionist models of learning and memory. *Psychological Review, 102*(3), 419.

McCrink, K., Dehaene, D., & Dehaene-Lambertz, G. (2007). Moving along the number line: Operational momentum in nonsymbolic arithmetic. *Perception and Psychophysics, 69,* 1324.

McCroskey, J. C. (1992). *An introduction to communication in the classroom*. Edina, MN: Burgess.

McCroskey, J. C., & McVetta, R. W. (1978). Classroom seating arrangements: Instructional communication theory versus student preferences. *Communication Education, 27*(2), 99–111. Retrieved 9 Aug 2013 from http://www.jamescmccroskey.com/publications/082.pdf

McCroskey, J. C., Sallinen, A., Fayer, J. M., Richmond, V. P., & Barraclough, R.A. (1996). Nonverbal immediacy and cognitive learning: A cross-cultural investigation. *Communication Education, 45*(3), 200–211.

McCroskey, J. C., Richmond, V.P., & Bennett, V.E. (2006). The relationship of student end-of-class motivation with teacher communication behaviors and instructional outcomes. *Communication Education, 55*(4), 403–414. doi:10.1080/03634520600702562

McCroskey, J. C., Valencic, K.M., & Richmond, V.P. (2004). Toward a general model of instructional communication. *Communication Quarterly, 52*(3), 197–210.

McDaniel, M. A., & Donnelly, C. M. (1996). Learning with analogy and elaborative integration. *Journal of Educational Psychology, 88*(3), 508–519. doi:10.1037/0022-0663.88.3.508

McGlone, E. L., & Anderson, L. J. (1973). The dimensions of teacher credibility. *The Speech Teacher, 22*(3), 196–200.

McGregor, D. (2007). *Developing thinking; developing learning.* New York, NY: McGraw-Hill International.

McLaren, I. (2009). Both rules and associations are required to predict human behaviour. *Behavioral and Brain Sciences, 32*(2), 216–217.

McNamara, D. S. (2006). Bringing cognitive science into education and back again: The value of interdisciplinary research. *Cognitive Science, 30*, 605–608.

McTighe, J., & Wiggins, G. (2013). *Essential questions: Opening doors to student understanding.* Alexandria, VA: Association for Supervision and Curriculum Development.

Meissner, W. (2006). The mind–brain relation and neuroscientific foundations: II. Neurobehavioral integrations. *Bulletin of the Menninger Clinic, 70*(2), 102–124.

Mekheiemer, M. A. A. (2012). Assessing aptitude and attitude development in a translation skills course. *CALICO Journal, 29*(2), 321–340.

Meltzer, L. (Ed.) (2011). *Executive function in education: From theory to practice.* New York, NY: Guilford.

Meltzoff, A. (1995). Understanding the intentions of others: Re-enactment of intended acts by 18-month-old children. *Developmental Psychology, 31*, 838–850.

Meltzoff, A., Kuhl, P. K., Movellan, J., & Sejnowski, T. J. (2009 July 17). Foundations for a new science of learning. *Science 325*(5938), 284–288.

Memmott, M. (2012). Minorities are now majority of U.S. births, Census says. *National Public Radio.* Retrieved 3 April 2013 from http://www.npr.org/blogs/thetwo-way/2012/05/17/152896230/minorities-are-now-majority-of-u-s-births-census-says. doi:10.1126/science.1175626

Mendler, A. (2009). *Motivating students who don't care: Successful techniques for educators.* Bloomington, IN: Solution Tree.

Menna-Barreto, L., & Wey, D. (2008). Time constraints in the school environment: What does a sleepy student tell us? *Mind, Brain, and Education, 2*(1), 24–28.

Mercer, S. H. & DeRosier, M. E. (2010). A prospective investigation of teacher preference and children's perceptions of the student–teacher relationship. *Psychology in the Schools, 47*(2), 184–192.

Mertens, D. M. (2009). *Research and evaluation in education and psychology: Integrating diversity with quantitative, qualitative, and mixed methods.* Thousand Oaks, CA: Sage.

Metiri Group. (2003). *enGauge 21st century skills for 21st century learners.* Retrieved October 29, 2010 from http://www.metiri.com/21/Metiri-NCREL21stSkills.pdf

Meyer, N. M., & Nulty, D.D. (2009). How to use (five) curriculum design principles to align authentic learning environments, assessment, students' approaches to thinking and learning outcomes. *Assessment & Evaluation in Higher Education, 34*(5), 565–577. doi:10.1080/02602930802226502

Meyer, P. J. (2003). *Attitude is everything: If you want to succeed above and beyond.* Monterrey, CA: Meyer Resource Group, Inc.

Michael, J. (2006). Where's the evidence that active learning works? *Advances in Physiology Education, 30*(4), 159–167.

Middlebrooks, P. G., & Sommer, M. A. (2012). Neuronal correlates of metacognition in primate frontal cortex. *Neuron, 75*(3), 517–530.

Milkie, M. A., Nomaguchi, K. M., & Denny, K.E. (2012). *How does the amount of time mothers spend with children matter?* Maryland: Bowling Green State University the Center for Family and Demographic Research.

Millar, R. (1991). Why is science hard to learn? *Journal of Computer Associated Learning, 7*(2), 66–74. doi:10.1111/j.1365-2729.1991.tb00229.x

Miller, T., & Geraci, L. (2011). Training metacognition in the classroom: the influence of incentives and feedback on exam predictions. *Metacognition and Learning, 6*(3), 303–314.

Miller, N. L., Shattuck, L. G., Matsangas, P., & Dyche, J. (2008). Sleep and academic performance in US military training and education programs. *Mind, Brain, and Education, 2*(1), 29–33.

Mills, C. M., Legare, C. H., Grant, M. G., & Landrum, A. R. (2011). Determining who to question, what to ask, and how much information to ask for: The development of inquiry in young children. *Journal of Experimental Child Psychology, 110*(4), 539–560.

Mills, D. L., Prat, C., Zangl, R., Stager, C. L., Neville, H. J., & Werker, J. F. (2004). Language experience and the organization of brain activity to phonetically similar words: ERP evidence from 14- and 20-month-olds. *Journal of Cognitive Neuroscience, 16*(8), 1452–1464.

Mindell, J., & Owens, J. A. (2009). *A clinical guide to pediatric sleep: Diagnosis and management of sleep problems.* Wolters Kluwer Health.

Miranda, L. (2010). On trends and rhythms in scientific and technological knowledge evolution: A quantitative analysis. *International Journal of Technology Intelligence and Planning, 6*(1), 76–109.

Mirochnik, E. & Sherman, D.C. (Eds.) (2002). *Passion and pedagogy: Relation, creation, and transformation in teaching.* Pieterlen, Switzerland: Peter Lang International Academic Publishers.

Mishra, P. & Kereluik, K. (2011). *What 21st century learning? A review and a synthesis.* Michigan State University. Paper submitted to the 2011, SITE Conference

Mitchell, M. M., Bradshaw, C. P., & Leaf, P. J. (2010). Student and teacher perceptions of school climate: A multilevel exploration of patterns of discrepancy. *Journal of School Health, 80*(6), 271–279. doi:10.1111/j.1746-1561.2010.00501.x

Mitru, G., Millrood, D., & Mateika, J. (2002). The impact of sleep on learning and behavior in adolescents. *Teachers College Record, 104*(4), 704–726.

Molder, H. T., & Potter, J. (2005). *Conversation and cognition.* Cambridge, UK: Cambridge University Press.

Molenaar, I., van Boxtel, C. A. M., & Sleegers, P. J. C. (2011). Metacognitive scaffolding in an innovative learning arrangement. *Instructional Science, 39*(6), 785–803. doi:10.1007/s11251-010-9154-1

Monaghan, P., & Rowson, C. (2008). The effect of repetition and similarity on sequence learning. *Memory and Cognition, 36*(8), 1509–1514. doi:10.3758/MC.36.8.1509.

Mondale, S. (2001). *School: The story of American public education.* New York, NY: Beacon.

Moon, J. (2004). *A handbook of reflective and experiential learning: Theory and practice.* London, UK: Routledge.

Moore, C. M., & Egeth H. (1997). Perception without attention: Evidence of grouping under conditions of inattention. *Journal of Experimental Psychology: Human Perception and Performance 23*, 339–352.

Moran, J. M., Macrae, C. N., Heatherton, T. F., Wyland, C. L., & Kelley, W. M. (2006). Neuroanatomical evidence for distinct cognitive and affective components of self. *Journal of Cognitive Neuroscience, 18*(9), 1586–1594. doi:10.1162/jocn.2006.18.9.1586

Morgan, K. (2011). *Mastery learning in the science classroom.* Arlington, VA: National Science Teachers Association Press.

Morita, K., Morishima, M., Sakai, K., & Kawaguchi, Y. (2013). Dopaminergic control of motivation and reinforcement learning: A closed-circuit account for reward-oriented behavior. *Journal of Neuroscience, 33*(20), 8866–8890. doi:10.1523/JNEUROSCI.4614-12.2013

Morocco, C. C., & Mata, C. A. (2002). Coteaching for content understanding: A school wide model. *Journal of Education and Psychological Consultation 13*(4), 315–347.

Morrison, F. J., Ponitz, C. C., & McClelland, M. M. (2010). Self-regulation and academic achievement in the transition to school. *Child development at the intersection of emotion and cognition,.* In M. Posner (Series Ed.) & S. Calkins & M. Bell (Vol. Eds.), *The developing human brain: Development at the intersection of emotion and* cognition (pp.203–224). Washington, D.C.: American Psychological Association.

Morrow, V., & Richards, M. (1996). The ethics of social research with children: An overview. *Children & Society, 10*(2), 90–105.

Morton, J. B. (2010). Language, bilingualism, and executive functioning in early development. *Psychological Reports, 107*(3), 888–890.

Morton, J. B., & Harper, S. N. (2007). What did Simon say? Revisiting the bilingual advantage. *Developmental Science, 10,* 719–726.

Moses, E. R. (2006). The art of questioning. *Today's Speech, 8*(4), 21–35.

Motschnig, R., & Cornelius-White, J. H. D. (2012). Experiential/Significant learning. *Encyclopedia of the Sciences of Learning,* 1219–1223.

Mottet, T. P., Richmond , V. P., & McCroskey, J. C. (Eds.) (2006). *Handbook of instructional communication: Rhetorical & relational perspectives.* Boston, MA: Pearson.

Mowszowski, L., Batchelor, J., & Naismith, S. L. (2010). Early intervention for cognitive decline: Can cognitive training be used as a selective prevention technique? *International Psychogeriatrics, 22*(4), 537.

Mozer, M. C., Pashler, H., Cepeda, N., Lindsey, R., & Vul, E. (2009). *Predicting the optimal spacing of study: A multiscale context model of memory.* Retrieved 1 Aug 2013 from http://machinelearning.wustl.edu/mlpapers/paper_files/NIPS2009_0736.pdf

Munakata, Y., Herd, S. A., Chatham, C. H., Depue, B. E., Banich, M. T., O'Reilly, R. C. (2011). A unified framework for inhibitory control. *Trends in Cognitive Neuroscience, 15*(10), 453–459.

Mundy, P., & Newell, L. (2007). Attention, joint attention, and social cognition. *Current Directions in Psychological Science, 16*(5), 269–274.

Murphy, J. V., & Miller, R. E. (1956). Spaced and massed practice with a methodological consideration of avoidance conditioning. *Journal of Experimental Psychology, 52*(2), 77–81. doi:10.1037/h0044969

Mustard, J. F. (2010). Early brain development and human development. *Encyclopedia on Early Childhood Development.* CEED / SKC-ECD. Retrieved 9 Aug 2013 from http://www.enfant-encyclopedie.com/pages/PDF/MustardANGxp.pdf

Myers, S. A. (1995). Student perceptions of teacher affinity-seeking and classroom climate. *Communication Research Reports, 12*(2), 192–199. doi:10.1080/08824099509362056

Myers, S. A. (2004). The relationship between perceived instructor credibility and college student in-class and out-of-class communication. *Communication Reports 17*(2), 129–137. doi:10.1080/08934210409389382

Myers, S. A., & Knox, R. L. (2000). Perceived instructor argumentativeness and verbal aggressiveness and student outcomes. *Communication Research Reports, 17,* 299–309.

Myers, S. A., & Rocca, K. A. (2001). Perceived instructor argumentativeness and verbal aggressiveness in the college classroom: Effects on student perceptions of climate, apprehension, and state motivation. *Western Journal of Communication, 65,* 113–127.

Myers, S. S., & Pianta, R. C. (2008). Developmental commentary: Individual and contextual influences on student teacher relationships and children's early problem behaviors. *Journal of Clinical Child and Adolescent Psychology, 37*(3), 600–608.

Mynard, J., & Navarro, D. (2010). Dialogue in self-access learning. In A. M. Stoke (Ed.), *JALT2009*

Conference Proceedings. Tokyo: JALT. Retrieved 9 Aug 2013 from http://jalt-publications.org/archive/proceedings/2009/E008.pdf

Naqib, F., Farah, C. A., Pack, C. C. & Sossin, W. S. (2011). The rates of protein synthesis and degradation account for the differential response of neurons to spaced and massed training protocols. *PLoS Computational Biology 7*(12), e1002324. doi:10.1371/journal.pcbi.1002324

National Board for Professional Teaching Standards. (2002). *Standards.* Arlington, VA: Author.

National Mathematics Advisory Panel. (2008). *Foundations for success: The final report of the National Mathematics Advisory Panel.* Washington, DC: U.S. Department of Education.

National Science Foundation. (2005). Cycle of innovation. In *Innovative technology experiences for students and teachers (ITEST).* Retrieved 9 Aug 2013 from http://www.nsf.gov/pubs/2009/nsf09506/nsf09506.htm

Nelkin, D. (1995 Sep 28). Biology is not destiny. *New York Times.*

Nelson, C. A., Thomas, K. M., & de Haan, M. (2012). *Neuroscience of cognitive development: The role of experience and the developing brain.* New York, NY: Wiley.

Nelson, J., Lynn, L., & Glenn, H. S. (1999). *Positive discipline* (2nd ed.). New York, NY: Prima Lifestyles.

Neumann, A. (2006). Professing passion: Emotion in the scholarship of professors at research universities. *American Educational Research Journal 43*(3), 381–424.

Newcombe, N. A. (2013). Educating to use evidence in thinking about education. *Mind, Brain, and Education, 7*(2), 147–150.

Newcombe, N. S. (2002). Biology is to medicine as psychology is to education: True or false?. *New Directions for Teaching and Learning, 2002*(89), 9–18.

Ng, P. T, & Tan, C. (2009). Community of practice for teachers: Sensemaking or critical reflective learning? *Reflective Practice: International and Multidisciplinary Perspectives, 10*(1), 37–44. doi: 10.1080/14623940802652730

Nicol, D. J., & Macdarlane-Dick, D. (2006). Formative assessment and self-regulation learning: A model and seven principles of good feedback practice. *Studies in Higher Education, 31*(2), 199–218. doi: 10.1080/03075070600572090

Nicolson, R. (2005). Dyslexia: Beyond the myth. *The Psychologist, 18*(11), 658–659.

Nie, Y., & Lau, S. (2009). Complementary roles of care and behavioral control in classroom management: The self-determination theory perspective. *Contemporary Educational Psychology, 34*(3), 185–194. doi:http://dx.doi.org/10.1016/j.cedpsych.2009.03.001

Nie, Y., & Lau, S. (2010). Differential relations of constructivist and didactic instruction to students' cognition, motivation, and achievement. *Learning and Instruction, 20*(5), 411–423.

Niemi, H. (2009). Why from teaching to learning? *European Educational Research Journal, 8*(1), ECER 2008 KEYNOTE. doi:http://dx.doi.org/10.2304/eerj.2009.8.1.1

Nilson, L.B. (2010). *Teaching at its best: A research-based resource for college instructors.* San Francisco, CA: Jossey-Bass.

Noddings, N. (2005 Sept). What does it mean to educate the whole child? *Educational Leadership, 63*(1), 8–13.

Noer, M. (2012). *One man, one computer, 10 million students: How Khan Academy is reinventing education.* Available on www.forbes.com/sites/michaelnoer/2012/11/02/one-man-one-computer-10-million-students-how-khan-academy-is-reinventing-education

Norton, A. (2013). The future of online higher education: Better but not necessarily faster or cheaper: Online educational technology could improve learning but that's not all students are looking for from higher education. *Policy, 29*(2), 10–14.

Northoff, G., Qin, P., & Nakao, T. (2010). Rest-stimulus interaction in the brain: A review. *Trends in Neuroscience, 33*(6), 277–284.

Northwest Regional Educational Laboratory. (2005). Nonlinguistic representations. *Focus on effectiveness: Research-based strategies.* Retrieved from http://www.netc.org/focus/strategies/nonl.php

Naqib, F., Farah, C. A., Pack, C. C., Sossin, W. S. (2011). The rates of protein synthesis and degradation account for the differential response of neurons to spaced and massed training protocols. *PLoS Computational Biology, 7*(12), e1002324. doi:10.1371/journal.pcbi.1002324.

Nihart, T., Lersch, K. M., Sellers, C., & Mieczkowski, T. (2005). Kids, cops, parents and teachers: Exploring juvenile attitudes toward authority figures. *Western Criminology Review, 6*(1), 79–88.

Niogi, S. N., & McCandliss, B. D. (2011). *U.S. Patent No. 8,077,937.* Washington, DC: U.S. Patent and Trademark Office.

Norman, D. A. (1968). Toward a theory of memory and attention. *Psychological Review, 75*(6), 522.

Nummela-Caine, R. & Caine, G. (1998). *Building a bridge between the neurosciences and education: Cautions and possibilities: Brain-based education.* Retrieved on September 10, 2007 from edc.gov.ab.ca/k_12/special/ aisi/pdfs/bbased_learning.pdf

Nummenmaa, L., Glerean, E., Viinikainen, M., Jääskeläinen, I. P., Hari, R., & Sams, M. (2012). Emotions promote social interaction by synchronizing brain activity across individuals. *Proceedings of the National Academy of Sciences, 109*(24), 9599–9604.

Nye, B., Konstantopoulous, S., & Hedges, L.V. (2004). How large are teacher effects? *Educational Evaluation and Policy Analysis, 26*(3), 237–257.

Obama, B. (2008 Feb 5). *Super Tuesday Speech*, Chicago, IL. Retrieved 7 June 2013 from http://obamaspeeches.com/E02-Barack-Obama-Super-Tuesday-Chicago-IL-February-5-2008.htm

Obradović, J., Bush, N. R., Stamperdahl, J., Adler, N. E., & Boyce, W. T. (2010). Biological sensitivity to context: The interactive effects of stress reactivity and family adversity on socioemotional behavior and school readiness. *Child Development, 81*(1), 270–289.

Ochsner, K.N., Knierim, K., Ludlow, D.H., Hanelin, J., Ramachandran, T., Glover, G., & Mackey, S.C. (2004). Reflecting upon feelings: An fMRI study of neural systems supporting the attribution of emotion to self and other. *Journal of Cognitive Neuroscience, 16*(10), 1746–1772. doi:10.1162/0898929042947829

O'Donnell, A. M., Dansereau, D. F., & Hall, R. H. (2002). Knowledge maps as scaffolds for cognitive processing. *Educational Psychology Review, 14*(1), 71–86.

O'Donnell, A., Reeve, J., & Smith, J. (2012). *Educational psychology: Reflection for action* (3rd ed.). Hoboken, NJ: John Wiley & Sons.

Office for Standards in Education of the UK, (2004). *Why colleges succeed.* London, UK: Crown Copyright. Retrieved 1 Aug 2013 from http://www.ofsted.gov.uk/resources/why-colleges-succeed.

Ohnishi, T., Matsuda, H., Asada, T., Aruga, M., Hirakata, M., Nishikawa, M., ... & Imabayashi, E. (2001). Functional anatomy of musical perception in musicians. *Cerebral Cortex, 11*(8), 754–760.

Olivera, A. W. (2010). Improving teacher questioning in science inquiry discussions through professional development. *Journal of Research in Science Teaching, 47*(4), 422–453.

O'Neill, S., & Stephenson, J. (2012). Does classroom management coursework influence pre-service teachers' perceived preparedness or confidence? *Teaching and Teacher Education.*

Organisation for Economic Co-Operation and Development. (2002). *Understanding the brain: Towards a new learning science.* Paris: OECD. Available online at *www.oecd.org*

Organisation for Economic Co-operation and Development. (2005). *Education at a glance.* Paris, France: Author.

Organisation for Economic Co-Operation and Development. (2007a). *The brain and learning.* Retrieved March 10, 2007 from *http://www.oecd.org/department /0,2688,en_2649_14935397_1_1_1_1_1,00.html.*

Organisation for Economic Co-Operation and Development. (2007b). *Understanding the brain: The birth of a new learning science.* Paris, France: Author.

Organización de Estados Iberoamericanos para la Educación, la Ciencia y la Cultura (OEI). (2011). *La importancia de la enseñanza de ciencias en la sociedad actual.* Downloaded on 8 March 2011de http://www.oei.es/oeivirt/curricie/curri01.htm

Organización de las Naciones Unidas para la Educación, la Ciencia y la Cultura (UNESCO). (2005). *¿Cómo promover el interés por la cultura científica?: una propuesta didáctica fundamentada para la educación científica de jóvenes de 15 a 18 años.* Santiago de Chile: Oficina Regional de Educación de la UNESCO para América Latina y el Caribe.

Orgill, M.K., & Thomas, M. (2007). *Analogies and the 5E model.* Washington, DC: National Science Teachers Association.

Ormrod, J.E. (2000). *Demonstrating the concepts "meaningful learning" and "elaboration."* Paper presented at the Annual Meeting of the American Educational Research Association (New Orleans, LA, April 24–28, 2000).

Ormrod, J. E., & Davis, K. M. (2004). *Human learning.* London, UK: Merrill.

Otmakhova, N., Duzel, E., Deutch, A. Y., & Lisman, J. (2013). The hippocampal-VTA loop: The role of novelty and motivation in controlling the entry of information into long-term memory. In G. Baldassrre & M. Mirolli (Eds.), *Intrinsically motivated learning in natural and artificial systems* (pp. 235–254). doi:10.1007/978-3-642-32375-1_10

Otten, L. J., Henson, R. N. A., & Rugg, M. D. (2001). Depth of processing effects on neural correlates of memory encoding. *Brain, 124*(2), 399–412. doi:10.1093/brain/124.2.399

Overholser, J. C. (1993). Elements of the Socratic Method: I. Systematic questioning. *Psychotherapy: Theory, Research, Practice, Training, 30*(1), 67–74. doi:10.1037/0033-3204.30.1.67

Ownsworth, T., Quinn, H., Fleming, J., Kendall, M., & Shum, D. (2010). Error self-regulation following traumatic brain injury: A single case study evaluation of metacognitive skills training and behavioural practice interventions. *Neuropsychological rRehabilitation, 20*(1), 59–80.

Paap, K. R., & Greenberg, Z. I. (2013 Mar). There is no coherent evidence for a bilingual advantage in executive processing. *Cognitive Psychology, 66*(2), 232–258.

Padak, N. (2002). *Strategies that work: What does the evidence tell us? Research to practice.* ERIC. Retrieved 9 Aug 2013 from http://eric.ed.gov/?id=ED476063

Palincsar, A. S. (1986). *Teaching reading as thinking.* Oak Brook, IL: North Central Regional Educational Laboratory.

Paller, K. A., & Gross, M. (1998). Brain potentials associated with perceptual priming vs explicit remembering during the repetition of visual word-form. *Neuropsychologia, 36*(6), 559–571.

Palmer, E. A., & Bemis, A. E. (1999). *Alternative calendars: Extended learning and year-round programs.* University of Minnesota, Center for Applied Research and Educational Improvement.

Palmer, P. J. (1997). *The courage to teach: Exploring the inner landscape of a teacher's life.* San Francisco, CA: Jossey-Bass.

Pang, K. (2010). Creating stimulating learning and thinking using new models of activity-based learning and metacognitive-based activities. *Journal of College Teaching and Learning, 17*(4).

Park, D. C. & Huang, C.-M. (2010). Culture wires the bran: A cognitive neuroscience perspective. *Perspectives on Psychological Science, 5*(4), 391–400.

Parrila, R., Kirby, J. R., & McQuarrie, L. (2004). Articulation rate, naming speed, verbal short-term memory, and phonological awareness: Longitudinal predictors of early reading development?. *Scientific Studies of Reading, 8*(1), 3–26.

Partnership for 21st Century Skills. (2007). *Framework for 21st century learning.* Retrieved October 29, 2010, from http://www.p21.org/documents/P21_Framework_Definitions.pdf

Pascual-Leone, A., Amedi, A., Fregni, F., & Merabet, L. B. (2005). The plastic human brain cortex. *Annual Review of Neuroscience, 28*, 377–401.

Pashler, H., Cepeda, N., Lindsey, R., Vul, E., & Mozer, M. C. (2009). Predicting the optimal spacing of study: A multiscale context model of memory. In *Advances in neural information processing systems* (pp. 1321–1329). Retrieved 10 Oct 2013 from http://machinelearning.wustl.edu/mlpapers/paper_files/NIPS2009_0736.pdf

Patrick, H., Kaplan, A., & Ryan, A. M. (2011). Positive classroom motivational environments: Convergence between mastery goal structure and classroom social climate. *Journal of Educational Psychology, 103*(2), 367–382.

Pashler, H., McDaniel, M., Rohrer, D., & Bjork, R. (2008). Learning styles: Concepts and evidence. *Psychological Science in the Public Interest, 9*(3), 105–119.

Patterson, K., Nestor, P. J., & Rogers, T. T. (2007 Dec). Where do you know what you know? The representation of semantic knowledge in the human brain. *Nature Reviews Neuroscience, 8,* 976–987. doi:10.1038/nrn2277

Paul, R. (1990). Critical thinking: What, why and how. In R. Paul, D. Weil and J.A. Binker's *Critical thinking: What every person needs to survive in a rapidly changing world* (pp.1–25). Sonoma State University Rohnert Park. CA: Center for Critical Thinking and Moral Critique.

Paul, R. (1992). Critical thinking: What, why and how. *New Directions for Community Colleges, 77,* 3–24. doi:10.1002/cc.36819927703.

Paul, R. (2012). Critical thinking: what every person needs to survive in a rapidly changing world (4th ed.). Tomales, CA: Foundation for Critical Thinking.

Paul, R., & Elder, L. (2001). *Critical thinking: Tools for taking charge of the learning in your life* (2nd ed.). New York, NY: Prentice Hall.

Paul, R., & Elder, L. (2007). *The thinker's guide to the art of Socratic questioning.* Tomales, CA: The Foundation for Critical Thinking.

Paul, R., & Elder, L. (2010). *The miniature guide to critical thinking concepts and tools.* Dillon Beach: Foundation for Critical Thinking Press. Available on http://louisville.edu/ideastoaction/about/criticalthinking/framework

Paulus, P. (2000). Groups, teams, and creativity: The creative potential of idea-generation groups. *Applied Psychology, 49*(2), 237–262. doi:10.1111/1464-0597.00013

Pavio, A (1971). *Imagery and verbal processes.* New York, NY: Holt, Rinehart, and Winston.

Pavio, A. (1976). Coding distinctions and repetition effects in memory. In G.H. Bower's *Psychology of learning and motivation* (pp. 179–212). New York, NY: Academic Press.

Pavio, A. (1990). *Mental representations.* New York, NY: Oxford University Press.

Pekrun, R., Goetz, T., Frenzel, A. C., Barchfeld, P., & Perry, R. P. (2011). Measuring emotions in students' learning and performance: The Achievement Emotions Questionnaire (AEQ). *Contemporary Educational Psychology, 36*(1), 36–48.

Pekrun, R., Goetz, T., Frenzel, A. C., Barchfeld, P., & Perry, R. P. (2011). Measuring emotions in students' learning and performance: The Achievement Emotions Questionnaire (AEQ). *Contemporary Educational Psychology, 36*(1), 36–48.

Pekrun, R., Goetz, T., Titz, W., & Perry R. (2002). Academic emotions in students self-regulated learning and achievement: A program of qualitative and quantitative research. *Educational Psychologist, 37*(2), 91–105. doi:10.1207/S15326985EP3702_4

Pellegrini, A. D., Symons, F., & Hoch, J. (2013). *Observing children in their natural worlds: A methodological primer* (3rd ed.). New York, NY: Taylor & Francis.

Pellegrino, J. W., & Hilton, M. L. (Eds.). (2012). *Education for life and work: Developing transferable knowledge and skills in the 21st century.* National Academies Press.

Pelphrey, K.A., Morris, J.P., & McCarthy, G. (2004). Grasping the intentions of others: The perceived intentionality of an action influences activity in the superior temporal sulcus during social perception. *Journal of Cognitive Science, 16*(10), 1706–1716.

Peña, A., Kayashima, M., Mizoguchi, R., & Dominguez, R. (2011). Improving students' meta-cognitive skills within intelligent educational systems: A review. *Foundations of Augmented Cognition, 6780*, 442–451.

Pennequin, V, Sorel, O., & Moainguy, M. (2010). Metacognition, executive functions and aging: The effect of training in the use of metacognitive skills to solve mathematical word problems. *Journal of Adult Development, 17*(3), 168–178.

Perkins, D. N. (1992). *Smart schools: From training memories to educating minds.* New York, NY: Free Press.

Perkins, D.N. (2010a). *Interview with David Perkins, Professor, Harvard Graduate School of Education.* 21 Foundation. Retrieved from http://www.youtube.com/watch?v=A7UnupF-uJk

Perkins, D. N. (2010b). *Making learning whole.* San Francisco, CA: Jossey-Bass.

Perrenoud, P. (1998). From formative evaluation to a controlled regulation of learning processes. Towards a wider conceptual field. Assessment in Education: *Principles, Policy & Practice, 5*(1), 85–102. doi:10.1080/0969595980050105

Perry, N. E., VanderKamp, K.O., Mercer, L. K., & Nordby, C. J. (2002). Investigating teacher-student interactions that foster self-regulated learning. *Educational Psychologist, 37*(1), 5–15. doi:10.1207/S15326985EP3701_2

Peterson, E. (2009). Teaching to think: Applying the Socratic Method outside of the law school setting. *Journal of College Teaching and Learning, 6*(5), 83–88.

Peterson, P. L. (1977). Interactive effects of student anxiety, achievement orientation, and teacher behavior on student achievement and attitude. *Journal of Educational Psychology, 69*(6), 779–792.

Petersen, S. E., & Posner, M. I. (2012). The attention system of the human brain: 20 years after. *Annual Review of Neuroscience, 35*, 73.

Piaget, J. (1950). *The psychology of intelligence.* New York, NY: Routledge.

Pickering, S. J., & Howard-Jones, P. (2007). Educators' views on the role of neuroscience in education: Findings from a study of UK and international perspectives. *Mind, Brain and Education, 1*(3), 109–113.

Pierce, W. P., Cameron, J., Banko, K. M., & So, S. (2003). Positive effects of rewards and performance standards on intrinsic motivation. *The Psychological Record, 53*(4). Retrieved from http://opensiuc.lib.siu.edu/tpr/vol53/iss4/4

Pilonieta, P. & Medina, A. (2011). Reciprocal teaching for the primary grades: "We can do it, too!" *The Reading Teacher, 63*(2), 120–129. doi:10.1598/RT.63.2.3

Pilzer, P. Z. (2007). *The new wellness revolution: How to make a fortune in the next trillion dollar industry* (2nd ed.). Hoboken, NJ: Wiley.

Pineda, J. A. (Ed.) (2008). *Mirror neuron systems: The role of mirroring processes in social cognition.* New York, NY: Springer.

Pinker, D. H. (2009). *Drive: The surprising truth about what motivates us.* New York, NY: Riverhead.

Pinker, S. (2002). *How the mind works.* New York, NY: Norton

Pintrich, P. R. (1995). Understanding self-regulated learning. *New Directions for Teaching and Learning, 63,* 3–12. doi:10.1002/tl.37219956304

Pitler, H. Hubbell, E. R. & Kuhn, M. (2012). *Using technology with classroom instruction that works* (2nd ed.). Alexandria, VA: Association for Supervision and Curriculum Development.

Plax, T. G., Kearney, P., McCroskey, J. P., & Richmond, V. P. (1986). Power in the classroom VI: Verbal control strategies, nonverbal immediacy, and affective learning. *Communication Education, 35,* 43–55.

Plaza, M., & Cohen, H. (2003). The interaction between phonological processing, syntactic awareness, and naming speed in the reading and spelling performance of first-grade children. *Brain and Cognition, 53*(2), 287–292.

Plotnik, R. & Kouyoumdjian, H. (2013). *Introduction to psychology* (10th ed.). Independence, KY: Cengage Learning.

Pogue, L. L. & Ahyun, K. (2006). The effect of teacher nonverbal immediacy and credibility on student motivation and affective learning. *Communication Education 55*(3), 331–344.

Popham, W. J. (2013). *Classroom assessment: What teachers need to know* (7th ed.). Boston, MA: Pearson.

Popp, A. J. (2004). Music, musicians and the brain: An exploration of musical genius. *Journal of Neurosurgery, 101*(6), 895–903.

Posner, M. I. (2011). *Cognitive neuroscience of attention.* New York, NY: Guilford.

Posner, M. I., & Fan, J. (2007). Attention as an organ system. In *Neurobiology of Perception and communication: From Synapse to Society,* De Lange Conference IV. Retrieved 17 Aug 2013 from http://citeseerx.ist.psu.edu/viewdoc/summary?doi=10.1.1.120.6937

Posner, M., & Rothbart, M. K. (1998). Attention, self-regulation and consciousness. *Philosophical Transactions of the Royal Society of London, 353*(1377), 1915–1927.

Posner, M., & Rothbart, M. K. (in press). Attention to learning of school subjects.

Posner, M. I., Sheese, B. E., Oldludas, Y., & Tang, Y. Y. (2006). Analyzing and shaping human attentional networks. *Neural Networks, 19,* 1422–1429. doi:10.1016/j.neunet.2006.08.004

Posner, R. (2009). *Lives of passion, school of hope: How one public school ignites a lifelong love of learning.* Boulder, CO: Sentient Publications.

Pouin-Dubois, D., Blayne, A, Coutya, J., & Bialystok, E. (2011). The effects of bilingualism on toddler's executive function. *Journal of Experimental Child Psychology, 108*(3), 567–579.

Powell, R. G. & Harville, B. (1990). The effects of teacher immediacy and clarity on instructional outcomes: An intercultural assessment. *Communication Education, 39*(4), 369–379. doi:10.1080/03634529009378816

Prawda, G. (2000). *Authenticity: Is it possible to be authentic?* Retrieved July 4, 2012 from http://www.philodialogue.com/Authenticity.htm

PREAL, Grupo FARO, Fundación Ecuador. (2010). *Informe de progreso educativo Ecuador 2009.* Principal investigators: Tracey Tokuhama-Espinosa y Daniela Bramwell. Washington, DC: PREAL.

Premack, D. G. & Woodruff, G. (1978). Does the chimpanzee have a theory of mind? *Behavioral and Brain Sciences, 1,* 515–52

Pressley, M. & McCormick, C. B. (1995). *Advanced educational psychology for educators, researchers, and policymakers.* New York, NY: Harper Collins.

Princeton University. (2013). *Prior knowledge and student learning.* The McGraw Center for Teaching and Learning. Retrieved from http://www.princeton.edu/mcgraw/library/sat-tipsheets/prior-knowledge/

Prior, A. & Gollan, T. H. (2011 Jul). Good language-switchers are good task-switchers: evidence from Spanish-English and Mandarin-English bilinguals. *Journal of the International Neuropsychological Society, 17*(4), 682–691.

Prior, A. & MacWhinney, B. (2010). A bilingual advantage in task switching. *Bilingualism: Language and Cognition 13*(2), 253–262.

Proctor, C. P. (1984, March). Teacher expectations: A model for school improvement. *The Elementary School Journal,* 469–481.

Puig, M. V. & Miller, E. K. (2012). The role of prefrontal dopamine D1 receptors in the neural mechanisms of associative learning. *Neuron, 74*(5), 874–886.

Pulvermüller, F., Shtyrov, Y., & Ilmoniemi, R. (2005). Brain signatures of meaning access in action word recognition. *Journal of Cognitive Neuroscience, 17*(6), 884–892.

Purves, A. C. & Elley, W. B. (1994). The role of the home and student differences. In W.B. Elley (Ed.), *The IEA study of reading literacy: Achievement and instruction in thirty-two school systems.* Oxford, England: Elsevier Science Ltd.

Pyc, M. A. & Dunlosky, J. (2010). Toward an understanding of students' allocation of study time: Why do they decide to mass or space their practice? *Memory & Cognition, 38*(4), 431–440. doi:10.3758/MC.38.4.431

Pyc, M. A., & Rawson, K. A. (2009). Testing the retrieval effort hypothesis: Does greater difficulty correctly recalling information lead to higher levels of memory? *Journal of Memory and Language, 60*(4), 437–447.

Quartz, S. R., & Sejnowski, T. J. (1997). The neural basis of cognitive development: A constructivist manifesto. *Behavioral and Brain Sciences, 20*(4), 537–556.

Quinn, P. (2013). *Instructional strategies that work.* Milwaukee, WI: Julian John.

Rabipour, S., & Raz, A. (2012). Training the brain: Fact and fad in cognitive and behavioral remediation. *Brain and Cognition, 79*(2), 159–179.

Rachlin, H. (2004). *The science of self control.* Cambridge, MA: Harvard University Press.

Raichle, M. E. (1998). The neural correlates of consciousness: An analysis of cognitive skill learning. *Philosophical Transactions of the Royal Society B, 353*(1377), 1889–1901.

Radel, R., Sarrazin, P., Legrain, P., & Wild, T. C. (2010). Social contagion of motivation between teacher and student: Analyzing underlying processes. *Journal of Educational Psychology, 102*(3), 577.

Radvansky, G. A. (2010). *Human memory* (2nd ed.). New York, NY: Pearson.

Rao, D. B. (2003). *Scientific attitude vis-à-vis scientific aptitude*. New Delhi, India: Discovery Publishing Pvt. Ltd

Rasmus, K. C., Wang, J. G., Varnell, A. L., Osterag, E. M., & Cooper, D. C. (2011). Sociability is decreased following deletion of the trpc4 gene. *Nature Precedings*. Retrieved from http://dx.doi.org/10.1038/npre.2011.6367.1

Ratcliff, R. (1978). A theory of memory retrieval. *Psychological Review, 85*(2), 59.

Raz, A. & Buhle, J. (2006, May). Typologies of attentional networks. *Nature Reviews Neuroscience, 7*, 367–379. doi:10.1038/nrn190

Redick, T. S. and Engle, R. W. (2006), Working memory capacity and attention network test performance. *Applied Cognitive Psychology, 20*, 713–721. doi: 10.1002/acp.1224

Reese, E., Sparks, A., & Leyva, D. (2010). A review of parent interventions for preschool children's language and emergent literacy. *Journal of Early Childhood Literacy, 10*(1), 97–117.

Reeve, J., & Reeve, J. (2001). *Understanding motivation and emotion*. New York, NY: Wiley.

Reeves, T. C., & Herrington, J. (2010). *Authentic tasks: The key to harnessing the drive to learn in members of "Generation Me"*. Retrieved 10 Oct 2013 from http://researchrepository.murdoch.edu.au/5148/1/Looking_toward_the_future.pdf

Reich, R. (2003 Fall). The Socratic Method: What it is and how to use it in the classroom. *Speaking of Teaching, 13*(1), 1–4.

Renner, J. W., Abraham, M. R., & Birnie, H. H. (1988). The necessity of each phase of the learning cycle in teaching high school physics. *Journal of Research in Science Teaching 25*(1), 39–58.

Rennie, L. J., & Johnston, D. J. (2004). The nature of learning and its implications for research on learning from museums. *Science Education, 88*(1), S4–S16.

Restak, R. (2009). *Think smart: Neuroscientist's prescription for improving your brain's performance*. New York, NY: Riverhead Trade.

Rhodewalt, F., Morf, C., Hazlett, S., & Fairfield, M. (1991). Self-handicapping: the role of discounting and augmentation in the preservation of self-esteem. *Journal of Personality and Social Psychology, 61*(1), 122–131.

Richard, J. M., Castro, D. C., DiFeliceantonio, A. G., Robinson, M. J. F., & Berridge, K. C. (2012). Mapping brain circuits of reward and motivation: In the footsteps of Ann Kelley. *Neuroscience and Behavioral* Reviews. doi:http://dx.doi.org/10.1016/j.neubiorev.2012.12.008

Richards, M., & Hatch, S. L. (2011). Good news about the ageing brain. *British Medical Journal, 343*, d6288.

Richardson, W. (2010). *Blogs, Wikis, Podcasts, and other powerful web tools for classrooms*. Thousand Oaks, CA: Corwin.

Richland, L. E., Zur, P., & Holyoak, K. J. (2007). Cognitive supports for analogies in the mathematics classroom. *Science, 316*, 1128–1129.

Riding, R. J., & Rayner, S. (2001). *Self-perception: International perspectives on individual differences*. Westport, CT: Greenwood.

Ripski, M. B., LoCasale-Crouch, J., & Decker, L. (2011). Pre-service teachers: Dispositional traits, emotional states, and quality of teacher-student interactions. *Teacher Education Quarterly, 38*(2), 77–96.

Rist, R. C. (1970). Student social class and teacher expectations: The self-fulfilling prophecy of ghetto education. *Harvard Educational Review, 40*(3), 411–51.

Ritchhart, R., Church, M., & Morrison, K. (2011). *Making thinking visible: How to promote engagement, understanding, and independence for all learners.* San Francisco, CA: Jossey-Bass.

Rivet, A.E. & Krajcik, J.S. (2008). Contextualizing instruction: Leveraging students' prior knowledge and experiences to foster understanding of middle school science. *Journal of Research in Science Teaching, 45*(1), 79–100.

Rizzolatti, G., & Craighero, L. (2004). The mirror-neuron system. *Annual Review of Neuroscience, 27,* 169–192.

Robinson, K. (2010). *Changing education paradigms.* RSA Animate. Retrieved from http://www.youtube.com/watch?v=zDZFcDGpL4U

Robinson, K. (2011). *Out of our minds: Learning to be creative.* Mankato, MN: Capstone.

Rocca, K.A. (2007). *Immediacy in the classroom: Research and practical implications.* Northfield, MN: St. John's University. Available on http://serc.carleton.edu/NAGTWorkshops/affective/immediacy.html

Roca, M., Parr, A., Thompson, R., Woolgar, A., Torralva, T., Antoun, N., ... & Duncan, J. (2010). Executive function and fluid intelligence after frontal lobe lesions. *Brain, 133*(1), 234–247.

Rodger, S., Murray, H.G., & Cummings, A.L. (2007). Effects of teacher clarity and student anxiety on student outcomes. *Teaching in Higher Education, 12*(1), 91–104. doi:10.1080/13562510601102255

Rodriguez, P. (2006). Talking brains: A cognitive semantic analysis of an emerging folk neuropsychology. *Public Understanding of Science, 15*(3), 301–330.

Rodriguez-Fornells, A., DeDiego Balaguer, R., & Münte, T.F. (2006). Executive control in bilingual language processing. *Language Learning, 56,* 133–190. doi:10.1111/j.1467-9922.2006.00359.x

Roe, M. F., & Egbert, J. (2010). Four faces of differentiation: Their attributes and potential. *Childhood Education 87*(2), 94–97. doi:10.1080/00094056.2011.10521452

Roediger, H. L., & Butler, A. C. (2010). The critical role of retrieval practice in long-term retention. *Trends in Cognitive Neuroscience, 15*(1), 20–27.

Roediger, H. L., Finn, B., & Weinstein, Y. (2012). Applications of cognitive science to education. In S. Della Sala and M. Anderson's *Neuroscience in education: The good, the bad, and the ugly* (pp.128–154). Oxford, UK: Oxford University Press.

Roediger, H. L., & Karpicke, J. D. (2006). Test-enhanced learning: Taking memory tests improves long-term retention. *Psychological Science, 17*(3), 249–255. doi:10.1111/j.1467-9280.2006.01693.x

Roediger, H. L., & Pyc, M. A. (2012). Inexpensive techniques to improve education: Applying cognitive psychology to enhance educational practice. *Journal of Applied Research in Memory and Cognition, 1,* 242–248.

Rogers, C. (2002). Seeing student learning: Teacher change and the role of reflection: Voices inside Schools. *Harvard Educational Review, 72*(2), 230–253.

Role, E. M. (2007). *The art of questioning.* Compiled by Jess Role UEAB. University of Eastern Africa, Baraton.

Ronis, D. L. (2007). *Problem-based learning for math and science: Integrating inquiry and the Internet.* Thousand Oaks: Corwin.

Roorda, D. L., Koomen, H.M.Y., Split, J. L., & Oort, F. J. (2011). The influence of affective teacher-student relationships on students' school engagement and achievement: A meta-analysis. *Review of Educational Research, 81*(4), 493–529. doi: 10.3102/0034654311421793

Rosales, F. J., Reznick, J. S., & Zeisel, S. H. (2009). Understanding the role of nutrition in the brain & behavioral development of toddlers and preschool children: Identifying and over-coming methodological barriers. *Nutritional Neuroscience, 12*(5), 190.

Rose, S. (2005). *The future of the brain: The promises and perils of tomorrow's neuroscience.* New York, NY: Oxford University Press.

Rosen, C. (2008). The myth of multitasking. *The New Atlantis, 20*, 105–110.

Rosenfield, P., Lambert, N. M., & Black, A. (1985). Desk arrangement effects on pupil classroom behavior. *Journal of Educational Psychology, 77*(1), 101.

Rosenfield, P., Lambert, N. M., & Black, A. (1985). Desk arrangement effects on pupil classroom behavior. *Journal of Educational Psychology, 77*(1), 101–108. Retrieved 9 Aug 2013 from http://www.summit.k12.co.us/cms/lib04/CO01001195/Centricity/Domain/72/Journal_of_Educational_Psychology.pdf

Rosenshine, B., & Meister, C. (1994). Reciprocal teaching: A review of the research. *Review of Educational Research. 64*(4), 479–530.

Rosenshine, B., & Stevens, R. (1986). Teaching function. In M. C. Wittrok (Ed.), *Handbook of research on teaching.* New York, NY: Macmillan.

Rosenthal, R. (1994). Interpersonal expectancy effects: A 30-year perspective. *Current Directions in Psychological Science, 3*(6), 176–179.

Rosenthal, R. (2002). The Pygmalion effect and its mediating mechanisms. In J. Aronson (Ed.), *Improving academic achievement: Impact of psychological factors on education.* San Diego, CA: Academic Press. doi:10.1016/B978-012064455-1/50005-1

Rosenthal, R., & Jacobson, L. (1966). Teachers' expectancies: Determinants of pupils' IQ gains. *Psychological Report, 19*, 115–118.

Rosenthal, R., & Jacobson, L. (1968). Pygmalion in the classroom. *The Urban Review, 3*(1), 16–20.

Rosenzweig, M. R., & Bennett, E. L. (1996). Psychobiology of plasticity: effects of training and experience on brain and behavior. *Behavioural Brain Research, 78*(1), 57–65.

Rosenzweig, M. R., Bennett, E. L., & Diamond, M. C. (1972 Feb). Brain changes in response to experience. *Scientific American, 226*(2), 22–29. doi: 10.1038/scientificamerican0272-22

Ross, J. A. (1992). Teacher efficacy and the effect of coaching on student achievement. *Canadian Journal of Education, 17*, 51–65.

Rothbart, M. K., Sheese, B. E., Rueda, M. R., & Posner, M. I. (2011). Developing mechanisms of self-regulation in early life. *Emotion Review, 3*(2), 207–213.

Rothman, S. M., & Mattson, M. P. (2013). Activity-dependent, stress-responsive BDNF signaling and the quest for optimal brain health and resilience throughout the lifespan. *Neuroscience, 239,* 228–240. doi:http://dx.doi.org/10.1016/j.neuroscience.2012.10.014

Rothstein, D., & Santana, L. (2011). *Make just one change: Teach students to ask their own questions.* Cambridge, MA: Harvard Education Press.

Rubie-Davies, C. M. (2010). Teacher expectations and perceptions of student attributes: Is there a relationship? *British Journal of Educational Psychology, 80*(1), 121–135.

Rudasill, K. M., Reio, T. G., Stipanovic, N. & Taylor, J. E. (2010). A longitudinal study of student teacher relationship quality, difficult temperament, and risky behavior from childhood to early adolescence. *Journal of School Psychology, 48*(5), 389–412. http://dx.doi.org/10.1016/j.jsp.2010.05.001

Rychen, D. S., & Salganik, L. H. (2000). *Definition and selection of key competencies.* THE INES COMPENDIUM (Fourth General Assembly of the OCDE Education Indicators programmme). Paris, France: OCDE, 61–73.

Ryve, A. (2011). Discourse research in mathematics education: A critical evaluation of 108 journal articles. *Journal of Research in Mathematics Education, 42*(2), 167–199.

Sadler, R. D. (1998). Formative assessment: Revisiting the territory. *Assessment in Education: Principle, Policy & Practice, 5*(1), 77–84. doi:10.1080/0969595980050104

Sahlberg, P. (2007). Education policies for raising student learning: the Finnish approach. *Journal of Education Policy, 22*(2), 147–171.

Sahlberg, P. (2011 Summer). Lessons from Finland. *American Educator,* 34–38.

Saito, S. (2001). The phonological loop and memory for rhythms: an individual differences approach. *Memory, 9*(4–6), 313–322.

Saleh, M., Lazonder, A. W., & Jong, T. D. (2007). Structuring collaboration in mixed-ability groups to promote verbal interaction, learning, and motivation of average-ability students. *Contemporary Educational Psychology, 32*(3), 314–331.

Salatas Waters, H., & Schneider, W. (Eds.) (2009). *Metacognition, strategy use and instruction.* New York, NY: Guilford.

Samson, D., Apperly, I. A., Chiavarino, C., & Humphreys, G.W. (2004). Left temporoparietal junction is necessary for representing someone else's belief. *Nature Neuroscience, 7*(5), 499–500.

Samuels, B. A. (2009). Can the difference between education and neuroscience be overcome by Mind, Brain, and Education? *Mind, Brain, and Education 3*(1), 45–55. doi:10.1111/j.1751-228X.2008.01052.x

Sanders, W. L., & Rivers, J. C. (1996). *Cumulative and residual effects of teachers on future students' academic achievement.* Knoxville, TN: University of Tennessee Value-Added Research and Assessment Center.

Sarina, V. & Namukasa, I. K. (2010). Nonmath analogies in teaching mathematics. *Procedia-Social and Behavioral Sciences, 2*(2), 5738–5743.

Savion, S. M., & Glisczinski, D. J. (2012). *Harnessing the power of emotionally cogent stimuli for optimal learning.* In Proceedings of the Fourth Annual Teachers College Educational Technology Conference, May 19–20th (pp.59–60). New York, NY: Teachers College, Columbia University.

Sawyer, K. (2011). The cognitive neuroscience of creativity: A critical review. *Creativity Research Journal, 23*(2), 137–154. doi:10.1080/10400419.2011.571191

Sawyer, A., Chittleborough, C., Mittinty, M., & Lynch, J. (2013). *The role of attention and emotion regulation in school readiness and school performance.* Retrieved 17 Aug 2013 from http://flosse.fahcsia.gov.au/fahcsiajspui/handle/10620/3804

Saxbe, D.E., Yang, X. F., Borofsky, L.A., & Immordino-Yang, M.H. (2012). The embodiment of emotion: Language use during the feeling of social emotions predicts cortical somatosensory activity. *Social Cognitive and Affective Neuroscience.* doi:10.1093/scan/nss075

Saxe, R. (2004). A region of right posterior superior temporal sulcus response to observed intentional actions. *Neuropsychologia 42,* 1435–1446

Saxe, R. & Powell, L. (2006). It's the thought that counts: Specific brain regions for one component of Theory of Mind. *Psychological Science 17*(8), 692–699.

Schacter, D. L. (1996). *Searching for memory: The brain, the mind, and the past.* New York, NY: Basic Books.

Schacter, D. L. (2002). *The seven sins of memory: How the mind forgets memory.* New York, NY: Mariner Books.

Scrhaw, G., & Dennison, R. S. (1994). Assessing metacognitive awareness. *Contemporary Educational Psychology, 19,* 460–475.

Schellenberg, S., Negishi, M., & Eggen, P. (2011). The effects of metacognition and concrete encoding strategies on depth of understanding in educational psychology. *Teaching Educational Psychology, 7*(2), 17–24.

Schmidt, L.A., Fox, N.A., Hu, S., & Hamer, D.H. (2002). Molecular genetics of shyness and aggression in preschoolers. *Personality and Individual Differences, 33*(2), 227–238.

Schneider, W. (2008). The development of metacognitive knowledge in children and adolescents: Major trends and implications for education. *Mind, Brain, and Education, 2*(3), 114–121. doi:10.1111/j.1751-228X.2008.00041.x

Schneider, W. (2010). The development of metacognitive competencies. *Towards a Theory of Thinking: Biomedical and Life Sciences,* 203–214. doi: 10.1007/978-3-642-03129-8_14

Scholz, J., Triantafyllou, C., Whitfield-Gabrieli, S., Brown, E.N., & Saxe, R. (2009). Distinct regions of right temporo-parietal junction are selective for theory of mind and exogenous attention. *PLoS One 4*(3), e4869. doi:10.1371/journal.pone.0004869. PMID 1929004

Schön, D. (1983). *The reflective practitioner.* New York, NY: Basic Books.

Schön, D. (1987). *Educating the reflective practitioner.* San Francisco, CA: Jossey-Bass.

Schooler, J. W., Fallshore, M., & Fiore, S. M. (1995). Epilogue: Putting insight into perspective. In R. J. Sternberg & J. E. Davidson (Eds.), *The nature of insight* (pp. 559–588). Cambridge, MA: The MIT Press.

Schorn, D. (Writer), & Ed Bradley (Reporter). (2009, February 11). *The Harlem Children's Zone: How one man's vision to revitalize Harlem starts with children* [Television broadcast]. New York, NY: CBS 60 Minutes.

Schrader, C., & Bastiaens, T. J. (2012). The influence of virtual presence: Effects on experienced cognitive load and learning outcomes in educational computer games. *Computers in Human Behavior, 28*(2), 648–658.

Schraw, G., & Moshman, D. (1995). Metacognitive theories. *Educational Psychology Review, 7*(4), 351–371.

Schrodt, P. (2003). Students' appraisals of instructors as a function of students' perceptions of instructors' aggressive communication. *Communication Education, 52*, 106–121.

Schrum, L. & Levin, B. B. (2009). *Leading 21st–century schools: Harnessing technology for engagement and achievement.* Thousand Oaks, CA: Corwin.

Schultz, R.T. (2003). The role of the fusiform face area in social cognition: Implications for the pathobiology of autism. *Philosophical Transactions of Royal Society of London, Series B: Biological Sciences, 358*(1430), 415–427.

Schunk, D. H. (1998). An educational psychologist's perspective on cognitive neuroscience. *Educational Psychology Review, 10*, 411–417.

Schunk, D.H., & Mullen, C.A. (2012). Self-efficacy as an engaged learner. In S.L. Christenson, A.L. Reschly & C. Wylie (Eds.), *Handbook of research on student engagement* (pp.219–235). New York, NY: Springer.

Schunk, D.H., & Pajares, F. (2002). The development of academic self-efficacy. In. A. Wigfield & J. Eccles (Eds.), *Development of achievement motivation* (pp.15–32). San Diego: Academic Press.

Schunk D. H., & Pajares, F. (2009). Self-efficacy theory. In Wentzel K. R., Wigfield A. (Eds.), *Handbook of motivation in school* (pp. 35–54). New York, NY: Taylor & Francis.

Schunk, D. H., & Zimmerman, B. J. (1994). *Self-regulation of learning and performance.* Hillsdale, NJ: Lawrence Erlbaum Associates.

Schwabe, L., & Wolf, O. T. (2012). Stress modulates the engagement of multiple memory systems in classification learning. *The Journal of Neuroscience, 32*(32), 11042–11049.

Schwarz, G. (2006 Jul). Expanding literacies through graphic novels. *The English Journal, 95*(6), 58–64.

Schwartz, M. S., & Gerlach, J. (2011a). Guiding principles for a research schools network: Successes and challenges. *Mind, Brain, and Education, 5*(4), 172–179.

Schwartz, M., & Gerlach, J. (2011b). The birth of a field and the rebirth of the laboratory school. *Educational Philosophy and Theory, 43*(1), 67–74.

Schwartz, M., Sadler, P. M., Sonnert, G., & Tai, R. H. (2009). Depth versus breadth: How content coverage in high school science courses relates to later success in college science coursework. *Science Education, 93*(5), 798–826.

Schwarzer, R., & Hallum, S. (2008). Perceived teacher self-efficacy as a predictor of job stress and burnout: Mediation analyses. *Applied Psychology: An International Review,* 57, 152–171 (Special Issue: Health and Well-Being). doi:10.1111/j.1464-0597.2008.00359.x

Schwartz, S. (2013). The future of higher education: Faster, cheaper, better: The Internet bullet train has left the station. *Policy, 29*(2), 3–9.

Seabrook, R., & Brown, G. D. A. (2005). Distributed and massed practice: From laboratory to classroom. *Applied Cognitive Psychology, 19*(1), 107–122. doi:10.1002/acp.1066

Sears, D. A., & Pai, H. H. (2012). Effects of cooperative versus individual study on learning and motivation after reward-removal. *The Journal of Experimental Education, 80*(3), 246–262.

SEDL. (2009). *Curriculum details for RAVE-O (retrieval, automaticity, vocabulary, engagement with language, orthography).* Retrieved May 30, 2009, from www.sedl.org/cgi-bin/mysql/after-school/curriculum-hoice.cgi?subj=l&resource=23.

Segalowitz, S. J. (2010). Neuroscience in theories of human development. In D. Coch, K.W. Fischer & G. Dawson's (Eds.), *Human behavior, learning, and the developing brain: Typical development* (pp.3–29). New York, NY: Guilford.

Senge, P., Cambron-McCabe, N., Lucus, T., Smith, B., Dutton, J., & Kleiner, A. (2000). *Schools that learn: A fifth discipline fieldbook for educators, parents, and everyone who cares about education.* New York, NY: Doubleday.

Sergiovanni, T. (1994). *Building community in schools.* San Francisco, CA: Jossey-Bass.

Settlage, J., Southerland, S. A., Smith, L., & Ceglie, R. (2009). Constructing a doubt–free teaching self: Self–efficacy, teacher identity, and science instruction within diverse settings. *Journal of Research in Science Teaching, 46*(1), 102–125.

Seung, S. (2013). *Connectome: How the brain's wiring makes us who we are.* New York, NY: Houghton Mifflin Harcourt.

Shakespeare, W. (1597). *Romeo and Juliet.* Act II scene II. First printed by John Danter.

Shanker, S. (2011). *The contribution of teacher beliefs and student motivation on the academic lives of different learners.* Available on: https://repositories.tdl.org/tdl-ir/handle/2152/ETD-UT-2010-12-2321

Shapiro, A. M. (2004). How including prior knowledge as a subject variable may change outcomes of learning research. *American Educational Research Journal, 41*(1), 159–189. doi:10.3102/00028312041001159

Shaywitz, B. A., Shaywitz, S. E., Blachman, B. A., Pugh, K. R., Fulbright, R. K., Skudlarski, P., ...& Gore, J. C. (2004). Development of left occipitotemporal systems for skilled reading in children after a phonologically-based intervention. *Biological Psychiatry, 55,* 926–933.

Shen, W. B., Liu, C., & Chen, J. J. (2010). Neural basis of creativity: Evidence from structural and functional imaging. *Advances in Psychological Science.* Retrieved from http://en.cnki.com.cn/Article_en/CJFDTOTAL-XLXD201009009.htm

Sheridan, K., Zinchenko, E., & Gardner, H. (2005). Neuroethics in education. In J. Illes, (Ed.), *Neuroethics* (pp.281–308). Oxford: Oxford University Press. Retrieved on September 10, 2007 from http://www.tc.umn.edu/~athe0007/BNEsig/papers/ NeuroethicsEducation.pdf

Shields, J. J. (2010). *Japanese schooling: Patterns of socialization, equality, and political control.* Philadelphia, PA: Penn State Press.

Shimamura, A. P. (2000). Towards a cognitive neuroscience of metacognition. *Consciousness and Cognition, 9*(2), 313–323. http://dx.doi.org/10.1006/ccog.2000.0450

Shonkoff, J. P., & Phillips, D. A. (Eds) (2000). *From neurons to neighborhoods: The science of early childhood development.* Washington, DC: National Academy Press.

Siegel, D. (2001). *The developing mind: How relationships and the brain interact to shape who we are.* New York, NY: Guilford.

Siegel, D. (2012). *The developing mind: how relationships and the brain interact to shape who we are* (2nd ed.). New York, NY: Guilford.

Simon, L. (2007). *Expanding literacies: Teachers' inquiry research and multigenre texts.* ERIC database. Retrieved 9 Aug 2013 from http://eric.ed.gov/?id=EJ776368

Simonds, C. J. (2007). Classroom understanding: An expanded notion of teacher clarity. *Communication Research Reports, 14*(3), 279–290. doi:10.1080/08824099709388671

Simons, D. J. & Chabris, C. F. (1999). Gorilla in our midst: sustained inattentional blindness for dynamic events. *Perception,* 28, 1059–1074.

Sjoberg, S., & Schreiner, C. (2008). *Young people, science and technology attitudes, values and interest and possible recruitment.* Brussels: ROSE.

Sisti, H. M., Glass, A. L., & Shors, T. J. (2007). Neurogenesis and the spacing effect: Lerning over time enhances memory and survival of neurons. *Learning and Memory, 14,* 368–375. doi:10.1101/lm.488707

Slater, W. H., & Horstman, F. R. (2002). Teaching reading and writing to struggling middle school and high school students: The case for reciprocal teaching. *Preventing School Failure, 46*(4), 163.

Slavin, R.E. (1987). Mastery learning reconsidered. *Review of Educational Research, 57*(2), 175–213.

Small, G. W., Moody, T. D., Siddarth, P., & Bookheimer, S. Y. (2009). Your brain on Google: Patterns of cerebral activation during Internet searching. *American Journal of Geriatric Psych, 17*(2), 116–126.

Smidt, S. (2006). *The developing child in the 21st century: A global perspective on child development.* New York, NY: Routledge.

Smith, G., & Throne, S. (2007). *Differentiating instruction with technology in K–5 classrooms.* Washington, DC: International Society for Technology in Education.

Smith, L. R. (1984 Nov–Dec). Effect of teacher vagueness and use of lecture notes on student performance. *Journal of Educational Research, 78*(2), 69–74.

Smith, L. R. (1985). Teacher clarifying behaviors: Effects on student achievement and perceptions. *Journal of Experimental Education, 53*(3), 162–169.

Smith, R. A. (2001 Winter). Formative evaluation and the scholarship of teaching and learning. *New Directions for Teaching and Learning, 88,* 51–62.

Smith, R. L., Skarbek, D., & Hurst, J. (Eds.) (2005). *The passion of teaching: Disposition in the schools.* Lanham, MD: Rowman & Littlefield.

Smithsonian Institution's Human Origins Program. (2013). *Bigger brain: Complex brains for a complex world.* Retrieved 30 April 2013 from http://humanorigins.si.edu/human-characteristics/brains

Sommers, F. G., & Dineen, T. (1984). *Curing nuclear madness.* London, UK: Methuen.

Son, L. K. (2004). Spacing one's study: Evidence for a metacognitive control strategy. *Journal of Experimental Psychology: Learning, Memory, and Cognition, 30*(3), 601–604. doi:10.1037/0278-7393.30.3.601

Son, L.K., & Simon, DA. (2012). Distributed learning: Data, metacognition, and educational implications. *Educational Psychology Review, 24*(3), 379–399.

Sousa, D. A., & Tomlinson, C. A. (2010). *Differentiation and the brain: How neuroscience supports the learner-friendly classroom.* Bloomington, IN: Solution Tree.

Sperling, R.A., Howard, B.C., Miller, L.A., & Murphy, c. (2002). Measures of children's knowledge and regulation of cognition. *Contemporary Educational Psychology, 27,* 51–79.

Spiro, R. J., Feltovich, P. J., Coulson, R. L., & Anderson, D. K. (1989). *Multiple analogies for complex concepts: Antidotes for analogy-induced misconception in advanced knowledge acquisition.* New York, NY: Cambridge University Press.

Spörer, N., Brunstein, J.C., & Kieschke, U. (2009). Improving students' reading comprehension skills: Effects of strategy instruction and reciprocal teaching. *Learning and Instruction, 19*(3), 272–286.

Sporns, O. (2010). *Networks of the brain.* Cambridge, MA: MIT Press.

Squire, K. (2011). Video games and learning: Teaching and participatory culture in the digital age. *Technology, Education—Connections (the TEC Series).* New York, NY: Teachers College Press.

Squire, L. (1987). *Memory and brain.* New York, NY: Oxford University Press.

Squire, L. R. (1992a). Declarative and nondeclarative memory: Multiple brain systems supporting learning and memory. *Journal of Cognitive Neuroscience, 4*(3), 232–243.

Squire, L. (1992b). *Encyclopedia of learning and memory.* New York, NY: Macmillan.

Squire, L., & Kandel, E. (2008). *Memory: From mind to molecules.* New York, NY: W. H. Freeman.

Squire, L. R., Knowlton, B. J., & Gazzaniga, M.J. (Eds.) (1995). Memory, hippocampus, and brain systems. In L.R. Squire, B.J. Knowton and M.J.Gazzaniga's *The cognitive neurosciences,* (pp. 825–837). Cambridge, MA, US: The MIT Press.

Stagg, C., Bachtiar, V., & Johansen-Berg, H. (2011). The role of GABA in human motor learning. *Current Biology, 21*(6), 480–484.

State of California. (2011 Oct). *California 5th grade curriculum guide.* Retrieved on 20 Mar 2013 fro, www.cde.ca.gov/ci/cr/cf/.../glc5thgradecurriculum.pdf

State of New York. (2011). *New York State P-12 common core learning standards for English language arts & literacy.* Albany, NY: Author.

Steele, J. R., & Ambady, N. (2006). "Math is hard!" The effect of gender priming on women's attitudes. *Journal of Experimental Social Psychology, 42*(4), 428–436. http://dx.doi.org/10.1016/j.jesp.2005.06.003

Stein, Z., & Fischer, K. (2011). Directions for Mind, Brain, and Education: Methods, models, and morality. *Educational Philosophy and Theory 43*(1), 56–66. doi:10.1111/j.1469-5812.2010.00708.x

Sternberg, R. J. (1981). Toward a unified componential theory of human intelligence: I. Fluid ability. In M. Friedman, J.P. Das & N. O'Connor's *Intelligence and learning* (pp. 327–344). New York, NY: Springer.

Sternberg, L. C., Varua, M. E., & Yong, J. (2012). Attitude, secondary schools and student success in a tertiary mathematics unit. *Journal of Modern Accounting and Auditing, 8*(4), 480–487.

Sticklin, K. (2011). Hands-on reciprocal teaching: A comprehension technique. *The Reading Teacher, 64*(8), 620–625. doi:10.1598/RT.64.8.8

Stickgold, R. (2005). Sleep-dependent memory consolidation. *Nature, 437*(7063), 1272–1278.

Stickgold, R., Hobson, J. A., Fosse, R., & Fosse, M. (2001). Sleep, learning, and dreams: Off-line memory reprocessing. *Science, 294*(5544), 1052–1057.

Stigler, J.W., & Hiebert, J. (1999). *The teaching gap.* New York, NY: Free Press.

Stigler, J.W., & Hiebert, J. (2009). *The teaching gap: Ten year anniversary.* New York, NY: Free Press.

Stillman, G., & Mevarech, Z. (2010). Metacognition research n mathematics education: from hot topic to mature field. *ZDM, 42*(2), 145–148.

Storbeck, J., & Clore, G. L. (2011). Affect influences false memories at encoding: Evidence from recognition data. *Emotion, 11*(4), 981–989.

Strauss, V., & Alexander, F. (2012). Survey: Teachers work 53 hours per week on average. *Washington Post blog.* Retrieved 7 Jan 2012 from http://www.washingtonpost.com/blogs/answer-sheet/post/survey-teachers-work-53-hours-per-week-on-average/2012/03/16/gIQAqGxYGS_blog.html

Stricklin, K. (2011). Hands-on reciprocal teaching: A comprehension technique. *The Reading Teacher, 64*(8). doi:10.1598/RT.64.8.8.

Strobel, J., & van Barneveld, A. (2009). When is PBL more effective? A meta-synthesis of meta-analyses comparing PBL to conventional classrooms. *Interdisciplinary Journal of Problem-based Learning, 3*(1). Available at: http://dx.doi.org/10.7771/1541-5015.1046

Sullivan, P. B., Hunt, S. K., & Lippert, L. S. (2004). Mediated immediacy: A language of affiliation in a technological age. *Journal of Language and Social Psychology, 23*(4), 464–490. doi:10.1177/0261927X04269588

Surgey, G. (2012). Bloom's Taxonomy: A practical approach for deeper learning. *Critical thinking.* Creative Commons. Retrieved from http://www.pedagoo.org/2012/09/blooms-taxonomy-a-practical-approach-for-deeper-learning/

Sutherland, K. A. (2013). The importance of critical reflection in and on academic development. *International Journal for Academic Development 18*(2), 111–113. doi:10.1080/13601 44X.2013.802074

Suzuki, S., Holloway, S. D., Yamamoto, Y., & Mindnich, J. D. (2009). Parenting self-efficacy and social support in Japan and the United States. *Journal of Family, 30*(11), 1505–1526.

Svinicki, M. (1993). What they don't know can hurt them: The role of prior knowledge in learning. In The Professional & Organizational Development Network in Higher Education, *Essays on Teaching Excellence: Toward the Best in the Academy*. Retrieved from http://www.podnetwork. org/publications/teachingexcellence/93-94/V5,%20N4%20Svinicki.pdf

Swanson, H. L. (2011). The influence of working memory growth on reading and math performance in children with math and/or reading disabilities. In Pierre Barrouillet and Vincaine Gaillard's *Cognitive development and working memory: A dialogue between neo-Piagetian and cognitive approaches* (pp. 203–231). Hove, UK: Psychology Press.

Sweet, C., Carpenter, R., Blythe, H., & Apostel, S. (2013). *Teaching applied creative thinking: A new pedagogy for the 21st century*. Stillwater, OK: New Forums Press.

Swing, E. L. (2008). *Attention abilities, media exposure, school performance, personality, and aggression*. Unpublished Master's thesis. Ames, Iowa: Iowa State University.

Taggart, G. L., & Wilson, A. P. (2005). *Promoting reflective thinking in teachers: 50 action strategies*. Thousand Oaks, CA: Corwin.

Tallal, S. (2010). The calculating brain. In D. Sousa (Ed.), *Mind, Brain, and Education: neuroscience implications for the classroom* (pp. 178–200). Bloomington, NI: Solution Tree Press.

Tan, H. Y., Chen, Q., Sust, S., Buckholtz, J. W., Meyers, J. D., Egan, M. F., …& Callicott, J. H. (2007). Epistasis between catechol-*O*-methyltransferase and type II metabotropic glutamate receptor 3 genes on working memory brain function. *Proceedings of the National Academy of Sciences of the United States of America, 104*(30). doi:10.1073/pnas.0610125104

Tang, Y., Zhang, W., Chen, K., Feng, S., Ji, Y., Shen, J., …& Liu, Y. (2006). Arithmetic processing in the brain shaped by cultures. *Proceedings of the National Academy of Sciences of the United States of America, 103*(28), 10775–10780.

Tanner, K. D. (2010). Order matters: Using the 5E model to align teaching with how people learn. The American Society for Cell Biology, *Life Sciences Education, 9*(3), 159–164. doi:10.1187/ cbe.10-06-0082

Tapscott, D. (2008). *Grown up digital: How the next generation is changing your world*. New York, NY: McGraw-Hill.

Tate, M. L. (2010). *Worksheets don't grow dendrites* (2nd ed.). Thousand Oaks, CA: Corwin.

Teaching As Leadership. (2011). *Critical thinking* (pp.56–57). Retrieved on 20 Mar 2013 from http://www.google.com.ec/url?sa=t&rct=j&q=&esrc=s&source=web&cd=9&ved=0CHYQFj AI&url=http%3A%2F%2Fteachingasleadership.org%2Fsites%2Fdefault%2Ffiles%2FRelated-Readings%2FLT_Ch5_2011.pdf&ei=aKw7Uen3Aszv0QGevYCYDg&usg=AFQjCNEn9s6d7 sTGftrV0llWVh8HtTD9CQ&sig2=_PDG1ZMpe5Pzh-01fUl-PA&bvm=bv.43287494,d.dmQ

Teven, J. A., & Hanson, T. L. (2004). The impact of teacher immediacy and perceived caring on teacher competence and trustworthiness. *Communication Quarterly 52*(1), 39–53. doi:10.1080/01463370409370177

Teven, J. J., & McCroskey, J. C. (1997). The relationship of perceived teacher caring with student learning and teacher evaluation. *Communication Education, 46,* 1–9.

Thomas, M. (2011). *Deconstructing digital natives: Young people, technology, and the new literacies.* London, UK: Routledge.

Thomson Reuters. (2011). *National science indicators.* Downloaded on 12 Jan 2011 de http://thomsonreuters.com/products_services/science/science_products/a-z/national_science_indicators/

Titti, K. (2011). Holistic school pedagogy and values: Finnish teachers' and students' perspectives. *International Journal of Educational Research, 50,* 159—165.

Titus, G. (2008). *U.S. competitiveness in science and technology.* Pittsburgh: Rand Corporation.

Tobias, S. (1994). Interest, prior knowledge, and learning. *Review of Educational Research, 64*(1), 37–54. doi:10.3102/00346543064001037

Tobin, R., & McInnes, A. (2008). Accommodating differences: Variations in differentiated literacy instruction in grade 2/3 classrooms. *Literacy, 42*(1), 3–9.

Tobin, R., & Trippet, C. D. (2013). Possibilities and potential barriers: Learning to plan for differentiated instruction in elementary science. *International Journal of Science and Mathematics Education.* doi:10.1007/s10763-013-9414-z

Tokuhama-Espinosa, T. (2008 Jul). *The scientifically substantiated art of teaching: A study in the development of standards in the new academic field of neuroeducation (Mind, Brain, and Education Science).* Dissertation (PhD), Capella University, Minnesota. AAT 3310716.

Tokuhama-Espinosa, T. (2010). *Applying mind, brain, and education science in the classroom.* New York, NY: Columbia University Press.

Tokuhama-Espinosa, T. (2011). *Mind, Brain, and Education Science: A comprehensive guide to the new brain-based teaching.* New York, NY: Norton.

Tokuhama-Espinosa, T., & Rivera, M. (2013). *Estudio del arte sobre conciencia fonológica en lenguaje y matemática.* Contratado por el gobierno de Costa Rica, CECC/SICA del Sistema de Integración Centroamericana.

Tomasello, M. (1999). *The cultural origins of human cognition.* Cambridge, MA: Harvard University Press.

Tomaszewski, J. (2012). Khan Academy part of "flipped" classroom trend. Meriden, CT: *Education World.* Retrieved on 6 Jan from http://www.educationworld.com/a_curr/vodcast-sites-enable-flipped-classroom.shtml

Tomlinson, C. A., & Edison, C. A. (2003). *Differentiation in practice: Grades 5–9: A resource guide for differentiating curriculum.* Alexandria, VA: Association for Supervision and Curriculum Development.

Tomlinson, C. A., & Strickland, C. A. (2005). *Differentiation in practice: A resource guide for dif-*

ferentiating curriculum, grades 9–12. Alexandria, VA: Association for Supervision and Curriculum Development.

Tononi, G., Sporns, O., & Edelman, G. M. (1994). A measure for brain complexity: relating functional segregation and integration in the nervous system. *Proceedings of the National Academy of Sciences, 91*(11), 5033–5037.

Tononi, G., Edelman, G. M., & Sporns, O. (1998). Complexity and coherency: integrating information in the brain. *Trends in Cognitive Sciences, 2*(12), 474–484.

Torey, Z. (2009). *The crucible of consciences: An integrated theory of mind and brain.* Cambridge, MA: The MIT Press.

Torp, L., & Sage, S. (1998). *Problems as possibilities: Problem-based learning for K–12 education.* Alexandria, VA: Association for Supervision and Curriculum Development.

Torrance, H., & Pryor, J. (1998). *Investigating formative assessment: Teaching, learning and assessment in the classroom.* Florence, KY: Taylor & Francis.

Torrente, J., Del Blanco, Á., Marchiori, E. J., Moreno-Ger, P., & Fernández-Manjón, B. (2010, April). Introducing educational games in the learning process. In *Education Engineering (EDUCON), 2010 IEEE* (pp. 1121–1126).

Tops, M., Boksem, M. A., Luu, P., & Tucker, D. M. (2010). Brain substrates of behavioral programs associated with self-regulation. *Frontiers in Psychology, 1.*

Tough, P. (2008). *Whatever it takes: Geoffrey Canada's quest to change Harlem and America.* Boston, MA: Houghton Mifflin Harcourt.

Tough, P. (2012). *How children succeed: Grit, curiosity and the hidden power of character.* Boston, MA: Houghton Mifflin Harcourt.

Trees, A. R., Kerssen-Griep, J., & Hess, J. A. (2009). Earning influence by communicating respect: Facework's contributions to effective instructional feedback. *Communication Education, 58,* 397–416.

Trilling, B. & Fadel, C. (2009). *21st century skills: Learning for life in our times.* San Francisco, CA: Jossy-Bass.

Trow, W. C. (1928 Jan). Recall vs. repetition in the learning of rote and meaningful material. *The American Journal of Psychology, 40*(1), 112–116.

Tsao, J. C. (1948). Studies in spaced and massed learning: II meaningfulness of material and distribution of practice. *Quarterly Journal of Experimental Psychology, 1*(2), 79–84. doi:10.1080/17470214808416748

Tschannen-Moran, M., & Barr, M. (2004). Fostering student learning: The relationship of collective teacher efficacy and student achievement. *Leadership and Policy in Schools, 3*(3), 189–209. doi:10.1080/15700760490503706

Tschannen-Moran, M. & Woolfolk-Hoy, A. (2001). Teacher efficacy: Capturing an elusive construct. *Teaching and Teacher Education, 17,* 783–805.

Tschannen-Moran, M., Woolfolk-Hoy, A. & Hoy, W. (1998). Teacher efficacy: Its meaning and measure. *Review of Educational Research, 68,* 202–248.

Tuchman, E., & Isaacs, J. (2011). The influence of formal and informal formative pre-service experiences on teacher self-efficacy. *Educational Psychology, 31*(4), 413–433.

Tun, P. A., & Lachman, M. E. (2010). The association between computer use and cognition across adulthood: Use it so you won't lose it?. *Psychology and Aging, 25*(3), 560.

Tuomi-Gröhn, T. (2007). Developmental transfer as a goal of collaboration between school and work. *Journal of Human Activity Theory, 1,* 41–62.

Tural, G., Akdeniz, A. R., & Alev, N. (2010). Effect of 5E teaching model on student teachers' understanding of weightlessness. *Journal of Science Education and Technology, 19,* 470–488.

Turner, J.C., Christensen, A., & Meyer, D.K. (2009). Teachers' beliefs about student learning and motivation. *International Handbook of Research on Teachers and Teaching, 21,* 361–371.

Tyler, W. J., Alonso, M., Bramham, C. R., & Pozzo-Miller, L. D. (2002). From acquisition to consolidation: On the role of brain-derived neurotrophic factor signaling in hippocampal-dependent learning. *Learning & Memory, 9*(5), 224–237.

Uprichard, E. (2010). Questioning research with children: Discrepancy between theory and practice?. *Children & Society, 24*(1), 3–13.

Ursache, A., Blair, C., & Raver, C. C. (2012). The promotion of self-regulation as a means of enhancing school readiness and early achievement in children at risk for school failure. *Child Development Perspectives, 6*(2), 122–128.

U.S. Department of Commerce, Census Bureau. (2010). *United States National Census.* Retrieved from http://www.census.gov

U.S. Department of Education.. (2004). *Meeting the highly qualified teachers challenge: The secretary's third annual report on teacher quality.* Washington, DC: Author.

Valdez, P., Reilly, T., & Waterhouse, J. (2008). Rhythms of mental performance. *Mind, Brain, and Education, 2*(1), 7–16.

Valerio, K. (2012). Intrinsic motivation in the classroom. *The Journal of Student Engagement: Education Matters, 2*(1), 30–35.

Valiande, S., & Tarman, B. (2011). *Differentiated teaching and constructive learning approach by the implication of ICT in mixed ability classrooms.* Ahi Evran Üniversitesi Eğitim Fakültesi Dergisi, Cilt 12, Sayı 1, Nisan, Sayfa 169–184.

Vallerand, R. J., Pelletier, L. G., Blais, M. R., Briere, N. M., Senecal, C., & Vallieres, E. (1993). On the assessment of intrinsic, extrinsic, and amotivation in education: Evidence on the concurrent and construct validity of the academic motivation scale. *Educational and Psychological Measurement, 53*(1), 159–172. doi:10.1177/0013164493053001018

Valtin, H. (2002). "Drink at least eight glasses of water a day." Really? Is there scientific evidence for "8x8"? *American Journal of Regulatory Comparative Physiology, 283,* 993–1004.

Vance, D. E., Roberson, A. J., McGuineess, T. M., & Fazeli, P. L. (2010). How neuroplasticity and cognitive reserve protect cognitive functioning. *Journal of Psychosocial Nursing and Mental Health Services, 48*(4), 23–30. doi:10.3928/02793695-20100302-01

Vandenberghe, R., Dupont, P., De Bruyn, B., Bormans, G., Michicls, J., Mortelmans, L., & Orban,

G. A. (1996). The influence of stimulus location on the brain activation pattern in detection and orientation discrimination A PET study of visual attention. *Brain, 119*(4), 1263–1276.

Van der Oord, S., Bögels, S. M., & Pejinenburg, D. (2012). The effectiveness of mindfulness training for children with ADHD and mindful parenting for the parents. *Journal of Family Studies, 21*(1), 139–147.

Van Hover, S., Hicks, D., & Washington, E. (2011 Winter). Multiple paths to testable content? Differentiation in high-stakes testing context. *Social Studies Research and Practice, 6*(3), 34–51.

Van Manen, M. (1995). On the epistemology of reflective practice. *Teachers and Teaching: Theory and Practice, 1*(1), 33–50. doi:10.1080/1354060950010104

Van Overwalle, F. (2009). Social cognition and the brain: A meta-analysis. *Human Brain Mapping, 30*(3), 829–858.

VanTassel-Baska, J. & Stambaugh, T. (2005). Challenges and possibilities for serving gifted learners in the regular classroom. *Theory Into Practice, 44*(3), 211–217.

Van Turennout, M., Bielamowicz, L., & Martin, A. (2003). Modulation of neural activity during object naming: Effects of time and practice. *Cerebral Cortex, 13*(4), 381–391. doi:10.1093/cercor/13.4.381

VanVoorhis, F.L. (2011). Maximum homework impact: Optimizing time, purpose, communication, and collaboration. In S. Redding, M. Murphy & P. Sheley's *Handbook on family and community engagement* (pp.105–112). Lincoln, IL: Academic Development Institute/Center for Innovation and Improvement.

Varma, S., McCandliss, B., & Schwartz, D. (2008, Apr). Scientific and pragmatic challenges for bridging education and neuroscience. *Educational Researcher, 37*(3),140–152.

Vartanian, O., & Mandel, D. R. (2011). *Neuroscience of decision making*. New York, NY: Psychology Press.

Vazire, T., & Wilson, T.D. (2012). *Handbook of self-knowledge*. New York, NY: Guilford.

Vega, I. (Producer) & Rose, C. (Host and Executive Producer). (2008). *Charlie Rose, guest: Geoffrey Canada*. New York, NY: PBS. Retrieved on 30 April 2013 from http://www.charlierose.com/guest/byname/geoffrey_canada

Virarouge, A., Hubbard, E. M., Dehaene, S., & Sackur, J. (2010). Number line comprehension and the illusory perception of random numbers. *Experimental Psychology, 57*, 446–454.

von Krogh, G., Ichijo, K., & Nonaka, I. (2000). *Enabling knowledge creation: How to unlock the mystery of tacit knowledge and release the power of innovation*. New York, NY: Oxford University Press.

Voss, J. F., Perkins, D. N., & Segal, J. W. (Eds.) (2012). *Informal reasoning and education*. New York, NY: Routledge.

Vul, E., Harris, C., Winkielman, P., & Pashler, H. (2009). Puzzlingly high correlations in fMRI studies of emotion, personality, and social cognition. *Perspectives on Psychological Science, 4*(3), 274–290.

Vygotsky. L. S. (1978). *Mind in society: The development of the higher psychological processes*. Cambridge, MA: The Harvard University Press.

Wadsworth, B. J. (1996). *Piaget's theory of cognitive and affective development: Foundations of constructivism*. London, UK: Longman Publishing.

Wahlheim, C. N., Dunlosky, J., & Jacoby, L. L. (2011). Spacing enhances the learning of natural concepts: An investigation of mechanisms, metacognition, and aging. *Memory & Cognition, 39*(5), 750–763. doi:10.3758/s13421-010-0063-y

Walker, N. J. (2003). The cultivation of student self-efficacy in reading and writing. *Reading and Writing Quarterly, 19*(2), 175–187.

Walker, S. O., & Plomin, R. (2005). The nature-nurture question: Teachers' perceptions of how genes and the environment influence educationally relevant behaviour. *Educational Psychology, 25*(5), 509–516.

Walsh, J. A., & Sattes, B. D. (2004). *Quality questioning: Research-based practice to engage every learner*. Thousand Oaks, CA: Corwin.

Wannarka, R., & Ruhl, K. (2008). Seating arrangements that promote positive academic and behavioural outcomes: A review of empirical research. *Support for Learning, 23*(2), 89–93.

Warren, A. D. (1989). *Mastery learning: A basic introduction*. Eastern Kentucky University. Retrieved 17 Aug 2013 from http://etc.buffalo.edu/eventResources/shopOfHorrorsResources/BloomTaxonomy.pdf

Waterhouse, L. (2006). Multiple intelligences, the Mozart effect, and emotional intelligence: A critical review. *Educational Psychologist, 41*(4), 207–225.

Waytz, A. (2009, December 8). The psychology of status: How the pursuit of status can lead to aggressive and self-defeating behavior. *Scientific American*. Retrieved 9 Aug 2013 from http://www.scientificamerican.com/article.cfm?id=the-psychology-of-social

Webster, J. (2010). *The 49 techniques from Teach Like a Champion*. Retrieved 30 December 2012 from http://specialed.about.com/od/managementstrategies/a/The-49-Techniques-From-Teach-Like-A-Champion_2.htm

Weinberger, N. M. (2011). Reconceptualizing the primary auditory cortex: Learning, memory and specific plasticity. In J.A. Winer and C.E. Screiner (Eds.), *The auditory cortex* (pp. 465–491). New York, NY: Springer.

Weierich, M. R., Wright, C. I., Negreira, A., Dickerson, B. C., & Barrett, L. F. (2010). Novelty as a dimension in the affective brain. *Neuroimage, 49*(3), 2871–2878.

Weisberg, D. S., Keil, F. C., Goodstein, J., Rawson, E., & Gray, J. (2008). The seductive lure of neuroscience explanations. *Journal of Cognitive Neuroscience, 20*(3), 470–477.

Welsh, J. A., Nix, R. L., Blair, C., Bierman, K. L., & Nelson, K. E. (2010). The development of cognitive skills and gains in academic school readiness for children from low-income families. *Journal of Educational Psychology, 102*(1), 43.

Wentzel, K. R., & Wigfield A. (Eds.) (2009). *Handbook of motivation in school*. New York, NY: Taylor & Francis.

Westermann, G., Mareschal, D., Johnson, M., Sirois, S., Spratling, M., & Thomas, M. (2007). Neuroconstructivism. *Developmental Science 10*(19), 75–83.

Westwood, P. (2001). Differentiation as a strategy for inclusive classroom practice: Some difficul-ties identified. *Australian Journal of Learning Disabilities, 6*(1), 5–11.

Wheatley, M., Salaam, A., & Bash, B. (2010). *Perseverance*. San Francisco, CA: Berrett-Koehler Publishers.

Whitebread, D., Anderson, H., Coltman, P., Page, C., Pino Pasternak, D. & Mehta, S. (2007). Developing independent learning in the early years. *Education 3–13: International Journal of Primary, Elementary and Early Years Education, 33*(1), 40–50. DOI:10.1080/03004270585200081

Whitebread, D., & Bingham, S. (2011). School readiness: A critical review of perspectives and evidence. *Occasional paper, 2.*

Whitebread, D., Bringham, S., Grau, V., Pino Pasternak, D., & Sangster, C. (2007). Development of metacognition and self-regulated learning in young children: Role of collaborative and peer-assisted learning. *Journal of Cognitive Education and Psychology, 6*(3), 433–455(23). doi:http://dx.doi.org/10.1891/194589507787382043

Whitebread, D., Coltman, P., Pasternak, D. P., Sangster, C., Grau, V., Bingham, S.…. & Demetriou, D. (2009). The development of two observational tools for assessing metacognition and self-regulated learning in young children. *Metacognition and Learning, 4*(1), 63–85.

Whitehurst, G. J., & Lonigan, C. J. (2001). Emergent literacy: Development from prereaders to readers. In S. B Neuman & D. K. Dickensen (Eds.), *Handbook of early literacy research* (pp. 11–29). New York, NY: Guilford.

Wiggins, G., & McTighe, J. (1998). Six facets of understanding. In G. Wiggins and J. McTighe, *Understanding by design*. Alexandria, VA: Association for Supervision and Curriculum Development.

Wiggins, G., & McTighe, J. (2005). *Understanding by design*. Alexandria, VA: Association for Supervision and Curriculum Development.

Wiggins, G., & McTighe, J. (2011). *UbD Introductory Paper*. Alexandria, VA: Association for Supervision and Curriculum Development.

Willcutt, E. G., Doyle A. E., Nigg, J. T., Faraone, S. V., & Pennington, B. F. (2005). Validity of the executive function theory of attention deficit/hyperactivity disorder: A meta-analytic review. *Biological Psychiatry, 57*(11), 1336–1346.

Wiliam, D. (2011). *Embedded, formative assessment*. Bloomington, IN: Solution Tree.

Williams, J. (2010). Taking on the role of questioner: Revisiting reciprocal teaching. *The Reading Teacher 64*(4), 278–281. doi:10.1598/RT.64.4.6.

Williams, J. (2011). Looking back, looking forward: Valuing post-compulsory mathematics education. *Research in Mathematics Education, 13*(2), 213–22. doi:10.1080/14794802.2011.585831

Williams, J. J. (2013). Improving learning in MOOCs with cognitive science. In Z. A. Prados and E. Schneider (Eds.), *Workshop on massive open online courses* (moocshop) (pp. 49–54). Retrieved 9 Aug 2013 http://ceur-ws.org/Vol-1009/aied2013ws_volume1.pdf#page=54

Williams, S. J., Higgs, P., & Katz, S. (2012). Neuroculture, active ageing and the "older brain": Problems, promises and prospects. *Sociology of Health & Illness, 34*(1), 64–78.

Willingham, D. T. (2007–2008 Winter). Should learning be its own reward? *American Educator*, 29–35.

Willingham, D. T. (2010). *Why students don't like school: a cognitive scientist answers questions about how the mind works and what it means for the classroom.* San Francisco, CA: Jossey-Bass.

Wilson, A. J., Revkin, S. K., Cohen, D., Cohen, L., & Dehaene, S. (2006). An open trial assessment of "The Number Race", an adaptive computer game for remediation of dyscalculia. *Behavioral and Brain Functions, 2*(1), 20.

Wingard, L. & Forsberg, L. (2009). Parent involvement in children's homework in American and Swedish dual-earner families. *Journal of Pragmatics, 41*(8), 1576–1595. http://dx.doi.org/10.1016/j.pragma.2007.09.010

Winston, J. S., Strange, B. A., O'Doherty, J., & Dolan, R. J. (2004). Automatic and intentional brain responses during evaluation of trustworthiness of faces. In J. T. Cacioppo and G. G. Berstein, *Social Neuroscience* (pp. 199–210). Sussex, UK: Psychology Press.

Witt, P. L., & Kerssen-Griep, J. (2011). Instructional feedback I: The interaction of facework and immediacy on students' perceptions of instructor credibility. *Communication Education, 60,* 75–94.

Witt, P. L., Wheeless, L. R., & Allen, M. (2006). The relationship between teacher immediacy and student learning: A meta-analysis. In B. M. Gayle, R. W. Preiss, N. Burrell & M. Allen (Eds.), *Classroom communication and instructional processes: Advances through metaanalysis* (pp.149–168). Mahwah, NJ: Erlbaum.

Wogan, M., & Waters, R.H. (1959). The role of repetition in learning. *American Journal of Psychology, 72,* 612–613.

Wolf, M., Miller, L., & Donnelly, K. (2000). Retrieval, automaticity, vocabulary elaboration, orthography (RAVE-O): A comprehensive, fluency-based reading intervention program. *Journal of Learning Disabilities, 33*(4), 375–386.

Wolfe, P. (2001). *Brain matters: Translating research into classroom practice.* Alexandria, VA: Association for Supervision and Curriculum Development.

Wolfson, A. R., & Carskadon, M. A. (1998). Sleep schedules and daytime functioning in adolescents. *Child Development, 69*(4), 875–887.

Wolfson, A. R., & Carskadon, M. A. (2003). Understanding adolescent's sleep patterns and school performance: A critical appraisal. *Sleep Medicine Reviews, 7*(6), 491–506.

Wong, E. (2008). *Reflective teaching in English as a second language classrooms.* Unpublished manuscript. Quito, Ecuador: Universidad San Francisco de Quito.

Wong, H. K. (2002). Induction: The best form of professional development. *Educational Leadership, 59*(6), 52–55.

Wood Daudelin, M. (1997). Learning from experience through reflection. *Organizational Dynamics, 24*(3), 36–48.

Woolley, A. W., Hackman, J. R., Jerde, T. E., Chabris, C. F., Bennett, S. L., & Kosslyn, S. M.

(2007). Using brain-based measures to compose teams: How individual capabilities and team collaboration strategies jointly shape performance. *Social Neuroscience, 2*(2), 96–105.

Wormeli, R. (2007). *Differentiation: from planning to practice, grades 6–12*. Portland, ME: Stenhouse Publishers.

Worobey, J., Tepper, B. J., & Kanarek, R. B. (2006). *Nutrition and behavior: a multidisciplinary approach*. Wallingford, UK: Cabi.

Wright, W. (1999). *Born that way: Genes, behavior and personality*. New York, NY: Routledge.

Wu, E.H. (2013). The path leading to differentiation: An interview with Carol Tomlinson. *Journal of Advanced Academics, 24*(2), 125–133. doi:10.1177/1932202X13483472

Xue, A. (2013). *Human experimentation: An analysis of the ethics of human experimentation*. Retrieved 7 Oct 2013 from http://newtoncaps.org/zool/wp-content/uploads/sites/38/2013/05/Human-Experimentation.pdf

Xue, G., Mei, L., Chen, C., Lu, Z. L., Poldrack, R., & Dong, Q. (2011). Spaced learning enhances subsequent recognition memory by reducing neural repetition suppression. *Journal of Cognitive Neuroscience, 23*(7), 1624–1633. doi:10.1162/jocn.2010.21532

Yamada, K., & Nabeshima, T. (2003). Brain-derived neurotrophic factor/TrkB signaling in memory processes. *Journal of Pharmacological Sciences 91*(4), 267–270. doi: 10.1254/jphs.91.267. doi:10.1254/jphs.91.267

Yano, K. (2013). The science of human interaction and teaching. *Mind, Brain, and Education, 7*(1), 19–29.

Yanowitz, K.L. (2010). Using analogies to improve elementary school students' inferential reasoning about scientific concepts. *School Science and Mathematics, 101*(3), 133–142. doi:10.1111/j.1949-8594.2001.tb18016.x

Yeager, M., & Yeager, D. (2013). *Executive function and child development*. New York, NY: Norton.

Yeates, K. O., Armstrong, K., Janusz, J., Taylor, H. G., Wade, S., Stancin, T., & Drotar, D. (2005). Long-term attention problems in children with traumatic brain injury. *Journal of the American Academy of Child & Adolescent Psychiatry, 44*(6), 574–584.

Yeh, S. S. (2001). Tests worth teaching to: Constructing state-mandated tests that emphasize critical thinking. *Educational Researcher, 30*(9), 12–17.

York-Barr, J., Sommers, W. A., Ghere, G. S., & Montie, J. K. (2001). *Reflective practice to improve schools*. Thousand Oaks, CA: Corwin.

Yorke, M. (2003). Formative assessment in higher education: Moves towards theory and the enhancement of pedagogic practice. *Higher Education, 45*(4), 477–501.

Yost, D. S., Sentner, S. M. & Forlenza-Bailey, A. (2000). An examination of the construct of critical reflection: Implications for teacher education programming in the 21st century. *Journal of Teacher Education, 51*(1), 39–49.

Young, M. (2010). The future of education in a knowledge society: The radical case for a subject-based curriculum. *Journal of the Pacific Circle Consortium for Education, 22*(1), 21–32.

Zago, L., Presenti, M., Mellet, E., Crivello, F., Mazoyer, B., & Tzourio—Mazoyer, N. (2011). Neural correlates of simple and complex mental calculation. *NeuroImage, 13,* 314–327. doi:10.1006/nimg.2000.0697

Zalazo, P. D., & Carlson, S. M. (2012). Hot and cold executive function in childhood and adolescence: Development and plasticity. *Child Development Perspectives, 6*(4), 354–360.

Zalla, T., Koechlin, E., Pietrini, P., Basso, G., Aquino, P., Sirigu, A., & Grafman, J. (2000). Differential amygdala responses to winning and losing: A functional magnetic resonance imaging study in humans. *European Journal of Neuroscience, 12*(5), 1764–1770.

Zamarian, L., Ischebeck, A., & Delazer, M. (2009). Neuroscience of learning arithmetic: Evidence from brain imaging studies. *Neuroscience and Biobehavioral Reviews 33*(6), 909–925.

Zanker, J. (2005). *Conceptual issues in psychology: Neuroscience.* Retrieved on 23 March 2007 from http://www.pc.rhul.ac.uk/staff/J.Zanker/teach/PS2080/L4/PS2080_4.htm.

Zatorre, R. J., Chen, J. L., & Penhune, V. B. (2007). When the brain plays music: Auditory–motor interactions in music perception and production. *Nature Reviews Neuroscience, 8*(7), 547–558.

Zatorre, R. J., Fields, R. D., & Johansen-Berg, H. (2012). Plasticity in gray and white: Neuroimaging changes in brain structure during earning. *Nature Neuroscience, 15,* 528–536. doi:10.1038/nn.3045

Zemelman, S., Daniels, H., & Hyde, A. (2005). *Best practice: new standards for teaching and learning in America's schools* (3rd ed.). New Hampshire: Heinemann.

Zhao, Y. (2012). *World class learners: Educating creative and entrepreneurial students.* Washington, DC: National Association of Elementary School Principals.

Ziegler, J. C., & Goswami, U. (2005). Reading acquisition, developmental dyslexia, and skilled reading across languages: A psycholinguistic grain size theory. *Psychological Bulletin, 131,* 3–29.

Zigarovich, K. L., & Myers, S. A. (2011 Mar). The relationship between perceived instructor communicative characteristics and college students' conflict-handling styles. *Journal of Instructional Psychology.* Available on http://findarticles.com/p/articles/mi_m0FCG/is_1_38/ai_n57826992/?tag=content;col1

Zimmerman, B. J., Bandura, A., & Martinez-Pons, M. (1992). Self-motivation for academic attainment: The role of self efficacy beliefs and personal goal setting. *American Educational Research Journal, 29*(3), 663–676.

Zimmerman, B. J., & Schunk, D. H. (Eds.) (2013). *Self-regulated learning and academic achievement: Theoretical perspectives.* New York, NY: Routledge.

Zotev, V., Krueger, F., Phillips, R., Alvarez, R. P., Simmons, W. K., Bellgowan, P., ... & Bodurka, J. (2011). Self-regulation of amygdala activation using real-time fMRI neurofeedback. *PLoS One, 6*(9), e24522.

Zwiers, J., & Crawford, M. (2011). *Academic conversations: Classroom talk that fosters critical thinking and content understandings.* Portland, ME: Stenhouse Publishers.

Zwozak-Myers, P. (2012). *The teacher's reflective practice handbook: Becoming an extended professional through capturing evidence-informed practice.* New York, NY: Routledge.

Index

Note: Page locators with *f* indicate figures; tables are noted with *t*.

Abramson, M. J., 253
accountability, 84, 242
actions, 159, 159*f*
active learning, 122
activities, 159, 159*f*, 172, 184*t*
Adams, H., 277
ADHD, xli, 16, 38–39
affect, 124–25, 230–33. *see also* emotions, 267–68
affective neuroscience, 21
ages and stages, paying attention to, 257–58
aging, MBE and, 28
Ahyun, K., 150
alerting system, 32, 39, 124
Allen, J, 239
Alvarez, D., 17
Alvidrez, J., 229
Ambady, N., 155
Amedi, A., 128
American Academy of Sciences, principles of learning and teaching, 273–74
American Educational Research Association, 14
amygdala, 30, 125
analogies, 128, 213, 214*f*, 215–16, 219, 222–23
Anderman, L. H., xxxi, 239
Andersen, J. F., 68

Anderson, D. K., 215
Andrzejewski, C., 239
Ansari, D., xxxviii, 17, 20, 279
anxiety, 36, 210
application, 96, 98, 98*f*, 99, 100*t*
Archer, A., 147
Arendal, L., 20
Aristotle, 28, 231
assessment, 58–60, 76–77, 139, 181
Association for Supervision and Curriculum Development, 15
Atherton, M., 279
attention, 31–32, 39, 121, 122–25
attentional networks, 242–43, 252
Attention Network Test, 39
attitude toward intervention, 51–53, 276–77
auditory memory, 34
authentic learning, 138–39, 173, 188, 203, 206

Bach, S., 20
backward design, xliv, 121*f*, 184
Baddeley, A. D., 132, 133, 133*f*
Baker, W., 163
Balata, D. A., 134
Bálint, R., 123
Bangasser, D. A., 52

Baron-Cohen, S., 104
Barr, M., 156
Barrett, R. A., 154
Battro, A., 279
BDNF. *see* brain-derived neurotrophic factor
    (BDNF)
behavior, 71, 72
Bergmann, J., 8, 255
Berman, L., 119
Berninger, V., 279
Bernstein, J., 20, 279
best practices
    activities, MBE and, 168*f*, 169*t*–171*t*
    complete list of, 275–76
Best Practice (Zemelman, Daniels, and Hyde),
    168, 184
Bialystok, E., 21
Biggs, J. B., 94
Biological Science Curriculum Study (BSCS),
    217, 217*f*
biology, xli–xlii, 26, 258
Black, P., 58
Blakemore, S. J., 18, 39, 279
Blakey, E., 164, 166*t*
block scheduling, 131
Bloom, B., 86, 90, 94, 95, 154, 155
Bloom's taxonomy, 84, 85*f*, 90–91, 94, 95*f*, 109
body language, 68, 155
Bollich, K. L., 162
Bonk, C., 264
brain, 12*t*, 13*t*, 14*t*, 25, 26–27, 28–29,
    32–33, 122
brain-based education, xxxiii
brain-derived neurotrophic factor (BDNF), 127
brain imaging, 11
Brain That Changes Itself, The (Doidge), 157
Brandeis, D., 20
Brekelmans, M., 67
Brem, S., 20
"Bridge Too Far," xxvi, 17–23, 40–41

Bruer, J. T., 17, 19, 21, 280
BSCS. *see* Biological Science Curriculum
    Study (BSCS)
Buccino, G., 104, 196

Callejas, A., 38
Canada, G., xliv
caring, 72, 96, 97, 114, 150
Carroll, J. B., 56
Carruthers, T., 111
case studies, 202, 211–12, 219, 222
categorization games, 91, 92*f*, 93
Cauley, K., 58
Cazden, C, 68
celebrating errors, 142, 235–37
Center for the Developing Child (Harvard
    University), 22
Centre for Educational Neuroscience (UK), 15
Chabirs, C., 123
challenging activities, 176–77
Changing Education Paradigms (video), 89
Cheseboro, J. L., 149
Chiesa, B. D., 280
chronobiology, 263
Church, M., 89, 248, 251
Claim-Support-Question, 251
Clark, R., xli
Classroom Instruction That Works (Marzano), 132
classroom management, 70–73, 78–79, 125,
    244–47
classrooms
    engaged, 242–44
    layout of, 260–61, 260*f*
    social and emotional climate of, 233
Coach Carter (film), xli
Coch, D., xxvii, 18, 280
cognition, 122, 232*f*
cognitive activities, 175
cognitive dissonance, 193, 240
cognitive neuropsychology, xxxiii

cognitive neuroscience, xxxiii, 274
cognitive preferences, 37
Cohen, H., 133
Coll, R. K., 215
collaborative environments, 84
collective teacher efficacy, 156
Collins, A., 58
Collis, K., 94
communication, 66, 67–69, 78, 149
communication immediacy, 149–51
community education initiatives, xliv–xlv
Compass Points, 249
competitive learning, 70
complex ideas, generating, 138
complex *versus* simple tasks, 131–32
concept maps, 249–50
concepts, in MBE, 23, 37
conceptual learning, memory pathways and, 129
Connectome: How the Brain's Wiring Makes Us Who We Are (Seung), xxv
conscious processes, learning and, 35–36
constructivism, 27, 53–54, 56–58, 93, 176, 238
context, learning embedded in, 35
cooperative learning, 69, 70, 202, 205f, 207–8, 219, 221
cooperative teaching, 69, 246
Corbett, D., xl
Costa, A., 101, 102, 164, 165f, 183, 226
Coulson, R. L., 215
Courage to Teach, The (Palmer), 241
Cousteau, J., 1
cramming, spreading out learning over time *versus,* 131
creativity, 84, 137
credibility, teacher, 48–51, 74
critical thinking, 90, 194
criticism, attitudes toward, 52–53
Crockett, L., 256, 257
cross-cultural approaches, 84

cultural neuroscience, xxxviii
culture, xxxviii–xxxix, 68–69, 71
cycle of innovation, 182, 182f
Czarnocha, B., 163

Damasio, A., 230
Daniel, D., xxxii, 17, 280
Daniels, H., 168
Davis, K. S., 233
debate, 66, 192
decision-making, 31, 173, 249
deep thinking, 84, 87, 90, 111–13
Dehaene, S., xxv, xxvi, 18, 20, 29, 280
Delazer, M., 20
Delphi Panel on Mind, Brain, and Education science, members of, 279–82
democratic activities, 174–75
Dennett, D., 104
Dennis, S., xli
depression, 36
depth *vs.* breadth, xxxix, 135
Dern, L., xli
De Smedt, B., 20
development, 13t
Developmental Cognitive Neuroscience Lab (University of British Columbia), 18
developmental stages, 56, 58
Devlin, J. T., 20
Dewey, J., 216, 219
diagnosis of learning status, 4–5, 6f, 7
dialogue, 193, 194, 195, 197, 200–201, 208
Diamond, A., 18
Diamond, M., 136, 280
differentiation, 2, 8, 37–39, 41–42, 140
digital generation, 90
digital literacy, 84
direct instruction, 132
disadvantaged children, xxxii, xlii, 26, 82, 225, 230, 262
discipline, 72, 246–47

disciplined mind, 105
discovery, 217, 217*t*
discovery learning, 66, 146, 219
distractions, 124, 246–47
Doidge, N., 157
Do no harm rule, of educators, xxvi, 14–15
Donovan, J. J., 131
dopaminergic loop, 180, 227
Dougherty, M., 183, 248
Drach-Zahavy, A., 126
dreaming, learning and, 36
Duchek, J. M., 134
Duit, R., 215
Dupper, D. R., 233
Dweck, C., 152
Dyer, W., 272
dyslexia, xli, 16, 20

early childhood development, xxxvii–xxxix
Eberly Center for Teaching Excellence
    (Carnegie Mellon), 123
education, as behind the times compared with
    other social institutions, 2, 2*f*
educational neuroscience, xxxiii, 277
educational psychology, xxxiii, xxxv, 7
"Education and the Brain: A Bridge Too Far"
    (Bruer), 17
effect sizes, xxxi, 47
Egbert, J., 37
Eggan, P. D., 213
Einstein, A., 84, 90, 136, 137
elaboration, 217*t*, 218
Elders, L., 197, 198, 199
elicit prior knowledge, 217*t*
embedded assessments, 141, 143
emotional intelligence, 230–31
emotional memory, 125
emotional regulation, 31
emotions, 13*t*, 21, 30–31, 97, 155, 230–34,
    232*f*, 241, 267–68

empathy, 86, 98, 98*f*, 99, 100*t*, 107, 241,
    243, 250–51
engagement, 216–17, 217*t*, 218, 242–44
environment, xxxviii, 13*t*, 26
Erez, M., 126
ergonomics, 260
errors, celebrating, 142, 235–37
Escalante, J., xl, xli
Etherington, M. B., 206
ethical mind, 107–9
ethical standards, 84
evaluations, 58–60, 76–77, 139–58, 184*t*,
    188–89, 217*t*, 218–19, 264
    clarity, immediacy and, 148–51
    feedback for mastery learning, 151–55
    formative, 141–43, 151, 156, 265
    nurturing teacher-student relationships,
        155–56
    plasticity and, 156–58
    product, process, and progress, 143
    role of, 140–41
    shared, explicit learning and, 145–48
    summative, 141, 144
    testing and, 144–45
executive control, 122
executive functions, 21, 32, 39, 42–44, 124,
    229–30
exercise, xlii, 36, 37
expectations, 227–29
experts *vs.* novices, 156
explanation, 98, 98*f*, 100*t*, 217*t*, 218
explicit instruction, 145–48, 219
exploration, 217, 217*t*, 218
extending knowledge, 217*t*

faces, 36, 150, 155, 245, 261
Faeth, M., 232, 233
Fallshore, M., 216
Farah, M. J., 152
Farrington, J., 178

Fast ForWord, 253
feedback, 33–34, 52, 60, 81, 132, 139, 142,
    144, 151–55, 162, 181, 225–26
Feltovich, P. J., 215
Fink, L. D., 86, 95, 96, 97f
Finland, community learning initiatives in,
    xlv
Fiore, S. M., 216
Fischer, K. W., xxxiii, 9, 10, 11, 16, 18, 20,
    280
Fisher, D., 52
5Es model, 216–19, 217t, 219, 223, 242
Five Minds for the Future, 90, 105–9, 108f
Fleming, S. M., 210
flipped classroom, 8–9, 254–56, 271
Flipped Learning Network, 255
Flip Your Classroom: Reach Every Student Every
    Class Every Day (Bergmann & Sams), 255
flow, 244
fluid intelligence, xlii, 158, 229–30, 267, 274
focused attention, 122–23
Fodor, I. E., 162
foreign language learning, 21, 27–28
formal education, goals of, 88f, 91f
formative evaluation, 58, 60, 141–43, 151,
    156, 265
foundational knowledge, 95–96
Foundation for Critical Thinking, 194, 195
Freeman, M., xli
Freiberg, H. J., 72
Frey, N., 52
Frith, C., 104, 151
Frith, U., 18, 39, 104
Fujimori, A., 107
Functions of Language in the Classroom (Cazden,
    Vera, & Hymes), 68

Gagliardi, J. L., 104
Galileo Galilei, 160
Gallese, V., 104, 196

gap analysis, 57
Gardner, H., 29, 89, 105, 106, 108, 109, 128,
    280
Garfield, J. A., 87
Gathercole, S., 133
Gazzaniga, M., 104
Geake, J., 281
gender, 12, 14t
gene potentiation, xxxviii
Generate-Sort-Connect-Elaborate, in concept
    maps, 249–50
genetics, xlii, 274
geriatric neurology, 28
Ghaye, T., 63
Ghesquiere, P., 20
Giard, M. H., 128
Giordano, P. J., 152
goals, 69, 146, 147
Godin, S., 242
Goleman, D., 230
Good, T. L., 228
Goodstein, J., 151
Goswami, U., 281
Gray, J., 151
Green, E., xl
group learning, 69–70
guided discovery, 146
guidelines, in MBE, 23, 25t
Guo, Y., 50
Guskey, T. R., 143

habits of mind, 89, 90, 101–3, 130, 152, 183,
    224, 226
habituation, xlii, 86–87
Hammer, D., 183
Hamre, B. K., 233
Hanushek, E., xl
Harlem Children's Zone, xxxvii, xliv
Harrison, A. G., 215
Hart, L., xxxiii

Hattie, J., xxxi, xxxii, xliii, xliv, 39, 46, 47, 57, 73, 81, 82, 111, 113, 119, 132, 139, 140, 146, 156, 157, 158, 192, 202, 215, 225, 228, 229, 230, 237, 238, 244, 261, 283, 289
headlines, 249
Hebart, J. F., 216, 217
Hebbian synapse model, 35, 239
Hefelbower, T., 244
Heinz dilemma, 107
Hennessey, M. G., 163
Hesse, M., 215
Higher Order Thinking *vs.* Lower Order Thinking, 90–94, 91*f*, 206
Highly Engaged Classroom, The (Marzano & Pickering), 72, 244
high-stakes testing, 242, 263, 265
hippocampus, 30, 125
Hitch, 132
Ho, H. Z., 229
home, 82, 227, 230, 254, 258
homework, 8, 9, 180–81
Hong, S., 229
Hook, C. J., 152
Hooker, K. E., 162
Howard-Jones, P., 18, 281
How We Think (Dewey), 217
Hughes, C. A., 147
Hulshof, H., 215
Human Behavior, Learning, and the Developing Brain (Coch, Fischer, & Dawson), 176
human dimension, 96
Hunt, S. K., 150
Hutchins, R. M., 90
Hyde, A., 168
Hymes, D., 68

Iacobini, M., 104, 196
Illinois Mathematics and Science Academy, 205
imagery, 132
IMBES (International Mind, Brain, and Education Society), 14, 16

immediacy, striving for, 148–51
Immordino-Yang, M. H., 18, 20, 97, 124, 125, 230, 232, 233, 281
inclusion, 37–38
inhibition, 21, 32
innovative environments, 84
inquiry, guiding, 248–49
instructional guidelines, in MBE, xxxvi–xxxvii, xxxvii*f*, 23, 25*t*, 37, 145
instructional immediacy, defined, 149
integration, 96
intellectual humility, 237, 250
interdisciplinarity, 84, 257
internal dialogue, 275. *see also* dialogue; reflection
International Brain Research Organization, 15
International Mind, Brain, and Education Society, 251–52
International Society for Technology and Education, 255
interpretation, 98, 98*f*, 100*t*, 248
interventions, 6*f*, 51–53
intrinsic motivators, 153
invention, 217, 217*t*
Ischebeck, A., 20

Jackson, R., 239
Jackson, S. L., xli
Jacobson, L., 228
Japan, community learning initiatives in, xlv
Jensen, E., 281
Johannet, P. M., 162
Jolles, J., 18, 281
Joubert, J., 61
journaling, 61, 62*t*, 63
Journal of Effective Teaching, 148
Journal of Positive Behavior Interventions, 72
Jukes, I., 193, 256, 257
Junior Metacognitive Awareness Inventory, 167
Justice, L. M., 50

Kabat-Zinn, J., 257
Kaderavek, J. N., 50
Kallick, B., 101, 102, 183, 226
Kandel, E., 127
Kauchak, D., 213
Keil, F. C., 151
Kelm, J. L., 51
Kennedy, John F., 81
Khan, S., 8, 255
Khan Academy, 255
Kirby, J. R., 133
Kline, K., xli
Klingberg, T., 127
Kohlberg, L., 107, 108
Koizumi, H., 18, 281
Koretz, D., 263
Kuhn, D., 163

labeling, 230
Lachman, M., 252
Lamb, S. M., 72
Lange, N., 183, 248
Langer, E., 162
Latin American School for Education, Cognitive
    and Neural Sciences, 19
learning, xlii, 12t–13t, 26–27, 33–35, 47–73,
    82–83, 121, 122, 267–68
  biology and, xli–xlii
  deep, 56
  in groups, 69–70
  life-long, 27–28, 58, 84, 90, 111, 142
  nutrition and, 258–59
  pattern seeking and, 29–30
  social nature of, 152
  spaced *versus* massed, 128–32
  teacher as most influential factor in, xxxix–
    xli, 82–83, 156–58
  testing to improve, 144–45
Learning and the Brain conference, 14
learning communities, xxxvii–xxxix
learning environment, 113–14, 203

learning how to learn, 95, 96
learning objectives, clearly articulated, 123–24
Lee, K., 20
Lemov, D., xxxiii
lesson planning. *see* planning lessons
Levine, M., 122, 125, 227
Levy, J., 67
life-long learning, 27–28, 58, 84, 90, 111, 142
Ligorio, M. B., 181
linguistic representations, 135, 136
Lippert, L. S., 150
listening, 207–8
Logan, J. M., 134
logistical problems, 245–46
long-term memory, 34, 35, 125, 126, 136
Lupianez, J., 38

Magg, J., 233
Making Thinking Visible (Ritchhart), 248
Mann, H., 258
Mann, V., 20
Martin, E., 20
Marzano, R. J., 72, 132, 172, 178, 179, 183,
    184, 207, 244
mastery learning, 86, 132, 151–55, 189–90, 258
math, xxxix, 20–21, 57–58, 79–80, 163–64,
    177t, 203, 205, 238, 244
Maxwell, K. J., 192
Mazur, E., 8, 255
Mazziotta, J. C., 104, 196
MBE, xxiii–xxiv, xxvii, xxxvi–xxxvii, xxxvif,
    2, 7, 7f, 10f, 15, 19–22, 28, 44–45, 86,
    241, 266
  complex, but not necessarily complicated,
    xxxiv–xxxv
  concepts, principles, tenets, and guidelines,
    23, 24t, 25t, 37
  content and, 16–17
  description of, xxxiii–xxxiv
  disciplines and subdisciplines in, 3f
  goals in, 291–93

MBE (*continued*)
　instructional guidelines in, 37
　levels of analysis, xxxv
　order and, 15–16
　teacher training in context of, 9–12, 14–17
　Visible Learning combined with, 46–47, 90
MBHE science, 9–10
McCain, T., 256, 257
McCroskey, J. C., 68, 149
McIntosh, K., 51
McMillan, J., 58
McQuarrie, L., 133
McTighe, J., 97, 98*f*, 99, 100, 109, 121*f*, 144, 145
meaning, human nature and search for, 27
Meltzoff, A., 21, 104
memory, 13*t*, 34–35, 52, 121, 125–28, 210
Memory and the Brain (Squire), 127
memory + attention, 35, 121–22, 184, 185–86, 274
memory consolidation, 125–27
mental energy control, 122
Mercer, L. K., 155
metacognition, 42–44, 60, 87, 160–62, 163–64, 165*f*, 166*t*, 250
Metacognition Awareness Inventory, 167
methodologies, appropriate, 64–67
methods, 159, 159*f*
microteaching, 50, 63
Mind, Brain, and Education, 17
mind-body connection, xlii
mindfulness, 162–63, 257
mindlessness, 257
mind maps, 65, 134, 134*f*
Mindset (Dweck), 152
minimal effort, law of, 239, 240
MINT project (Switzerland), 18
mirror neurons, 104, 196, 234, 241
mistakes, 236, 237
Molnar-Szakacs, I., 104, 196
Montessori-style education, 258

MOOCs (massive open online courses), 255
Morrison, K., 89, 248, 251
Morton, J. B., 21
motivation, 36, 81, 143, 146*f*, 153, 205, 215, 228, 237–39, 241, 244, 258, 269
multiple intelligences theory, 128
multitasking, 11
Mynard, J., 181

Nabeshima, T., 127
National Board for Professional Teaching Standards (NBPTS), 61
National Mathematics Advisory Panel, xxxix
National Science Foundation, 217
natural interests, 243–44
Navarro, D., 181
NBPTS. *see* National Board for Professional Teaching Standards (NBPTS)
negative, extrinsic motivators, 153
negative attention, 247
negative disturbances, 244–45
Nelkin, D., xlii
neural pathways, 19–20, 34
neuroconstructivism, xxxiv
neuroeducation, xxxiii
neurogenesis, 258
neuromotor functions, 122
neuromyths, 11, 12*t*–14*t*, 14–15, 37
neuronal networks, 122
neuroplasticity, xxv, 27–28, 142, 157–58, 210, 237
neuropsychology, xxxv, 7
neuroscience literacy, improving, 12
Neuroscience of Learning, The: Beyond the Hebbian Synapse (Gallistel & Matzel), 177
neurotransmitters, 22, 31, 34, 52, 127
Never Work Harder Than Your Students (Jackson), 239
Newcombe, N., 18
Ng, P. T., 63

"Nine Instructional Strategies," 90
nonlinguistic representations, 135–36
nonverbal communication, 149
nonverbal immediacy, 149
Nordby, C. J., 155
Northwest Regional Educational Laboratory, 135
Norton, R. W., 68
note taking, 179
novelty, 29–30, 126, 178, 256
Number Race, 253
Numerical Cognition Laboratory (University of Western Ontario), 17
Nummela-Caine, R., 281
Nussbaum, J. F., 68
nutrition, xlii, 14t, 36, 37, 258–59

objectives, 146, 147
O'Donnell, A., 61
OECD. see Organisation for Economic Co-operation and Development (OECD)
online teaching, 150–51
openness to experiences, 235–36, 237
Organisation for Economic Co-operation and Development (OECD), xxxiv
Orgill, M. K., 216
orienting system, 124
Outward Bound, 237
Ovemyer, J., 255

Pajares, F., 48
Palmer, P. J., 241
Papagno, C., 133
parallel teaching, 246
parents, 82, 83, 227, 228, 229, 258
Parrila, R., 133
passion (in or for teaching), 146, 158, 240–42, 268–69
pattern detection, 29–30, 126, 178
Paul, R., 197, 198, 199
Pavio, A., 132, 133

peer-tutoring, 132
perceptions, 249–50
Performance Checklist: Metacognition, 165f
performance goals, 154
performance verbs, for learning outcomes, 85f
peripheral perception, 31, 32, 123
Perkins, D., 4, 87, 264
Peronnet, F., 128
Perry, N. E., 155
perseverance, 235–37, 268
personal objectives, 181
perspective, 98, 98f, 99, 100t
Pfeiffer, M., xli
phonological loop, 132, 133f, 134
Piaget, J., 53, 56
Piata, R. C., 233
Pickering, D. J., 72, 178, 183, 244
Pineda, J., 104
Pinker, S., 104
planning lessons, 121–39, 184t
Plasta, S. B., 50
Plaza, M., 133
Pogue, L. L., 150
Poitier, S., xli
Pollock, E., 178, 183
positive, intrinsic motivators, 153
positive learning environment, 72
Posner, M., 32, 39, 124, 125, 242, 281
praise, 72, 137, 152, 180, 227
preferences, attention and, 128
Premack, D. G., 104
presumptions, 251
primacy-recency phenomenon, 66
principles
    in MBE, xxxvi, xxxvif, 23, 24t, 37
    that great teachers follow, 25–36
problem-based learning (PBL), 142, 203–6, 205f, 219, 221
problem-solving, 84
process evaluations, 143

processing control, 122
Proctor, P., 227–28
product evaluations, 143
production control, 122
productivity, 84
progress evaluations, 143
Project Zero, 4, 163
"Pygmalion effect," 228

questioning, 66, 101–2, 192, 194, 195, 196–200,
    201–2, 220–21
Quinn, D., 46

Radosevich, D. J., 131
rational-emotive therapy, 233
RAVE-O, 253
Rawson, E., 151
reading, 20, 22–23, 82, 253
Reading Brains Lab (Dartmouth), 18
recall, variation and, 135
reciprocal teaching, 69, 202, 208–10, 219, 222
recognition, providing, 179–80
reflection, 60, 101, 102, 111, 192, 217
reflective activities, 173–74
reflective journal, 62t
Reich, R., 192, 193
reinforcing effort, 179–80
relational knowledge understanding, analogies
    and, 213
relationships, 82–83
REM sleep, 35, 36
repetition, 132–34, 187–88
"research school" design, xxvii
resilience, 235
respectful mind, 106–7
responsibility, 84
review practice, 145
revisiting ideas and concepts, 130
rewards for learning, 153
Richardson, U., 20

Richland, L. E., 215
Ritchhardt, R., 89, 248, 250, 251
Roberts, J., xli
Robinson, K., 89
Roe, M. F., 37
Role of Emotion and Skilled Intuition in Learning,
    The (Immordino-Yang & Faeth), 233
Rosenthal, R., 155, 228
Rossier School of Education (University of
    Southern California), 18
Rothbart, M. K., 32, 124

Sage, S., 204
saliency control system, 122
Sams, A., 8, 255
Sanders, W., xl
scaffolding, 93
scaling up interventions, gradual, 6f
Schacter, Daniel, 230
Schön, D., 61
school, 238, 242
Schooler, J. W., 216
school readiness, 258
school start times, 263
Schumacher, R., 18
Schunk, D. H., 48
Schwatz, M., 281
science, 19–22, 57–58, 79–80, 205, 217,
    219, 238
Science Curriculum Improvement Study
    (SCIS), 217, 217t
scientists, teachers' unquestioning trust in, 16
SCIS. see Science Curriculum Improvement
    Study (SCIS)
See-Think-Wonder, 248
Segalowitz, S., 176
selective attention, 123
self-assessment, 98, 98f
self-concept, 48
self-correction, 28–29, 142, 236

self-efficacy, 47–48, 49, 50, 51, 63, 73–74, 225–27, 235, 266
self-esteem, xxxii, 226, 235
self-image, 48
self-knowledge, 100t, 103, 104
self-perception, 103, 235
self-reflection, 61, 62t, 63–64, 77–78, 162, 163
self-regulation, 21, 42–44, 105, 156, 265
Senge, P., 63
sensory input, 30, 34
sensory perception, 125–26
Sentence-Phrase-Word, 249
SES. see socioeconomic status (SES)
Seung, S., xxv
7Es model, 217, 217f, 219
Shakespeare, W., 19
Shaw, G. B., 276
Shors, T. J., 52
short-term memory, 125
Siegel, D., 104
significant learning, 90, 95–97, 97f, 121–22
similarities and differences, 178–79
Simons, D. J., 123
singing about math, 177t
sitting students in rows, 201, 245, 260–61
"Six Facets of Understanding," 97, 98–100, 98f, 100t
sleep, xlii, 35, 36, 37, 96
Small, G., 253
small-group learning, 202–3
SMART goals, characteristics of, 147–48
Smilkstein, R., 282
Smith, L. R., 150
social activities, 174
social affect, 97
social brain, 104
Social Brain, The (Gazzaniga), 104
social cognition, 104, 105, 122, 234
social contagion, 234–35
social interaction, 234–35

social media, 103
social neuroscience, 234–35, 241
social status, 82
Society for Neuroscience, 15
socioeconomic status (SES), 82, 225
Socratic classroom, 200–201
Socratic method, 191–201, 219, 220
SOLO. see Structured Observed Learning Outcomes (SOLO)
Sousa, D., 282
space versus massed practice, xxviii, 128–32, 186–87
Spence, S., 164, 166t
"spiraling up" activities, 129–30
Spiro, R. J., 215
Squire, K., 252
Squire, L., 127
standardized tests, 89, 142, 201, 235, 264
Stein, Z., 9, 10, 11, 16
STEM education, 252
Stern, E., 18
Stop Stealing Dreams (Godin), 242
strategies, 159, 159f
Strategies for Developing Metacognitive Behaviors (Blakey and Spence), 164
stress, xlii, 36, 52, 210
Structured Observed Learning Outcomes (SOLO), 94
student-centered activities, 172
student-teacher relationships, 51–53, 190
Successful Classroom Management (Eyster and Martin), 72
Sullivan, P. B., 150
summarizing, 179, 249
summative evaluation, 58, 141, 144
Surgey, G., 94, 95f
survival mechanisms, teaching moments vs., 39
Swank, H., xli
Swanson, H. L., 133
Swiss Federal Institute of Technology (Zurich), 18

symbol systems, xxxviii
synapses, 22–23, 35
synthesizing information, 249
synthesizing mind, 105–6

Taggart, G. L., 63
Tan, C., 63
Tan, H. Y., 127
taxonomy of learning objectives, 84, 85*f,*
    90–91, 94, 95*f,* 109
TCSI. *see* Teacher Clarity Short Inventory (TCSI)
teacher clarity, 67, 78, 146*f,* 148–51
Teacher Clarity Short Inventory (TCSI), 149
teacher credibility, 48–51, 74
teacher education, as lifelong process, 11
teacher formation. *see* teacher education
teacher quality, xxxiii, 49
teachers, xxxii, xli, 47–73
    experts *vs.* novices, 156
    great, characteristics of, 114
    learning to think like MBE scientists, 16
    list of habits, 224–25
    as most influential factor in learning,
        xxxix–xli, 82–83, 156–58
    self-reflection by, 61, 62*t,* 63–64
teacher-student relationships, 155–56, 234
teacher training, in context of MBE, 9–12,
    14–17
teaching
    great, goals of, 83–84, 86–90
    neuromyths about, 12*t*–13*t*
    recommended films about, xli, xlv–xlvi
    as science and art, 15
Teaching Gap, The (Stigler & Hiebert), 111, 112
teaching methodologies, 64–67
teaching models, 90–91, 93–111, 113–14, 113*f*
"Teaching the Digital Generation," 90
teaching to the test, 155, 264
team teaching, 246
teamwork, 213, 219

techniques, 159, 159*f*
technology, 9, 19, 22, 84, 238, 251–54, 270,
    277
teenagers, xlii, 234, 263
temporal-sequential ordering, 122
tenets, in MBE, xxxvi, xxxvi*f,* 23, 24*t,* 37
testing, 144–45, 263–65
testing hypotheses, 181–83, 248
theory of mind, 33, 90, 103–5, 151, 210
thinking, 84, 86–87, 109–10, 114–16, 193,
    194, 247–48, 264
Think-Puzzle-Explore, 248
Thomas, M., 216
Thomas, R., 183, 248
threats, 31, 155, 231
time, 86–87
timing, 103–4
tone of voice, 36, 149, 155
Torp, L., 204
transdisciplinarity, xxv, xxxv, 7, 7*f,* 17, 23, 45,
    136–38, 184, 264
transfer, 130, 135, 203
Tschannen-Moran, M., 156
Tuleda, P., 38
Tun, P., 252
21st century skills, 84, 89, 242, 261, 264

unconscious processes, learning and, 35–36
Understanding by Design (Wiggins &
    McTighe), 98
*Understanding the Brain: The Birth of a New
    Learning Science* (OECD), xxxvi
University College of London, 18
Usable Knowledge digital newsletter, 10–11

VanderKamp, K. O., 155
variation, 134–36
Vazire, S., 162
Vera, J. P., 68
verbal processes, 132, 149

Verloop, N., 215
Verschaffel, L., 20
videos, 254, 255
visible learning, coining of term, xxxi
Visible Learning (Hattie), xliii, xliv, 39, 46–47,
      158, 266
   interventions interpreted to be within
      teacher's realm of influence, 289–90
   150 influences that impact student learning
      outcomes, 283–88
visible thinking, 248
voices, 39, 149, 150, 155
Vygotsky, L. S., 209

Warren, A. D., 56
Washington, D., xli
Weinstein, R. S., 229
Weisbert, D. S., 151
wellness, 162
Whitebread, D., 152
Why Don't Students Like School? (Willingham), 238

Wiggins, G., 97, 98*f*, 99, 100, 109, 121*f*, 144, 145
William, D., 58
Williams, R., xli
Willingham, D. T., 153, 238
Willis, J., 282
Wilson, A. P., 63
Wilson, B., xl
Wolfe, P., 18, 282
Woodruff, G., 104
working memory, 125, 126, 133
World Declaration on Education for All, 83
writing, 173, 178, 179
Wubbels, T., 67

Yamada, K., 127
year-round schooling, 261–62, 262*f*
Yeh, S., 89

Zago, L., 20
Zamarian, L., 20
Zemelman, S., 168, 184